ArtScroll Mishnah Series®

משנה

A rabbinic commentary to the Six Orders of the Mishnah

Rabbi Nosson Scherman / Rabbi Meir Zlotowitz

General Editors

A PROJECT OF THE

Mesorah Heritage Foundation

ששה סדרי משנה

THE COMMENTARY HAS BEEN NAMED **YAD AVRAHAM**
AS AN EVERLASTING MEMORIAL AND SOURCE OF MERIT
FOR THE *NESHAMAH* OF
אברהם יוסף ע״ה בן הר״ר אליעזר הכהן גליק נ״י
AVRAHAM YOSEF GLICK ע״ה
WHOSE LIFE WAS CUT SHORT ON 3 TEVES, 5735

Published by
Mesorah Publications, ltd

the mishnah

ARTSCROLL MISHNAH SERIES / A NEW TRANSLATION WITH A COMMENTARY **YAD AVRAHAM** ANTHOLOGIZED FROM TALMUDIC SOURCES AND CLASSIC COMMENTATORS.

INCLUDES THE COMPLETE HEBREW TEXT OF THE COMMENTARY OF **RAV OVADIAH BERTINORO**

FIRST EDITION
Three Impressions . . . June 1985 — February 1995

REVISED EDITION
Seven Impressions . . . June 2004 — November 2021
Eighth Impression . . . January 2024

Published and Distributed by
MESORAH PUBLICATIONS, Ltd.
313 Regina Avenue / Rahway, N.J. 07065

Distributed in Europe by
LEHMANNS
Unit E, Viking Business Park
Rolling Mill Road
Jarrow, Tyne & Wear NE32 3DP
England

Distributed in Australia & New Zealand by
GOLDS WORLD OF JUDAICA
3-13 William Street
Balaclava, Melbourne 3183
Victoria Australia

Distributed in Israel by
SIFRIATI / A. GITLER — BOOKS
POB 2351
Bnei Brak 51122

Distributed in South Africa by
KOLLEL BOOKSHOP
Northfield Centre, 17 Northfield Avenue
Glenhazel 2192, Johannesburg, South Africa

THE ARTSCROLL® MISHNAH SERIES
SEDER NASHIM Vol. III; *GITTIN / KIDDUSHIN*

ISBN 10: 0-89906-283-0 / ISBN 13: 978-0-89906-283-9
ITEM CODE: NA3H

Typography by Compuscribe at ArtScroll Studios, Ltd.

Printed in the United States of America
Bound by Sefercraft, Quality Bookbinders, Ltd. Rahway, NJ

Seder Nashim Vol. III:

מסכת גיטין
Tractate Gittin

מסכת קידושין
Tractate Kiddushin

The Publishers are grateful to

YAD AVRAHAM INSTITUTE

and the

MESORAH HERITAGE FOUNDATION

for their efforts in the publication of the

ARTSCROLL MISHNAH SERIES

בָּרוּךְ אֲשֶׁר יָקִים אֶת דִּבְרֵי הַתּוֹרָה הַזֹּאת

Blessed is he who maintains the words of this Torah

This Volume is dedicated by

ר׳ אברהם ברוך בן ר׳ יששכר רפופורט

ורעיתו הכבודה רות בת ר׳ אברהם שיחיו

Mr. & Mrs. Bruce Rappaport

of Haifa, Israel and
Geneva, Switzerland

in loving memory of his parents

ר׳ יששכר בן ר׳ יעקב ע״ה

ט״ו תמוז

מרת בלומא שושנה בת ר׳ ברוך ע״ה

ט״ו אייר

They handed down a legacy of integrity and kindness,
of loyalty to their tradition
and concern for the future.
This legacy has been lovingly adopted and fostered
by their offspring;
a legacy that flourishes
thanks to the vision and generosity of

Bruce and Ruth Rappaport

תנצב״ה

PATRONS OF THE MISHNAH

With generosity, vision, and devotion to the perpetuation of Torah study, the following patrons have dedicated individual volumes of the Mishnah.

SEDER ZERAIM

BERACHOS:

In memory of

ר׳ אברהם יוסף ז״ל ב״ר אליעזר הכהן ודבורה נ״י

Avraham Yosef Glick ז״ל

PEAH:

In memory of

הגאון הרב ר׳ אהרן ב״ר מאיר יעקב זצ״ל

Rabbi Aron Zlotowitz זצ״ל

והרבנית פרומא בת ר׳ חיים צבי ע״ה

Rebbetzin Fruma Zlotowitz ע״ה

DEMAI:

Chesky and Sheindy Paneth and family

In memory of their parents

ר׳ אברהם מרדכי בן ר׳ שרגא פייוועל ז״ל – Avrohom Mordechai Mendlowitz ז״ל

ר׳ יעקב חיים בן ר׳ יחזקאל ז״ל – Yaakov Chaim Paneth ז״ל

and in memory of his brother

ר׳ משולם בן ר׳ יעקב חיים ז״ל – Meshulam Paneth ז״ל

Moshe and Esther Beinhorn and family

In memory of their grandparents

ר׳ ישראל מרדכי ב״ר חיים צבי הי״ד וזוג׳ פעסיל ב״ר משה הי״ד

ר׳ משה ב״ר שלום יוסף הי״ד וזוג׳ איידיל ב״ר יהודה אריה ע״ה

ר׳ יחיאל מיכל ב״ר אברהם זאב הי״ד וזוג׳ שיינדל ב״ר יוסף הי״ד

ר׳ יצחק ב״ר משה הי״ד וזוג׳ לאה גיטל ב״ר חיים עזרא הי״ד

KILAYIM:

Mr. and Mrs. Louis Glick

In memory of

יעקב מאיר חיים בן אפרים אליעזר הכהן ז״ל – Jerome Schottenstein ז״ל

SHEVIIS:

In memory of

ר׳ אריה לייב בן שמואל יוסף ז״ל

Aryeh Leib Pluchenik ז״ל

TERUMOS:

Benzi and Esther Dunner

In memory of their grandparents

ר׳ אורי יהודה ב״ר אברהם אריה ז״ל וזוג׳ מרת רבקה בת שרה ע״ה

PATRONS OF THE MISHNAH

MAASROS, MAASER SHENI:

Barry and Sipora Buls and Family

In memory of our parents

אברהם בן מרדכי ז״ל   חיה שיינדל בת חיים צבי ע״ה

Abraham and Jeanette Buls ע״ה

אלטר חיים משולם בן יעקב ז״ל   אסתר בת ראובן ע״ה

Meshulam and Esther Kluger ע״ה

and in memory of our grandparents

מרדכי בן אברהם יצחק ז״ל וזוג׳ רבקה בת אברהם ע״ה – בולס

חיים צבי בן דוד ז״ל וזוג׳ פיגא בת יצחק ע״ה – מאשקאוויטש

יעקב ז״ל הי״ד וזוג׳ טאבא ע״ה הי״ד – קלוגר

ראובן ז״ל הי״ד וזוג׳ פיגא בת יחזקאל נתן ע״ה הי״ד – שעכטר־בירנבוים

CHALLAH, ORLAH, BIKKURIM:

Yossi and Linda Segel   Danny and Shani Segel   and families

In memory of their father

ר׳ ברוך בן ר׳ יוסף הלוי ז״ל – Baruch Segel ז״ל

Chesky and Sheindy Paneth and family

In memory of their parents

ר׳ אברהם מרדכי בן ר׳ שרגא פייוועל ז״ל – Avrohom Mordechai Mendlowitz ז״ל

ר׳ יעקב חיים בן ר׳ יחזקאל ז״ל – Yaakov Chaim Paneth ז״ל

and in memory of his brother

ר׳ משולם בן ר׳ יעקב חיים ז״ל – Meshulam Paneth ז״ל

Moshe and Esther Beinhorn and family

In memory of their uncle

ר׳ אברהם זאב בן ר׳ יחיאל מיכל ז״ל – Avrohom Beinhorn ז״ל

SEDER MOED

SHABBOS:

Mr. and Mrs. Philip Amin
Mr. and Mrs. Lee R. Furman

In memory of their son and brother

קלמן בן ר׳ פסח ז״ל – Kalman Amin ז״ל

ERUVIN:

Mr. and Mrs. Lawrence M. Rosenberg

In honor of their parents

ר׳ גרשון בן ר׳ יהודה ומרת שרה שיינא בת דוב בערל עמו״ש

Judge and Mrs. Gustave Rosenberg עמו״ש

and in memory of their brother and sister

אברהם דוד ודבורה חאשא חוה בני ר׳ גרשון

PATRONS OF THE MISHNAH

BEITZAH:

Mr. and Mrs. Herman Wouk

In memory of their בכור and ילד שעשועים

אברהם יצחק ע״ה בן חיים אביעזר זעליג נ״י

PESACHIM:

Mr. and Mrs. Leonard A. Kestenbaum

In memory of their father ר׳ דוד ב״ר אליהו זצ״ל – David Kestenbaum זצ״ל

SHEKALIM:

In memory of **ר׳ יוסף דוד ב״ר משה גאלדווארם זללה״ה**

ROSH HASHANAH, YOMA, SUCCAH:

ר׳ יוסף שמעון בן חיים ע״ה – 1st Lt. Joseph Simon Bravin ע״ה

TAANIS, MEGILLAH, MOED KATAN, CHAGIGAH:

In memory of

מו״ר הרה״ג ר׳ גדליה הלוי שארר זצ״ל

HaGaon HaRav Gedalia Halevi Schorr זצ״ל

SEDER NASHIM

YEVAMOS:

David and Rochelle Hirsch

In memory of their father Mr. Henry Hirsch ז״ל

KESUBOS:

In memory of

מרת בילא בת ר׳ צבי מאיר ע״ה – Mrs. Bertha Steinmetz ע״ה

NEDARIM:

The Knoll Family (Israel and Venezuela)

In memory of their parents

ר׳ צבי הירש בן ר׳ שרגא פייוול ע״ה

ומרת פעסיא דבורה בת ר׳ יעקב דוד ע״ה

NAZIR:

In memory of

יוטא ע״ה בת ר׳ יקותיאל יהודה לאי״ט – Yitty Leibel ע״ה

SOTAH:

In honor of the

Fifth Avenue Synagogue

GITTIN, KIDDUSHIN:

Bruce and Ruth Rappaport

In memory of his parents

ר׳ יששכר ב״ר יעקב ז״ל

ומרת בלומא שושנה בת ר׳ ברוך ע״ה

PATRONS OF THE MISHNAH

SEDER NEZIKIN

BAVA KAMMA:

In memory of

הרב שמעון ב״ר נחמיה הלוי ז״ל

Rabbi Shimon Zweig ז״ל

BAVA METZIA:

The Steinmetz family

In memory of their parents

ר׳ שמעון ב״ר שאול יהודה ז״ל

וזוגתו בילא בת ר׳ צבי מאיר ע״ה

BAVA BASRA:

In memory of

ר׳ יצחק מאיר ב״ר משה ז״ל – Mr. Irving Bunim ז״ל

SANHEDRIN:

The Zweig and Steinmetz families

In memory of

סימא בת ר׳ שמעון ע״ה – Sima Rabinowitz ע״ה

MAKKOS, SHEVUOS:

In memory of

יהושע יצחק ז״ל בן אברהם מאיר נ״י – Joshua Waitman ז״ל

EDUYOS:

Mr. and Mrs. Woli and
Chaja Stern (Saō Paulo, Brazil)

In honor of their children

Jacques and Ariane Stern   Jaime and Ariela Landau

Michael and Annete Kierszenbaum

AVODAH ZARAH, HORAYOS:

In memory of our Rebbe

מור״ר שרגא פייבל בן ר׳ משה זצ״ל

Reb Shraga Feivel Mendlowitz זצ״ל

AVOS:

Mr. Louis Glick   Mr. and Mrs. Sidney Glick

Mr. and Mrs. Mortimer Sklarin

In memory of their beloved mother

מרת רבקה בת ר׳ משה גליק ע״ה – Mrs. Regina Glick ע״ה

Mr. Louis Glick   Shimon and Mina Glick and family

Shimon and Esti Pluchenik and family

In memory of their beloved wife, mother and grandmother

מרת דבורה בת ר׳ שמעון גליק ע״ה – Mrs. Doris Glick ע״ה

PATRONS OF THE MISHNAH

SEDER KODASHIM

ZEVACHIM:

Mr. and Mrs. Richard Hirsch

In memory of their son

הילד אליעזר ז״ל בן יהודה זליג שיחי׳ — Lawrence A. Hirsch ז״ל

MENACHOS:

In memory of

שמעון בן משה עמוס ז״ל – Simon Amos ז״ל

CHULLIN:

The Steinmetz and Barouch families

In memory of

רבקה עטיה בת ר׳ שמעון ע״ה — Ruth Barouch ע״ה

BECHOROS:

Yad Avraham Institute

In honor of

Bruce and Ruth Rappaport

ARACHIN:

In memory of

גילה מסעודה ע״ה בת ר׳ יעקב נ״י

Gillah Amoch ע״ה

דפנה ע״ה בת ר׳ יעקב נ״י

Amy Amoch ע״ה

KEREISOS:

In memory of

ר׳ דוד ז״ל בן ר׳ שמעון נ״י – David Litman ז״ל

TEMURAH, MEILAH:

Baruch and Susie Singer and Yitzchak Ahron

Rabbi Eli Hersh and Rivky Singer

Rabbi Nussie and Ruchy Singer

Yossie and Surie Singer

Sruly Singer and Leah

In honor of

Rebbetzin Bluma Singer שתחי׳

In memory of

הרה״ג ר׳ יצחק אהרן בן הרה״ג ר׳ אליהו זינגער זצ״ל

נפ׳ י״ג טבת תשס״א

הרה״ג ר׳ אליהו בן הרה״ג ר׳ שמעון זינגער זצ״ל

וזוגתו הרבנית רייזל בת הרה״ח ר׳ יששכר דוב ע״ה

הרה״צ ר׳ ישראל אריה ליב האלפערן בן הרה״צ ר׳ ברוך מסאקאליוווקא זצ״ל

וזוגתו הרבנית שבע בת הרה״ג ר׳ אריה ליבוש ע״ה

TAMID, MIDDOS, KINNIM:

Hashi and Miriam Herzka **Moishe and Channie Stern**
Avi and Freidi Waldman **Benzi and Esti Dunner**
Dovid and Didi Stern **Avrumi and Esti Stern**

In honor of our dear parents

William and Shoshana Stern שיחי׳

London, England

SEDER TOHOROS

KEILIM I-II:

Leslie Westreich

Adam and Dayna Westreich **Ezra and Rayna Rosenzweig**
Daniel and Dina Lieberman **and families**

In memory of

ז״ל Larry Westreich – אריה לייב ב״ר יהושע ז״ל

and in memory of our parents and grandparents

הרב יהושע בן מו״ר הרב הגאון יוסף יאסקא ז״ל
גיטל בת זאב וואלף ע״ה

OHOLOS:

In memory of

הרב יהושע בן מו״ר הרב הגאון יוסף יאסקא ז״ל
Rabbi Yehoshua Westreich ז״ל

and

ע״ה Gerda Westreich – גיטל בת זאב וואלף ע״ה

NEGAIM:

Moshe and Esther Beinhorn and family

In memory of

יוסף דוד ז״ל בן יצחק אייזיק
Yosef Dovid Beinhorn ז״ל

PARAH:

Moshe and Esther Beinhorn and family

In memory of their uncles and aunts

אברהם צבי, חוה, רחל, חיים עזרא, אריה לייביש,
ישראל ברוך, שמואל דוד, ומשה הי״ד, והילד שלמה ע״ה

children of

יצחק בן משה שטיינבערגער ז״ל וזוג׳ לאה גיטל בת חיים עזרא ע״ה הי״ד

Chesky and Sheindy Paneth and family

In memory of their grandparents

הרב יחזקאל ב״ר יעקב חיים פאנעטה ז״ל הי״ד וזוג׳ רחל לאה בת ר׳ אשר לעמל ע״ה
הרב חיים יהודה ב״ר משולם ווייס ז״ל וזוג׳ שרה רחל בת ר׳ נתן קארפל ע״ה
הרב שרגא פייוועל ב״ר משה מענדלאוויטש זצ״ל וזוג׳ בלומא רחל בת ר׳ שמעון הלוי ע״ה
ר׳ ישכר בעריש ב״ר אברהם הלוי לאמפערט ז״ל וזוג׳ גיטל פערל בת ר׳ בצלאל ע״ה

PATRONS OF THE MISHNAH

MIKVAOS:

Mr. and Mrs. Louis Glick

In memory of his father

ר׳ אברהם יוסף בן ר׳ יהושע העשיל הכהן ז״ל

Abraham Joseph Glick ז״ל

NIDDAH:

Moshe and Esther Beinhorn and family

In memory of his beloved mother

טילא בת ר׳ יצחק ע״ה

Mrs. Tilli Beinhorn ע״ה

נפ׳ כ״ו טבת תשס״ח

MACHSHIRIN, ZAVIM:

David and Joan Tepper and family

In memory of their parents

ר׳ מנחם מענדל ב״ר יעקב ז״ל ומרת מינדל בת ר׳ אריה ליב ע״ה

Milton and Minnie Tepper ז״ל

ר׳ ראובן ב״ר נחמיה ז״ל ומרת עטיל בת ר׳ ישראל נתן נטע ע״ה

Rubin and Etta Gralla ז״ל

TEVUL YOM, YADAYIM, UKTZIN:

Barry and Tova Kohn and family

In memory of their beloved brother

הרב מנחם מנדל בן ר׳ יוסף יצחק אייזיק זצ״ל

HaRav Menachem Kohn זצ״ל

נפ׳ כ״ז מנחם אב תשס״ו

And in memory of their fathers, and grandfathers

ר׳ יוסף יצחק אייזיק ב״ר בן ציון ז״ל, נפ׳ י׳ שבט תשנ״ח — Josef Kohn ז״ל

ר׳ בנימין אלכסנדר ב״ר דוד ז״ל, נפ׳ ל׳ שבט תשס״א — Benjamin Wiederman ז״ל

and יבל״ח in honor of their mothers and grandmothers שתחי׳ לאוי״ט

Helene Kohn Sylvia Wiederman

הדרן עלך ששה סדרי משנה

הסכמה

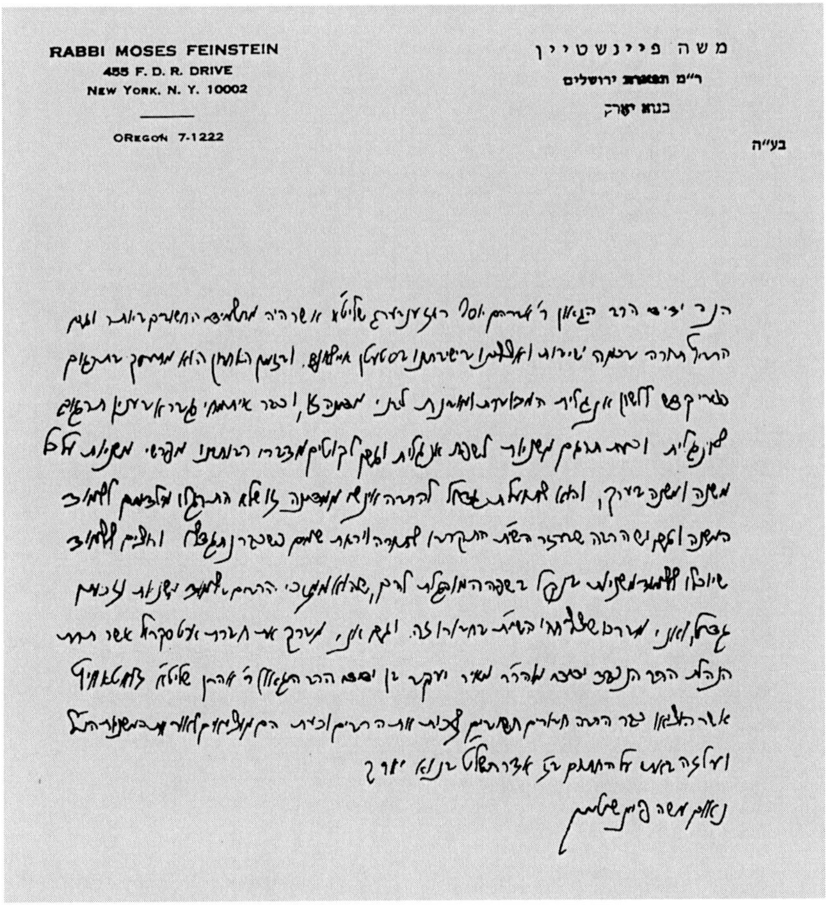
RABBI MOSES FEINSTEIN
455 F. D. R. DRIVE
NEW YORK, N. Y. 10002
ORegon 7-1222

משה פיינשטיין
ר"מ תפארת ירושלים
בנוא יארק

בע"ה

הנה ידידי הרב הגאון ר' אברהם יוסף ראזענבערג שליט"א אשר היה מתלמידי החשובים ביותר וגם הרביץ תורה בכמה ישיבות ואצלינו בישיבתנו בסטעטן איילאנד, ובזמן האחרון הוא מתעסק בתרגום ספרי קדש ללשון אנגלית המדוברת ומובנת לבני מדינה זו, וכבר איתמחי גברא בענין תרגום לאנגלית וכעת תרגם משניות לשפת אנגלית וגם לקוטים מדברי רבותינו מפרשי משניות על כל משנה ומשנה בערך, והוא לתועלת גדול להרבה אינשי ממדינה זו שלא התרגלו מילדותם ללמוד המשנה וגם יש הרבה שבעזר השי"ת התקרבו לתורה ויראת שמים כשכבר נתגדלו ורוצים ללמוד שיוכלו ללמוד משניות בנקל בשפה המורגלת להם, שהוא ממזכי הרבים בלמוד משניות וזכותו גדול. ואני מברכו שיצליחהו השי"ת בחבורו זה. וגם אני מברך את חברת ארטסקרול אשר תחת הנהלת הרב הנכבד ידידי מוהר"ר מאיר יעקב בן ידידי הרב הגאון ר' אהרן שליט"א זלאטאוויץ אשר הוציאו כבר הרבה חבורים חשובים לזכות את הרבים וכעת הם מוציאים לאור את המשניות הנ"ל.

ועל זה באתי על החתום בז' אדר תשל"ט בנוא יארק.

נאום משה פיינשטיין

מכתב ברכה

יעקב קמנצקי
RABBI J. KAMENECKI
38 SADDLE RIVER ROAD
MONSEY, NEW YORK 10952

בע"ה

יום ה' ערב חג השבועות תשל"ט, פה מאנסי.

כבוד הרבני איש החסד שוע ונדיב מוקיר רבנן מר אלעזר נ"י גליק שלו' וברכת כל טוב.

מה מאד שמחתי בהודעי כי כבודו רכש לעצמו הזכות שייקרא ע"ש בנו המנוח הפירוש מבואר על כל ששת סדרי משנה ע"י "ארטסקראל" והנה חברה זו יצאה לה מוניטין בפירושה על תנ"ך, והנה נקוה שכשם שהצליחה בתורה שבכתב כן תצליח בתורה שבע"פ. ובהיות שאותיות "משנה" הן כאותיות "נשמה" לפיכך טוב עשה בכוונתו לעשות זאת לעילוי נשמת בנו המנוח אברהם יוסף ע"ה, ומאד מתאים השם "יד אברהם" לזה הפירוש, כדמצינו במקרא (ש"ב י"ח) כי אמר אין לי בן בעבור הזכיר שמי וגו'. ואין לך דבר גדול מזה להפיץ ידיעת תורה שבע"פ בקרב אחינו שאינם רגילים בלשון הקדש. וד' הטוב יהי' בעזרו ויוכל לברך על המוגמר. ויראה רוב נחת מכל אשר אתו כנפש מברכו.

יעקב קמנצקי

מכתב ברכה

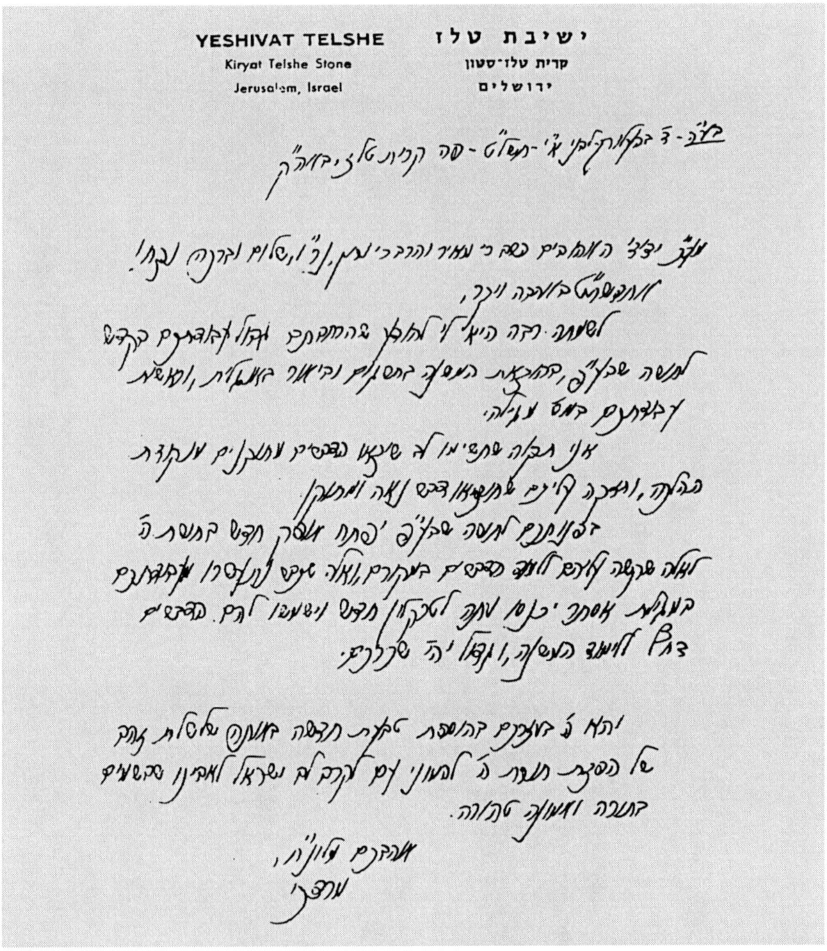

בע״ה — ד׳ בהעלותך — לבני א״י — תשל״ט — פה קרית טלז, באה״ק

מע״כ ידידי האהובים הרב ר׳ מאיר והרב ר׳ נתן, נר״ו, שלום וברכה נצח!

אחדשה״ט באהבה ויקר,

לשמחה רבה היא לי להודע שהרחבתם גבול עבודתכם בקדש לתורה שבע״פ, בהוצאת המשנה בתרגום וביאור באנגלית, וראשית עבודתכם במס׳ מגילה.

אני תקוה שתשימו לב שיצאו הדברים מתוקנים מנקודת ההלכה, וחזקה עליכם שתוציאו דבר נאה ומתוקן.

בפנותכם לתורה שבע״פ יפתח אופק חדש בתורת ה׳ לאלה שקשה עליהם ללמוד הדברים במקורם, ואלה שכבר נתעשרו מעבודתכם במגילת אסתר יכנסו עתה לטרקלין חדש וישמשו להם הדברים דחף ללימוד המשנה, וגדול יהי׳ שכרכם.

יהא ה׳ בעזרכם בהוספת טבעת חדשה באותה שלשלת זהב של הפצת תורת ה׳ להמוני עם לקרב לב ישראל לאבינו שבשמים בתורה ואמונה טהורה.

אוהבכם מלונ״ח,
מרדכי

מכתב ברכה

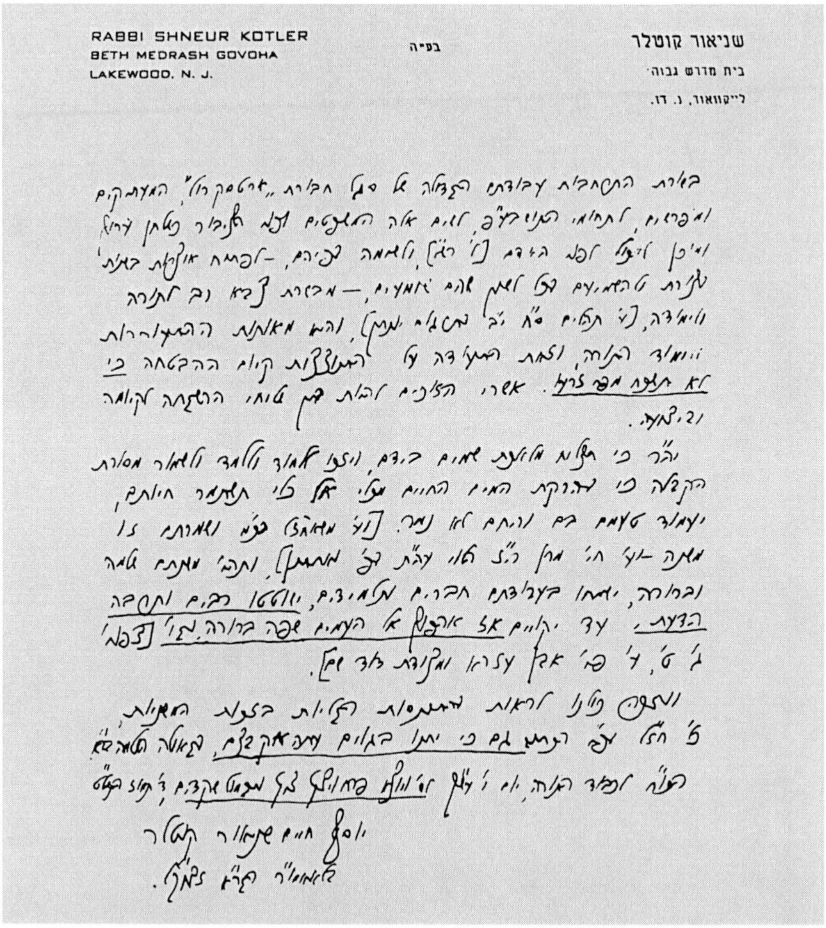
RABBI SHNEUR KOTLER
BETH MEDRASH GOVOHA
LAKEWOOD, N. J.

בס״ה

שניאור קוטלר
בית מדרש גבוה
לייקוואוד, נ. דז.

בשורת התרחבות עבודתם הגדולה של סגל חבורת ,,ארטסקרול״, המעתיקים ומפרשים, לתחומי התושבע״פ, לשים אלה המשפטים לפני הציבור כשלחן ערוך ומוכן לאכול לפני האדם [ל׳ רש״י], ולשימה בפיהם – לפתוח אוצרות בשנות בצורת ולהשמיעם בכל לשון שהם שומעים – מבשרת צבא רב לתורה ולימודה [ע׳ תהלים ס״ח י״ב בתרגום יונתן], והיא מאותות ההתעוררות ללימוד התורה, וזאת התעודה על התנוצצות קיום ההבטחה ,,כי לא תשכח מפי זרעו״. אשרי הזוכים להיות בין שלוחי ההשגחה לקיומה וביצועה.

יה״ר כי תצליח מלאכת שמים בידם, ויזכו ללמוד וללמד ולשמור מסורת הקבלה כי בהרקת המים החיים מכלי אל כלי תשתמר חיותם, יעמוד טעמם בם וריחם לא נמר. [וע׳ משאחז״ל בכ״מ ושמרתם זו משנה – וע׳ חי׳ מרן רי״ז הלוי עה״ת בפ׳ ואתחנן]. ותהי׳ משנתם שלמה וברורה, ישמחו בעבודתם חברים ותלמידים, ,,ישוטטו רבים ותרבה הדעת״, עד יקויים ,,אז אהפוך אל העמים שפה ברורה וגו׳ ״ [צפני׳ ג׳ ט׳, ע׳ פי׳ אבן עזרא ומצודת דוד שם].

ונזכה כולנו לראות בהתכנסות הגליות בזכות המשניות, כל׳ חז״ל עפ״י הכתוב ,,גם כי יתנו בגוים עתה אקבצם״, בגאולה השלמה בב״א.

הכו״ח לכבוד התורה, יום ו׳ עש״ק לס׳ ,,ויוצא פרח ויצץ ציץ ויגמול שקדים״, ד׳ תמוז התשל״ט

יוסף חיים שניאור קוטלר
בלאאמו״ר הגר״א זצוק״ל

מכתב ברכה

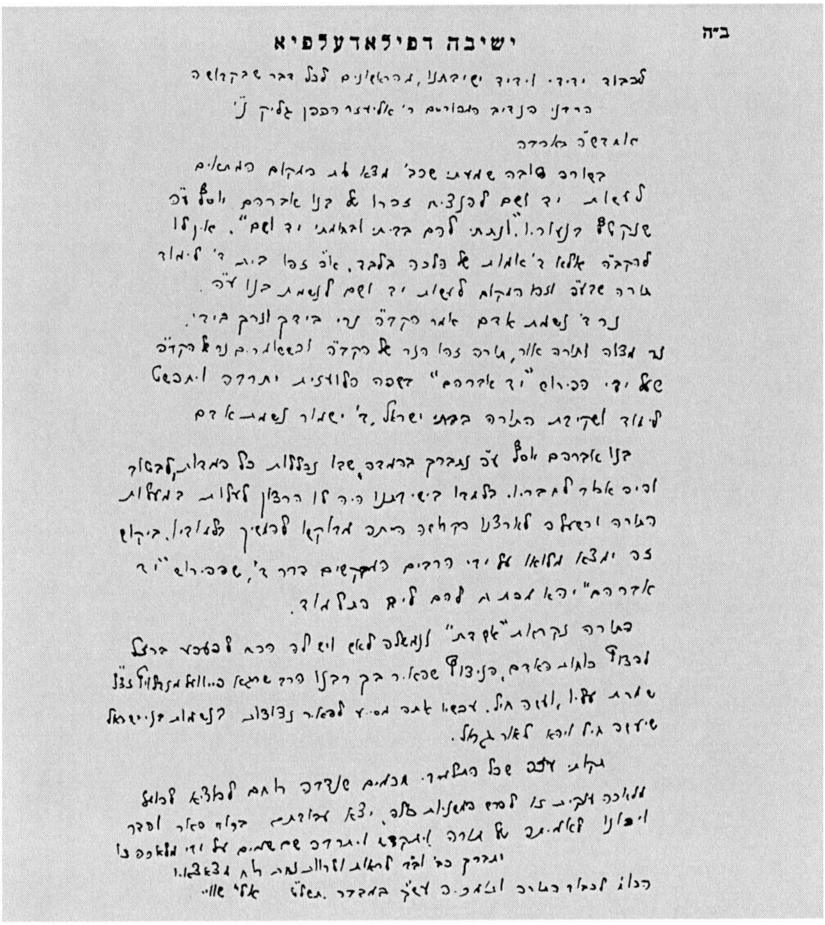

ב״ה
לכבוד ידידי וידיד ישיבתנו, מהראשונים לכל דבר שבקדושה
הרבני הנדיב המפורסם ר׳ אליעזר הכהן גליק נ״י
אחדש״ה באהבה

בשורה טובה שמעתי שכב׳ מצא את המקום המתאים לעשות יד ושם להנציח זכרו של בנו **אברהם יוסף ע״ה** שנקטף בנעוריו. ,,ונתתי להם בביתי ובחומתי יד ושם״. אין לו להקב״ה אלא ד׳ אמות של הלכה בלבד. א״כ זהו בית ד׳ לימוד תורה שבע״פ וזהו המקום לעשות יד ושם לנשמת בנו ע״ה.

נר ד׳ נשמת אדם אמר הקב״ה נרי בידך ונרך בידי. נר מצוה ותורה אור, תורה זהו הנר של הקב״ה וכששומרים נר של הקב״ה שעל ידי הפירוש ,,**יד אברהם**״ בשפה הלועזית יתרבה ויתפשט לימוד ושקידת התורה בבתי ישראל. ד׳ ישמור נשמת אדם.

בנו אברהם יוסף ע״ה נתברך בהמדה שבו נכללות כל המדות, לב טוב והיה אהוב לחבריו. בלמדו בישיבתנו היה לו הרצון לעלות במעלות התורה וכשעלה לארצנו הקדושה היתה מבוקשו להמשיך בלמודיו. ביקוש זה ימצא מלואו על ידי הרבים המבקשים דבר ד׳, שהפירוש ,,**יד אברהם**״ יהא מפתח להם לים התלמוד.

התורה נקראת ,,אש דת״ ונמשלה לאש ויש לה הכח לפעפע ברזל לקצוץ כוחות האדם, הניצוץ שהאיר בך רבנו הרב שרגא פייוועל מנדלויץ זצ״ל שמרת עליו, ועשה חיל. עכשיו אתה מסייע להאיר נצוצות בנשמות בני ישראל שיעשה חיל ויהא לאור גדול.

תקותי עזה שכל התלמידי חכמים שנדבה רוחם להוציא לפועל מלאכה ענקית זו לפרש המשניות כולה, יצא עבודתם ברוב פאר והדר ויכונו לאמיתה של תורה ויתקדש ויתרבה שם שמים על ידי מלאכה זו.

יתברך כב׳ וב״ב לראות ולרוות נחת רוח מצאצאיו.
הכו״ח לכבוד התורה ותומכיה עש״ק במדבר תשל״ט

אלי׳ שוויי

מכתב ברכה

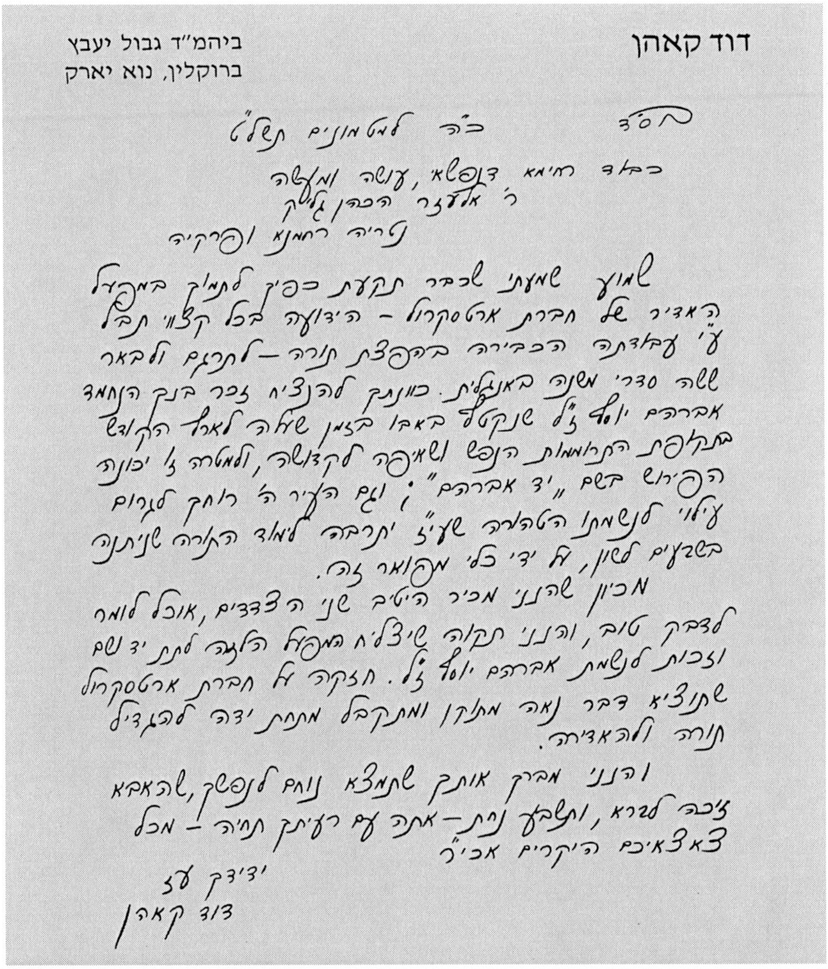
דוד קאהן

ביהמ"ד גבול יעבץ
ברוקלין, נוא יארק

בס"ד
כ"ה למטמונים תשל"ט

כבוד רחימא דנפשאי, עושה ומעשה
ר' אלעזר הכהן גליק
נטריה רחמנא ופרקיה

שמוע שמעתי שכבר תקעת כפיך לתמוך במפעל
האדיר של חברת ארטסקרול – הידועה בכל קצווי תבל
ע"י עבודתה הכבירה בהפצת תורה – לתרגם ולבאר
ששה סדרי משנה באנגלית. כוונתך להנציח זכר בנך הנחמד
אברהם יוסף ז"ל שנקטף באבו בזמן שעלה לארץ הקודש
בתקופת התרוממות הנפש ושאיפה לקדושה, ולמטרה זו יכונה
הפירוש בשם „יד אברהם"; וגם האיר ה' רוחך לגרום
עילוי לנשמתו הטהורה שע"ז יתרבה לימוד התורה שניתנה
בשבעים לשון, על ידי כלי מפואר זה.
מכיון שהנני מכיר היטיב שני הצדדים, אוכל לומר
לדבק טוב, והנני תקוה שיצליח המפעל הלזה לתת יד ושם
וזכות לנשמת אברהם יוסף ז"ל. חזקה על חברת ארטסקרול
שתוציא דבר נאה מתוקן ומתקבל מתחת ידה להגדיל
תורה ולהאדירה.
והנני מברך אותך שתמצא נוחם לנפשך, שהאבא
זוכה לברא, ותשבע נחת – אתה עם רעיתך תחיה – מכל
צאצאיכם היקרים אכי"ר
ידידך עז
דוד קאהן

בס״ד כ״ה למטמונים תשל״ט

כבוד רחימא דנפשאי, עושה ומעשה
ר׳ אלעזר הכהן גליק נטריה רחמנא ופרקיה

שמוע שמעתי שכבר תקעת כפיך לתמוך במפעל האדיר של חברת ארטסקרול – הידוע בכל קצווי תבל ע״י עבודתה הכבירה בהפצת תורה – לתרגם ולבאר ששה סדרי משנה באנגלית. כוונתך להנציח זכר בנך הנחמד אברהם יוסף ז״ל שנקטף באבו בזמן שעלה לארץ הקודש בתקופת התרוממות הנפש ושאיפה לקדושה, ולמטרה זו יכונה הפירוש בשם ,,**יד אברהם**״; וגם האיר ה׳ רוחך לגרום עילוי לנשמתו הטהורה שעי״ז יתרבה לימוד התורה שניתנה בשבעים לשון, על ידי כלי מפואר זה.

מכיון שהנני מכיר היטיב שני הצדדים, אוכל לומר לדבק טוב, והנני תקוה שיצליח המפעל הלזה לתת יד ושם וזכות לנשמת אברהם יוסף ז״ל. חזקה על חברת ארטסקרול שתוציא דבר נאה מתוקן ומתקבל מתחת ידה להגדיל תורה ולהאדירה.

והנני מברך אותך שתמצא נוחם לנפשך, שהאבא זוכה לברא, ותשבע נחת – אתה עם רעיתך תחיה – מכל צאצאיכם היקרים אכי״ר

ידידך עז
דוד קאהן

◆§ Publisher's Preface

אָמַר ר' יוֹחָנָן: לֹא כָּרַת הקב"ה בְּרִית עִם יִשְׂרָאֵל אֶלָּא עַל־תּוֹרָה שֶׁבְּעַל
פֶּה שֶׁנֶּאֱמַר: „כִּי עַל־פִּי הַדְּבָרִים הָאֵלֶּה כָּרַתִּי אִתְּךָ בְּרִית . . ."

R' Yochanan said: The Holy One, Blessed is He, sealed a covenant with Israel only because of the Oral Torah, as it is said [Exodus 34:27]: For according to these words have I sealed a covenant with you . . . (Gittin 60b).

With gratitude to *Hashem Yisborach* we present the Jewish public with *Masechtos Gittin* and *Kiddushin*. Work continues by various authors not only on the remainder of *Nashim*, but on *Nezikin* and *Taharos* as well. Thanks to the vision and commitment of MR. AND MRS. LOUIS GLICK, the future of the ArtScroll Mishnah Series is assured בעזהי"ת. In their quiet, self-effacing way, the Glicks have been a major force for the propagation of Torah knowledge and the enhancement of Jewish life for a generation.

By dedicating the ArtScroll Mishnah Series, they have added a new dimension to their tradition of service. The many study groups in synagogues and congregations throughout the English-speaking world are the most eloquent testimony to the fact that thousands of people thirst for Torah learning that is presented in a challenging, comprehensive, yet comprehensible manner.

The commentary bears the name YAD AVRAHAM, in memory of their son AVRAHAM YOSEF GLICK ע"ה. An appreciation of the niftar will appear in Tractate *Berachos*. May this dissemination of the Mishnah in his memory be a source of merit for his soul. תנצב"ה.

We are proud and grateful that such venerable luminaries as MARAN HAGAON HARAV YAAKOV KAMENECKI שליט"א and MARAN HAGAON HARAV MORDECHAI GIFTER זצ"ל have declared that this series should be translated into Hebrew. *Baruch Hashem*, it has stimulated readers to echo the words of King David: גַּל עֵינַי וְאַבִּיטָה נִפְלָאוֹת מִתּוֹרָתֶךָ, Uncover my eyes that I may see wonders of Your Torah (Psalms 119:18).

May we inject two words of caution:

First, although the Mishnah, by definition, is a compendium of laws, the final *halachah* does not necessarily follow the Mishnah. The development of *halachah* proceeds through the Gemara, commentators, codifiers, responsa, and the acknowledged poskim. Even when our commentary cites the *Shulchan Aruch*, the intention is to sharpen the reader's understanding of the Mishnah, but not to be a basis for actual practice. In short, this work is meant

as a first step in the study of our recorded Oral Law — no more.

Second, as we have stressed in our other books, the ArtScroll commentary is not meant as a substitute for the study of the sources. While this commentary, like others in the various series, will be immensely useful even to accomplished scholars and will often bring to light ideas and sources they may have overlooked, we strongly urge those who are able to study the classic sefarim in the original to do so. It has been said that every droplet of ink coming from *Rashi's* pen is worthy of seven days' contemplation. Despite the exceptional caliber of our authors, none of us pretends to take the place of the study of the greatest minds in Jewish history.

Tractate *Gittin* is devoted to the laws of divorce beginning with the rules governing a bill of divorce, such as its delivery by the husband or an agent; witnesses; conditions affecting its validity; and various enactments of the Sages on an assortment of divorce matters.

The first chapter of Tractate *Kiddushin* deals with the methods and property by which a man legally "consecrates" his intended wife; and also the means of formal acquisition of property. The rest of the tractate discusses conditions placed on the consecration, the kind of evidence needed to decide cases of doubtful *kiddushin*, and the children of prohibited unions.

With this volume we have the honor of introducing a new author in the Mishnah Series: RABBI MATIS ROBERTS of Yeshivas Kol Yaakov in Monsey, New York. He combines scholarship with an unusual ability to present complex ideas in a readily accessible manner. We look forward to his continued participation in the Series. This volume was edited by RABBI TZVI ZEV AREM, who continues the standard he set with his work on Tractates *Kesubos* and *Nedarim*.

We are grateful to REB DANIEL FLEISCHMANN for his very fine graphics production of this volume. He carries on the tradition established by our colleague, REB SHEAH BRANDER, who remains a leader in bringing beauty of presentation to Torah literature.

We are also grateful to the staff of Mesorah Publications: RABBI HERSH GOLDWURM, whose encyclopedic knowledge was always available; RABBI YEHEZKEL DANZIGER, RABBI AVIE GOLD, STEPHEN BLITZ, YOSAIF TIMINSKY, MICHAEL ZIVITZ, LEAH FREIER, CHANEE FREIER, MRS. ESTHER FEIERSTEIN, SIMIE GLUCK, MALKY GLATZER, MRS. FAYGIE WEINBAUM, MRS. JUDI DICK and MRS. SHONNIE FRIEDMAN.

Finally, our gratitude goes to RABBI DAVID FEINSTEIN שליט״א and RABBI DAVID COHEN שליט״א, whose concern, interest, and guidance have been essential to the success of the ArtScroll series since its inception.

Rabbis Nosson Scherman / Meir Zlotowitz

ב׳ תמוז תשמ״ה / June 21, 1985
Brooklyn, New York

מסכת גיטין
Tractate Gittin

Translation and anthologized commentary by
Rabbi Matis Roberts

Edited by
Rabbi Tzvi Arem

General Introduction to Gittin

כִּי יִקַּח אִישׁ אִשָּׁה וּבְעָלָהּ, וְהָיָה אִם לֹא תִמְצָא חֵן בְּעֵינָיו כִּי מָצָא בָהּ עֶרְוַת דָּבָר, וְכָתַב לָהּ סֵפֶר כְּרִיתֻת וְנָתַן בְּיָדָהּ וְשִׁלְּחָהּ מִבֵּיתוֹ (דברים כד: א).

When a man takes a wife and has relations with her, and it comes to pass that she does not find favor in his eyes because he found in her an adulterous thing, he shall write for her a document of severance, and he shall place [it] in her hand, and he shall send her from his house (Deuteronomy 24:1).

☙ The Get / Divorce Document

From the above verse we learn that in order to divorce his wife, a man must give her a document which states that she is being sent away from him, and which totally severs the marital relationship between them (*Rambam, Hilchos Gerushin* 1:1*ff.*).

This document is referred to in the Talmud as a *get* (pl. *gittin*); hence, the name of this tractate. Actually, the term *get* can refer to any type of legal document, but its common usage is in reference to divorce documents, and that connotation is assumed wherever the term is found unless otherwise indicated[1] (*Tosafos* 2 s.v. המביא).

A *get* is divided into two sections — the תֹּרֶף, *toref*, and the טֹפֶס, *tofes*. The first section, the *toref*, includes the date, the names of the man and woman, and the place where the *get* was drawn up (*Meiri* to 2:4), along with the basic declaration of divorce (*Gemara* 26a). This is followed by the *tofes*, the remaining text, most of which is identical in all *gittin* and which elaborates on the ramifications of the *get*.

The *toref* is the essential portion of the *get*, and thus, all Biblical regulations governing the *get* pertain to it alone. Nevertheless, the Rabbis extended many of these regulations to include the *tofes*, as well as including it in many of their own Rabbinical ordinances.

By law, a *get* may be written in any language, but the accepted custom is to write it in Aramaic using כְּתַב אַשּׁוּרִית, the Hebrew lettering which is used in Torah Scrolls. [This is why a scribe is usually the one who writes the *get*.] A *get* written in any other manner may not be used except in pressing circumstances (*Even HaEzer* 126:1).

1. *Tosafos* add that a *get* is customarily written in twelve lines, because the numerical value of the word גֵּט, *get*, is twelve (see also *Shiltei Giborim*).

The term *get* is not found in Biblical Hebrew, but was adopted in Talmudic times. *Vilna Gaon* makes the ingenious observation that in the entire Torah the two letters ג and ט are never next to each other — neither within one word, nor even as the last and first letter of adjacent words. Since these letters are always separated from one another, they are an appropriate title for an instrument that separates husband and wife from one another (see *Divrei Eliyahu*).

☙§ The rule of לִשְׁמָהּ/ Specific Intent

Among the Biblical prerequisites for the validity of a *get* is the requirement that, at the time it is made, it must be intended specifically for the divorce of the particular woman to whom it is subsequently given. This requirement is referred to as לִשְׁמָהּ, *specific intent for her* (mishnah 3:1). It is derived from the words וְכָתַב לָהּ — *an he shall write for her* — which means that it must be written with her in mind (*Gem.* 24b).

☙§ The Divorce Process

The divorce is executed when the husband gives the *get* to his wife for the sake of divorce — as indicated by the words, *and he shall place it in her hand, and he shall send her from his house* (*Rambam* loc. cit.). If the wife takes the *get* from her husband, rather than passively receiving it from him, it does not take effect (*Gem.* 78a).

From the Torah's choice of the word וְשִׁלְּחָהּ — *and he will send her* — rather than *he will divorce her,* we deduce that the husband can send the *get* to his wife through an agent, whose delivery on the husband's behalf constitutes a legitimate act of divorce. Any competent adult, male or female, is qualified to serve in this capacity (2:5,7). Also, from that word — which, without the דָגֵשׁ, *dagesh* (dot) in the letter ה is translated: *and she shall send,*[2] we derive exegetically that if an agent appointed by the woman receives the *get* on her behalf, it takes effect (*Kiddushin* 41a; *Rashi* ad loc.). Scripture repeats the words, *and he places [it] in her hand* (*Deut.* 24:3), to indicate that even placing the *get* into the wife's property is sufficient to execute the divorce (*Gem.* 77a ad loc.).

A divorce is valid only if the husband gives the *get* of his own volition (*Yevamos* 14:1), as indicated by Scripture's reason for the husband's divorcing her: *she does not find favor in his eyes* (*Rambam* loc. cit.). The woman's acquiescence is not required by law, but Rabbeinu Gershom Meor Hagolah, a medieval Jewish leader (c. 960-1040), decreed a *cherem* (ban) against anyone who divorces his wife against her will.

☙§ The Witnesses

From the word דָּבָר, *thing,* in the above verse, it is exegetically derived that the verse (*Deut.* 19:15), *By the mouths of two witnesses ... a thing shall be established* — which is stated in reference to punitive and monetary judgments made by the courts — applies to *gittin* as well. However, in monetary law, two witnesses are necessary only for purposes of evidence, whereas for *gittin* they are a prerequisite to the validity of the process itself (*Kiddushin* 65b; see *Rashba* ad loc.).

Accordingly, a *get,* which is imbued with the capacity to effect a divorce, must include the testimony of two witnesses in order to be valid. The nature of this testimony is the subject of a dispute between R' Meir and R' Elazar.

2. Although the word is written with a *dagesh,* which means *and he shall send her,* the ordinary way to write it would have been וְשִׁלַּח אוֹתָהּ, rather than contracting it into one word (cf. *Genesis* 27:6, ibid. 45:8, *Exodus* 3:20). The Torah writes it in one word to allow for the allusion to her sending an agent (*Torah Temimah, Deut.* ad loc.).

R′ Meir maintains that the testimony which validates a *get* is the signatures of two witnesses on the document. Some commentators rule that two witnesses must also be present at the time of delivery in order to validate the divorce itself (*Tos.* 4a s.v. דקיי״ל). Others contend that the signatures on the *get* alone are sufficient to validate its delivery as well (*Rif* to 76b).

R′ Elazar, however, is of the opinion that the *get* is validated by the witnesses who observe its delivery, and that signatures of witnesses on the document are not necessary for its effectuality (9:4). Whether or not he agrees that signed witnesses also serve to validate a *get* is controversial among the commentators (see commentary ad loc.).

A major application of the dispute between R′ Meir and R′ Elazar is the meaning of the word וְכָתַב — *and he shall write* — in the above verse, from which many of the laws of *gittin* are derived. According to R′ Meir, the most important writing on the *get* is the signatures of the witnesses which validate it; hence, that is the writing to which the verse refers. R′ Elazar, however, maintains that such signatures are not required; thus, the verse refers to the text of the *get* itself — i.e., the *toref* [see above, s.v. *The Get*] (*Gem.* 34b).

The *Gemara* (86b) concludes that the *halachah* follows the view of R′ Elazar.

☙ *Rabbinic Annulment*

In certain cases, the Rabbis found it necessary to validate a divorce which is void by Biblical law (see commentary to 4:2 s.v. הִתְקִין). This presents a problem, since the Rabbis do not have the authority to permit the active transgression of a Biblical prohibition (*Yevamos* 89b), and the validation of such a divorce would allow another man to live with this woman, who is still married according to Biblical law.

Therefore, the Rabbis instituted a stipulation to every Jewish marriage that it be bound to their continued acquiescence. Thus, when circumstances demand the validation of a divorce which is Biblically void, the Rabbis retroactively annul the marriage in accordance with the original stipulation (*Gem.* 33a). This stipulation is the basis for the words כְּדַת מֹשֶׁה וְיִשְׂרָאֵל, *like the law of Moses and Israel*, which every man adds to his declaration of marriage [see ArtScroll Siddur (*Ashkenaz* ed.), p. 204] (*Tos.* ad loc. s.v. כל).

Notes Regarding the Commentary

As in the previous volumes of the Mishnah Series, every entry in the commentary has been carefully documented. Where the author has inserted a comment of his own, it is surrounded by brackets.

Untranslated Hebrew terms found in the Commentary are defined in the glossary at the end of the tractate.

Acknowledgments

This work has been written in commemoration of my dear father, Rabbi Yehuda Roberts, ז״ל, whose deep love of Torah and lifelong involvement in its dissemination inspired me to undertake this type of endeavor. His *Ahavas Hashem* (love of God), his unwavering faith in the face of the most trying circumstances, and his uncompromising commitment to the truth continue to serve as an inspiration — as well as a challenge — to his entire family. יְהִי זִכְרוֹ בָּרוּךְ — *May his memory be blessed.*

Although many people have shared in bringing this work to fruition, there are two whose contributions have been immeasurable: Rabbi Tzvi Zev Arem, who has been a patient guide and mentor, as well as an editor; and my wife, Leah, whose support and encouragement have been constant sources of strength.

Matis Roberts
Rosh Chodesh Sivan, 5745
Monsey, New York

פרק ראשון

Chapter One

[א] הַמֵּבִיא גֵט מִמְּדִינַת הַיָּם צָרִיךְ שֶׁיֹּאמַר: „בְּפָנַי נִכְתַּב וּבְפָנַי נֶחְתַּם".

ר' עובדיה מברטנורא

פרק ראשון – המביא גט. (א) המביא גט ממדינת הים. כל חוצה לארץ קרי מדינת הים: **צריך לומר בפני נכתב ובפני נחתם.** אית דאמרי טעמא, לפי שאין בני מדינת הים בני תורה, ואין יודעין שצריך לכתוב הגט לשם האשה, הלכך אומר השליח בפני נכתב ובפני נחתם, וממילא שיילינן ליה אם נכתב לשמה, והוא אומר אין. ואית דאמרי טעמא, לפי שאין שיירות מצויות משם לכאן, שאם יבא הבעל ויערער לומר לא כתבתיו, שיהיו עדים מצויין להכיר חתימת העדים, והאמינוהו רבנן לשליח כבתרי, ושוב לא יועיל ערעור הבעל:

יד אברהם

1.

הַמֵּבִיא גֵט — *One who brings a get*

[A man sent a *get* (bill of divorce) to his wife through an agent.]

Although it is the husband's act of giving the *get* to his wife which effects the divorce, he can nevertheless send it to her through an agent, whose delivery of the *get* on his behalf constitutes a valid act of divorce. The *Gemara* (*Kiddushin* 41a) derives this from the verse (*Deuteronomy* 24:1) which describes the divorce procedure with the expression *and he will send her from his house* rather than *he will divorce her* (*Tosafos Yov*).

מִמְּדִינַת הַיָּם — *from overseas*

[The agent brought the *get* to the wife in Eretz Yisrael (the Land of Israel) from the husband who was overseas (*Tiferes Yisrael*).]

All lands outside Eretz Yisrael are referred to as *overseas* (*Rav, Rashi*) [with the exception of Babylonia[1] (*Rashi*)].

Others comment that the term denotes distant lands and is used here to exclude cities along the border of the Holy Land. According to this *Tanna*, divorces brought from such cities do not require this testimony, as explained further in the mishnah (*Tosafos*).

צָרִיךְ שֶׁיֹּאמַר: „בְּפָנַי נִכְתַּב וּבְפָנַי נֶחְתַּם". — *must state: "It was written in my presence and signed in my presence."*

The agent delivering the *get* must testify before two men that he witnessed its writing and signing (*Rambam, Hilchos Gerushin* 7:5 from *Gem.* 5b).

The Rabbis required this testimony because they feared that a man who had a *get* prepared and sent to his wife might later deny that he had done so and declare it a forgery. If the *get* had been sent from a distant place, there would be no way for the woman to confirm the authenticity of the signatures. The Rabbis therefore ordained that the agent must attest to the validity of the *get* upon delivery, thus avoiding subsequent complications (*Gem.* 2b).

Actually, any legal document signed by two witnesses, which is presented in court, is considered fully validated by Biblical law, and no unsupported claim of forgery can be made against it. However, the Rabbis

1. Because there was a constant flow of travelers between Eretz Yisrael and Babylonia, the problem which necessitated the enactment in our mishnah — as explained below — was not pertinent to Babylonia (*Gem.* 6a).

1. **O**ne who brings a *get* from overseas must state: "It was written in my presence and signed

YAD AVRAHAM

enacted that the signatures of the witnesses must be confirmed[1] (*Gem.* 3a; see 1:3) [because they were concerned with the possibility of forgeries].

Although the mishnah implies that the agent must witness the writing of the *get*, it is sufficient if he hears the sound of writing on the parchment, as long as it was done at the behest of the husband (*Gem.* 6a). He must, however, actually observe the signing of the *get* by its witnesses (*Rambam, Hil. Gerushin* 7:12).

In the *Gemara* (2a), Rabbah maintains that there was another factor in addition to that of confirmation of the signatures which prompted the Rabbinic enactment requiring the agent's testimony. The mishnah (3:1) states that at the time a *get* is made, it must be intended specifically for the divorce of the particular woman to whom it is subsequently given. The *Gemara* (24b) derives this from the verse (*Deut.* 24:1): *And he shall write for her a document of divorce*, which means that it must be written with her in mind. This requirement is referred to as לִשְׁמָהּ, *with specific intent for her*, and the lack of it invalidates the *get*.

In communities of the Diaspora, there were those who were unaware of this requirement.[2] Therefore, the Rabbis ordained that an agent bringing a *get* from there must witness its

1. Whereas all other documents require two witnesses in order to validate them, a *get* need be validated only by the agent who delivers it. The reason for this is that since the very need to validate documents is due only to a Rabbinic enactment, the Rabbis were lenient in this case to avoid a situation in which a woman would be prevented from remarrying because she could not find two witnesses. However, in order to prevent people from mistakenly applying this leniency to other cases, they required that the agent also testify about the writing of the document, in addition to the signatures, thus indicating the singularity of this case (*Gem.* 3a).

Although a legal document must be validated by a court of law, which consists of at least three men, the agent need testify to its authenticity before only two men, because he can also be considered a member of the court which validates it. However, if a woman was the agent of delivery she would have to attest to having witnessed its writing and signing before three men, since she cannot be a member of a court of Jewish law (*Gem.* 5b).

2. The commentators note that among all the prerequisites for the validity of a *get*, the only one regarding which the Rabbis feared lack of compliance was that of specific intent. The explanation for this is based upon the *Gemara* (2b), which states that the possibility of laxity in a *get* is in reality, very remote, because *gittin* are written by professional scribes who know all of the laws and are unlikely to err. The only cause for concern is that the husband may have found a discarded *get*, written for a couple whose names are the same as his and his wife's (*Rashi* ad loc., s.v. ורבנן). [Since, on *gittin* and many other legal documents, family names are usually not used, and people are referred to only by their given name and that of their father (e.g. *Yitzchak, the son of Avraham*), this possibility is not as remote as it may appear.] In such a case, the only flaw in the *get* is the lack of specific intent (*Meiri*).

Another approach is that the laxity outside Eretz Yisrael in complying with the rule of specific intent was not due to ignorance, but rather because there were those who disagreed with the exegetical basis for the entire concept. No other facet of the laws of *gittin* aroused a similar controversy (*Tos.*).

גיטין
א/א

רַבָּן גַּמְלִיאֵל אוֹמֵר: אַף הַמֵּבִיא מִן הָרֶקֶם וּמִן הַחֶגֶר. רַבִּי אֱלִיעֶזֶר אוֹמֵר: אֲפִלּוּ מִכְּפַר לוּדִים לְלוּד. וַחֲכָמִים אוֹמְרִים: אֵינוֹ צָרִיךְ שֶׁיֹּאמַר: ,,בְּפָנַי נִכְתַּב וּבְפָנַי נֶחְתַּם״, אֶלָּא הַמֵּבִיא מִמְּדִינַת הַיָּם וְהַמּוֹלִיךְ.

ר׳ עובדיה מברטנורא

מן הרקם ומן החגר. בין קדש ובין ברד (בראשית טז,יד), מתרגמינן בין רקם ובין חגרא: **אפילו מכפר לודים.** שהיא מחוצה לארץ, ללוד, שהיא סמוכה לה והיא מארץ ישראל:

יד אברהם

writing and signing[1] so that he can then be asked if they were done with specific intent[2] (*Rav* from *Gem.* 2b, *Rashi*). According to this, the need for testimony is extended also to a case of delivery of a *get* within a foreign land. In such a case, confirmation of the signatures is readily available, but the question of specific intent still exists (*Gem.* 4b).

Neither the Mishnah nor the *Gemara* makes any explicit reference to the agent being asked about specific intent. This leads some commentators to the conclusion that once the agent has testified to having witnessed the writing of the *get*, we can assume that it was done with specific intent (*Tos.*). The reason for this is that the agent will understand that he is being relied upon to attest to the *get's* validity, and will therefore mention any deviation from normal procedure which occurred. Alternatively, the possibility that the *get* was written for one man's wife in this agent's presence and then was discarded or lost and found by another, who then chose this same person as an agent, is too unlikely to merit serious concern (*Ran*).

The Rabbis could have required the agent to say: "It was written in my presence with specific intent and signed in my presence with specific intent." However, they felt that making the required testimony this lengthy would increase the likelihood that the agent would abbreviate his words and leave out the information regarding specific intent (*Gem.*

1. The word לָהּ, *for her*, from which the requirement for specific intent is derived, refers to the word וְכָתַב, *and he shall write*, which immediately precedes it. Therefore, according to R' Meir, who holds that the signatures of the witnesses validate the *get* and thus, the writing to which the verse refers (see General Introduction, s.v. *The Witnesses*), only they must be written with specific intent but not the text of the *get* itself. The mishnah, which requires specific intent for the writing of the text of the *get*, as well as its signatures, must be following the opinion of R' Elazar, who maintains that signed witnesses are not necessary for a *get* and, thus, the verse refers to the writing of the text of the *get* itself (ibid.). Despite the fact that the witnesses' signatures are not necessary, if they do appear on the *get* they are considered part of the document itself and must therefore be in compliance with all of its regulations (*Gem.* 3a).

2. Although testimony regarding marital status always requires two witnesses, in this case we rely solely upon this agent to grant the woman a divorce. This is because the possibility of the *get* having been written without specific intent is really too remote to demand consideration, yet the Rabbis decided nonetheless to safeguard against it. Consequently, they were lenient in their requirements for testimony to avoid preventing the woman from remarrying because she could not find two witnesses to testify that the *get* had been written with specific intent (*Gem.* 2b).

1 in my presence." Rabban Gamliel says: Also one who
1 brings [it] from Rekem or from Cheger. R' Eliezer says: Even from Kefar Ludim to Lud. The Sages, however, say: One is not required to state: "It was written in my presence and signed in my presence,' unless he is bringing it from overseas or taking it [overseas].

3a).[1] Were this to occur, it would invalidate the divorce, even if he subsequently clarified that the *get* was written with specific intent, because the divorce process is bound to the Rabbinic ordinances which regulate it. Therefore, if explicit testimony about specific intent were required at the time of delivery, failure to provide it would constitute a violation of the laws governing the divorce and would thus invalidate it (*Rashi* ad loc. s.v. אתי למיגזייה).

רַבָּן גַּמְלִיאֵל אוֹמֵר: אַף הַמֵּבִיא מִן הָרֶקֶם וּמִן הַחֶגֶר. — *Rabban Gamliel says: Also one who brings [it] from Rekem or from Cheger.*

[An agent bringing a *get* from Rekem or Cheger must attest to its having been written and signed in his presence.]

Rekem and Cheger are the Aramaic names for the towns of Kadesh and Bered [mentioned in *Genesis* 16:14] (*Rav; Rashi*).

Rabban Gamliel disagrees with the first, anonymous *Tanna*, who maintains that these cities do not require this testimony because they border Eretz Yisrael, and witnesses to confirm the signatures were therefore readily available. Rabban Gamliel, however, maintains that the availability of witnesses was not certain enough to be relied upon (*Gem.* 44a).

According to the opinion of Rabbah (discussed above), the first *Tanna's* reason is that, due to their proximity to Eretz Yisrael, the populace of these towns was well aware of the rule of specific intent (ibid.).

רַבִּי אֱלִיעֶזֶר אוֹמֵר: אֲפִלּוּ מִכְּפַר לוּדִים לְלוּד. — *R' Eliezer says: Even from Kefar Ludim to Lud.*

The borderline of Eretz Yisrael is irregular, with areas which extend farther outward than others. Kefar Ludim was just outside the border at a point between two of these protrusions. It was thus "swallowed up" within the extensions of the border. Because of this, both the first *Tanna* and Rabban Gamliel agree that it has all of the advantages of the Land in regard to the delivery of a *get*, and no testimony is required. R' Eliezer, however, maintains that the Rabbis did not differentiate among cities outside of Eretz Yisrael, and — in order to avoid confusion — included in their enactment even those areas where it was not really necessary (*Gem.* 6a).

The mishnah specifies Lud as the destination of the *get* to teach us that, although Kefar Ludim was named for its proximity to Lud and for the fact that the citizens of Lud were constantly there, it is nevertheless not considered a part of Lud itself. Thus, R' Eliezer still requires the agent to testify when bringing the *get* (*Tos.*).

וַחֲכָמִים אוֹמְרִים: אֵינוֹ צָרִיךְ שֶׁיֹּאמַר: „בְּפָנַי נִכְתַּב וּבְפָנַי נֶחְתַּם", אֶלָּא הַמֵּבִיא מִמְּדִינַת הַיָּם וְהַמּוֹלִיךְ. — *The Sages, however,*

1. [Since there are no specifications given for the two men before whom the agent testifies, we cannot assume that they will be sufficiently learned to make certain that he presents his testimony properly.]

וְהַמֵּבִיא מִמְּדִינָה לִמְדִינָה בִּמְדִינַת הַיָּם צָרִיךְ שֶׁיֹּאמַר: ,,בְּפָנַי נִכְתַּב וּבְפָנַי נֶחְתַּם״. רַבָּן שִׁמְעוֹן בֶּן גַּמְלִיאֵל אוֹמֵר: אֲפִלּוּ מֵהֶגְמוֹנְיָא לְהֶגְמוֹנְיָא.

[ב] **רַבִּי** יְהוּדָה אוֹמֵר: מֵרֶקֶם לַמִּזְרָח, וְרֶקֶם כַּמִּזְרָח; מֵאַשְׁקְלוֹן לַדָּרוֹם, וְאַשְׁקְלוֹן כַּדָּרוֹם; מֵעַכּוֹ לַצָּפוֹן, וְעַכּוֹ כַּצָּפוֹן.

ר׳ עובדיה מברטנורא

מהגמוניא להגמוניא. שני הגמונים בעיר אחת, ומקפידים זה על זה: **(ב) מרקם למזרח.** מרקם עד סוף העולם למזרחו, קרוי חוצה לארץ. ורקם עצמה נדונה כמזרח העולם ולא כארץ ישראל:

יד אברהם

say: One is not required to state: "It was written in my presence and signed in my presence," unless he is bringing it from overseas or taking it [overseas].

[I.e., from overseas to Eretz Yisrael or vice versa.]

It is clear that the first *Tanna* also does not distinguish between bringing a *get* to or from the Holy Land, since the availability of witnesses to confirm the signatures depends upon the amount of travel between the two areas. Thus, the Sages are not contesting the statement of the first *Tanna*, but are rather explaining that it applies equally if the *get* is sent overseas from Eretz Yisrael (*Gem.* 4b).

וְהַמֵּבִיא מִמְּדִינָה לִמְדִינָה בִּמְדִינַת הַיָּם צָרִיךְ שֶׁיֹּאמַר: ,,בְּפָנַי נִכְתַּב וּבְפָנַי נֶחְתַּם״. — *One who brings [a get] from province to province overseas must say: "It was written in my presence and signed in my presence."*

This is because, outside of the Holy Land, if a *get* is brought from one province to another, there exists the same concern for the availability of document confirmation as when one is brought from foreign lands to Eretz Yisrael.

The wording of the mishnah implies that even in foreign lands, testimony is required only when delivering a *get* between provinces, and not within one province. According to Rabbah, however, testimony is always required within foreign lands because of the fear that the *get* had not been made with specific intent. Accordingly, the case of delivery between provinces is stated only to imply that in Eretz Yisrael it is not required even in such an instance. Although the mishnah says this explicitly below, we might think that, initially, the agent must testify that he witnessed the writing and signing of the *get* even when he delivers it within the Land, and that only expost facto, if he did not witness them, may he still deliver the *get*. The *Tanna* therefore adds this implication to indicate that testimony is not required even from the outset (*Gem.* 4b; *Tos.* ad loc. s.v. אי; cf. *Rashi*).

רַבָּן שִׁמְעוֹן בֶּן גַּמְלִיאֵל אוֹמֵר: אֲפִלּוּ מֵהֶגְמוֹנְיָא לְהֶגְמוֹנְיָא. — *Rabban Shimon ben Gamliel says: Even from rulership to rulership.*

This refers to one city divided into two rulerships which maintain a closed border between them (*Rav* from *Gem.* 4b).

One who brings [a *get*] from province to province overseas must say: "It was written in my presence and signed in my presence." Rabban Shimon ben Gamliel says: Even from rulership to rulership.

2. **R**' Yehudah says: From Rekem eastward [is considered outside *Eretz Yisrael]*, and Rekem is like the East; from Ashkelon southward, and Ashkelon is like the South; form Acco northward, and Acco is like the North.

YAD AVRAHAM

[An agent delivering a *get* from one of these rulerships to the other must testify that he witnessed its writing and signing.]

The specific example which prompted the mention of this case was in Eretz Yisrael, and it is thus clear that the enactment was due to the need for signature confirmation, since in Eretz Yisrael there was full compliance with the rule of specific intent. This is the source for the *Gemara's* conclusion that Rabbah agrees that this is the issue of primary concern to the mishnah; he maintains only that the concern of specific intent was an additional reason for the enactment.

If the agent presented the *get* without saying: "It was written in my presence and signed in my presence," there is a disagreement cited in *Gemara* (5b) as to its validity. R' Meir holds that it is totally void. The Sages opine that the agent should take it back and redeliver it in the prescribed manner. If he does not, the *get* cannot take effect unless the signatures on it are confirmed from other sources (*Rambam, Hil. Gerushin* 7:17; *Rosh* 5).

2.

This mishnah is a continuation of the previous one, which states that an agent who delivers a *get* from outside Eretz Yisrael must attest to having witnessed its writing and signing. The *Tanna* now defines the borders of the Holy Land.

רַבִּי יְהוּדָה אוֹמֵר: מֵרֶקֶם לַמִּזְרָח, וְרֶקֶם כַּמִּזְרָח; — *R' Yehudah says: From Rekem eastward [is considered outside Eretz Yisrael], and Rekem is like the East;*

From Rekem to the easternmost ends of the world is considered outside of the Holy Land. Rekem itself is considered part of this section, and not a part of Eretz Yisrael (*Rav; Rashi*). Therefore, one who brings a *get* from Rekem and eastward to the Holy Land [or any other province (mishnah 1; and commentary ad loc. s.v. (וְהַמֵּבִיא))] must testify: "It was written in my presence and signed in my presence" (*Rashi*).

מֵאַשְׁקְלוֹן לַדָּרוֹם, וְאַשְׁקְלוֹן כַּדָּרוֹם; מֵעַכּוֹ לַצָּפוֹן, וְעַכּוֹ כַּצָּפוֹן. — *from Ashkelon southward, and Ashkelon is like the South; from Acco northward, and Acco is like the North.*

These towns, too, are considered outside Eretz Yisrael, and one who brings a *get* from them to the Holy Land must state this testimony (*Rashi*).

רַבִּי מֵאִיר אוֹמֵר: עַכּוֹ כְּאֶרֶץ יִשְׂרָאֵל לְגִטִּין.

[ג] **הַמֵּבִיא** גֵּט בְּאֶרֶץ יִשְׂרָאֵל אֵינוֹ צָרִיךְ שֶׁיֹּאמַר: ,,בְּפָנַי נִכְתַּב וּבְפָנַי נֶחְתַּם". אִם יֵשׁ עָלָיו עוֹרְרִים — יִתְקַיֵּם בְּחוֹתְמָיו.

ר' עובדיה מברטנורא

(ג) **ואם יש עליו עוררים.** שהבעל מערער שהוא מזוייף: **יתקיים בחותמיו.** אם יעידו העדים על חתימת ידיהם, או עדים אחרים יכירו חתימתם, כשר. ובזמן הזה, המביא גט בין בארץ ישראל בין בחוצה לארץ צריך ליתנו לה בפני שנים, וצריך לומר בפני נכתב ובפני נחתם, ואם חתימת העדים נכרת במקום נתינת הגט ונתקיים הגט בחותמיו, אין צריך לומר בפני נכתב ובפני נחתם:

יד אברהם

The western border is not mentioned here because Eretz Yisrael is bordered on that side by the Mediterranean Sea (*Rashi*). Others interpret the mishnah as defining the corner borders of the Holy Land with Rekem to the northeast, Ashkelon to the southwest, and Acco to the northwest. It was well known that the southeastern border was the Dead Sea, and therefore it did not require mention (*Tos. Yom Tov* quoting *Kaftor Vaferach*).

Although all three of these cities are mentioned either in Scripture or the Talmud as being within Eretz Yisrael, the mishnah lists them as being outside the borders — each for a different reason. Ashkelon, though part of the Land in Biblical times, was not reconquered during the era of the Second Temple, and its inhabitants were neither available for signature confirmation nor reliable in regard to the rule of specific intent. Thus, *gittin* coming from there to Eretz Yisrael required the testimony of the agent (*Tos.*). Although we find reference to the capture of the crossroads of Ashkelon during the resettlement of the Land in that period, this could refer to a crossroad nearby Ashkelon and not one within the city itself (*Ran*).

In regard to Rekem, *Rabbeinu Tam* asserts that there are two sets of twin cities referred to in Scripture as Kadesh and Bered, or — in Aramaic — Rekem and Cheger. One of these sets was within Eretz Yisrael, and one was outside the border. It is this latter pair outside the border which is referred to in our mishnah. Acco, on the other hand, was half within the Holy Land and half without; the outer half is the area our mishnah is discussing.

Ri suggests that all of these towns were within the borders of Eretz Yisrael, but were far from the main settlements, and their inhabitants were not readily available for signature confirmation nor totally aware of the requirement of specific intent. Therefore, a *get* delivered from one of them required the testimony of the agent.

רַבִּי מֵאִיר אוֹמֵר: עַכּוֹ כְּאֶרֶץ יִשְׂרָאֵל לַגִּטִּין — *R' Meir says: Acco is like Eretz Yisrael regarding gittin.*

There is no cause for concern in regard to signature confirmation or specific intent in Acco (*Rashi* 8a s.v. לגיטין אין). [Consequently, an agent bringing a *get* from there is not required to say, "It was written in my presence and signed in my presence." Assumedly, R' Meir drew his opinion from his knowledge of the situation in Acco.]

3.

הַמֵּבִיא גֵט בְּאֶרֶץ יִשְׂרָאֵל אֵינוֹ צָרִיךְ שֶׁיֹּאמַר: ,,בְּפָנַי נִכְתַּב וּבְפָנַי נֶחְתַּם". — *One who brings a get within Eretz Yisrael is not required to say: "It was written in my*

R' Meir says: Acco is like *Eretz Yisrael* regarding *gittin.*

3. **O**ne who brings a *get* within *Eretz Yisrael* is not required to say: "It was written in my presence and signed in my presence." If there are protesters against it, it should be validated through its signatures.

YAD AVRAHAM

presence and signed in my presence."

In Eretz Yisrael, the flow of travel was sufficiently heavy so as to ensure the availability of confirmation of signatures even between provinces, and the rule of specific intent was universally complied with. It was therefore unnecessary for the agent delivering the *get* to testify regarding these facts (*Gem.* 4b).

However, if the agent did testify to that effect, his testimony is accepted, just as with a *get* coming from a foreign land, and the validity of the *get* can no longer be challenged by the husband (*Gem.* 6b).

— אִם יֵשׁ עָלָיו עוֹרְרִים — *If there are protesters against it,*

This refers to the dissent of the husband, who claims it was forged (*Rav* from *Gem.* 9a).

However, if the husband is silent and one witness claims it was forged, the latter is ignored. On the other hand, if two witnesses are dissenters, they are not overruled by the confirmation of the signatures, and the woman retains her status of a married woman. Therefore, this cannot be the case referred to in the mishnah, which states that confirmation validates the *get* (*Gem.* 9a).

Tosafos point out that if the woman tries to collect the amount of her *kesubah* (the marriage contract, which requires every husband to pay his wife a dower upon his death or their divorce) from possessors of fields upon which she has a lien by virtue of the *kesubah,* they, too, have the right to demand validation of the *get* before she can collect. This would explain the plural form of the word *protesters* in the mishnah (*Tos. Yom Tov*).

Ran, however, maintains that even without any protest from the owners of the fields, the courts will stay her lien until confirmation of the signatures is obtained. According to this opinion, the only possible protestor referred to in the mishnah is the husband, and the use of the plural form seems inappropriate. However, since the words of any other sole dissenter are ignored, yet the dissent of the husband is heeded, the mishnah uses the plural form in reference to the husband to emphasize his special capacity (ibid.).

.יִתְקַיֵּם בְּחוֹתְמָיו — *it should be validated through its signatures.*

[If the husband claims that the *get* was forged, the signatures on the *get* must be confirmed in order for it to be validated.]

This is done either by the witnesses themselves confirming their signatures or by other witnesses who recognize them (*Rav*). Another method is to compare the signatures on the *get* with the signatures of these same witnesses on another document which has been certified as valid by the courts (*Kesubos* 2:2, see *Rashi*).

If the husband claimed that the *get* was a forgery, and it could not be validated, the woman retains her status as this man's wife (*Rambam, Hil. Gerushin* 7:2; *Even Haezer* 141:53).

הַמֵּבִיא גֵט מִמְּדִינַת הַיָּם וְאֵינוֹ יָכוֹל לוֹמַר: "בְּפָנַי נִכְתַּב וּבְפָנַי נֶחְתַּם" — אִם יֵשׁ עָלָיו עֵדִים יִתְקַיֵּם בְּחוֹתְמָיו.

[ד] **אֶחָד** גִּטֵּי נָשִׁים וְאֶחָד שִׁחְרוּרֵי עֲבָדִים שָׁוו לַמּוֹלִיךְ וְלַמֵּבִיא. וְזוֹ אֶחָד

ר' עובדיה מברטנורא

ואינו יכול לומר. כגון שנתנו [לה] כשהוא פקח, ולא הספיק לומר בפני נכתב ובפני נחתם עד שנתחרש: (ד) **שוין למוליך ולמביא.** לומר בפני נכתב ובפני נחתם:

יד אברהם

The implication of the mishnah is that as long as the husband did not protest, the *get* is accepted as valid. Some commentaries derive from this that confirmation of a legal document is required only when there is a claim of forgery (*Ran* citing *Tos.*). Others say that only in regard to *gittin* were the Rabbis lenient, so as not to put the woman in a situation that would prevent her from remarrying (*Tos.*).

הַמֵּבִיא גֵט מִמְּדִינַת הַיָּם וְאֵינוֹ יָכוֹל לוֹמַר: "בְּפָנַי נִכְתַּב וּבְפָנַי נֶחְתַּם" — *One who brings a get from overseas and is unable to say: "It was written in my presence and signed in my presence"* —

This refers to a deaf-mute, who is unable to give testimony. The mishnah is speaking of a case in which he was stricken with this condition immediately upon delivering the *get*, before he had the opportunity to testify. Otherwise, he would not be legally qualified to serve as an agent for the delivery of the *get*, since a deaf-mute is considered mentally incompetent[1] (*Rav* from *Gem.* 9a, *Rashi* ad loc.; see comm. to 2:5).

The agent must state his testimony at the time he delivers the *get*. From the *Gemara's* language in qualifying our mishnah, it is obvious that he may also do so if he begins saying it תּוֹךְ כְּדֵי דִיבּוּר, *within the time it takes to say three words*,[2] after he has handed over the *get*. Since the *Gemara* says that the agent was stricken with the condition *before he had the opportunity to testify*, it is clear that had he not been stricken, he would have had an opportunity to testify even after delivering the *get*. [It is assumed that this grace period is limited to the time it takes to say three words, because this is the duration within which a speaker is still considered to be making the same statement.] *Ri* is undecided what the *halachah* would be if the agent testified after this amount of time — but while they were still involved with the divorce — or if he testified before he handed over

1. Although a mute who is not deaf is not considered mentally incompetent (*Rambam, Hil. Ishus* 2:26), the *Gemara* could not interpret the mishnah to be discussing a case where a mute brought the *get*. This is because he could still testify that he witnessed the writing and signing of the *get* by way of body motions or writing (*Tiferes Yaakov;* cf. commentary to 7:1, s.v. וְהִרְכִּין).

2. Specifically, these three words: שָׁלוֹם עָלֶיךָ, רַבִּי (*Rambam, Hil. Shevuos* 2:17).

1
4

One who brings a *get* from overseas and is unable to say: "It was written in my presence and signed in my presence" — if there are witnesses on it, it should be validated through its signatures.

4. Both *gittin* and [documents of] emancipation of slaves correspond in regard to being taken [from *Eretz Yisrael*] and being brought [there]. This

the *get* (*Tos.* 5b s.v. יטלנו).

אִם יֵשׁ עָלָיו עֵדִים יִתְקַיֵּם בְּחוֹתְמָיו. — *if there are witnesses on it, it should be validated through its signatures.*

[Since the agent is unable to supply the required testimony that it was written and signed in his presence, the *get* cannot take effect unless the signatures on the document are verified.]

According to Rabbah, who maintains that the mishnah is concerned also about specific intent, the confirmation of the signatures alone should not suffice to allay our fears that the *get* is invalid. The *Gemara* (5a) explains, however, that the principle of specific intent was eventually complied with universally, even outside Eretz Yisrael. The requirement of the agent's testimony was only retained for fear of a relapse to the original neglect but it was not extended to include unusual circumstances, such as those of our mishnah.

4.

אֶחָד גִּטֵּי נָשִׁים וְאֶחָד שִׁחְרוּרֵי עֲבָדִים — *Both gittin* (lit., *documents of women) and [documents of] emancipation of slaves*

The Torah (*Leviticus* 25:44) permits the acquisition of non-Jewish slaves by Jewish owners. The mishnah (*Kiddushin* 1:3) states that one of the means of freeing such a slave is with a document of emancipation.

שָׁוו לַמּוֹלִיךְ וְלַמֵּבִיא. — *correspond in regard to being taken [from Eretz Yisrael] and being brought [there].*

They are alike in the respect that in both cases, the agent who delivers them must say, "It was written in my presence and signed in my presence" (*Rav, Rashi*).

[A document of emancipation requires confirmation of the signatures on it, just like any other legal document. Therefore, one which is brought from a foreign land requires this testimony from the agent in order to confirm its validity.]

Concerning the issue of specific intent, its requirement in a *get* is derived from the word לָהּ, *[for] her*, in the verse (*Deut.* 24:1) which prescribes the *get's* requisites (see mishnah 1). The same word is used by the Torah (*Lev.* 19:20) regarding a document of emancipation; therefore, the same law is derived (*Rambam, Hil. Avadim* 6:6).

Just as the Rabbis were lenient in their enactment for the sake of preventing a difficult situation for the woman (*Gem.* 3a, see footnote to mishnah 1, s.v. צָרִיךְ), and relied upon one witness to validate the *get*, so too were they lenient for the sake of a slave. Since the document of emancipation has been delivered, but not confirmed, the slave's status is in doubt, for if the document is valid and he is free, he becomes a full-fledged Jew (see *Rambam, Hil. Issurei*

מִן הַדְּרָכִים שֶׁשָׁווּ גִּטֵי נָשִׁים לְשִׁחְרוּרֵי עֲבָדִים.

[ה] **כָּל** גֵּט שֶׁיֵּשׁ עָלָיו עֵד כּוּתִי פָּסוּל, חוּץ מִגִּטֵי נָשִׁים וְשִׁחְרוּרֵי עֲבָדִים. מַעֲשֶׂה

━━━━━━━━━━ **ר' עובדיה מברטנורא** ━━━━━━━━━━

(ה) **חוץ מגיטי נשים.** שָׁאִם יֵשׁ עָלָיו עֵד כּוּתִי אֶחָד, כָּשֵׁר. אֲבָל שְׁנֵיהֶם כּוּתִים, פּוֹסֵל תַּנָּא קַמָּא אֲפִילוּ בְּגִטֵּי נָשִׁים. וְרַבָּן (שִׁמְעוֹן בֶּן) גַּמְלִיאֵל עָשָׂה מַעֲשֶׂה וְהִכְשִׁיר אֲפִילוּ כְּשֶׁשְׁנֵיהֶם כּוּתִים. וְהָאִידְנָא דְּגָזְרוּ עַל הַכּוּתִים שֶׁיִּהְיוּ כַגּוֹיִם לְכָל דִּבְרֵיהֶם, לֹא שְׁנָא שְׁאָר שְׁטָרוֹת וְלֹא שְׁנָא גִּטֵּי נָשִׁים אֲפִילוּ עֵד אֶחָד כּוּתִי פָּסוּל:

יד אברהם

Biah 13:12). Under these circumstances, he cannot marry either a slave — since he might be a bona fide Jew — or a Jewess — since he might be a slave. Such a situation is considered sufficient hardship to warrant the leniency of this enactment (Ran; Meiri).

וְזוֹ אֶחָד מִן הַדְּרָכִים שֶׁשָׁווּ גִּטֵי נָשִׁים לְשִׁחְרוּרֵי עֲבָדִים. — *This is one of the ways in which gittin correspond to [documents of] emancipation of slaves.*

[Several other parallels will be enumerated in the following mishnayos.]

It would have been more precise to say that documents of emancipation correspond to *gittin*, since it is in regard to the latter that the law of the agent's testimony was initially stated. However, the mishnah stated the analogy in this manner, because *gittin* is the topic discussed up to now (*Tos.*).

5.

◆§ **Cutheans**

The Cutheans (Samaritans), or Cuthites, were a group of peoples from different lands, including Cuthah, whom the king of Assyria settled in the land of Samaria during the era of the First Temple. Initially, they did not fear God, and He sent lions who began to attack and kill them. Upon hearing of this, the king sent one of the *Kohanim* who had been exiled from the Land to teach them the Jewish tradition. Under his guidance, they converted to Judaism — although they continued to worship their own idols as well — and the danger passed (*II Kings* 17:24ff.).

There is a dispute among the *Tannaim* as to whether their conversion was valid (*Kiddushin* 75b; *Niddah* 66b; *Tos.* to *Chullin* 3b). Even among those who maintain that they were properly converted, some consider them unfit for many functions in Jewish law. This is because they did not accept the Rabbinic interpretation of the Torah, and thus could not be relied upon to fulfill the commandments correctly (*Gem.* 10a).

כָּל גֵּט שֶׁיֵּשׁ עָלָיו עֵד כּוּתִי פָּסוּל, — *Every document which has a Cuthean witness on it is void,*

The *Gemara* (10a) explains that the *Tanna* of the mishnah is R' Elazar, who forbids eating matzah made by

Cutheans, because they are not careful in the details of Jewish laws. Likewise, their testimonies are not to be trusted. Therefore, if even one of the witnesses on a document is a Cuthean, it lacks the required two valid wit-

is one of the ways in which *gittin* correspond to [documents of] emancipation of slaves.

5. Every document which has a Cuthean witness on it is void, except for *gittin* and [documents of] emancipation of slaves. It once occurred that

YAD AVRAHAM

nesses and is thus void.

.חוּץ מִגִּטֵּי נָשִׁים וְשִׁחְרוּרֵי עֲבָדִים — *except for gittin and [documents of] emancipation of slaves.*

[Either of these is valid even if one of the witnesses who signed it is a Cuthean.]

The mishnah is speaking of a case in which the first witness who signed on the document is a Cuthean, and the second is a Jew. Were the Cuthean not recognized by the Jew as one who is reliable in his performance of the commandments, he would not have accorded him the honor of allowing him to sign first on the document. Therefore, the testimony of the Cuthean is accepted. This assumption, however, is valid only when dealing with a *get* or a document of emancipation, because there is a Rabbinic law regarding these documents which requires the two witnesses to sign in each other's presence. Other documents, however, do not require this, and it is therefore possible that the Jewish witness signed on the bottom to leave room for the signature of an older witness whom he assumed would be signing. Instead, the owner of the document had the Cuthean sign, thus invalidating the document (*Gem.* 10a-b).

The reason for requiring the witnesses of a *get* or document of emancipation to sign in each other's presence is as follows:

If a man tells a group of people: "I want all of you to write a *get* for my wife" (6:7), this is considered a stipulation to the *get* and they all must sign on the document in order for it to be effective. If the witnesses would be allowed to sign separately, the wife or slave might possibly receive the *get* before it is signed by the entire group. Seeing two or more witnesses signed upon the document, the recipient will think that it is valid when it is really not, and act accordingly. Because of the stringency of the laws involved, the Rabbis decreed that each of the witnesses must sign in the presence of all the others so as to preclude this possibility. As an extra precaution, the Rabbis required that all *gittin* and documents of emancipation — even those which had no such stipulation — be signed by each of their witnesses in the presence of the other (*Gem.* 10b; *Rashi* ad loc.; *Tos. Yom Tov*).

Since it is the signature of the Jewish witness beneath it which legitimizes that of the Cuthean, the validity of the *get*, in reality, rests solely on the credibility of one witness. This being the case, the *get* would seem to be invalid, since it must derive its effectiveness from the testimony of two witnesses. However, the *Tanna* of the mishnah is among those who assume that the Cutheans were properly converted, and he therefore considers their testimony to be legally valid (*Tos.* 10b s.v. אי לאו). [The Rabbis required a greater degree of caution in using Cutheans due to their lapses in fulfilling the commandments, but in a case such as ours where there is corroboration from another source, they retain their status as legal witnesses.]

In later times, the Rabbis decreed that the Cutheans were to be considered as gentiles in all matters because they reverted to idolatry (*Rav; Chullin* 6a). Therefore, they are no longer valid as witnesses, even on *gittin* or documents of emancipation (*Rav*).

שֶׁהֵבִיאוּ לִפְנֵי רַבָּן גַּמְלִיאֵל לִכְפַר עוֹתְנַאי גֵּט אִשָּׁה, וְהָיוּ עֵדָיו עֵדֵי כוּתִים, וְהִכְשִׁיר.

כָּל הַשְּׁטָרוֹת הָעוֹלִים בְּעַרְכָּאוֹת שֶׁל גּוֹיִם, אַף עַל פִּי שֶׁחוֹתְמֵיהֶם גּוֹיִם, כְּשֵׁרִים, חוּץ מִגִּטֵּי נָשִׁים

ר׳ עובדיה מברטנורא

בערכאות של גוים. שהעידו העדים עדותם לפני השופט במקום מושב משפטיהם. והוא שידענו בהותו שופט ובהותם עדים דלה מקבלי שוחדה. ודוקה בשטרי הלוהות ושטרי מקח וממכר, שהעדים רהו בנתינת הממון, הבל שטרי הודהות וגיטי נשים, וכל דבר שהוה מעשה בית דין, בערכהות שלהם, הכל פסול:

יד אברהם

מַעֲשֶׂה שֶׁהֵבִיאוּ לִפְנֵי רַבָּן גַּמְלִיאֵל לִכְפַר עוֹתְנַאי גֵּט אִשָּׁה, וְהָיוּ עֵדָיו עֵדֵי כוּתִים, וְהִכְשִׁיר. — *It once occurred that they brought before Rabban Gamliel in Kefar Usnai a get whose witnesses were Cutheans, and he validated [it].*

R' Gamliel accepted the *get* even though both of the witnesses were Cutheans. This does not correspond to the previous statement in the mishnah, which only validates a *get* with one Cuthean witness.

It is thus evident that the mishnah has been abridged, and should read as follows: *Rabban Gamliel, however, validates [a get or a document of emancipation] with [even] two [Cuthean witnesses]. It once occurred that they brought before ...* (*Gem.* 10b).

Rabban Gamliel agrees with the view of Rabban Shimon ben Gamliel, who is of the opinion that those laws which the Cutheans accepted upon themselves, they fulfilled more meticulously than other Jews (*Gem.* 10a). Rabban Gamliel maintains that the Cutheans accepted the laws of *gittin* and emancipation, but not the regulations of other legal documents. Therefore, they are totally reliable with regard to the former two types of documents, and these are valid with even two Cuthean witnesses. For other documents, however, they are not to be relied upon at all (*Tos.*).

An alternative explanation offered by the *Gemara* for the connection between the incident of Rabban Gamliel and the previous statement of the mishnah is that the text of the mishnah should be emended to read *whose witness was a Cuthean,* in the singular form. Accordingly, the event depicted is simply an illustration of the previous *halachah.*

☙ Gentile Witnesses

Since legal documents must be signed by two qualified Jewish witnesses in order to be valid in Jewish law, one signed by gentiles is totally void. Nevertheless, the Rabbis ascribed validity to such documents under the circumstances described in this mishnah.

כָּל הַשְּׁטָרוֹת הָעוֹלִים בְּעַרְכָּאוֹת שֶׁל גּוֹיִם, — *All documents which are processed* (lit., *go up*) *in gentile courts,*

Witnesses testified about them before a non-Jewish court of law, and it is known that both the judges and witnesses do not accept bribes (*Rav*).

אַף עַל פִּי שֶׁחוֹתְמֵיהֶם גּוֹיִם, כְּשֵׁרִים, —

they brought before Rabban Gamliel in Kefar Usnai a *get* whose witnesses were Cutheans, and he validated [it].

All documents which are processed in gentile courts, although their signatories are gentiles, are valid, except for *gittin* and [documents of] emanci-

YAD AVRAHAM

although their signatories are gentiles, are valid,

This refers to documents which attest to the transactions of sales or gifts (*Rav; Gem.* 10b). We can safely rely upon the integrity of these witnesses because they would be willing to perjure themselves (*Gem.* ibid.). The Rabbis therefore enacted to accept these as valid documents, even though, in Biblical law, they lack legitimate witnesses and cannot be used (*Ran*).

Another version in the *Gemara* explains the mishnah to include even those documents of sales of gifts which are used for actually effecting the transfer of property, not only for evidence thereof. This is based upon the principle of דִּינָא דְּמַלְכוּתָא דִּינָא, *the law of the land is binding according to Jewish law* — i.e., that monetary laws set by a government are binding by Jewish law (*Rambam, Hil. Zechiyah* 1:15), as long as they are applied equally to all citizens of the land (*Choshen Mishpat* 369:8). [Therefore, transactions which are executed with these documents are halachically valid.]

The first opinion rejects the application in our mishnah of the universally accepted principle that the law of the land is binding. This is because the principle is applicable only when the law involved is enacted for the benefit of the king, but does not apply to other laws of the government. In the case of our mishnah however, the king has no vested interest in the *halachah* of the document's validity. Alternatively, this view in the *Gemara* construes the mishnah to include those cases in which the courts are not officially designated by the government; hence, the aforementioned principle does not apply (*Ran*).

There is a dispute among the authorities concerning the *halachah* of a document upon which a loan is recorded, according to the first opinion that documents signed by gentile witnesses are valid only to serve as evidence, but not to effect a transaction. Some maintain that since a documented loan is dealt with differently in several aspects than one attested to orally, the former is considered as one which effects a transaction,[1] and consequently, gentile witnesses cannot be used. Others maintain that since the basic debt is due to the loan itself and is not brought about by the fact that it was recorded, the document is primarily considered one for purposes of evidence, and gentile witnesses are valid if the requirements stated in this mishnah are met (*Rambam, Hil. Malveh* 27:1; *Maggid Mishneh* ad loc.).

.חוּץ מִגִּטֵּי נָשִׁים וְשִׁחְרוּרֵי עֲבָדִים — *except for gittin and [documents of] emancipation of slaves.*

[*Gittin* and emancipation documents which are processed in gentile courts with gentile witnesses are not valid in Jewish law.]

Since only documents of evidence are acceptable in this manner, but not those which effect a transaction, *gittin*

1. Since it causes changes in the laws regarding the loan. For example, one who borrows money without recording the loan on a document is believed to say that he paid, whereas if it was recorded, the borrower can no longer claim that he paid (*Rambam, Hil. Malveh* 11:1).

וְשִׁחְרוּרֵי עֲבָדִים. רַבִּי שִׁמְעוֹן אוֹמֵר: אַף אֵלּוּ כְּשֵׁרִין; לֹא הֻזְכְּרוּ אֶלָּא בִזְמַן שֶׁנַּעֲשׂוּ בַהֶדְיוֹט.

ר׳ עובדיה מברטנורא

רבי שמעון אומר כשרים. לא הוזכרו בבית המדרש להפסל, אלא בזמן שנעשו בהדיוט, על ידי גוים הדיוטות שאינם דיינים. ואין הלכה כרבי שמעון:

יד אברהם

and documents of emancipation are not different than any other documents in the latter category. Therefore, the text must be emended to read: *except for documents like gittin ...,* referring to all those which effect a transaction (*Gem.* 10b).

According to the opinion that transactions can be effected even by documents signed by gentile witnesses, *gittin* and documents of emancipation are singled out as exceptions, because gentiles are not affected by the laws of divorce as defined in the Torah, and can therefore not be active parties in their execution. Contrastingly, all other types of transactions are relevant to gentiles because דִּינִים, *justice,* is one of the seven Noachide laws applying to all gentiles (see footnote to 5:8, s.v. אֵין מְמַחִין). The only other exception is a document of emancipation, since it is hermeneutically derived from the laws of *gittin* that gentiles are excluded from their execution as well (*Rashi* 9b).

רַבִּי שִׁמְעוֹן אוֹמֵר: אַף אֵלּוּ כְּשֵׁרִין; — *R' Shimon says: These are also valid;*

R' Shimon maintains that even *gittin* and documents of emancipation which are processed by gentile courts and are signed by gentile witnesses are qualified as long as two valid Jewish witnesses observed their delivery to their recipients.

R' Shimon follows the opinion of R' Elazar (see General Introduction, s.v. *The Witnesses*), who maintains that the vital testimony of a document is not its signatures, but the testimony that the witnesses had observed the document being given to the recipient, thereby effecting the transaction. Therefore, the witnesses signed on the document do not affect its validity. However, even R' Elazar invalidates a document which has unqualified witnesses signed upon it, because people may come to rely on their testimony rather than that of the witnesses to the handing over of the *get*. Therefore, R' Shimon must be dealing with a case in which the names signed on the *get* are unmistakably gentile, and thus, no one will mistake them for legitimate witnesses (*Gem.* 10b-11a).

The first, anonymous *Tanna* would seem to agree with R' Meir that the witnesses signed on the document provide vital testimony and must therefore be legitimate Jewish witnesses. However, the *Gemara* (10a) concludes that the first *Tanna,* too, accepts the opinion of R' Elazar, that the vital witnesses are those who observe the giving of the document. He maintains, however, that the Rabbis prohibited obviously gentile names, nonetheless, because they were apprehensive that the use of such documents would spread to cases in which the names were not so obviously gentile, and could be mistaken for legitimate witnesses (*Ran*).

לֹא הֻזְכְּרוּ אֶלָּא בִזְמַן שֶׁנַּעֲשׂוּ בַהֶדְיוֹט. — *they were not mentioned [as being void], except when they were made by private individuals.*

This refers to *gittin* and documents of emancipation, which — if drawn up privately — do not become publicized. Therefore, R' Shimon holds

pation of slaves. R' Shimon says: These are also valid; they were not mentioned [as being void], except when they were made by private individuals.

YAD AVRAHAM

that even when obviously gentile names are signed upon them, there is a concern that people might still think that the witnesses are Jewish. They could thereby come to rely upon the document itself for proof of the divorce or emancipation, without the valid witnesses who observed the giving of the document. However, documents that are drawn up by the courts generate publicity, and therefore, everyone is aware that the witnesses signed upon them are gentiles and are not to be relied upon (*Ran; Tos. Yom Tov*).

Other commentators maintain that with regard to a *get* or a document of emancipation, it makes no difference whether it was drawn up privately or by the courts. This is because we are depending upon the witnesses to the giving of the document for validity, and upon the unmistakably gentile names to prevent reliance on the document itself. Accordingly, the distinction between the documents processed by the courts and those made privately applies to monetary documents used for evidence. Because the reliance on the credibility of the gentile witnesses in these documents is based upon their fear of perjury, it is applicable only to those documents which are processed by the courts. R' Shimon means to say that *gittin* and documents of emancipation which were written by gentiles were mentioned as being void only when the names are not unmistakably gentile, in which case they are as unacceptable as monetary documents processed by private individuals, which are void (*Gem.* 11a; *Rashi* ad loc., s.v. אבל שמות).

Tosafos (ad loc., s.v. נעשו) interpret the mishnah similarly to *Rashi* — i.e., that the distinction between documents processed by the courts and those made by private individuals applies only to monetary documents. However, they explain the reason for this distinction in a different manner [which applies to documents which effect transactions as well as those used only for evidence — and is thus applicable to both opinions in the *Gemara* (see above, s.v. אַף עַל פִּי)].

Since monetary documents which are processed by gentile courts are valid even without Jewish witnesses to the transaction, the Rabbis feared that if documents made by private individuals would be acceptable in any form whatsoever, people would assume that they are the same as those of the courts, and would come to rely on them also, even without Jewish witnesses to the transaction. Therefore, they disqualified such documents in all cases even where there were Jewish witnesses to the transaction and the signatures are unmistakably gentile names. In the cases of *gittin* and documents of emancipation, however, such a decree was unnecessary, because even those processed by the courts are valid only with Jewish witnesses to the transaction and unmistakably gentile names signed on the document (see *Tos. R' Akiva*).

The *Gemara* offers a second explanation of this final phrase in the mishnah: that it was said by the first *Tanna*, rather than R' Shimon. According to this interpretation, the earlier statement of the first *Tanna* — that documents drawn up in gentile courts are acceptable — refers to documents which are used solely for evidence, not to effect transactions; they are valid because the witnesses are afraid to perjure themselves. The mishnah now tells us that this reasoning applies only to those documents which are processed in the courts, but privately processed documents with gentile signatories are not acceptable as evidence.

[ו] **הָאוֹמֵר:** ,,תֵּן גֵּט זֶה לְאִשְׁתִּי" וּ,,שְׁטָר שִׁחְרוּר זֶה לְעַבְדִּי" — אִם רָצָה לַחֲזוֹר בִּשְׁנֵיהֶן, יַחֲזוֹר; דִּבְרֵי רַבִּי מֵאִיר. וַחֲכָמִים אוֹמְרִים: בְּגִטֵּי נָשִׁים, אֲבָל לֹא בְשִׁחְרוּרֵי עֲבָדִים, לְפִי שֶׁזָּכִין לָאָדָם שֶׁלֹּא בְּפָנָיו, וְאֵין חָבִין לוֹ אֶלָּא בְּפָנָיו; שֶׁאִם יִרְצָה

ר' עובדיה מברטנורא

(ו) **רצה לחזור בשניהן.** קודם שיגיע ליד האשה והעבד: **יחזור.** ואין השליח יכול לזכות בהם לצרכן, דחוב הוא להן, שמאבדין מזונותיהן: **וחכמים אומרים בגטי נשים.** יכול לחזור, אבל לא בשחרורי עבדים. והלכה כחכמים:

יד אברהם

6.

Just as a man can appoint an agent to deliver a *get* to his wife, so can a woman appoint one to receive a *get* on her behalf. When this occurs, she becomes divorced as soon as the *get* is given to her agent (6:1).

If a man tells an agent, "Give this *get* to my wife," he is understood to be directing him to receive it on her behalf (*Gem.* 11b). However, since he was not appointed by the woman, the capacity of his receipt of the *get* to effect the divorce depends upon whether it is considered beneficial or detrimental to her, as explained in the mishnah.

הָאוֹמֵר: ,,תֵּן גֵּט זֶה לְאִשְׁתִּי" וּ,,שְׁטָר שִׁחְרוּר זֶה לְעַבְדִּי" — *One who says: "Give this get to my wife" or "this document of emancipation to my slave"* —

The *Gemara* (11b) states that these words are tantamount to saying: "Acquire this document on behalf of my wife (or slave)." This means that the messenger should accept the document from the husband (or master) as an agent of the wife (or slave) for the sake of effecting the divorce (or emancipation), and not merely for the purpose of delivering it.

אִם רָצָה לַחֲזוֹר בִּשְׁנֵיהֶן, — *if he wants to retract in both of those [cases],*

If he seeks to retract the *get* or document of emancipation before it reaches his wife or slave (*Rav*).

יַחֲזוֹר; דִּבְרֵי רַבִּי מֵאִיר. — *he can retract; [these are] the words of R' Meir.*

He may change his mind, since the agent cannot acquire these documents on behalf of the wife or slave for immediate divorce or emancipation because they are considered detrimental to them [as explained below] (*Rav*).

וַחֲכָמִים אוֹמְרִים: בְּגִטֵּי נָשִׁים, אֲבָל לֹא בְשִׁחְרוּרֵי עֲבָדִים, — *The Sages, however, say: In [cases of] gittin, but not in [cases of documents of] emancipation of slaves,*

[If a man tells an agent: "Give this *get* to my wife," he can retract his instructions as long as the document has not been delivered. However, if he says: "Give this document of emancipation to my slave," once the agent

1
6

6. One who says: "Give this *get* to my wife" or "this document of emancipation to my slave" — if he wants to retract in both of those [cases], he can retract; [these are] the words of R' Meir. The Sages, however, say: In [cases of] *gittin*, but not in [cases of documents of] emancipation of slaves, because [we] can benefit a person in his absence, but [we] cannot cause detriment to a person, except in his presence; for if he wants to

YAD AVRAHAM

accepts the document on behalf of the slave, the master can no longer change his mind. This is because the Sages maintain that divorce is considered detrimental to the wife, whereas emancipation is considered beneficial to the slave, as explained below.]

According to some authorities, even though the master can no longer nullify the document of emancipation once the agent has received it, the slave does not become free until the document is actually in his possession (*Rif; Rambam, Hil. Avadim* 6:1). By using the term *give* instead of saying "Acquire this for my slave," the master indicates to the agent that he does not want the actual emancipation to take effect until the slave has received the document. Nonetheless, since his instructions are construed to mean that the agent should acquire the document on behalf of the recipient, a total commitment has been made, and he can no longer change his mind (*Lechem Mishneh* ibid.).

לְפִי שֶׁזָּכִין לָאָדָם שֶׁלֹּא בְּפָנָיו, — *because [we] can benefit a person in his absence,*

This is derived from the Scriptural account (*Num.* 34:18) in which representatives from each tribe drew lots to acquire a portion in the Holy Land for all the members of their tribes (*Kiddushin* 42a).

There is a discussion among the commentators as to whether this is a subcategory of the general principle that an agent can act on another's behalf or a new category of its own which is not subject to the laws of representation by an agent (see *Ran* ad loc.).

[Despite the fact that acceptance of the document of emancipation is considered by the Sages to be beneficial to the slave (see below), the agent cannot act on his behalf without the master's instruction that he do so. This is because the emancipation of a slave is the prerogative of the master and can be effected only in accordance with his wishes, similar to a woman's divorce, which is bound to the will of the husband (see 6:1).]

וְאֵין חָבִין לוֹ אֶלָּא בְּפָנָיו; — *but [we] cannot cause detriment to a person* (lit., *to him*), *except in his presence;*

[It is clear that the terminology of absence and presence is used loosely, because if a person appoints an agent to do something for him — even if it turns out to be to his detriment — it takes effect although it is not done in his presence. On the other hand, if a man performs an act on behalf of another which is detrimental to the latter, it is not valid even if done in his presence unless he instructed him to do so. Rather, the mishnah is discussing only those things which are done without the sanction of the person in whose behalf they are undertaken. In

שֶׁלֹּא לָזוּן אֶת עַבְדּוֹ — רַשַּׁאי, וְשֶׁלֹּא לָזוּן אֶת אִשְׁתּוֹ — אֵינוֹ רַשַּׁאי. אָמַר לָהֶם: וַהֲרֵי הוּא פּוֹסֵל אֶת עַבְדּוֹ מִן הַתְּרוּמָה כְּשֵׁם שֶׁהוּא פּוֹסֵל אֶת אִשְׁתּוֹ! אָמְרוּ לוֹ: מִפְּנֵי שֶׁהוּא קִנְיָנוֹ.

ר׳ עובדיה מברטנורא

שאם ירצה שלא לזון את עבדו רשאי. הלכך כי משחרר ליה לא מפסיד ליה מזוני. אבל שלא לזון את אשתו אינו רשאי, הלכך כי מגרש לה מפסיד לה מזוני: **מפני שהוא קנינו.** כלומר הא דהוא אכיל בתרומה כשהוא עבד כהן, אינו אלא מפני שהוא קנינו של כהן, מידי דהוה אבהמתו של כהן שאוכלת בכרשיני תרומה, ולאו משום מעליותא היא, הלכך כי משחרר ליה אף על פי שמפסידו מלאכול בתרומה, אין זו חובה לעבד:

יד אברהם

receiving those profits, nor may he tell her to keep the profits of her work and assume responsibility for her own support, unless those profits are sufficient to meet her needs (*Gem.* 12a). Thus [in any case that her handiwork will not suffice to support her, which was apparently considered to be the norm], her divorce causes her a loss of support and is considered a detriment (*Rav*). [Therefore, the agent cannot accept the *get* on her behalf without her consent.]

אָמַר לָהֶם: — *He said to them:*
[R' Meir said to the Sages.]

וַהֲרֵי הוּא פּוֹסֵל אֶת עַבְדּוֹ מִן הַתְּרוּמָה כְּשֵׁם שֶׁהוּא פּוֹסֵל אֶת אִשְׁתּוֹ! — *But he is disqualifying his slave from [eating] terumah, just as he is disqualifying his wife!*

The *Gemara* (12b) explains that R' Meir accepted the Sages' argument concerning the issue of support, but retained his position that emancipation is a detriment for another reason. The owner of crops grown in *Eretz Yisrael* is required to separate a small portion of them, and give it to a *Kohen* (*Num.* 18:12; *Deut.* 18:4). This is called *terumah,* and it is imbued with a degree of sanctity which limits its

such a case, only matters which benefit him can be accomplished on his behalf, not detriments.]

שֶׁאִם יִרְצֶה שֶׁלֹּא לָזוּן אֶת עַבְדּוֹ — רַשַּׁאי, — *for if he wants to refrain from supporting his slave, he is permitted,*

A master can refrain from providing his slave with support and still demand that he continue to work for him (*Gem.* 12a), thus compelling the slave to beg for sustenance (*Rashi; Rambam, Hil. Avadim* 9:7). This is based upon the *halachah* that Jews are obligated to support the slaves living among them with charity (*Rambam* ibid.). Thus, a slave loses nothing when he is freed, for even the support of his master had never been guaranteed him. Therefore, his emancipation is considered a benefit, and it may be brought about without his knowledge (*Rav*).

וְשֶׁלֹּא לָזוּן אֶת אִשְׁתּוֹ — אֵינוֹ רַשַּׁאי. — *but to refrain from supporting his wife, he is not permitted.*

A man is obligated to support his wife (*Kesubos* 4:4); in return, he receives the profits from her work (ibid., 47b; see *Tos.* ad loc. s.v. תיקנו). As long as they are married, he may not refrain from supporting her while still

1
6
refrain from supporting his slave, he is permitted, but to refrain from supporting his wife, he is not permitted. He said to them: But he is disqualifying his slave from [eating] *terumah,* just as he is disqualifying his wife! They said to him: [This is] because he is his possession.

YAD AVRAHAM

consumption to *Kohanim* and their households, including their slaves (*Lev.* 22:10*ff.*). Because only a limited number of people are allowed to eat *terumah,* it is relatively inexpensive (*Tos.* ibid. s.v. השבתוני). In addition, there are those who maintain that when the owner is apportioning his *terumah,* he may give it to the slave of a *Kohen,* even if his master is not there (ibid.). When the slave is freed, he loses these advantages, and it must therefore be considered a detriment.[1]

This reason obviously applies only to the slave of a *Kohen.* Regarding the slave of any other Jew, R' Meir maintains that since his liberation — which makes him a full-fledged Jew (see *Yevamos* 47b) — causes that intimacy with female slaves is now forbidden to him, it is considered a detriment, although he also becomes permitted to marry a free Jewess. This is because female slaves tend to be less chaste, and thus, more readily available for the satiation of his desires (*Gem.* 13a).

In this mishnah, R' Meir chose to state the reason which pertains only to the slaves of *Kohanim* rather than one which includes all slaves, because he realized that the Sages contend that the slave would prefer the permissibility to marry a free Jewess rather than a relationship with a female slave. However, he considered his argument regarding slaves of *Kohanim* to be irrefutable (*Tos.* 12b s.v. שאם).

.אָמְרוּ לוֹ: מִפְּנֵי שֶׁהוּא קִנְיָנוֹ — *They said to him: [This is] because he is his possession.*

The Sages consider emancipation a benefit even to a *Kohen's* slave because the slave is the master's possession and he can sell him to a non-*Kohen* at any time, thereby disqualifying him from eating *terumah.* Therefore, this advantage of being able to eat *terumah* is insignificant, and its negation is not considered a detriment (*Gem.* 13a).

Another explanation is that since his right to eat *terumah* is due to his lowly status as a monetary possession, its loss cannot be considered a detriment (*Rav; Rambam Commentary;* see *Tos. Yom Tov*).

As mentioned above regarding the slave of a non-*Kohen,* the Sages maintain that the prohibition of marriage to female slaves which comes with emancipation is outweighed by the right to marry a free Jewess, and it is therefore considered a benefit (*Tos.* 12b s.v. שאם). Alternatively, the entire issue is negligible in the face of the overriding benefit of the emancipation itself (*Tos.* 13a s.v. עבדא).

Yerushalmi wonders why the nature of the husband or master in these cases is not taken into consideration when determining whether divorce or emancipation from them is a benefit or detriment. *Yerushalmi's* answer is somewhat ambiguous and is discussed by the commentators on the

1. The idea that this minor detriment should outweigh the overall benefit of emancipation appears ludicrous. However, even an act which is mostly beneficial cannot be performed on another's behalf without his consent if there is any aspect of detriment involved (*Toras Gittin* to *Tos.* 11b, s.v. בגיטי נשים).

גיטין
א/ו

הָאוֹמֵר: „תְּנוּ גֵט זֶה לְאִשְׁתִּי" וּ„שְׁטָר שִׁחְרוּר זֶה לְעַבְדִּי", וָמֵת — לֹא יִתְּנוּ לְאַחַר מִיתָה. „תְּנוּ מָנֶה לְאִישׁ פְּלוֹנִי", וָמֵת — יִתְּנוּ לְאַחַר מִיתָה.

ר' עובדיה מברטנורא

לא יתנו לאחר מיתה. דגיטא לא הוי עד דמטי לידה, וכי מטי לידה הא מית, ואין גט לאחר מיתה. ושטר שחרור נמי, כי מטא לידיה הא מית ופקע רשותיה מיניה: **יתנו לאחר מיתה.** ואף על גב דלא אמר מנה זה, דדברי שכיב מרע ככתובין וכמסורין דמו:

יד אברהם

Mishnah. One explanation is that a slave can be sold to another owner against his will, and is therefore better off being free than remaining in the possession of even the most benevolent master, because he may sell the slave at any time to another who is not so kind. A woman, however, prefers to be married under any circumstances rather than to be on her own (*Yevamos* 118b); hence, her divorce is always considered a detriment (*Tos. HaRosh* to 11b). [For other explanations to *Yerushalmi's* comment, see *Maharsha* and *Toras Gittin* to *Tos.* ad loc. s.v. בגיטי נשים.]

הָאוֹמֵר: „תְּנוּ גֵט זֶה לְאִשְׁתִּי" וּ„שְׁטָר שִׁחְרוּר זֶה לְעַבְדִּי", וָמֵת — *If someone says: "Give this get to my wife" or "this document of emancipation to my slave," and he dies,*

The mishnah uses the plural form, תְּנוּ, for the word *give* rather than the singular form, תֵּן, used previously, to denote that he did not hand over the *get* to a specific agent of delivery prior to his death, but rather instructed a group of people to see to it that the divorce or emancipation is taken care of (*Rashi*). [The significance of this distinction will be clarified below.]

לֹא יִתְּנוּ לְאַחַר מִיתָה. — *they shall not give [it] after [his] death.*

The agents appointed to deliver the *get* or document of emancipation may no longer carry out his instructions if he dies before they do so, because these documents do not take effect until they are given, which — in this case — is after the death of the husband or master. At that time, his marriage or ownership is no longer in effect for a divorce or emancipation from him to be pertinent (*Rav; Rashi*).

Although a similar *halachah* is also stated in a later mishnah (7:3), it is not a mere redundancy, because in this instance — unlike the later case — the husband appointed an agent as his surrogate to carry out the divorce on his behalf. We might therefore think that he retains that status even after the husband dies (*Tos.*).

This *halachah* — that the document of emancipation must be delivered before the death of the master in order to be valid — is no contradiction to the mishnah's earlier statement that the document is effective as soon as the agent accepts it. As explained above by *Rashi*, the plural terminology here denotes that at the time the master issued his instructions there was no document handed over to the agent to enable him to accept it in behalf of the slave.

In *Rif's* version of the text, however, there are no differences between the wordings of the two cases of the mishnah. Therefore, he, along with *Rambam* (*Hil. Avadim* 6:1), proposes a different solution to this apparent contradiction. They maintain that the words *Give to* ... are equated with *Acquire for* ... only to the extent that the master can no longer rescind the

1
6

If someone says: "Give this *get* to my wife" or "this document of emancipation to my slave," and he dies, they shall not give [it] after [his] death.

[If one says:] "Give a hundred [*zuz*] to So-and-So," and he dies, they shall give [it] after [his] death.

YAD AVRAHAM

document. The slave does not go free, however, until it reaches his possession. Thus, although the Sages maintain that the agent can accept the document in the slave's behalf, they admit that if the master dies before the slave receives it, it is no longer valid, and the slave does not go free (see *Lechem Mishneh* ibid.).

Tosafos bring several other resolutions for this apparent contradiction in the mishnah. One possibility is simply that the author of this opinion that the document is void if given after the master's death is R' Meir, who holds that emancipation is a detriment, and cannot take effect prior to delivery. Another approach is that the instructions *Give to* ... are construed as meaning *Acquire for* ... only when the object under discussion is handed over at the time these instructions are given. In the case of the mishnah, however, this did not occur. Therefore, the agent is authorized only to deliver the document to the slave, but not to accept it in his behalf. Consequently, the slave does not go free unless he receives the document prior to his master's death. *Rabbeinu Tam* maintains that the word *this* should be deleted from the text of the mishnah, which then reads: "*Give a document of emancipation to my slave.*" This wording clearly denotes that the master is not referring to a document on hand, but rather dictating the preparation and delivery of such a document. This concurs with the explanation of *Rashi*, cited above.

,,תְּנוּ מָנֶה לְאִישׁ פְּלוֹנִי״, וָמֵת — יִתְּנוּ לְאַחַר מִיתָה. - *[If one says:] "Give a hundred [zuz] to So-and-so," and he dies, they shall give [it] after [his] death.*

[A man instructed an agent to give a sum of money to another, but did not give it over to the agent, which would enable him to acquire it on the recipient's behalf. The agent can carry out his instructions and give over the money even after the death of the owner.]

The mishnah is speaking about someone so enfeebled by sickness that he is bedridden (*Rav* from *Gem.* 13a). Although a transfer of ownership normally requires an act of acquisition, the Rabbis ordained that the instructions of such a person have the legal validity of a document which was written and handed over. This was done to prevent any deterioration of the person's condition resulting from the fear that his instructions would not be carried out (*Bava Basra* 147b; *Rambam, Hil. Zechiyah* 8:2). Accordingly, his directive to give a sum of money in itself constitutes a valid transfer of ownership, and no document is required. Even if no specific money was set aside, the agent can carry out his instructions [since one who is bedridden can obligate himself in payment with mere words as well as effecting a transaction] (*Gem.* ibid.).

An alternative interpretation offered in the *Gemara* (ad loc.) is that the mishnah is discussing a case in which the owner, the agent, and the recipient are together at the time the instructions are issued. The Rabbis ordained that a directive to give something over from one person to another which is issued in this manner constitutes a legal act of acquisition. Therefore, the transfer takes place immediately, and not after his death.

פרק שני

Chapter Two

[א] **הַמֵּבִיא** גֵט מִמְּדִינַת הַיָּם, וְאָמַר: „בְּפָנַי נִכְתַּב", אֲבָל לֹא: „בְּפָנַי נֶחְתַּם"; „בְּפָנַי נֶחְתַּם", אֲבָל לֹא: „בְּפָנַי נִכְתַּב"; „בְּפָנַי נִכְתַּב כֻּלּוֹ, וּבְפָנַי נֶחְתַּם חֶצְיוֹ", „בְּפָנַי נִכְתַּב חֶצְיוֹ, וּבְפָנַי נֶחְתַּם כֻּלּוֹ" — פָּסוּל. אֶחָד אוֹמֵר: „בְּפָנַי נִכְתַּב", וְאֶחָד אוֹמֵר: „בְּפָנַי נֶחְתַּם" — פָּסוּל.

ר' עובדיה מברטנורא

פרק שני – המביא גט. (א) המביא. נחתם חציו. אחד מן העדים חתם: **בפני נכתב חציו וכו' פסול.** ודוקא חציו האחרון, אבל בפני נכתב חציו הראשון, שהוא שם האיש והאשה והזמן, כשר. וחציו הראשון נמי לא צריך שיראה הכתיבה עצמה, אלא אם שמע קול הקולמוס בלבד עובר על הנייר בשעת כתיבה, תו לא צריך: **אחד אומר בפני נכתב ואחד אומר בפני נחתם פסול.** בזמן שהגט יוצא מתחת יד אחד מהם, דאצרכוהו רבנן לשליח המביא גט למימר תרווייהו. אבל אם הגט יוצא מתחת יד שניהם, כשר, ששנים שהביאו גט אין צריך שיאמרו בפנינו נכתב ובפנינו נחתם:

יד אברהם

1.

הַמֵּבִיא גֵט מִמְּדִינַת הַיָּם, וְאָמַר: „בְּפָנַי נִכְתַּב", אֲבָל לֹא: „בְּפָנַי נֶחְתַּם"; „בְּפָנַי נֶחְתַּם", אֲבָל לֹא: „בְּפָנַי נִכְתַּב"; — *[If] one brought a get from overseas, and said: "It was written in my presence," but not: "It was signed in my presence"; [or] "It was signed in my presence," but not: "It was written in my presence";*

An agent who delivers a *get* from a foreign land must testify that it was written and signed in his presence in order to confirm its signatures, and thereby avoid subsequent difficulties if the validity of the *get* should be challenged (1:1). [If he witnessed only the writing of the *get* or only its signing, his delivery of the *get* is not valid, and the divorce does not take effect.]

„בְּפָנַי נִכְתַּב כֻּלּוֹ, וּבְפָנַי נֶחְתַּם חֶצְיוֹ"; — *[or] "All of it was written in my presence, and half of it was signed in my presence";*

[The agent had witnessed the writing of the entire *get*, but only one of the witnesses had signed in his presence.]

Even if the agent testifies that he himself is the other witness signed on the *get*, the divorce does not take effect. This is because the attestation of two witnesses to their own signatures is one of the standard methods of confirming a document, while the lone testimony of the agent that it had been written and signed in his presence is an unconventional form of document confirmation, which is ordinarily insufficient, and was only allowed in the cases of our mishnayos. The Rabbis required that the confirmation should be done either through the standard process or through this special procedure, but a combination of the two is not acceptable (*Gem.* 15b), because the agent's word was accepted as confirmation only in a case in which it is complete (*Tos. Rid* ad loc.).

Although the agent is, in effect, confirming both signatures, and is usually believed under such circumstances, the fact that he himself served as a witness makes it appear that he is prejudiced in verifying the other signature, because he wishes to

2
1

1. [If] one brought a *get* from overseas, and said: "It was written in my presence," but not: "It was signed in my presence"; [or] "It was signed in my presence," but not: "It was written in my presence"; [or] "All of it was written in my presence, and half of it was signed in my presence"; [or] "Half of it was written in my presence, and all of it was signed in my presence," it is void. [If] one says: "It was written in my presence," and one says: "It was signed in my presence," it is void.

YAD AVRAHAM

confirm the testimony to which he had signed (*Tos.* ibid. s.v. אני הוא).

However, if the second signature is identified by two other witnesses, or by the agent and another witness, the divorce takes effect. This is based upon an axiom that the testimony of one witness cannot be more effective than the same testimony given by two witnesses (*Gem.* 15a-b).

,,בְּפָנַי נִכְתַּב חֶצְיוֹ, וּבְפָנַי נֶחְתַּם כֻּלּוֹ" — *[or] "Half of it was written in my presence, and all of it was signed in my presence,"*

The agent testifies that the second half of the *get* — the טֹפֶס, *tofes* — which contains the nonessential, standard wording common to all *gittin*, was written in his presence. However, he did not witness the writing of the first half — the תֹּרֶף, *toref* — which contains the basic declaration of divorce as well as the specific information pertinent to this divorce (i.e., the names of the husband and wife, etc.; see General Introduction, s.v. *The Get*). [If, however, he witnessed the writing of only the *toref*, it is tantamount to witnessing the entire writing, because that is the essential portion of the *get* (*Gem.* 15a).]

The only reason the agent is required to testify about the writing of the *get* in addition to its signatures is to emphasize the unique nature of this case of signature confirmation. This is to prevent observers from erroneously concluding that confirmation of all documents can be accomplished with the testimony of a single witness (*Gem.* 3a; see commentary to 1:1 s.v. צָרִיךְ). Nevertheless, this emphasis is effective only if the testimony is of significance. Therefore, it is the first half of the *get*, which contains its vital information, that must be dealt with in the agent's testimony (*Tos.* 3a s.v. אי לאחלופי).

פָּסוּל. — *it is void.*

In all cases, since the agent did not attest to having witnessed both the writing and signing of the entire *get*, his confirmation of the *get* is not accepted, and the woman is not divorced.

However, if other witnesses are found to confirm the signatures on the *get*, it can then take effect (*Rambam, Hil. Gerushin* 7:17; *Even Haezer* 141:53).

אֶחָד אוֹמֵר: ,,בְּפָנַי נִכְתַּב", וְאֶחָד אוֹמֵר: ,,בְּפָנַי נֶחְתַּם" — פָּסוּל. — *[If] one says: "It was written in my presence," and one says: "It was signed in my presence," it is void.*

One witness testified to having observed the writing of the *get*, and another to its signing, but only one of

שְׁנַיִם אוֹמְרִים: "בְּפָנֵינוּ נִכְתַּב", וְאֶחָד אוֹמֵר: "בְּפָנַי נֶחְתַּם" — פָּסוּל; וְרַבִּי יְהוּדָה מַכְשִׁיר. אֶחָד אוֹמֵר: "בְּפָנַי נִכְתַּב", וּשְׁנַיִם אוֹמְרִים: "בְּפָנֵינוּ נֶחְתַּם" — כָּשֵׁר.

ר' עובדיה מברטנורא

שנים אומרים בפנינו נכתב ואחד אומר בפני נחתם פסול. בזמן שהגט יוצא מתחת יד אחד מהם. אבל אם יוצא מתחת יד שניהם, כשר: **ורבי יהודה מכשיר.** ואפילו יוצא מתחת ידו של אחד מהם. ואין הלכה כרבי יהודה:

יד אברהם

them was appointed an agent to deliver the *get*. In such a case, the confirmation is not sufficient. If the agent was the one who witnessed the writing, the testimony of the other regarding the signing is not acceptable, because only the agent who delivered the *get* is granted the credibility to confirm its legitimacy on his own, not any other single witness (*Rav; Rashi*). If the agent attested only to the signing of the *get*, the testimony of the other witness regarding its writing is of no value. Since the agent himself is not the one testifying about the writing of the *get*, an observer may assume that his testimony about the signing is a standard form of signature confirmation (see commentary to 1:1 s.v. צָרִיךְ, and footnote there). He could thereby draw the erroneous conclusion that all documents can be confirmed by only one witness. Therefore, the Rabbis insisted that the agent himself testify to the writing of the *get* as well as its signing (*Gem.* 16b).

If two agents are appointed to deliver the *get*, one of whom testifies to having witnessed its writing and the other its signing, the *get* is valid, and the woman is divorced.[1] This is because when two witnesses bring a *get*, there is no need for the agent's testimony, since the witnesses are available if the need arises to confirm the validity of the document (*Rav* from *Gem.* 16b; *Rashi* ad loc. s.v. כשר).

Tosafos (2b s.v. דאתייה בי תרי) disagree with this because there is no guarantee that the agents will still be available when the question of forgery arises. Instead, *Riva* (ibid.) offers another explanation as to why the *get* in this case is valid. Once the two witnesses testify that the husband sent them, the latter can no longer claim otherwise. This leaves only the possibility of a deliberate forgery arranged by the husband himself, which we do not suspect him of doing. Therefore, the two witnesses delivering the *get* are not even required to testify that they witnessed its writing and signing.

There is another opinion that even when two agents bring the *get*, at least one of them must testify to having witnessed both its writing and signing. This follows the approach of Rabbah in the *Gemara*, that the purpose of the agent's testimony is to ensure that the *get* was written and signed with specific intent for this woman's divorce (see commentary to 1:1 s.v. צָרִיךְ), which the mere presence of the witnesses does not accomplish.

However, the witness who testifies about its signing is, in fact, confirming the *get's* signatures along with the compliance with the rule of specific intent. Therefore, he

1. *Rashi* (16a s.v. מתחת ידי שניהם) states that the two agents must both be holding the *get* at the time of delivery. *Tosafos* (16a s.v. אבל גט) maintain that as long as both testify that the husband appointed them agents of delivery, it is sufficient.

2
1 If two say: "It was written in our presence," and one says: "It was signed in my presence," it is void. R' Yehudah, however, validates [it]. If one says: "It was written in my presence," and two say: "It was signed in our presence," it is valid.

YAD AVRAHAM

himself must also testify to its writing, because otherwise, an observer may conclude that all signature confirmations require only one witness[1] (*Gem.* 16b).

שְׁנַיִם אוֹמְרִים: „בְּפָנֵינוּ נִכְתַּב", וְאֶחָד אוֹמֵר: „בְּפָנַי נֶחְתַּם" — פָּסוּל. — *If two say: "It was written in our presence," and one says: "It was signed in my presence," it is void.*

If an agent delivers a *get* from a foreign land and attests only that he saw the *get* being signed, while two other witnesses testify that they observed its writing, the *get* is not confirmed (*Rashi*). Because the agent himself, who is the one confirming the authenticity of the signature, did not testify about the writing of the *get*, an observer may conclude that all signature confirmations require only one signature (*Gem.* 16b).

If the situation is reversed, and the agents are the two witnesses who testify about the writing of the *get*, the confirmation is valid. This is because a *get* delivered by two agents was not included in the enactment requiring the agent's testimony, as explained above (*Rav* from *Gem.* ibid.).

וְרַבִּי יְהוּדָה מַכְשִׁיר. — *R' Yehudah, however, validates [it].*

R' Yehudah maintains that if the agent who delivers the *get* testifies that he saw its signing, and two other witnesses assert that it was written in their presence, the *get* is valid. Since there is testimony about the writing of the *get* as well as its signing, an observer will realize that it is a unique case and will not draw any conclusions regarding the standard procedure for document confirmation (*Gem.* 16b).

For the same reason, R' Yehudah also disagrees with the previous statement of the mishnah and maintains that one witness testifying about the writing of the *get*, and another about its signing is sufficient to validate the *get* (ibid.).

אֶחָד אוֹמֵר: „בְּפָנַי נִכְתַּב", וּשְׁנַיִם אוֹמְרִים: „בְּפָנֵינוּ נֶחְתַּם" — כָּשֵׁר. — *If one says: "It was written in my presence," and two say: "It was signed in our presence," it is valid.*

If a *get* is delivered to a woman with one witness testifying that he had viewed its writing and two others its signing, the *get* is confirmed and the woman is divorced. If the two witnesses are the agents of delivery, the *get* is valid because no testimony is required at all, as explained above. If the agent is the single witness to the *get's* writing, it is also valid, because the confirmation of the signatures by the two witnesses makes his testi-

1. However, Rabbah is not bound to this opinion, and can still hold that when two agents deliver the *get*, there is no requirement for testimony, because the rule of specific intent eventually achieved universal compliance. Although it was still maintained as a factor in the enactment in order to prevent future lapses, it was no longer extended to include unusual cases such as the delivery of a *get* by two witnesses (*Gem.* 16b; *Rashi* ad loc. s.v. ורבה; see 1:3).

[ב] **נִכְתַּב** בַּיּוֹם וְנֶחְתַּם בַּיּוֹם, בַּלַּיְלָה וְנֶחְתַּם בַּלַּיְלָה, בַּלַּיְלָה וְנֶחְתַּם בַּיּוֹם — כָּשֵׁר. בַּיּוֹם וְנֶחְתַּם בַּלַּיְלָה — פָּסוּל. רַבִּי שִׁמְעוֹן מַכְשִׁיר, שֶׁהָיָה רַבִּי שִׁמְעוֹן אוֹמֵר: כָּל הַגִּטִּין

ר׳ עובדיה מברטנורא

(ב) **בלילה ונחתם ביום כשר.** שהיום הולך אחר הלילה, ואין זה מוקדם: **ביום ונחתם בלילה פסול.** שהרי מוקדם הוא. ותקנו חכמים זמן בגיטין, גזירה שמא יהיה נשוי עם בת אחותו, ותזנה עליו וחס עליה שלא תחנק, ונותן לה גט בלא זמן, וכשמעידים עליה בבית דין, מוליאה גיטה ואומרת גרושה הייתי ופנויה באותה שעה: **ורבי שמעון מכשיר.** דסבר רבי שמעון דחכמים תקנו זמן בגיטין משום פירי, שאם לא יהיה זמן בגט, יהיה הבעל מוכר והולך פירות נכסי מלוג של אשתו לאחר גרושין, וכשתתבע בדין יאמר, קודם גירושין מכרתי. ולהכי מכשיר רבי שמעון בנכתב ביום ונחתם בלילה, אף על פי שהוא מוקדם, דסבר משעה שנתן עיניו לגרש, אף על פי שלא גירש, שוב אין לו לבעל פירות. ואין הלכה כרבי שמעון:

יד אברהם

mony unnecessary (*Gem.* 17a).

According to the opinion that the agent's testimony that he witnessed the writing and signing of the *get* is required even in a case in which the *get* is delivered by two witnesses, their testimony would have to include the writing of the *get*, as well as its signing. Otherwise, the presence of a single witness testifying to its writing would not suffice to give it validity, since he is not the agent of delivery, and his testimony is thus not acceptable without the corroboration of a second witness. Therefore, the ruling of the mishnah applies only to a case in which the witness to the writing of the *get* was the appointed agent, and two other witnesses testified about its signing. Because the agent is given credibility, it is the equivalent of having two witnesses for the writing and two for the signing (ibid.).

2.

The Rabbis decreed that a *get* must be dated to be valid, as explained below. The mishnah discusses a case in which a *get* was written and dated prior to the date on which it was signed.

נִכְתַּב בַּיּוֹם וְנֶחְתַּם בַּיּוֹם, בַּלַּיְלָה וְנֶחְתַּם בַּלַּיְלָה, — *[If] it was written by day and signed by day, [or written] by night and signed by night.*

If a *get* was written and dated on a specific day or night and was signed by witnesses on that same day or night, it is valid (*Gem.* 17a).

בַּלַּיְלָה וְנֶחְתַּם בַּיּוֹם — כָּשֵׁר. — *[or written] by night and signed by day, it is valid.*

If a *get* was written and dated at night and signed by witnesses the following day, it is valid. Since, in Jewish law, the new day begins with nightfall, this *get* is considered to have been written and signed on the same day (*Rav*).

בַּיּוֹם וְנֶחְתַּם בַּלַּיְלָה — פָּסוּל. — *[If it was written] by day and signed by night, it is void.*

[A *get* which was written and dated by day and signed the following night is invalid, because the date upon which the *get* should take effect is not the date written on it.]

The Rabbis required that a *get* be dated because they were apprehensive that if a man married his niece [or

2. [If] it was written by day and signed by day, [or written] by night and signed by night, [or written] by night and signed by day, it is valid. [If it was written] by day and signed by night, it is void. R' Shimon [however] validates it, for R' Shimon used to say: All documents which

YAD AVRAHAM

other relative (see *Tos. Yom Tov*)] and she committed adultery, he might decide to help her escape punishment by giving her an undated *get*, so that she could claim to having been divorced before the act of adultery took place[1] (*Gem.* 17a, *Rashi* ad loc.). Therefore, a *get* which was written and dated by day, but signed the following night — or any predated *get* — is also void, because if she committed adultery between the time it was written and the time it was signed, she could use it to circumvent punishment (*Gem.* 17b, *Rashi* ad loc.).

The Rabbis were not concerned that a man might have a *get* written and signed on one day and given to his wife on a later date, because a person would not retain an object of such detrimental potential — i.e., the potential to dissolve his marriage — unless he had irrevocably decided to give it to her. Therefore, once it is written, he will certainly use it to divorce her immediately (*Gem.* 18a).

The possibility does exist of a man having a *get* written, signed, and dated in one place, and then sent with an agent to his wife in a different place, resulting in a time lapse between the date on the *get* and the true date of divorce. However, in such a case, the witness to the delivery of the *get* will note the discrepancy and will make sure to remember the correct date of the divorce (*Gem.* 18a; *Tos.* ad loc. s.v. הנהו קלא).

רַבִּי שִׁמְעוֹן מַכְשִׁיר, — *R' Shimon [however] validates it,*

[R' Shimon maintains that a *get* which is dated from the time it was written is valid even if signed on a later date.]

R' Shimon construes the Rabbinic ordinance requiring a date on every *get* as a means of protecting the wife. When a woman is married, the husband receives any benefits derived from her possessions (*Kesubos* 4:4). If he sells any of these benefits — such as the produce of her fields — the sale is valid. Accordingly, if a *get* has no date, a woman's former husband could continue to sell the produce of her fields even after the divorce. When she would claim the produce from the buyers, she would have no proof that her divorce had preceded the sale.

1. Generally, when there is doubt if a woman had already been divorced at a certain time, the legal principle of *chazakah* (presumptive status) applies. Since we know that the woman had been married before that time, but are uncertain if the divorce had taken place, the *chazakah* principle dictates that we assume she was still married until proven otherwise. In this case, however, we would not presume that the woman was still married on the date in question — when she committed adultery — because at the present moment she is definitely divorced, which weakens the assumption that she was married at any given time. In addition, there is a presumptive status to the contrary: every Jew is assumed to be law abiding unless proven otherwise. We therefore assume that this woman did not commit adultery (*Tos.* 17a s.v. משום בת אחותו), because these two factors combined are enough to negate the effect of her presumptive married status (*Pnei Yehoshua* ad loc.).

שֶׁנִּכְתְּבוּ בַיּוֹם וְנֶחְתְּמוּ בַלַּיְלָה — פְּסוּלִין, חוּץ מִגִּטֵּי נָשִׁים.

[ג] **בַּכֹּל** כּוֹתְבִין: בִּדְיוֹ, בְּסַם, בְּסִקְרָא, וּבְקוֹמוֹס, וּבְקַנְקַנְתּוֹם, וּבְכָל דָּבָר שֶׁהוּא שֶׁל קַיָּמָא. אֵין כּוֹתְבִין לֹא בְמַשְׁקִים,

ר׳ עובדיה מברטנורא

(ג) **בדיו.** אלמיד״ר בערבי: **סיקרא.** צבע אדום: **קומוס.** שרף האילן: **קנקנתום.** וידריאול״ו בלע״ז:

יד אברהם

recording a debt would allow the bearer to collect from buyers even those fields which were bought from the debtor before the document actually took effect. Similarly, a bill of sale which is predated would enable the bearer to take possession of a field which was actually sold to someone else first. Accordingly, such documents which were written and dated on one day and signed the following night are not valid (*Rashi*).

חוּץ מִגִּטֵּי נָשִׁים. — *except for gittin.*

Gittin which were written and dated by day and signed the following night are valid according to R' Shimon, as explained above.

Some authorities state that R' Shimon's opinion can be replied upon in pressing situations. Therefore, if a woman remarried after receiving such a *get*, or the husband left the country and cannot be reached, the *get* is valid (*Rosh* from *Gem.* 19a). Others maintain that even under these circumstances the *get* is not valid (*Rosh* from *Gem.* 19a). Others maintain that even under these circumstances the *get* is not valid (*Rif; Rambam, Hil. Gerushin* 1:25).

Resh Lakish offers a different explanation of the dispute between the first, anonymous *Tanna* and R' Shimon. He maintains that adultery is too infrequent an occurrence to necessitate the requirement of a date on a *get*. Thus, even the first

Therefore, the Rabbis decreed that every *get* have a date indicating the day of divorce (*Rav* from *Gem.* 17a).

According to this approach, the prohibition of predating a *get* is for the protection of those who had bought produce before the divorce, because the wife could use the predated *get* to prove that she was divorced before the produce was sold, and thereby confiscate it illicitly (*Tos.* 17a s.v. נכתב).

However, R' Shimon is of the opinion that from the moment a man decides to divorce his wife, he loses his rights to the benefits from her possessions. Accordingly, from the day the *get* is written, the woman regains the rights to the produce of her fields, and can legitimately claim them from any subsequent buyers. Therefore, a *get* dated from the time it was written is valid (*Rav* from *Gem.* 18a).

שֶׁהָיָה רַבִּי שִׁמְעוֹן אוֹמֵר: כָּל הַגִּטִּין שֶׁנִּכְתְּבוּ בַיּוֹם וְנֶחְתְּמוּ בַלַּיְלָה — פְּסוּלִין, — *for R' Shimon used to say: All documents which were written by day and signed by night are void,*

A debt recorded in a legal document is collectible from any real property belonging to the debtor at the time the document took effect, even if he later sold it. Thus, a predated document

were written by day and signed by night are void, except for *gittin*.

3. [We] write [it] with anything: with ink, with orpiment, with red pigment, with gum, with ferrous sulfate, or with anything which is lasting. [We] do not write [it] with liquids,

YAD AVRAHAM

Tanna agrees with R' Shimon that the need for the date is to protect the woman from the illegal sale of the produce of her fields, and a predated *get* is invalid because it would enable her to cheat the buyers. However, the first *Tanna* maintains that the husband does not lose his rights to the benefits from his wife's possessions until the *get* is signed and rendered effective. Accordingly, she has no rights to any produce which was sold between the time of the writing of the *get* and its signing. Consequently, a *get* written and dated by day and signed the following night that would enable her to unlawfully collect such produce is void (*Gem.* 17a-b).

3.

The *Tanna* now focuses on the laws governing the writing of a *get*. In this mishnah, he discusses the types of ink with which one may write a *get* and the objects upon which it may be written.

בַּכֹּל כּוֹתְבִין: — *[We] write [it] with anything:*

A *get* may be written with any of the following:

בִּדְיוֹ, — *with ink,*

Black ink, which maintains its color on parchment (*Tif. Yis.* to *Megillah* 2:2).

Nowadays, it is customary to make ink for sacred use from a combination of ferrous sulfate, gallnuts, and gum arabic, which form a stable, thick, black compound (*Mishnah Berurah* 32:8).

בְּסַם, — *with orpiment,*

Orpiment is a yellow arsenic. This translation follows *Rashi* and *Aruch*. *Rambam* and *Rav* (to *Megillah* loc. cit.) render it as an ink derived from a grass root.

בְּסִקְרָא, — *with red pigment,*

Rav and *Rashi* translate this as a red dye. *Tiferes Yisrael* maintains that it is a red chalk (cf. *Rav* to *Megillah* loc. cit.).

וּבְקוֹמוֹס, — *with gum,*

Rav and *Rashi* render this as gum arabic, which is used in the manufacture of ink. According to *Rambam*, it is a type of yellow earth.

וּבְקַנְקַנְתּוֹם, — *with ferrous sulfate,*

This is also known as copperas or vitriol (*Rav; Tos.*).

וּבְכָל דָּבָר שֶׁהוּא שֶׁל קַיָּמָא. — *or with anything which is lasting.*

I.e., anything which makes a permanent mark (*Rambam, Hil. Gerushin* 4:1).

The *Gemara* (19a) notes that this includes lead and מֵי טְרַיָא, which means either rain water which collected on the roofs, or water in which gallnuts have soaked (*Rashi; Tos. Yom Tov*).

אֵין כּוֹתְבִין לֹא בְמַשְׁקִים, — *[We] do not write [it] with liquids,*

A *get* may not be written with mulberry juice or other liquids which

וְלֹא בְמֵי פֵרוֹת, וְלֹא בְכָל דָּבָר שֶׁאֵינוֹ מִתְקַיֵּם. עַל הַכֹּל כּוֹתְבִין: עַל הֶעָלֶה שֶׁל זַיִת; וְעַל הַקֶּרֶן שֶׁל פָּרָה, וְנוֹתֵן לָהּ אֶת הַפָּרָה; עַל הַיָּד שֶׁל עֶבֶד, וְנוֹתֵן לָהּ אֶת הָעֶבֶד. רַבִּי יוֹסֵי הַגְּלִילִי אוֹמֵר: אֵין כּוֹתְבִין לֹא עַל דָּבָר שֶׁיֵּשׁ בּוֹ רוּחַ חַיִּים, וְלֹא עַל הָאֳכָלִים.

[ד] **אֵין** כּוֹתְבִין בִּמְחֻבָּר לַקַּרְקַע. כְּתָבוֹ

ר׳ עובדיה מברטנורא

על העלה של זית. תלושה: **ונותן לה את הפרה.** שאינו יכול לקצצו אחר כתיבה, דכתיב (דברים כד, ג) וכתב לה ספר כריתות ונתן בידה, מי שאינו מחוסר אלא כתיבה ונתינה, יצא זה שמחוסר כתיבה קצירה ונתינה: **רבי יוסי הגלילי אומר כו׳.** דרחמנא קרייה לגט ספר (שם), מה ספר מיוחד שאין בו רוח חיים ואינו אוכל, אף כל שאין בו רוח חיים ואינו אוכל. ורבנן אמרי, אי כתב בספר כדקאמרת, השתא דכתיב ספר, לספירת דברים הוא דאתא. והלכה כחכמים: **(ד) אין כותבין במחובר.** מפני שמחוסר קצירה:

יד אברהם

produce a black effect (*Rav* to *Shabbos* 12:5; *Rashi* ibid. 104b).

וְלֹא בְמֵי פֵרוֹת, — *nor with fruit juice,*

I.e., juices of other fruits which do not produce a black effect (ibid.).

Tiferes Yisrael explains that מַשְׁקִים refers to extracts of fruits which are commonly squeezed, and מֵי פֵרוֹת refers to extracts of fruits which are not normally squeezed.

וְלֹא בְכָל דָּבָר שֶׁאֵינוֹ מִתְקַיֵּם. — *nor with anything which is not lasting.*

[These substances and others like them which do not leave a permanent mark cannot be used to write a *get.*]

עַל הַכֹּל כּוֹתְבִין: — *[We] write [it] upon anything:*

A *get* may be written on any material, as long as it is lasting. It cannot be written on something which will wither (*Tos.* 21b s.v. על עלה).

עַל הֶעָלֶה שֶׁל זַיִת; — *on the leaf of an olive tree;*

If the leaf is already detached from the tree (*Rav* to 2:4). [Attached items are discussed in the next mishnah.] Although the value of an olive leaf is negligible, it is acceptable for a *get,* because it can be combined with other leaves, thereby taking on some value. In addition, a *get* is not required to have any monetary value and is valid even if written on something which is forbidden for any benefit [and thus has no monetary value whatsoever] (*Gem.* 20a).

וְעַל הַקֶּרֶן שֶׁל פָּרָה, וְנוֹתֵן לָהּ אֶת הַפָּרָה; — *or on the horn of a cow, and he gives her the cow;*

If a *get* is written on the horn of a cow which is still attached, it must be given together with the entire cow. The *Gemara* (21b) derives exegetically from the verse (*Deut.* 24:1), *He shall write ... and he shall give,* that a *get* must be something which need only be written and given in order to effect the divorce. When another process —

nor with fruit juice, nor with anything which is not lasting.

[We] write [it] upon anything: on the leaf of an olive tree; or on the horn of a cow, and he gives her the cow; or on the hand of a slave, and he gives her the slave. R' Yose the Galilean says: [We] do not write [it] on a living creature, nor on food.

4. [We] do not write [it] on something attached to the ground. [If] he wrote it

YAD AVRAHAM

such as detachment — is necessary to execute the *get*, it is not valid (*Rav;* see 2:4).

This requirement, that a *get* be written on something unattached, applies only to the writing and/or signing of the *get* (see mishnah 4 and commentary ad loc.); if it is attached to something afterward it may be detached again and given to the woman. In our case, when the *get* was written, it was not yet disqualified by virtue of being attached, because he was still able to give her the entire cow. Nevertheless, he cannot detach the horn and give it to her because once he gives her the detached horn, the *get* is defined as being the horn alone, and not the entire cow. Since at the time the *get* was written, the horn required detachment in order to be given alone, it is void (*Rashba* loc. cit. s.v. רבי יהודה פוסל).

עַל הַיָּד שֶׁל עֶבֶד, וְנוֹתֵן לָהּ אֶת הָעֶבֶד. — *or on the hand of a slave, and he gives her the slave.*

[If a *get* is written on the hand of a slave, the husband must give the wife the entire slave, in order for the *get* to be effective.].

רַבִּי יוֹסֵי הַגְּלִילִי אוֹמֵר: אֵין כּוֹתְבִין לֹא עַל דָּבָר שֶׁיֵּשׁ בּוֹ רוּחַ חַיִּים, וְלֹא עַל הָאֳכָלִים. — *R' Yose the Galilean says: [We] do not write [it] on a living creature, nor on food.*

R' Yose disagrees with the first *Tanna*, and maintains that a *get* cannot be written on the horn of a cow, nor on the leaf of an olive tree, because neither a living creature nor food may be used for a *get*. He derives this from the Torah's reference (*Deut.* 24:1) to a *get* as a סֵפֶר, *a book*, which is not made from either of these (*Rav* from *Gem.* 21b).

The leaf of an olive tree is considered food, because it is eaten by doves, as is evident from the story of Noah [*Gem.* 8:11] (*Tos. Yom Tov*).

The first, anonymous *Tanna* construes the Biblical reference to a book as denoting that the *get* tells a tale by describing the divorce process. However, it is not meant to prescribe the material upon which the *get* should be written (*Rav* from *Gem.* loc. cit.).

4.

אֵין כּוֹתְבִין בִּמְחֻבָּר לַקַּרְקַע. — *[We] do not write [it] on something attached to the ground.*

A *get* may not be written on something attached to the ground (e.g., a leaf), because it must then be detached before being given. As explained in the commentary to the previous mishnah, the Torah requires that a *get* be written in a form in which it can be

בִּמְחֻבָּר, תְּלָשׁוֹ, וַחֲתָמוֹ, וּנְתָנוֹ לָהּ — כָּשֵׁר. רַבִּי יְהוּדָה פּוֹסֵל, עַד שֶׁתְּהֵא כְתִיבָתוֹ וַחֲתִימָתוֹ בְּתָלוּשׁ.

רַבִּי יְהוּדָה בֶּן בְּתֵירָה אוֹמֵר: אֵין כּוֹתְבִין לֹא עַל הַנְּיָר הַמָּחוּק, וְלֹא עַל

ר׳ עובדיה מברטנורא

כתבו על המחובר וכו׳. הכי קאמר, כתב במחובר הטופס, שהוא כל הגט כולו חוץ ממקום האיש ומקום האשה והזמן, ותלשו וחתמו, כלומר שכתב התורף, שהוא מקום האיש והאשה והזמן, אחר שתלשו, כשר, דכיון שנכתב התורף בתלוש, אף על פי שהטופס נכתב במחובר, כשר: **על הנייר המחוק.** שיכול לחזור ולמוחקו עד העדים, ולכתוב עליו מה שירצה, ולא מנכרא מלתא, שהרי עדים נמי על המחק הם חתומים:

יד אברהם

given immediately with no necessity for detachment in the interim (*Rav* from *Gem.* 21b). It cannot be given together with the ground to which it is attached, because the Torah states (*Deut.* 24:1): *and he shall give [it] in her hand,* which denotes that a *get* must be fitting to be handed over. This disqualifies anything attached to the ground (*Rosh; Meiri*).

There is a dispute among the commentators as to the extend of this requirement. Some maintain that it applies only to those things which are attached to the source from which they grew, such as a plant or a cow's horn. However, to write a *get* on a small portion of a large sheet of parchment, and then detach it from the remainder of the sheet, is not considered a detachment of sufficient significance to invalidate the *get*. Others maintain that any detachment whatsoever invalidates the *get*, but even they agree that cutting off small pieces of parchment from the *get* (e.g., to make it look nicer) is not considered detaching the *get* from a different object and is permissible (*Tos.* 21b s.v. יצא זה). Nevertheless, it is recommended that the parchment of the *get* be cut to its desired measurements before the *get* is written on it (*Even Haezer* 124:3).

כְּתָבוֹ בִּמְחֻבָּר, תְּלָשׁוֹ, וַחֲתָמוֹ, וּנְתָנוֹ לָהּ — כָּשֵׁר. — *[If] he wrote it on something attached, and [then] detached it, completed it, and gave it to her, it is valid.*

This statement of the *Tanna* seems to directly contradict his previous words, that a *get* cannot be written on something attached. The *Gemara* (21b) explains that the first statement is discussing a Rabbinic ruling — discussed below — which only prohibits such a *get* initially, but accepts its validity if it was used for divorce. The second statement is discussing the Biblical law, which applies ex post facto.

According to R' Elazar, who maintains that the writing of the *get* discussed in the Torah is the text of the *get* and not its signatures (see General Introduction, s.v. *The Witnesses*), the verse disqualifying a *get* which was written when attached refers to the text of the *get*. However, that includes only the *toref*, but not the *tofes* (see commentary to mishnah 1 s.v. בְּפָנַי נִכְתַּב חֶצְיוֹ). Accordingly, if R' Elazar is the first *Tanna* of the mishnah, he is stating that it is prohibited by Rabbinic law to write even the *tofes* on something attached to the ground, as a preventive measure

on something attached, and [then] detached it, completed it, and gave it to her, it is valid. R' Yehudah invalidates [it], unless its writing and completion are done when [it is] detached.

R' Yehudah ben Beseira says: [We] do not write [it] on paper which has been erased, nor on

YAD AVRAHAM

against the possibility of someone writing the *toref* in that manner. However, if he went ahead and wrote the *tofes* while the *get* was attached, but detached it before writing the *toref*, and he gave it to the woman for divorce, it is valid (*Gem.* 21b).

Another opinion in the *Gemara* is that the author of the mishnah is R' Meir, who maintains that the witnesses signed on the *get* are the ones who validate it. Therefore, their signatures constitute the primary writing in the *get*, and hence, the writing to which the Torah refers. According to this view, the mishnah is understood as follows: The Rabbis invalidated a *get* whose specifics were written on something attached to the ground, in order to prevent the possibility of having it signed when still attached. However, if one did write the *get* when it was attached, it is still valid, as long as the witnesses signed after it was detached (*Gem.* loc. cit.).

According to this explanation, the word וַחֲתָמוֹ in the mishnah is translated as *and he had it signed* (*Meiri*).

רַבִּי יְהוּדָה פּוֹסֵל, עַד שֶׁתְּהֵא כְתִיבָתוֹ וַחֲתִימָתוֹ בְּתָלוּשׁ. — *R' Yehudah invalidates [it], unless its writing and completion are done when [it is] detached.*

R' Yehudah maintains that both the *tores* and the *toref* of the *get* must be written after the *get* is detached in order for it to be valid. R' Yehudah agrees that the requirement for the *toref* to be written on something detached is of Rabbinic origin. However, he maintains that the Rabbis reinforced their enactment by invalidating any *get* which does not comply with it. This explanation follows those who attribute the mishnah to R' Elazar (*Tos.* 3b s.v. דתנן).

According to those who attribute it to R' Meir and understand וַחֲתָמוֹ in the mishnah to refer to the witnesses' signatures, R' Yehudah is stating that both the writing of the *get* and its signing must be done after it is detached. This is because he maintains that the writing of the *get* discussed in the Torah refers to both the wording of the *get* itself and the signing of the witnesses. Thus, both are bound by the *get's* regulation (*Rashba* from *Gem.* 4a).

רַבִּי יְהוּדָה בֶּן בְּתֵירָה אוֹמֵר: אֵין כּוֹתְבִין לֹא עַל הַנְּיָר הַמָּחוּק, — *R' Yehudah ben Beseira says: [We] do not write [it] on paper which has been erased,*

A *get* may not be written on paper from which writing has been erased, because anyone can erase it again and write whatever he wants without the changes being noticed (*Rav; Rashi*). Although the difference between the single erasure under the witnesses' signatures and the double erasure under the wording of the *get* is generally discernible, the Rabbis were apprehensive that it might sometimes be similar enough to escape notice (*Tos. Yom Tov* citing *Baal HaIttur*).

Others explain that the mishnah is discussing a case in which the witnesses sign on an erasure, but the text of the *get* is written on a clean section. This is disallowed, because if the *get* would be erased later to make changes, it would be similar to

הַדִּפְתְּרָא, מִפְּנֵי שֶׁהוּא יָכוֹל לְהִזְדַּיֵּף; וַחֲכָמִים מַכְשִׁירִין.

[ה] **הַכֹּל** כְּשֵׁרִין לִכְתּוֹב אֶת הַגֵּט, אֲפִלּוּ חֵרֵשׁ, שׁוֹטֶה, וְקָטָן. הָאִשָּׁה

ר׳ עובדיה מברטנורא

ודפתרא. אין המחק שלו ניכר. דיפתרא, דמליח וקמיח ולא עפיץ: **וחכמים מכשירין.** בגיטין בלבד, דסבירא להו עדי מסירה כרתי, והעדים שהגט נמסר בפניהם הם עיקר הגרושין, לא עדי חתימה. אבל בשאר שטרות דסמכינן אעדי חתימה, מודים חכמים שאין נכתבים לא על נייר מחוק ולא על דיפתרא. והלכה כחכמים: (ה) **ואפילו חרש שוטה וקטן.** והוא שגדול עומד על גביו ואומר לו כתוב לשם פלוני. אבל נכרי ועבד, אפילו גדול עומד על גביו, לכתחלה לא יכתוב גט, מפני שהם בני דעת ואדעתא דנפשייהו עבדי, שאפילו גדול אומר לו כתוב לשם פלוני, הוא לא יכתוב אלא לדעת עצמו. ואם נכרי ועבד כתבו טופס הגט, וישראל בן דעת כתב התורף, שהוא שם האיש והאשה והזמן, שכל אלו צריכין לשמן, הגט כשר. וכן חרש שוטה וקטן דאמרינן במתניתין שכשרים לכתוב את הגט, הני מילי טופס, אבל תורף אינו כשר אלא שיכתבנו ישראל גדול ובן דעת:

יד אברהם

the witnesses' signatures, and would not be discerned (*Tos.* 22a s.v. לא). Another approach is that the text of the *get* is written on a previous erasure, but the signatures are on a clean section of the paper. In such a case, a double erasure in the *get* would not be noticed, because there is no single erasure with which to compare it (*Ran*).

וְלֹא עַל הַדִּפְתְּרָא, — *nor on unfinished parchment,*

Parchment is treated in three stages — with salt, with flour, and with gallnut. דִּפְתְּרָא refers to parchment which has been treated with salt and flour, but not with gallnut (*Rav* from *Gem.* 22a). [Even at this point] it may not be used for a *get* because erasures upon it are [still] not discernible (*Rav*).

מִפְּנֵי שֶׁהוּא יָכוֹל לְהִזְדַּיֵּף; — *because it can be forged;*

[R' Yehudah ben Beseira maintains that any *get* which can be forged or altered is not valid from the outset.]

וַחֲכָמִים מַכְשִׁירִין. — *the Sages, however, validate [these].*

They maintain that even a *get* which is susceptible to forgery is valid, because they accept R' Elazar's view that the witnesses to the giving of the *get* are the ones who validate it, and not those signed on the document. Therefore, even when the *get* can be forged, and thus, cannot be relied upon for evidence, we can call upon the witnesses to the giving of the *get* to provide any necessary testimony (*Rav* from *Gem.*22a-b; *Rashi*). According to R' Meir, however, the *get* is validated by the testimony of the witnesses signed upon it. Therefore, if the information in the *get* to which they signed cannot be relied upon, their testimony is not efficacious, and thus, the *get* is not valid (*Tos.* 22a s.v. מאן חכמים).

The Sages were lenient regarding a *get* which can be forged, because the woman needs to bring it to court only once to establish her unmarried status, and we can therefore rely upon the witness who saw it being given over to notice any change. However, a monetary document which is kept for purposes of evidence is void if

unfinished parchment, because it can be forged; the Sages, however, validate [these].

5. **A**ll are qualified to write a *get*, even a deaf-mute, a mentally deranged person, and a minor.

YAD AVRAHAM

it can be forged, because the witnesses to the transaction will forget the details in the course of time, and the document will be relied upon for evidence. Therefore, the possibility of forgery is of concern, even according to the Sages (*Rav* from *Gem.* 22b; *Rashi;* cf. *Tos.* ad loc, s.v. אבל; *Ran*).

5.

הַכֹּל כְּשֵׁרִין לִכְתּוֹב אֶת הַגֵּט, — *All are qualified to write a get,*

No special qualifications are necessary to write the *tofes* of a *get* without including the *toref* (see commentary to mishnah 1 s.v. בְּפָנַי נִכְתַּב חֶצְיוֹ) (*Rav* from *Gem.* 23a).

אֲפִלּוּ חֵרֵשׁ, — *even a deaf-mute,*

Who is considered to be mentally incompetent (*Gem.* 22b).

Technically, the term חֵרֵשׁ signifies a deaf person. But throughout the Talmud (see *Chagigah* 2b-3a, *Terumos* 1:2), wherever the term is juxtaposed with שׁוֹטֶה וְקָטָן, *a deranged person and a minor,* it denotes a deaf person who is deemed mentally incompetent. As the *Gemara* (ibid.) makes clear, this refers to a deaf-mute who, because of his condition, lacks the ability to communicate and is therefore not obligated in the performance of the commandments. Hence, one who was born deaf and is, as a result, a deaf-mute is included in this category.[1]

שׁוֹטֶה, — *a mentally deranged person,*

One who is deranged to the extent that he is no longer obligated to observe *mitzvos,* because he is not considered responsible for his actions. The exact criteria for judging a deranged person are discussed in the *Gemara* (*Chagigah* 3b) and at length by the halachic authorities, and do not lend themselves to synopsis (see *Rambam, Hil. Eidus* 9:9ff.; *Even Haezer* 121; *Yoreh Deah* 1:5; *Choshen Mishpat* 35:8-10). *Rambam* adds: "The very feeble-minded ... are included in the category of deranged."

וְקָטָן. — *and a minor.*

[This refers to a child who has not yet reached the age of legal responsibility and competence in Jewish law. A girl is considered a minor until her twelfth birthday, and a boy until his thirteenth.]

Even the three types enumerated here are qualified to write the *tofes* of a *get,* provided that a competent adult oversees them and instructs them to write it with specific intent for the particular man and woman involved. This is because the *tofes* requires specific intent only by virtue of Rabbinic enactment. Such supervision is not sufficient for the *toref,* however, which requires specific in-

1. The halachic status of a deaf-mute who has been taught to talk by modern methods is extensively discussed in the responsa of the later authorities. See *Teshuvos Divrei Chaim* (*Even Haezer* 72), *Maharam Schick* (ibid. 79), *Igros Moshe* (ibid. 3:33), *Maharsham* 2:140), *Teshuvos HaGri Steif* (239).

כּוֹתֶבֶת אֶת גִּטָּהּ, וְהָאִישׁ כּוֹתֵב אֶת שׁוֹבָרוֹ, שֶׁאֵין קִיּוּם הַגֵּט אֶלָּא בְחוֹתְמָיו.

הַכֹּל כְּשֵׁרִין לְהָבִיא אֶת הַגֵּט, חוּץ מֵחֵרֵשׁ, שׁוֹטֶה, וְקָטָן, וְסוּמָא, וְנָכְרִי.

ר' עובדיה מברטנורא

חוץ מחרש שוטה וקטן. דלאו בני דעה נינהו: **וסומא.** פסול להביא גט מחוצה לארץ, שאינו יכול לומר בפני נכתב ובפני נחתם. אבל להביא גט בארץ ישראל, שאין צריך לומר בפני נכתב ובפני נחתם, או אפילו בחוצה לארץ, אם הגט מקויים בחותמיו, או להיות שליח של אשה לקבל גטה, לכל אלו הסומא כשר: **ונכרי.** דליתיה בתורת גיטין וקדושין, ובמידי דלנפשיה לא חזי לא מצי למעבד שליחותא לאחריני:

יד אברהם

tent by Biblical law (*Rav* from *Gem.* 23a; *Rambam, Hil. Gerushin* 3:18; *Rosh*).

A gentile cannot write even the *tofes* of a *get,* despite the presence of a Jewish adult instructing him to write with specific intent, because he does not negate his will to that of the instructor, and we therefore cannot assume that he had specific intent (*Rav* from *Gem.* 23a).

Regarding a slave, there is a dispute among the commentators. Some maintain that he is totally disqualified, even with a free adult supervising, because he is not a participant in the laws of Jewish marriage and divorce, and can therefore not play a role in executing them (*Rav; Rambam, Hil. Gerushin* 3:15*f.*; see *Tos. R' Akiva*). Others maintain that to write the *tofes* of the *get* does not require any legal qualifications, as long as it is written with specific intent. Therefore, a slave can write it even with no free adult supervising (*Rambam; Rashba*).

All of these requirements for the writing of the *tofes* of the *get* apply only at the outset. However, if a deaf-mute, mentally deranged person, or minor did write it without the supervision of a competent adult — or even if it was written by a gentile or a slave — the *get* is valid (*Rav; Rambam, Hil. Gerushin* 3:17).

Other commentators maintain that the Rabbis did not extend the rule of specific intent to the *tofes* of the *get* at all, and it may therefore be written by anyone, even a gentile. The *Gemara,* which states that a deaf-mute, a mentally deranged person, and a minor can write a *get* only under the supervision of a capable adult, is referring to the *toref.* Such supervision is considered effective even when specific intent is required by Biblical law, but it is of no avail when the writer of the *get* is a gentile, because the latter does not negate his will to that of the overseer, as explained above (*Ran; Meiri*).

There is another approach to this mishnah which attributes it to R' Meir, who maintains that the signatures of the witnesses are the only portion of the *get* governed by its regulations. Hence, a deaf-mute, a mentally deranged person, a minor, or a gentile can write the entire *get,* including its particulars, without the supervision of a competent Jewish adult. Only the signatures of the witnesses requires specific intent (*Gem.* 23a).

הָאִשָּׁה כּוֹתֶבֶת אֶת גִּטָּהּ, — *A woman may write her own get,*

And give it to her husband to assume ownership. He can then return it to her, and thereby divorce her (*Rashi*).

At the time of its writing, this *get* was not ready for immediate use, because it first required transfer to the husband's possession. Nevertheless, it is not comparable to a *get* that is attached to the ground — which is invalid because it must be detached before being given (see previous mishnah) — since

2
5

A woman may write her own *get*, and a man may write his own receipt, for the validity of the document is [dependent] only upon those who sign it.

All are qualified to bring a *get*, except a deaf-mute, mentally deranged person, a minor, a blind person, and a gentile.

YAD AVRAHAM

the transfer of ownership to the husband is not an act done to the body of the *get* itself, and is therefore a less significant interruption between the writing and giving of the document than its detachment (*Ran*).

וְהָאִישׁ כּוֹתֵב אֶת שׁוֹבָרוֹ, — *and a man may write his own receipt,*

The receipt for the payment of the *kesubah* (marriage contract), which should really be written by the woman and given to the man upon payment, may be written by the man himself (*Rashi*).

שֶׁאֵין קִיּוּם הַגֵּט אֶלָּא בְחוֹתְמָיו. — *for the validity of the document is [dependent] only upon those who sign it.*

[According to R' Meir, it is the witnesses to the document who grant it validity. Therefore, the *get* is valid as long as it is in the possession of the husband at the time it is validated. Also, the receipt for the *Kesubah* is valid as long as it is signed at the behest of the woman.]

According to R' Elazar, it is the witnesses who observe the giving of the *get* that grant it validity, not those signed upon it. Nevertheless, the mishnah refers to them as the signatories of the *get* because it is generally the witnesses signed upon the document who are requested to observe it being given over (*Rashi* 23a s.v. והוא שהיה; *Meiri*).

הַכֹּל כְּשֵׁרִין לְהָבִיא אֶת הַגֵּט, חוּץ מֵחֵרֵשׁ, שׁוֹטֶה, וְקָטָן, — *All are qualified to bring a get, except a deaf-mute, mentally deranged person, a minor,*

These are not qualified to be agents of the husband to deliver a *get* to his wife, because they are considered mentally incompetent, and are therefore not legally qualified to act as agents (*Rav* from *Gem.* 23a).

וְסוּמָא, — *a blind person,*

Although a blind person is considered legally competent, he cannot be an agent to bring a *get* from a foreign land, because such an agent must testify to having witnessed its writing and signing (see 1:1), and a blind person cannot do this (*Rav* from *Gem.* 23a). However, in those cases where such testimony is not required — such as the delivery of a *get* within Eretz Yisrael (see 1:3) or delivery of a *get* whose signatures have been confirmed by witnesses (see mishnah 1) — a blind person can be the agent of delivery (ibid.).

Although it is sufficient for the agent to testify that he heard the sound of the pen writing upon the paper at the behest of the husband (see 1:1), this is because the scribe knows that the witness can check what he is doing and will therefore certainly follow instructions. Obviously, this assumption is not valid when the witness is blind (*Ran*).

וְנָכְרִי. — *and a gentile.*

Since a gentile is not a participant in the laws of Jewish marriage and divorce, he cannot be an agent to deliver a *get*. This is based on the axiom that one can be a legal agent

[ו] **קִבֵּל** הַקָּטָן, וְהִגְדִּיל; חֵרֵשׁ, וְנִתְפַּקַּח; סוּמָא, וְנִתְפַּתַּח; שׁוֹטֶה, וְנִשְׁתַּפָּה; נָכְרִי, וְנִתְגַּיֵּר — פָּסוּל. אֲבָל פִּקֵּחַ, וְנִתְחָרֵשׁ, וְחָזַר וְנִתְפַּקַּח; פִּתֵּחַ, וְנִסְתַּמָּא, וְחָזַר וְנִתְפַּתַּח;

ר' עובדיה מברטנורא

(ו) קבל הקטן. הגט מיד הבעל: **והגדיל.** קודם שמסרו לה: **פתוח ונסתמא וחזר ונתפתח.** אפילו לא חזר ונתפתח, הואיל והיה פתוח בשעת קבלת הגט, שפיר מצי למיהוי שליח, דהא יכול לומר בפני נכתב ובפני נחתם, אלא איידי דבעי למתנא סיפא וחזר ונשתפה, שצריך שיהיה בן דעת בשעת נתינה, תנא נמי רישא וחזר ונתפתח. וכל פסולי עדות בעבירה, פסולין להביא את הגט, שאין נאמנים לומר בפני נכתב ובפני נחתם, ואם הגט מקויים בחותמיו, כשרים להביאו:

יד אברהם

only for something he is capable of doing in his own behalf (*Rav* from *Gem.* 23a).

The *Gemara* (23b) states that a slave cannot be an agent to receive a *get* on behalf of a woman because, like a gentile, he is not a participant in the laws of Jewish marriage and divorce. Most commentators maintain that he is likewise disqualified from being an agent to deliver the *get* (*Tos.* 23b s.v. אין העבד; *Rif; Rambam, Hil. Gerushin* 6:6; *Meiri*). The reason the mishnah mentions gentiles as an example of this rather than slaves is to tell us that even if he intends to convert, and is thus on his way to becoming a participant, he is still not qualified. This point is not applicable to a slave who can take no initiative regarding his freedom (*Tos.* ibid.).

There is another opinion that a slave is disqualified only from receiving the *get* for the woman, but not from delivering it to her. This is because the execution of the *get* takes place when it enters the agent's hand, and since a slave is not a participant in the laws of Jewish marriage and divorce, the delivery of a *get* into his hand cannot effect a divorce. To deliver the *get*, however, he need only act as an agent for the husband, and a slave is qualified to do that.[1] Only a gentile is excluded even from this role because he is disqualified from any agency in Jewish law (*Ran* citing *Ri Migash*).

6.

קִבֵּל הַקָּטָן, וְהִגְדִּיל; — *[If] a minor received [it], and [then] became of age;*

A minor was given a *get* by the husband to give to his wife, and he came of age before delivering the *get* (*Ran*).

חֵרֵשׁ, וְנִתְפַּקַּח; — *[or] a deaf-mute, and he [then] became able to hear;*

1. The distinction made here is quite obscure and requires explanation. The role of an agent who delivers a *get* is an active one. The reason for the validity of his delivery can therefore be defined as follows: His act on behalf of the husband is considered as if it were done by the husband himself. The woman, however, plays a passive role; the fact that the *get* has been placed in her hand validates the divorce. Accordingly, her agent can be effective only if a *get* placed in his hand is considered as if it were in hers (*Pnei Yehoshua* to *Kiddushin* 41a). [Thus, the role of the husband's agent requires only that his action execute the *get* for which his eligibility to be an agent is sufficient. That of her agent, however, necessitates that his hand itself be instrumental in the divorce, and for that purpose, one must have the legal capacity to be a participant in a divorce.]

2
6

6. [If] a minor received [it], and [then] became of age; [or] a deaf-mute, and he [then] became able to hear; [or] a blind person, and he [then] became able to see; [or] a mentally deranged person, and he [then] became sane; [or] a gentile, and he [then] became a proselyte — [he is] not valid. However, [if it was] a hearing person [who received it], and he [then] became a deaf-mute, and then regained his hearing; [or] a seeing person, and he [then] became blind, and [then] regained his sight;

YAD AVRAHAM

[He was a deaf-mute when he received the *get* from the husband, but gained the ability to hear before delivering it.[1]]

סוּמָא, וְנִתְפַּתַּח; — *[or] a blind person, and he [then] became able to see;*

This refers to an agent of delivery from a foreign land, who must testify to having witnessed the writing and signing of the *get* when he delivers it (see comm. to previous mishnah s.v. וְסוּמָא). In this case, the agent was blind when he was given the *get* and was thus incapable of witnessing its writing and signing. However, by the time he delivered the *get*, he had gained the ability to see (*Gem.* 23a).

שׁוֹטֶה וְנִשְׁתַּפָּה; נָכְרִי, וְנִתְגַּיֵּר — *[or] a mentally deranged person, and he [then] became sane; [or] a gentile, and he [then] became a proselyte —*

[In these cases, too, he received the *get* at a time when he was not qualified to be an agent of delivery, and became qualified before he delivered it to the wife.]

פָּסוּל. — *[he is] not valid.*

[Since these persons were not qualified to be agents of delivery at the time they received the *get*, their agency is null and the delivery of the *get* void. In the case of the blind person, confirmation of the authenticity of the *get* by two witnesses would validate the divorce] (see commentary to 1:1 s.v. רַבָּן שִׁמְעוֹן בֶּן גַּמְלִיאֵל.)]

אֲבָל פִּקֵּחַ, וְנִתְחָרֵשׁ, וְחָזַר וְנִתְפַּקַּח; — *However, [if it was] a hearing person [who received it], and he [then] became a deaf-mute, and then regained his hearing;*

[After a normal person had been given a *get* by the husband to deliver to his wife, he became a deaf-mute. However, he regained his hearing before actually delivering the *get*.]

פִּתֵּחַ, וְנִסְתַּמָּא, וְחָזַר וְנִתְפַּתַּח; — *[or] a seeing person, and he [then] became*

1. Even if he did not gain the power of speech, he would still be considered a qualified agent at the time of delivery, since a mute who is not deaf is assumed to be mentally competent (see *Rambam, Hil. Ishus* 2:26). He could even testify to having witnessed the writing and signing of the *get*, by conveying his testimony with body motions or by writing it (see commentary to 1:3 s.v. הַמֵּבִיא ... וְאֵינוֹ יָכוֹל לוֹמַר).

שָׁפוּי, וְנִשְׁתַּטָּה, וְחָזַר וְנִשְׁתַּפָּה — כָּשֵׁר. זֶה
הַכְּלָל: כָּל שֶׁתְּחִלָּתוֹ וְסוֹפוֹ בְּדַעַת — כָּשֵׁר.

[ז] **אַף** הַנָּשִׁים שֶׁאֵינָן נֶאֱמָנוֹת לוֹמַר
"מֵת בַּעְלָהּ" נֶאֱמָנוֹת לְהָבִיא
אֶת גִּטָּהּ: חֲמוֹתָהּ, וּבַת חֲמוֹתָהּ,

ר' עובדיה מברטנורא

(ז) **חמותה ובת חמותה כו'.** אֵינָן נֶאֱמָנוֹת לוֹמַר מֵת בַּעְלָהּ, מִשּׁוּם דְּסָנְיָין לָהּ וּמְכַוְּונִין לְקַלְקְלָהּ:

יד אברהם

blind, and [then] regained his sight;

[A person who could see was given a *get* by the husband in a foreign land to deliver to his wife. He then became blind, but regained his sight before delivering the *get*.]

Even if he did not regain his vision, he could deliver the *get* because a blind person is considered legally competent, and thus, his ability to testify to having witnessed the writing and signing of the *get* depends solely on the state of his vision at the time it was written. The mishnah mentions his regaining vision only for the sake of uniformity with the other cases[1] (*Gem.* 23a).

שָׁפוּי, וְנִשְׁתַּטָּה, וְחָזַר וְנִשְׁתַּפָּה — *[or] a sane person, and he [then] became mentally deranged, and [then] regained his sanity —*

[He became an imbecile after receiving the *get* from the husband, but regained his sanity before delivering it.]

כָּשֵׁר. — *[he is] valid.*

[All of these persons are valid agents to deliver the *get*, as will be explained below.]

זֶה הַכְּלָל: כָּל שֶׁתְּחִלָּתוֹ וְסוֹפוֹ בְּדַעַת — כָּשֵׁר. — *This is the general rule: Anyone who is mentally competent at the beginning and at the end is valid.*

[An agent who was mentally competent both upon receiving the *get* from the husband and upon delivering it to the wife is considered qualified even if there was a period in between when he was not qualified.]

The mishnah does not state: Anyone who is qualified at the beginning and at the end [which would seem more appropriate for a general rule about the validity of witnesses]. This is to indicate that only those defects which revolve around mental competence must be corrected before the *get* is delivered. But one who became blind after receiving the *get* can deliver it while he is blind, because he is considered mentally competent [as mentioned above] (*Gem.* 23a).

1. The *Gemara*, in other places (e.g., *Bava Basra* 128a), disqualifies a blind person from testimony even where there is no specific requirement for visual observation. Nevertheless, in our mishnah, where the standard prerequisites for valid testimony are not required (i.e., two male witnesses), a blind man is also acceptable, as long as he can testify that the *get* had been written and signed in his presence (*Tos.* 23a s.v. הוא הדין). Others maintain that a blind person is always qualified to testify. Those places in the *Gemara* which state otherwise are dealing with cases in which information is needed which cannot be acquired without being able to see (*Meiri*).

2
7

[or] a sane person, and he [then] became mentally deranged, and [then] regained his sanity — [he is] valid. This is the general rule: Anyone who is mentally competent at the beginning and at the end is valid.

7. Even those women who are not trusted to say: "Her husband died" are trusted to bring her *get:* her mother-in-law, her mother-in-law's

YAD AVRAHAM

7.

אַף הַנָּשִׁים שֶׁאֵינָן נֶאֱמָנוֹת לוֹמַר: "מֵת בַּעְלָהּ" — *Even those women who are not trusted to say: "Her husband died"*

Although one witness is believed to testify that a man died and to thereby permit his wife to remarry (*Yevamos* 87b), the women listed below are not. This is because they are assumed to bear enmity toward the wife, and are therefore suspected of fabricating the story of the husband's death so that the wife will remarry. Upon her original husband's return, she would become forbidden to both men and subject to all the penalties enumerated in *Yevamos* 10:1 (*Rav* ibid. 15:4).

נֶאֱמָנוֹת לְהָבִיא אֶת גִּטָּהּ: — *are trusted to bring her get:*

Even these women are trusted to bring her *get* from a foreign land and testify to having witnessed its writing and signing. There is no fear of a plot against the wife, because her husband would not be believed to later deny having sent the *get* (see 1:1), and she would thus remain married to her new husband — without being subject to any penalties (*Gem.* 23b). We are not afraid that they would lie about a *get* in order to cause her to leave the first husband and marry another, because only the powerful passion of hatred which incites them to cause her harm would be a strong enough incentive to lie about a *get* [and bring about the violation of such a stringent Biblical prohibition as that of adultery] (*Meiri*).

However, if they bring a *get* within Eretz Yisrael, where they are not required to testify to having witnessed its writing and signing, the husband is able to later dispute the validity of the *get* (see 1:2). Therefore, the possibility of a plot against the wife must be considered, and they are not believed (*Gem.* loc. cit.).

If any of these women brought a *get* from within Eretz Yisrael and did testify that it had been written and signed in her presence, the husband can no longer dispute the *get*, and they are therefore believed (*Rambam*). Others maintain that they are not believed because they may not be aware that the husband's protest will be disregarded, and could still be plotting against the wife (*Rashba*).

חֲמוֹתָהּ, — *her mother-in-law,*

It is presumed that a mother-in-law hates her daughter-in-law because she feels that the latter will reap the fruits of her labor (*Rav* to *Yevamos* 15:4) [i.e., that her daughter-in-law will share in her son's inheritance of his father, which includes those possessions she brought into the marriage from her

וְצָרָתָהּ, וִיבִמְתָּהּ, וּבַת בַּעְלָהּ. מַה בֵּין גֵּט לְמִיתָה? שֶׁהַכְּתָב מוֹכִיחַ.

הָאִשָּׁה עַצְמָהּ מְבִיאָה אֶת גִּטָּהּ, וּבִלְבַד שֶׁהִיא צְרִיכָה לוֹמַר: „בְּפָנַי נִכְתַּב וּבְפָנַי נֶחְתַּם״.

ר׳ עובדיה מברטנורא

ובלבד שהיא צריכה לומר בפני נכתב ובפני נחתם. ודוקא כשהתנה הבעל עמה בשעה שמסר הגט לידה, ואמר לה לא תתגרשי אלא בבית דינו של פלוני ותאמרי בפני נכתב ובפני נחתם, והבית דין לוקחין אותו מידה אחר שאמרה בפני נכתב ובפני נחתם, וממנין שליח שיחזור ויתן אותו לה. אבל אשה שגטה יוצא מתחת ידה בכל מקום שהיא, הרי זו מגורשת, ואפילו שאין הגט מקוים בחותמיו, ואינה צריכה שתאמר בפני נכתב ובפני נחתם:

יד אברהם

depriving her of the husband's affection (*Yevamos* 118a; see ibid. 15:6).

וִיבִמְתָּהּ, — *her husband's brother's wife,*

We assume that these sisters-in-law hate each other because each knows that if her own husband dies, her brother-in-law may perform *yibum*,[1] and they will become co-wives. This can cause hatred even before it occurs (*Rav* to *Yevamos* 15:4; see *Tos. Yom Tov*).

This applies even if the two women were sisters [in which case neither brother may marry both of them (*Lev.* 18:18)] or had children, when *yibum* is not applicable. The Sages disqualified even these in order to have a single uniform law for all brothers' wives. Another explanation is that even sisters-in-law with children may hate each other because of the possibility that their children may die, and they will then become eligible for *yibum* (*Tos. R' Akiva* to *Yevamos* ibid.).

וּבַת בַּעְלָהּ. — *and her husband's daughter.*

A stepdaughter usually hates her stepmother for assuming her mother's father's house (*Rashi* ibid. 117a)].

A daughter-in-law is also disqualified from testifying about her father-in-law's death since it is assumed that she harbors enmity toward her mother-in-law. This is because the latter reports her daughter-in-law's activities to her son (*Yevamos* 117a). The same also applies to the other women enumerated below as invalid witnesses; their counterparts are also disqualified (*Tos. R' Akiva* ibid. 15:4).

וּבַת חֲמוֹתָהּ, — *her mother-in-law's daughter,*

Her mother-in-law's daughter may not testify for her because she resents her sister-in-law, who will eventually inherit her parents' wealth [Her husband will inherit from his parents and pass it on to his wife] (*Rav* loc. cit.). Similarly, a father-in-law's daughter may not testify (*Yevamos* 117a).

וְצָרָתָהּ, — *her co-wife,*

[According to Biblical law, a man may have more than one wife. If he does, each wife is said to be the co-wife of the others.]

Each co-wife hates the others for

1. [This is the process dictated by the Torah (*Deut.* 25:5), whereby a woman whose husband dies without children is married to his brother, unless they perform an alternative ceremony known as *chalitzah* which releases her to remarry (see General Introduction to ArtScroll *Yevamos*).]

daughter, her co-wife, her husband's brother's wife, and her husband's daughter. What is the difference between a *get* and [testimony of] death? That the written document is evidence.

The woman herself may bring her own *get*, only she must say: "It was written in my presence and signed in my presence."

YAD AVRAHAM

place and reaping the profits of her work (*Rav* loc. cit.).

מַה בֵּין גֵּט לְמִיתָה? שֶׁהַכְּתָב מוֹכִיחַ. — *What is the difference between a get and [testimony of] death? That the written document is evidence.*

The presence of the *get* in these women's hands adds to their credibility, and we can therefore assume that they are telling the truth (*Rav* ibid.; *Rashi* to *Yevamos* 117a).

This statement of the mishnah would seem to be unnecessary, since the reason for their credibility in this case has already been sufficiently explained. However, even when these women bring the *get* from a foreign land, and testify to having witnessed its writing and signing, the possibility of a plot cannot be ruled out completely. For, although the husband is not believed to dispute the *get* in such a case, the women might produce witnesses or other forms of proof that he did not send it (*Tos.* 23b s.v. אדרבה). It is therefore necessary for the mishnah to add that their credibility is enhanced by the presence of the *get* in their hands, and that is why they are believed (*Maharam Shif* ibid. s.v. אדרבה).

An alternative interpretation is that the reason any agent of delivery is relied upon to the point of rejecting the husband's subsequent protest is because the *get* in the agent's hands strengthens his credibility. Since the reason we are not concerned about a plot in our case is due to the fact that the husband would not be believed to dispute the *get*, it is ultimately the presence of the *get* in the women's hands which rules out any suspicion of a plot against the wife (*Meiri*).

הָאִשָּׁה עַצְמָהּ מְבִיאָה אֶת גִּטָּהּ, וּבִלְבַד שֶׁהִיא צְרִיכָה לוֹמַר: ,,בְּפָנַי נִכְתַּב וּבְפָנַי נֶחְתַּם". — *The woman herself may bring her own get, only she must say: "It was written in my presence and signed in my presence."*

A man gave his wife a *get* with the following stipulation: She must be his agent to deliver it to the court in a specific place, and the court will then appoint another agent to divorce her by handing her the *get*. Under these circumstances, the woman, in bringing the *get* to the court, is like any other agent for delivery, and must therefore testify to having witnessed its writing and signing (*Gem.* 24a; *Rambam Commentary* and *Hil. Gerushin* 7:23; *Meiri*).

However, if a woman comes to court with a *get* in her hands, and claims she was divorced, she is fully believed, even without testifying to having witnessed its writing and signing. She is not suspected of lying in this matter, since she would only be causing her own transgression if she remarried illicitly (*Rambam, Hil. Gerushin* 7:24; *Meiri*).

[The above is only one of several instances cited in the *Gemara,* in which her testimony would be required. The common factor in all of them is that her husband stipulated that she be an agent for delivery until reaching a designated place where the divorce should be executed.]

פרק שלישי

Chapter Three

[א] **כָּל** גֵּט שֶׁנִּכְתַּב שֶׁלֹּא לְשׁוּם אִשָּׁה — פָּסוּל. כֵּיצַד? הָיָה עוֹבֵר בַּשּׁוּק וְשָׁמַע קוֹל סוֹפְרִים מַקְרִין: „אִישׁ פְּלוֹנִי מְגָרֵשׁ אֶת פְּלוֹנִית מִמָּקוֹם פְּלוֹנִי”, וְאָמַר: „זֶה שְׁמִי וְזֶה שֵׁם אִשְׁתִּי” — פָּסוּל לְגָרֵשׁ בּוֹ.

יָתֵר מִכֵּן, כָּתַב לְגָרֵשׁ בּוֹ אֶת אִשְׁתּוֹ, וְנִמְלַךְ; מְצָאוֹ בֶּן עִירוֹ וְאָמַר לוֹ: „שְׁמִי כִּשְׁמְךָ, וְשֵׁם אִשְׁתִּי כְּשֵׁם אִשְׁתְּךָ” — פָּסוּל לְגָרֵשׁ בּוֹ.

ר׳ עובדיה מברטנורא

פרק שלישי – כל הגט. (א) כל הגט. קול סופרים מקרין. הגדולים מקרין לתלמידיהם, כשיבא גט לפניך כתבהו כך, והזכירו שם איש בעלמא: **יותר מכן.** ולא זה בלבד שנכתב שלא לשם גירושין אלא להתלמד, אלא אף זה שנכתב לשם גירושין גמורים ונמלך, פסול:

יד אברהם

The mishnah now proceeds to teach us the requisite of specific intent and elaborates upon its application.

1.

כָּל גֵּט שֶׁנִּכְתַּב שֶׁלֹּא לְשׁוּם אִשָּׁה — פָּסוּל. — *Any get which is written without specific intent for a particular woman is void.*

A *get* must be written with specific intent for the divorce of the particular woman to whom it is subsequently given in order to be valid. This is derived from the verse (*Deut.* 24:1): *he shall write for her a document of severance,* which means that it must be written with her in mind. This requirement is referred to as לִשְׁמָהּ, *with specific intent for her* (*Gem.* 24b).

This version of the mishnah is correct only if the author is R' Elazar, who holds that the reference in the Torah to the writing of the *get* means the wording of the *get* itself and not the signatures of the witnesses (see General Introduction, s.v. *The Witnesses*). Accordingly, the rule of specific intent mentioned in the same verse applies also to the actual writing of the *get*. According to R' Meir, however, even a *get* that had been discarded by another may be used for divorce as long as the witnesses sign with specific intent. Therefore, those who assume that R' Meir is the author of the mishnah emend the text to read: *Any bill of get which was signed without specific intent ...* (*Gem.* 23a).

כֵּיצַד? — *How [is this exemplified]?*

[The mishnah uses examples to illustrate a step-by-step development of the principle of specific intent and the extent to which it is applied.]

הָיָה עוֹבֵר בַּשּׁוּק וְשָׁמַע קוֹל סוֹפְרִים מַקְרִין: — *[If a man] was passing through the street and heard the sound of scribes dictating:*

He heard professional scribes teaching their students by dictating the proper wording of a *get* to them (*Rav*).

„אִישׁ פְּלוֹנִי מְגָרֵשׁ אֶת פְּלוֹנִית מִמָּקוֹם פְּלוֹנִי”, — *"So-and-so is divorcing So-and-so from such and such a place,"*

In dictating the wording of the *get,*

3
1

1. **A**ny *get* which is written without specific intent for a particular woman is void. How [is this exemplified]? [If a man] was passing through the street and heard the sound of scribes dictating: "So-and-so is divorcing So-and-so from such and such a place," and he said: "That is my name and that is my wife's name," it is void for executing a divorce with it.

Moreover, [if] he wrote [a *get*] with which to divorce his wife, and he changed his mind, [and] a man of his city met him and said to him: "My name is like your name, and my wife's name is like your wife's name," it is void for executing a divorce with it.

YAD AVRAHAM

the scribe used specific names for the man, woman, and place, as examples (*Rav*).

וְאָמַר: ,,זֶה שְׁמִי וְזֶה שֵׁם אִשְׁתִּי" — *and he said: "That is my name and that is my wife's name,"*

[The names used as examples by the scribe were the same as those of this man and his wife, and he decided to use the *get* written by those students to divorce his wife.]

פָּסוּל לְגָרֵשׁ בּוֹ. — *it is void for executing a divorce with it.*

He cannot use the *get* to divorce his wife because it was written for practice, not for the purpose of divorce. This is disqualified by virtue of the verse cited above: *he shall write for her a document of severance,* which indicates that it must be written for the sake of divorce (*Gem.* 24b).

According to those who attribute the authorship of this mishnah to R' Meir (as discussed above), it must be assumed that students of scribes who wrote *gittin* for practice used to sign those *gittin* as well. Thus, such *gittin* are void, for they were not even signed for the sake of divorce (*Tos.* 23a s.v. אימא).

יָתֵר מִכֵּן, — *Moreover,*

Not only is a *get* which was written for practice void, but even one which was written for the sake of divorce can be disqualified by virtue of the requirement for specific intent (*Rav*).

כָּתַב לְגָרֵשׁ בּוֹ אֶת אִשְׁתּוֹ, וְנִמְלַךְ; — *[if] he wrote [a get] with which to divorce his wife, and he changed his mind,*

[If a man had a *get* drawn up for the sake of divorcing his wife, and he decided not to use it.]

מְצָאוֹ בֶּן עִירוֹ וְאָמַר לוֹ: ,,שְׁמִי כְּשִׁמְךָ, וְשֵׁם אִשְׁתִּי כְּשֵׁם אִשְׁתְּךָ" — *[and] a man of his city met him and said to him: "My name is like your name, and my wife's name is like your wife's name,"*

[Another man from the same town and with the same name as the man for whom the *get* was written, who had a wife with the same name as the first man's wife, requested to use the *get* for the divorce of his wife.]

פָּסוּל לְגָרֵשׁ בּוֹ. — *it is void for executing a divorce with it.*

The *get* cannot be used by the second man to divorce his wife, because the verse says, *And he shall*

יָתֵר מִכֵּן, הָיוּ לוֹ שְׁתֵּי נָשִׁים וּשְׁמוֹתֵיהֶן שָׁוִים; כָּתַב לְגָרֵשׁ בּוֹ אֶת הַגְּדוֹלָה — לֹא יְגָרֵשׁ בּוֹ אֶת הַקְּטַנָּה.

יָתֵר מִכֵּן, אָמַר לַלַּבְלָר: ,,כְּתֹב; לְאֵיזוֹ שֶׁאֶרְצֶה אֲגָרֵשׁ״ — פָּסוּל לְגָרֵשׁ בּוֹ.

ר׳ עובדיה מברטנורא

יתר מכן היו לו שתי נשים כו׳. ולא זה בלבד שנכתב שלא לשם גירושין של אדם זה, פסול, אלא אף זה שהיו לו שתי נשים שנכתב לשם גירושין דהאי גברא, פסול, כיון שנכתב שלא לשם גירושיה של זו: **גדולה וקטנה.** לאו דוקא: **יתר מכן אמר ללבלר וכו׳.** הא קא משמע לן דלא אמרינן הוברר הדבר למפרע דבשעת כתיבה נמי דעתיה אהא ואיכא גירושין דידיה ודידה:

יד אברהם

which of the couples bearing those names it is referring, it can still be used by the couple for whom it was written (*Rambam; Ran; Meiri*). However, it cannot be used by the woman as evidence of her divorce unless there are witnesses that she is the one to whom it was given. Otherwise, we suspect that the *get* may have been written for the other couple bearing those names; the husband changed his mind and discarded it; and this woman then found it (*Gem.* 24b; see *Rashi* ad loc. s.v. הא גדולה and s.v. הא דאמרינן).

יָתֵר מִכֵּן, — *Moreover,*

Not only is a *get* written for one man invalid for another, but even a man with two wives cannot use a *get* for one of them if it had been written for the other (*Rav*).

הָיוּ לוֹ שְׁתֵּי נָשִׁים וּשְׁמוֹתֵיהֶן שָׁוִים; כָּתַב לְגָרֵשׁ בּוֹ אֶת הַגְּדוֹלָה — לֹא יְגָרֵשׁ בּוֹ אֶת הַקְּטַנָּה. — *[if] he had two wives whose names were alike, [and] he wrote [a get] to divorce the elder, he cannot divorce the younger with it.*

This is derived from the expression *for her* in the verse, which indicates that it must be written with specific *write it*, which indicates that the man who uses the *get* to divorce his wife must be the one for whom the *get* was written[1] (*Gem.* 24b).

The statement that the second man may not use this *get* implies that the first man, for whom it was written, can use it to divorce his wife (*Gem.* 24b). This holds true only according to R' Elazar (see General Introduction s.v. *The Witnesses*), who maintains that the witnesses who validate the *get* are those who observe its delivery to the wife, and they may be relied upon to provide any necessary information not clarified in the *get*. According to R' Meir, however, it is the witnesses signed on the *get* who grant it validity. Therefore, any information vital to the *get* must be contained in the *get* upon which they are signed, in order for it to be included in their testimony. Thus, in a case where two couples with the same names live in the same city, a *get* bearing these names does not fully specify the principles involved and is therefore null unless it gave more specific information [e.g., that he is a *Kohen*] (*Tos.* 24b s.v. בעדי מסירה). Others contend that even according to R' Meir, outside sources may be relied upon to clarify the information in the *get*. Therefore, even if the *get* does not specify to

1. The verse would seem to imply that the husband or his legal agent must write the *get*, but evidence from the *Gemara* indicates that it is required only that the *get* be written for the sake of his divorce (*Tos.* 22b s.v. והא; see below commentary to mishnah 2 s.v. צריך שיניח).

3
1

Moreover, [if] he had two wives whose names were alike, [and] he wrote [a *get*] to divorce the elder, he cannot divorce the younger with it.

Moreover, [if] he said to the scribe: "Write [a *get*]; I will divorce whichever one I will want," it is void for executing a divorce with it.

YAD AVRAHAM

intent for the woman to whom it is subsequently given (*Gem.* 24b).

The statement disallowing this *get's* use for the second wife implies that it is valid for divorcing the first wife for whom it was written (*Gem.* 24b). Here, too, there are those who contend that this holds true only according to R' Elazar, who maintains that we rely on the witnesses who observe the delivery of the *get* to clarify which of the women received it (see above, s.v. פָּסוּל לְגָרֵשׁ בּוֹ). According to R' Meir, however, all vital information must be contained in the *get* itself, and a *get* which does not specify which of two wives is intended is not valid (*Tos.* 24b s.v. בעדי מסירה). Others dispute this assumption and hold that even R' Meir does not require full specification in the *get* (*Ramban; Ran; Meiri*). In this case, the *get* can even be used by the woman as evidence of her divorce, because the possibility that it had originally been given to the other wife, was subsequently lost, and then found by this wife of the same man, is considered too remote to merit concern (*Meiri* to 24b s.v. בבר בארנו).

,יָתֵר מִכֵּן — *Moreover,*

[In addition to the basic requirement for specific intent, the mishnah states a further application of that principle.]

אָמַר לַלַּבְלָר: ,,כְּתֹב; לְאֵיזוֹ שֶׁאֶרְצֶה אֲגָרֵשׁ" — *[if] he said to the scribe: "Write [a get]; I will divorce whichever one I will want,"*

[A man who had two wives with the same name directed a scribe to write a *get* with the intent that the husband can use it to divorce whichever wife he chooses.]

.פָּסוּל לְגָרֵשׁ בּוֹ — *it is void for executing a divorce with it.*

Such a *get* is not specifically designated for either of the two wives, because the husband's eventual choice is not considered to have retroactively defined his original intention; therefore, the *get* is not valid[1] (*Rav*).

Some opinions in the *Gemara* hold that the *gittin* disqualified in the mishnah for not complying with the rule of specific intent are included among those which — due to their similarity to a legitimate *get* — nevertheless disqualify the woman from

1. *Ri* maintains that even those who, in other areas of Jewish law, rely upon the final resolution of an unclear situation to retroactively define its original status (see *Gem.* 25a-b) agree that the specific intent of a *get* cannot be defined in such a manner. This is because of the verse which states, *and he shall write for her a document of severance,* which indicates that the specific intent must be defined at the time the *get* is written (*Tos.* 24b s.v. לאיזו). Others contend that the question of retroactive definition is the same in regard to *gittin* as it is regarding all other areas of Jewish law (*Meiri*). The *halachah* follows this opinion, and since the issue of retroactive definition is not resolved, if he delivered this *get* to either of his wives its validity would remain in doubt (*Even HaEzer* 130:4; *Beis Shmuel* ibid. 4).

[ב] **הַכּוֹתֵב** טָפְסֵי גִטִּין – צָרִיךְ שֶׁיַּנִּיחַ מְקוֹם הָאִישׁ, וּמְקוֹם הָאִשָּׁה, וּמְקוֹם הַזְּמַן; שִׁטְרֵי מִלְוָה – צָרִיךְ שֶׁיַּנִּיחַ מְקוֹם הַמַּלְוֶה, מְקוֹם הַלֹּוֶה, מְקוֹם הַמָּעוֹת, מְקוֹם הַזְּמַן; שִׁטְרֵי מֶקַח – צָרִיךְ שֶׁיַּנִּיחַ מְקוֹם הַלּוֹקֵחַ, וּמְקוֹם הַמּוֹכֵר, וּמְקוֹם הַמָּעוֹת, וּמְקוֹם הַשָּׂדֶה, וּמְקוֹם הַזְּמַן,

ר׳ עובדיה מברטנורא

(ב) **הכותב טופסי גיטין.** סופר שרולה שיהיו מזומנין אללו, שפעמים אדם בא לשכרו והוא טרוד בשטרות אחרים: **צריך שיניח מקום האיש ומקום האשה ומקום הזמן.** ובגמרא (כו, א) מוסיף אף מקום הרי את מותרת לכל אדם:

יד אברהם

subsequently marrying a *Kohen* (to whom a divorcee is forbidden) by Rabbinic decree and prohibit her to her own husband if he is a *Kohen* (see 8:8). Others disagree in regard to the first case — a *get* written only for practice — and contend that such a *get* is completely null, and does not prohibit her to a *Kohen.* A third opinion is that all *gittin* without specific intent are totally invalid and have no effect whatsoever. However, the mishnah's decision in the final case, that the husband's eventual choice does not retroactively define his original intention, is not certain enough to be relied upon for leniency. Therefore, in the final case of the mishnah, the woman to whom the *get* is given is forbidden to a *Kohen.* Others state that even in such a case, the *get* is totally null, because the decision which precludes retroactive definition is to be relied upon completely (*Gem.* 25b-25a; *Rashi* ad loc.).

2.

As explained in the General Introduction, every *get* consists of two sections: the *toref* and the *tofes.* The *toref* is the essential portion of the *get* which includes the date, the names of the man and woman, the place where the *get* was made, and the basic declaration of divorce. The *tofes* is the remainder of the *get,* containing the general wording standard to all *gittin,* which elaborates on the ramifications of the divorce. By Biblical law, any requisites for the writing of the text of the *get* apply only to the *toref.*

הַכּוֹתֵב טָפְסֵי גִטִּין — *One who writes tofsim of gittin*

A scribe who prepares *tofsim* (pl. of *tofes*) — forms for *gittin* — so they should be readily available if they are needed when he is busy with other documents (*Rav*).

צָרִיךְ שֶׁיַּנִּיחַ מְקוֹם הָאִישׁ, וּמְקוֹם הָאִשָּׁה, — *must leave [blank] the space for [the name of] the man, and the space for [the name of] the woman,*

Even if he knows that a specific marriage is heading toward divorce, and he prepares a *get* for that eventuality, he may not fill in the names of the man and woman on his own initiative (*Rashi*). This is because these must be written with specific intent for a particular woman's divorce (*Gem.* 26a), and since a married woman is not designated for divorce without the decision of her husband,

3 **2.** One who writes *tofsim* of *gittin* must leave
2 [blank] the space for [the name of] the man, and the space for [the name of] the woman, and the space for the date; [on] documents of loans, he must leave [blank] the space for [the name of] the lender, the space for [the name of] the borrower, the space for the [amount of] money, [and] the space for the date; [on] bills of sale, he must leave [blank] the space for [the name of] the buyer, the space for [the name of] the seller, the space for the [amount of] money, the space for the field, and the space for the date,

YAD AVRAHAM

only he can designate a *get* to be specifically intended for that purpose (*Zevachim* 2b).

וּמְקוֹם הַזְּמַן; — *and the space for the date;*

He may not date the *get* until it is signed by witnesses, because a predated *get* is not valid (*Meiri;* see commentary to 2:2).

He must also leave space for the words, *You are hereby permitted to every man,* which is the essence of the *get,* and must therefore be written with specific intent (*Gem.* 26b).

The exclusion from this list of the names of the cities in which the husband and wife are located indicates that this information may be filled in by the scribe in advance (*Tos. Yom Tov*).

שְׁטָרֵי מִלְוָה — *[on] documents of loans,*

[A scribe who prepares forms for documents of loans so that they will be available upon request.]

צָרִיךְ שֶׁיַּנִּיחַ מְקוֹם הַמַּלְוֶה, מְקוֹם הַלֹּוֶה, מְקוֹם הַמָּעוֹת, — *he must leave [blank] the space for [the name of] the lender, the space for the [name of] the borrower, the space for the [amount of] money,*

Even if he is aware that a loan is about to take place, he may not fill in the names of the lender and the borrower, nor the sum of money to be borrowed, on his own initiative (*Rashi*). Although monetary documents are not required to be made with specific intent, the law requiring it for *gittin* was extended to include all legal documents as a precautionary measure, so that people not be led to think that *gittin,* too, do not need it (*Rav* from *Gem.* 26a).

מְקוֹם הַזְּמַן; — *[and] the space for the date;*

The scribe may not date the document at the time he prepares it, because a predated monetary document is invalid (see commentary to 2:2 s.v. כָּל הַגִּטִּין).

שְׁטָרֵי מֶקַח — צָרִיךְ שֶׁיַּנִּיחַ מְקוֹם הַלּוֹקֵחַ, וּמְקוֹם הַמּוֹכֵר, וּמְקוֹם הַמָּעוֹת, וּמְקוֹם הַשָּׂדֶה, וּמְקוֹם הַזְּמַן, — *[on] bills of sale, he must leave [blank] the space for [the name of] the buyer, the space for [the name of] the seller, the space for the [amount of] money, the space for the field, and the space for the date,*

A scribe who prepares forms for bills of sale to be available upon request may not, on his own initiative,

מִפְּנֵי הַתַּקָּנָה. רַבִּי יְהוּדָה פּוֹסֵל בְּכֻלָּן. רַבִּי אֶלְעָזָר מַכְשִׁיר בְּכֻלָּן, חוּץ מִגִּטֵּי נָשִׁים, שֶׁנֶּאֱמַר: „וְכָתַב לָהּ", לִשְׁמָהּ:

ר' עובדיה מברטנורא

מפני התקנה. התירו לכתוב טופסי גיטין ושטרות שלא לשמן, מפני תקנת הסופר, שיהיו מזומנים לו, ובלבד שישייר תורף לכתבו לשמה, וגזרינן תורף שאר שטרות אטו תורף דגיטין: **רבי יהודה פוסל בכולן.** דגזר טופס אטו תורף, ושאר שטרות אטו גיטין: **רבי אלעזר מכשיר בכולן.** דלא גזר שאר שטרות אטו גיטין: **חוץ מגטי נשים שנאמר וכתב לה לשמה.** וגזרינן טופס אטו תורף. והלכה כרבי אלעזר:

יד אברהם

fill in the names of the buyer and seller, the amount involved in the sale, or the specifications of the field being sold even if he knows that such a sale is about to take place. As mentioned above, this is because the prohibition on prewritten *gittin* was extended to include all legal documents as a precautionary measure. The scribe also should not date the document when he prepares it, because a predated bill of sale is null (*Meiri;* see commentary to 2:2 loc. cit.).

.מִפְּנֵי הַתַּקָּנָה — *for the sake of the benefit involved.*

This cannot mean that the ruling stated in the mishnah is for the sake of the benefit involved, because one of the cases to which it refers is that of *gittin,* which require specific intent by Biblical law. Therefore, the mishnah must be understood as follows: The reason the Rabbis did not extend their decree to prohibit preparing even the *tofsim* of these documents in advance was for the benefit of the scribes, so that they should be free to prepare these forms in order to have them readily available (*Rav* from *Gem.* 26a).

An alternative explanation of the benefit involved is that the Rabbis were concerned about the possibility of a man who is forced to take a sudden trip to a distant land and wants to divorce his wife before he goes, so that she should not be left without knowing if he is alive, and thus, whether she is still married. If prepared forms were prohibited, such a person might not be able to acquire a *get* before leaving, and his wife would be left in uncertainty as to her marital status (*Gem.* 26b).

This approach to the mishnah is based on the assumption that the first, anonymous *Tanna* is R' Elazar, who holds that the writing of the *get* mentioned in the Torah refers to the specifics of the *get* itself and not the signatures of the witnesses (see General Introduction, s.v. *The Witnesses*). Others maintain that the author of the mishnah up to this point is R' Meir, who maintains that the writing discussed in the verse, and thus that which is bound by the regulations described therein, is the signing of the witnesses. Accordingly, Biblical law would allow the scribe to fill in the entire *get* on his own initiative as long as it is signed by the witnesses at the behest of the husband. However, the Rabbis prohibited him from filling in the particulars of the *get,* because a woman might overhear the scribe mentioning her name and that of her husband while writing. She would thereby conclude that her husband had instructed him to write a *get* for her, thus causing marital strife. Alter-

for the sake of the benefit involved. R' Yehudah invalidates all of them. R' Elazar validates all of them, except for *gittin*, for it is written (*Deut.* 24:1): *He shall write for her* — with specific intent for her.

natively, they did not want *gittin* made so readily available that a man could procure one instantly and divorce his wife in a fit of temper. Thus, if the author of the mishnah is R' Meir, the words *for the sake of the benefit involved* explain the reason for the prohibition of preparing the *toref* of a *get*, rather than the reason the preparation of the *tofes* is permitted (*Gem.* 26b).

רַבִּי יְהוּדָה פּוֹסֵל בְּכֻלָּן. — *R' Yehudah invalidates all of them.*

R' Yehudah maintains that the Rabbis extended the prohibition of writing a *get* in advance to include the *tofes* of the *get*, and further extended it to include monetary documents as well (*Rav* from *Gem.* 26a).

רַבִּי אֶלְעָזָר מַכְשִׁיר בְּכֻלָּן, — *R' Elazar validates all of them,*

R' Elazar holds that the Rabbis did not prohibit the preparation of the *tofsim* of other documents as a precautionary measure for those of *gittin* (ibid.). Therefore, a document of a loan or a bill of sale may be prepared in advance, as long as the specifics listed in the mishnah are not included (*Rashi*).

Others contend that R' Elazar permits the preparation of monetary documents in their entirety, even including the particulars listed in the mishnah (*Tos.; Rosh; Ramban*). Only the date must be omitted according to all opinions, because its inclusion would render the document predated, and consequently, null (*Meiri*).

According to those who hold that the first, anonymous *Tanna* of the mishnah is R' Elazar, the apparent contradiction between his two statements in the mishnah is due to a dispute among *Tannaim* as to his actual position (*Gem.* 26b).

חוּץ מִגִּטֵּי נָשִׁים, — *except for gittin,*

R' Elazar, too, prohibits the preparation of *gittin* in advance, even that of the *tofes* alone (*Rav* from *Gem.* 26a).

There is a dispute among the commentators as to the stringency of the prohibition against using a *get* whose *tofes* was prepared in advance. Some maintain that it is only prohibited initially, but ex post facto if a man had already given a *get* written in such a manner to his wife, the divorce takes effect. However, if the husband is still available, he should be coerced to give her another *get* (*Rosh*). Others contend that the *get* is totally invalid, and the divorce is null (*Ramban; Ran* to 21b). According to this latter opinion, the Rabbis were stricter in this case than in the case of a *get* whose *tofes* was written on an attached object, which they prohibited only initially (see 2:4). This is because that situation is unusual, and thus requires fewer precautionary measures, whereas the acceptance of any part of a *get* written without compliance with the rule of specific intent could easily lead to entire *gittin* being written without specific intent (*Ramban*).

שֶׁנֶּאֱמַר: ,,וְכָתַב לָהּ״, לִשְׁמָהּ. — *for it is written* (*Deut.* 24:1): *"He shall write for her"* (lit., *for her name*) — *with specific intent for her.*

Since Biblical law requires that the *toref* of the *get* be written with specific intent, the Rabbis extended the requirement to include the *tofes* of the *get* as a precautionary measure (*Gem.* 26a).

[ג] הַמֵּבִיא גֵּט וְאָבַד הֵימֶנּוּ, מְצָאוֹ לְאַלְתַּר — כָּשֵׁר; וְאִם לָאו — פָּסוּל. מְצָאוֹ בַּחֲפִיסָה אוֹ בִּדְלֻסְקְמָא, אִם מַכִּירוֹ — כָּשֵׁר.

ר׳ עובדיה מברטנורא

(ג) **לאלתר**. מיד, כשר: **ואם לאו פסול**. ודוקא שאבד במקום שהשיירות מצויות, דאיכא למימר מעוברים ושבים נפל, אבל אם אבד במקום שאין השיירות מצויות, אפילו לאחר זמן מרובה, כשר. ואפילו אבד במקום שהשיירות מצויות, אם יש לעדים בו סימן מובהק, כגון שיאמרו נקב יש בו בצד אות פלונית, או שיאמרו מעולם לא נתמנו בגט באלו השמות אלא בזה בלבד, כשר, ואפילו לאחר זמן מרובה: **בחפיסא או בדלוסקמא**. אמתחות שרגילין לתת בהם שטרות, ויש בהן סימן שהם שלו: **אם מכירו בשר**. מלתא באנפי נפשה היא. והכי קאמר, מצאו בחפיסה או בדלוסקמא אף על פי שאינו מכירו לגט, או שמכירו לגט אף על פי שמצאו בכל מקום, כשר:

יד אברהם

3.

הַמֵּבִיא גֵּט וְאָבַד הֵימֶנּוּ, — *[If] one was bringing a get and lost it* —

[An agent of the husband was bringing a *get* to the wife, and he lost it.]

מְצָאוֹ לְאַלְתַּר — *[if] he found it immediately,*

From the time he lost it until he found it, there was someone standing nearby who saw that no one had passed by the place where it was found (*Rif* from *Gem.* 28a).

Others maintain that as long as he attests that no one tarried in that place, the *get* is still considered to have been found immediately (*Gem.* ibid.).

כָּשֵׁר; — *it is valid;*

[He can assume that the *get* which he found is the one he had lost, and can now deliver it to the wife.]

וְאִם לָאו — פָּסוּל. — *if not, it is void.*

It may not be used to divorce the wife, because it may be the *get* of a different couple who have the same names and come from a town with the same name as the couple whose *get* the agent was carrying and who dropped it in traveling[1] (*Rashi* to mishnah and 27a s.v. ואפילו).

The case of the mishnah is that a *get* was found in a place where caravans pass by often, and there is a realistic possibility that it was dropped by one of its members. However, if the *get* was found in a place where caravans are rare, the agent can assume it is the one he dropped, even if he did not find it immediately (*Rav* from *Gem.* 27a-b). Even where caravans are not common, if it has been established that there is another couple with the same names as this couple in the same city, the possibility that it is their *get* that was found must be considered, and the *get* may not be used (*Rosh*).

Another opinion holds that only if both of these conditions exist — i.e., that there is a

1. [As mentioned above, many legal documents in Jewish law generally bear only the given names of the principals and those of their fathers (e.g., *Reuven, the son of Shimon*) as identification. Thus, the possibility of duplication with which the mishnah is concerned is not as farfetched as it may seem.]

3. [If] one was bringing a *get* and lost it — [if] he found it immediately, it is valid; if not, it is void. [If] he found it in a pouch or in a case, [and] he recognizes it, it is valid.

YAD AVRAHAM

known couple in the city with the same names as this couple, and caravans are common in the area in which the *get* was found — do we suspect the possibility of this being a different *get* than the one the agent dropped (*Baal Halachos Gedolos* and *R' Chananel*, cited by *Ran*).

Others maintain that if the only source of concern is the frequency of caravans, the *get* is considered to have been found immediately and is therefore valid, as long as it can be established that no one tarried in that area between the time the *get* was lost and when it was found. However, if there is the additional factor of another couple in town with the same names as this couple, it must be ascertained that no one had passed through this area at all in the intervening period in order to consider the *get* as having been found immediately, and thus valid (*Rif*, see *Ran; Rambam, Hil. Gerushun* 3:9f.).

Even where caravans pass by frequently, if the witnesses who are signed on the *get* can identify it based on a distinct earmark (such as a hole in the parchment near a specific letter), the *get* is valid (*Rav* from *Gem.* 27b).

The agent is also trusted to identify the *get* based on a distinct earmark, but he is only relied upon if he mentions the mark before seeing the *get;* whereas witnesses are relied upon to identify it even after they have seen it (*Tos.* 27b s.v. כגון).

According to *Rashi* (27b s.v. מעולם), this helps only if they testify that the husband who sent this agent is the one for whom they signed. Otherwise, we are concerned that another couple with the same names as this couple may have had a *get* signed by witnesses with the same names as these. *Tosafos* (ibid.) contends that even if the witnesses merely testify that they signed only one such *get*, but they do not know if this man is the one for whom they signed, the husband is believed to say that it had been for him. This is because he is not suspected of deliberately seeking to harm his wife by causing her to be erroneously assumed a divorcee [and thus permitted by the courts to remarry illicitly]. Nevertheless, when there are no witnesses, the husband's claim that this is the *get* which he had sent is not believed. This is because the Rabbis feared that he may take for granted that no other *get* with the same names had been written and therefore conclude too hastily that the *get* which was found is the one he had sent.

מְצָאוֹ בַּחֲפִיסָה אוֹ בִדְלֻסְקְמָא, — *[If] he found it in a pouch or in a case,*

If the agent who dropped the *get* found it in a pouch or case which have earmarks identifying it as his (*Rav; Rashi*).

The mishnah is speaking of a situation in which he either knows that he did not lend this pouch or case to someone else, or he remembers having lost the *get* when it was in the pouch or case. Otherwise, we would have to consider the possibility that he lent his pouch or case to someone else who lost a different *get* in it (*Tos.* 28a s.v. מצאו).

אִם מַכִּירוֹ — כָּשֵׁר. — *[and] he recognizes it, it is valid.*

Alternatively, there are no earmarks to identify the pouch, but the agent recognizes the *get* as being the one he dropped. In either case, he may now deliver it to the wife (*Rav; Rashi*).

Although only a Torah scholar is relied upon to identify something based on his own recognition without identifying any earmarks, that is because anyone else is suspected of lying. In this case, however, the agent is above suspicion, because he could

הַמֵּבִיא גֵט וְהִנִּיחוֹ זָקֵן אוֹ חוֹלֶה — נוֹתְנוֹ לָהּ בְּחֶזְקַת שֶׁהוּא קַיָּם. בַּת יִשְׂרָאֵל הַנְּשׂוּאָה לְכֹהֵן, וְהָלַךְ בַּעְלָהּ לִמְדִינַת הַיָּם — אוֹכֶלֶת בִּתְרוּמָה בְּחֶזְקַת שֶׁהוּא קַיָּם. הַשּׁוֹלֵחַ חַטָּאתוֹ מִמְּדִינַת הַיָּם — מַקְרִיבִין אוֹתָהּ בְּחֶזְקַת שֶׁהוּא קַיָּם.

[ד] **שְׁלֹשָׁה** דְּבָרִים אָמַר רַבִּי אֶלְעָזָר בֶּן פַּרְטָא לִפְנֵי חֲכָמִים, וְקִיְּמוּ אֶת דְּבָרָיו:

ר׳ עובדיה מברטנורא

נותנו לה בחזקת שהוא קיים. ולא חיישינן שמא מת, ובטל שליחותו, דאמרינן העמד דבר על חזקתו. אבל אם נודע שמת קודם שהגיע גט לידה, הגט בטל, דאין גט לאחר מיתה: **מקריבין אותה.** ולא חיישינן שמא מתו בעליה, וחטאת שמתו בעליה למיתה עומדת:

יד אברהם

have delivered the *get* without revealing that it had ever been lost (*Tos.* loc. cit.).

Others explain the words, *he recognizes it,* to be referring to the pouch or case rather than the *get* itself. According to this interpretation, this is part of the previous case, and not a new statement on its own [i.e., *he found it in a pouch or in a case which he recognizes*] (ibid.).

הַמֵּבִיא גֵט וְהִנִּיחוֹ זָקֵן אוֹ חוֹלֶה — *One who brings a get and had left him old or ill*

[An agent brought a *get* to a woman whose husband had been old or sick when he left him.]

נוֹתְנוֹ לָהּ בְּחֶזְקַת שֶׁהוּא קַיָּם. — *may give it to her on the assumption that he is alive.*

The agent may give the *get* to the wife, and she is assumed to be divorced, because the status quo of the husband being alive is assumed to have been maintained. Were he to have died prior to the delivery of the *get,* she would be a widow rather than a divorcee [which has ramifications in regard to *yibum* (see commentary to 2:7 s.v. וִיבַמְתָּהּ) and marriage to a *Kohen,* to whom a divorcee is forbidden] (*Rav*). This principle of *chazakah* — that the status quo is assumed to have been maintained — is derived hermeneutically in *Chullin* 10b (*Rashi*).

If the husband was near death when he sent the *get,* the assumption that he is still alive is not valid, because most people in that condition do not survive (*Gem.* 28a).

There is an opinion in the *Gemara* (ibid.) that a man over 80 is no longer assumed to be alive at any point in question, unless he has reached the age of 100 (according to *Rashi,* 90), in which case he has established himself as enjoying an unusual degree of longevity. Others contend that a man's age does not have any effect on the assumption that he is alive (ibid.).

Having mentioned the principle of *chazakah* concerning *gittin,* the *Tanna* now goes on to discuss this subject in regard to other areas of Jewish law.

בַּת יִשְׂרָאֵל הַנְּשׂוּאָה לְכֹהֵן, — *The daughter of a non-Kohen who was married to a Kohen —*

And may therefore eat *terumah* as

One who brings a *get* and had left him old or ill may give it to her on the assumption that he is alive. The daughter of a non-*Kohen* who was married to a *Kohen* — and her husband went overseas — may eat *terumah* on the assumption that he is alive. [If] one sends his sin-offering from overseas, it may be offered on the assumption that he is alive.

4. R' Elazar ben Parta said three things before the Sages, and they confirmed his words:

YAD AVRAHAM

long as she is his wife (*Kesubos* 5:2; see commentary to 1:6, s.v. וַהֲרֵי).

וְהָלַךְ בַּעֲלָהּ לִמְדִינַת הַיָּם — *and her husband went overseas —*

[And we do not know if he is still alive.]

אוֹכֶלֶת בַּתְּרוּמָה בְּחֶזְקַת שֶׁהוּא קַיָּם. — *may eat terumah on the assumption that he is alive.*

Although it is possible for her to avoid any doubts by eating other food, she is allowed to rely on the status quo to assume that her husband is alive, and eat *terumah* (*Gem.* 28b).

הַשּׁוֹלֵחַ חַטָּאתוֹ מִמְּדִינַת הַיָּם — *[If] one sends his sin-offering from overseas,*

[Someone from a foreign country has sent a sin-offering to the Temple to atone for a transgression] and we do not know if he has died, in which case his offering may not be brought on the Altar (*Rav*).

מַקְרִיבִין אוֹתָהּ בְּחֶזְקַת שֶׁהוּא קַיָּם. — *it may be offered on the assumption that he is alive.*

We are not concerned with the possibility that the sacrifice is no longer fitting to be offered because its sender may have died, even though the offering of an unfit animal on the Altar is prohibited (*Gem.* 28b).

The mishnah is discussing a sin-offering which is a bird, or one which was sent by a woman. Otherwise, the offering may not be brought, because the sender is obligated to offer it himself so as to perform the required rite of סְמִיכָה, *semichah* [leaning his hands upon the head of the animal, see *Lev.* 1:4] (ibid.).

4.

The mishnah continues the discussion of the *chazakah* (presumptive status) that one has remained alive, which was begun in the previous mishnah.

שְׁלֹשָׁה דְבָרִים אָמַר רַבִּי אֶלְעָזָר בֶּן פַּרְטָא לִפְנֵי חֲכָמִים, — *R' Elazar ben Parta said three things before the Sages,*

[R' Elazar ben Parta stated before the Sages the law for three pairs of contrasting cases regarding the assumption that the person involved was still alive.]

וְקִיְּמוּ אֶת דְּבָרָיו: — *and they confirmed his words:*

גיטין ג/ד

עַל עִיר שֶׁהִקִּיפָהּ כַּרְקוֹם, וְעַל הַסְּפִינָה הַמִּטָּרֶפֶת בַּיָּם, וְעַל הַיּוֹצֵא לִדּוֹן — שֶׁהֵן בְּחֶזְקַת קַיָּמִין. אֲבָל עִיר שֶׁכְּבָשָׁהּ כַּרְקוֹם, וּסְפִינָה שֶׁאָבְדָה בַּיָּם, וְהַיּוֹצֵא לֵהָרֵג — נוֹתְנִין עֲלֵיהֶן חֻמְרֵי חַיִּים וְחֻמְרֵי מֵתִים: בַּת יִשְׂרָאֵל לְכֹהֵן, וּבַת כֹּהֵן לְיִשְׂרָאֵל — לֹא תֹאכַל בִּתְרוּמָה.

ר׳ עובדיה מברטנורא

(ד) כרקום. תרגום מצור (דברים כ, כ) כרכומין: **המטרפת.** ועדיין לא טבעה: **לידון.** בדיני נפשות: **בת ישראל לכהן. בת כהן לישראל.** חומרי מתים: חומרי חיים:

יד אברהם

[The Sages accepted R' Elazar's decisions for these cases.]

עַל עִיר שֶׁהִקִּיפָהּ כַּרְקוֹם, — *Concerning [the people in] a city besieged by an army,*

An army besieged a city and it is not known if it has been captured (*Meiri*) [and the question arises whether a certain person in the city is still alive].

וְעַל הַסְּפִינָה הַמִּטָּרֶפֶת בַּיָּם, — *and [those in] a ship storm tossed at sea,*

Which is not yet known to have sunk[1] (*Rav; Rashi*) [and the question arises if a particular individual on the ship is still alive].

Others explain this as a ship which is caught in a storm and is out of control, but its steering implements are still intact (*Rambam Commentary; Meiri*).

וְעַל הַיּוֹצֵא לִדּוֹן — — *and one who goes* (lit., *goes out*) *to be tried* —

For a capital crime (*Rav*).

שֶׁהֵן בְּחֶזְקַת קַיָּמִין. — *they are presumed to be alive.*

The *chazakah* dictates that in each of these cases, the status quo has been maintained, and that the city was not captured, the ship was not sunk, and the defendant was not sentenced to death (*Meiri*).

אֲבָל עִיר שֶׁכְּבָשָׁהּ כַּרְקוֹם, — *But [concerning people in] a city captured by an army,*

[And the question arises whether a particular person has survived.]

וּסְפִינָה שֶׁאָבְדָה בַּיָּם, — *and [those in] a ship lost at sea,*

I.e., it has sunk. Nevertheless, the possibility of survivors must be considered (*Tos. Yom Tov*).

Others explain this as a ship whose steering implements had been destroyed in the storm, but which was still afloat in the water [when last sighted] (*Rambam Commentary, Meiri*).

וְהַיּוֹצֵא לֵהָרֵג — — *and one who goes to be executed* —

Someone who was sentenced to death in a gentile court and has gone forth to receive his sentence (*Gem.* 28b; *Rambam, Hil. Gerushin* 6:29; *Even HaEzer* 141:69).

1. [Although *Rav* and *Rashi* use the words, *which has not yet sunk*, they are speaking only in contrast to the second case in which the ship is known to have sunk (see *Tos. Yom Tov*). If it is known for certain that the ship has not sunk, there is no reason to even consider the question as to whether anyone on the ship has died.]

Concerning [the people in] a city besieged by an army, and [those in] a ship storm tossed at sea, and one who goes to be tried — they are presumed to be alive. But [concerning people in] a city captured by an army, and [those in] a ship lost at sea, and one who goes to be executed — the stringencies of the living and the stringencies of the dead are applied to them: The daughter of a non-*Kohen* [married] to a *Kohen* and the daughter of a *Kohen* [married] to a non-*Kohen* may not eat of *terumah.*

YAD AVRAHAM

Because of the possibility of bribery, his death is not considered a certainty (*Rashi* 28b s.v. לא שנו; *Meiri*). However, if he was sentenced in a Jewish court, his death is considered a foregone conclusion (*Gem.* ibid.; *Rambam, Hil. Terumos* 9:20), since the possibility of new evidence being introduced in his favor at this late stage is too remote to merit concern (*Tos.* 29a s.v. אבל) [and bribery is not a realistic possibility].

There is another opinion to the contrary — that only in a Jewish court is the possibility of survival considered, because new evidence in his favor is always accepted. Someone sentenced in a supreme gentile court (see *Tos.* s.v. פורסי; *Meiri; Tos. Yom Tov*), however, is certain to be put to death[1] (*Gem.* 28b-29a; *Rosh*).

There is a third view that calls for the stringency stated below in the mishnah to be applied to both one who is sentenced in a Jewish court and one who is sentenced in a gentile court (*Rashba*).

נוֹתְנִין עֲלֵיהֶן חֻמְרֵי חַיִּים וְחֻמְרֵי מֵתִים: — *the stringencies of the living and the stringencies of the dead are applied to them*:

[The probability of death is too great to allow for reliance on the status quo; it is also not yet certain that he is dead. Therefore, both the stringencies which would apply if he were known to be living, and those which would be applicable if he were known to be dead, are in effect, as the mishnah explains.]

בַּת יִשְׂרָאֵל לְכֹהֵן, — *The daughter of a non-Kohen [married] to a Kohen*

Who may eat *terumah* only if her husband is presumed to be alive (*Rav; Lev.* 22:23).

וּבַת כֹּהֵן לְיִשְׂרָאֵל — *and the daughter of a Kohen [married] to a non-Kohen*

Who may eat *terumah* only if her husband is presumed dead (*Rav; Lev.* ibid. vs. 12,13).

לֹא תֹאכַל בַּתְּרוּמָה. — *may not eat of terumah.*

[If the husband of either of these women was in one of the three situations described above, his wife may not eat *terumah* because we apply the dual stringency, as explained above.]

1. [Assumedly, in a country with a legal system such as that in the U.S., where new evidence is accepted in the defendant's favor, the law would be the same as in a Jewish court.]

[ה] **הַמֵּבִיא** גֵט בְּאֶרֶץ יִשְׂרָאֵל וְחָלָה — הֲרֵי זֶה מְשַׁלְּחוֹ בְּיַד אַחֵר. וְאִם אָמַר לוֹ: „טוֹל לִי הֵימֶנָּה חֵפֶץ פְּלוֹנִי" — לֹא יְשַׁלְּחֶנּוּ בְּיַד אַחֵר, שֶׁאֵין רְצוֹנוֹ שֶׁיְּהֵא פִּקְדוֹנוֹ בְּיַד אַחֵר.

ר' עובדיה מברטנורא

(ה) **המביא גט בארץ ישראל.** שאין צריך לומר בפני נכתב ובפני נחתם: **משלחו ביד אחר.** ועושה שליח מאליו ולא בבית דין. ודוקא חלה: **ואם אמר לו.** בעל לשליח: **טול לי הימנה חפץ פלוני.** כשתתן לה את הגט, לא ישלחנו ביד אחר:

יד אברהם

Certainly, a woman whose husband was in these circumstances may not remarry (*Tos. Yom Tov*).

If an agent was carrying a *get* for a man who was in one of these situations, he may not deliver it to the wife. If he did, she remains in a state of doubt as to whether she is divorced until she receives another *get* (*Rambam, Hil. Gerushin* 6:29; *Even HaEzer* 141:69).

5.

The *Tanna* now returns to the topic of an agent who was sent by a man to deliver a *get* to his wife, and prescribes the proper course of action if the agent became ill and could not carry out his mission. This mishnah discusses such a case when the agent was bringing the *get* within Eretz Yisrael.

הַמֵּבִיא גֵט בְּאֶרֶץ יִשְׂרָאֵל — *One who was bringing a get within Eretz Yisrael*

An agent brought a *get* from one place to another in the Holy Land, where he need not testify: "It was written in my presence and signed in my presence" (*Rav;* see 1:3).

— וְחָלָה — *and became ill*

The agent became ill, or was otherwise unable to deliver the *get* to the wife (*Meiri*).

הֲרֵי זֶה מְשַׁלְּחוֹ בְּיַד אַחֵר. — *may send it with* (lit., *in the hand of*) *another.*

Because he is ill, he may — on his own authority — appoint another agent to deliver the *get*, and he does not need to do so before a court (*Rav* from *Gem.* 19a). The authority of an agent to appoint another agent in his place is derived hermeneutically by the *Gemara* (*Kiddushin* 41a).

The Rabbis did not allow an agent of delivery who is healthy to appoint another in his place, because the husband may not agree to the change of agents and would therefore revoke his instructions to deliver the *get* (*Ran*). [This would create considerable difficulty, because the woman receiving the *get* would not know if her husband had agreed to the change of agents or not.]

Another opinion maintains that the mishnah is dealing with a case in which the husband specifically told the agent: "You can deliver the *get*." Therefore, he can appoint another agent to replace him only if he is sick, in which case it is assumed that the husband would agree to the switch. However, if the husband did not make this

3
5

5. One who was bringing a *get* within Eretz Yisrael and became ill may send it with another. But if he had said to him: "Take from her such and such a thing for me," he may not send it with another, for he does not want his deposit to be in the hand of another.

YAD AVRAHAM

specification, the agent delivering the *get* may appoint a second agent, even if he is not ill (*Gem.* 29a).

וְאִם אָמַר לוֹ: ,,טוֹל לִי הֵימֶנָּה חֵפֶץ פְּלוֹנִי" — — *But if he had said to him: "Take from her such and such a thing for me,"*

The husband instructed the agent that when he delivers the *get*, he should take a certain article for him from his wife (*Rav*).

לֹא יְשַׁלְּחֶנּוּ בְּיַד אַחֵר, — *he may not send it with another,*

The agent may not appoint another to bring the *get* instead of him, even if he became ill (*Meiri*).

שֶׁאֵין רְצוֹנוֹ שֶׁיְּהֵא פִקְדוֹנוֹ בְּיַד אַחֵר. — *for he does not want his deposit to be in the hand of another.*

The husband specified that he wants his article placed in the care of this agent. Therefore, the wife — who has been the guardian of the item up to this point — may not give it to another agent, for a depositary of someone's article is not allowed to give it to another person without the sanction of the owner (*Gem.* 29a).

In addition, the agent may not appoint another to replace him, because it could jeopardize the validity of the *get*, as follows: If the husband had instructed the agent to first take the deposit from his wife, and then give her the *get*, he would be understood as stipulating that the divorce is valid only if the agent takes the deposit first. Thus, if the agent were to deliver the *get* prior to taking the deposit, it would invalidate the divorce. Therefore, the Rabbis prohibited the appointment of a second agent, for fear that the instructions would not be transmitted clearly and the second agent would deliver the *get* before collecting the deposit, thus nullifying the divorce (*Rashi* 29b s.v. ואזל; *Rambam, Hil. Gerushin* 9:35; *Even HaEzer* 151:51). [This would be an undesirable consequence because the woman, unaware of these facts, would assume that she is divorced and remarry illicitly.]

Others maintain that if the husband told the agent to take the deposit and then deliver the *get*, delivery by a second agent would not be valid, even if he obeyed the instructions and collected the deposit before delivering the *get*. Since the husband made delivery of the *get* dependent upon collection of the deposit, any violation of the husband's wishes regarding the deposit, including the appointment of another agent, would nullify the divorce. Only if he had told the agent to deliver the *get* and then collect the deposit would the divorce be valid. Because he did not make the divorce contingent upon receiving the deposit, the appointment of a second agent, which is contrary to the husband's instructions only in regard to the deposit, would not affect the *get* (*Tos.* 29b s.v. רבי יוחנן).

[ו] **הַמֵּבִיא** גֵט מִמְּדִינַת הַיָּם וְחָלָה — עוֹשֶׂה בֵית דִּין וּמְשַׁלְּחוֹ, וְאוֹמֵר לִפְנֵיהֶם: „בְּפָנַי נִכְתַּב וּבְפָנַי נֶחְתַּם". וְאֵין הַשָּׁלִיחַ הָאַחֲרוֹן צָרִיךְ שֶׁיֹּאמַר: „בְּפָנַי נִכְתַּב וּבְפָנַי נֶחְתַּם", אֶלָּא אוֹמֵר: „שְׁלִיחַ בֵּית דִּין אֲנִי".

[ז] **הַמַּלְוֶה** מָעוֹת אֶת הַכֹּהֵן, וְאֶת הַלֵּוִי, וְאֶת

ר' עובדיה מברטנורא

(ו) **עושה ב"ד.** שליח, ומשלחו: **שליח בית דין אני.** ומסתמא בית דין עשו הדבר בהכשרו. ושליח שני ממנה שליח שלישי, עד מאה, וכולן בבית דין, מדתנן במתניתין אין השליח האחרון כו' אלא אומר שליח בית דין אני:

יד אברהם

6.

הַמֵּבִיא גֵט מִמְּדִינַת הַיָּם — *[If] one was bringing a get from overseas*

An agent was delivering a *get* from a foreign country, in which case he is required to testify: "It was written in my presence and signed in my presence" [1:1] (*Meiri*).

וְחָלָה — — *and became ill,*

The agent became ill, or was otherwise unable to deliver the *get* to the wife (*Meiri*).

עוֹשֶׂה בֵית דִּין וּמְשַׁלְּחוֹ, — *the court appoints [another] and sends him,*

The court appoints a second agent to replace the first. The agent himself cannot appoint another instead of him, because the second agent cannot give the required testimony of having witnessed the writing and signing of the *get* (*Meiri*).

וְאוֹמֵר לִפְנֵיהֶם: „בְּפָנַי נִכְתַּב וּבְפָנַי נֶחְתַּם". — *and he says before them: "It was written in my presence and signed in my presence."*

[The first agent testifies before the court which is going to appoint a replacement that he witnessed the writing and signing of the *get*, thus placing the matter in their hands.]

וְאֵין הַשָּׁלִיחַ הָאַחֲרוֹן צָרִיךְ שֶׁיֹּאמַר: „בְּפָנַי נִכְתַּב וּבְפָנַי נֶחְתַּם", — *The latter agent need not say: "It was written in my presence and signed in my presence";*

[The second agent is not required to testify to having witnessed the writing and signing of the *get* (which he would not be able to do); therefore, he may deliver the *get*.]

From the mishnah's use of the term "latter" rather than "second," the *Gemara* (29b) derives that the second agent may appoint a third and the third a fourth, and so on, as long as each appointment is done with the sanction of the court (*Rav*). However, they may do this only if they themselves are unable to deliver the *get* (*Tif; Rambam, Hil. Gerushin* 6:4; *Rosh; Ran; Meiri*).

If the *get* is being delivered within Eretz Yisrael, where the participation of the court is not required (see mishnah 5), each of the agents — if he is ill — may appoint another to replace him, even without the court's sanction (*Gem.* 29b).

אֶלָּא אוֹמֵר: „שְׁלִיחַ בֵּית דִּין אֲנִי". — *rather, he says: "I am an agent of the court."*

Upon delivering the *get* to his wife,

6. [If] one was bringing a *get* from overseas and became ill, the court appoints [another] and sends him, and he says before them: "It was written in my presence and signed in my presence." The latter agent need not say: "It was written in my presence and signed in my presence"; rather, he says: "I am an agent of the court."

7. One who lends money to a *Kohen*, a *Levi*, or a

YAD AVRAHAM

the agent declares himself to be an agent of the court. It is then assumed that the proper procedure was followed (*Rashi*).

7.

Terumah and Tithes

The Mishnah now returns to the topic, discussed earlier [mishnayos 3,4) of relying upon the חֲזָקָה, *presumptive status*, of a person being alive. Among the subjects involved in this discussion is that of *terumah* and tithes.

When a person grows produce in Eretz Yisrael, he becomes obligated to separate certain portions from his crop and give them to their appropriate recipients.

The first portion separated is תְּרוּמָה, *terumah* (usually between a fortieth and a sixtieth of the total), which must be given to a *Kohen* (*Deut.* 18:4) and is forbidden to a non-*Kohen* (*Lev.* 22:10; see *Rashi* ad loc.).

מַעֲשֵׂר רִאשׁוֹן, *the first tithe*, which is exactly a tenth of the remainder, is then separated and given to a *Levi* (*Num.* 18:24). This may be eaten by ordinary Jews as well (*Rambam, Hil. Maaser* 1:2).

The *Levi* must separate a tenth of his tithe and give it to a *Kohen*. This portion is called תְּרוּמַת מַעֲשֵׂר, *terumah of the tithe*, and it has the same status as regular *terumah* (*Num.* 18:26).

In the first, second, fourth, and fifth years of the Sabbatical cycle, a second tithe is separated from what remains of the produce after the shares of the *Kohen* and *Levi* have been removed. This tithe must be brought to Jerusalem by the owner and there by him, his household, and his guests. Alternatively, he may redeem the produce for money, which he takes to Jerusalem and uses there for the purchase of food. This is called מַעֲשֵׂר שֵׁנִי, *the second tithe* (*Deut.* 14:22-26).

In the third and sixth years of the Sabbatical cycle, the second tithe is separated for distribution to the poor. This is referred to as מַעֲשֵׂר עָנִי, *the poor man's tithe* (*Deut.* 14:29; see *Rashi* ad loc.).

הַמַּלְוֶה מָעוֹת אֶת הַכֹּהֵן, וְאֶת הַלֵּוִי, וְאֶת הֶעָנִי, — *One who lends money to a Kohen, a Levi, or a poor person,*

A person lent money to one of these

גיטין
ג/ז

הֶעָנִי, לִהְיוֹת מַפְרִישׁ עֲלֵיהֶן מֵחֶלְקָן — מַפְרִישׁ עֲלֵיהֶן בְּחֶזְקַת שֶׁהֵן קַיָּמִין, וְאֵינוֹ חוֹשֵׁשׁ שֶׁמָּא מֵת הַכֹּהֵן אוֹ הַלֵּוִי, אוֹ הֶעֱשִׁיר הֶעָנִי. מֵתוּ — צָרִיךְ לִטּוֹל רְשׁוּת מִן הַיּוֹרְשִׁין.

ר׳ עובדיה מברטנורא

(ז) **להיות מפריש עליהן מחלקן.** כשיפריש התרומה ימכרנה, ויעכב הדמים לעצמו בשביל חובו שיש לו על הכהן. ומעשר ראשון ומעשר עני יעכב ויאכל בשביל החוב שיש לו על הלוי ועל העני. אלא שמפריש ממעשר ראשון תרומת מעשר לכהן. ואם הוא רגיל ליתן תרומותיו ומעשרותיו לזה הכהן או הלוי או העני שהלוה להן, אין צריך לזכות להם מעשרותיו ותרומותיו על יד אחר, אלא לוקחן לעצמו מיד אחר שיפרישם. אבל אם רגיל ליתן תרומותיו ומעשרותיו לאחרים, אינו יכול לעכבן בחובו, עד שיזכה להם על ידי אחר תחילה, ואחר כך יחזור ויטלם בחובו: **צריך ליטול רשות מן היורשים.** שירשו מהם קרקע משועבדת לבעל חוב, צריך ליטול מהם רשות אם רוצים לפרוע חוב זה מתרומות ומעשרות הללו, דשמא רוצים הם ליקח מתנותיהן ולפרוע חוב מורישם ממקום אחר:

יד אברהם

types of people, without imposing upon them any obligation to repay except in the manner described below (*Gem.* 30a).

לִהְיוֹת מַפְרִישׁ עֲלֵיהֶן מֵחֶלְקָן — *[on the condition] to separate from their portions in its stead* (lit., *in their stead*),[1]

As payment of the loan, the lender wishes to retain for himself the *terumah*, tithe, or poor man's tithe, which he is obligated to separate from his produce to give to the *Kohen, Levi,* or poor man respectively. Although a non-*Kohen* may not eat *terumah*, in this case he wishes to retain it as payment after he has separated it, and sell it to a *Kohen.* After he has separated the *Levi's* tithe, he may eat it himself as long as he first separates one-tenth of it to give to a *Kohen.* He may eat the poor man's tithe as soon as he has separated it (*Rav*).

If this *Kohen, Levi,* and poor man are those to whom he generally gives his *terumah* and tithes, it can be assumed that all other eligible recipients have already abandoned hope of receiving these portions (*Rashi* s.v. במכרי). Accordingly, when he separates these allotments with the intent that they be designated for these specific individuals, it is considered as if they actually received them (ibid.), and he may therefore collect his debts from them (*Rav* from *Gem.* 23a). If he does not consistently allot his portions to these individuals, they have no more claim to them than any other *Kohen, Levi,* or poor man. Therefore, the portions belong to all members of these eligible groups, and the owner may not take them as payment of his loan, until a third party acquires them on behalf of these borrowers, and then returns them to the lender (*Rav* from *Gem.* 30a).

There is another opinion in the *Gemara* (ibid.) that in this instance, the Rabbis granted the lender the right to acquire the portions directly, without the standard

1. [The plural form is used because מָעוֹת, *money*, is construed as plural.]

3 poor person, [on the condition] to separate from
7 their portions in its stead, may separate in its stead on the assumption that they are alive, and he need not be concerned that the *Kohen* or *Levi* may have died, or that the poor man become wealthy. [If] they died, he must obtain permission from the heirs.

YAD AVRAHAM

procedure necessary for acquisition [in order to make loans to *Kohanim, Leviim,* and poor people easier to collect and thus, easier for them to obtain].

Others translate the words לִהְיוֹת מַפְרִישׁ עֲלֵיהֶן, *to separate on their behalf*, meaning to separate the allotments with the intention of designating them for these specific individuals (*Meiri*). [However, the owner must still acquire the portions through a third party if these individuals are not his standard recipients, because his intentions alone do not nullify the rights that the other *Kohanim, Leviim,* and poor people have to them.]

מַפְרִישׁ עֲלֵיהֶן בְּחֶזְקַת שֶׁהֵן קַיָּמִין, — *may separate in its stead on the assumption that they are alive,*

[Even if the borrowers are not present, the lender may separate their portions for the sake of collecting their debts, with the assumption that they are still alive.]

וְאֵינוֹ חוֹשֵׁשׁ שֶׁמָּא מֵת הַכֹּהֵן אוֹ הַלֵּוִי, אוֹ הֶעֱשִׁיר הֶעָנִי. — *and he need not be concerned that the Kohen or Levi may have died, or that the poor man became wealthy.*

[The lender can rely on the status quo to assume that the *Kohen* or *Levi* is still alive, and that the poor man is still impoverished, and take their allotments as payment. Obviously, the assumption regarding the poor man also includes the fact that he is still alive.]

If the poor man became wealthy, he is no longer entitled to the tithe, and consequently the lender may not collect his debt with it. He also cannot collect from the former's possessions because their original agreement stipulated that he would not collect from him directly (*Gem.* 30b).

מֵתוּ — צָרִיךְ לִטּוֹל רְשׁוּת מִן הַיּוֹרְשִׁין. — *[If] they died, he must obtain permission from the heirs.*

The mishnah is dealing with a case in which (a) the debt had been recorded on a document, and (b) the heirs had inherited real property. [Jewish law provides for an automatic lien on all real estate in a person's possession when he incurs a debt, as long as the debt is recorded on a legal document (*Bava Metzia* 13b).]

If the borrowers die, the lender must receive permission from the heirs before he can take the allotments as payment of his debt, because the heirs may wish to retain the allotments for themselves and repay the lender some other way (*Rav*).

Rashi, on the other hand, comments that in the mishnah's case, the heirs are not obligated to pay the debt. [Obviously, *Rashi* construes the case as one in which either the debt had not been recorded on a document or the heirs had not inherited any real property.]

Therefore, only if the heirs grant the lender permission may he take those portions for himself. The reason they might desire to do so is because Jewish law encourages the repayment

אִם הִלְוָן בִּפְנֵי בֵית דִּין — אֵינוֹ צָרִיךְ לִטּוֹל רְשׁוּת מִן הַיּוֹרְשִׁין.

[ח] **הַמַּנִּיחַ** פֵּרוֹת לִהְיוֹת מַפְרִישׁ עֲלֵיהֶן תְּרוּמָה וּמַעַשְׂרוֹת, מָעוֹת לִהְיוֹת מַפְרִישׁ עֲלֵיהֶן מַעֲשֵׂר שֵׁנִי — מַפְרִישׁ עֲלֵיהֶן בְּחֶזְקַת שֶׁהֵן קַיָּמִין. אִם אָבְדוּ — הֲרֵי זֶה

ר׳ עובדיה מברטנורא

(ח) **המניח פירות להיות מפריש עליהן כו׳.** סומך על אלו, ואוכל טבלים אחרים שיש לו, ואומר, הרי תרומתן באותן פירות שהקליתי לכך: **ואם אבדו.** הלך לבדקן ומלאן שאבדו:

יד אברהם

of a dead man's debts by his heirs, even if they are not obligated to do so (see *Meiri*).

אִם הִלְוָן בִּפְנֵי בֵית דִּין — *If he lent them before the court,*

A man lent money to a *Kohen*, *Levi*, or poor man before a Jewish court, with the explicit stipulation that he collect the debt from the *terumah* or tithes, as explained above (*Meiri*).

אֵינוֹ צָרִיךְ לִטּוֹל רְשׁוּת מִן הַיּוֹרְשִׁים. — *he need not obtain permission from the heirs.*

In case any of these borrowers died, the lender may collect his debt from the *terumah* or tithes, even without the permission of the heirs.[1] Although the borrower is no longer alive, and thus the lender has no more legal right to these portions, his collection of the portions as payment is allowed by the courts when the loan was made under their jurisdiction. This is because it is in the interest of *Kohanim*, *Leviim*, and poor people that repayment of such loans be ensured, so that they will continue to be forthcoming (*Rashi*). However, if the poor man became wealthy, the lender may not collect from his poor man's tithe, even if payment was stipulated before the courts. This is because it is unusual for poor people to acquire wealth, and the Rabbis did not concern themselves in their decree with so rare an occurrence (*Gem.* 30b; *Rashi*).

This Rabbinic decree — allowing the lender to collect the debt from the *terumah* and tithes even after the borrower dies — is in effect only if the borrower's heirs inherited real property from him. Since the heirs are responsible for the borrower's debts because of the property, there is still a debt to the lender for which he may collect from *terumah* or tithes by virtue of the Rabbinic decree. Even if his claim is greater than the value of the property, he may still

1. When the lender separates the *terumah* or tithes, he must do so with the express intent that it be designated for the dead man's heirs, and therefore collectible for his debt. Regarding the poor man's title, however, this would not suffice, because his heirs may be wealthy and thus not entitled to this tithe. Therefore, he must keep in mind that he is separating the tithe on behalf of all those poor who are entitled to it. Although they are in no way liable for the debt, the Rabbis allowed him to collect from their tithe, because it is in the best interest of the poor that such loans be repaid in order to ensure their continued availability (*Gem.* 30a).

If he lent them before the court, he need not obtain permission from the heirs.

8. One who puts aside produce to separate *terumah* and tithes with them, [or] money to separate the second tithe with them, may separate with them on the assumption that they are still in existence. If they were lost, he must be

YAD AVRAHAM

collect the entire debt from *terumah* or tithes. This is due to a law which states that if one seizes property from heirs to cover part of a debt, and the heirs buy back the land, the creditor may seize it a second time to cover the balance of the debt. Thus, theoretically, he could collect the entire debt from this one field by means of successive seizures; therefore, the entire debt is still extant. However, if the heirs did not inherit any real property, the debt is nullified with the death of the borrower, and the lender may no longer collect from *terumah* or tithes (*Gem.* 30b).

8.

Any produce which requires the separation of *terumah* or any of the tithes is forbidden to be eaten by Biblical law until those portions are separated (*Deut.* 22:15; *Sanhedrin* 83a). Produce which is prohibited in this manner is called *tevel* (see ArtScroll commentary to *Pesachim* 2:5).

הַמַּנִּיחַ פֵּרוֹת לִהְיוֹת מַפְרִישׁ עֲלֵיהֶן תְּרוּמָה וּמַעַשְׂרוֹת, — *One who puts aside produce to separate terumah and tithes with them* (lit., *on them*),

A person put aside produce, with the intent that it will subsequently serve as *terumah* or tithes for *tevel* which he has elsewhere, thus enabling him to partake of the latter (*Rav*).

Although one may designate produce as *terumah* or tithes only if it is near the produce from which it is being separated (*Bikkurim* 2:5), if the Sabbath or a festival [when tithing is forbidden] is drawing near, and there is no time for proper tithing, it is permitted to tithe from produce which is found elsewhere. This is the case to which the mishnah is referring (*Tos.*).

Others explain the mishnah to be speaking of one who transgressed and tithed from distant produce, in which case it takes effect ex post facto (*Rambam, Hil. Terumos* 5:26; *Meiri*).

מָעוֹת לִהְיוֹת מַפְרִישׁ עֲלֵיהֶן מַעֲשֵׂר שֵׁנִי — — [*or*] *money to separate the second tithe with them,*

A man set aside money to be available for redeeming the produce of the second tithe when it will be necessary (see preface to mishnah 7).

מַפְרִישׁ עֲלֵיהֶן בְּחֶזְקַת שֶׁהֵן קַיָּמִין. — *may separate with them on the assumption that they are still in existence.*

[Even when the designated produce or money is not before him, he may rely upon the assumption of its continued existence to eat the produce for which he designated the former as *terumah* or tithe, or to eat the second tithe for which the money was designated as its redemption.]

אִם אָבְדוּ — — *If they were lost,*

If after he had relied upon the designated produce for tithing (or the designated money for redemption

חוֹשֵׁשׁ מֵעֵת לְעֵת; דִּבְרֵי רַבִּי אֶלְעָזָר בֶּן שַׁמּוּעַ. רַבִּי יְהוּדָה אוֹמֵר: בִּשְׁלֹשָׁה פְרָקִים בּוֹדְקִין אֶת הַיַּיִן: בְּקָדִים שֶׁל מוֹצָאֵי הֶחָג, וּבְהוֹצָאַת סְמָדַר, וּבִשְׁעַת כְּנִיסַת מַיִם בַּבֹּסֶר.

ר׳ עובדיה מברטנורא

הרי זה חושש. לאותן טבלים שתקן בהבטחתן של אלו, ואם לא אכלן צריך להפריש מהם, שמא כשאמר הרי תרומתן בפירות שהקציתי, כבר היו אבודין: **מעת לעת.** של בדיקה. כשבדקן ומצאן אבודין חושש שמא מאתמול בעת הזאת אבדו, ואם עשאן מעשר תוך מעת לעת על פירות אחרים, צריך להפריש עליהם מספק. ועפי מהכי לא אחמור רבנן למיחש, אלא סומכין אחזקה: **בודקין את היין.** שהניחו להיות מפריש עליו, צריך לבדקו, שמא החמיץ, ואין תורמין מן החומץ על היין: **בקדים של מוצאי החג.** כשמנשבת רוח קדים במוצאי החג: **ובשעת כניסת מים.** כשהן כפול הלבן נקראים בוסר. וכשהלחלוחית נכנסת וגדילה בתוכו שיכול לעצור מהן כל שהוא, היינו כניסת מים. פירוש אחר, היו כותשים הענבים כשהן בוסר ונותנים לתוכו מים ועושים חומץ לטבול. והלכה כרבי יהודה:

יד אברהם

of the second tithe), he found them to be missing (*Rav*).

הֲרֵי זֶה חוֹשֵׁשׁ מֵעֵת לְעֵת; — *he must be cautious regarding a period of twenty-four hours —*

Any produce not yet eaten,[1] for which he had used the designated produce as *terumah* or tithe (or any second tithe for which he had used the designated money as redemption) within the twenty-four hours before it was discovered missing, must have *terumah* or tithe separated from it again. This is due to the fear that the designated produce was already lost at the time that he decided to use it as *terumah* or tithes (*Rav; Rashi*).

1. This implies that any produce which had already been eaten when the designated fruits were discovered missing requires no further separation [even though if one eats untithed fruits he must still separate an amount equivalent to its *terumah* and tithes and give it to the *Kohen, Levi,* and poor man]. The reason for this is that where the only concern is the separation and allocation of the *terumah* and tithes, but not the possibility of eating *tevel,* he may rely on the assumption that the designated *terumah* and tithes were lost after the produce had been eaten.

Rambam (*Hil. Terumos* 5:26), on the other hand, does not draw this distinction, thus implying that the caution required by the mishnah is necessary even where the food has already been eaten in order to be certain that he fulfills his obligation to give the portions to their appropriate recipients. However, it is possible that there is no dispute between *Rambam* and *Rashi,* since *Rashi* is explaining the opinion of R' Elazar ben Shamua — whose approach to this case is the more lenient one (see below) — whereas *Rambam* rules according to the prevailing opinion of the Sages — who demand a greater degree of caution (*Tos. Yom Tov*).

3
8 cautious regarding a period of twenty-four hours — [these are] the words of R′ Elazar ben Shamua.

R′ Yehudah says: At three points in time the wine must be examined: at the time of the east wind [which is] after the Festival, with the emergence of the budding berries, and at the time that liquid enters the unripe grapes.

YAD AVRAHAM

דִּבְרֵי רַבִּי אֶלְעָזָר בֶּן שַׁמּוּעַ. — *[these are] the words of R′ Elazar ben Shamua.*

The Sages, however, disagree, maintaining that since the designated produce could have disappeared any time after they were last seen, all crops for which they were used as *terumah* or tithes since that time may still be *tevel*, and their *terumah* and tithes must be taken again (*Gem.* 31b).

רַבִּי יְהוּדָה אוֹמֵר: בִּשְׁלֹשָׁה פְרָקִים בּוֹדְקִין אֶת הַיַּיִן: — *R′ Yehudah says: At three points in time the wine must be examined:*

Wine which has been put aside to be available for tithing — similar to the previous case — must be checked at three specific times [when the wine tends to sour] to make certain that it has not turned into vinegar, which may not be designated as *terumah* or tithes for wine (*Rav*).

בְּקָדִים שֶׁל מוֹצָאֵי הֶחָג, — *at the time of the east wind [which is] after the Festival,*

The wine must be checked in the season of the east wind, which is immediately after the holiday of Succos (*Rav*).

This is necessary only if autumn has already begun at that time. However, in the event that the coordination between the solar and lunar calendars was off, and Succos took place before autumn, the wine need not be checked (*Gem.* 31b; *Rashi* ad loc.; *Meiri;* see *Tos. Yom Tov*).

וּבְהוֹצָאַת סְמָדַר, — *with the emergence of the budding berries,*

When the leaves of the vine fall off, and the grapes first appear in the cluster (*Rashi*).

וּבִשְׁעַת כְּנִיסַת מַיִם בַּבֹּסֶר. — *and at the time that liquid enters the unripe grapes.*

I.e., when there is enough moisture in the unripe grapes so that it is possible to squeeze some out (*Rav*).

Alternatively, when tbe unripe grapes reach the stage when it is customary to crush them and place them in water to make vinegar (*Rav*).

פרק רביעי

Chapter Four

[א] **הַשּׁוֹלֵחַ** גֵּט לְאִשְׁתּוֹ, וְהִגִּיעַ בַּשָּׁלִיחַ, אוֹ שֶׁשָּׁלַח אַחֲרָיו שָׁלִיחַ, וְאָמַר לוֹ: „גֵּט שֶׁנָּתַתִּי לָךְ בָּטֵל הוּא" — הֲרֵי זֶה בָּטֵל. קָדַם אֵצֶל אִשְׁתּוֹ אוֹ שֶׁשָּׁלַח אֶצְלָהּ שָׁלִיחַ, וְאָמַר לָהּ: „גֵּט שֶׁשָּׁלַחְתִּי לִיךְ בָּטֵל הוּא" — הֲרֵי זֶה בָּטֵל. אִם מִשֶּׁהִגִּיעַ הַגֵּט לְיָדָהּ — שׁוּב אֵינוֹ יָכוֹל לְבַטְּלוֹ.

ר' עובדיה מברטנורא

פרק רביעי – השולח. (א) השולח. והגיע בשליח. שלא היה מתכוין לרדוף אחריו להשיגו, אלא שנשתהה השליח בדרך, והיה לו לזה דרך לשם וראהו וביטל הגט, אפילו הכי בטל, ולא אמרינן לגטורא בעלמא מכוין, שאם היה בדעתו לבטלו היה רודף אחריו: **אינו יכול לבטלו.** הא קא משמע לן דאף על פי דחזינן ליה דמהדר עליה מעיקרא לבטוליה, לא אמרינן אגלאי מלתא למפרע דבטולי בטליה. והיכא דיהיב איניש גיטא לדביתהו לזמן או על תנאי, אי אמר לה הרי זה גיטך מעכשיו ולזמן פלוני או אם יתקיים תנאי פלוני, מכי מטי גטה לידה לא מצי תו לבטוליה, ותהיה מגורשת לאותו זמן או כשיתקיים התנאי, ואי לא אמר לה מעכשיו, אפילו לבתר דמטא גטה לידה מצי מבטל ליה:

יד אברהם

1.

As noted above (1:6), when a man gives an agent a *get* to deliver to his wife, the divorce does not take effect until the woman receives the *get*. This being the case, the husband can retract the authorization of the agent, and thereby negate the subsequent execution of the *get*, as long as it has not been delivered. The following mishnah dwells on this principle, and discusses the acceptable methods whereby he can nullify the divorce.

,הַשּׁוֹלֵחַ גֵּט לְאִשְׁתּוֹ — *[If] one sent a get to his wife,*

[A man sent his wife a *get* through an agent.]

,וְהִגִּיעַ בַּשָּׁלִיחַ — *and encountered the agent,*

The husband was not seeking the agent, but met him by chance (Rav; see below).

,אוֹ שֶׁשָּׁלַח אַחֲרָיו שָׁלִיחַ — *or sent an agent after him,*

[The husband sent a second agent to recall the first.]

— וְאָמַר לוֹ: „גֵּט שֶׁנָּתַתִּי לָךְ בָּטֵל הוּא" — *and he said to him: "The get that I gave you is void,"*

[The husband or the second agent told the first agent that the *get* is void, and should not be delivered.]

.הֲרֵי זֶה בָּטֵל — *it is void.*

The authorization of the agent to deliver the *get* to the wife is revoked, and even if he proceeds to do so, she is not divorced. In the first case — that the husband merely chanced upon the agent — we do not assume that since the husband did not seek him out, it proves that he does not really want to void the *get*, but is only taking advantage of the encounter to torment his wife by delaying her divorce.

1. [If] one sent a *get* to his wife, and encountered the agent, or sent an agent after him, and he said to him: "The *get* that I gave you is void," it is void. [If] he reached his wife first or sent an agent to her, and he said to her: "The *get* that I sent you is void," it is void. If [the above occurred] after she received the *get*, he can no longer nullify it.

YAD AVRAHAM

In the second case, the mishnah reveals that the second agent has the authority to revoke the agency of the first (*Rav* from *Gem.* 32a).

Nevertheless, the husband can use this same *get* to divorce her another time, because the product of a physical act — such as the writing of a *get* — cannot be nullified by mere words (*Gem.* 32a).

קָדַם אֵצֶל אִשְׁתּוֹ — *[If] he reached his wife first*

If the husband did not encounter the agent but rather reached the wife before the agent (*Meiri*).

אוֹ שֶׁשָּׁלַח אֶצְלָהּ שָׁלִיחַ, — *or sent an agent to her,*

[Or even if he sent a second agent, who reached the wife before the agent of delivery.]

וְאָמַר לָהּ: ,,גֵּט שֶׁשָּׁלַחְתִּי לִיךְ בָּטֵל הוּא" — — *and he said to her: "The get that I sent you is void,"*

[The husband or agent declared the *get* to be void.] Any statement which indicates that he is thereby nullifying the *get* is equivalent to declaring it void, but one which denotes a previous loss of validity has no effect. Thus, for example, if he says: "This *get* shall not be effective," it is tantamount to nullification. If, however, he says: "This *get* is not effective," it implies an already existing lack of validity which we do not know to be the case. Therefore, the *get* remains unaffected (*Gem.* 32a-b).

הֲרֵי זֶה בָּטֵל. — *it is void.*

[If the husband or agent declared to the wife that the *get* is void, it can no longer take effect when delivered by the first agent.]

Since the husband gave this message to his wife rather than to the agent of delivery, it seems likely that his intention is only to torment her. Certainly, when he sends an agent to deliver this message rather than troubling himself to do so, such an interpretation is appropriate. Nevertheless, his words are taken at face value and the divorce is voided (*Gem.* 32a), because intentions which are not explicitly stated have no effect in Jewish law [*Kiddushin* 50a] (*Tos.* 32a s.v. מהו דתימא).

— אִם מִשֶּׁהִגִּיעַ הַגֵּט לְיָדָהּ — *If [the above occurred] after she received the get* (lit., *after the get reached her hand*),

If the husband declared the *get* void after it was received by his wife, or by an agent appointed to receive it on her behalf (*Meiri*).

שׁוּב אֵינוֹ יָכוֹל לְבַטְּלוֹ. — *he can no longer nullify it.*

[Because the divorce has already taken effect.] Even if he was seen trying to reach her before she received the *get*, his subsequent declaration that it is void cannot retroactively

[ב] **בָּרִאשׁוֹנָה,** הָיָה עוֹשֶׂה בֵית דִּין בְּמָקוֹם אַחֵר וּמְבַטְּלוֹ. הִתְקִין רַבָּן גַּמְלִיאֵל הַזָּקֵן שֶׁלֹּא יְהוּ עוֹשִׂין כֵּן, מִפְּנֵי תִקּוּן הָעוֹלָם.

בָּרִאשׁוֹנָה, הָיָה מְשַׁנֶּה שְׁמוֹ וּשְׁמָהּ, שֵׁם עִירוֹ

ר' עובדיה מברטנורא

(ב) **בראשונה.** לא היה מבטלו בפני האשה ולא בפני השליח, אלא במקום שהיה עומד היה מבטלו בפני שלשה: **מפני תקון העולם.** שהשליח שאינו יודע בדבר מוליכו לה והיא נישאת בו. ומכח תקנת רבן גמליאל, מלקין על מי שמבטל הגט או מוסר מודעא על הגט: **בראשונה היה משנה שמו ושמה.** כשהיו לו שני שמות, אחד כאן ואחד במדינת הים, היה מגרשה בשם הנוהג במקום כתיבת הגט, ולא היה מקפיד לכתוב את שניהם:

יד אברהם

render his pursuit tantamount to a declaration of nullification, and the divorce takes effect (*Rav* from *Gem.* 32a). Since his intentions were not understood until after the *get* was delivered, they have no effect on its validity (*Tos.* loc. cit.).

Since he did everything in his power to express his intentions, explaining them subsequently should render them effective retroactively. However, the Rabbis decreed the *get* is nullified, because he did not actually express his intentions (ibid.). *Ri* maintains that intentions that are not expressed are not even effective in Biblical law, despite the fact that everything possible was done to reveal them (ibid.).

If the *get* was given with the stipulation that it cannot take effect until a certain time, or until a specific condition has been met, the husband can nullify it even after it is in his wife's possession, as long as the stated time has not arrived or the condition has not been met. However, if he stipulated that upon the arrival of that time or the fulfillment of that condition, the *get* should take effect retroactively from the time it was given to the wife, he can no longer nullify it once it is in her hands (*Rav* from *Gem.* 34a).

2.

בָּרִאשׁוֹנָה, הָיָה עוֹשֶׂה בֵית דִּין בְּמָקוֹם אַחֵר וּמְבַטְּלוֹ. — *Originally, he would convene a court elsewhere and nullify it.*

In earlier times, a man who had sent an agent to deliver a *get* to his wife would declare the *get* null in the presence of two men, despite the absence of his wife and the agent of delivery (*Gem.* 32b; *Meiri; Even HaEzer* 141:60).

Although a Jewish court generally consists of at least three men, two can also serve as a court for nonmonetary matters (*Gem.* 32b). Therefore, the two men necessary to ratify the nullification can legitimately be referred to as a court. The reason they are required is because any legal act which is part of the process of marriage or divorce must be performed in the presence of two witnesses in order to be valid (*Ran*). Since, unlike most witnesses, their function here is to ratify and not only to testify, the mishnah refers to them as a court rather than as witnesses (*Tos. Yom Tov*).

There is another opinion in the *Gemara* (32b) that a standard court of three men is required in this case. Since the woman must be informed of the nullification in order to avoid remarrying illicitly, it is necessary to convene a formal court of three men so that

2. Originally, he would convene a court elsewhere and nullify it. Rabban Gamliel the Elder decreed that they should not do this, for the sake of the general good.

Originally, he would change his name and her name, the name of his town and the name of her

YAD AVRAHAM

the act will be publicized (*Ran*).

הִתְקִין רַבָּן גַּמְלִיאֵל הַזָּקֵן שֶׁלֹּא יְהוּ עוֹשִׂין כֵּן, — *Rabban Gamliel the Elder decreed that they should not do this,*

Rabban Gamliel decreed that the husband may nullify the *get* only in the presence of his wife or the agent of delivery (*Meiri*). However, if the husband transgressed this decree and declared the *get* null before two men, the nullification takes effect (*Gem.* 33a-34a), but the husband is punished in court with forty lashes (*Rav*).

There is a second opinion in the *Gemara* (33a) that the Rabbis prevented the nullification from taking effect if it was not done in the presence of his wife or the agent of delivery. Although they cannot reinstate a divorce which is Biblically void, they can retroactively invalidate the original marriage. This is because the validity of every Jewish marriage is subject to the continued acquiescence of the Rabbinic authorities (ibid.; see General Introduction, s.v. *Rabbinic annulment*).

מִפְּנֵי תִקּוּן הָעוֹלָם. — *for the sake of the general good* (lit., *for the sake of an improvement of the world*).

The reason for the decree requiring the husband to nullify the *get* in the presence of his wife or the agent of delivery is to prevent the woman from mistakenly believing that she is divorced, in which case she might remarry illicitly, and any children born of that marriage would be illegitimate (*Gem.* 33a). This could actually be avoided by requiring nullification in the presence of a formal court of three men which would generate publicity. Nevertheless, Rabban Gamliel designed the decree in this manner in order to make it more difficult for the husband to nullify the *get*, and thus help bring about the wife's freedom to remarry, rather than be stuck in marriage with a husband who intends to divorce her, but is delaying for the sake of tormenting her (*Tos.* 33a s.v. ובי תרי).

According to those who maintain that even before Rabban Gamliel's decree, the husband could nullify the *get* only before a court of three, the likelihood of publicity which this creates negates the concern for the possibility of the wife's illicit remarriage due to her mistaken assumption that she is divorced. Thus, making it difficult for the husband to nullify the *get* is the entire reason for the decree (*Gem.* 33a).

There is a third approach to the mishnah which also assumes that even before Rabban Gamliel's decree the *get* could be nullified only before a court of three. Nevertheless, the possibility that the nullification would not be well publicized and that the woman would mistakenly presume herself divorced and remarry illicitly could not be ruled out completely. This concern induced Rabban Gamliel to require that the *get* be nullified in the presence of the wife or the agent of delivery (*Rav; Rashi;* see *Mishneh LaMelech* to *Hil. Gerushin* 6:18).

בָּרִאשׁוֹנָה, הָיָה מְשַׁנֶּה שְׁמוֹ וּשְׁמָהּ, — *Originally, he would change his name and her name,*

If a man or his wife were called

וְשֵׁם עִירָהּ, וְהִתְקִין רַבָּן גַּמְלִיאֵל הַזָּקֵן שֶׁיְּהֵא כוֹתֵב: „אִישׁ פְּלוֹנִי וְכָל שֵׁם שֶׁיֵּשׁ לוֹ", „אִשָּׁה פְּלוֹנִית וְכָל שׁוּם שֶׁיֵּשׁ לָהּ", מִפְּנֵי תִקּוּן הָעוֹלָם.

[ג] **אֵין** אַלְמָנָה נִפְרַעַת מִנִּכְסֵי יְתוֹמִים אֶלָּא בִשְׁבוּעָה. נִמְנְעוּ

ר' עובדיה מברטנורא

מפני תיקון העולם. שלא יוציאו לעז על בניה מן השני, לאמר לא גרשה בעלה, שאין זה שמו. ואדם שהוחזק בשני שמות בשני מקומות, אחד במקום הכתיבה ואחד במקום הנתינה, אינה מגורשת עד שיכתוב שם של מקום הנתינה ושם של מקום הכתיבה עמו, אבל אם הוחזק בשני שמות במקום אחד, וכתב אחד מן השמות, בדיעבד הגט כשר, מיהו לכתחילה צריך לכתוב שניהם. והיכא דשינה שמו או שמה בגט, אף על פי שכתב אחר כך וכל שם שיש לי, הגט בטל: (ג) **אין אלמנה נפרעת.** כתובתה: **מנכסי יתומים, אלא בשבועה.** שלא נתקבלה כלום:

יד אברהם

different names in different places, the husband would include in the *get* only the names which were used in the town where he wrote the *get* (*Rav; Meiri*).

שֵׁם עִירוֹ וְשֵׁם עִירָהּ, — *the name of his town and the name of her town,*

Similarly, if their town had several names they would list only one of them (*Tos.* 80a s.v. שינה).

Other commentators explain this to mean that if the husband or wife had changed their place of residence, the *get* would include only the name of the town in which they resided at that time (*Ran; Meiri*).

וְהִתְקִין רַבָּן גַּמְלִיאֵל הַזָּקֵן שֶׁיְּהֵא כוֹתֵב: „אִישׁ פְּלוֹנִי וְכָל שֵׁם שֶׁיֵּשׁ לוֹ", „אִשָּׁה פְּלוֹנִית וְכָל שׁוּם שֶׁיֵּשׁ לָהּ", — *but Rabban Gamliel the Elder decreed that he write: "The man, So-and-so, and any name he has"; "the woman, So-and-so, and any name she has,"*

Rabban Gamliel decreed that the husband first write the name which he is called in the place where the *get* shall be given to the wife (*Rav; Tos.* 31b s.v. והוא; *Rosh; Ran; Even HaEzer* 129:4), and then add any other name which he is called in the town where the *get* is being written, or elsewhere (*Rav; Rabbeinu Tam* cited by *Tos.* loc. cit. s.v. וכל שום; *Rama, Even HaEzer* 129:1). Otherwise, the *get* is null (*Rav*). By the same token, when writing their place of residence, he must list all names which that place is called (*Rama* ibid., 128:3).

If — in the town where the *get* is being written — it is not known that he is called by a different name elsewhere, he need only use the name by which he is known in that place (*Gem.* 34b). Nevertheless, it is preferable that he include all his names even in this case (*Tos.* loc. cit. s.v. והוא; *Ran*).

If he wrote a name by which he is not called at all, the *get* is null, even if he added: *and any name which he has* (*Rav*).

Others contend that the opposite is true; the names which they are called in the place the *get* is written are the primary names, which should be listed first, and those which they are called in the place where it

town, but Rabban Gamliel the Elder decreed that he write: "The man, So-and-so, and any name he has"; "the woman, So-and-so, and any name she has," for the sake of the general good.

3. A widow is not paid from the property of orphans except with an oath. They ceased

YAD AVRAHAM

is to be given are secondary (*Tosefta*, cited in *Tos.* loc. cit.; *Meiri*).

A third opinion maintains that the only names mentioned in the *get* are the primary names; all others are included in the phrase, *and any names he/she has* (*Rashi* 34b s.v. *Bahag*, quoted by *Tos.* 34b s.v. וכל; *Rosh; Ran; Meiri; Even HaEzer* 129:1). Similarly, only the primary name of the town is listed, with all the others included in the phrase, *and any name which it has* (*Rosh, Nussach HaGet; Even HaEzer* 128:3). According to the view that the issue concerning the name of the town was the mention of their present location alone without reference to any previous residence (see above), the decree of Rabban Gamliel was that the name of the town where they had previously resided should also be included (*Ran; Meiri*).

There is another view that if he is called two different names in the city where the *get* is being written, he writes the primary name and adds, *and any name he has.* However, if he is called different names in different places, he must list all of his names in the *get* (*Ravad* in *Hasagos* to *Rif*).

.מִפְּנֵי תִקּוּן הָעוֹלָם — *for the sake of the general good.*

All of these names must be listed so that there should not later arise any doubt whether the *get* she received was really for her husband and herself, and thus, whether her children from a second marriage are legitimate (*Rav; Rashi*). Accordingly, if the husband or wife is known by several names in the same town, and the *get* mentions only one of them, it is still valid, because — in this instance — there is no doubt as to their correct identities (*Rav; Tos.* 34b s.v. והוא).

Others contend that it is even permitted to do so initially (*Rashba;* see *Maggid Mishneh, Hil. Gerushin* 3:13).

3.

[Following the Mishnah's mention of two decrees enacted *for the sake of the general good,* it continues in this chapter and the next to list other such enactments and also those promulgated *for the sake of peace,* although most of them are totally unrelated to the subject of *gittin.*]

אֵין אַלְמָנָה נִפְרַעַת מִנִּכְסֵי יְתוֹמִים אֶלָּא .בִּשְׁבוּעָה — *A widow is not paid from the property of orphans except with an oath.*

A widow who claims her *kesubah* (marriage settlement; see General Introduction to ArtScroll *Kesubos*) from her husband's orphans (i.e., from the properties they inherited from him, see *Choshen Mishpat* 107:1) is prevented from collecting it from them without an oath, because she may have already received some or all of the *kesubah* during her husband's lifetime. She must therefore swear that she has not received any part of

גיטין
ד/ג

מִלְּהַשְׁבִּיעָהּ, הִתְקִין רַבָּן גַּמְלִיאֵל הַזָּקֵן שֶׁתְּהֵא נוֹדֶרֶת לַיְתוֹמִים כָּל מַה שֶּׁיִּרְצוּ, וְגוֹבָה כְתֻבָּתָהּ. הָעֵדִים חוֹתְמִין עַל הַגֵּט מִפְּנֵי תִקּוּן הָעוֹלָם.

ר׳ עובדיה מברטנורא

נמנעו מלהשביעה. שמפני שהיא טורחת לפני היתומים, מורה התירא לעצמה ליֵשבע שלא לקחה כלום. ואף על פי שלקחה דבר מועט, סבורה שבשכר טרחה נוטלתו ואינו מפרעון כתובתה. ולפיכך נמנעו מלהשביעה, והיתה מפסדת כתובתה: **התקין רבן גמליאל שתהא נודרת ליתומים כל מה שירצו.** כגון קונם מיני מזונות עלי אם נהניתי מכתובתי, וגובה כתובתה. ואם נשאת לאחר קודם שהדירוה היתומים על כתובתה, ואם ידירוה אחר שנשאת, שמא יפר לה בעלה, כיצד יעשו, משביעין אותה חוץ לבית דין שבועה דרבנן, שאין ענשה מרובה, ונוטלת כתובתה אחר שנשאת. וכשבאת לגבות כתובתה קודם שתנשא לאחר, הרשות ביד היתומים, רצו משביעין אותה חוץ לבית דין, או מדירים אותה בבית דין: **העדים חותמים על הגט מפני תקון העולם.** אתרווייהו קאי, גבי אלמנה שתהא נודרת ליורשים כל מה שירצו, מפני תקון העולם, שיהיו הנשים נשאות לבעליהן ולא תדאגנה להפסיד כתובתן. וגבי עדים חותמים על הגט, מפני תיקון העולם, דהואיל ועדי מסירה כרתי, שהעדים שנמסר הגט בפניהם לאשה הם עיקר הגירושין, לא היה צריך שיחתמו עדים בגט, אלא מפני תיקון העולם, דחיישינן שמא ימות אחד מן העדים שנמסר הגט בפניהם, ונמצא הגט שבידה בלא עדים כחספא בעלמא:

יד אברהם

the *kesubah* before she can collect it (*Rav*).

Notwithstanding that this law pertains to all who seek to collect from the possessions of orphans, the mishnah singles out a widow, because one might think that the Rabbis were more lenient in her case so that women would feel more secure about their future financial welfare, and thus be more willing to marry in the first place (*Gem.* 35a).

Although a *kesubah* is not designed to be collected until after divorce or death, and there is a principle that we assume that a person does not pay his debts or obligations until they are due, we are nevertheless apprehensive that a woman may have received all or part of the *kesubah* during her husband's lifetime. This is because there is a tendency for the husband to guarantee payment in advance by placing the money in the wife's possession for safekeeping due to the fact that the obligation of *kesubah* is imposed upon him by the courts [and it is therefore more stringent in his eyes] (*Tos.* 34b s.v. אין).

נִמְנְעוּ מִלְּהַשְׁבִּיעָהּ, — *They ceased from imposing an oath upon her,*

The Rabbis stopped imposing an oath upon the widow, for fear that she had indeed received some small part of the *kesubah*, but would nevertheless swear to the contrary, rationalizing that she deserved this amount for her efforts in caring for the orphans. As a result, no widow was able to collect her *kesubah* (*Rav* from *Gem.* 35a).

הִתְקִין רַבָּן גַּמְלִיאֵל הַזָּקֵן שֶׁתְּהֵא נוֹדֶרֶת לַיְתוֹמִים כָּל מַה שֶּׁיִּרְצוּ, — *[so] Rabban Gamliel the Elder decreed that she should make a neder prohibiting whatever the orphans wish,*

[Rabban Gamliel decreed that the orphans can demand from the widow that, instead of an oath, she make a *neder* (loosely, *vow*) forswearing whatever item the orphans choose if she has collected any part of her *kesubah*. [The difference between a *neder* and an oath is that a *neder* is used to forbid an object to a person,

from imposing an oath upon her, [so] Rabban Gamliel the Elder decreed that she should make a *neder* prohibiting whatever the orphans wish, and collect her *kesubah.*

Witnesses sign on a *get* for the sake of the general

YAD AVRAHAM

whereas an oath forbids the person to use the object. Several halachic consequences result from the distinction (see *Nedarim* 2:1*ff.* and General Introduction to ArtScroll *Nedarim*).]

There are several reasons why a *neder* is considered preferable to an oath. First of all, one who swears falsely incurs very severe punishment, much greater than one who transgresses a *neder* (*Ran*). Secondly, since a *neder* involves forbidding an item, the orphans are likely to demand that she forswear something which is constantly needed, such as food, thus assuring that every time she eats from that food she will be reminded of her *neder* (*Meiri*). In addition, women tended to be more afraid of transgressing a *neder* than of swearing falsely (*Yerushalmi*, cited by *Ran*) [perhaps because a *neder* is transgressed by deed, whereas a false oath is made merely by speech].

Alternatively, the orphans may demand that the widow swear outside the court that she has not received any of her *kesubah* (*Rav* from *Gem.* 35a). An oath sworn outside of court is made without holding a Torah scroll, and is less consequential than one sworn in court (*Rashi*). [Therefore, the Rabbis were willing to allow such an oath despite the concern that she may swear falsely.]

וְגוֹבָה כְּתֻבָּתָהּ. — *and collect her kesubah.*

[Upon making the *neder* demanded by the orphans, she collects her *kesubah.*]

If the widow was already remarried when she claimed her *kesubah*, a *neder* is no longer a viable option since her new husband can nullify it (see *Kesubos* 4:4). Therefore, she can collect only if she swears outside of court that she has not received any payment for her *kesubah* (*Rav* from *Gem.* 35b). If she was not yet married, there is no concern that she will subsequently remarry and then have her new husband nullify the vow, because a man can nullify only those vows which his wife made after they were married (*Gem.* ibid.).

The commentators discuss several options for avoiding the possibility of her husband nullifying her *neder*, but rule them all out. Despite the fact that one is permitted to nullify a *neder* only in the presence of the person to whom it was made [which would guarantee the orphans the opportunity to protest it], if he transgresses and nullifies it in their absence it takes effect nonetheless (*Tos.* 35b s.v. ליחוש). If she were to make a *neder* prohibiting something which does not involve self-denial, her husband could not nullify it (see *Nedarim* 10:1 and ArtScroll commentary ibid.), but such a *neder* would not guarantee her truthfulness (*Rosh*). The orphans could demand that she make a *neder* not to eat bread if she received any payment, and then have her eat bread immediately, thus ensuring the violation of the *neder*, if she had already collected the *kesubah*. However, this, too, would not prove her veracity, because she is not concerned about the single transgression of a *neder* (*Tos.* loc. cit.).

הָעֵדִים חוֹתְמִין עַל הַגֵּט מִפְּנֵי תִקּוּן הָעוֹלָם. — *Witnesses sign on a get for the sake of the general good.*

Rashi states that this enactment, too, is attributed to Rabban Gamliel

הִלֵּל הִתְקִין פְּרוֹזְבּוּל מִפְּנֵי תִקּוּן הָעוֹלָם.

[ד] עֶבֶד שֶׁנִּשְׁבָּה וּפְדָאוּהוּ אִם לְשׁוּם עֶבֶד —

ר' עובדיה מברטנורא

הִלֵּל הִתְקִין פְּרוֹזְבּוּל. שֶׁרָאָה אֶת הָעָם שֶׁנִּמְנְעוּ מִלְּהַלְווֹת זֶה אֶת זֶה, וְעָבְרוּ עַל מַה שֶׁכָּתוּב
בַּתּוֹרָה (דברים טו, ט) הִשָּׁמֶר לְךָ פֶּן יִהְיֶה דָבָר עִם לְבָבְךָ בְלִיַּעַל, עָמַד וְהִתְקִין פְּרוֹזְבּוּל. וְזֶה גוּפוֹ
שֶׁל פְּרוֹזְבּוּל, מוֹסֵר אֲנִי לָכֶם פְּלוֹנִי וּפְלוֹנִי דַּיָּינִים, שֶׁכָּל חוֹב שֶׁיֵּשׁ לִי אֵצֶל פְּלוֹנִי, שֶׁאֶגְבֶּנּוּ כָּל זְמַן
שֶׁאֶרְצֶה: (ד) עֶבֶד שֶׁנִּשְׁבָּה וּפְדָאוּהוּ. יִשְׂרְאֵלִים אֲחֵרִים, לְאַחַר שֶׁנִּתְיָאֵשׁ רַבּוֹ מִמֶּנּוּ:

יד אברהם

the Elder. *Tosafos* (36a s.v. וְהָעֵדִים)
disagree because of an implication of
the *Gemara* that the enactment of
witnesses signing on a *get* predated
Rabban Gamliel.

Although it is the witnesses obser-
ving the delivery of the *get* who
legitimize it, the Rabbis nonetheless
enacted that witnesses sign on the *get*
itself. This was due to the possibility
that one of the witnesses to the
delivery may die, and the woman
would then have no proof of her
divorce (*Rav* from *Gem.* 36a). This
enactment was not decreed as an
obligation, but only as a recommen-
dation in order to avoid difficulties
(*Rosh*; *Tos.* 3b s.v. רבי אלעזר).

This explanation assumes that the mishnah follows the view of R' Elazar, who
maintains that the vital witnesses to a *get*
are those who observe its delivery (see
General Introduction). Others contend that
the mishnah is in accordance with the
opinion of R' Meir, who attributes the
legitimacy of a *get* to its signed witnesses.
The enactment described in the mishnah is
not the basic prerequisite of the witnesses'
signatures, which is required by Biblical
law, but the requirement that they identify
themselves by signing with their names,
rather than merely writing, "I signed as a
witness," without specifying their names.
This was enacted to facilitate confirmation
of the document's validity (*Gem.* 36a; see
Tosefta 7:11).

הִלֵּל הִתְקִין פְּרוֹזְבּוּל מִפְּנֵי תִקּוּן הָעוֹלָם. —
*Hillel decreed [the] prozbul for the sake
of the general good.*

At the end of *Shemittah*, the Sabbatical year, any debts outstanding
between two Jews are automatically
nullified (*Deut.* 15:2; *Sheviis* 10:1; see
Rosh 18). Because of this, people
became reluctant to lend money to
others, and thus transgressed the
Biblical injunction (*Deut.* 15:9) against
refraining from lending money for
that reason (*Rav* from *Gem.* 36a;
Sheviis 10:3). Therefore, Hillel the
Elder ordained the writing of a
prozbul, which states that the creditor
is placing all debts owed him into the
hands of the courts (*Meiri*). Once the
debts have been transferred to the
court for collection, they are not
nullified by *Shemittah* (*Sheviis* 10:2),
as derived hermeneutically from
Scripture (*Yerushalmi*, cited by *Rashi*
ad loc.).

The word *prozbul* is a contraction of
the words פְּרוֹס בּוּלֵי בּוּטֵי, *an enactment
for rich and poor* (*Gem.* 36b-37a). It
benefits the rich by enabling them to
collect their loans, thereby encouraging them to continue lending to the
poor (*Rashi* ad loc.).

Although, even before the advent of the
prozbul, creditors could have avoided this
predicament by giving over their documents to the courts for collection, many

good. Hillel decreed [the] *prozbul* for the sake of the general good.

4. **A** slave who was taken captive and they redeemed him — if to be a slave, he shall be

YAD AVRAHAM

were reluctant to lose possession of these documents. Also, *prozbul* is effective even for loans which were not recorded in legal documents (*Rav; Meiri*). Another option for creditors would be to stipulate at the time of the loan that it is not to be revoked by the Sabbatical year. However, if that practice were to become universal, the laws of *Shemittah* regarding the nullification of debts would become forgotten entirely. Therefore, Hillel enacted the *prozbul*, which requires the participation of the courts and emphasizes the fact that the debt stands to be annulled by the Sabbatical year (*Meiri*).

Although the nullification of loans during *Shemittah* is a Biblical law, its implementation when the laws of *Yovel* (Jubilee) are not in effect is of Rabbinic origin (*Rashi* 36a s.v. בשביעית הזמן הזה).[1] It is only for such an era that Hillel enacted *prozbul*, since he would not have instituted a means to negate a Biblical law (*Gem.* 36a; *Tos.* ad loc. s.v. מי איכא; *Rambam, Hil. Shemittah* 9:16; *Meiri*).

Others contend that the decree of *prozbul* applies even to a time when the Biblical laws of *Shemittah* are in effect. This is because the courts have total authority over all monetary possessions and can revoke private ownership when necessary (*Gem.* 36b). Thus, in enacting *prozbul*, Hillel circumvented the Biblical law of *Shemittah* by revoking the debtor's ownership of the money involved (*Rashi* 36b s.v. רבא אמר).

4.

עֶבֶד שֶׁנִּשְׁבָּה — *A slave who was taken captive*

A non-Jewish slave belonging to a Jew was taken captive by gentiles (*Gem.* 37b, *Rashi; Tif. Yis.*).

,וּפְדָאוּהוּ — *and they redeemed him —*

He was ransomed by another Jew after his original master had given up hope of recovering him (*Rav* from *Gem.* 37b). [When the owner of a lost object despairs of retrieving it, it becomes permissible for anyone to take it and assume possession of it (*Bava Kamma* 2:1; see *Rashi* here).]

,אִם לְשׁוּם עֶבֶד — *if to be a slave,*

If the Jew who redeemed him did so with the intent of acquiring him as his own slave (*Meiri*).

;יִשְׁתַּעְבֵּד — *he shall be subjugated;*

The slave becomes subjugated to the one who redeemed him (*Rav* from *Gem.* 37b). Although a gentile can acquire only the rights to the profits that a slave produces, but not full possession of his person (*Gem.* 37b), the Jew who redeems him from the gentile assumes full possession of him by having him immersed in a *mikveh* (ritual pool) for the purpose of enslaving him. The slave thereby becomes a partial Jew and is obligated by the laws of the Torah to the same extent as a Jewish woman (*Rashi* 37b s.v. למעשה).

Others contend that the second Jewish master automatically assumes the full ownership which had been enjoyed by the original owner. This is because the gentile's lack of full ownership was due only to his

1. According to *Rashi*, the laws of *Yovel* were not in effect even during the time of the Second Temple; according to *Tosafos* (36a s.v. בזמן), they were.

יִשְׁתַּעְבֵּד; אִם לְשׁוּם בֶּן חוֹרִין — לֹא יִשְׁתַּעְבֵּד. רַבָּן שִׁמְעוֹן בֶּן גַּמְלִיאֵל אוֹמֵר: בֵּין כָּךְ וּבֵין כָּךְ — יִשְׁתַּעְבֵּד.

עֶבֶד שֶׁעֲשָׂאוֹ רַבּוֹ אַפּוֹתִיקִי לַאֲחֵרִים וְשִׁחְרְרוֹ — שׁוּרַת הַדִּין, אֵין הָעֶבֶד חַיָּב כְּלוּם; אֶלָּא, מִפְּנֵי תִקּוּן הָעוֹלָם,

ר׳ עובדיה מברטנורא

אם לשום עבד ישתעבד. לרבו שני: **לשום בן חורין לא ישתעבד.** לא לרבו ראשון, ולא לרבו שני. לרבו שני לא, דהא לשום בן חורין פרקיה. לרבו ראשון לא, דלמא ממנעי ולא פרקי: **רבן שמעון בן גמליאל אומר בין כך ובין כך ישתעבד.** לרבו ראשון, שלא יהא כל אחד ואחד הולך ומפיל עצמו לגייסות ומפקיע עצמו מיד רבו: **אפותיקי.** פה תהא קאי, מזה תגבה חובך ולא ממקום אחר: **ושחררו.** רבו ראשון: **שורת הדין אין העבד חייב כלום.** לרבו שני, שהשחרור ששחררו רבו ראשון מפקיעו מידי שעבוד: **אלא מפני תקון העולם.** שמא ימצאנו רבו שני בשוק, ויאמר לו עבדי אתה, ויוציא לעז על בניו:

יד אברהם

Rabbis granted him freedom — despite the fact that he actually still belongs to the first owner — for fear that otherwise, people would not redeem him at all, because they obviously do so for the *mitzvah* of ransoming a slave (see *Tos.* s.v. דלמא), as the *Gemara* (37b) tells us: Just as it is a *mitzvah* to redeem free people, so is it a *mitzvah* to redeem slaves [owned by Jews].

רַבָּן שִׁמְעוֹן בֶּן גַּמְלִיאֵל אוֹמֵר: בֵּין כָּךְ וּבֵין כָּךְ — יִשְׁתַּעְבֵּד. — *Rabban Shimon ben Gamliel says: In either case, he shall be subjugated.*

He maintains that whether the one who redeemed the slave did so for the sake of acquiring him for himself or in order to set him free, the slave is returned to his original master. This was decreed by the Rabbis to prevent slaves from allowing themselves to become captives in order to escape from their masters' possession (*Rav* from *Gem.* 37b). However, if the one who ransomed the slave did so with the intent of acquiring him for him-

limited capacity to possess a slave, and not because the slave acquired any degree of possession of his own person which would limit the scope of the second Jew's ownership[1] (*Meiri*).

אִם לְשׁוּם בֶּן חוֹרִין — *if to be a free man,*

[If the Jew who ransomed him did so with the intent of freeing him.]

לֹא יִשְׁתַּעְבֵּד. — *he shall not be subjugated.*

The slave is not subjugated to the one who redeemed him, since he intended to free him (*Rav* from *Gem.* 37b). He is not enslaved to his original master because the latter had already despaired of regaining him, thus losing his ownership (*Gem.* ibid.).

Another interpretation is that the mishnah is speaking of a slave whose master had not yet despaired of recovering him. If the one who redeemed him did so with the intent of retrieving him for his master, he returns to the latter's subjugation. If he ransomed him so that he could go free, the

1. *Meiri* wonders why *Rashi* maintains that the slave needs immersion.

4
4

subjugated; if to be a free man, he shall not be subjugated. Rabban Shimon ben Gamliels says: In either case, he shall be subjugated.

A slave whose master designated him as payment for a debt to another and [then] freed him — by right of law, the slave should not be liable at all; but, for the sake of the general good,

YAD AVRAHAM

self, the original owner must pay him the slave's value upon regaining possession of him (*Tosefta*, cited by *Ran; Rambam, Hil. Avadim* 8:15).

The reason the slave must return to the original master, rather than the one who redeemed him, is because otherwise, slaves unhappy with their masters might allow themselves to fall into captivity in order to be redeemed and thus acquired by a different master (*Tos.* 37b s.v. בין כך).

Others maintain that only if he was redeemed for the sake of being freed does he return to his original master. If he was redeemed for the sake of acquisition, he becomes subjugated to the one who redeemed him (*Rosh; Meiri*).

According to the interpretation that in the case of the mishnah, the original master did not yet give up hope of recovering the slave and thus retains his ownership, the first *Tanna* agrees that if he is ransomed for the sake of subjugation, he is returned to the original master. Accordingly, Rabban Shimon ben Gamliel's view is only in dispute with the second statement of the first *Tanna* — that if he was redeemed for the sake of being freed he goes free. Rabban Shimon ben Gamliel maintains that even when the slave is redeemed for the sake of being set free, he is returned to his original master. This is because he considers the obligation to redeem a captive applicable to a slave as well as a free man. Therefore, the first *Tanna's* concern that people will not redeem him if he does not go free is unwarranted (*Gem.* 37b).

עֶבֶד שֶׁעֲשָׂאוֹ רַבּוֹ אַפּוֹתִיקִי לַאֲחֵרִים — *A slave whose master designated him as payment for a debt to another*

A person designated his slave as the sole form of payment for a specific debt. The word אַפּוֹתִיקִי, *aposiki*, is a contraction of the words פֹּה תְּהֵא קָאֵי, *here you shall be*, meaning that only from here shall you collect your debt (*Rav*). Its origin is from the Greek word for *collateral* [cf. the English word, *hypothecate*] (*Tif. Yis.*).

וְשִׁחְרְרוֹ — *and [then] freed him* —

His master set him free (*Rav*). This effectively releases the master from his debt, since the slave had been designated as the sole form of payment (*Meiri*).

שׁוּרַת הַדִּין, אֵין הָעֶבֶד חַיָּב כְּלוּם; — *by right of law, the slave should not be liable at all;*

The slave should no longer be bound to the creditor, because the emancipation of a slave negates the lien of any creditor (*Rav* from *Gem.* 40b).

אֶלָּא, מִפְּנֵי תִקּוּן הָעוֹלָם, — *but, for the sake of the general good,*

I.e., to avoid the possibility of the creditor confronting him publicly and proclaiming that he is his slave, thereby causing others to question the status of his children (*Rav* from *Gem.* 41a), since the daughter of a slave is disqualified from marrying a *Kohen* (*Tos. R' Akiva*).

גיטין
ד/ה

כּוֹפִין אֶת רַבּוֹ וְעוֹשֶׂה אוֹתוֹ בֶּן חוֹרִין, וְכוֹתֵב שְׁטָר עַל דָּמָיו. רַבָּן שִׁמְעוֹן בֶּן גַּמְלִיאֵל אוֹמֵר: אֵינוֹ כוֹתֵב; אֶלָּא מְשַׁחְרֵר.

[ה] **מִי** שֶׁחֶצְיוֹ עֶבֶד וְחֶצְיוֹ בֶּן חוֹרִין — עוֹבֵד אֶת רַבּוֹ יוֹם אֶחָד וְאֶת עַצְמוֹ יוֹם אֶחָד; דִּבְרֵי בֵית הִלֵּל. אָמְרוּ לָהֶם בֵּית שַׁמַּאי:

ר׳ עובדיה מברטנורא

כופין את רבו. שני, ועושהו בן חורין. וכותב לו העבד שטר חוב על דמיו, כלומר כפי מה שהוא שוה לימכר בשוק, לא כפי החוב, אם היה החוב יתר על דמיו: **רבן שמעון בן גמליאל אמר אין העבד כותב.** שטר חוב, שהוא אינו חייב כלום, אלא רבו ראשון שהזיק שעבודו של זה, הוא שצריך לשלם לו דמיו, שהמזיק שעבודו של חברו חייב. והלכה כרבן שמעון בן גמליאל: **(ה) מי שחציו עבד וחציו בן חורין.** כגון עבד של שני שותפים ושחררו אחד מהם. אי נמי, שקבל רבו ממנו חצי דמיו ושחרר חציו באותם הדמים:

יד אברהם

כּוֹפִין אֶת רַבּוֹ וְעוֹשֶׂה בֶּן חוֹרִין, — *they compel his master to free him* (lit., *and he makes him a free man*),

The creditor who had an *aposiki* on the slave and was, to a limited degree, his master, is compelled to write him a document of emancipation [thus avoiding any question about his status] (*Rav* from *Gem.* 41a).

וְכוֹתֵב שְׁטָר עַל דָּמָיו. — *and he writes a bond for his value.*

The slave writes a bond to the creditor for the amount of his market value which was pledged to the original debt [but not his full value if it exceeds the amount of the debt] (*Rav* from *Gem.* 41a).

There is a second approach to the mishnah which explains that it was the creditor who gave the slave a document of emancipation. Since the creditor is not his master, the slave is not freed and retains his current status, which includes being obligated to perform only those commandments that are required of Jewish women. A freed slave, on the other hand, attains the status of a bona fide Jew, and like every Jewish man, is required to fulfill all the commandments. Thus, the words אֵין הָעֶבֶד חַיָּב כְּלוּם mean *the slave should not be obligated at all* — i.e., he shall not be obligated in the additional commandments which a legitimate emancipation would impose upon him. However, since the creditor's act may generate rumors that the slave has been freed, his master is compelled to grant him his freedom, and the slave writes the master a bond for the amount that his market value exceeds the debt (*Gem.* 41a, *Rashi* ad loc. s.v. על דמיו).

רַבָּן שִׁמְעוֹן בֶּן גַּמְלִיאֵל אוֹמֵר: אֵינוֹ כוֹתֵב; אֶלָּא מְשַׁחְרֵר. — *Rabban Shimon ben Gamliel says: He does not write; only the one who freed [him].*

Rabban Shimon ben Gamliel contends that since the master is the one who nullified the pledge of his creditor, he — and not the slave — must compensate for the loss incurred (*Rav* from *Gem.* 51a). The first, anonymous opinion, however, holds that nullification of a pledge is not considered direct damage, but rather,

4
5 they compel his master to free him, and he writes a bond for his value. Rabban Shimon ben Gamliel says: He does not write; only the one who freed [him].

5. **O**ne who is half-slave and half-free works one day for his master and one day for himself; [these are] the words of Beis Hillel. Beis Shammai

YAD AVRAHAM

an indirect cause of loss for which a person is not liable in court (*Gem.* 51a). Therefore, he maintains that the Rabbis imposed payment on the slave, who is the beneficiary of the emancipation (see *Rashi* 41a s.v. היזק שאינו ניכר).

According to those who interpret the mishnah to be discussing a case in which the creditor gave the slave the document of emancipation, Rabban Shimon ben Gamliel is of the opinion that since the creditor caused the slave to be set free, he must pay the master the amount that the slave's value exceeds the debt. The first *Tanna,* however, contends that a person is not liable for damage that he causes which is not discernible. In this case, too, there is no physical change in the slave to indicate his emancipation (*Gem.* 41a).

5.

מִי שֶׁחֶצְיוֹ עֶבֶד וְחֶצְיוֹ בֶּן חוֹרִין — *One who is half-slave and half-free*

This refers to a slave who belonged to two partners — one of whom freed his half — or a slave whose master received payment for half of his value and freed him halfway in exchange for that money [since one of the ways a slave is freed is by the payment of his value (*Kiddushin* 1:3)] (*Rav* from *Gem.* 41b).

The mention of a half is only an example; the same laws apply when any percentage of a slave is freed (*Meiri; Rav* s.v. כופין את רבו).

Only when being freed for money can a slave be partially manumitted by a master who owns him completely. This is because the legitimacy of a document of emancipation for only part of a slave is the subject of a dispute among the *Tannaim,* and the ruling is that it does not take effect (*Tos. R' Akiva Eiger* citing *Gem.* 41b). However, if the master freed one half of his slave and sold or gave away the other half at the same time, the partial emancipation is legitimate even if it was effected with a document (*Gem.* 43a; *Rambam, Hil. Avadim* 7:4).

עוֹבֵד אֶת רַבּוֹ יוֹם אֶחָד וְאֶת עַצְמוֹ יוֹם אֶחָד; דִּבְרֵי בֵית הִלֵּל. — *works one day for his master and one day for himself; [these are] the words of Beis Hillel.*

The partnership of the master and slave is administered by dividing the rights to the slave according to time, each of them enjoying full monetary proprietorship on the day that the slave is in his possession. This includes not only the profits from the labor of that day, but also any articles the slave finds and any payment awarded for damage which was done to him on that day. They do not divide the profits from all days equally, because the master would consider it an affront to his authority to share his profits with the slave himself (*Tos. Rid*).

גיטין
ד/ה

תִּקַּנְתֶּם אֶת רַבּוֹ, וְאֶת עַצְמוֹ לֹא תִקַּנְתֶּם: לִשָּׂא שִׁפְחָה אִי אֶפְשָׁר, שֶׁכְּבָר חֶצְיוֹ בֶּן חוֹרִין; בַּת חוֹרִין אִי אֶפְשָׁר, שֶׁכְּבָר חֶצְיוֹ עֶבֶד; יִבָּטֵל? וַהֲלֹא לֹא נִבְרָא הָעוֹלָם אֶלָּא לִפְרִיָּה וְרִבְיָה, שֶׁנֶּאֱמַר: „לֹא תֹהוּ בְרָאָהּ; לָשֶׁבֶת יְצָרָהּ". אֶלָּא, מִפְּנֵי תִקּוּן הָעוֹלָם, כּוֹפִין אֶת רַבּוֹ וְעוֹשֶׂה אוֹתוֹ בֶּן חוֹרִין, וְכוֹתֵב שְׁטָר עַל חֲצִי דָמָיו. וְחָזְרוּ בֵית הִלֵּל לְהוֹרוֹת כְּדִבְרֵי בֵית שַׁמַּאי.

ר' עובדיה מברטנורא

תקנתם את רבו. שאינו חסר כלום: **לישא שפחה אינו יכול.** מפני לד חירות שבו: **בת חורין אינו יכול.** מפני לד עבדות שבו: **כופין את רבו ועושהו בן חורין.** והוא הדין אם היה עבד של מאה שותפין, ואחד מהם שחררו, שכופין את כלם לשחררו:

יד אברהם

אָמְרוּ לָהֶם בֵּית שַׁמַּאי: תִּקַּנְתֶּם אֶת רַבּוֹ, וְאֶת עַצְמוֹ לֹא תִקַּנְתֶּם: — *Beis Shammai said to them: You have provided a solution for his master, but for [him] himself you have not provided a solution:*

You have provided for the needs of the master by seeing to it that he does not lose from his share of the slave's profits (*Rav*) [but you have not provided for the needs of the slave, as explained below].

An alternative interpretation is: You have complied with the master's desire of not wanting to be a partner with his slave, by granting him full proprietorship on the days in which the slave is in his possession (*Tos. Rid*).

לִשָּׂא שִׁפְחָה אִי אֶפְשָׁר, שֶׁכְּבָר חֶצְיוֹ בֶּן חוֹרִין; — *He cannot marry a slave, because he is half-free;*

And a free Jew is forbidden to marry a female slave (*Deut.* 3:18; *Targum Onkelos* ad loc.).

Even if he were to marry a slave and have children, he would still not fulfill the Biblical commandment (*Gen.* 1:29) to be fruitful and multiply, because the paternity of slaves has no validity in Jewish law. Nevertheless, since he would at least be able to fulfill the Scriptural exhortation to propagate the human race (see below), the Rabbis would not have forced his master to free him (*Tos.* 41a s.v. לישא).

בַּת חוֹרִין אִי אֶפְשָׁר, שֶׁכְּבָר חֶצְיוֹ עֶבֶד; — *[and he cannot marry] a free woman, because he is half-slave;*

And a slave is forbidden to a free Jewish woman (*Deut.* loc. cit.; *Targum Onkelos* ad loc.).

The positive commandment to have children cannot supersede the prohibition of marrying a female slave, because the alternative of freeing the male slave is available. Actually, he could marry a *mamzer* (the product of illicit relations), since the latter is permitted to both a slave and a former slave. However, the Rabbis rejected this possibility because the children of such a union would also have the status of *mamzerim*, and they did not wish to increase the illegitimate population among the Jewish people (*Tos.* loc. cit.).

יִבָּטֵל? — *Shall he remain idle?*

I.e., from marrying.

וַהֲלֹא לֹא נִבְרָא הָעוֹלָם אֶלָּא לִפְרִיָּה וְרִבְיָה, שֶׁנֶּאֱמַר: „לֹא תֹהוּ בְרָאָהּ; לָשֶׁבֶת יְצָרָהּ". —

4 said to them: You have provided a solution for his
5 master, but for [him] himself you have not provided a solution: He cannot marry a slave, because he is half-free; [and he cannot marry] a free woman, because he is half-slave. Shall he remain idle? But was not the world created only for propagation, as it says (*Isaiah* 45:18): *He created it not a waste; he formed it to be inhabited.* Rather, for the sake of the general good, his master is compelled to free him, and he writes a bond for half his value. [Subsequently] Beis Hillel retracted, and taught in accordance with the words of Beis Shammai.

YAD AVRAHAM

But was not the world created only for propagation, as it says (*Isaiah* 45:18): *"He created it not a waste; he formed it to be inhabited."*

[A situation which negates the possibility of the slave being allowed to marry is unacceptable, because the charge to have children is a primary precept and may not be ignored.]

The reason this verse, rather than the Biblical commandment to be fruitful and multiply (*Gen.* 1:28), is applied is that even if the directive stated in this verse were fulfilled, the Rabbis would not have compelled the master to free the slave (*Tos. Yom Tov;* see commentary above, s.v. לִשָּׂא שִׁפְחָה).

Alternatively, the mishnah chose a verse which applies to the enslaved half as well as the free half. The Biblical verse does not apply to a slave, because a slave is included only in those commandments which include women, and the verse, *Be fruitful and multiply*, obligates only men (*Tos. Yom Tov*).

אֶלָּא, מִפְּנֵי תִקּוּן הָעוֹלָם, כּוֹפִין אֶת רַבּוֹ וְעוֹשֶׂה אוֹתוֹ בֶּן חוֹרִין, — *Rather, for the sake of the general good, his master is compelled to free him,*

[For the sake of the fulfillment of the commandment to be fruitful and multiply, the slave's master is compelled to free him completely, thus allowing him to marry a free Jewess.]

וְכוֹתֵב שְׁטָר עַל חֲצִי דָמָיו. — *and he writes a bond for half his value.*

[The slave becomes indebted to the master for the amount of his market value which the master owned and is now losing by freeing him.]

וְחָזְרוּ בֵית הִלֵּל לְהוֹרוֹת כְּדִבְרֵי בֵית שַׁמַּאי. — *[Subsequently] Beis Hillel retracted, and taught in accordance with the words of Beis Shammai.*

[The ruling in this case is like Beis Shammai, because Beis Hillel accepted their opinion.]

If a female slave was half-freed, her master would not be compelled to free her completely because a woman is not obligated by the commandment of being fruitful and multiplying. Therefore, she would work for her master one day and for herself, the other, as prescribed by Beis Hillel. However, if she indulged in promiscuous behavior, the master must free her so as to enable her to marry (*Meiri* from *Gem.* 43b).

[ו] **הַמּוֹכֵר** עַבְדּוֹ לְגוֹי אוֹ לְחוּצָה לָאָרֶץ, יָצָא בֶן חוֹרִין. אֵין פּוֹדִין אֶת הַשְּׁבוּיִים יוֹתֵר עַל כְּדֵי דְמֵיהֶן, מִפְּנֵי תִקּוּן הָעוֹלָם. וְאֵין מַבְרִיחִין אֶת הַשְּׁבוּיִין, מִפְּנֵי תִקּוּן הָעוֹלָם. רַבָּן שִׁמְעוֹן בֶּן גַּמְלִיאֵל אוֹמֵר:

ר׳ עובדיה מברטנורא

(ו) **יצא בן חורין.** אם ברח מן הנכרי, או שקנסו אותו בית דין לפדותו מן הנכרים, כדאמרינן (מד, א) כופין אותו לפדותו, ואחר שפדאו, לא ישתעבד בו. וקנס חכמים הוא, לפי שהפקיעו מן המצות. וכן לחוצה לארץ, יצא לחירות, לפי שהוציאו מארץ ישראל: **מפני תקון העולם.** שלא ימסרו הנכרים עצמן להרבות להביא שבויין, כשרואין שמוכרין אותם ביותר מכדי דמיהם: **ואין מבריחין את השבויין מפני תקון העולם.** שמא יקפצו על השבויין העתידים לבא לידם ויתנום בשלשלאות וישימו בסד רגלם:

יד אברהם

6.

הַמּוֹכֵר עַבְדּוֹ לְגוֹי — *[If] one sells his slave to a gentile*

A man sold his slave to a gentile, an act which is prohibited, because the slave will not be able to fulfill the commandments incumbent upon him. The slave subsequently escaped, or his original master redeemed him (*Rav*) in compliance with the latter's obligation to redeem the slave for up to ten times his market value (*Meiri; Rambam, Hil. Avadim* 8:1 from *Gem.* 44a).

אוֹ לְחוּצָה לָאָרֶץ, — *or to [someone] outside Eretz Yisrael,*

A Jew living in the Holy Land sold his slave to someone, even another Jew, living outside the Land (*Meiri*), which is a Rabbinic prohibition (*Gem.* 44a), because he will not be able to fulfill the commandments which are applicable only in Eretz Yisrael (*Tos. Rid*).

יָצָא בֶן חוֹרִין. — *he goes free* (lit., *he went out a freedman*).

In both of these cases, the Rabbis fined the master and obligated him to set the slave free (*Rav*). If the slave was sold to a gentile, and he escaped or was redeemed, he must obtain a document of emancipation from the original master (*Gem.* 43b). If he was sold to a Jew living outside Eretz Yisrael, the second master must grant him a document of emancipation, and cannot demand remuneration from the seller. Although both the buyer and the seller participated in the transgression, the Rabbis imposed the fine upon the buyer because the forbidden article — i.e., the slave who was transferred out of the Land — is in his possession (*Gem.* 45a; *Rosh*).

Despite the fact that a slave in Eretz Yisrael sold to someone outside the Land may refuse to move (*Kesubos* 110b), if he does not do so, the Rabbis compelled the buyer to free the slave in order to prevent him from convincing the slave to accept the transaction and enter his possession (*Ritva* to 44a, s.v. ת״ר).

Tosafos (44b s.v. לחוצה לארץ) maintain that if the slave accepts the sale and moves outside Eretz Yisrael, he relinquishes his right to be freed. The mishnah is discussing a case in which the sale was transacted, but

6. [If] one sells his slave to a gentile or to [someone] outside Eretz Yisrael, he goes free. Captives may not be redeemed for more than their value, for the sake of the general good. And captives may not be helped to escape, for the sake of the general good. Rabban Shimon ben Gamliel says:

YAD AVRAHAM

the slave was not yet transferred. *Ritva,* however, contends that in the mishnah's case, the transfer must have already taken place, because the *Gemara* (45a; see commentary above) states explicitly that the forbidden article is in the buyer's possession. [Perhaps *Tosafos* construe this as referring to the buyer's legal ownership, which takes effect as soon as the sale is transacted.]

If the owner of a slave gave him to a gentile as collateral for a loan, he is also obligated to set him free. Even if he only designated him as collateral, without giving him over to the gentile, when the deadline for payment arrives, and the gentile has the right to possess the slave, the owner is obligated to free him. However, if the gentile took the slave as payment for a debt, without the master having so specified, or if the master offered the slave as a bribe to a gentile who was threatening his life, he is not obligated to free the slave if he subsequently ransoms him or the slave escapes (*Gem.* 43b-44a).

If a slave moves outside of Eretz Yisrael with his master, he relinquishes his right to be freed if sold there, since he willingly left the Holy Land to live outside of it. However, if they only went temporarily, the slave retains his right to be freed if the master sells him there (*Gem.* 44b).

אֵין פּוֹדִין אֶת הַשְּׁבוּיִים יוֹתֵר עַל כְּדֵי דְמֵיהֶן, מִפְּנֵי תִקּוּן הָעוֹלָם. — *Captives may not be redeemed for more than their value, for the sake of the general good.*

I.e., so that the abductors should not be encouraged to take other captives for exorbitant ransoms (*Rav* from *Gem.* 45a). Therefore, even if the family of the captive is wealthy, they may not redeem their relative for an exorbitant price (*Meiri; Ran*). There is a dispute as to whether the captive's value is assessed according to the slave market, or if it is based upon his wealth and standing in the community (*Meiri*).

A husband is permitted to redeem his wife for an exorbitant price because a man and wife are considered as one, and no limits are set on the rights of a person to ransom himself. Also, if the captive is an eminent Torah scholar — or even shows unusual promise of developing into such a scholar — there are no limits on his ransom (*Tos.* 45a s.v. דלא; *Rosh*). In a time of war or the like, when gentiles are abducting Jews freely, there is no obligation to refrain from ransoming at exorbitant prices, since it would not help as a deterrent in any case (*Tos.* ibid.; *Meiri* to 45a s.v. ככר בארנו). If the captives are in danger, there are also no limits set on efforts to ransom them (*Tos.* 58a s.v. כל ממון; *Meiri* loc. cit.).

וְאֵין מַבְרִיחִין אֶת הַשְּׁבוּיִין, מִפְּנֵי תִקּוּן הָעוֹלָם. — *And captives may not be helped to escape, for the sake of the general good.*

It is prohibited to help captives escape their abductors, because they are likely to take out their anger on other captives by treating them very harshly. Even if there are no others in their hands at the present moment, we are apprehensive that they will abduct others in the future and mistreat them (*Rav* from *Gem.* 45a).

מִפְּנֵי תַקָּנַת הַשְּׁבוּיִין. וְאֵין לוֹקְחִים סְפָרִים, תְּפִלִּין, וּמְזוּזוֹת מִן הַגּוֹיִם יוֹתֵר עַל כְּדֵי דְמֵיהֶן, מִפְּנֵי תִקּוּן הָעוֹלָם.

[ז] **הַמּוֹצִיא** אֶת אִשְׁתּוֹ מִשּׁוּם שֵׁם רָע — לֹא יַחֲזִיר; מִשּׁוּם נֶדֶר — לֹא יַחֲזִיר.

ר׳ עובדיה מברטנורא

רבן שמעון בן גמליאל אומר מפני תקנת השבויין. דלא קיים רבן שמעון בן גמליאל על העתידים לבא בשביה, אלא על אותם שהם שבויים עתה עמו, שאם אין שבוי אלא הוא יחידי, מבריחין אותו, ואין לחוש כאן מפני תקנת שבויים אחרים, כשאין שבויים אחרים עמו. והלכה כרבן שמעון בן גמליאל: **(ז) משום שם רע.** שיצא עליה לעז זנות: **משום נדר.** שנדרה, והוא אומר אי אפשי באשה נדרנית: **לא יחזיר.** ואפילו נמצאו הדברים שקר, או הנדר התירו חכם. שמא תלך ותנשא לאחר, וימצא הלעז של זנות שקר, והנדר יתירנו חכם, והיא לא תהיה פרוצה בנדרים, ויאמר אלו הייתי יודע שכן, אפילו היו נותנים לי מאה מנה לא הייתי מגרשה, ונמצא גט בטל ובניה ממזרים. לפיכך אומרים לו, הוי יודע שהמוציא את אשתו משום שם רע ומשום נדר לא יחזיר עולמית, ומתוך הדברים הללו, הוא גומר ומגרש גירושין גמורים, ולא אתי תו לקלקלה:

יד אברהם

הַגּוֹיִם יוֹתֵר עַל כְּדֵי דְמֵיהֶן, מִפְּנֵי תִקּוּן הָעוֹלָם. — *Torah scrolls, phylacteries, and mezuzos may not be bought from gentiles for more than their value, for the sake of the general good.*

I.e., to discourage gentiles from stealing these articles in order to sell them for exorbitant prices (*Meiri*). Nevertheless, only excessively high prices are prohibited; to overpay slightly, however, is permitted (*Gem.* 45b; *Tif. Yis.*).

רַבָּן שִׁמְעוֹן בֶּן גַּמְלִיאֵל אוֹמֵר: מִפְּנֵי תַקָּנַת הַשְּׁבוּיִין. — *Rabban Shimon ben Gamliel says: For the benefit of the captives.*

Only if there are other captives in the hands of these abductors is it prohibited to help some of them escape. However, to refrain from aiding their escape for fear of future captives being taken and mistreated is not required (*Rav*).

וְאֵין לוֹקְחִים סְפָרִים, תְּפִלִּין, וּמְזוּזוֹת מִן

7.

הַמּוֹצִיא אֶת אִשְׁתּוֹ מִשּׁוּם שֵׁם רָע — *One who divorces his wife because of a bad reputation*

A woman was rumored to have committed adultery, and her husband divorced her (*Rav* from *Gem.* 45b), specifying that he was doing so because of that rumor (*Gem.* ibid.).

לֹא יַחֲזִיר; — *may not take [her] back;*

Even if the rumor is proven unfounded, the husband may not take her back. The Rabbis feared that after she would marry another man and have children from him, the first husband might discover her innocence, and claim that he would never have divorced her had he known the truth (*Rav* from *Gem.* 46a). Although his claim would not actually affect the divorce, since he never made his reason for divorcing her a condition to the validity of the *get*, it could

For the benefit of the captives. Torah scrolls, phylacteries, and *mezuzos* may not be bought from gentiles for more than their value, for the sake of the general good.

7. One who divorces his wife because of a bad reputation may not take [her] back; because of a *neder*, he may not take [her] back.

YAD AVRAHAM

nevertheless cast aspersion on the legitimacy of her second marriage and any children thereof (*Tos.* ad loc. s.v. אי). Therefore, the Rabbis decreed that if he divorces her because of this rumor, he may never remarry her, even if it is proven untrue. Thus forewarned, he no longer has any basis for a subsequent protest (*Rav* from *Gem.* 46a; *Meiri*).

Others contend that since he stated explicitly that he was divorcing her because of her reputation, it is tantamount to a stipulation to the divorce. Thus, were it not for the decree which precludes his option for protest, if it were later discovered that the rumors had been false, the divorce would actually be null, and her second marriage invalidated (*Ritva*).

— מִשּׁוּם נֶדֶר — *because of a neder,*

Her husband divorced her because she made a *neder*, and he explained his reason to be that he does not want to be married to a woman who makes *nedarim* (*Rav; Rashi*).

.לֹא יַחֲזִיר — *he may not take [her] back.*

Even if the *neder* is nullified,[1] he is forbidden to remarry her in order to prevent any subsequent claim that he would not have divorced her had he known that her *neder* could be annulled, since such a claim would asperse the validity of her second marriage to another and any children thereof (*Rav* from *Gem.* 46a).

If, after divorcing her because of her bad reputation, he remarried her despite the prohibition, he is not obligated to divorce her (*Rambam, Hil. Gerushin* 10:12; *Rosh*).

If he did not specify that he was divorcing her because of the rumor of adultery or because of the *neder*, he is permitted to remarry her, if she had not married anyone else in the interim. This is because even if she had married someone else, the first husband's subsequent claim that he had divorced her only due to the rumor of the *neder*, and that her second marriage to another man is therefore void would not be given credence, and her children's validity would not be doubted (*Gem.* 45b, *Rashi* ad loc.).

Another approach to the mishnah is that the reason he may not remarry her is to prevent women from being reckless in the areas of chastity and vows by increasing the severity of their repercussions. According to this explanation, he is forbidden to remarry her whether or not he specified these as his reasons for the divorce. Nevertheless, the Rabbis decreed that he specify the reason for his action in order to set an example for others (*Gem.* 46a; *Meiri*).

1. In general, a sage or panel of three knowledgeable laymen is authorized to annul a *neder* once they ascertain that there exists a sufficient basis for annulment (*Bechoros* 36b). The details of what constitutes such a basis is discussed in *Nedarim*, Chapter 9 (see General Introduction to ArtScroll *Nedarim*, p. 4, s.v. *Cancellation of Nedarim*).

רַבִּי יְהוּדָה אוֹמֵר: כָּל נֶדֶר שֶׁיָּדְעוּ בוֹ רַבִּים — לֹא יַחֲזִיר, וְשֶׁלֹּא יָדְעוּ בוֹ רַבִּים — יַחֲזִיר. רַבִּי מֵאִיר אוֹמֵר: כָּל נֶדֶר שֶׁצָּרִיךְ חֲקִירַת חָכָם — לֹא יַחֲזִיר, וְשֶׁאֵינוֹ צָרִיךְ חֲקִירַת חָכָם — יַחֲזִיר. אָמַר רַבִּי אֶלְעָזָר: לֹא אָסְרוּ זֶה אֶלָּא מִפְּנֵי זֶה.

ר׳ עובדיה מברטנורא

רבי יהודה אומר כל נדר שידעו בו רבים לא יחזיר. רבי יהודה סבר, דטעמא דאמור רבנן המוציא את אשתו משום שם רע ומשום נדר לא יחזיר, כדי שלא תהיינה בנות ישראל פרוצות בעריות ובנדרים. ומשום הכי קאמר דנדר שידעו בו רבים, עשרה מישראל או יותר, איכא פריצותא טפי, וקנסוה ולא יחזיר, ושלא ידעו בו רבים, ליכא פריצותא כולי האי, ולא קנסוה: **לא יחזיר.** דרבי מאיר סבר, טעמא משום קלקולא, הלכך נדר שאינו יכול להפר אבל חכם יכול להתיר, יכול הוא לקלקל את הגט לאחר, שתנשא לאחר ויאמר אלו הייתי יודע שחכם יכול להתיר, לא הייתי מגרשה. ושאינו צריך חקירת חכם, אלא הוא יכול להפר, לא הוצרכו חכמים לאסור עליו מלהחזירה, לפי שאינו יכול לקלקלה ולומר אילו הייתי יודע כו׳, שהרי נדר פתוח הוא והיה לו להפר ולא הפר: **לא אסרו זה.** שצריך חקירת חכם, להחזיר: **אלא מפני זה.** שאינו צריך, דבצריך לא היה לנו לחוש לקלקולא, לפי שאינו יכול לומר אילו הייתי יודע שחכם יכול להתירו לא הייתי מגרש, דאנן סהדי שאף על פי כן היה מגרש, שאין אדם רוצה שתתבזה אשתו בבית דין בפני חכם לילך לבית דינו ולשאול על נדרה. אלא מפני נדר שאינו צריך חכם, ובעל יכול להפר, אסרו את כולן, שלא יאמר אילו הייתי יודע שהייתי יכול להפר לא הייתי מגרשה:

יד אברהם

רַבִּי יְהוּדָה אוֹמֵר: כָּל נֶדֶר שֶׁיָּדְעוּ בוֹ רַבִּים — לֹא יַחֲזִיר, — *R' Yehudah says: [If because of] any neder which was known to the public, he may not take [her] back,*

R' Yehudah holds that the reason he may not remarry his wife if he divorced her because of a *neder* is to prevent women from being reckless with *nedarim.* However, he maintains that only if a *neder* is known to the public — i.e., it is made publicly (*Rashi*) — is it considered sufficiently reckless to warrant this decree (*Rav*).

There is a dispute in the *Gemara* (46a) whether a *neder* is considered public if made before three people or only if made before ten.

וְשֶׁלֹּא יָדְעוּ בוֹ רַבִּים — יַחֲזִיר. — *but [if because of a neder] not known to the public, he may take [her] back.*

If he divorced his wife for making a *neder* privately, he may remarry her, because vowing in private is not considered sufficiently reckless to warrant a prohibitive decree (*Rav*).

Others contend that a *neder* made in public is considered particularly reckless not because of the increased publicity, but because such a *neder* cannot be annulled (*Tos. R' Akiva Eiger*).

רַבִּי מֵאִיר אוֹמֵר: כָּל נֶדֶר שֶׁצָּרִיךְ חֲקִירַת חָכָם — לֹא יַחֲזִיר, — *R' Meir says: [If he divorced her because of] any neder which requires the inquiry of a sage, he may not take [her] back,*

If a man divorced his wife for making a *neder* which only a sage can nullify, but not the husband [i.e., a *neder* which does not involve self-denial and does not affect their marital relationship (*Nedarim* 11:1; 79b)], he may not take her back. R' Meir holds that the reason for the decree was to

R′ Yehudah says: [If because of] any *neder* which was known to the public, he may not take [her] back, but [if because of a *neder*] not known to the public, he may take [her] back.

R′ Meir says: [If he divorced her because of] any *neder* which requires the inquiry of a sage, he may not take [her] back, but [if because of a *neder*] which does not require the inquiry of a sage, he may take [her] back. Said R′ Elazar: They prohibited this only because of the other.

YAD AVRAHAM

protect the wife from aspersions cast on her second marriage by the protest of the first husband. Thus, if the *neder* can be nullified only by a sage, the husband may claim that he was not aware that such a *neder* could be nullified at all, and he would not have divorced her had he known about it (*Rav* from *Gem.* 46a).

[The term *inquiry* is used because a sage questions the person who made the *neder* in order to find a legitimate basis for annulment.]

וְשֶׁאֵינוֹ צָרִיךְ חֲקִירַת חָכָם — יַחֲזִיר. — *but [if because of a neder] which does not require the inquiry of a sage, he may take [her] back.*

If the husband could have nullified the *neder* himself, his claim that he was unaware of this would not be believed, and there is no need for the decree (*Rav*).

There is a view that the possibility of the husband not being aware that a *neder* can be nullified by a sage is also not credible. However, as long as he could not revoke it himself, he could claim that he did not think she had any intention of presenting her vow to a sage for annulment, since she had made no move in that direction (*Rashba* to 46b s.v. פשיטא; see commentary below s.v. מפני תקון העולם).

אָמַר רַבִּי אֶלְעָזָר: לֹא אָסְרוּ זֶה אֶלָּא מִפְּנֵי זֶה. — *Said R′ Elazar: They prohibited this only because of the other.*

[The Rabbis prohibited remarrying one's wife if he had divorced her because of a *neder* which requires the inquiry of a sage only as a precautionary measure to the prohibition of remarrying her if he had divorced her because of a *neder* which does not require such an inquiry.]

R′ Elazar contends that only a *neder* which the husband himself can nullify can cause difficulties for the woman, because the husband can subsequently claim that he would have nullified the *neder* and not divorced her, had he known that he was able to do so. However, a *neder* which requires nullification by a sage cannot cause any such problems, because a man would not want his wife to undergo the humiliation of presenting her *neder* to a sage or court for nullification. Therefore, any claim that he would have done so would not be believed. Nevertheless, the Rabbis prohibited him from remarrying her even in such a case as a precautionary measure for the case of a *neder* which the husband can nullify himself (*Rav* from *Gem.* 46a).

אָמַר רַבִּי יוֹסֵי בַּר יְהוּדָה: מַעֲשֶׂה בְצִידָן בְּאֶחָד שֶׁאָמַר לְאִשְׁתּוֹ: „קוֹנָם אִם אֵינִי מְגָרְשִׁיךְ״, וְגֵרְשָׁהּ, וְהִתִּירוּ לוֹ חֲכָמִים שֶׁיַּחֲזִירֶנָּה, מִפְּנֵי תִקּוּן הָעוֹלָם.

[ח] **הַמּוֹצִיא** אֶת אִשְׁתּוֹ מִשּׁוּם אַיְלוֹנִית — רַבִּי יְהוּדָה אוֹמֵר: לֹא יַחֲזִיר,

ר׳ עובדיה מברטנורא

אמר רבי יוסי ברבי יהודה כו׳. בגמרא (מו, א) מפרש, דחסורי מחסרא והכי קתני, במה דברים אמורים כשנדרה היא, אבל נדר הוא שיגרשנה, וגרשה, יחזיר, ולא חיישינן לקלקולא. ואמר רבי יוסי ברבי יהודה, מעשה נמי בצידן, באחד שאמר לאשתו קונם אם איני מגרשך, כלומר יאסרו כל פירות שבעולם עלי אם איני מגרשך, וגרשה, והתירו לו חכמים שיחזירנה: **מפני תקון העולם.** כלומר שלא אמרו חכמים המגרש את אשתו משום נדר לא יחזירנה, אלא מפני תקון העולם, דחיישינן לקלקולא, והא לא שייך אלא משום נדר דידה, אבל כשנדר הוא שאין כאן משום תקון העולם, התירו להחזיר. והלכה כרבי יוסי: **(ח) רבי יהודה אומר לא יחזיר.** שמא תנשא ותלד, ויאמר אילו הייתי יודע שכן, אפילו היו נותנים לי מאה מנה לא הייתי מגרשך:

יד אברהם

אָמַר רַבִּי יוֹסֵי בַּר יְהוּדָה: מַעֲשֶׂה בְצִידָן — *Said R' Yose bar Yehudah: It occurred in Sidon*

The text of the mishnah has been abridged and should be emended to read as follows: *When is this stated* [that a man may not remarry his wife if he divorced her because of a *neder*]? *When she vowed. But if he vowed to divorce her, and he did so, he may take her back. And R' Yose bar Yehudah said: Indeed it occurred in Sidon ...* (*Rav* from *Gem.* 46a).

בְּאֶחָד שֶׁאָמַר לְאִשְׁתּוֹ: „קוֹנָם אִם אֵינִי מְגָרְשִׁיךְ״, — *that one said to his wife: "Konam, if I do not divorce you,"*

[*Konam* is a word used as a substitute for the term of *korban* (offering), a common reference for a *neder*, in which one prohibits a person or thing to himself like a sacrificial offering (see General Introduction to ArtScroll *Nedarim*, p. 3).]

A man said to his wife: "I forbid myself all of the world's produce like an offering, if I do not divorce you" (*Rav* from *Gem.* 46b).

וְגֵרְשָׁהּ, וְהִתִּירוּ לוֹ חֲכָמִים שֶׁיַּחֲזִירֶנָּה, — *and he divorced her, and the Sages allowed him to take her back,*

The Sages allowed him to remarry her, and did not punish him for disregarding the severity of unnecessary *nedarim* (*Gem.* 46b).

מִפְּנֵי תִקּוּן הָעוֹלָם. — *for the sake of the general good.*

The reason the Sages allowed him to do so is that they maintain that the prohibition against remarrying one's wife if he divorced her because of her *neder* was enacted for the sake of the general good, i.e., to protect her from difficulties resulting from his subsequent protest. This reason is not applicable in the case of his own *neder* (*Rav* from *Gem.*

Said R' Yose bar Yehudah: It occurred in Sidon that one said to his wife: "*Konam,* if I do not divorce you," and he divorced her, and the Sages allowed him to take her back, for the sake of the general good.

8. [If] one divorces his wife because [she is] an *ailonis,* R' Yehudah says: He may not take

YAD AVRAHAM

46b), because the laws regarding the nullification of a man's *nedarim* are simple and well understood, unlike those regarding the *nedarim* of a married woman, which are complex and confusing, and he would not be able to claim that he was unaware that his *neder* could be annulled (*Meiri*).

Others explain that everyone is aware of the fact that a *neder* can be annulled by a sage. However, in regard to his wife's *neder,* he could claim that he did not think she intended to go to a sage for annulment since she gave no indication of planning to do so. Obviously, this reasoning does not apply to a *neder* made by the man himself (*Rashba*).

Another interpretation of these final words in the mishnah is that they refer back to the beginning, as an explanation for the decree forbidding a man from remarrying his wife if he divorced her because of her bad reputation or her *neder* (*Gem.* 46b). [It was prohibited *for the sake of the general good* — either to prevent the husband from aspersing the legitimacy of the woman's children or to discourage women from making *nedarim* (*Rashi* ad loc.), as explained above.]

8.

— הַמּוֹצִיא אֶת אִשְׁתּוֹ מִשּׁוּם אַיְלוֹנִית — *[If] one divorces his wife because [she is] an ailonis,*

A man divorced his wife upon concluding that she was an *ailonis,* a sexually underdeveloped woman who is incapable of giving birth. Although the marriage was based on a false premise — that she could bear him children — he must still give her a *get,* because a man does not allow his marital relations to be illicit, and therefore bears in mind at the time of their intimacy that it should serve as an act of *kiddushin* if necessary (*Rashi;* see *Kiddushin* 1:1).

Others contend that the mishnah is speaking of a case in which the husband was not certain that his wife was barren, but had sufficient basis for suspicion that such was the case, and he therefore decided to divorce her (*Tos.*).

The *Gemara* (*Kesubos* 11a) derives the term *ailonis* from אַיִל, *a ram,* which cannot give birth because it is a male (*Rashi* ad loc.). The term is applied to this type of woman because she exhibits certain male characteristics. The symptoms of this condition are underdeveloped female organs and a masculine-sounding voice (*Rambam Commentary* to *Yevamos* 8:5; *Rav* ibid. 1:11). [Such a woman does not have a womb or the form of a normal woman.]

,רַבִּי יְהוּדָה אוֹמֵר: לֹא יַחֲזִיר — *R' Yehudah says: He may not take [her] back,*

If his conclusion is disproved, and she turns out to be fertile, he may not remarry her. This is because if she were to marry another man and have children, he might claim that his divorce was based on a false premise and is therefore null, thus aspersing

וַחֲכָמִים אוֹמְרִים: יַחֲזִיר. נִשֵּׂאת לְאַחֵר וְהָיוּ לָהּ בָּנִים הֵימֶנּוּ, וְהִיא תוֹבַעַת כְּתֻבָּתָהּ — אָמַר רַבִּי יְהוּדָה: אוֹמֵר לָהּ: „שְׁתִיקוּתֵיךְ יָפָה לִיךְ מִדִּבּוּרֵיךְ".

ר' עובדיה מברטנורא

וחכמים אומרים יחזיר. דלא חיישינן לקלקולא. ובגמרא (מו, ב) מפרש, מאן חכמים, רבי מאיר, דאמר בעינן תנאי כפול. והכא במאי עסקינן, דלא כפליה לתנאיה, שלא אמר לה הוי יודעת שמשום אילונית אני מוציאך, ואם אין את אילונית לא יהא גט, דהשתא הוי גט אפילו אינה אילונית: **והיא תובעת כתובתה.** שהאילונית אין לה כתובה, ועכשיו שנמצא שאינה אילונית, תובעת כתובתה: **שתיקותיך יפה ליך מדבוריך.** שיאמר אילו ידעתי שסופי ליתן לך כתובה לא גרשתיך, נמצא גט בטל ובניה ממזרים:

יד אברהם

credible, R' Yehudah maintains that a decree was enacted for the protection of the wife.

There is another opinion in the *Gemara* (ibid.) that the mishnah should be emended, attributing the first statement that he may not remarry her to the Sages, and the second opinion that there is no need for protective measures to R' Yehudah, in accordance with his view in the previous mishnah.

וַחֲכָמִים אוֹמְרִים: יַחֲזִיר. — *but the Sages say: He may take [her] back.*

The Sages do not agree with the need for a decree to protect the wife from the husband's protest. The *Gemara* (46b) attributes this statement to R' Meir, who maintains that a stipulation must be expressed in a dual manner (e.g., "if this occurs, the *get* is valid; if not, it is not") in order to be effective (*Kiddushin* 3:4). The mishnah is discussing a case in which the husband said only that he is divorcing her because she is an *ailonis*, but did not add: "and if she is not an *ailonis*, I do not want this divorce." In such a case, the stipulation does not take effect. Therefore, there can be no doubt as to the legitimacy of her second marriage and the children thereof. Therefore, the Rabbis decreed that he may not remarry her in any event, thus finalizing the divorce and foreclosing any options of protest on his part (*Rav*).

In the previous mishnah, R' Yehudah was understood as interpreting the decree against remarrying a wife whom one divorced for making a *neder* as a punitive measure which was instituted to prevent reckless *nedarim*, and not as a protection for the wife against the possibilities of her husband's protest. Obviously, the former reason does not apply to the case of *ailonis*. The *Gemara* (46b) explains that in the case of *nedarim*, R' Yehudah agrees with R' Meir (see mishnah 7) that a *neder* which the husband can nullify presents no threat to the wife, because he would not be believed to say that he was unaware that he could annul it. He also agrees with R' Elazar that a man would not want his wife to undergo the humiliation of presenting her *neder* to a sage for annulment, and any claim to the contrary would not be given credence. Therefore, he holds that the only reason for the decree in the case of a *neder* is as a punitive measure. Regarding the case of *ailonis*, however, in which the husband's subsequent protest would be

4 [her] back, but the Sages say: He may take [her]
8 back. [If] she was married to another and had children from him, and she demands her *kesubah,* R' Yehudah said: He says to her: "Your silence is better for you than your speech."

YAD AVRAHAM

validity of the *get,* even if she turns out to be fertile, and any protest by the husband to the contrary would be disregarded (*Rav*).

In the previous mishnah, R' Meir explained the decree regarding the wife's *neder* to be a protection against the possibility of the husband's protest. Therefore, he must be discussing a case in which the husband expressed his reason for divorcing her in a dual manner [i.e., "I am divorcing you because of your *neder;* were it not for the *neder,* I would not divorce you"]. Accordingly, the husband's subsequent claim that the divorce was based on the irreversibility of the *neder* would be accepted by anyone who considered his statement at the time of the divorce to be a valid stipulation (*Rosh; Tos.* 46a s.v. אי).

נִשֵּׂאת לְאַחֵר וְהָיוּ לָהּ בָּנִים הֵימֶנּוּ, וְהִיא תוֹבַעַת כְּתֻבָּתָהּ — *[If] she was married to another and had children from him, and she demands her kesubah,*

The wife remarried and had children, and then claimed the payment of her *kesubah* from her first husband. This payment had been denied her up to now because she had been assumed to be an *ailonis,* in which case she would not get a *kesubah* (*Rav;* see *Kesubos* 11:6). [Her having children from the second husband obviously disproved the assumption that she was infertile.]

אָמַר רַבִּי יְהוּדָה: אוֹמֵר לָהּ: ,,שְׁתִיקוּתֵיךְ יָפָה לִיךְ מִדִּבּוּרֵיךְ״. — *R' Yehudah said: He says to her: "Your silence is better for you than your speech."*

"It is wiser for you to remain silent and not request the payment of your *kesubah,* because if you do, I will respond: 'Had I known that I would have to pay your *kesubah,* I would not have divorced you,' in which case the divorce is annulled, and your children are *mamzerim*" (*Rav*).[1]

Although the Rabbis decreed that the divorce is final even if the husband's motive for giving it turns out to be baseless, that pertains only if the motive concerned her fertility, but not if it concerned her eligibility for receiving payment of the *kesubah.* Hence, if he claims that he would not have divorced her had he known that he would have to pay it, the divorce is indeed retroactively voided (*Meiri*). [Therefore, the woman is better off not bringing up the issue of her *kesubah.*]

1. [The amount specified in the *kesubah* is usually two hundred *zuz* (see General Introduction to ArtScroll *Kesubos,* p. 3). this was considered a large sum in those days (ibid.). Indeed, we are told (*Peah* 8:3, *Rav* ad loc.) that two hundred *zuz* is sufficient for a person to purchase food and clothes for one year! Consequently, it is plausible for a man to claim that he would not have divorced his wife had he known that he would have to pay her *kesubah.*]

[ט] **הַמּוֹכֵר** אֶת עַצְמוֹ וְאֶת בָּנָיו לְגוֹי — אֵין פּוֹדִין אוֹתוֹ, אֲבָל פּוֹדִין אֶת הַבָּנִים לְאַחַר מִיתַת אֲבִיהֶן.
הַמּוֹכֵר אֶת שָׂדֵהוּ לְגוֹי — לוֹקֵחַ וּמֵבִיא מִמֶּנּוּ בִּכּוּרִים, מִפְּנֵי תִקּוּן הָעוֹלָם.

ר׳ עובדיה מברטנורא

(ט) **אין פודין אותו.** והוא שרגיל בכך, כגון שמכר ושנה ושלש: **לוקח ומביא ביכורים.** בכל שנה צריך ליקח מהנכרי ביכורי פירותיה בדמים, ומביאן לירושלים: **מפני תקון העולם.** שלא יהא רגיל למכור קרקע בארץ ישראל לנכרים. ואם מכר, יטרח לחזור ולפדות:

יד אברהם

9.

הַמּוֹכֵר אֶת עַצְמוֹ וְאֶת בָּנָיו לְגוֹי — *[If] one sells himself and his children to a gentile,*

This refers to someone who has already sold himself and his children as slaves to a gentile a number of times (*Rav* from *Gem.* 46b).

אֵין פּוֹדִין אוֹתוֹ, — *he is not to be redeemed* (lit., *they do not redeem him*),

It is forbidden to redeem them a third time because such a practice should not be encouraged (*Meiri*). However, if there is a question of their lives being endangered, they are to be redeemed (*Meiri* from *Gem.* 47a).

אֲבָל פּוֹדִין אֶת הַבָּנִים לְאַחַר מִיתַת אֲבִיהֶן. — *but the children are to be redeemed after the death of their father.*

If their father dies, the children must be ransomed, because without their father looking after them, they are likely to assimilate among the gentiles (*Gem.* 47a; *Rashi*, s.v. מקום קלקולא).

הַמּוֹכֵר אֶת שָׂדֵהוּ לְגוֹי — *One who sells his field to a gentile*

[A Jew sold a field in Eretz Yisrael to a gentile.]

לוֹקֵחַ וּמֵבִיא מִמֶּנּוּ בִּכּוּרִים, — *must buy and bring first-fruits from it,*

The seller is obligated to buy the first-fruits from that field every year and to fulfill with them the commandment (*Deut.* 26:1) of bringing the *bikkurim* (first-fruits) to Jerusalem [where they are brought as an offering before the Altar, and then given to the *Kohen*] (*Rav; Rashi*).

Others maintain that the seller is not obligated to buy the fruits. The mishnah is only telling us that if a Jew does buy the produce of that field from the gentile, he is required to bring the *bikkurim,* even though they grew while in the possession of the gentile, who is not obligated to bring them. According to this interpretation, the mishnah should read: לוֹקֵחַ מֵבִיא מִמֶּנּוּ בִּכּוּרִים, *a buyer brings first-fruits from it* (*Tos.; Ran*).

Another version of the text is: וְחָזַר וְלְקָחָה מִמֶּנּוּ יִשְׂרָאֵל, הַלּוֹקֵחַ מֵבִיא מִמֶּנּוּ בִּכּוּרִים, *and a Jew bought it back from him, the buyer brings first-fruits from it.* According to this version, the mishnah is discussing a case in which another Jew bought the field itself from the gentile after the fruits in question had already ripened, and it tells us that the buyer is obligated to bring the *bikkurim,* although the land belonged to the gentile when the fruits ripened (*Rambam Commentary; Meiri*). According to this version, if a Jew had bought the fruits alone, he would not be required to bring the *bikkurim,* because the gentile's ownership of the land in which they grew was still in effect when the fruits were harvested (*Tos. Yom Tov*).

9. [If] one sells himself and his children to a gentile, he is not to be redeemed, but the children are to be redeemed after the death of their father.

One who sells his field to a gentile must buy and bring first-fruits from it, for the sake of the general good.

YAD AVRAHAM

מִפְּנֵי תִּקּוּן הָעוֹלָם. — *for the sake of the general good.*

The obligation of the seller to buy the first-fruits and to bring them to Jerusalem is a Rabbinic decree enacted for the sake of discouraging Jewish landowners in Eretz Yisrael from selling their fields to gentiles [thereby downgrading their sanctity (*Rambam Commentary*)] and to motivate those who do sell them to repurchase them (*Rav; Rashi*).

According to those who maintain that the seller is not obligated to repurchase the land, the general benefit is that people will note the fact that the buyer is required to bring *bikkurim,* and they will thereby realize that the land has retained its sanctity. This will motivate them to purchase it from the gentile (*Maharam*).

This explanation of *the general good* mentioned in the mishnah concurs with the opinion in the *Gemara* (47a) that a gentile can attain full ownership of land in Eretz Yisrael, even to the extent of eliminating from the fruits of that field the special obligation regarding produce from the Holy Land. Thus, there is no Biblical obligation to bring the *bikkurim* of this field — which belongs to a gentile — to Jerusalem, and it is only required by Rabbinic decree (*Tos. Yom Tov*).

According to those who maintain that a gentile cannot attain that level of ownership of land in Eretz Yisrael, and the fruits retain their sanctity which obligates the fulfillment of these commandments, a Jew buying this field or its produce is required to bring the first-fruits by Biblical law — not only by Rabbinic decree. They interpret the Rabbinic decree to be the following: Originally, the Rabbis freed the buyer from his Biblical obligation to bring the *bikkurim* so that people would take note of the fact that selling land in Eretz Yisrael to a gentile downgrades its holiness, and they would therefore refrain from doing so. Eventually, the fact that they were not obligated to bring the *bikkurim* led many to assume that land in Eretz Yisrael which is in the hands of a gentile is void of any sanctity whatsoever, and they did not bother buying it back from them. Consequently, the Rabbis reinstated the Biblical law requiring the buyer to bring the first-fruits[1] (*Gem.* 47b; *Meiri*).

1. *Tosafos* (47a s.v. לוקח) derives from this that the mishnah does not obligate the seller of the field to bsuy back its first-fruits every year, because if that were the case, the enactment of the mishnah could be explained as referring to that obligation, which is definitely of Rabbinic origin, rather than the Biblical requirement that the buyer bring the *bikkurim.* If so, the *Gemara* would not need to assume that there had been two Rabbinic enactments in order to identify the Rabbinic ordinance cited in the mishnah. However, *Rashi* (47b s.v. לא מדאורייתא) maintains that if the gentile's acquisition of the field does not remove the obligations concerning its fruits, the field is still considered the property of the original Jewish owner in regard to those obligations since the gentile is not bound by them. Accordingly, the Jew is required by Biblical law to do whatever is necessary to fulfill his obligations, even to buy the first-fruits in order to bring them to Jerusalem. Thus, if no Rabbinic decree is necessary to require the bringing of the *bikkurim,* neither is one necessary to require their purchase (cf. *Maharsha* to *Tos.* loc. cit.).

פרק חמישי

Chapter Five

[א] **הַנִּזָּקִין** — שָׁמִין לָהֶם בָּעִדִּית; וּבַעַל חוֹב — בַּבֵּינוֹנִית; וּכְתֻבַּת אִשָּׁה —

ר' עובדיה מברטנורא

פרק חמישי – הנזקין. (א) הנזקין שמין להם בעידית. אף על גב דמדאורייתא היא, דכתיב (שמות כב, ד) מיטב שדהו ומיטב כרמו ישלם, האי תנא סבר דמיטב שדהו דניזק קאמר קרא, ומפני תקון העולם, אמרו חכמים, שישלם המזיק מעידית שבנכסיו, אף על פי שהם טובים מעידית של ניזק, כדי שיהו נזהרים מלהזיק: **ובעל חוב בבינונית.** דמדאורייתא לא גבי אלא מזיבורית, דכתיב (דברים כד, יא) והאיש אשר אתה נושה בו יוציא אליך את העבוט החוצה, ואין דרכו של אדם להוציא אלא הפחות שבנכסיו, ומפני תקון העולם, אמרו בעל חוב בבינונית, כדי שלא תנעול דלת בפני לווין: **וכתובת אשה בזבורית.** דליכא למיחש בה לנעילת דלת, דיותר ממה שהאיש רוצה לישא, אשה רוצה להנשא:

יד אברהם

1.

Although this chapter does not deal with *gittin,* it was included in this tractate because it concludes a list of Rabbinic ordinances enacted for the general good which was begun in the previous chapter (*Tos.; Meiri*).

This mishnah deals with enactments for the general good involving collection of debts. It focuses on three types of payments: those of damages, loans, and women's *kesubos* (marriage contracts). The subject of the discussion is the nature of payment when one collects the debt from the debtor's land. The *Gemara* divides land into three basic categories: עִדִּית, *superior fields;* בֵּינוֹנִית, *fields of medium quality;* and זִבּוּרִית, *inferior fields.* The mishnah discusses which grade of land may be collected for each of the categories of debts.

In approaching the mishnah, it is necessary to bear in mind that the breakdown of these three grades of land is not based on any absolute criterion, but rather on the relative quality of each person's fields. This allows for the dispute, stated below, whether payment is set according to the quality of the fields of the debtor or of the creditor.

הַנִּזָּקִין — שָׁמִין לָהֶם בָּעִדִּית; — *Victims of damages are [paid by] assessing for them the superior fields;*

One who is responsible for damage done to another, and has no money or chattels with which to pay him (see *Bava Kamma* 9a), must pay from the best fields in his possession (*Meiri; Gem.* 48b).

Although the total value of the land given in payment will be the same regardless of the quality, a smaller and better field is considered preferable to a larger and poorer field (*Rashi*).

In mishnah 3, we are told that this was enacted for the sake of the general good — to encourage people to exercise greater caution in avoiding damage to others. *A person will say to himself: "Why should I steal or buy with force? Tomorrow, the court will come and take my best field from me"* (*Gem.* 49b). Although the Torah (*Ex.* 22:4) explicitly requires the payment of the best fields for damages, R' Yishmael explains that this refers to the best fields of the victim. Thus, if

5
1

1. Victims of damages are [paid by] assessing for them the superior fields; lenders, with fields of medium quality; and a woman's *kesubah,* with fields of the poorest quality.

YAD AVRAHAM

the damager's poorest fields were similar in quality to the best fields of the victim, they would be acceptable for payment. The Rabbis, however, decreed that the damager must pay from his own best fields for the sake of the general good (*Rav* from *Gem.* 48*ff.*).

Another interpretation of the mishnah is that it follows the view of R' Akiva that even Biblical law requires the damager to pay with the best fields in his own possession. The *general good* cited in the mishnah is the basis upon which the Rabbis relied in interpreting the verse to be referring to the best fields of the damager rather than those of the victim. This is in accordance with R' Shimon's opinion that explanations may be given for Biblical laws for the sake of deriving legal decisions thereby (*Gem.* 49b; *Tos.* s.v. ורבי שמעון).

וּבַעַל חוֹב — בְּבֵינוֹנִית; — *lenders* (lit., *a lender*), *with fields of medium quality;*

[One who borrows money from another, and has no money or movables with which to repay, must pay him with fields which are at least of medium quality among those that he owns.] Biblical law allows him to pay with his poorest fields, as derived from the verse, *And the man to whom you did lend shall bring forth the pledge* (*Deut.* 14:11). *What does a man usually bring forth in such a case? His worst articles* (*Gem.* 50a). However, the Rabbis required him to pay from his medium-quality fields so that people should not be deterred from lending money for fear of receiving inferior fields as payment (ibid.).

Another opinion is that Biblical law dictates payment of loans from the best fields, because it is being given in exchange for money borrowed, and money is the prime form of payment (see *Bava Kamma* 9a). However, the Rabbis allowed the debtor to pay from his medium-quality fields, because they were apprehensive that people would exploit others in need and offer them loans for the sake of acquiring their best fields as payment. Actually, for this reason, they would have allowed the debtor to pay with even his poorest fields were it not for the fear that it would discourage people from lending money altogether (*Gem.* 49b).

וּכְתֻבַּת אִשָּׁה — בְּזִבּוּרִית. — *and a woman's kesubah, with fields of the poorest quality.*

A woman who collects her *kesubah* from her husband's land can do so only from his poorest fields. Since a woman desires marriage even more than a man does, there was no need for the Rabbis to change the nature of payment as they did for payment of a loan (*Rav* from *Gem.* 49b).

There is an opinion that the *kesubah* is a Biblical obligation (*Kesubos* 10a; see General Introduction to ArtScroll *Kesubos,* p. 3), which must be paid from the husband's best fields. Nevertheless, the Rabbis revoked this right in order to prevent the woman from provoking her husband to divorce her for the sake of acquiring those fields. Once the Biblical requirement to pay with the best fields was no longer in effect, they decided to limit her to his poorest fields, rather than his medium ones. This is because a woman desires marriage more than a man does, and it is therefore more important to make the prospect of marriage attractive to men, who would otherwise be discouraged from marrying because of their financial obligation in case of divorce (*Tos.* 48b).

בַּזִּבּוּרִית. רַבִּי מֵאִיר אוֹמֵר: אַף כְּתֻבַּת אִשָּׁה, בַּבֵּינוֹנִית.

[ב] **אֵין** נִפְרָעִין מִנְּכָסִים מְשֻׁעְבָּדִים בִּמְקוֹם שֶׁיֵּשׁ נְכָסִים בְּנֵי חוֹרִין, וַאֲפִלּוּ הֵן זִבּוּרִית. אֵין נִפְרָעִין מִנִּכְסֵי יְתוֹמִים אֶלָּא מִן הַזִּבּוּרִית.

ר׳ עובדיה מברטנורא

רבי מאיר אומר כו׳. ואין הלכה כרבי מאיר: **(ב) אין נפרעים מנכסים משועבדים.** כגון לוה שמכר בינונית שלו שהיא משועבדת לבעל חוב, אין הבעל חוב יכול לטרוף אותה מן הלוקח, אם נשאר אצל הלוה נכסים בני חורין, ואף על פי שאינן אלא זבורית:

יד אברהם

רַבִּי מֵאִיר אוֹמֵר: אַף כְּתֻבַּת אִשָּׁה בַּבֵּינוֹנִית. — *R' Meir says: Also a woman's kesubah [is paid] with fields of medium quality.*

[R' Meir equates the collection of *kesubah* to that of a loan, and allows the wife to collect from her husband's medium-quality fields.]

There is a dispute regarding the possessions which a woman brings into her marriage with the stipulation that in the event of divorce or the husband's death she be reimbursed for their value as it stood at the time of marriage. These are known as נִכְסֵי צֹאן בַּרְזֶל, *fixed-value property* (see General Introduction to ArtScroll *Yevamos*, p. 13). Some say that these, too, may be repaid from his poorest-quality fields, because the accepted view is that a lender may be paid from the husband's poorest fields by Biblical law, and is given the right to collect from those of medium quality only for the sake of encouraging the lending of money (see commentary above). Since a woman desires to marry, this concern is not pertinent in regard to her reimbursement. Others contend that if those possessions which women themselves brought into marriage would be repaid with inferior fields, it would be sufficient cause to discourage them from marrying (*Ran*).

2.

When a person becomes indebted to another by damaging him or by borrowing money and recording the loan on a document, any real property which he owns becomes mortgaged to the creditor. The same applies to the financial obligations written in the *kesubah*. Therefore, if the debtor subsequently sold these fields, the creditor can collect them from the buyers, who return to the seller for reimbursement.

אֵין נִפְרָעִין מִנְּכָסִים מְשֻׁעְבָּדִים בִּמְקוֹם שֶׁיֵּשׁ נְכָסִים בְּנֵי חוֹרִין, — *Payment may not be taken from assigned property if there is unassigned property available,*

The field of a debtor, which was mortgaged to a creditor, was subsequently sold. As long as the debtor has other possessions from which to collect, the creditor may not seize the field that was sold (*Rav*).

The mishnah also refers to the victim of damages. He may not collect from fields that have been sold — even if they were sold after the

R′ Meir says: Also a woman's *kesubah* [is paid] with fields of medium quality.

2. **P**ayment may not be taken from assigned property if there is unassigned property available, even if they are of the poorest quality. Payment from the property of orphans may be taken only from fields of the poorest quality.

YAD AVRAHAM

damage had been done — as long as there are unencumbered properties available (*Meiri*).

וַאֲפִלּוּ הֵן זִבּוּרִית. — *even if they are of the poorest quality.*

Although the creditor has the right to collect from the debtor's medium-quality fields [and the victim, from the damager's superior fields (*Meiri*)], he may not take these from the buyers if there are any fields — even those of the poorest quality — left in the hands of the debtor that are sufficient to pay the amount of the debt (*Rav*). Despite the Rabbis' commitment to enhance the position of creditors whenever possible, for the sake of maintaining the availability of loans (see commentary to mishnah 1 s.v. וּבַעַל חוֹב בְּבֵינוֹנִית), the protection of buyers of fields was an overriding concern in this case (*Gem.* 50b; *Tos.* 48b, s.v. אין נפרעין מנכסים משעובדים).

The same law applies if the debtor gave superior fields away as a gift, rather than selling them. Since he would not have given this gift had he not derived some sort of benefit from the recipient, the Rabbis saw fit to protect the recipient in the same manner as a buyer (*Gem.* 50b; *Rosh; Meiri; Rambam, Hil. Malveh* 19:2).

If the debtor sold his poorest-quality fields after selling all the others, the creditor must still collect from that field which was sold last (*Meiri* from *Gem.* 50b). If the debtor's unsold field was washed away, the creditor may then collect from the assigned property (*Rif, Meiri* from *Kesubos* 95a).

אֵין נִפְרָעִין מִנִּכְסֵי יְתוֹמִים אֶלָּא מִן הַזִּבּוּרִית. — *Payment from the property of orphans may be taken only from fields of the poorest quality.*

A creditor, whose debtor died, may collect only from the poorest fields which were left to the orphans, even if they are no longer minors. This is because one who lends money does not anticipate the death of the borrower, and thus, there was no need to upgrade the rights of the lender in this case for the sake of maintaining the availability of loans (*Gem.* 50a). If someone damaged another person and subsequently died, the one who was damaged may also collect only from the poorest-quality fields which the orphans inherited, even though his right to collect from the superior fields is of Biblical origin, because the Rabbis wanted to maintain uniformity in the laws of collection from orphans (*Tos.* loc. cit. and 50a s.v. כיון).

Others contend that this uniformity is maintained only when the orphans are still minors, and hence, under the protection of the courts. However, if they are already of age, there is no reason to prevent the victim of their father's damage from collecting from the best fields (*Rabbeinu Yonah*, cited by *Rosh; Ran; Meiri*).

[ג] אֵין מוֹצִיאִין לַאֲכִילַת פֵּרוֹת, וְלִשְׁבַח קַרְקָעוֹת, וְלִמְזוֹן הָאִשָּׁה וְהַבָּנוֹת מִנְּכָסִים מְשֻׁעְבָּדִים, מִפְּנֵי תִקּוּן הָעוֹלָם. וְהַמּוֹצֵא

ר' עובדיה מברטנורא

(ג) **אין מוציאין לאכילת פירות ולשבח קרקעות.** הגוזל שדה ומכרה לאחר, וזרעה ולמחה ועשאה פירות, ובא נגזל וגבאה עם פירותיה מן הלוקח, ואינו משלם ללוקח כי אם היליאה, חוזר הלוקח על המוכר, וגובה דמי הקרקע מנכסים משועבדים, שהרי מכרה לו באחריות וכתב לו שטר מכירה והרי היא מלוה בשטר, ואת הפירות מנכסים בני חורין ולא ממשועבדים. וכן לשבח קרקעות, אם השביחה הלוקח בנטיעת האילנות או בזבל וכיולא בזה: **ולמזון האשה והבנות.** דתנאי כתובה הוא, ואת תהא יתבא בביתי ומתזנא מנכסי, ובנן נוקבין דיהויין ליכי מנאי, יהוויין יתבין בביתי ומתזנין מנכסאי וכו', כשבאות לגבות מזונותיהן, אין גובים אלא מנכסים בני חורין ולא ממשועבדים: **מפני תקון העולם.** שהם דברים שאין להם קצבה, ולא ידע כמה הם ולא מלי מזדהר:

יד אברהם

3.

This mishnah cites cases where, by Biblical law, one should be able to collect from assigned properties, but is prevented from doing so by Rabbinic decree *for the sake of the general good.*

אֵין מוֹצִיאִין לַאֲכִילַת פֵּרוֹת, — *Payment may not be collected — for the consumption of produce,*

A man unwittingly bought a stolen field and cultivated it. Eventually, the true owner reclaimed the field along with its produce. The seller must return the money which the buyer paid him for the field, and he must also reimburse him for the produce which was taken from him. However, whereas the buyer can collect the amount of the price of the field even from mortgaged property, he cannot do so in regard to recompense for the produce, as will be explained below (*Rav; Rashi; Ran*).

Others explain the mishnah to be discussing a man who stole a field which was full of fruits. [He was convicted for the theft of the field, which generated publicity about the field, but not about the fruits (*Bava Metzia* 15a).] Subsequently, he consumed the fruit and ruined the field. The owner can collect for the field from assigned property [since buyers were forewarned by the publicity (ibid.)], but he can collect only from unmortgaged property for the fruits which were consumed (*Rambam Commentary* from *Bava Metzia* 14b-15a).

וְלִשְׁבַח קַרְקָעוֹת, — *or for the improvement of property,*

If the buyer of the stolen property improved it, the owner need reimburse him only for his expenses. The buyer can recoup from the seller the amount that the value of the improvement exceeds the expenses, but only from property which is free and clear (*Rav; Meiri*).

Others explain this to be dealing with a field which was taken from the buyer by a creditor of the seller who had been unable to obtain payment from the seller himself. If the buyer had made improvements in the field, the creditor has rights to one half the value of those improvements [the other half belonging to the buyer, who may take it by

5
3

3. **P**ayment may not be collected — for the consumption of produce, or for the improvement of property, or for the support of the wife and daughters — from assigned property, for the sake of the general good. One who finds a lost

retaining a portion of the field or by collecting money from the creditor (*Meiri* to *Bava Metzia* 14b)] and the seller must reimburse the buyer for that amount. However, that reimbursement cannot be collected from assigned property (*Rambam Commentary; Meiri;* see *Bava Metzia,* loc. cit.).

וְלִמְזוֹן הָאִשָּׁה וְהַבָּנוֹת — *or for the support of the wife and daughters —*

It is stipulated in the *kesubah* that if the husband dies, his wife and daughters are to be supported from his possessions until they marry (*Rav* from *Kesubos* 4:11*ff.*).

מִנְּכָסִים מְשֻׁעְבָּדִים, — *from assigned property,*

[All of the above cannot be collected from assigned property.]

מִפְּנֵי תִקּוּן הָעוֹלָם. — *for the sake of the general good.*

All of these claims are unpredictable as to their amount, and a buyer has no way of protecting himself from them. Therefore, the Rabbis decreed that they cannot be collected from assigned property (*Rav* from *Gem.* 50b).

Another explanation is that the produce of the field and its improvements were not in existence at the time the document of sale was written, and they are thus not included in the publicity which accompanies a documented transaction. Consequently, buyers of the field were not aware of the existence of these claims or the possibility that they will have to pay them. Therefore, the Rabbis exempted them from responsibility for their payment (*Gem.* 50b; *Rashi* s.v. לפי). Regarding the support of one's wife and daughters, this obligation is stipulated by the courts — and thus knowledge of the marriage includes awareness of these responsibilities — but that stipulation is so ordained as to limit their payment to unassigned property (*Gem.* 50b). This is because no one would buy a field from another if it meant bearing responsibility for the continuous support of the seller's wife and daughters (*Rashi,* s.v. מעיקרא).

According to the explanation that the first case, regarding a field and its produce, is discussing the owner's right to collect from the thief, the distinction between the field and its produce would seem to be dictated by law — and not merely by Rabbinic decree — since the thief was convicted for the field alone and thus only the theft of the field has been publicized. However, once publicity is generated about the field, knowledge about the produce tends to follow, and the owner would be able to collect from assigned property were it not for the Rabbinic enactment (*Tos.* to *Bava Metzia* 15a s.v. כשעמד). Others explain that the words *for the general good* refer only to the other cases in the mishnah: collection for the improvement of property and the support of one's wife and daughters. However, payment for a field's produce which was consumed by the thief could not be collected from mortgaged properties by law (*Ramban, Rashba* ibid.).

וְהַמּוֹצֵא מְצִיאָה — *One who finds a lost article*

A man who lost two articles which were attached together observed from a distance as someone recovered them.

מְצִיאָה לֹא יִשָּׁבַע, מִפְּנֵי תִקּוּן הָעוֹלָם.

[ד] **יְתוֹמִים** שֶׁסָּמְכוּ אֵצֶל בַּעַל הַבַּיִת, אוֹ שֶׁמִּנָּה לָהֶן אֲבִיהֶן אַפּוֹטְרוֹפּוֹס — חַיָּב לְעַשֵּׂר פֵּרוֹתֵיהֶן. אַפּוֹטְרוֹפּוֹס שֶׁמִּנָּהוּ אֲבִי יְתוֹמִים — יִשָּׁבַע; מִנָּהוּ בֵית דִּין — לֹא יִשָּׁבַע.

ר׳ עובדיה מברטנורא

והמוצא מציאה. והחזירה, והבעלים אומרים שלא החזיר כולה: **לא ישבע מפני תקון העולם.** שאם אתה אומר ישבע, אין לך אדם שמטפל במציאה להחזירה: **(ד) יתומים שסמכו אצל בעל הבית.** לעשות מעשיהם על פיו, ולא שנתמנה להם אפטרופוס, אפילו הכי כאפטרופוס הוא. אפטרופוס, בלשון רומי קורין לאב פאט״ר ולקטנים פוטו״ס. ופירוש אפטרופוס, אביהן של קטנים: **שמינהו אבי יתומים ישבע.** דאי לאו דאית ליה הנאה מיניה לא הוה ליה אפטרופוס, ומשום שבועה לא אתי לאמנועי: **מנוהו בית דין לא ישבע.** דטובת חנם היא שזה עושה לבית דין לקבל דבריהם ולטרוח חנם, ואי רמית עליה שבועה אתי לאמנועי:

יד אברהם

He could not see clearly if the finder picked up one item or two, but claimed that he must have picked up both, since they were attached. The finder, however, claimed that he found only one (*Rashba* to *Gem.* 51a; *Tos. R' Akiva Eiger*).

Others describe the case in the following manner. A man announced publicly that he had found a certain article, and its owner claimed it by identifying specific earmarks. The owner claimed that two of them had been attached together, and that the finder must have stolen one, whereas the finder insisted that he had found only one (*Meiri* to *Gem.* 51a; *Ran* ibid.).

לֹא יִשָּׁבַע, מִפְּנֵי תִקּוּן הָעוֹלָם. — *need not swear, for the sake of the general good.*

Although the owner has a valid claim, and the finder should have to take an oath just like any other defendant who admits to part of the plaintiff's claim (see *Gem.* 51b), the Rabbis freed him from this oath so that people should not refrain from returning lost articles for fear of being required to swear (*Rav*).

If the owner knew that the article had been found only because the finder informed him of it, there would be no obligation to swear, even according to Biblical law. Since he could have retained the article for himself without anyone knowing about it, his returning it attests to his truthfulness (*Rashba* to *Gem.* 51a; *Ran* ibid.).

If the owner claims that he clearly saw the finder pick up both of the lost articles, the Rabbinic enactment would not apply, and the finder would have to swear to the contrary (*Rashba*).

4.

יְתוֹמִים שֶׁסָּמְכוּ אֵצֶל בַּעַל הַבַּיִת, — *Orphans who relied upon a householder,*

Orphans relied upon someone who had not been appointed by their father or the courts to assume responsibility for the administration of their possessions (*Rav*).

5 article need not swear, for the sake of the general
4 good.

4. **O**rphans who relied upon a householder, or if their father appointed an administrator for them — he is obligated to tithe their produce. An administrator appointed by the orphans' father must swear; [if] appointed by the court, he need not swear.

YAD AVRAHAM

Some authorities maintain that only if the orphans are 9 years old or older does their designation of an administrator have any significance (*Ramah*, cited by *Rosh*).

או שֶׁמִּנָּה לָהֶן אֲבִיהֶן אַפּוֹטְרוֹפּוֹס — *or if their father appointed an administrator for them —*

Their father appointed an administrator for the orphans' possessions before he died, or the courts appointed one after his death (*Tos. Yom Tov*). The word אַפּוֹטְרוֹפּוֹס is derived from the Latin words *pater* (father) and *fotos* (minors), meaning *father of minors* (*Rav*).

Others explain that it is the Greek word for *administrator* (*Tif. Yis.*).

חַיָּב לְעַשֵּׂר פֵּרוֹתֵיהֶן. — *he is obligated to tithe their produce.*

The administrator of the orphans' possessions must tithe their produce which they are going to eat (*Gem.* 52a), because the act of tithing by a minor is not valid (*Tos. Rid*). However, he may not tithe produce which is left in storage, because they can do so for themselves when they come of age. Although an administrator is precluded by Biblical law from tithing from produce in his trust, since it is not his own produce (*Gem.* ibid.), the Rabbis removed the produce from the possession of the orphans — thus allowing the administrator to acquire it and tithe it — for the benefit of the orphans so that they may eat it if they so desire (*Tos. Rid*).

אַפּוֹטְרוֹפּוֹס שֶׁמִּנָּהוּ אֲבִי יְתוֹמִים — יִשָּׁבַע; — *An administrator appointed by the orphans' father must swear;*

When orphans come of age and take over the administration of their possessions from the administrator appointed by their father, he must swear that he has not retained any of their belongings in his possession (*Rashi*). His acceptance of responsibility for their possessions is assumed to have been due to some benefit he had received from their father. Therefore, the requirement that he take an oath would not deter him from accepting that responsibility (*Rav* from *Gem.* 52b).

מִנָּהוּ בֵּית דִּין — לֹא יִשָּׁבַע. — *[if] appointed by the court, he need not swear.*

An administrator appointed by the court is not required to take an oath that he has not stolen any of the orphans' possessions [unless someone claims that he did] because such an obligation would deter people from accepting this responsibility (ibid.) [since righteous people refrained as much as possible from taking oaths, even if they were true].

אַבָּא שָׁאוּל אוֹמֵר: חִלּוּף הַדְּבָרִים.
הַמְטַמֵּא, וְהַמְדַמֵּעַ, וְהַמְנַסֵּךְ: בְּשׁוֹגֵג — פָּטוּר; בְּמֵזִיד — חַיָּב. הַכֹּהֲנִים שֶׁפִּגְּלוּ בַמִּקְדָּשׁ מְזִידִין חַיָּבִין.

ר׳ עובדיה מברטנורא

אבא שאול אומר חלוף הדברים. מנוהו בית דין ישבע, דבההיא הנאה דקא נפיק עליה קלא דאינש מהימנא הוא, דהא סמכי עליה בי דינא, משום שבועה לא אתי לאמנועי. מינהו אבי יתומים לא ישבע, דטובת חנם עושה לו לטרוח עם בניו, ואי רמית עליה שבועה אתי לאמנועי. והלכה כאבא שאול: **המטמא.** טהרותיו של חברו: **והמדמע.** מערב תרומה בחולין של חברו, ומפסידו, שצריך למכרו לכהנים בזול: **והמנסך.** שמערב יין נסך ביין כשר, ואוסרו בהנאה: **במזיד חייב.** ובדין הוא שיהא פטור, דהיזק שאינו ניכר לאו שמיה היזק, אלא מפני תקון העולם, שלא יהא כל אחד ואחד הולך ומטמא טהרותיו של חברו ואומר פטור אני: **הכהנים שפגלו.** קרבנות ששחטו וזרקו דמם במחשבת לאכול מהם חוץ לזמנו, ולא הורצו לבעלים: **מזידים.** שידעו שפסולים בכך: **חייבים.** לשלם דמיהן לבעלים, שהרי צריכין להביא אחרים. ואי נמי נדבה היא, שאינו חייב בתשלומין, מכל מקום קשה בעיניו שלא הקריב קרבנו, שהרי להביא דורון היה מבקש:

יד אברהם

אַבָּא שָׁאוּל אוֹמֵר: חִלּוּף הַדְּבָרִים. — *Abba Shaul says: The reverse [is true].*

He maintains that an administrator appointed by the courts is required to swear, because the prestige of being chosen by the court for a position which attests to his integrity will suffice to induce people to accept that responsibility, despite the obligation to take an oath. However, an administrator appointed by the father often accepts the position as a favor, and may be discouraged from doing so if he knows that he will be required to swear. Therefore, the Rabbis freed him from the oath (*Rav* from *Gem.* 52b).

An administrator chosen by the orphans themselves is certainly freed from the obligation to swear, so that he should be willing to accept the position (*Ravad,* cited by *Ramban; Ritva; Ran*). Others maintain that the fear of an unscrupulous person gaining the orphans' trust and robbing them is an overriding concern. Therefore, an administrator whom they chose is required to swear (*Rosh*).

The *Gemara's* ruling follows Abba Shaul's view. Some authorities maintain that, by the same token, if an administrator appointed by the father caused a loss to the orphans through his negligence, the Rabbis absolved him of liability, for fear that otherwise he would not accept the position (*Tos.* 52b s.v. הלכה; *Ramban*). Others contend that he is liable, because the risk of his own negligence would not deter him from assuming responsibility (*Tos.* ibid.; *Rabbeinu Tam,* cited by *Ran*).

The mishnah now proceeds to give other laws enacted by the Rabbis for the sake of the general good.

הַמְטַמֵּא, — *One who ritually contaminates [another's food],*

A man ritually contaminated the food of another. If it is *terumah,* it becomes forbidden to eat; thus, the loss involved is the value of the food. If it is ordinary food, and the owner is careful to keep it ritually pure, its contamination causes a loss in value, because it can no longer be sold to those who eat only ritually pure food (*Meiri*).

5
4

Abba Shaul says: The reverse [is true].

One who ritually contaminates [another's food], or one who mixes [it] with *terumah*, or one who offers [another's wine as] a libation [for idol-worship], if [he did it] inadvertently, he is not liable; if deliberately, he is liable. *Kohanim* who deliberately rendered [an offering] in the Sanctuary *piggul* are liable.

YAD AVRAHAM

וְהַמְדַמֵּעַ, — *or one who mixes [it] with terumah,*

A man mixed *terumah* into the nonconsecrated food of a non-*Kohen*, thus making it forbidden to all non-*Kohanim*, and forcing the owner to sell it for a cheaper price to the limited market of *Kohanim* (*Rav*).

וְהַמְנַסֵּךְ: — *or one who offers [another's wine as] a libation [for idol-worship],*

A man mixed wine, from which some had been offered as a libation for idol-worship, into someone else's wine, thus rendering the mixture forbidden for any benefit (*Rav* from *Gem.* 52b).

If he used the other's wine as a libation for idol-worship, the remaining wine would not become prohibited, because a Jew who commits such an act is assumed to be doing it to torment the owner, and not with actual intention for idolatry. However, if he is known to be an idolater, or he is a partner in the wine [and it is unlikely that he is tormenting the other at his own expense], it does become prohibited (*Meiri; Rambam, Hil. Chovel Umazik* 6:7).

— בְּשׁוֹגֵג — *[if he did it] inadvertently,*

He did these acts without realizing that he was causing damage. For example, he thought that contaminated *terumah* is permitted to a contaminated person, or he did not realize that ordinary food mixed with *terumah* is forbidden to a non-*Kohen*, or that the wine which he mixed into that of the other person was left over from wine used as a libation for idol worship (*Meiri*).

פָּטוּר; — *he is not liable;*

This is because damage which is not discernible is not included in the legal definition of damage for which one is culpable (*Gem.* 53a).

According to those who contend that one who causes indiscernible damage is liable, the Rabbis absolved him of liability in this case, for fear that he would not inform the owner of what had occurred, thus causing him to eat forbidden food (ibid.).

בְּמֵזִיד — חַיָּב. — *if deliberately, he is liable.*

The Rabbis fined him by having him pay for the damage in order to discourage such acts (*Rav* from *Gem.* 53a).

Although — in the case of contaminating ordinary food — the damage is minimal, the Rabbis nevertheless fined him, because it is forbidden to contaminate even nonconsecrated food in *Eretz Yisrael* (*Meiri* from *Gem.* 53a; see *Sotah* 30b).

הַכֹּהֲנִים שֶׁפִּגְּלוּ בַמִּקְדָּשׁ מְזִידִין חַיָּבִין. — *Kohanim who deliberately rendered [an offering] in the Sanctuary piggul are liable.*

If a *Kohen* either slaughtered an

[ה] **הֵעִיד** רַבִּי יוֹחָנָן בֶּן גֻּדְגְּדָה עַל הַחֵרֶשֶׁת שֶׁהִשִּׂיאָהּ אָבִיהָ, שֶׁהִיא יוֹצְאָה בְגֵט; וְעַל קְטַנָּה בַת יִשְׂרָאֵל שֶׁנִּשֵּׂאת לְכֹהֵן, שֶׁאוֹכֶלֶת בַּתְּרוּמָה; וְאִם מֵתָה — בַּעְלָהּ יוֹרְשָׁהּ; וְעַל הַמָּרִישׁ הַגָּזוּל שֶׁבְּנָאוֹ בַבִּירָה,

ר׳ עובדיה מברטנורא

(ה) **על החרשת שהשיאה אביה.** ואף על גב דהויא אשת איש גמורה, שהרי קבל אביה קדושיה כשהיא קטנה, אפילו הכי יוצאה בגט, ומקבלת את גטה כשהיא חרשת, ואף על גב דלית בה דעתא, דאשה מתגרשת בעל כרחה, הלכך לא בעינן דעתה: **ועל קטנה בת ישראל שנשאת לכהן.** והיא יתומה, דלא הוי נשואים אלא מדרבנן: **שאוכלת בתרומה.** דרבנן, ולא גזרינן תרומה דרבנן אטו תרומה דאורייתא: **מריש.** קורה: **בירה.** בית גדול:

יד אברהם

offering on behalf of another person, received its blood, brought the blood to the Altar, or offered the blood on the Altar, with intention to eat the meat after the time allotted to do so will have passed — thus invalidating the offering — he is liable to the other person (*Rav; Tos. Yom Tov*).

The same law would apply if he had intention to burn the animal on the Altar after the allotted time (*Tif. Yis.*).

Although the damage is not discernible, and the *Kohen* should therefore not be liable, the Rabbis obligated him to reimburse the owner as a preventive measure for the sake of the general good (*Meiri* from *Gem.* 53a). Even if the offering was voluntary, and the owner is not required to replace it, the *Kohen* is still liable, because the owner has lost the offering which he sought to bring (*Rav; Meiri*).

According to those who maintain that one who causes indiscernible damage is liable, the *Kohen* is responsible by law — not merely as a preventive measure. However, if he did it inadvertently, the Rabbis absolved him of liability for the sake of the general good, so that he should not hesitate to inform the owner of what occurred (*Gem.* 53a).

5.

הֵעִיד רַבִּי יוֹחָנָן בֶּן גֻּדְגְּדָה — *R' Yochanan ben Gudgedah testified*

This mishnah [also found in *Eduyos* (7:9)] is recorded here for the sake of its last two cases, which are also Rabbinic decrees enacted for the general good (*Rashi*).

עַל הַחֵרֶשֶׁת שֶׁהִשִּׂיאָהּ אָבִיהָ, — *that a deaf-mute girl, whose father married her off,*

A deaf-mute girl was married off by her father when she was a minor and still under his legal jurisdiction (*Kesubos* 4:4); hence, her marriage is valid by Biblical law (*Rav*).

שֶׁהִיא יוֹצְאָה בְגֵט; — *can be divorced* (lit. *she goes out*) *with a get;*

Although she is not considered mentally competent, she can receive a *get*, and the divorce is valid. Since a divorce does not require the consent of the wife, her mental competence is not necessary for its validity (*Rav*), only that she be capable of understanding

5. R' Yochanan ben Gudgedah testified that a deaf-mute girl, whose father married her off, can be divorced with a *get;* and that a minor, the daughter of a non-*Kohen* who was married to a *Kohen,* may eat *terumah;* and if she dies, her husband inherits her; and that for a stolen beam which was built into a large building,

YAD AVRAHAM

that she is no longer married to this man, and is not to return to his home (*Meiri; Tos. Rif* from *Gem.* 64b).

וְעַל קְטַנָּה בַּת יִשְׂרָאֵל שֶׁנִּשֵּׂאת לְכֹהֵן, — *and that a minor, the daughter of a non-Kohen who was married to a Kohen,*

An orphan girl whose father was not a *Kohen* was married off to a *Kohen* by her mother or brother — a marriage which is valid only by Rabbinic law (*Rav*).

שֶׁאוֹכֶלֶת בַּתְּרוּמָה; — *may eat terumah;*

She is permitted to eat the type of *terumah* which is only consecrated as such by Rabbinic law [e.g., vegetables; see *Rambam, Hil. Terumos* 2:6]. We do not fear that she may thereby be led to also eat *terumah* which is consecrated by Biblical law [and is forbidden to her because her marriage to the *Kohen* is not Biblically valid, as noted above] (*Rav*).

From the fact that the mishnah changed the subject from a deaf-mute to a minor in order to discuss the case of a Rabbinically valid marriage to a *Kohen,* it is apparent that a deaf-mute who was married to a *Kohen* on her own accord — another case of a marriage that is valid only by Rabbinic law — would not be permitted to eat even Rabbinical *terumah.* This was prohibited because such a case could easily be confused with that of a mentally competent girl married to a deaf-mute *Kohen* — also a Rabbinic-law marriage — in which case she is prohibited to eat even Rabbinical *terumah* because we fear she may be led to eat Biblical *terumah.* Therefore, to avoid confusion, the Rabbis also prohibited the deaf-mute married to a *Kohen* from eating any *terumah* whatsoever (*Gem.* 55a). The Rabbis did not impose this precautionary measure on a minor, because even if she eats *terumah* consecrated by Biblical law, there is no transgression, since she is only a minor. Nevertheless, they did not permit her to eat Biblical *terumah* from the outset, because the permissibility of allowing a minor to eat forbidden food is an unresolved issue in the *Gemara* (*Tos.;* see *Yevamos* 113b-114b).

וְאִם מֵתָה — בַּעְלָהּ יוֹרְשָׁהּ; — *and if she dies, her husband inherits her;*

The Rabbinical courts have jurisdiction over the possessions of Jews (*Gem.* 36b), and they decreed, in the case of Rabbinic-law marriage, that the husband inherits the wife just as he does in a Biblical marriage (*Tos. Rid*).

וְעַל הַמָּרִישׁ הַגָּזוּל שֶׁבְּנָאוֹ בְּבִירָה, — *and that for a stolen beam which was built into a large building,*

A man stole a large beam and built it into a building without making any changes in the beam. Had he altered the stolen item, it would have become his, and he would be obligated to repay the owner for its value (*Tos. Rid*).

שֶׁיִּטּוֹל אֶת דָּמָיו, מִפְּנֵי תַקָּנַת הַשָּׁבִים; וְעַל הַחַטָּאת הַגְּזוּלָה שֶׁלֹּא נוֹדְעָה לָרַבִּים, שֶׁהִיא מְכַפֶּרֶת, מִפְּנֵי תִקּוּן הַמִּזְבֵּחַ.

[ו] **לֹא** הָיָה סִיקְרִיקוֹן בִּיהוּדָה בַּהֲרוּגֵי

ר' עובדיה מברטנורא

מפני תקנת השבים. שאם אתה מצריכו לקעקע בירתו ולהחזיר המריש עצמו, ימנע מלעשות תשובה: **שלא נודעה לרבים.** שהיא גזולה: **שהיא מכפרת.** ואין צריך להביא אחרת: **מפני תקון מזבח.** שלא יהיו כהנים עצבים, שאכלו חולין שנשחטו בעזרה, ונמצא מזבח בטל, שנמנעים מלעבוד עבודה: **(ו) לא היה סקריקון.** נכרי רוצח. כלומר לא דנו דין סקריקון, לומר שהקונה קרקע של ישראל מיד הנכרי רוצח, יהיה חייב לדון עם הבעלים:

יד אברהם

שֶׁיִּטּוֹל אֶת דָּמָיו, — *he shall take its value,*

[Although the thief is required by law to return the beam itself, the Rabbis decreed that he may keep the beam and reimburse the owner for its value.]

מִפְּנֵי תַקָּנַת הַשָּׁבִים; — *for the sake of penitents;*

The Rabbis feared that the obligation to demolish his building in order to return the beam would deter the thief from repenting (*Rav*).

וְעַל הַחַטָּאת הַגְּזוּלָה שֶׁלֹּא נוֹדְעָה לָרַבִּים, — *and that a stolen sin-offering, [whose status] was not known to the public,*

[An animal which had been stolen was offered on the Altar as a sin-offering. People were not aware that it had been stolen.]

The expression *not known to the public* here means that it was not known to even three people (*Meiri* from *Yerushalmi; Kesef Mishneh, Hil. Issurei Mizbe'ach* 5:7).

Others contend that in this instance, it does not refer to the awareness of three people, but that each situation is different, and the judge must determine how many people must be aware of these particular circumstances in order for it to be considered *known to the public* (*Tos. Yom Tov*).

שֶׁהִיא מְכַפֶּרֶת, — *atones,*

Although a stolen animal is generally invalid as an offering (*Bava Kamma* 66b), in this case the Rabbis decreed that it be effective, and he need not bring another sacrifice in its place (*Rav*). The Rabbis did this in accordance with their authority to require the passive negation of a Biblical commandment (*Rashi* 55a s.v. נמצא מזבח בטל). However, if the *Kohanim* discovered the animal's status before eating its meat or bringing its entrails on the Altar, they may no longer do so (*Tos. R' Akiva Eiger*).

Others contend that the Rabbis employed their jurisdiction over Jewish possessions to remove the animal from the possession of its owner and place it in the possession of the thief who offered it, in order to enable it to achieve atonement for him (*Meiri; Rashba*), for the reason stated below.

If the animal's status was known to the public, the Rabbis did not validate the offering. This was based on an exegetically derived implication that an offering whose disqualification is known is not valid (*Yerushalmi*).

Another explanation is that the thief is unlikely to bring an animal which is known

5
6 he shall take its value, for the sake of penitents; and that a stolen sin-offering, [whose status] was not known to the public, atones, for the sake of the Altar.

6. There were no extortionists of land in Judea in

to be stolen as an offering, and the Rabbis did not extend their enactment to deal with such an unlikely event (*Tos. Yom Tov*).

מִפְּנֵי תִקּוּן הַמִּזְבֵּחַ, — *for the sake of the Altar.*

If the offering would not be valid, the *Kohanim* would be upset that they had unwittingly eaten nonconsecrated food which was slaughtered in the Temple courtyard [and is forbidden (*Rashi*)], and would therefore refrain from bringing other offerings (*Rav* from *Gem.* 55a).

Even in a case in which the original owner despaired of recovering the animal (see commentary to 4:4 s.v. וּפְדָאוּהוּ), the offering is valid only because of the Rabbinic enactment. This is because the despair of the owner of recovering a stolen object does not enable a thief to acquire it unless there is also a change of proprietorship after the owner despaired [in which case the stolen article is acquired, and the thief becomes obligated to reimburse the owner for its loss] (*Gem.* 55a).

Although the animal's change of status from nonconsecrated to consecrated is considered a change of proprietorship (*Bava Kamma* 67a), the animal may not be brought as an offering by Biblical law, because the fulfillment of a *mitzvah* through the transgression of a prohibition is not valid. Nevertheless, if the owner's despair of recovery would in itself enable the thief to acquire the animal, its consecration and subsequent offering would not be considered as resulting from a transgression [because the connection to the transgression has been severed by the intervening acquisition of the animal] (*Tos.* 55a s.v. מאי טעמא).

Others explain the mishnah to be discussing an instance in which the animal had already been consecrated before it was stolen (*Meiri*).

There is another opinion that the owner's despair of recovering the animal is enough to enable the thief to acquire it [and that is the case discussed in the mishnah]. According to this view, the Rabbinical decree in the mishnah was not the acceptance of the stolen offering when its status is not public knowledge, which is required by law, but its invalidation when its status is known, which was enacted so that people should not say, "The Altar consumes stolen animals" (*Gem.* 55a; *Rambam, Hil. Issurei Mizbe'ach* 5:7).

6.

This mishnah deals with the issue of purchasing land which gentiles extorted from Jewish owners. Its inclusion in this chapter is apparently due to the decree of R' Judah the Prince, which was enacted to encourage Jews to purchase land in Eretz Yisrael from gentiles, as explained below.

לֹא הָיָה סִיקָרִיקוֹן בִּיהוּדָה בַּהֲרוּגֵי הַמִּלְחָמָה — *There were no extortionists of land in Judea in [the time of] those slain at war.*

הַמִּלְחָמָה. מֵהֲרוּגֵי הַמִּלְחָמָה וְאֵילָךְ, יֵשׁ בָּהּ סִיקְרִיקוֹן. כֵּיצַד? לָקַח מִסִּיקְרִיקוֹן, וְחָזַר וְלָקַח מִבַּעַל הַבַּיִת — מִקָּחוֹ בָטֵל; מִבַּעַל הַבַּיִת, וְחָזַר וְלָקַח מִסִּיקְרִיקוֹן — מִקָּחוֹ קַיָּם. לָקַח מִן הָאִישׁ, וְחָזַר וְלָקַח מִן הָאִשָּׁה — מִקָּחוֹ בָטֵל; מִן הָאִשָּׁה, וְחָזַר וְלָקַח מִן הָאִישׁ — מִקָּחוֹ קַיָּם. זוֹ מִשְׁנָה רִאשׁוֹנָה.

ר׳ עובדיה מברטנורא

בשעת הרוגי המלחמה. בשעה שהיתה הגזירה קשה על ישראל ליהרג במלחמה. שהלוקח ממנו באותה שעה, היה מקחו קיים, ולא היה צריך לדון עם הישראל בעל הקרקע, משום דאגב אונסיה דישראל הוה גמר ומקני לסיקריקון, וקיימא לן (בבא בתרא מז, ב) תלוהו וזבין זביניה זביני: **אבל מהרוגי המלחמה ואילך.** שלא היתה הגזירה ליהרג, דנו דין סקריקון, לומר שהקונה ממנו יעשה דין עם הבעלים, כמו שמפורש במשנה: **מקחו בטל.** דאמרינן מירא עבד: **לקח מן האיש.** קרקע המיוחד לכתובת אשתו: **מקחו בטל.** דאמרה נחת רוח עשיתי לבעלי:

יד אברהם

The law discussed below, regarding buying land from a gentile who confiscated it from a Jew by threatening his life, did not apply at the time of Titus' war on Jerusalem and Judea. Since soldiers were then encouraged to kill Jews whenever possible, if a Jew bought off a Roman with his land, he was sincere about the transaction and lost all rights to the land (*Rav* from *Gem.* 55b, *Rashi*).

Others explain the specification of Judea for this decree as being due to a special hatred for the descendants of Judah — the son of Jacob — by the Romans because of a tradition that it was he who killed their ancestor Esau (*Yerushalmi*, cited in *Tos.*).[1]

The word סִיקְרִיקוֹן is a contraction for שָׂא קַרְקַע וְהַנִּיחֵנִי, *take the field and leave me* (*Rav* to *Bikkurim* 1:2).

מֵהֲרוּגֵי הַמִּלְחָמָה וְאֵילָךְ, — *From [the time of] the slain at war and onward,*

When the wrath of the Romans had subsided (*Meiri*), it was declared illegal to kill innocent Jews. Therefore, if a Roman forced a Jew to give him his land, the Jew did not comply sincerely, but rather did so with the intention of subsequently recovering his land in court (*Rav* from *Gem.* 55b).

יֵשׁ בָּהּ סִיקְרִיקוֹן. — *there are extortionists there.*

The laws regarding the confiscation of land do not apply, and a Jew who buys land from a gentile, which was acquired from another Jew by extortion, must deal with the original owner of the field, as explained below (*Rav* from *Gem.* 55b).

Although the *Gemara* in *Bava Basra* (57b) states that a transaction imposed by force is valid, that is true only when the owner receives payment for his land; in this case, he did not (*Rosh*; *Meiri*).

כֵּיצַד? — *How?*

[What is the law regarding land

1. See *Tosafos*, who seek to reconcile this tradition with the opinion (*Sotah* 13a) that Chushim, son of Dan, beheaded Esau.

5
6 [the time of] those slain at war. From [the time of] the slain at war and onward, there are extortionists there. How? [If] one bought from the extortionist, and then bought from the owner, his purchase is void; from the owner, and then from the extortionist, his purchase is valid. [If] he bought from the husband, and then bought from the wife, his purchase is void; from the wife, and then from the husband, his purchase is valid. This is the original ruling.

YAD AVRAHAM

seized from a Jew by a gentile?]

לָקַח מִסִּיקְרִיקוֹן, וְחָזַר וְלָקַח מִבַּעַל הַבַּיִת — *— [If] one bought from the extortionist, and then bought from the owner* (lit., *householder*),

[If a Jew bought a stolen field from the extortionist, and then from the owner.]

מִקָּחוֹ בָטֵל; — *his purchase is void;*

The owner can recover the field from the buyer in court, because his acquiescence to the sale was for fear of the gentile (*Rav*). Even if he wrote a bill of sale to the buyer, he can recoup the field. However, if he accepted responsibility to reimburse the buyer if the field will be taken from him by the seller's creditors, the sale is valid, because that degree of responsibility is not likely to be demanded by the extortionist and is therefore an indication of a sincere decision to sell (*Meiri* from *Gem.* 58a).

Others contend that even drawing up a bill of sale indicates the seller's sincerity, and he can no longer recover the field (*Gem.* 58a).

מִבַּעַל הַבַּיִת, וְחָזַר וְלָקַח מִסִּיקְרִיקוֹן — מִקָּחוֹ קַיָּם. — *from the owner, and then from the extortionist, his purchase is valid.*

[If the buyer purchased the field from the owner and then from the extortionist — so that the latter should not cause him problems — the sale is valid, because the owner was under no pressure from the gentile to agree to the sale, and his decision to do so was obviously sincere.]

לָקַח מִן הָאִישׁ, וְחָזַר וְלָקַח מִן הָאִשָּׁה — *[If] he bought from the husband, and then bought from the wife,*

A man sold land which had been designated for the payment of his wife's *kesubah* (*Rav*), or land which was specified in the *kesubah* itself, or נִכְסֵי צֹאן בַּרְזֶל, *fixed-value property,* which the wife brought into the marriage with the stipulation that in the event of divorce or the husband's death, she be reimbursed for its value as it stood at the time of marriage (*Rashi* from *Bava Basra* 49b). Afterwards, the buyer paid the wife to relinquish her right to collect the *kesubah* from this field (*Rashbam* ibid. s.v. וחזר).

מִקָּחוֹ בָטֵל; — *his purchase is void;*

The purchase from the wife is void, even if she wrote a separate bill of sale (*Meiri*), because she can claim that she

בֵּית דִּין שֶׁל אַחֲרֵיהֶם אָמְרוּ: הַלּוֹקֵחַ מִסִּיקְרִיקוֹן נוֹתֵן לַבְּעָלִים רְבִיעַ. אֵימָתַי? בִּזְמַן שֶׁאֵין בְּיָדָן לִקַּח. אֲבָל יֵשׁ בְּיָדָן לִקַּח — הֵן קוֹדְמִין לְכָל אָדָם.

רַבִּי הוֹשִׁיב בֵּית דִּין, וְנִמְנוּ שֶׁאִם שֶׁהֲתָה בִּפְנֵי סִיקְרִיקוֹן שְׁנֵים עָשָׂר חֹדֶשׁ — כָּל הַקּוֹדֵם לִקַּח זוֹכֶה, אֲבָל נוֹתֵן לַבְּעָלִים רְבִיעַ.

ר' עובדיה מברטנורא

נותן לבעלים רביע. שסיתרו, דסיקריקון מתוך שנכנס בה לידו מוזיל גביה רבעה:

יד אברהם

agreed only in order to please her husband (*Rav* from *Bava Basra* 49b). Therefore, although the actual purchase of the field is valid, if the woman's husband dies or divorces her, she can still collect her *kesubah* from this field (*Meiri; Rashbam* loc. cit. s.v. מקחו בטל; *Tos.* ibid. 50a s.v. אילימא; *Even HaEzer* 90:17).

Others maintain that the entire sale is null from the onset, and the buyer does not take possession of the field at all (*Rambam, Hil. Mechirah* 30:3; *Geonim,* cited in *Meiri*), because the woman is not expected to litigate with buyers in order to collect her *kesubah* [and thus the designation of specific fields for the *kesubah* includes a commitment not to sell them] (*Maggid Mishneh* ad loc.).

If the husband sold other fields in his possession [all the husband's property is mortgaged to the wife's *kesubah* (*Kesubos* 4:7)], her consent is certainly not binding, because she can claim to have been afraid that any protest on her part could incite her husband to accuse her of anticipating their divorce or his demise (*Tos. Yom Tov* from *Bava Basra* 50a). In this case, however, since the field was not specifically designated for the *kesubah,* the original sale is definitely valid and only the wife's surrender of her right to collect the *kesubah* from that field is null (*Meiri; Tos. Yom Tov*).

מִן הָאִשָּׁה, וְחָזַר וְלָקַח מִן הָאִישׁ — מִקָּחוֹ קַיָּם. — *from the wife, and then from the husband, his purchase is valid.*

[If the wife sold her rights to the field before the husband sold the field itself, she cannot claim that she did so to please her husband, and the sale is invalid.]

זוֹ מִשְׁנָה רִאשׁוֹנָה. — *This is the original ruling.*

The nullification of the purchase of land from an extortionist was the original decision of the Rabbis (*Meiri*).

בֵּית דִּין שֶׁל אַחֲרֵיהֶם אָמְרוּ: הַלּוֹקֵחַ מִסִּיקְרִיקוֹן נוֹתֵן לַבְּעָלִים רְבִיעַ. — *The court that came after them said: One who buys from an extortionist gives the owner one-fourth.*

A later court decreed that the purchase of land from the extortionist is valid, but the buyer must return one-fourth of the land to the original owner, or else pay him one-third of the price which he paid the extortionist, if that is what the owner prefers (*Meiri* from *Gem.* 58b). This is based on the assumption that the extortionist reduced the price of the

The court that came after them said: One who buys from an extortionist gives the owner one-fourth. When [is this]? When they do not have [with what] to buy. But if they have [with what] to buy, they take precedence over any person.

Rabbi convened a court, and they voted and enacted that if it remained with the extortionist twelve months, whoever is first to buy it acquires [it], but he gives the owner one-fourth.

field by one-fourth, because he acquired it without payment (*Rav*).

There is another opinion that the owner receives either one-fourth of the price paid to the extortionist or one-fifth of the field (*Gem.* 58b).

אֵימָתַי? — *When [is this]?*

[When may the buyer retain the field if he gives the owner one-fourth?]

בִּזְמַן שֶׁאֵין בְּיָדָן לִקַּח. — *When they do not have [with what] to buy.*

[If the original owner cannot afford to buy the field from the extortionist, another man may buy it and give the owner one-fourth.]

אֲבָל יֵשׁ בְּיָדָן לִקַּח — הֵן קוֹדְמִין לְכָל אָדָם. — *But if they have [with what] to buy, they take precedence over any person.*

If the owner has the means, he has the right to buy his field back from the extortionist, and no one else may purchase it (*Rambam, Hil. Gezeilah* 10:3).

Others explain that even if someone else purchased the field from the gentile at a time when the original owner could not afford it, he is obligated to sell it back to the owner whenever he attains the means to purchase it (*Meiri; Tur Choshen Mishpat* 236; see *Tos. Yom Tov*).

רַבִּי הוֹשִׁיב בֵּית דִּין, — *Rabbi convened a court,*

R' Judah the Prince convened a court to deal with this issue in order to prevent land in Eretz Yisrael from being left in the hands of gentiles [as people refrained from buying this land because of the original owner's claim] (*Meiri*).

וְנִמְנוּ שֶׁאִם שֶׁהָתָה בִּפְנֵי סִיקְרִיקוֹן שְׁנֵים עָשָׂר חֹדֶשׁ — כָּל הַקּוֹדֵם לִקַּח זוֹכֶה, — *and they voted* (lit., *were counted*) *and enacted that if it remained with the extortionist twelve months, whoever is first to buy it acquires [it],*

[Once the field has remained in the hands of the extortionist for twelve months and the owner has not bought it back, he loses his right of precedence, and anyone may purchase it.]

אֲבָל נוֹתֵן לַבְּעָלִים רְבִיעַ. — *but he gives the owner one-fourth.*

[The owner does not lose the right granted him by Rabbinic decree to take one-fourth of the field or one-third of its price from the buyer.]

[ז] **חֵרֵשׁ** — רוֹמֵז וְנִרְמָז; וּבֶן בְּתֵירָה אוֹמֵר: קוֹפֵץ וְנִקְפָּץ בְּמִטַּלְטְלִין. הַפָּעוֹטוֹת — מִקָּחָן מִקָּח וּמִמְכָּרָן מִמְכָּר בְּמִטַּלְטְלִין.

ר׳ עובדיה מברטנורא

(ז) **רומז ונרמז.** מה שהוא רומז, או שאחרים רומזים לו ונתרצה, הכל קיים. רמיזה, בידיו ובראשו. קפיצה, עקימת שפתים, שנאמר (איוב ה, טז) קפצה פיה, ואינו סימן ניכר כמו רמיזה: **במטלטלין.** אם מכר מטלטלין. ואין הלכה כבן בתירה: **הפעוטות.** הקטנים כבן שבע כבן שמונה, אם הוא חריף ויודע בטיב משא ומתן, או כבן תשע ובן עשר, אם אינו חריף כל כך: **מקחן [מקח] וממכרן ממכר במטלטלין.** ומתנתן מתנה, אחת מתנת בריא, ואחת מתנת שכיב מרע, אחת מתנה מרובה, ואחת מתנה מועטת:

יד אברהם

7.

This mishnah follows the previous one in discussing enactments for the sake of the general good. According to Biblical law, the transactions of a deaf-mute, mentally deranged person, and a minor are void, since these persons are deemed mentally incompetent and thus incapable of executing a legal act. However, the Rabbis validated the transactions of a deaf-mute and a minor, as described in the mishnah, to enable them to take care of their basic needs. [Apparently, a mentally deranged person was not considered capable of implementing such an enactment.]

חֵרֵשׁ — רוֹמֵז וְנִרְמָז; — *A deaf-mute gestures and is gestured to;*

If a deaf-mute gestures with his hands and head to convey his intention to execute a transaction, or he signals his agreement to the gestures of another which indicate as much, the transaction takes effect (*Rav*). Although this does not comply with the normal requirements for executing a transaction, the Rabbis decreed that it is effective in order to enable a deaf-mute to take care of his basic needs (*Tos. Rid; Rash;* 59a s.v. קמ״ל).

The same law applies to one who is totally deaf but not mute. However, one who is mute but not deaf has the status of a legally competent adult (*Meiri; Rambam, Hil. Mechirah* 29:2; *Choshen Mishpat* 235:17).

וּבֶן בְּתֵירָה אוֹמֵר: קוֹפֵץ וְנִקְפָּץ — *Ben Beseirah, however, says: He moves his lips and is communicated with by means of lip-movements*

Even if he moves only his lips to indicate his intention to execute a transaction, or he responds to a signal conveyed only by lip-movement, the transaction takes effect (*Rav; Rashi*).

Others maintain that קְפִיצָה means to actually exchange the money for the object purchased. Only then is his intention sufficiently clear, and this act replaces speech as the means of conveying his intent. Thus Ben Beseirah's view is stricter than the first anonymous opinion (*Rambam Commentary;* see *Meiri*).

בְּמִטַּלְטְלִין. — *in [transactions involving] chattels.*

According to both Ben Beseirah and

7. **A** deaf-mute gestures and is gestured to; Ben Beseirah, however, says: He moves his lips and is communicated with by means of lip-movements, in [transactions involving] chattels. Young children's purchases are purchases and their sales are sales in [transactions involving] chattels.

YAD AVRAHAM

the first, anonymous *Tanna*, the gestures of a deaf-mute suffice only for the transaction of movable possessions, but not for that of real property (*Meiri; Tos. Rid; Rashi* 59a, s.v. קמ״ל; *Rambam, Hil. Mechirah* 29:2).

Others contend that the words *in chattels* are part of Ben Beseirah's statement — i.e., that lip-movements are a valid means of conducting transactions of movables. Gestures of the hands and head, however, are effective even for transactions of real property (*Ravad* ad loc.; see *Meiri*).

There is a dispute in the *Gemara* (59a), if, in the case of a divorce executed by a deaf-mute through gestures (see *Yevamos* 14:1), Ben Beseirah concedes to the first *Tanna* that full gestures are required, or if he maintains that lip-movements are sufficient there, too, because the marriage itself was brought about only through gestures (*Tos. Rid*).

הַפָּעוֹטוֹת — מִקָּחָן מִקָּח וּמִמְכָּרָן מִמְכָּר בְּמִטַּלְטְלִין. — *Young children's purchases are purchases and their sales are sales in [transactions involving] chattels.*

This refers to young children at the age of 7 or 8 if they are sufficiently intelligent to understand the workings of a transaction, or at the age of 9 or 10, if they are not so astute (*Rav*).

[Even the age of 9 or 10 is given only as a norm.] Basically, from the time a child is 6 until he reaches adulthood, he must be assessed as to whether he understands the workings of a transaction in order for his sales and purchases to be valid (*Meiri; Rambam, Hil. Mechinah* 29:6).

The Rabbis validated their transactions in order to enable them to attend to their basic needs (*Gem.* 59a). [This would seem to apply only to children who have lost both of their parents.] However, if an administrator was appointed to take care of their needs, their transactions are no longer valid (*Meiri* from *Kesubos* 70a).

Gifts which these children give are also valid, no matter what the extent of the gifts (*Rav* from *Gem.* 59a), because their decision to give them is generally due to benefits they have received from the recipient [and the Rabbis wanted to encourage people to benefit them] (*Rashi* ad loc., s.v. מתנתו). Some authorities maintain that their gifts are valid even if an administrator was appointed to see to their needs, because the validity of their gifts was not granted for the sake of their basic needs (*Rabbeinu Chananel* cited in *Tos.* to *Kesubos* 70a, s.v. אבל; see *Meiri*). Others disagree (*Meiri; Rambam, Hil. Mechirah* 29:6*ff.*).

There are those who hold that the only transactions which are valid are those which involve the children's basic needs, since that is the only reason for their legitimization (*R' Hai Gaon, Mekach Umemkar 3, cited by Rosh, Ran, Meiri).* Others contend that once the Rabbis empowered these children to buy and sell, they included all transactions in the enactment (*Ramban; Meiri; Rambam, Hil. Mechirah* 29:6).

[ח] **וְאֵלּוּ** דְבָרִים אָמְרוּ מִפְּנֵי דַרְכֵי שָׁלוֹם: כֹּהֵן קוֹרֵא רִאשׁוֹן, וְאַחֲרָיו לֵוִי, וְאַחֲרָיו יִשְׂרָאֵל, מִפְּנֵי דַרְכֵי שָׁלוֹם. מְעָרְבִין בְּבַיִת יָשָׁן,

ר׳ עובדיה מברטנורא

(ח) **כהן קורא ראשון וכו׳.** כשהן שוין בחכמה, אבל אם הישראל גדול בחכמה, קודם לכהן וללוי, דממזר תלמיד חכם קודם לכהן גדול עם הארץ. הדין הוא דינא דגמרא (הוריות יג, א). והאידנא נהוג, שכהן אפילו עם הארץ קודם לחכם גדול שבישראל: **מפני דרכי שלום.** דמדאורייתא יכול הכהן לתת רשות למי שירצה שיקרא בתורה לפניו, ומפני דרכי שלום אמרו שיקרא הוא ראשון, ולא יתן רשות לאחר שיקרא, דלא ליתי לאנצויי ולומר מפני מה הרשה לזה ולא לאחר. ולא שנא בשבתות וימים טובים דשכיחי רבים, ולא שנא בשני ובחמישי בזמן הזה, לעולם כהן קורא ראשון, ואינו יכול לתת רשות לישראל שיקרא לפניו, כי היכי דלא ליתו לאנצויי. ואם אין שם כהן, נתפרדה החבילה, ולא יקרא לוי שני אלא כפי חשיבותו, ואית דאמרי לא יקרא לוי בתורה כלל, וכן המנהג: **מערבין בבית ישן.** בני חצר שרגילים ליתן עירובן בכל שבת בבית אחד, אין

יד אברהם

8.

[Following the earlier mishnayos which discussed decrees instituted *for the sake of the general good*, the next two mishnayos deal with enactments instituted *in the interests of peace.*]

וְאֵלּוּ דְבָרִים אָמְרוּ מִפְּנֵי דַרְכֵי שָׁלוֹם: — *These things were declared in the interests of peace* (lit., *for the ways of peace*):

[The following laws were decreed by the Rabbis in order to avoid conflict and promote harmony.]

✤ Reading of the Torah

כֹּהֵן קוֹרֵא רִאשׁוֹן, — *A Kohen reads first,*

When the Torah is read in the synagogue, the first portion must be read by a *Kohen,*[1] and he may not waive his privilege and allow a non-*Kohen* to precede him (*Rav* from *Gem.* 59b). This only applies when the *Kohen* and non-*Kohen* are of equal status. However, a non-*Kohen* who is a Torah scholar takes precedence over a *Kohen* who is ignorant (*Rav*) or even a lesser scholar (*Rambam Commentary*). Nevertheless, the prevailing custom is for the *Kohen* to read first in all cases (*Rav*), because the comparative stature of Torah scholars is no longer clearly defined, and any attempt to single out specific individuals to precede the *Kohen* would lead to discord (*Tos. Yom Tov*).

Others contend that only a Torah scholar who is of greater stature than any *Kohen* known to be living takes precedence over a *Kohen* (*Tos.* 59b s.v. דאפי׳; see *Meiri*), because the entire tribe of *Kohanim* is obligated to honor him (*Meiri*).

The decree requiring the prece-

1. Originally, it was the practice for each one who was called to the Torah to read his own portion. Subsequently, when ignorance became more widespread, it became customary for a reader to read the portion on behalf of all those called to the Torah, so as not to embarrass those who could not read it themselves (*Tos.* to *Megillah* 21b, s.v. תנא). [This, however, does not affect the law that a *Kohen* must be called to the Torah first (see *Orach Chaim* 139:2).]

8. These things were declared in the interests of peace: a *Kohen* reads first, and after him a *Levi*, and after him a *Yisrael*, in the interests of peace. An *eruv* is placed in the [same] house as before,

dence of a *Kohen* was stated only concerning the reading of the Torah on the Sabbath and Festivals, when many people are in attendance, and it is likely that there will be arguments as to who should read first. However, for the Torah reading on Monday and Thursday, a non-*Kohen* may read first (*Gem.* 59b). Nevertheless, the prevailing custom is to require that a *Kohen* read first even on Monday and Thursday (*Rav*), because there are often many people in attendance on these days as well (*Rabbeinu Chananel*, cited in *Tos.* 59b s.v. אבל).

וְאַחֲרָיו לֵוִי, וְאַחֲרָיו יִשְׂרָאֵל, — *and after him a Levi, and after him a Yisrael,*

[After the *Kohen*, a *Levi* reads, and only then may a *Yisrael* be called to read.] However, if there is no *Kohen*, a *Levi* no longer takes precedence over a *Yisrael* (*Rav* from *Gem.* 59b).

Some authorities hold that when there is no *Kohen*, a *Levi* is not called upon to read from the Torah at all (*Rav; Rashi* 59b s.v. נתפרדה).

[For a fuller discussion of the *halachos* regarding these laws, see *Orach Chaim* 135:3-13 and the commentators there.]

מִפְּנֵי דַרְכֵי שָׁלוֹם. — *in the interests of peace.*

The obligation to honor a *Kohen* and call upon him to read first is of Biblical origin, as it is included in the commentary (*Lev.* 21:8), *You shall sanctify him.* However, in all other matters to which this verse pertains, a *Kohen* may waive his privilege and honor another if he so desires. The Rabbis prohibited him from doing so with regard to being called first to the Torah in order to avoid arguments among non-*Kohanim* as to who is fitting to read first in his stead (*Rav* from *Gem.* 59b).

☙ Eruv Chatzeiros

On the Sabbath it is Rabbinically forbidden to carry from one's private domain to a communal courtyard. The Sages, however, provided a procedure by which carrying would be permitted. This method allows us to view all the houses opening into the courtyard as owned by a single consortium composed of all the residents of the courtyard. This is accomplished by collecting a loaf of bread (or a matzah) before the Sabbath from each of the dwellings which open into that yard, and placing it in one of those dwellings for the duration of the Sabbath. This then symbolizes that all the contributing residents are legally residing in one dwelling (the house in which their bread was placed), and the yard is therefore the province of only one dwelling (the one in which they have merged) rather than several of them. Since the yard and the house are all the property of one ownership, there is no prohibition to carry from one to the other (see *Rambam, Hil. Eruvin* 1:1,2,6, and General Introduction to ArtScroll *Eruvin* pp. 6-8).

מְעָרְבִין בְּבַיִת יָשָׁן, — *An eruv is placed in the [same] house as before* (lit., *in an old house*),

A group of people whose homes

מִפְּנֵי דַרְכֵי שָׁלוֹם. בּוֹר שֶׁהוּא קָרוֹב לָאַמָּה מִתְמַלֵּא רִאשׁוֹן, מִפְּנֵי דַרְכֵי שָׁלוֹם.

מְצוּדוֹת חַיָּה, וְעוֹפוֹת, וְדָגִים יֵשׁ בָּהֶם מִשּׁוּם גָּזֵל, מִפְּנֵי דַרְכֵי שָׁלוֹם. רַבִּי יוֹסֵי אוֹמֵר: גָּזֵל גָּמוּר.

מְצִיאַת חֵרֵשׁ, שׁוֹטֶה, וְקָטָן יֵשׁ בָּהֶן מִשּׁוּם גָּזֵל, מִפְּנֵי דַרְכֵי שָׁלוֹם. רַבִּי יוֹסֵי אוֹמֵר: גָּזֵל גָּמוּר.

ר׳ עובדיה מברטנורא

משנין את מקומן ליתנו בבית אחר: **מפני דרכי שלום.** שבני אדם שהיו רגילים לראות העירוב באותו בית, עכשיו שאין רואים אותו, יאמרו שמטלטלין בלא עירוב, ואיכא חשדא: **בור שהוא קרוב.** למולא אמת המים הבא מן הנהר, מתמלא ראשון, ואחריו יתמלאו התחתונים: **מצודות חיה.** שאין להם תוך, דליקני ליה כליו: **יש בהן גזל מפני דרכי שלום.** ולא נפיק בדיינים: **רבי יוסי אומר גזל גמור.** מדבריהם, ונפיק בדיינים. ומיהו מודה רבי יוסי דלא הוי גזל דאורייתא לעבור עליו בלאו. ואין הלכה כרבי יוסי:

יד אברהם

runs alongside a series of fields, and the owners of the fields irrigate them from this channel. To avoid the possibility of the channel drying out before the fields are sufficiently irrigated, the owners dug cisterns on the edges of their fields to collect the water from the channel (*Meiri*).

מִתְמַלֵּא רִאשׁוֹן, — *is filled first,*

If it is necessary to stop the flow of the channel in order to divert its water into cisterns, the owner of the field which is nearest to the beginning of the channel has the right to divert the water to his cistern first, and the other fields continue in the order of their proximity to the first (*Rav; Meiri*).

Others contend that the order of precedence is the reverse — the cistern of the last field is to be filled first, and so on. This is because the channel must be left to its natural flow as much as possible. They interpret the mishnah to be stating that in a

share a common courtyard and who are accustomed to placing their *eruv* in the same house every Friday may not move its location to a different house (*Rav*), even if the original owner of the first house had died, and a new owner now lives there (*Meiri*).

מִפְּנֵי דַרְכֵי שָׁלוֹם. — *in the interests of peace.*

The Rabbis feared that people who were accustomed to seeing the *eruv* in the same home every week, and noticed it missing on the week it was moved, would suspect the dwellers of that courtyard of ignoring the prohibition of carrying between the house and the courtyard without an *eruv* [and hostility borne of suspicion and false accusations would ensue] (*Rav* from *Gem.* 60b; *Rashi*).

בּוֹר שֶׁהוּא קָרוֹב לָאַמָּה — *The cistern nearest to the channel*

A channel which flows from a river

in the interests of peace. The cistern nearest to the channel is filled first, in the interests of peace.

Traps for beasts, birds, and fish are covered by the laws of theft, in the interests of peace. R' Yose says: [It is] actual theft.

An article found by a deaf-mute, a mentally deranged person, or a minor is covered by the laws of theft, in the interests of peace. R' Yose says: [It is] actual theft.

YAD AVRAHAM

case in which the channel flows directly over the cistern of the first field, its owner may allow it to collect the water, and he is not required to cover it so as not to impede the flow of the channel (*Gem.* 60b).

מִפְּנֵי דַרְכֵי שָׁלוֹם. — *in the interests of peace.*

I.e., to avoid constant bickering as to who takes precedence in taking from the channel to fill his cistern (*Rashi*).

מְצוּדוֹת חַיָּה, וְעוֹפוֹת, וְדָגִים — *Traps for beasts, birds, and fish*

Traps which are set for these animals, even if they cannot hold the trapped animal within them so as to allow for their owner's acquisition of the animal by virtue of it being in his utensil (*Rav* from *Gem.* 60b-61a).

יֵשׁ בָּהֶם מִשּׁוּם גָּזֵל, מִפְּנֵי דַרְכֵי שָׁלוֹם. — *are covered by the laws of theft, in the interests of peace.*

The Rabbis prohibited anyone else to remove the animals from these traps in order to avoid discord. However, if someone did remove them, he cannot be held liable in court (*Rav*).

רַבִּי יוֹסֵי אוֹמֵר: גָּזֵל גָּמוּר. — *R' Yose says: [It is] actual theft.*

R' Yose contends that the Rabbis gave the capture of these animals in the traps the status of legal acquisition (*Rashi*). Therefore, one who removes them is actually stealing from the owner of the trap, who can then retrieve the animal in court (*Rav*).

מְצִיאַת חֵרֵשׁ, שׁוֹטֶה, וְקָטָן — *An article found by a deaf-mute, a mentally deranged person, or a minor*

[I.e., who are considered mentally incompetent and are incapable of effecting a legal acquisition (see commentary to 2:5).] A minor is capable of acquiring an item only if an adult transfers it to him (*Meiri*).

יֵשׁ בָּהֶן מִשּׁוּם גָּזֵל, מִפְּנֵי דַרְכֵי שָׁלוֹם. — *is covered by the laws of theft, in the interests of peace.*

[The Rabbis prohibited taking items that they have found away from them in order to avoid conflict.]

רַבִּי יוֹסֵי אוֹמֵר: גָּזֵל גָּמוּר. — *R' Yose says: [It is] actual theft.*

[Here, too, R' Yose disagrees, maintaining that the Rabbis legally awarded the findings of these individuals to them.]

עָנִי הַמְנַקֵּף בְּרֹאשׁ הַזַּיִת — מַה שֶּׁתַּחְתָּיו גָּזֵל, מִפְּנֵי דַרְכֵי שָׁלוֹם. רַבִּי יוֹסֵי אוֹמֵר: גָּזֵל גָּמוּר. אֵין מְמַחִין בְּיַד עֲנִיֵּי גוֹיִם בַּלֶּקֶט, וּבַשִּׁכְחָה, וּבַפֵּאָה, מִפְּנֵי דַרְכֵי שָׁלוֹם.

[ט] **מַשְׁאֶלֶת** אִשָּׁה לַחֲבֶרְתָּהּ הַחֲשׁוּדָה עַל הַשְּׁבִיעִית נָפָה, וּכְבָרָה,

ר' עובדיה מברטנורא

המנקף. חותך, כמו ונקף סבכי היער (ישעיה י, לד): (ט) **החשודה על השביעית.** לשמור פירות שביעית, ולהכניס מן הביעור ואילך:

יד אברהם

עָנִי הַמְנַקֵּף בְּרֹאשׁ הַזַּיִת — *[If] a poor man is cutting at the top of an olive tree,*

From the top of an olive tree, a poor man was cutting the fruits which were left unpicked by the owner, and are thus designated for the poor (*Meiri;* see *Deut.* 24:19).

מַה שֶּׁתַּחְתָּיו גָּזֵל, מִפְּנֵי דַרְכֵי שָׁלוֹם. — *[to take] what [lies] below him is [considered] theft, in the interests of peace.*

The Rabbis prohibited someone else from taking the fruits which were cut off and fell to the ground, in order to avoid conflicts (*Meiri*).

If the poor man picked them with his hand and they then fell, their removal is actual theft by Biblical law, because his grasping them effects a legal acquisition (*Gem.* 61a), even though he held them only with the intent of subsequently dropping them (*Tos.* 61a s.v. ליקט).

רַבִּי יוֹסֵי אוֹמֵר: גָּזֵל גָּמוּר. — *R' Yose says: [It is] actual theft.*

[As explained above.]

אֵין מְמַחִין בְּיַד עֲנִיֵּי גוֹיִם — *Poor gentiles are not prevented from [collecting]*

Even those gentiles who do not keep the Noachide[1] laws are not prevented from collecting the produce of fields owned by Jews that is allocated to the poor (*Meiri*).

בַּלֶּקֶט, — *gleanings,*

Single ears of grain, or pairs thereof, which were dropped during reaping may not be retrieved, but must be left for the poor to gather (*Lev.* 19:9; *Rashi*).

וּבַשִּׁכְחָה, — *forgotten sheaves,*

The same applies to grain which is inadvertently left unpicked in the fields during reaping (*Deut.* 24:19).

וּבַפֵּאָה, — *or the unpicked corners of fields,*

A landowner is obligated to intentionally leave a portion of his field unpicked, so the poor can come pick it for themselves (*Lev.* loc. cit.).

מִפְּנֵי דַרְכֵי שָׁלוֹם. — *in the interests of peace.*

[I.e., for the sake of peaceful rela-

1. I.e., the seven commandments that are binding upon all of mankind. These include the prohibition of idolatry, cursing God's Name, murder, illicit sexual relations, theft, eating the limb of a live animal, and the responsibility to establish a judicial system (*Rambam, Hil. Melachim* 9:1*ff.;* cf. *Ramban* to *Gen.* 34:11).

[If] a poor man is cutting at the top of an olive tree, [to take] what [lies] below him is [considered] theft, in the interests of peace. R' Yose says: [It is] actual theft. Poor gentiles are not prevented from [collecting] gleanings, forgotten sheaves, or the unpicked corners of fields, in the interests of peace.

9. A woman may lend to her friend who is suspect regarding produce of the Sabbatical year a sifter, a sieve, a handmill, or an

YAD AVRAHAM

tions with gentile neighbors.]

By the same token, the Rabbis decreed that gentile poor are to be supported along with Jewish poor; their sick are to be visited along with the Jews who are ill; and their unattended dead are to be buried as well as the unattended Jewish dead (*Gem.* 61a), but not in the same cemeteries (*Rashi; Meiri*).

9.

Shemittah/The Sabbatical Year

The Torah (*Lev.* 25:2*ff.*) designates every seventh year as *Shemittah,* the Sabbatical year, in Eretz Yisrael. During that year, the owner of a field has no proprietorship over his produce, and he may only bring them into his house when they are needed for consumption. Similarly, when any given crop is no longer to be found in the fields, the owner may no longer retain any of it in his possession (*Taanis* 6a).

מַשְׁאֶלֶת אִשָּׁה לַחֲבֶרְתָּהּ הַחֲשׁוּדָה עַל הַשְּׁבִיעִית — *A woman may lend to her friend who is suspect regarding produce of the Sabbatical year*

[This mishnah is a repetition of *Sheviis* 5:9.]

A woman who has a friend that is suspected of keeping produce of *Shemittah,* after the time when it must be removed from one's possession, is permitted to lend to her the utensils listed here (*Rav*). She is not considered to be facilitating a transgression, because she may assume that the borrower will use them in a permissible manner. However, if the borrower states explicitly that she intends to use them for produce of the Sabbatical year, it is forbidden to lend her the utensils (*Rambam Commentary; Meiri* citing *Yerushalmi*).

The mishnah specifies that she may lend them to a friend, because only then is the need for peaceful relations vital enough to warrant such a degree of leniency (*Tos. Anshei Shem* to *Sheviis* ibid.).

נָפָה, — *a sifter,*

A utensil used to sift flour (*Rambam Commentary* to *Sheviis* ibid.). The lender may assume that her friend will use it only to count money in it (*Meiri* from *Yerushalmi*).

וּכְבָרָה, — *a sieve,*

A utensil used to sift grain (*Ram-*

וְרֵחַיִם, וְתַנּוּר; אֲבָל לֹא תָבוֹר וְלֹא תִטְחַן עִמָּהּ.
אֵשֶׁת חָבֵר מַשְׁאֶלֶת לְאֵשֶׁת עַם הָאָרֶץ נָפָה וּכְבָרָה; וּבוֹרֶרֶת, וְטוֹחֶנֶת, וּמַרְקֶדֶת עִמָּהּ. אֲבָל מִשֶּׁתַּטִּיל הַמַּיִם — לֹא תִגַּע עִמָּהּ, לְפִי שֶׁאֵין מַחֲזִיקִין יְדֵי עוֹבְרֵי עֲבֵרָה. וְכֻלָּן לֹא אָמְרוּ

ר׳ עובדיה מברטנורא

לא תבור ולא תטחון עמה. לסייעה, מפני שאסור לסייע בידים ידי עוברי עבירה בשעת העבירה: **לאשת עם הארץ.** החשודה על המעשרות: **ובוררת וטוחנת.** לפי שרוב עמי הארץ מעשרין הן: **אבל משתטיל המים.** בעיסה: **לא תגע עמה.** לפי שמשנגלגלה הוטבלה לחלה, וקא מיטמאה מחמת כלים טמאים, שהרי הוכשרה לקבל טומאה, וזו מסייעתה לגלגל, ואסור לגרום טומאה לחלה:

יד אברהם

bam loc. cit.). It can also be used to sift sand, and the lender may assume that this is the purpose for which it is being borrowed (*Meiri* from *Yerushalmi*).

וְרֵחַיִם, — *a handmill,*

This can be used to grind spices as well as grain (ibid.).

וְתַנּוּר; — *or an oven,*

She may be borrowing this to dry out flax rather than to bake bread from *Shemittah* grain (ibid.).

There are those who maintain that the mishnah is speaking of a case in which the lender knows that the borrower has no produce save that of the Sabbatical year. This is because the mishnah later gives the reason for this leniency as being for the sake of peace; if the borrower had other produce for which she might need these utensils, it would be permitted to lend them to her by law. On the other hand, if there would be no possibility whatsoever of her needing the utensils for any other purpose, the Rabbis would not have allowed the woman to lend them to her even in the interests of peace. Thus, *Yerushalmi* suggests an alternative use for each utensil which is unlikely but possible, and it is therefore permissible to lend them in the interests of peace (*Tos.* s.v. משאלת; *Rash* to *Sheviis* ibid.).

Others contend that the alternative uses cited in *Yerushalmi* are not far-fetched, and are parallel to a case in which the borrower had non-*Shemittah* products to bake. However, if one sells these utensils to such a person, he may assume that they will not be used for *Shemittah* products — even without the consideration of peace — because the Rabbis were more lenient for the sake of one's livelihood (*Ramban*). In addition, the utensils are totally severed from any connection with the seller once they have been sold (*Meiri*), unlike those which have been borrowed (*Rambam Commentary; Rambam; Rashba; Meiri*).

אֲבָל לֹא תָבוֹר וְלֹא תִטְחַן עִמָּהּ. — *but she may not winnow or grind with her.*

And take the risk of joining her in the actual transgression of the laws of *Shemittah* (*Rav*).

אֵשֶׁת חָבֵר מַשְׁאֶלֶת לְאֵשֶׁת עַם הָאָרֶץ נָפָה וּכְבָרָה; — *The wife of a scholar may lend a sifter or a sieve to the wife of an unlearned person;*

The wife of a scholar may lend these utensils to the wife of an *am haaretz,* a person unlearned in Torah, whose observance of the laws of tithing is suspect (*Rav*).

Here the mishnah does not specify a *friend.* Since the majority of *amei haaretz* are careful with tithing (see below), there is

5 oven, but she may not winnow or grind with her.
9 The wife of a scholar may lend a sifter or a sieve to the wife of an unlearned person; and she may winnow, grind, and sift with her. But from when she pours the water — she may not help her, because it is forbidden to assist transgressors. All of these

a greater basis for leniency, and the need for peaceful relations with any acquaintance is enough to warrant it (*Tos. Anshei Shem* to *Sheviis* ibid.).

This part of the mishnah does not mention a handmill and an oven again, but they are obviously included in this category, just as above (*Tos.*). Others contend that only a sifter and sieve are permitted, because she can purify them by immersion in a *mikveh* (ritual pool) when they are returned, in the event that the borrower had ritually contaminated them (see below). However, a handmill is bulky and difficult to immerse, and an earthen oven cannot be purified. Therefore, these may not be lent to the wife of an *am haaretz* (*Tif. Yis.*).

וּבוֹרֶרֶת, וְטוֹחֶנֶת, וּמַרְקֶדֶת עִמָּהּ. — *and she may winnow, grind, and sift with her.*

She may even assist her in processing her food, because most *amei haaretz* adhere to the laws of tithing, and it is unlikely that she is involved in a transgression (*Rav* from *Gem.* 61a).

Another interpretation is that the mishnah is discussing the wife of a person whom R' Meir refers to as an *am haaretz* — i.e., one who is careful with tithing, but does not make sure to keep nonconsecrated foods free of contamination. The mishnah is of the opinion that it is forbidden to cause the contamination of even nonconsecrated foods in *Eretz Yisrael* (see *Sotah* 30b), but since it is only a Rabbinic prohibition, the Rabbis were lenient in this case in the interests of peace. However, according to this opinion, it would be forbidden to assist a woman who is suspect of eating untithed food, which is a Biblical prohibition, even in the interests of peace (*Gem.* 61a).

The mishnah mentions *sifting* in this case, as opposed to the previous case, because it goes on to discuss the next step of pouring water into the flour (*Tos. Yom Tov* to *Sheviis* ibid.).

אֲבָל מִשֶּׁתַּטִּיל הַמַּיִם — — *But from when she pours the water —*

Once she has poured water into the flour for the sake of kneading the dough (*Rav*), at which time the dough becomes subject to contamination (see *Lev.* 11:38).

לֹא תִגַּע עִמָּהּ, לְפִי שֶׁאֵין מַחֲזִיקִין יְדֵי עוֹבְרֵי עֲבֵרָה. — *she may not help* (lit., *touch with*) *her, because it is forbidden to assist transgressors.*

She may not assist the wife of the *am haaretz*, because when the dough is kneaded, the requirement to separate *challah*[1] takes effect, and by assisting with the kneading, she is helping cause the contamination of

1. This is the portion from one's dough which must be offered to a *Kohen* as stated in the verse (*Num.* 15:20): *The first of your dough you shall separate for terumah; like the terumah of grain so you shall separate it.* No specific amount is required by Biblical law, but the Rabbis decreed that from dough made for personal use, one must separate one twenty-fourth, and from dough made for commercial use, one forty-eighth (*Rambam, Hil. Bikkurim* 5:1).

אֶלָּא מִפְּנֵי דַרְכֵי שָׁלוֹם.
וּמַחֲזִיקִין יְדֵי גוֹיִם בַּשְּׁבִיעִית — אֲבָל לֹא יְדֵי יִשְׂרָאֵל — וְשׁוֹאֲלִין בִּשְׁלוֹמָן, מִפְּנֵי דַרְכֵי שָׁלוֹם.

ר' עובדיה מברטנורא

וכולן לא אמרו בו'. לא התירו להשאילם כלים ולסייעם בלא שעת עבירה עצמה, אלא משום דרכי שלום: **ומחזיקין ידי גוים.** לומר להם תחזקנה ידיכם: **ושואלים בשלומם.** כל הימים, ואפילו ביום חגם. ואף על פי שמטיל שם שמים על הנכרי, ששלום אחד משמותיו של הקדוש ברוך הוא:

יד אברהם

the *challah* dough, which is forbidden by Biblical law (*Rav; Rashi* 61a s.v. וסיפא בטומאת חלה).

Once the dough is kneaded, she may again assist with further preparation, because if the wife of the *am haaretz* or her utensils were contaminated, the *challah* dough has already been affected, and no further transgression will take place (*Mishnah Rabbah* to *Sheviis* 5:9).

וְכֻלָּן לֹא אָמְרוּ אֶלָּא מִפְּנֵי דַרְכֵי שָׁלוֹם. — *All of these were stated only in the interests of peace.*

All of the examples mentioned in this mishnah — in which a woman takes the chance of facilitating a transgression — were permitted only in the interests of peace (*Rav*).

וּמַחֲזִיקִין יְדֵי גוֹיִם בַּשְּׁבִיעִית — *Gentiles may be encouraged* (lit., *supported*) *during the Sabbatical year* —

It is permitted to give encouragement to a gentile who is tending his

5
9 were stated only in the interest of peace.

Gentiles may be encouraged during the Sabbatical year — but not a Jew — and they may be greeted, in the interests of peace.

YAD AVRAHAM

field during the Sabbatical year, because he is not bound to the laws of *Shemittah* (*Meiri*).

אֲבָל לֹא יְדֵי יִשְׂרָאֵל — — *but not a Jew* —

[It is forbidden to encourage a Jew who is transgressing the law.]

וְשׁוֹאֲלִין בִּשְׁלוֹמָן, — *and they may be greeted,*

One may greet a gentile with the traditional greeting of *Shalom* (peace), even though it is also one of the Names of God, and he is thus invoking His Name to greet a gentile (*Rav*). Even when encountering them on their religious holiday, this is permitted (*Rav* from *Gem.* 62a), but it should be done in a subdued manner (*Gem.* ibid.).

Nevertheless, one should not greet them extensively (*Gem.* ibid.), because it can lead to a greater depth of relationship between the Jew and the gentile than is desirable (*Meiri*). However, this refers only to gentiles who are idolatrous, and there is a fear of the Jew being drawn to their idolatry (ibid.).

מִפְּנֵי דַרְכֵי שָׁלוֹם. — *in the interests of peace.*

[The reason these exchanges with a gentile are permitted is for the sake of peaceful coexistence with them.]

פרק ששי

Chapter Six

[א] **הָאוֹמֵר:** „הִתְקַבֵּל גֵּט זֶה לְאִשְׁתִּי״, אוֹ: „הוֹלֵךְ גֵּט זֶה לְאִשְׁתִּי״ — אִם רָצָה לַחֲזוֹר — יַחֲזוֹר. הָאִשָּׁה שֶׁאָמְרָה: „הִתְקַבֵּל לִי גִּטִּי״ — אִם רָצָה לַחֲזוֹר לֹא יַחֲזוֹר. לְפִיכָךְ, אִם אָמַר לוֹ הַבַּעַל: „אִי אֶפְשִׁי שֶׁתְּקַבֵּל לָהּ, אֶלָּא הוֹלֵךְ וְתֵן לָהּ״ — אִם רָצָה לַחֲזוֹר

ר׳ עובדיה מברטנורא

פרק ששי – האומר התקבל. (א) האומר התקבל. אם רצה לחזור יחזור. דגט חוב הוא לה, ואין חבין לאדם שלא מדעתו: **לא יחזור.** דכיון דאיהי שויתיה שליח, הרי הוא כידה, ונתגרשה מיד בקבלתו של זה:

יד אברהם

1.

After concluding its discussion of Rabbinic enactments which were ordained for the sake of the general good, the mishnah returns to the topic of agents for divorce, upon which it focused in the fourth chapter (*Tos.; Ran* to 67a). There are those who contend that the next chapter precedes this one (*Rosh; Meiri*).

As noted earlier (1:6, 4:1), an agent can participate in the delivery of a *get* in one of two ways: He can deliver the *get* on behalf of the husband, or he can receive it on behalf of the wife. In the former case, the divorce does not take effect until the woman receives the *get;* therefore, the husband can retract it up to that time. In the latter case, the *get* is executed by the agent's receipt of it, and the husband can no longer change his mind. However, in order for this to be valid, the husband must consent to this man's serving as the wife's agent. This is because a *get* must be given by the will of the husband (*Rambam, Hil. Gerushin* 1:4f.), and its execution must therefore comply with his wishes.

הָאוֹמֵר: „הִתְקַבֵּל גֵּט זֶה לְאִשְׁתִּי״, — *[If] one says: "Accept this get for my wife,"*

A husband gave a *get* to someone who had not been appointed by the wife as an agent to receive it, and instructed him to accept it on his wife's behalf (*Meiri*).

אוֹ: „הוֹלֵךְ גֵּט זֶה לְאִשְׁתִּי״, — *or: "Take this get to my wife,"*

The husband used the word הוֹלֵךְ, *take,* which is the subject of an unresolved dispute in the *Gemara* (63a,b) as to whether it denotes delivering the *get* as an agent of the husband or receiving it as an agent of the wife (*Meiri*).

אִם רָצָה לַחֲזוֹר, יַחֲזוֹר. — *if he wants to retract, he can retract.*

The husband can retract the *get* as long as his wife has not received it (*Meiri*), because it is considered to be detrimental to the wife, and only an agent whom she appointed can receive it on her behalf (*Rav;* see 1:6).

Even if the wife had expressed her

1. [If] one says: "Accept this *get* for my wife," or: "Take this *get* to my wife," if he wants to retract, he can retract. [If] a woman said: "Receive my *get* for me," if [the husband] wants to retract, he cannot retract. Therefore, if the husband said to him: "I do not want you to accept [it] for her; rather, take [it] and give [it] to her," if he wants to retract,

YAD AVRAHAM

desire to be divorced, the agent cannot accept a *get* on her behalf, because she may have changed her mind (*Yerushalmi; Ran; Meiri*).

Although the husband told the agent to accept the *get* on behalf of his wife, he is aware of his inability to give the agent such an assignment, and it is therefore understood that he merely wants him to be an agent of delivery (*Gem.* 63a).

According to the opinion that the term הוֹלֵךְ, *take,* denotes delivery, it is obvious that the *get* does not take effect until the wife receives it, since the agent was never instructed by the husband to receive it on her behalf. The mishnah mentions this case only to establish a frame of reference for the previous case in which the husband said, "Accept this *get*" — i.e., to indicate that when the agent was not appointed by the wife, the word הִתְקַבֵּל, *accept,* is construed to mean the same as הוֹלֵךְ, *take* (*Gem.* 62b).

הָאִשָּׁה שֶׁאָמְרָה: ,,הִתְקַבֵּל לִי גִטִּי״, — *[If] a woman said: "Receive my get for me,"*

A woman appointed an agent to receive a *get* on her behalf, and thereby cause the divorce to become effective immediately (*Meiri*). Her ability to do so is derived from the verse (*Deut.* 24:1), *and he shall send her from his house,* which is exegetically interpreted as teaching us that she can appoint an agent to act on her behalf (*Kiddushin* 41a; see General Introduction, s.v. *The Divorce Process*).

אִם רָצָה לַחֲזוֹר, לֹא יַחֲזוֹר. — *if [the husband] wants to retract, he cannot retract.*

If, following the wife's appointment, the husband gave the *get* to the agent to accept it for the wife, he can no longer change his mind, because the divorce has already taken effect (*Rav*).

לְפִיכָךְ, — *Therefore,*

Since the husband can no longer retract after the wife's agent receives it on her behalf, the only way for him to keep his options open, when the agent was appointed by the wife to receive it for her, is as follows (*Rashi*).

אִם אָמַר לוֹ הַבַּעַל: ,,אִי אֶפְשִׁי שֶׁתְּקַבֵּל לָהּ, אֶלָּא הוֹלֵךְ וְתֵן לָהּ״, — *if the husband said to him: "I do not want you to accept [it] for her; rather, take [it] and give [it] to her,"*

[The husband refused to allow the agent to accept the *get* in his role as the wife's agent, but rather appointed him as his own agent to deliver the *get.*]

The implication of the mishnah is that if he said: "Take it and give it to her," without saying, "I do not want you to accept it for her," the agent would retain his role as the wife's agent. However, according to the opinion that הוֹלֵךְ denotes delivery, the use of the word הוֹלֵךְ itself would suffice to indicate the agent's reassignment as an

יַחֲזֹר. רַבָּן שִׁמְעוֹן בֶּן גַּמְלִיאֵל אוֹמֵר: אַף הָאוֹמֶרֶת:
„טוֹל לִי גִּטִּי" — אִם רָצָה לַחֲזֹר לֹא יַחֲזֹר.

[ב] **הָאִשָּׁה** שֶׁאָמְרָה: „הִתְקַבֵּל לִי גִּטִּי" —
צְרִיכָה שְׁתֵּי כִתֵּי עֵדִים: שְׁנַיִם
שֶׁאוֹמְרִים: „בְּפָנֵינוּ אָמְרָה", וּשְׁנַיִם שֶׁאוֹמְרִים:

─────────── ר' עובדיה מברטנורא ───────────

אַף הָאוֹמֶרֶת טוֹל לִי גִּטִּי. לְשׁוֹן קַבָּלָה הוּא. וַהֲלָכָה כְּרַבָּן שִׁמְעוֹן בֶּן גַּמְלִיאֵל: **(ב) צְרִיכָה.**
לְהָבִיא לְפָנֵינוּ שְׁתֵּי כִתֵּי עֵדִים: **שְׁנַיִם שֶׁיֹּאמְרוּ בְּפָנֵינוּ אָמְרָה.** לוֹ לְקַבְּלוֹ:

יד אברהם

agent of delivery. Therefore, according to that view, the text of the mishnah must read הֵילֵךְ, rather than הוֹלֵךְ, since the word הֵילֵךְ is a directive to take it in accordance with the wife's instructions [because הֵילֵךְ is similar to saying, "Here, take it," whereas הוֹלֵךְ indicates more strongly the issuing of new instructions] (*Meiri* from *Gem.* 62b).

אִם רָצָה לַחֲזֹר, יַחֲזֹר. — *if he wants to retract, he can retract.*

Since the *get* can take effect only in accordance with the husband's wishes, this agent can take it only for the sake of delivery, but not as an agent to accept it for the wife. Therefore, as long as it has not yet been delivered to the wife, the husband can change his mind (*Rashi*).

Others maintain that this statement of the husband might be interpreted to mean that he agrees that the agent may receive the *get* on his wife's behalf but he insists that it be he who designates him for the role, rather than his wife. Since the wife has indicated her desire for divorce by appointing the agent, the *get* could be considered to be to her benefit, and the agent could therefore accept it on her behalf without her explicit consent. Nevertheless, the mishnah states that she cannot be divorced in

this manner, because she may have changed her mind about the divorce, in which case the *get* would still be considered a detriment, as explained above. Therefore, the husband's instructions to the agent are understood to be appointing him as an agent of delivery, rather than one of receipt.

According to this approach, the transition conveyed by the word *therefore* refers back to the first case in the mishnah, and is understood as follows: Since a *get* is considered a detriment to the wife, it cannot be assumed that she still desires to be divorced. Therefore, even when she has indicated this desire by appointing an agent to accept it for her, he cannot be instructed to receive the *get* on the husband's authority, rather than the wife's, on the assumption that it is an agency which is for her benefit (*Ran*).

רַבָּן שִׁמְעוֹן בֶּן גַּמְלִיאֵל אוֹמֵר: אַף הָאוֹמֶרֶת: „טוֹל לִי גִּטִּי" — אִם רָצָה לַחֲזֹר לֹא יַחֲזֹר. — *Rabban Shimon ben Gamliel says: Also, [if] she says: "Take my get for me," if he wants to retract, he cannot retract.*

The word טוֹל also denotes the act of receiving rather than that of delivery [and the *get* is thus executed as soon as it is given to the agent] (*Rav*).

2.

הָאִשָּׁה שֶׁאָמְרָה: „הִתְקַבֵּל לִי גִּטִּי" — [If] a woman said: "Receive my get for me,"

A woman appointed an agent to receive a *get* on her behalf, and he returned and said that he did so (*Rashi*).

he can retract. Rabban Shimon ben Gamliel says: Also, [if] she says: "Take my *get* for me," if he wants to retract, he cannot retract.

2. [If] a woman said: "Receive my *get* for me," she needs two pairs of witnesses: Two who say: "She said [so] in our presence," and two who say:

YAD AVRAHAM

צְרִיכָה שְׁתֵּי כִתֵּי עֵדִים: — *she needs two pairs of witnesses:*

She needs the two pairs of witnesses described below in order to establish her divorce so that her husband cannot contest it (*Meiri*).

There is a dispute in the *Gemara* concerning a case in which a married couple's *get* is in the possession of a third person, who claims that he received this *get* from the husband on behalf of the wife, and she was thereby divorced. The husband, however, insists that he gave it to him for safekeeping, not for divorce. R' Huna says that the husband is believed, because if he wanted to divorce her, he would have given it to her himself [since the case in question is one in which they were all in the same town (*Tos.* ibid., s.v. בעל)]. R' Chisda maintains that the other man is believed, since the husband trusted him by placing the *get* in his possession (see *Tos.*, s.v. שליש).

According to R' Huna, the witnesses required by our mishnah are clearly necessary since the agent's testimony will not prevail if the husband protests. According to R' Chisda, however, the ruling of the mishnah is puzzling, and will be explained below.

שְׁנַיִם שֶׁאוֹמְרִים: ,,בְּפָנֵינוּ אָמְרָה" — *Two who say: "She said* [so] *in our presence,"*

Two witnesses must testify that she appointed the agent to receive the *get*.

Even according to R' Chisda, who holds that the agent is believed to say that he received the *get* on the woman's behalf, that is only when the *get* is still in his possession (*Gem.* 64a). In such a case [although the husband's trust in him is sufficient only to prove his statement that he was an agent for divorce, but not to specify that he was the wife's agent of receipt, since it is not in the husband's power to appoint him for that], he could have given the *get* to the woman and she would have been divorced. Therefore, he is believed to say she was divorced with his receipt of the *get*, because of the principle of מִגּוֹ, *miggo* — i.e., since he could have accomplished his objective in an easier or more advantageous manner, the fact that he did not do so attests to his veracity. In the case of the mishnah, however, the agent does not possess the *get*, since — as stated below — it has been torn up. Therefore, he is not believed to establish himself as an agent of receipt, and the testimony of two witnesses is necessary (*Rashi* ad loc. s.v. מי קא נפיק).

Others contend that even if he has the *get* in his hands he is not believed that he was appointed an agent by the wife (*Tos.* ad loc. s.v. ולהימניה), because she may not be willing to accept a *get* which is disputed by the husband, and he therefore has no *miggo* to prove his claim (*Tos.* ibid., s.v. שליש).

„בְּפָנֵינוּ קִבֵּל, וְקָרַע", אֲפִלּוּ הֵן הָרִאשׁוֹנִים וְהֵן הָאַחֲרוֹנִים, אוֹ אֶחָד מִן הָרִאשׁוֹנִים וְאֶחָד מִן הָאַחֲרוֹנִים וְאֶחָד מִצְטָרֵף עִמָּהֶן.
נַעֲרָה הַמְאֹרָסָה — הִיא וְאָבִיהָ מְקַבְּלִין

ר' עובדיה מברטנורא

ושנים שיאמרו בפנינו קבל וקרע. ובשעת השמד שנו, שגזרו על המצות, והיו קורעים הגט מיד, שלא יראה: **ואפילו הן כו'.** שהשנים שאמרה בפניהם הם עצמם ראו כשקבלו: **או אחד מן הראשונים ואחד מן האחרונים ואחד.** שלישי, שנעשה עד בזו ובזו, מצטרף עמהם: **היא ואביה.** או היא או אביה. היא יש לה יד, דהא גדולה היא, ואביה נמי זכאי לקבלו:

יד אברהם

וּשְׁנַיִם שֶׁאוֹמְרִים: „בְּפָנֵינוּ קִבֵּל, — *and two who say: "He received [it] in our presence,*

Two witnesses must testify that the agent received the *get* on behalf of the wife in their presence. Although, according to R' Chisda's view — that the agent is believed about his assignment — it should be sufficient for the witnesses to attest to having seen the *get* in his possession before it was torn up, and for the agent to state that he received it on behalf of the wife, the *Gemara* explains that the author of the mishnah is R' Elazar, who holds that testimony to the delivery of a *get* is necessary to establish its validity.

R' Elazar agrees that a *get* signed by two witnesses, which is in the possession of the woman, is accepted as valid (see 4:3), because it is assumed to have been delivered in the presence of two witnesses. However, the mishnah is discussing a case in which the *get* is not signed by witnesses (*Tos.* 64a,s.v. רבי אלעזר), or where the signatures on the *get* cannot be confirmed (*Tur Even HaEzer* 141).

Others contend that R' Elazar requires the testimony of witnesses to the delivery in all cases (*Rashi* 64a s.v. ר' אלעזר; *Tos. Rid;* see 9:4).

וְקָרַע", — *and he tore [it] up,"*

The agent ripped up the *get* without delivering it to the wife, because it was during the time of a decree against Judaism, and *gittin* were torn up immediately after they were handed over in order to avoid discovery (*Rav*).

This fact was included in the witnesses' testimony (*Rambam Commentary*), because otherwise people might assume that he would have taken the risk of delivering the *get* had he really received it, and his failure to do so refutes the testimony of the witnesses (*Tos. Yom Tov*). Others explain that the words *and he tore it up* are not part of the witnesses' testimony, but rather a note of explanation — that once testimony has been rendered that the agent received the *get*, it is to be assumed that he tore it up (*Meiri*).

The testimony of each of these pairs of witnesses is not disqualified for being only half of a testimony — i.e., one which does not disclose all of the information required for a specific issue (see *Bava Kamma* 70a, *Bava Basra* 56b), because each pair attests to all that was possible to witness at the time of the event which they observed (*Tos.* to *Bava Kamma* 70b s.v. למעוטי).

אֲפִלּוּ הֵן הָרִאשׁוֹנִים וְהֵן הָאַחֲרוֹנִים, — *even [if] the first witnesses are the same ones as the second witnesses*

Even if the same witnesses testify to the appointment of the agent and to his receipt of the *get*, they are believed. It is not considered too unlikely that the witnesses should happen to be first in the vicinity of the wife, and then in

6
2

"He received [it] in our presence, and he tore [it] up," even [if] the first witnesses are the same ones as the second witnesses or [if] one is from the first [pair] and one from the second, and another joined with each of them.

[If] a *naarah* is betrothed, she or her father [can]

YAD AVRAHAM

that of the husband at the same times as the agent (*Tos.; Ran*).

Others explain that the word *even* is used in reference to the amount of witnesses; i.e., that this testimony can be attained even without the involvement of two separate pairs of witnesses (*Meiri*).

אוֹ אֶחָד מִן הָרִאשׁוֹנִים וְאֶחָד מִן הָאַחֲרוֹנִים וְאֶחָד מִצְטָרֵף עִמָּהֶן. — *or [if] one is from the first [pair] and one from the second, and another joined with each of them.*

[If there is one witness to the appointment of the agent, one to his receipt of the *get*, and a third witness to both, the testimony is valid.]

The mishnah is adding that even in this case, we do not suspect fraud, although it seems highly unlikely that the third witness just happened to be present at the appointment as well as at the receipt of the *get* [and being only one witness, he does not have the same credibility that two witnesses have in similar circumstances] (*Tos. Yom Tov*).

The mishnah is discussing a case in which the agent himself is a relative of the husband or wife [or is otherwise disqualified as a witness]. If he were a valid witness, he could testify to both the appointment and the delivery, and only one more witness would be needed for each (*Yerushalmi*, cited by *Meiri; Even HaEzer* 141:8). Others contend that since he represents the wife in this transaction, he cannot be a witness (*Beis Yosef* ad loc. citing *Rosh*).

נַעֲרָה — *[If] a naarah*

A girl who reaches twelve years and a day[1] — and has grown two pubic hairs, as is usually the case — is classified as a *naarah* for the next six months, after which she is known as a *bogeres*[2] (*Tos. Rid*).

הַמְאֹרָסָה — *is betrothed,*

[She has undergone the initial phase of the marriage process called *erusin* or *kiddushin* (see *Kiddushin* 1:1 and preface to 8:9), but has not been fully married through the process of *chupah*. Nevertheless, the only way to dissolve such a marriage is with a *get*.]

1. This wording is from a mishnah in *Niddah* (5:6). It means that the twelve years must be complete, unlike other areas of Jewish law, for which a portion of the final years counts as a full year (*Mishneh LaMelech, Hil. Ishus* 2:21).

There is a dispute among the authorities as to what constitutes completion of the final year. Some maintain that it must be measured to the hour, and a girl who was born at midday does not become a *naarah* until midday of her twelfth birthday (*Rashi* to *Arachin* 18b s.v. לפרקין; *Tos.* ibid. 31a s.v. מיום). Others contend that with the onset of nightfall on her twelfth birthday, the year is considered completed and she becomes a *naarah* (*Tos.* ibid. citing *R' Elchanan; Rashba* to *Niddah* 47b). The latter opinion is universally accepted as the halachah (*Sma* to *Choshen Mishpat* 35:1; *Shach* ad loc.; *Bach* to *Tur Orach Chaim* 53; *Taz* ibid. 6; *Magen Avraham* ibid. 13; *Mishnah Berurah* ibid. 33).

2. If she grows the two pubic hairs later than usual, the time of her becoming a *bogeres* is a subject of dispute (see footnote to ArtScroll *Kesubos* 3:1, p. 49).

אֶת גִּטָּהּ. אָמַר רַבִּי יְהוּדָה: אֵין שְׁתֵּי יָדַיִם זוֹכוֹת כְּאֶחָת; אֶלָּא, אָבִיהָ מְקַבֵּל אֶת גִּטָּהּ בִּלְבָד.

וְכָל שֶׁאֵינָהּ יְכוֹלָה לִשְׁמוֹר אֶת גִּטָּהּ — אֵינָהּ יְכוֹלָה לְהִתְגָּרֵשׁ.

[ג] **קְטַנָּה** שֶׁאָמְרָה: ,,הִתְקַבֵּל לִי גִּטִּי״ — אֵינוֹ גֵט עַד שֶׁיַּגִּיעַ גֵּט לְיָדָהּ. לְפִיכָךְ, אִם רָצָה הַבַּעַל לַחֲזוֹר — יַחֲזוֹר, שֶׁאֵין קָטָן עוֹשֶׂה

ר׳ עובדיה מברטנורא

אינה מתגרשת. ואפילו בקבלת אביה, דכתיב (דברים כד, א) ושלחה מביתו, מי שמשלחה ואינה חוזרת, יצאה זו שמשלחה וחוזרת:

יד אברהם

הִיא וְאָבִיהָ מְקַבְּלִין אֶת גִּטָּהּ. — *she or her father [can] receive her get.*

She can receive her own *get* [without her father's knowledge (*Meiri*)], because a *naarah* is considered an adult in all areas of Jewish law. Her father can also receive it [without her knowledge (ibid.)], because she is still under his legal jurisdiction until she becomes a *bogeres* (*Rav;* see *Kesubos* 4:4). Once she is fully married, however, she is no longer under her father's jurisdiction, and only she [or her agent] can receive her *get* (*Ran;* see *Kesubos* 4:5).

Some authorities maintain that the mishnah's specification of a *naarah*, as opposed to a minor, is due to the fact that only a *naarah* is authorized to receive her own *get*, whereas a minor who has a father can be divorced only by delivery of the *get* into his possession (*Rashi; Rif* to *Gem.* 65a; *Meiri; Tos. Rid; Rambam, Hil. Gerushin* 2:18).

Others contend that a minor who is capable of properly guarding her *get* (see below) can receive it even when her father is alive (*Tos.; Rashi* to *Kiddushin* 43b; *Baal HaMaor; Rosh*). According to this view, the mishnah specifies *naarah* only in order to emphasize the father's authority over her despite her status as an adult (*Meiri*).

אָמַר רַבִּי יְהוּדָה: אֵין שְׁתֵּי יָדַיִם זוֹכוֹת כְּאֶחָת; אֶלָּא, אָבִיהָ מְקַבֵּל אֶת גִּטָּהּ בִּלְבָד. — *R' Yehudah said: Two hands cannot make acquisitions as one; rather, her father alone receives her get.*

R' Yehudah maintains that there cannot be dual jurisdiction over a person's status, and since the Torah gave the father jurisdiction over his daughter when she is a *naarah*, she has no right to receive her *get* (*Gem.* 64b).

וְכָל שֶׁאֵינָהּ יְכוֹלָה לִשְׁמֹר אֶת גִּטָּהּ — *Anyone who is unable to take care of her get*

This refers to a girl who cannot distinguish between her *get* and another document, and, if given a document to watch, might return the *get* in its place when asked to give it back (*Meiri*).

There are two versions to the further elaboration of the *Gemara* (65a) as to when a girl is considered old enough to guard her *get*. According to one version, this is described as the age of פָּעוֹטוֹת (see commentary to 5:7) — from 6 to 8 — when a child's purchases and sales are considered

receive her *get*. R' Yehudah said: Two hands cannot make acquisitions as one; rather, her father alone receives her *get*.

Anyone who is unable to take care of her *get* cannot be divorced.

3. [If] a minor girl said: "Receive my *get* for me," it is not a *get* until it reaches her hand. Therefore, if the husband wants to retract, he can retract, because a minor cannot appoint an

YAD AVRAHAM

valid (*Rashi*). The other version states that it is as soon as she is discerning enough to choose correctly between a nut and a stone (*Rif*).

אֵינָהּ יְכוֹלָה לְהִתְגָּרֵשׁ. — *cannot be divorced.*

She cannot be divorced, even by her father's receipt of her *get* (*Rav; Rashi*). This is derived exegetically from the verse (*Deut.* 24:1), *and he shall send her from his house*, which is exegetically interpreted to mean that only a woman who understands the concept of divorce well enough to refrain from returning to her husband's house [which is apparently the same stage of intellectual development as that mentioned above] can be divorced (*Rav* from *Yevamos* 113b).

Others contend that this refers only to a *get* which is delivered to the girl herself; if, however, it is given to her father, she can be divorced at any age (*Rif; Rambam, Hil. Gerushin* 2:18; *Tos.; Rosh; Meiri; Tos. Rid*), because he will see to it that she does not return to her husband (*Tos.*).

3.

קְטַנָּה שֶׁאָמְרָה: ,,הִתְקַבֵּל לִי גִּטִּי״ — *[If] a minor girl said: "Receive my get for me,"*

A girl who is a minor but has no father [and can therefore receive her own *get*] appointed an agent to receive a *get* on her behalf (*Rav* from *Kiddushin* 44b).

אֵינוֹ גֵט עַד שֶׁיַּגִּיעַ גֵּט לְיָדָהּ. — *it is not a get until it reaches her hand.*

[The agent cannot receive the *get* on behalf of the girl, but can only execute the divorce by delivering it into her hands, for the reason explained below.]

Once it reaches her hand, however, the divorce takes effect, even if the husband did not explicitly instruct the agent to deliver the *get*, rather than to receive it on her behalf. This is because the husband is assumed to realize that a minor cannot appoint an agent, and a husband cannot appoint an agent for receipt. Therefore, his only possible intent in appointing the agent was for the sake of delivery. Accordingly, even if he said, "Accept this *get*," he is understood to have meant: "Accept this *get* and deliver it" (*Gem.* 63a).

לְפִיכָךְ, אִם רָצָה הַבַּעַל לַחֲזוֹר — יַחֲזוֹר, — *Therefore, if the husband wants to retract, he can retract,*

[Since the *get* cannot take effect until the girl receives it, her husband can retract it at any time until then.]

שָׁלִיחַ. אֲבָל אִם אָמַר לוֹ אָבִיהָ: ,,צֵא וְהִתְקַבֵּל לְבִתִּי גִּטָּהּ'' — אִם רָצָה לְהַחֲזִיר לֹא יַחֲזִיר.

הָאוֹמֵר: ,,תֵּן גֵּט זֶה לְאִשְׁתִּי בְּמָקוֹם פְּלוֹנִי'', וּנְתָנוֹ לָהּ בְּמָקוֹם אַחֵר — פָּסוּל; ,,הֲרֵי הִיא בְּמָקוֹם פְּלוֹנִי'', וּנְתָנוֹ לָהּ בְּמָקוֹם אַחֵר — כָּשֵׁר.

הָאִשָּׁה שֶׁאָמְרָה: ,,הִתְקַבֵּל לִי גִּטִּי בְּמָקוֹם פְּלוֹנִי'', וְקִבְּלוֹ לָהּ בְּמָקוֹם אַחֵר — פָּסוּל. רַבִּי אֱלִיעֶזֶר מַכְשִׁיר. ,,הָבֵא לִי גִּטִּי מִמָּקוֹם פְּלוֹנִי'', וֶהֱבִיאוֹ לָהּ מִמָּקוֹם אַחֵר — כָּשֵׁר.

ר' עובדיה מברטנורא

(ג) **במקום אחר פסול.** שהבעל מקפיד, שאין רצונו שילעיזו עליו שם: **הרי היא במקום פלוני.** אינו אלא כמראה מקום, שם תמצאנה: **ורבי אליעזר מכשיר.** דסבר, איהו דמדעתיה מגרש, איכא קפידא, איהי דבעל כרחה מתגרשת, מראה מקום הוא לו. ואין הלכה כרבי אליעזר:

יד אברהם

שֶׁאֵין קָטָן עוֹשֶׂה שָׁלִיחַ. — *because a minor cannot appoint an agent.*

A minor is not authorized to appoint an agent [even for those things which he may do for himself], because the verse from which it is derived that one can authorize an agent to act in his place is speaking only of an adult [and a minor, whose legal authority is limited, cannot be assumed to have the same ability] (*Rashi* to *Bava Metzia* 71b).

אֲבָל אִם אָמַר לוֹ אָבִיהָ: ,,צֵא וְהִתְקַבֵּל לְבִתִּי גִּטָּהּ'' — *But if her father said to him: "Go receive my daughter's get for her,"*

The girl's father was still alive, and he appointed an agent to receive her *get* in his stead (*Kiddushin* 44b).

אִם רָצָה לְהַחֲזִיר לֹא יַחֲזִיר. — *if he wants to retract, he cannot retract.*

[Once the agent receives the *get*, the divorce takes effect, and her husband can no longer cancel it.]

הָאוֹמֵר: ,,תֵּן גֵּט זֶה לְאִשְׁתִּי בְּמָקוֹם פְּלוֹנִי'', וּנְתָנוֹ לָהּ בְּמָקוֹם אַחֵר — פָּסוּל; — *[If] one says: "Give this get to my wife in such and such a place," and he gave it to her in a different place, it is void;*

If the husband designated a specific place for the delivery of the *get* to his wife, this is interpreted as a stipulation that the divorce should take effect only upon its delivery in that place because he does not want the people of another place to malign him (*Rav*).

,,הֲרֵי הִיא בְּמָקוֹם פְּלוֹנִי'', וּנְתָנוֹ לָהּ בְּמָקוֹם אַחֵר — כָּשֵׁר. — *[If he said:] "She is in such and such a place," and he gave it to her in a different place, it is valid.*

If the husband only specified the place where he assumed his wife to be, he is understood to be merely giving the agent directions, rather than making a stipulation to the divorce [and the *get* takes effect regardless of where it is delivered] (*Rav*).

הָאִשָּׁה שֶׁאָמְרָה: ,,הִתְקַבֵּל לִי גִּטִּי בְּמָקוֹם פְּלוֹנִי'', וְקִבְּלוֹ לָהּ בְּמָקוֹם אַחֵר — פָּסוּל. *[If] a woman said: "Receive my get for*

agent. But if her father said to him: "Go receive my daughter's *get* for her," if he wants to retract, he cannot retract.

[If] one says: "Give this *get* to my wife in such-and such a place," and he gave it to her in a different place, it is void. [If he said:] "She is in such and such a place," and he gave it to her in a different place, it is valid.

[If] a woman said: "Receive my *get* for me in such and such a place," and he received it for her in a different place, it is void. R' Eliezer validates [it]. [If she said:] "Bring my *get* from such and such a place," and he brought it to her from a different place, it is valid.

YAD AVRAHAM

me in such and such a place," and he received it for her in a different place, it is void.

A woman who designates a specific place for the receipt of her *get* is also understood to be making a stipulation to her appointment of the agent to act on her behalf. Therefore, if he receives it elsewhere, it does not take effect (*Meiri*).

רַבִּי אֱלִיעֶזֶר מַכְשִׁיר. — *R' Eliezer validates [it].*

R' Eliezer holds that since a woman has no choice with regard to her divorce, she is not assumed to be making stipulations to the execution of the *get* (*Rav* from *Gem.* 65a).

,,הָבֵא לִי גִטִּי מִמָּקוֹם פְּלוֹנִי״, וֶהֱבִיאוֹ לָהּ מִמָּקוֹם אַחֵר — כָּשֵׁר. — *[If she said:] "Bring my get from such and such a place," and he brought it to her from a different place, it is valid.*

If she told the agent to bring her *get* from a specific place, this is interpreted as merely having given him directions. Since he is only an agent for delivery, and not for receipt, the *get* does not take effect until it reaches the woman. Therefore, the husband does not have to give it to the agent in front of two witnesses, and there is thus no publicity involved which would warrant the wife's insistence on a specific place (*Ran; Meiri*).

Another reason given is that the woman cannot appoint an agent to deliver the *get*, since that is not something she can do for herself. Therefore, she is only providing the husband with an agent of delivery, and it is not in her power to stipulate regarding the agent's assignment (*Tos. Rid; Meiri*).

Others contend that a woman is able to appoint an agent to deliver the *get* to her (*Rambam, Hil. Gerushin* 6:4[1]) by assigning

1. This mishnah seems to support *Rambam's* opinion, because if the wife is not the one who is appointing the agent, it is obvious that she cannot make stipulations regarding his commission, and the mishnah is superfluous (*Ran* ibid.; *Maggid Mishneh* to *Rambam* loc. cit.).

[ד] ,,הָבֵא לִי גִטִּי" — אוֹכֶלֶת בַּתְּרוּמָה עַד שֶׁיַּגִּיעַ גֵּט לְיָדָהּ. ,,הִתְקַבֵּל לִי גִטִּי" — אֲסוּרָה לֶאֱכוֹל בַּתְּרוּמָה מִיָּד. ,,הִתְקַבֵּל לִי גִטִּי בְּמָקוֹם פְּלוֹנִי" — אוֹכֶלֶת בַּתְּרוּמָה עַד שֶׁיַּגִּיעַ גֵּט לְאוֹתוֹ מָקוֹם. רַבִּי אֱלִיעֶזֶר אוֹסֵר מִיָּד.

ר' עובדיה מברטנורא

(ד) **הבא לי גטי אוכלת בתרומה.** אם אשת כהן היא, עד שיגיע גט לידה: **לאותו מקום.** שכך אמרה לו, לא תהא שלוחי אלא שם: **ורבי אליעזר אוסר מיד.** משפירש מאצלה. ורבי אליעזר לטעמיה (במשנה ג), דמכשר כשקבלו במקום אחר, דמראה מקום היא לו, ומשעת קבלה איגרשה לה, לפיכך משעה שפירש מלפניה אסורה, שמא מצאו חוץ לעיר וקבלו הימנו. ואין הלכה כרבי אליעזר:

יד אברהם

him to receive the *get* on her behalf with the stipulation that it not take effect until she receives it (*Rav* to *Gem.* 63b). Nevertheless, since the *get* does not take effect when the agent receives it, she does not care where it is given to him (*Tos. R' Akiva Eiger*).

4.

A non-*Kohen* is prohibited by Biblical law from eating *terumah* (*Lev.* 22:10). However, the passage says (ibid. v. 11), *And a Kohen, if he will acquire a soul* [*as*] *the acquisition of his money, he shall eat it,* which includes his wife (*Kiddushin* 5a), who can be acquired for *erusin* — the first step of marriage — with money (ibid. 1:1).

,,הָבֵא לִי גִטִּי" — *[If a woman said:] "Bring me my get,"*

The daughter of a non-*Kohen,* who was married to a *Kohen* [and may eat *terumah* only as long as she remains married to him], sent an agent to bring her *get* to her (*Rav*).

.אוֹכֶלֶת בַּתְּרוּמָה עַד שֶׁיַּגִּיעַ גֵּט לְיָדָהּ — *she may eat terumah until the get reaches her hand.*

Since the agent is not authorized to receive the *get* on her behalf, there is no possibility of it taking effect before she receives it. Therefore, she may continue to eat *terumah* until that occurs (*Meiri*).

.,,הִתְקַבֵּל לִי גִטִּי" — אֲסוּרָה לֶאֱכוֹל בַּתְּרוּמָה מִיָּד — *[If she said:] "Receive my get for me," she is forbidden to eat terumah immediately.*

If she authorized the agent to receive the *get* on her behalf, she may no longer eat *terumah,* because once he leaves her presence the possibility exists that he has already received the *get* for her and she is divorced (*Meiri*).

Although the principle of *chazakah* (presumptive status) dictates that, unless proven otherwise, a person is presumed to have retained his previous status, and in our case that she is still assumed to be married until we know for certain that the agent received the *get*, the Rabbis prohibited her to eat *terumah* because of another *chazakah* — that an agent fulfills his assignment. Despite the fact that the matter is not entirely in his hands, since the husband's consent to grant the divorce is not guaranteed, the Rabbis considered it enough of a probability to

4. [If a woman said:] "Bring me my *get*," she may eat *terumah* until the *get* reaches her hand. [If she said:] "Receive my *get* for me," she is forbidden to eat *terumah* immediately. [If she said:] "Receive my *get* for me in such and such a place," she may eat *terumah* until the *get* reaches that place. R' Eliezer prohibits [it] immediately.

YAD AVRAHAM

warrant the prohibition (*Tos.*).

"הִתְקַבֵּל לִי גִּטִּי בְּמָקוֹם פְּלוֹנִי" — *[If she said:] "Receive my get for me in such and such a place,"*

She told the agent: "Receive my *get* for me in city A, but sometimes you will find my husband in city B." This is understood to mean that he may receive it anywhere, but the divorce cannot take effect until he brings it to city A (*Gem.* 65a-b).

אוֹכֶלֶת בַּתְּרוּמָה עַד שֶׁיַּגִּיעַ גֵּט לְאוֹתוֹ מָקוֹם. — *she may eat terumah until the get reaches that place.*

She may eat *terumah* for as long as it should take the agent to reach city A [after which it is prohibited, because of the possibility that the *get* was given and then brought there] (*Meiri*).

Although the *get* did not yet take effect when it was given to the agent, the divorce is valid. This is because the wife's directive is understood to be a stipulation that the agent's receipt on her behalf is valid only if he brings the *get* to city A. This is similar to a case in which a man gives his wife a *get* and stipulates that it not take effect until after a set time — which is valid.

Alternatively, the mishnah is discussing a case in which she told the agent to take the *get* from the husband and bring it to city A, where he should appoint a second agent of delivery and receive it from him in her behalf (*Tos.* 65b s.v. גיטא).

רַבִּי אֱלִיעֶזֶר אוֹסֵר מִיָּד. — *R' Eliezer prohibits [it] immediately.*

R' Eliezer holds that she is forbidden to eat *terumah* immediately, in accordance with his opinion (mishnah 3) that her specification of a place for the receipt of the *get* is not meant as a binding stipulation and the *get* takes effect wherever he receives it (*Rav*). Even if she told the agent to go east where the husband is to be found, and he went west, she is prohibited to eat *terumah* immediately. This is because of the possibility that he may have encountered the husband as he was leaving, and received the *get* (ibid. from *Gem.* 65b).

5.

As noted earlier (commentary to 2:5), a *get* can only be designated as specifically intended for a particular woman at the behest of her husband. Similarly, an agent may deliver the *get* only in accordance with the husband's wishes (4:1), since the legitimacy of the *get* requires his consent (*Rambam, Hil. Gerushin* 1:2). Accordingly, it must be written, signed, and delivered upon the husband's instructions in order to be valid. The mishnah now discusses the laws governing these instructions.

[ה] **הָאוֹמֵר:** ,,כִּתְבוּ גֵט וּתְנוּ לְאִשְׁתִּי״, ,,גָּרְשׁוּהָ״, ,,כִּתְבוּ אִגֶּרֶת וּתְנוּ לָהּ״ — הֲרֵי אֵלּוּ יִכְתְּבוּ וְיִתְּנוּ. ,,פִּטְרוּהָ״, ,,פַּרְנְסוּהָ״, ,,עֲשׂוּ לָהּ כַּנִּמּוּס״, ,,עֲשׂוּ לָהּ כָּרָאוּי״ — לֹא אָמַר כְּלוּם.

בָּרִאשׁוֹנָה הָיוּ אוֹמְרִים: הַיּוֹצֵא בַקּוֹלָר וְאָמַר: ,,כִּתְבוּ גֵט לְאִשְׁתִּי״ — הֲרֵי אֵלּוּ יִכְתְּבוּ וְיִתְּנוּ. חָזְרוּ לוֹמַר: אַף הַמְפָרֵשׁ וְהַיּוֹצֵא בְשַׁיָּרָא.

ר׳ עובדיה מברטנורא

(ה) **כתבו אגרת וכו׳.** שהגט קרוי אגרת, שכך כתוב בו ואגרת שבוקין: **פטרוה לא אמר כלום.** דלמא לשון פטור וחובה קאמר, להקל מעליה חובות שחייבת: **פרנסוה.** לשון עשיית צרכיה כמו מוציאים לפרנסה וכו׳ (כתובות סט, א). הלכך לא ידעינן אי צרכי הגט הוא, שלא תהא זקוקה ליבם, אי צרכי מלבוש וכסות הוא: **בנימוס.** כחוק. לא ידעינן אי חק גט, אי חק מזון וכסות. וכן כראוי: **היוצא בקולר.** ליהרג בדין המלכות: **ואמר כתבו.** אף על פי שלא אמר תנו: **יכתבו ויתנו.** דאגב פחדיה טריד ולא פריש: **המפרש.** לים: **והיוצא בשיירא.** למדבריות:

יד אברהם

הָאוֹמֵר: ,,כִּתְבוּ גֵט וּתְנוּ לְאִשְׁתִּי״, — *[If] one says: "Write a get and give [it] to my wife,"*

A man told two people to write a *"get"* — a word which, although it literally refers to any document (such as גֵט שִׁחְרוּר, *a bill of emancipation*), when used alone, generally is understood to mean a divorce document — and give it to his wife (*Meiri*).

[Two people are necessary because, in preparing the *get*, they must sign as witnesses.]

,,גָּרְשׁוּהָ״, — *"Divorce her,"*

He used a term derived from גֵרוּשִׁין, which literally means *banishment*, but is commonly used to refer to a divorce (*Rashi*).

,,כִּתְבוּ אִגֶּרֶת וּתְנוּ לָהּ״ — *[or] "Write a letter and give [it] to her,"*

He referred to the *get* as a letter, which is the term used in the wording of the *get* itself: אִגֶּרֶת שְׁבוּקִין, *a letter of release* (*Rashi*).

הֲרֵי אֵלּוּ יִכְתְּבוּ וְיִתְּנוּ. — *they may write and give [it].*

[The witnesses may legitimately conclude that the husband is appointing them as agents to write a *get* for his wife and deliver it to her.] However, this is only if he had been discussing the topic of divorce prior to issuing these instructions. If not, the agents cannot be certain that his intention is for divorce (*Hasagos HaRavad* to *Rif; Beis Shmuel* to *Even HaEzer* 141:20).

,,פִּטְרוּהָ״, — *[If he said:] "Release her,"*

The husband told the agents to release his wife, which could mean from a debt, rather than from the marriage (*Rav*).

,,פַּרְנְסוּהָ״, — *"Provide for her,"*

This is another case, in which the husband told the agents to provide for his wife. This could mean to provide for her needs by having her divorced, thus preventing her from falling to *yibum* [the Biblically ordained marriage of a woman to the brother of her

5. [If] one says: "Write a *get* and give [it] to my wife," "Divorce her," [or] "Write a letter and give [it] to her," they may write and give [it]. [If he said:] "Release her," "Provide for her," "Do for her as is customary," [or] "Do for her as is proper," he did not say anything.

Originally, they said: [If] one goes out in chains and says: "Write a *get* for my wife," they write and give [it]. They later said: Also one who sets out [to sea] and one who leaves in a caravan.

YAD AVRAHAM

late husband, who died and left no children], or it could mean to provide for such needs as clothing (*Rav*).

,,עֲשׂוּ לָהּ כַּנִּמּוּס", ,,עֲשׂוּ לָהּ כָּרָאוּי" — *"Do for her as is customary," [or] "Do for her as is proper,"*

Here, too, the husband could be referring to a *get*, or to food and clothing (*Rav*).

לֹא אָמַר כְּלוּם. — *he did not say anything.*

It cannot be assumed that he appointed them to write and give a *get*, and if they do so, it is null (*Rambam, Hil. Gerushin* 2:10).

Other commentators seem to imply that if they write and deliver a *get* in response to any of these instructions, its validity would remain in doubt (*Rashi; Ran;* see *Beis Shmuel* to *Even HaEzer* 141:21).

בָּרִאשׁוֹנָה הָיוּ אוֹמְרִים: — *Originally, they said:*

This is mentioned in reference to the following mishnah, which states that if a healthy man instructed two people to write a *get* for his wife, they cannot assume that he also means that they should deliver it (*Meiri*).

הַיּוֹצֵא בַקּוֹלָר — *[If] one goes out in chains*

A man going out in chains to be put to death by the government (*Rav; Rashi; Tos. Rid; Meiri*).

The same law applies to one who is imprisoned for monetary offenses (*Yerushalmi*, cited in *Meiri; Rambam, Hil. Gerushin* 2:12; *Even HaEzer* 141:16).

וְאָמַר: ,,כִּתְבוּ גֵט לְאִשְׁתִּי" — *and says: "Write a get for my wife,"*

He issued instructions for the writing of a *get*, but not for its delivery (*Rav*).

הֲרֵי אֵלּוּ יִכְתְּבוּ וְיִתְּנוּ. — *they write and give [it].*

It is assumed that he meant that the *get* should be written and delivered, but that he did not express himself clearly because of his fear and confusion (*Rashi; Meiri*).

חָזְרוּ לוֹמַר: אַף הַמְפָרֵשׁ וְהַיּוֹצֵא בְשַׁיָּרָא. — *They later said: Also one who sets out [to sea] and one who leaves in a caravan.*

[The Rabbis subsequently added that one who sets out for a journey at sea or in the desert (*Rav*) is also assumed to be frightened and confused. Therefore, his instructions to write a *get* are also understood to include its delivery.]

רַבִּי שִׁמְעוֹן שְׁזוּרִי אוֹמֵר: אַף הַמְסֻכָּן.

[ו] **מִי** שֶׁהָיָה מֻשְׁלָךְ לַבּוֹר, וְאָמַר כָּל הַשּׁוֹמֵעַ אֶת קוֹלוֹ יִכְתֹּב גֵּט לְאִשְׁתּוֹ — הֲרֵי אֵלּוּ יִכְתְּבוּ וְיִתְּנוּ.

הַבָּרִיא שֶׁאָמַר: „כִּתְבוּ גֵט לְאִשְׁתִּי", רָצָה לְשַׂחֵק בָּהּ. מַעֲשֶׂה בְּבָרִיא אֶחָד שֶׁאָמַר: „כִּתְבוּ גֵט לְאִשְׁתִּי",

ר' עובדיה מברטנורא

המסוכן. חולה. והלכה כרבי שמעון שזורי:(ו) **ואמר כל השומע את קולו.** ופירש שמו ושם עירו: **רצה לשחק בה.** הואיל ולא אמר תנו: **מעשה בבריא.** מפרש בגמרא, דחסורי מחסרא והכי קתני, ואם הוכיח סופו על תחלתו, הרי זה גט, ומעשה נמי בבריא וכו'. והלכה כרבן שמעון בן גמליאל:

יד אברהם

רַבִּי שִׁמְעוֹן שְׁזוּרִי אוֹמֵר: אַף הַמְסֻכָּן. — *R' Shimon Shezuri says: Also one who is endangered.*

One who is ill (*Rav; Rashi*) is considered to be in danger (*Meiri; Tos. Yom Tov*) [and is thus assumed to be frightened and confused. Therefore, his directive to write a *get* for his wife is also understood to mean that they should write and deliver it].

Some authorities maintain that the mishnah refers only to one who became extremely ill very quickly (*Rambam, Hil. Gerushin* 2:12; *Even HaEzer* 141:16). Others contend that it also includes one who was ill for three days (*Tur Even HaEzer* 141; *Beis Shmuel* ibid. 22; *Taz* ibid. 13), and one who affirms that he is dangerously ill (*Ran*).

6.

מִי שֶׁהָיָה מֻשְׁלָךְ לַבּוֹר, — *[If] someone was thrown into a pit,*

[A man was in a pit, and could not be seen in order to be identified.]

וְאָמַר כָּל הַשּׁוֹמֵעַ אֶת קוֹלוֹ יִכְתֹּב גֵּט לְאִשְׁתּוֹ — — *and he said that whoever hears his voice should write a get for his wife,*

He instructed whoever hears his voice to write a *get* for his wife, specifying his name and the town where he lived (*Rav*), and her name and the town where she lived (*Meiri*), thereby appointing the listener an agent to write the *get* (*Meiri* from *Kesubos* 70b).

Some commentators hold that if he said, "Whoever wants to should write a *get* for my wife," it is not considered an appointment to be an agent, but only a statement of permission. Therefore, a *get* written in response to such a declaration would not be valid (*Rambam; Tos.*). Others contend that such a statement would also be understood as assigning the listener to be an agent (*Ran; Tos.*).

הֲרֵי אֵלּוּ יִכְתְּבוּ וְיִתְּנוּ. — *they shall write and give [it].*

Although those who hear his voice cannot see or recognize him, they may heed his instructions and write the *get*, because — under such pressing circumstances — we do not concern ourselves with the possibility of someone else [such as another wife of this

R' Shimon Shezuri says: Also one who is endangered.

6. [If] someone was thrown into a pit, and he said that whoever hears his voice should write a *get* for his wife, they shall write and give [it].

[If] a healthy man said: "Write a *get* for my wife," he desired to taunt her. It happened that a healthy man said: "Write a *get* for my wife,"

YAD AVRAHAM

man (*Gem.* 66a)] posing as him in order to cause this wife's divorce (*Meiri* from *Gem.* ibid.). The agents may also deliver the *get*, since these are circumstances similar to those of the previous mishnah, in which it is assumed that he meant to dictate the delivery of the *get*, as well as its writing, but forgot to do so in the confusion of the situation (*Tos. R' Akiva Eiger*).

Some authorities maintain that the possibility that they are hearing the voice of a demon must be considered, since they are wont to lurk in pits. Therefore, those present must see his shadow and a shadow of that shadow [since demons do not have a double shadow (*Gem.* 66a)] (*Rach* cited by *Ran; Rosh; Tur, Even HaEzer* 141). Others contend that this concern, too, is overridden by the urgency of the situation (*Rambam, Hil. Gerushin* 2:13).

הַבָּרִיא שֶׁאָמַר: ,,כִּתְבוּ גֵט לְאִשְׁתִּי״, — *[If] a healthy man said: "Write a get for my wife,"*

[A healthy man, who was under no pressure which would warrant confusion, told two people to write a *get* for his wife, but did not tell them to deliver it.]

רָצָה לְשַׂחֵק בָּהּ. — *he desired to taunt her.*[1]

It cannot be assumed that he wants the *get* delivered. However, it may be written and signed (*Meiri* to mishnah 5).

מַעֲשֶׂה בְּבָרִיא אֶחָד שֶׁאָמַר: — *It happened that a healthy man said:*

The text of the mishnah is defective and should read: *But if the end attests to the beginning* [i.e., subsequent events demonstrate that, at the time of the husband's instructions, he intended to commit suicide and was therefore in a state of confusion (*Meiri*)], *it is a get. Indeed, it happened that ...* (*Rav* from *Gem.* 66a).

,,כִּתְבוּ גֵט לְאִשְׁתִּי״, — *"Write a get for my wife,"*

[But he did not ask them to deliver it.]

1. The statement of the mishnah, *he desired to taunt her*, seems puzzling because that which he directed is taken seriously, and it is only the delivery of the *get* — which he did not dictate — that is not carried out (*Tos. R' Akiva Eiger*). [Perhaps we can answer this with the *Gemara* (18a) which states that a man does not write a *get* unless he intends to deliver it to his wife immediately. Thus, as long as it cannot be assumed that he wants it delivered, the only possible reason for his having it written is in order to taunt her.]

וְעָלָה לְרֹאשׁ הַגַּג, וְנָפַל וָמֵת. אָמַר רַבָּן שִׁמְעוֹן בֶּן גַּמְלִיאֵל: אָמְרוּ חֲכָמִים: אִם מֵעַצְמוֹ נָפַל — הֲרֵי זֶה גֵּט; אִם הָרוּחַ דְּחָאַתּוּ — אֵינוֹ גֵט.

[ז] **אָמַר** לִשְׁנַיִם: ,,תְּנוּ גֵט לְאִשְׁתִּי״, אוֹ לִשְׁלֹשָׁה: ,,כִּתְבוּ גֵט וּתְנוּ לְאִשְׁתִּי״, הֲרֵי אֵלּוּ יִכְתְּבוּ וְיִתְּנוּ.

אָמַר לִשְׁלֹשָׁה: ,,תְּנוּ גֵט לְאִשְׁתִּי״ — הֲרֵי אֵלּוּ יֹאמְרוּ לַאֲחֵרִים וְיִכְתְּבוּ, מִפְּנֵי שֶׁעֲשָׂאָן בֵּית דִּין; דִּבְרֵי רַבִּי מֵאִיר. וְזוֹ הֲלָכָה הֶעֱלָה רַבִּי חֲנִינָא אִישׁ

ר׳ עובדיה מברטנורא

(ז) **אמר לשנים תנו גט לאשתי.** אף על גב דלא אמר כתבו ותנו, הרי אלו יכתבו בעצמן, ולא יאמרו לסופר אחר שיכתוב, ולא לעדים לחתום, דלאו בית דין נינהו לצוות על אחרים אלא עדים נינהו, והן הן שלוחיו הן הן עדיו. ואם אמר לשלשה כתבו ותנו גט לאשתי, אף על פי שהן ראוין ליעשות בית דין, כיון דבהדיא אמר להו כתבו, לאו בית דין נינהו אלא עדים: **אמר לשלשה תנו.** ולא אמר כתבו: **הרי אלו יאמרו.** לעדים אחרים לכתוב ולחתום וליתן, מפני שעשאן בית דין:

יד אברהם

אִם הָרוּחַ דְּחָאַתּוּ — אֵינוֹ גֵט. — *if the wind pushed him, it is not a get.*

[If his fall was an accident, it cannot be assumed that he intended suicide when he issued his instructions. Therefore, his words must be interpreted strictly as dictating the writing of the *get*, but not its delivery.]

If it is unclear whether his fall was intentional, the sequence of events leads us to assume that it was, and if the *get* was delivered before he died, it takes effect (*Rambam, Hil. Gerushin* 2:13; see *Kesef Mishneh* ad loc.). However, if the fall occurred sometime after he issued his instructions, this assumption is no longer valid, and the *get* is null (*Kesef Mishneh* ibid.; *Meiri*).

וְעָלָה לְרֹאשׁ הַגַּג, וְנָפַל וָמֵת. — *and he went up to the top of the roof, and he fell and died.*

Immediately after issuing these instructions, he went up on a roof and fell off (*Rambam, Hil. Gerushin* 2:13; *Meiri*).

אָמַר רַבִּי שִׁמְעוֹן בֶּן גַּמְלִיאֵל: אָמְרוּ חֲכָמִים: אִם מֵעַצְמוֹ נָפַל — הֲרֵי זֶה גֵּט; — *Said Rabban Shimon ben Gamliel: The Sages said: If he fell on his own, it is a get;*

If he fell purposely, it is clear that this was his intention when he issued the instructions. Therefore, it can be assumed that his failure to specifically mention the delivery of the *get* was only due to his confusion because of the situation (*Meiri*).

7.

Although the husband's instructions to write a *get* do not include its delivery (mishnah 6), his instructions to deliver a *get* are understood to be a directive to write it as well [if there is none already written].

6
7

and he went up to the top of the roof, and he fell and died. Said Rabban Shimon ben Gamliel: The Sages said: If he fell on his own, it is a *get;* if the wind pushed him, it is not a *get.*

7. [If] someone said to two [persons]: "Give a *get* to my wife," or to three: "Write a *get* and give [it] to my wife," they shall write and give [it].

[If] he said to three: "Give a *get* to my wife," they may tell others to write [it], because he designated them as a court; [these are] the words of R' Meir. R' Chanina of Ono brought this law

YAD AVRAHAM

As explained previously (preface to mishnah 5), it is the husband's instructions which validate the writing, signing, and delivering of a *get.* Therefore, they must be done in strict accordance with those instructions.

אָמַר לִשְׁנַיִם: ,,תְּנוּ גֵט לְאִשְׁתִּי״, — *[If] someone said to two [persons]: "Give a get to my wife,"*

If a man instructed two others to give his wife a *get* — which means that they should write, sign, and give it (*Meiri*), since that is the only way to fulfill his directive (*Tos. Rid*).

אוֹ לִשְׁלֹשָׁה: ,,כִּתְבוּ גֵט וּתְנוּ לְאִשְׁתִּי״, — *or to three: "Write a get and give [it] to my wife,"*

[He explicitly told a group of three people to write a *get* and give it to his wife.]

הֲרֵי אֵלּוּ יִכְתְּבוּ וְיִתְּנוּ. — *they shall write and give [it].*

They themselves must write, sign, and deliver the *get* [i.e., one of them must write it, two must sign it, and one deliver it (*Meiri*)], because the husband only appointed them as witnesses to sign the *get* and agents to write and deliver it, but not as a court to see that it be executed by appointing others to perform those functions (*Rav; Meiri*) [and a *get* must be executed by order of the husband's instructions so as to be valid].

Others maintain that only the signing and delivery of the *get* must be done by the appointed witnesses, but they may appoint another to write it. This is because the writing to which he refers is the signing of the *get* (*Tos.* 67a s.v. מתניתין).

אָמַר לִשְׁלֹשָׁה: ,,תְּנוּ גֵט לְאִשְׁתִּי״ — *[If] he said to three: "Give a get to my wife,"*

He instructed a group of three people to give a *get* to his wife, but did not specify to them that they must also write it (*Rav*).

הֲרֵי אֵלּוּ יֹאמְרוּ לַאֲחֵרִים וְיִכְתְּבוּ, מִפְּנֵי שֶׁעֲשָׂאָן בֵּית דִּין; דִּבְרֵי רַבִּי מֵאִיר. — *they may tell others to write [it], because he designated them as a court; [these are] the words of R' Meir.*

They may appoint others to write, sign, and deliver the *get,* because he meant to appoint them as a court only to see that the *get* be executed, but not to specify that they must personally perform these functions (*Meiri*).

אונו מבֵּית הָאֲסוּרִין: מְקֻבָּל אֲנִי בְּאוֹמֵר לִשְׁלֹשָׁה: ,,תְּנוּ גֵט לְאִשְׁתִּי״, שֶׁיֹּאמְרוּ לַאֲחֵרִים וְיִכְתְּבוּ, מִפְּנֵי שֶׁעֲשָׂאָן בֵּית דִּין. אָמַר רַבִּי יוֹסֵי: נוֹמֵינוּ לַשָּׁלִיחַ: אַף אָנוּ מְקֻבָּלִין, שֶׁאֲפִלּוּ אָמַר לְבֵית דִּין הַגָּדוֹל שֶׁבִּירוּשָׁלַיִם: ,,תְּנוּ גֵט לְאִשְׁתִּי״, שֶׁיִּלְמְדוּ, וְיִכְתְּבוּ, וְיִתֵּנוּ.

אָמַר לַעֲשָׂרָה: ,,כִּתְבוּ גֵט לְאִשְׁתִּי״ — אֶחָד כּוֹתֵב וּשְׁנַיִם חוֹתְמִין. ,,כֻּלְּכֶם כִּתְבוּ״ — אֶחָד כּוֹתֵב וְכֻלָּם חוֹתְמִין. לְפִיכָךְ, אִם מֵת אֶחָד מֵהֶן — הֲרֵי זֶה גֵּט בָּטֵל.

ר׳ עובדיה מברטנורא

מבית האסורים. משמו של רבי עקיבא שהיה חבוש בבית האסורים: **נומינו לשליח.** אמרנו לרבי חנינא, שנעשה שליח בהלכה זו לאמרה בבית המדרש: **ילמדו.** אם אינם יודעים לכתוב, ילמדו לכתוב עד שיכתבוהו הן בעצמן:

יד אברהם

וְזוֹ הֲלָכָה הֶעֱלָה רַבִּי חֲנִינָא אִישׁ אוֹנוֹ מִבֵּית הָאֲסוּרִין: מְקֻבָּל אֲנִי בְּאוֹמֵר לִשְׁלֹשָׁה: ,,תְּנוּ גֵט לְאִשְׁתִּי״, שֶׁיֹּאמְרוּ לַאֲחֵרִים וְיִכְתְּבוּ, מִפְּנֵי שֶׁעֲשָׂאָן בֵּית דִּין. — *R′ Chanina of Ono brought this law from prison: I have a tradition concerning one who says to three: "Give a get to my wife," that they may tell others to write [it], because he designated them as a court.*

He had heard this law from R′ Akiva, who stated it while in prison[1] (*Rav*).

אָמַר רַבִּי יוֹסֵי: נוֹמֵינוּ לַשָּׁלִיחַ: — *Said R′ Yose: We said to the messenger:*

We told R′ Chanina, who had been sent to state this law in the study hall (*Rav*).

אַף אָנוּ מְקֻבָּלִין, שֶׁאֲפִלּוּ אָמַר לְבֵית דִּין הַגָּדוֹל שֶׁבִּירוּשָׁלַיִם: ,,תְּנוּ גֵט לְאִשְׁתִּי״, שֶׁיִּלְמְדוּ, וְיִכְתְּבוּ, וְיִתֵּנוּ. — *We also have a tradition that even if he said to the Great Court in Jerusalem: "Give a get to my wife," they must learn, and write, and give [it].*

Even if the husband instructed a court of law to give a *get* to his wife, they themselves must write, sign, and deliver it. If they do not know how to write [which is not an outlandish case, since the qualifications of a judge do not include the ability to write (*Rambam Commentary*)], *they learn how to do so, and then write it* (*Meiri*). This is because an agent who was instructed to carry out an assignment without being given any tangible object with which to fulfill it [such as in this case, in which the *get* has not yet been written] cannot appoint another

1. [R′ Akiva was incarcerated by the Romans for teaching Torah in defiance of their edict.]

6 from prison: I have a tradition concerning one who
7 says to three: "Give a *get* to my wife," that they may tell others to write [it], because he designated them as a court. Said R' Yose: We said to the messenger: We also have a tradition that even if he said to the Great Court in Jerusalem: "Give a *get* to my wife," they must learn, and write, and give [it].

[If] he said to ten: "Write a *get* for my wife," one writes and two sign. [If he said:] "All of you write," one writes and they all sign. Therefore, if one of them died, the *get* is null.

YAD AVRAHAM

agent to replace him (*Gem.* 66b; *Rashi* ad loc.).

Others explain that any assignment for an incomplete function — such as the writing of a *get*, which does not effect a divorce until it is delivered — cannot be transferred to another agent. Although the agents in this case were also appointed to deliver the *get*, that is a separate assignment from its writing (*Mordechai* 120; see *Tif. Yis.* 1).

Even if the husband told them explicitly to tell a scribe to write a *get*, they cannot do so, because the assignment to write a *get* cannot be transferred to another agent, even on the husband's request (*Gem.* 66b-67a).

אָמַר לַעֲשָׂרָה: „כִּתְבוּ גֵט לְאִשְׁתִּי" — *[If] he said to ten: "Write a get for my wife,"*

A man told a group of ten people to write a *get* for his wife and sign it (*Tif. Yis.*).

אֶחָד כּוֹתֵב וּשְׁנַיִם חוֹתְמִין. — *one writes and two sign.*

He is understood to mean that any of those present should write and sign the *get*, not that they must all participate (*Meiri*).

„כֻּלְּכֶם כִּתְבוּ" — אֶחָד כּוֹתֵב וְכֻלָּם חוֹתְמִין. — *[If he said:] "All of you write," one writes and they all sign.*

If he specified that they must all write the *get*, he means that one of them should write it and all should sign (*Meiri*). His intention is that only two must serve as witnesses, but the others must sign for the sake of fulfilling his stipulation. Therefore, if one of them signed on a later date than the others, or one turned out to be an unqualified witness [which would normally invalidate the entire group (*Sanhedrin* 9a)], the *get* is still valid (*Gem.* 18b).

לְפִיכָךְ, אִם מֵת אֶחָד מֵהֶן — הֲרֵי זֶה גֵט בָּטֵל. — *Therefore, if one of them died, the get is null.*

If one of them died before he signed the *get*, it is null (*Rav*), because the husband's stipulation to its validity was not met (*Tos. Rid*).

פרק שביעי

Chapter Seven

[א] **מִי** שֶׁאֲחָזוֹ קֻרְדְּיָקוֹס וְאָמַר: ,,כִּתְבוּ גֵט לְאִשְׁתִּי" — לֹא אָמַר כְּלוּם. אָמַר: ,,כִּתְבוּ גֵט לְאִשְׁתִּי" וַאֲחָזוֹ קֻרְדְּיָקוֹס, וְחָזַר וְאָמַר: ,,אַל תִּכְתְּבוּ" — אֵין דְּבָרָיו הָאַחֲרוֹנִים כְּלוּם.

נִשְׁתַּתֵּק, וְאָמְרוּ לוֹ: ,,נִכְתֹּב גֵּט לְאִשְׁתְּךָ?" וְהִרְכִּין בְּרֹאשׁוֹ — בּוֹדְקִין אוֹתוֹ שְׁלֹשָׁה

ר' עובדיה מברטנורא

פרק שביעי – מי שאחזו. (א) מי שאחזו קורדייקוס. שנתבלבלה דעתו מחמת שד השולט על השותה יין חדש: **אין בדבריו האחרונים כלום.** ואין צריך לחזור ולשאלו אחר שנתישבה דעתו, אלא כותבים הגט וסומכים על דבריו הראשונים. ומיהו, כל זמן שדעתו מבולבלת אין כותבין הגט: **הרכין.** הטה: **בודקין אותו.** בדברים אחרים:

יד אברהם

1.

מִי שֶׁאֲחָזוֹ קֻרְדְּיָקוֹס — *One who was seized by delirium*

He was affected by a type of delirium caused by a demon that has power over one who drinks new wine (*Rav* from *Gem.* 67b) or by any similar state of mental disorder (*Meiri;* cf. *Rambam*).

וְאָמַר: ,,כִּתְבוּ גֵט לְאִשְׁתִּי" — *and said: "Write a get for my wife,"*

The same is true even if he said: "Write a *get* for my wife and give it to her" (*Tos.* 67b).

לֹא אָמַר כְּלוּם. — *did not say anything.*

His instructions are not to be followed, because he issued them when he was mentally incompetent (*Rambam, Hil. Gerushin* 2:14). If a *get* was written in response to these instructions, it is not valid (*Beis Shmuel* to *Even HaEzer* 121:1).

אָמַר: ,,כִּתְבוּ גֵט לְאִשְׁתִּי" וַאֲחָזוֹ קֻרְדְּיָקוֹס, — *[If] he said: "Write a get for my wife," and was seized by delirium,*

This is another case. A healthy man instructed an agent to write and give a *get* to his wife; he then became delirious. [Had he merely told the agent to write it, the agent cannot give it to her even if the husband remains healthy, because the fact that he did not instruct the agent to do so indicates that he wants the *get* written only for the sake of taunting her (see 6:6).]

Others interpret the mishnah as meaning that the man who is giving these instructions is gravely ill; thus, his directive to write a *get* is construed to mean that it should also be delivered, since it is presumed that he became confused due to the illness and therefore expressed himself unclearly (see commentary to 6:5). Subsequently, he was seized by delirium (*Meiri*).

וְחָזַר וְאָמַר: ,,אַל תִּכְתְּבוּ" — *and he then said: "Do not write it,"*

[While in the grip of his mental disorder, he retracted his instructions to write the *get*.]

אֵין דְּבָרָיו הָאַחֲרוֹנִים כְּלוּם. — *his latter words are worthless.*

7
1

1. One who was seized by delirium and said: "Write a *get* for my wife," did not say anything. [If] he said: "Write a *get* for my wife," and was seized by delirium, and he then said: "Do not write it," his latter words are worthless.

[If one] became mute, and they said to him: "Shall we write a *get* for your wife?" and he nodded with his head, they test him three

YAD AVRAHAM

When he is cured from the delirium, the *get* may be written and delivered, and he need not reiterate his instructions (*Rav* from *Gem.* 70b). [However, his instructions should not be carried out as long as he is still delirious.]

On the other hand, if a healthy person issued such instructions and then fell asleep, the *get* may be written and delivered even while he is sleeping. Since sleep is a state from which a person awakens on his own, he is considered even then to be in a state of mental competence, unlike the delirious person, who needs a special cure to recover (*Gem.* ibid.).

If the *get* was written and delivered before he recovered from his mental disorder, its status is a subject of controversy among the authorities. Some hold that it is void under Rabbinic law [i.e., his wife may not remarry; however, if she does, the marriage is valid] (*Rambam, Hil. Gerushin* 2:15, explained by *Maggid Mishneh* ibid. 7; see *Rambam* ad loc.), but is Biblically valid, because the husband was sane when he issued his instructions, and those who write and deliver the *get* are thus duly authorized (*Bach* to *Even HaEzer* 121; *Chelkas Mechokek* ibid. 2; *Beis Shmuel* ad loc. 4; *Or Same'ach* to *Hil. Gerushin* 2:14).

Others contend that if the *get* was written or delivered when the husband was mentally incompetent, it is totally void even by Biblical law (*Tur, Even HaEzer* 121; *Perishah* ad loc. 5). A third opinion is that if the delirium is curable, a *get* written or delivered while he is in that state is void only by Rabbinic law; but, if it is incurable, the *get* is null even according to Biblical law (*Shulchan Aruch* ibid. 2).

נִשְׁתַּתֵּק, — *[If one] became mute,*

A man was in possession of his faculties, but was struck dumb (*Rashi*).

This does not refer only to the case of delirium above; it applies to any husband who suddenly became mute (*Meiri*).

וְאָמְרוּ לוֹ: ,,נִכְתֹּב גֵּט לְאִשְׁתְּךָ?״ — *and they said to him: "Shall we write a get for your wife?"*

A mute is likened to a gravely ill man (*Meiri*) [in that when he gives instructions to write a *get*, it is automatically understood that he also wants it delivered to his wife, as explained above. Therefore, they need not explicitly ask him about the delivery (ibid.)].

וְהִרְכִּין בְּרֹאשׁוֹ — *and he nodded with his head,*

Indicating his assent (ibid.). Although there is a rule that instructions to write a *get* must be transmitted vocally (*Gem.* 72a), physical movements which indicate the husband's approval are considered the equivalent of oral communication (*Tos.* 72a, s.v. קולו), since he transmits his instructions directly rather than

פְּעָמִים: אִם אָמַר עַל „לָאו״ „לָאו״, וְעַל „הֵן״ „הֵן״ — הֲרֵי אֵלּוּ יִכְתְּבוּ וְיִתְּנוּ.

[ב] **אָמְרוּ** לוֹ: „נִכְתֹּב גֵּט לְאִשְׁתְּךָ?״ וְאָמַר לָהֶם: „כְּתֹבוּ״; אָמְרוּ לַסּוֹפֵר, וְכָתַב, וְלָעֵדִים, וְחָתְמוּ; אַף עַל פִּי שֶׁכְּתָבוּהוּ וַחֲתָמוּהוּ וּנְתָנוּהוּ לוֹ, וְחָזַר וּנְתָנוֹ לָהּ — הֲרֵי הַגֵּט בָּטֵל, עַד שֶׁיֹּאמַר לַסּוֹפֵר: „כְּתֹב״, וְלָעֵדִים: „חֲתֹמוּ״.

ר׳ עובדיה מברטנורא

הרי אלו יכתבו ויתנו. אם הרכין על הגט הרכנת הין: **(ב) אמרו לו.** לבריא או לשכיב מרע חכם: **נכתוב גט לאשתך.** שלא תזקק ליבם:

יד אברהם

through the medium of a written statement (*Rosh* to 66b).

Some maintain that instructions written by one who can speak are also tantamount to an oral directive, while others contend that all written instructions are inefficacious. Another opinion is that even instructions issued by nodding are generally ineffective, but that the Rabbis were lenient in the case of a mute (*Rosh* ibid.).

There is another view that distinguishes between a deaf-mute and a mute who can hear. The communications of the former [who is considered mentally incompetent (see commentary to 2:5)] are not acceptable in writing or by body motion, whereas the latter may communicate in either way and it is tantamount to speaking (see *Beis Shmuel* to *Even HaEzer* 120:5).

בּוֹדְקִין אוֹתוֹ שְׁלֹשָׁה פְּעָמִים: — *they test him three times.*

To confirm his lucidity, he is tested by being asked three questions to which the correct answer is "yes" and three others whose answer ought to be "no," totaling six questions. The correct answers to the questions are arranged in the following order to make them more difficult: (1) no (2) yes (3) yes (4) no (5) no (6) yes (*Gem.* 70b). If one jumbled the questions in a different order, it is also sufficient (*Beur HaGra; Even HaEzer* 121 9).

An approach recommended by the *Gemara* (70b) is to ask him if he would like them to pick for him specific fruits which are known to be out-of-season at that time (*Tos.* 71a s.v. אלא). This type of question is considered to be difficult for him to answer, and it is sufficient to consecutively ask three such questions whose answers should be "yes" and three which should be "no" (*Tos.* 70b s.v. דבר ר׳ ישמעאל). Others contend that even these questions must be asked out of order (*Tur, Even HaEzer* 121).

The same system may be used to test anyone whose mental competence is under question (*Meiri*).

אִם אָמַר עַל „לָאו״ „לָאו״, וְעַל „הֵן״ „הֵן״ — הֲרֵי אֵלּוּ יִכְתְּבוּ וְיִתְּנוּ. — *If he said "no" for a "no," and "yes" for a "yes," they may write and give [it].*

If he had nodded to the question of whether a *get* should be written [and established his lucidity by correctly responding to each of the questions], the *get* may be written and delivered (*Rav*).

7 times. If he said "no" for a "no," and "yes" for
2 a "yes," they may write and give [it].

2. [If] they said to him: "Shall we write a *get* for your wife?" and he said to them: "Write," [and] they told a scribe, and he wrote; or witnesses, and they signed, although they wrote it, signed it, and gave it to him, and he, in turn, gave it to her, the *get* is void unless he says to the scribe: "Write," and to the witnesses: "Sign."

YAD AVRAHAM

2.

As stated previously (6:7), if a man tells two people to give a *get* to his wife, they themselves must write, sign, and deliver it in order for the divorce to be valid. If he said this to a group of three men, R' Meir maintains that they become designated as a court to oversee the execution of the *get*, and it is not necessary that they perform these functions themselves. R' Yose, however, maintains that even in such a case they must do it themselves, because an appointment to write and give a *get* cannot be transferred to another agent.

אָמְרוּ לוֹ: „נִכְתֹּב גֵּט לְאִשְׁתְּךָ?" — *[If] they said to him: "Shall we write a get for your wife?"*

Two or three men (*Rambam, Hil. Gerushin* 2:5 from *Gem.* 72a; see below s.v. הרי) asked a man who was healthy — or gravely ill, but mentally sound — if he wants them to write a *get* for his wife (*Rav*).

If the man was healthy, the case is that he was leaving on a long, dangerous trip with a caravan. In either case, the man must have been childless, and is doing so to benefit his wife by divorcing her, so that in the event of his death, she need not marry his brother in accordance with the laws of *yibum* (see footnote to 2:7 s.v. וִיבִמְתָּהּ) (*Meiri*).

וְאָמַר לָהֶם: „כִּתְבוּ"; — *and he said to them: "Write,"*

The husband told them to write it — or even to write and deliver it (*Gem.* 72a; *Rashi* ad loc. s.v. כולה ר' יוסי).

אָמְרוּ לַסּוֹפֵר, וְכָתַב, וְלָעֵדִים, וְחָתְמוּ; — *[and] they told* (lit. *said to*) *a scribe, and he wrote; or witnesses, and they signed,*

They told a scribe to write it, or other witnesses to sign it, rather than doing it themselves (*Meiri*).

אַף עַל פִּי שֶׁכְּתָבוּהוּ, וַחֲתָמוּהוּ, וּנְתָנוּהוּ לוֹ, וְחָזַר וּנְתָנוֹ לָהּ — *although they wrote it, signed it, and gave it to him, and he, in turn, gave it to her,*

[The scribe wrote the *get*, or the witnesses signed it, and the husband gave it to his wife, thereby indicating that he approved of the manner in which his instructions were carried out.]

הֲרֵי הַגֵּט בָּטֵל, עַד שֶׁיֹּאמַר לַסּוֹפֵר: „כְּתֹב", וְלָעֵדִים: „חֲתֹמוּ". — *the get is void unless he says to the scribe: "Write," and to the witnesses: "Sign."*

[ג] ,,זֶה גִּטֵּךְ אִם מַתִּי״, ,,זֶה גִּטֵּךְ אִם מַתִּי מֵחֹלִי זֶה״, ,,זֶה גִּטֵּךְ לְאַחַר מִיתָה״ — לֹא אָמַר כְּלוּם.

,,מֵהַיּוֹם אִם מַתִּי״, ,,מֵעַכְשָׁיו אִם מַתִּי״ — הֲרֵי זֶה גֵּט; ,,מֵהַיּוֹם וּלְאַחַר מִיתָה״ — גֵּט וְאֵינוֹ גֵּט. אִם מֵת — חוֹלֶצֶת, וְלֹא מִתְיַבֶּמֶת.

ר׳ עובדיה מברטנורא

(ג) **זה גטך אם מתי.** לא אמר כלום. דמשמע לכשאמות, ואין גט לאחר מיתה: **מחולי זה.** משמע מחולי זה ואילך, וכיון שמת מתוך החולי, נמצא שאין הגט חל אלא לאחר מיתה: **מהיום ולאחר מיתה גט ואינו גט.** מספקא לן אי תנאה הוי, מהיום אם אמות, וכיון שמת נתקיים התנאי ונמצא שהוא גט משעת נתינתו, אי חזרה הוי, שחזר בו ממאי דאמר מהיום, ואמר לאחר מיתה יהא גט, ואינו כלום, כיון דלא אמר מהיום אם מתי: **חולצת.** שמא אינו גט: **ולא מתיבמת.** שמא גט הוא, והויא לה גרושת אחיו, וקיימא עליה באסור כרת:

יד אברהם

Only those whom the husband appoints personally may carry out his assignment to write and deliver the *get*. This is in accordance with the view of R' Yose, who maintains that agents who are instructed to write and deliver a *get* may not appoint someone else in their place, since there is no tangible object for them to give over to the second pair (*Gem.* 72a; see commentary to 6:7).

Others opine that the mishnah rules out the substitution of another pair of agents only in a case in which there were only two agents, or the husband had told them explicitly to write the *get*. However, if he told three agents to deliver the *get*, they may appoint others to carry out his instructions in their place, in accordance with the view of R' Meir (6:7), that it is as if he had made them a court to attend to the execution of the *get*. Nevertheless, the last statement of the mishnah — that the *get* is void unless he personally instructs the scribe and the witnesses — definitely follows the opinion of R' Yose, because according to R' Meir, it should have said that the *get* is void unless he tells three people to give a *get* to his wife (*Gem.* 71b).

3.

The discussion in this mishnah is based upon the *halachah*, stated earlier (1:6), that a *get* cannot take effect after the husband's death. The mishnah analyzes specific cases to determine if the *get* is disqualified by this rule.

,,זֶה גִּטֵּךְ אִם מַתִּי״, — *[If a man said:] "This is your get if I die,"*

A healthy man gave his wife a *get* and stipulated that it should take effect if he dies (*Rambam, Hil. Gerushin* 9:12), which is tantamount to saying that it be operative only after his death (*Rav* from *Gem.* 72a).

,,זֶה גִּטֵּךְ אִם מַתִּי מֵחֹלִי זֶה״, — *"This is your get if I die from this illness of mine,"*

A sick man stipulated that the *get* should take effect if he dies from his current illness (*Rambam* ibid.).

7
3

3. [If a man said:] "This is your *get* if I die," "This is your *get* if I die from this illness of mine," [or] "This is your *get* after [my] death," he has not said anything.

[If he said:] "[The *get* should take effect] from today if I die," [or] "from now if I die," it is a *get;* "from today and after [my death]," it is a *get* and not a *get.* If he dies, she performs *chalitzah,* but not *yibum.*

YAD AVRAHAM

In other versions, the text reads: זֶה גִּטֵּךְ מֵחֹלִי זֶה — *This is your get from this illness of mine;* i.e., he stipulates that the *get* should take effect after his illness. Since he died from that illness, the consequence of his stipulation would be that the *get* should take effect after his death (*Rav*).

,,זֶה גִּטֵּךְ לְאַחַר מִיתָה'' — *[or] "This is your get after [my] death,"*

These cases are comparable to the husband dictating explicitly that the *get* take effect only after his death (*Tos. Yom Tov*).

These stipulations are binding whether they were written in the *get* or stated orally at the time of delivery (*Meiri* from *Gem.* 72b).

לֹא אָמַר כְּלוּם. — *he has not said anything.*

The *get* is void, because it cannot take effect after the husband's death (*Rav;* see 1:6).

R' Yose maintains that the date written on the *get* is tantamount to a directive that it take effect beginning that day (*Bava Basra* 7:8). Therefore, all the instructions listed above are understood to be stipulations to the *get's* retroactive effectiveness from the date written upon it, and they are thus analogous to the following cases in the mishnah, in which this was stated explicitly (*Gem.* 72a).

,,מֵהַיּוֹם אִם מַתִּי'', ,,מֵעַכְשָׁיו אִם מַתִּי'' — הֲרֵי זֶה גֵּט; — *[If he said:] "[The get should take effect] from today if I die," [or] "from now if I die," it is a get;*

If he said explicitly that the *get* should take effect immediately, the words *if I die* are understood as stipulating the *get's* retroactivity at the time of his death, and not as designating when the divorce should take effect (*Gem.* 72a).

If he said, "... from today if I die," it is possible that he might have meant that it should take effect only after that day, and thus, if he dies on that day itself, it is questionable whether the *get* takes effect at all (*Tos.* 72a s.v. מהיום).

,,מֵהַיּוֹם וּלְאַחַר מִיתָה'' — *"from today and after [my] death,"*

If he worded his instructions in this manner, it is unclear whether the designated time for the divorce is that day, and the words *and after death* are meant as a stipulation — so that if he dies, the *get* takes retroactively — or whether the latter phrase was meant to reject the first, and to set the time for divorce after his death — which is not valid (*Rav*).

The same is true if he said: "from now and after [my] death" (*Tos. R' Akiva Eiger*).

גֵּט וְאֵינוֹ גֵּט. — *it is a get and not a get.*

[The *get* is considered valid in certain respects, but not in others.]

אִם מֵת — חוֹלֶצֶת, וְלֹא מִתְיַבֶּמֶת. — *If he dies, she performs chalitzah, but not yibum.*

"זֶה גִּטֵּךְ מֵהַיּוֹם אִם מַתִּי מֵחֹלִי זֶה", וְעָמַד וְהָלַךְ בַּשּׁוּק, וְחָלָה וָמֵת — אוֹמְדִין אוֹתוֹ: אִם מֵחֲמַת חֹלִי הָרִאשׁוֹן מֵת — הֲרֵי זֶה גֵּט; וְאִם לָאו — אֵינוֹ גֵּט.

[ד] **לֹא** תִתְיַחֵד עִמּוֹ אֶלָּא בִּפְנֵי עֵדִים, אֲפִלּוּ עֶבֶד, אֲפִלּוּ שִׁפְחָה, חוּץ מִשִּׁפְחָתָהּ, מִפְּנֵי שֶׁלִּבָּהּ גַּס בָּהּ בְּשִׁפְחָתָהּ.

ר' עובדיה מברטנורא

(ד) **לא תתיחד עמו.** זה שנתן גט ואמר לה מהיום אם מתי, לא תתייחד עמו, שמא יבא עליה ותהא צריכה גט שני, דחיישינן שמא בעל לשם קדושין:

יד אברהם

[Generally, when a husband dies childless, his wife is subject to *yibum* — marrying her husband's brother — until he releases her through the ceremony of *chalitzah* (*Deut.* 25:5).] In our case, however, the brother may not marry her, because the *get* may have been valid, thus rendering her his brother's divorcee, who is forbidden to him. She may also not marry anyone else, because the *get* may have been ineffective, and she is therefore bound to the husband's brother for *yibum* or *chalitzah*. Consequently, she has no choice but to perform *chalitzah* (*Rav*).

"זֶה גִּטֵּךְ מֵהַיּוֹם אִם מַתִּי מֵחֹלִי זֶה", — *[If he said:] "This is your get from today if I die from this illness of mine,"*

[A man who was dangerously ill gave his wife a *get* with the provision that it take effect only if he dies from that sickness.]

וְעָמַד וְהָלַךְ בַּשּׁוּק, וְחָלָה וָמֵת — *and then he rose and went in the marketplace, and became ill and died,*

[He recovered from his illness enough to go out, but then became sick again and died.]

אוֹמְדִין אוֹתוֹ: אִם מֵחֲמַת חֹלִי הָרִאשׁוֹן מֵת — הֲרֵי זֶה גֵּט; — *we assess him: if he died from his first illness, it is a get;*

If he died without fully recovering from his first illness, the stipulation *if I die from this illness* has been fulfilled, because the words *from this illness* mean while still stricken by the illness, and not that the illness must be the cause of death. Therefore, the *get* takes effect (*Rashi* 73a s.v. מאי שנא רישא).

Others contend that it must be concluded that the first illness was the actual cause of death in order for his condition to be met and the *get* to be valid (*Rashba* to 73a; *Ran* ad loc.; see *Tos. R' Akiva Eiger*).

וְאִם לָאו — אֵינוֹ גֵּט. — *if not, it is not a get.*

[If he had fully recovered from the first illness, the stipulation that he die from that illness has not been met and the *get* is ineffective.]

Some commentators maintain that if he walked on his own without support, it is assumed that he has recovered from his first illness, and the *get* is invalid. Only if he was walking with a support is there a question whether he has recovered, thus requiring an assessment (*Rashi* 73a s.v. לא סבירא להו; *Ran; Meiri*). Others contend that the assessment is required even if he walked on his own (*Tos.* 72b s.v. אמר ר' הונא;

7
4

[If he said:] "This is your *get* from today if I die from this illness of mine," and then he rose and went in the marketplace, and became ill and died, we assess him: if he died from his first illness, it is a *get;* if not, it is not a *get.*

4. She should not be alone with him unless [it is] in the presence of witnesses — even a slave, even a female slave — except her female slave, because she is comfortable with her.

YAD AVRAHAM

Ramban ibid.; *Rambam, Hil. Gerushin* 9:18).

If he had not recovered from the first illness, the *get* takes effect even if it was cured while he was bedridden and he died from a second illness [because it is understood that he wanted the *get* to be effective in such a case] (*Gem.* 72b; see *Meiri; Rambam* loc. cit.).

4.

לֹא תִתְיַחֵד עִמּוֹ — *She should not be alone with him*

This refers to the man discussed in the previous mishnah, who gave his wife a *get* and said that it should take effect retroactively from that day if he dies. She should not be alone with him from the time he gives the *get* until he recovers from his illness or dies, because this may lead them to have relations. Such relations would be suspected of having been done for the purpose of *erusin.* Therefore, if two men observed them secluding themselves, they would serve as witnesses to that *erusin,* and a new *get* would be required. Even if there are no witnesses, intimacy between them is forbidden, because the *get* may take effect when he dies, and revoke their first marriage retroactively (*Rashi; Meiri*).

Others contend that if they did live together it would nullify the original *get* (*Rambam, Hil. Gerushin* 8:2), because it would be a clear indication of a decision to revoke it (*Tos. Rid* to 76b).

אֶלָּא בִּפְנֵי עֵדִים, — *unless [it is] in the presence of witnesses* —

[If there is someone else with them, there is no fear that they will have relations. Although the mishnah uses the word *witnesses* in the plural, this is not to imply that two qualified male witnesses or even that two people are required. Rather, the term witnesses is a generic word meaning whatever testimony is required for the situation under discussion. In this case, one witness is sufficient to allay the fear that the woman and her husband may engage in intimacy (*Tos. Yom Tov*).

אֲפִלּוּ עֶבֶד, אֲפִלּוּ שִׁפְחָה, — *even a slave, even a female slave* —

[Even the presence of a male or female slave is sufficient to deter them from intimacy.]

Someone who can enter and leave their room at will is also considered an adequate deterrent (*Tif. Yis.*).

חוּץ מִשִּׁפְחָתָהּ, מִפְּנֵי שֶׁלִּבָּהּ גַּס בָּהּ בְּשִׁפְחָתָהּ. — *except her female slave, because she is comfortable with her* (lit., *her heart is close to her*).

[The presence of the wife's female

גיטין
ז/ה

מַה הִיא בְּאוֹתָן הַיָּמִים? רַבִּי יְהוּדָה אוֹמֵר: כְּאֵשֶׁת אִישׁ לְכָל דְּבָרֶיהָ. רַבִּי יוֹסֵי אוֹמֵר: מְגֹרֶשֶׁת וְאֵינָהּ מְגֹרֶשֶׁת.

[ה] **,,הֲרֵי** זֶה גִּטֵּךְ עַל מְנָת שֶׁתִּתְּנִי לִי מָאתַיִם זוּז" — הֲרֵי זוֹ מְגֹרֶשֶׁת, וְתִתֵּן.

ר׳ עובדיה מברטנורא

מה היא באותן הימים. לאו ארישא קאי באומר מהיום אם מתי, דההיא ודאי לכי מיית אגלאי מלתא דהוי גט משעת נתינה, והבא עליה פטור. אלא באומר לה במסירת הגט הרי זה גטך והתגרשי בו מעת שאני בעולם אם מתי, רבי יהודה סבר, סמוך למיתה הוא דהוי גט, ומקמי הכי אשת איש היא, ורבי יוסי סבר, מכי יהיב לה גיטא כל שעתא מספקא לן דלמא זו היא שעה הסמוכה למיתה, והוי גט ספק, ואף על גב דחי טפי, אין ברירה, הלכך ספיקא היא, והבא עליה באשם תלוי: (ה) **הרי זו מגורשת ותתן.** מגורשת מעכשיו משעת קבלת הגט, וחייבת ליתן מה שהתנה עמה. ואם אבד הגט או נקרע קודם שתתן, אינה צריכה גט אחר, דכל האומר על מנת כאומר מעכשיו:

יד אברהם

slave in the room is not an effective deterrent from intimacy, because she has no shame before her.] The same applies to her minor son (*Tosefta* 5:4).

Regarding translation of the word גַּס, see *Aruch*.

מַה הִיא בְּאוֹתָן הַיָּמִים? — *What is she in those days?*

I.e., if a man gave his wife a *get* and said, "Here is your *get*, effective from the time I am still alive, if I die," what is her status from the time he gives the *get* until he dies? In the cases of the previous mishnah, in which he stated explicitly that the divorce should be retroactively effective from the time of delivery, her retroactive status as a divorced woman is unquestionable (*Rav; Rashi*).

Others contend that this indeed refers to the cases of the previous mishnah as implied by the mishnah's wording here. Nevertheless, there is a question as to her status in the interim period, as will be explained below (*Tos.* 73b s.v. אמר רבה; *Rosh; Tos. Rid; Meiri*).

רַבִּי יְהוּדָה אוֹמֵר: כְּאֵשֶׁת אִישׁ לְכָל דְּבָרֶיהָ. — *R' Yehudah says: Like a married woman in all respects.*

R' Yehudah maintains that the *get* does not take effect until the moment before death, as stipulated. Therefore, she remains fully married until that time, and her husband retains all of the rights which he assumed with their marriage (*Gem.* 74a; see *Kesubos* 4:4). Accordingly, if another man lives with her in the interim, he is judged in accordance with the laws of adultery (*Rashi*).

According to the opinion that the mishnah is referring to the cases of the previous mishnah, R' Yehudah holds that since it is only the possibility of his death which prompted him to give her the *get* [in order to prevent her from falling to *yibum*], he wants the divorce delayed as much as possible while he is alive. Therefore, we construe his words to mean that it should take effect in the final moment of his life (*Tos.* ibid.).

According to this interpretation of R' Yehudah, the prohibition, stated above,

What is she in those days? R' Yehudah says: Like a married woman in all respects. R' Yose says: She is divorced and not divorced.

5. [If a man said:] "Here is your *get* on condition that you give me two hundred *zuz*," she is divorced and she shall gave [it].

YAD AVRAHAM

against their being alone together, cannot be for fear of interdicted relations, because their married status is not under question until the moment before his death. Rather, the prohibition is for the purpose of protecting them against rumors that the *get* took effect when it was given, and that any children conceived afterward are illegitimate (*Tos.* 73a s.v. לא תתיחד; see 8:4).

רַבִּי יוֹסֵי אוֹמֵר: מְגֹרֶשֶׁת וְאֵינָהּ מְגֹרֶשֶׁת. — *R' Yose says: She is divorced and not divorced.*

R' Yose maintains that as long as the husband is alive, her marital status remains in question because, at any given moment, it is possible that he will die and render her retroactively divorced from that moment. Therefore, one who lives with her cannot be judged as having committed adultery, but only as having indulged in an act of uncertain permissibility. Accordingly, he must bring an אָשָׁם תָּלוּי, *guilt-offering in case of doubt* (see *Lev.* 5:17). The fact that the husband did not die immediately afterward cannot retroactively define the act as illicit, because R' Yose is a proponent of אֵין בְּרֵירָה [lit., *there is no (subsequent) selection*] — i.e., that such retroactive clarification is not legally valid [see commentary to 3:1 s.v. פסול לגרש בו] (*Rav; Rashi* 73b s.v. ומשני אמר רבה; *Tos. Rid;* see *Tos. HaRosh* s.v. רש״י הקשה).

According to those who opine that this mishnah is referring back to the cases of the previous one, R' Yose considers it uncertain whether or not the words *from today if I die* can be understood to mean *from the moment before I die.* Thus, when the husband dies, it is unclear whether the *get* took effect retroactively from the time of delivery or only from the moment before death (*Tos.* ibid.; *Rosh; Meiri*).

The wording *divorced and not divorced* is used to indicate that the husband is obligated to support her during the period in question (*Tos. Yom Tov* from *Gem.* 74a).

5.

„הֲרֵי זֶה גִּטֵּךְ עַל מְנָת שֶׁתִּתְּנִי לִי מָאתַיִם זוּז" — הֲרֵי זוֹ מְגֹרֶשֶׁת, וְתִתֵּן. — *[If a man said:] "Here is your get on condition that you give me two hundred zuz," she is divorced and she shall give [it].*

If a man gave his wife a *get* on condition that she must give him two hundred *zuz,* the *get* takes effect when she gives him the money, retroactive to the time of delivery, because the words עַל מְנָת, *on condition,* are construed to mean that it should take effect from now if the condition is met (*Meiri* from *Gem.* 74a). Therefore, even if the *get* is lost before she gives him the money, the divorce is valid (*Rav* from *Gem.* ibid.).

For the same reason, once the *get* has been given, the husband can no

„עַל מְנָת שֶׁתִּתְּנִי לִי מִכָּאן וְעַד שְׁלֹשִׁים יוֹם״: אִם נָתְנָה לוֹ בְּתוֹךְ שְׁלֹשִׁים יוֹם — מְגֹרֶשֶׁת; וְאִם לָאו — אֵינָהּ מְגֹרֶשֶׁת. אָמַר רַבָּן שִׁמְעוֹן בֶּן גַּמְלִיאֵל: מַעֲשֶׂה בְּצִידוֹן בְּאֶחָד שֶׁאָמַר לְאִשְׁתּוֹ: „הֲרֵי זֶה גִּטֵּךְ עַל מְנָת שֶׁתִּתְּנִי לִי אִצְטְלִיתִי״, וְאָבְדָה אִצְטְלִיתוֹ, וְאָמְרוּ חֲכָמִים: תִּתֵּן לוֹ אֶת דָּמֶיהָ.

ר׳ עובדיה מברטנורא

אמר רבן שמעון בן גמליאל מעשה בצידן. בגמרא (עד, ב) מפרש דחסורי מחסרא והכי קתני, אם אמר לה על מנת שתתני לי איצטליתי ואבדה איצטליתו, איצטלית דוקא קאמר לה. רבן שמעון בן גמליאל אומר תתן לו את דמיה, שלא נתכוין הבעל אלא להרווחה דידיה, ומעשה נמי בצידן באחד שאמר לאשתו וכו׳, ואמרו חכמים תתן לו את דמיה. ואין הלכה כרבן שמעון בן גמליאל:

יד אברהם

longer nullify it (*Meiri* to 74b; *Rambam, Hil. Gerushin* 8:1).

Nevertheless, the wife may not remarry until she gives him the money (*Gem.* ibid.), even if she plans to give it, because her plans may not materialize, and the *get* will thus be null (*Rashi*).

If he refused to accept the money, but his wife gave it to him against his will, there is a dispute in the *Gemara* whether or not the assignment of the money is valid, thereby effecting the *get.* Some authorities maintain that the issue remains unresolved, and her marital status is in doubt (*Rosh; Rashba*). Others contend that the assignment — and thus the *get* — is Biblically valid, but is void by Rabbinic law (*Rambam, Hil. Gerushin* 8:21; *Even HaEzer* 143:4; see commentary to mishnah 1).

The stipulation as stated in the mishnah was not expressed in a dual manner — viz., that if the condition is met, the *get* takes effect; if not, it does not take effect (see *Kiddushin* 3:4) — nor was the condition mentioned before the divorce itself — i.e., "On condition that you give me two hundred *zuz,* here is your *get.*" For both of these reasons, the manner in which this provision was expressed is contrary to the general rules governing stipulations to a *get* (see *Rambam, Hil. Ishus* 6:2; *Maggid Mishneh,* ad loc.). However, these rules do not apply when the *get* takes effect retroactively (*Rif* to 76a; *R' Hai Gaon,* cited by *Rosh; Rambam* loc. cit. 17; *Meiri* to 75a). This is because a stipulation which does not delay the effectuality of the *get* until the condition is met, but rather takes effect retroactively from the time of delivery, is considered only partially effective and is therefore not governed by the regular rules for stipulations (*Ravad,* cited by *Rosh* and *Ran*).

Others dispute this distinction and contend that all stipulations to a *get* must be expressed in a dual manner prior to the mention of the divorce (*Rosh; Ran*). Accordingly, the stipulation stated in our mishnah is abridged, and in order to be valid must meet these conditions (*Tos.* 75a s.v. לאפוקי; *Rashba* ad loc.; *Ran* ad loc.).

There is another opinion that the words *on condition* do not indicate that the *get* should take effect retroactively, and thus it is only valid from the time the wife gives

7
5 "On condition that you give [it] to me between now and thirty days" — if she gave [it] to him within thirty days, she is divorced; if not, she is not divorced. Said Rabban Shimon ben Gamliel: It occurred in Sidon that one said to his wife: "Here is your *get* on condition that you give me my cloak," and she lost his cloak, and the Sages said: She shall give him its value.

the husband the money. Therefore, if the *get* is lost before this occurs, the divorce is null (*Gem.* 74a).

„עַל מְנָת שֶׁתִּתְּנִי לִי מִכָּאן וְעַד שְׁלֹשִׁים יוֹם", אִם נָתְנָה לוֹ בְּתוֹךְ שְׁלֹשִׁים יוֹם — מְגֹרֶשֶׁת; וְאִם לָאו — אֵינָהּ מְגֹרֶשֶׁת. — *"On condition that you give [it] to me between now and thirty days" — if she gave [it] to him within thirty days, she is divorced; if not, she is not divorced.*

We do not assume that he said it only to induce her to give the money quickly, but did not really mean it to be a provision to the legitimacy of the *get* (*Gem.* 74b).

אָמַר רַבָּן שִׁמְעוֹן בֶּן גַּמְלִיאֵל: מַעֲשֶׂה בְצִידוֹן — *Said Rabban Shimon ben Gamliel: It occurred in Sidon*

The mishnah should be emended to read as follows: *If he said to her: "[This is your get] on condition that you give me my cloak," and she lost his cloak, the get is not valid* [because he is interested only in retrieving his cloak, and will not accept its monetary value instead]. *Rabban Shimon ben Gamliel says: She should give him its value* [because the husband intended only to benefit by the *get*, whether it be by retrieving his cloak or its value (*Rav; Rashi*)]. *Indeed, it occurred in Sidon …* (*Rav* from *Gem.* 74b).

בְּאֶחָד שֶׁאָמַר לְאִשְׁתּוֹ: „הֲרֵי זֶה גִּטֵּךְ עַל מְנָת שֶׁתִּתְּנִי לִי אִצְטְלִיתִי", וְאָבְדָה אִצְטְלִיתוֹ, וְאָמְרוּ חֲכָמִים: תִּתֵּן לוֹ אֶת דָּמֶיהָ. — *that one said to his wife: "Here is your get on condition that you give me my cloak," and she lost his cloak, and the Sages said: She shall give him its value.*

The *halachah* follows the view of the first, anonymous *Tanna* (*Rav* from *Gem.* ibid.).

If the husband stipulated that she give him money, and then waived his stipulation, we do not consider the waiver to be tantamount to having received the money, and the *get* is not valid. This is because he did not merely intend to gain the money — which he is now willing to forgo — but also meant to cause her anguish [and had set this as a condition to the *get*], and this did not occur (*Gem.* ibid.).

In the case of the mishnah, if the husband agreed to accept the money in lieu of the cloak, the *get* is valid, because he fulfilled his intention of anguishing her by causing her a monetary loss (*Rosh*). Others opine that even if he accepted the money in place of the cloak, the *get* is void because the condition was not met as stated (*Tos.* to *Arachin* 32a s.v. מדאצטריך; see *Tos. R' Akiva Eiger*).

[ו] ,,הֲרֵי זֶה גִּטֵּךְ עַל מְנָת שֶׁתְּשַׁמְּשִׁי אֶת אַבָּא'', ,,עַל מְנָת שֶׁתָּנִיקִי אֶת בְּנִי'': כַּמָּה הִיא מְנִיקָתוֹ? שְׁתֵּי שָׁנִים; רַבִּי יְהוּדָה אוֹמֵר: שְׁמוֹנָה עָשָׂר חֹדֶשׁ. מֵת הַבֵּן, אוֹ שֶׁמֵּת הָאָב — הֲרֵי זֶה גֵּט. ,,הֲרֵי זֶה גִּטֵּךְ עַל מְנָת שֶׁתְּשַׁמְּשִׁי אֶת אַבָּא שְׁתֵּי שָׁנִים'', ,,עַל מְנָת שֶׁתָּנִיקִי אֶת בְּנִי שְׁתֵּי שָׁנִים'': מֵת הַבֵּן, אוֹ שֶׁמֵּת הָאָב, אוֹ שֶׁאָמַר הָאָב: ,,אִי אֶפְשִׁי שֶׁתְּשַׁמְּשֵׁנִי'' שֶׁלֹּא בְהַקְפָּדָה — אֵינוֹ

ר' עובדיה מברטנורא

(ו) **על מנת שתשמשי את אבא על מנת שתניקי את בני.** בגמרא (עה, ב) מוכח דכל סתם שלא קבע זמן כמה תשמש את אביו או כמה תניק את בנו, כמפרש יום אחד דמי, ונתקיים התנאי אם תשמש את אביו או תניק את בנו יום אחד בלבד: **כמה היא מניקתו.** כלומר כמה הוא זמן היניקה, שאם הניקתו יום אחד בזה הזמן נתקיים התנאי, שתי שנים. רבי יהודה אומר שמונה עשר חדש. אבל אם הניקה אותו אחר שכלו שתי שנים לרבנן, ושמונה עשר חדש לרבי יהודה, אין זו יניקה, ולא נתקיים התנאי. ואין הלכה כרבי יהודה: **מת הבן.** ולא הניקתו כלל: **או מת האב.** ולא שמשתו: **הרי זה גט.** דלאו לצעורה אכוין בתנאו אלא להרווחה דידיה, והא לא אצטריך. ואם היה יודע שימות אביו או בנו, לא היה מתנה: **שלא בהקפדה.** אף על פי שהיא לא הכעיסתו, ואין העכבה ממנה, אינו גט. וכל שכן אם היה בהקפדה:

יד אברהם

6.

,,הֲרֵי זֶה גִּטֵּךְ עַל מְנָת שֶׁתְּשַׁמְּשִׁי אֶת אַבָּא'', ,,עַל מְנָת שֶׁתָּנִיקִי אֶת בְּנִי'': — *[If one said:] "Here is your get on condition that you serve my father," [or] "on condition that you nurse my son,"*

A man gave his wife a *get*, stipulating that she must serve his father or nurse his son, but did not specify how long she must do so (*Meiri* from *Gem.* 75b). If she performs these services for any length of time, she is considered to have met his condition, and the *get* is valid (*Rav* from *Gem.* ibid.; *Rif; Rambam, Hil. Gerushin* 8:19; see *Tos.* loc. cit. s.v. ורמיהנו; *Ran* ibid.; *Beis Shmuel* to *Even HaEzer* 143:18; *Turei Zahav* ad loc. 14).

Others contend that if he does not specify a time period, we assume that he wishes her to nurse for the amount of time stated below (*Gem.* ad loc.; *Rif; Rosh; Tos Rid*) and to serve his father as long as he lives (*Rashi; Meiri; Tos. Rid*).

כַּמָּה הִיא מְנִיקָתוֹ? — *how long must she nurse him?*

What is the time period during which she can nurse his son, and thereby fulfill his stipulation? (*Rav* from *Gem.* ad loc.).

According to the opinion that we assume that he wishes her to nurse for a specific period of time, the mishnah is now explaining what that time period is (*Meiri*).

שְׁתֵּי שָׁנִים; רַבִּי יְהוּדָה אוֹמֵר: שְׁמוֹנָה עָשָׂר חֹדֶשׁ. — *Two years; R' Yehudah says: Eighteen months.*

The first, anonymous opinion maintains that the normal nursing period is two years, and that is

7
6

6. [If one said:] "Here is your *get* on condition that you serve my father," [or] "on condition that you nurse my son," how long must she nurse him? Two years; R' Yehudah says: Eighteen months. If the son died, or the father died, it is a *get*. [If he said:] "Here is your *get* on condition that you serve my father for two years," [or] "on condition that you nurse my son for two years" — and the son died, or the father died, or the father said: "I do not want you to serve me" when [he was] not in anger, it is not a

YAD AVRAHAM

assumed to be his intent. R' Yehudah maintains that it is eighteen months (*Rashi;* see *Kesubos* 60b).

מֵת הַבֵּן, אוֹ שֶׁמֵּת הָאָב — הֲרֵי זֶה גֵּט. — *[If] the son died, or the father died, it is a get.*

If the son died before the wife had nursed him at all, or the father died before she served him at all, the *get* is still valid, because the husband's stipulation was made for the sake of meeting the stated need, and if the need ceases to exist, the stipulation is no longer binding (*Rav; Rashi; Tos.*).

Others maintain that if she did not nurse the son or serve the father at all, the condition has not been met, and the *get* is null. The mishnah is discussing a case in which she had already performed somewhat of the services (*Rambam, Hil. Gerushin* 8:19; *Meiri*), and it teaches us that even a minimal amount of service suffices to meet the condition (*Rav*).

Although this part of the mishnah is written in accordance with the view of the Sages, who maintain that the husband's conditions are assumed to be for the sake of tormenting his wife (see commentary to mishnah 5) and must therefore be met in full (*Gem.* 74b), in this case it is the combination of the factors of his wife's anguish and his son's or father's need which motivated the stipulation. Therefore, if the need is no longer existent, the stipulation is null and the *get* is valid (*Tos.* 75b s.v. מתניתין).

„הֲרֵי זֶה גִּטֵּךְ עַל מְנָת שֶׁתְּשַׁמְּשִׁי אֶת אַבָּא שְׁתֵּי שָׁנִים", „עַל מְנָת שֶׁתָּנִיקִי אֶת בְּנִי שְׁתֵּי שָׁנִים": — *[If he said:] "Here is your get on condition that you serve my father for two years," [or] "on condition that you nurse my son for two years"* —

The husband stated explicitly that his wife must serve his father or nurse his son for a period of two years in order for the *get* to be valid (*Meiri*).

מֵת הַבֵּן, אוֹ שֶׁמֵּת הָאָב, — *[and] the son died, or the father died,*

The wife was not able to fulfill the stipulation because the son or father died before the allotted time had elapsed (*Meiri*).

In the version of this mishnah printed in the *Gemara*, the words *or the father died* are omitted [since the mishnah divides the examples of the son and the father, applying the former to this case and the latter to the one mentioned below].

אוֹ שֶׁאָמַר הָאָב: „אִי אֶפְשִׁי שֶׁתְּשַׁמְּשֵׁנִי" שֶׁלֹּא בְהַקְפָּדָה — — *or the father said: "I do not want you to serve me" when [he was] not in anger,*

גֵט. רַבָּן שִׁמְעוֹן בֶּן גַּמְלִיאֵל אוֹמֵר: כָּזֶה גֵט.
כְּלָל אָמַר רַבָּן שִׁמְעוֹן בֶּן גַּמְלִיאֵל: כָּל עַכָּבָה
שֶׁאֵינָה הֵימֶנָּה — הֲרֵי זֶה גֵט.

[ז] ,,הֲרֵי זֶה גִטֵּךְ אִם לֹא בָאתִי מִכָּאן וְעַד
שְׁלֹשִׁים יוֹם", וְהָיָה הוֹלֵךְ מִיהוּדָה
לַגָּלִיל: הִגִּיעַ לְאַנְטִיפַּטְרֶס וְחָזַר — בָּטֵל תְּנָאוֹ.

ר' עובדיה מברטנורא

כָזֶה גֵט. הוֹאִיל וְלֹא הִקְפִּידְתּוּ, וְאֵין הָעַכָּבָה מִמֶּנָּה. וְאֵין הֲלָכָה כְּרַבָּן שִׁמְעוֹן בֶּן גַּמְלִיאֵל: **(ז) הִגִּיעַ לְאַנְטִיפַּטְרֶס.** מְפָרֵשׁ בַּגְּמָרָא (עו, ב) מִשְׁנָה זוֹ, כְּגוֹן דְּאַתְנֵי שְׁנֵי תְנָאִים, אִי מְטֵינָא לַגָּלִיל, לַאֲלַתַּר לֶיהֱוֵי גִּיטָּא. וְאִי לֹא מְטֵינָא לַגָּלִיל, אִי מִשְׁתַּהֵין תְּלָתִין יוֹמִין וְלֹא אֲתֵינָא, לֶיהֱוֵי גִּיטָּא, לֶיהֱוֵי גִּיטָּא, וְאִי לֹא, לֹא לֶיהֱוֵי גִּיטָּא. וְהָלַךְ וְהִגִּיעַ לְאַנְטִיפַּטְרֶס שֶׁהוּא סוֹף אֶרֶץ יְהוּדָה, וְחָזַר קוֹדֶם שְׁלֹשִׁים יוֹם, בָּטֵל הַגֵּט. דְּלֹא לַגָּלִיל מָטָא, וְלֹא אִשְׁתַּהֵי תְּלָתִין יוֹמִין: **וְכֵן אִם הָיָה הוֹלֵךְ מִגָּלִיל לִיהוּדָה וְהִגִּיעַ לַכְּפָר**

יד אברהם

The husband's father refused the service of the wife, although she had not angered him in any way (*Rav*).

אֵינוֹ גֵט. — *it is not a get.*

The *get* is not valid despite the fact that it was not the wife's fault that the condition had not been met, because the husband made the provision in order to torment her, and is therefore insistent that it be fully met (see *Ran; Tos.* 76a s.v. בשלמא). This is certainly so if she had caused the father's anger, and was thus responsible for the negation of the condition (*Rav*).

The *Gemara* (76a) poses the question why this case is different than the previous case — in which the wife's inability to meet the husband's condition does not invalidate the *get* — and leaves the question unresolved.

However, according to those who interpret the previous case to be one in which she had nursed the son or served the father before they died, the difference between those cases and this one is clear. In the former, the husband did not specify an amount of time for her service, and thus, if she fills the specified need until it ceases to exist, she has met his condition. In this case,

on the other hand, he specified an amount of time for her service, and his stipulation was not fulfilled.

רַבָּן שִׁמְעוֹן בֶּן גַּמְלִיאֵל אוֹמֵר: כָּזֶה גֵט. — *Rabban Shimon ben Gamliel says: [In a case] like this it is a get.*

Since the negation of the husband's stipulation was not caused by his wife, it does not invalidate the *get* (*Rav*), because his intention in making the condition was solely for the sake of the stated need. Once the need is no longer existent, the stipulation is null (*Tos.* 75b s.v. כלל).

כְּלָל אָמַר רַבָּן שִׁמְעוֹן בֶּן גַּמְלִיאֵל: כָּל עַכָּבָה שֶׁאֵינָה הֵימֶנָּה — הֲרֵי זֶה גֵט. — *A rule was stated by Rabban Shimon ben Gamliel: [In] any [case of an] impediment which is not because of her, it is a get.*

[He maintains that the stipulation to a *get* which remains unfulfilled through no fault of the wife does not invalidate the *get*.]

The *halachah* follows the view of the first, anonymous *Tanna* (*Rav*). Therefore, if he specified a period of

get. Rabban Shimon ben Gamliel says: [In a case] like this it is a *get*.

A rule was stated by Rabban Shimon ben Gamliel: [In] any [case of an] impediment which is not because of her, it is a *get*.

7. [If one said:] "Here is your *get* if I do not come within thirty days," and he was going from Judea to Galilee — [if] he reached Antipatris and returned, his condition is null.

YAD AVRAHAM

time for her service, and the son or father died, the *get* is void (*Rif; Rambam, Hil. Gerushin* 8:20; *Meiri*).

Others contend that the ruling is like Rabban Shimon ben Gamliel (*Tos.* 75b s.v. כלל). Although the *Gemara* states that if the husband stipulated that the wife give him a sum of money, and then waived his condition, the *get* is null (74b; see commentary to mishnah 5 s.v. באחד שאמר), that is because his original intention to receive the money was never fulfilled. The intention behind the condition to serve his father or son, however, is solely *for the fulfillment of* that need, and if it ceases to exist, it is tantamount to the condition being met (*Tos.* ibid.). Although, when the husband's father refuses to be served by the wife, the *get* is valid despite the need not being met, that is because it is not the husband who changed his mind, but the father (*Pnei Yehoshua*) [and this is considered a change in the situation surrounding the condition and, thus, the equivalent of fulfillment. The husband's change of heart, however, is a negation of the stipulation itself].

7.

,,הֲרֵי זֶה גִּטֵּךְ אִם לֹא בָאתִי מִכָּאן עַד שְׁלֹשִׁים יוֹם,'' — *[If one said:] "Here is your get if I do no come within* (lit., *from now until*) *thirty days,"*

[A man gave his wife a *get*, stipulating that it should take effect if he does not return within thirty days.]

וְהָיָה הוֹלֵךְ מִיהוּדָה לַגָּלִיל: — *and he was going from Judea to Galilee —*

This means that he also stated that if he should reach Galilee, the *get* should take effect even if he returns within thirty days (*Rav* from *Gem.* 76b).

הִגִּיעַ לְאַנְטִיפַּטְרַס וְחָזַר — *[if] he reached Antipatris and returned,*

He reached Antipatris, a town on the Judean side of the border between Judea and Galilee, and returned within thirty days of his departure (*Rav* from *Gem.*).

בָּטֵל תְּנָאוֹ. — *his condition is null.*

And the *get* is void, because neither did he reach Galilee, nor did he stay away thirty days (*Rav, Meiri* from *Gem.*). Even if he later fulfilled either of the conditions, the *get* does not take effect, because the stipulations were made in reference to the first trip and were broken by his return from it (*Rashi; Ran*). Nevertheless, if he takes back the *get* from his wife, he can use it to divorce her, by giving it to her once again (*Tos. Rid*).

If he said that he was going to Galilee and

„הֲרֵי זֶה גִּטֵּךְ אִם לֹא בָאתִי מִכָּאן עַד שְׁלֹשִׁים יוֹם״, וְהָיָה הוֹלֵךְ מִגָּלִיל לִיהוּדָה, וְהִגִּיעַ לִכְפַר עוֹתְנַאי וְחָזַר — בָּטֵל תְּנָאוֹ.

„הֲרֵי זֶה גִּטֵּךְ אִם לֹא בָאתִי מִכָּאן עַד שְׁלֹשִׁים יוֹם״, וְהָיָה הוֹלֵךְ לִמְדִינַת הַיָּם, וְהִגִּיעַ לְעַכּוֹ וְחָזַר — בָּטֵל תְּנָאוֹ.

„הֲרֵי זֶה גִּטֵּךְ כָּל זְמַן שֶׁאֶעֱבֹר מִכְּנֶגֶד פָּנַיִךְ שְׁלֹשִׁים יוֹם״: הָיָה הוֹלֵךְ וּבָא, הוֹלֵךְ וּבָא — הוֹאִיל וְלֹא נִתְיַחֵד עִמָּהּ, הֲרֵי זֶה גֵּט.

ר׳ עובדיה מברטנורא

עותנאי. שהוא בקצה גבול הגליל: **וכן אם היה הולך למדינת הים והגיע לעכו.** שהוא בקצה גבולה של ארץ ישראל, וחזר בתוך שלשים יום, בטל הגט. שהרי לא הלך למדינת הים, וגם לא נשתהה שלשים יום: **כל זמן שאעבור מנגד פניך שלשים יום.** כשאשתהה שלשים יום עובר מנגד פניך, אז יהא גט: **והיה הולך ובא וכו׳.** לאחר מכאן כשישתהה שלשים יום עובר מנגד פניה, יהא גט. ולא אמרינן הואיל ומעיקרא היה הולך ובא, ניחוש שמא פייס קטטה שביניהם ובטל גיטא, דמאחר שלא נתייחד עמה בשעה שהיה הולך ובא, לא חיישינן שמא פייס. ולכי מקיים תנאיה ושהה שלשים יום עובר מנגד פניה, הוי גיטא. ובגמרא מוקי לה באומר בשעת התנאי על מנת כן אני מוסר לה הגט, שתהא נאמנת עלי כמאה עדים כל זמן שתאמר שלא באתי ונתיחדתי ופייסתי. וכן הלכה, שאם לא אמר כן בשעת התנאי, חיישינן שמא יבא בעל ויערער ויאמר פייסתי:

יד אברהם

stipulated that the *get* take effect if he does not return within thirty days, his subsequent return without having reached Galilee would not nullify the *get*, because the condition was dependent upon a trip to Galilee, and the thirty-day period begins only if and when he arrives there (*Gem.* 76b; *Rashi* ad loc.).

Others contend that if when giving her the *get* he mentioned that he is going from Judah to Galilee we interpret his statement to mean that the *get* should take effect if he reaches Galilee even if he does not stay away for thirty days (*Meiri*).

„הֲרֵי זֶה גִּטֵּךְ אִם לֹא בָאתִי מִכָּאן עַד שְׁלֹשִׁים — יוֹם״, וְהָיָה הוֹלֵךְ מִגָּלִיל לִיהוּדָה, *[If he said:] "Here is your get if I do not come within thirty days," and he was going from Galilee to Judea,*

[A man gave his wife a *get* before setting out on a journey from Galilee to Judea, and he stipulated that it should take effect if he either reaches Judea or remains away for thirty days.]

וְהִגִּיעַ לִכְפַר עוֹתְנַאי וְחָזַר — *and he reached Kefar Osnai and returned,*

He reached Kefar Osnai, which is on the Galilean side of the border, and returned within thirty days (*Rav* from *Gem.* ibid.).

בָּטֵל תְּנָאוֹ. — *his condition is null.*

[And the *get* is void.]

The mishnah mentions this case to teach us that although the province of Judea —

7
7 [If he said:] "Here is your *get* if I do not come within thirty days," and he was going from Galilee to Judea, and he reached Kefar Osnai and returned, his condition is null.

[If he said:] "Here is your *get* if I do not come within thirty days," and he was going overseas, and he reached Acco and returned, his condition is null.

[If he said:] "Here is your *get* any time that I shall be away from your presence [for] thirty days," [and] he was going and coming, [and] going and coming — since he was not alone with her, it is a *get*.

YAD AVRAHAM

because it included Jerusalem — was of greater stature than that of Galilee, the Galilean towns on the border were not considered extensions of Judea; hence, his trip to Kefar Osnai is not regarded as a fulfillment of the stipulation that he reach Judea (*Tif. Yis.*).

,,הֲרֵי זֶה גִּטֵּךְ אִם לֹא בָאתִי מִכָּאן עַד שְׁלֹשִׁים יוֹם'', וְהָיָה הוֹלֵךְ לִמְדִינַת הַיָּם, — *[If he said:] "Here is your get if I do not come within thirty days," and he was going overseas,*

A man about to set out on a journey from *Eretz Yisrael* gave his wife a *get* and stipulated that it take effect if he either leaves the Holy Land or does not return from his journey within thirty days (*Gem.* ibid.).

וְהִגִּיעַ לְעַכּוֹ וְחָזַר — בָּטֵל תְּנָאוֹ. — *and he reached Acco and returned, his condition is null.*

If he reached Acco, which is a border town within *Eretz Yisrael*, and returned within thirty days, the condition has not been fulfilled, and the *get* is void (*Rav* from *Gem.* ibid.).

The mishnah teaches us that although Acco is considered to be outside the border of the Holy Land with regard to the laws of an agent who delivers a *get* (1:2), it is actually within its borders (*Tif. Yis.*; see commentary to 1:1 s.v. מאשקלון לדרום).

,,הֲרֵי זֶה גִּטֵּךְ כָּל זְמַן שֶׁאֶעֱבֹר מִכְּנֶגֶד פָּנַיִךְ שְׁלֹשִׁים יוֹם'': — *[If he said:] "Here is your get any time that I shall be away from your presence* (lit., *from before your face*) *[for] thirty days,"*

A man gave his wife a *get* and stipulated that it should take effect if and when he is separated from her for thirty days (*Rav*).

הָיָה הוֹלֵךְ וּבָא, הוֹלֵךְ וּבָא — *[and] he was going and coming, [and] going and coming —*

The husband came and went, but was not away for thirty days consecutively (*Gem.* 76b).

הוֹאִיל וְלֹא נִתְיַחֵד עִמָּהּ, הֲרֵי זֶה גֵּט. — *since he was not alone with her, it is a get.*

Although the *get* is not operative since he has not yet been away for thirty days, it retains its validity and can still effect divorce if the condition is subsequently met. We do not consider this analogous to the case of a גֵּט יָשָׁן, *"outdated" get*, in which a husband and wife were alone together

[ח] "הֲרֵי זֶה גִּטֵּךְ אִם לֹא בָאתִי מִכָּאן וְעַד שְׁנֵים עָשָׂר חֹדֶשׁ", וּמֵת בְּתוֹךְ שְׁנֵים עָשָׂר חֹדֶשׁ — אֵינוֹ גֵט.
"הֲרֵי זֶה גִּטֵּךְ מֵעַכְשָׁיו אִם לֹא בָאתִי מִכָּאן וְעַד שְׁנֵים עָשָׂר חֹדֶשׁ", וּמֵת בְּתוֹךְ שְׁנֵים עָשָׂר חֹדֶשׁ — הֲרֵי זֶה גֵט.

ר' עובדיה מברטנורא

(ח) אינו גט. דכיון דלא אמר מעכשיו, משמע לאחר שנים עשר חדש יהא גט, והרי מת בתוך הזמן וצריכה ליבם:

יד אברהם

between the writing of their *get* and its delivery. In the latter case, the *get* is Rabbinically void, because it might be rumored that a child conceived during such a seclusion had been conceived after the *get* was given; i.e., out of wedlock (*Rashi* 76b s.v. גט ישן from 8:4); in our case, however, the husband and wife were never alone together during these brief meetings (*Gem.* ibid.).

We are not concerned that the husband will later claim that he had spent time alone with her and that he settled the argument between them and nullified the *get*, because the mishnah is discussing a case in which the husband stipulated that the wife be believed about that issue (*Rav* from *Gem.* ibid.).

Another view is that the concern under discussion is that he will claim that he appeased her and had marital relations with her, thus rendering the *get* "outdated" [as explained above]. The mishnah is telling us that we are not apprehensive of such a claim (*Rashi* 18b s.v. שמא פייס; see *Tos.* ad loc. s.v. שמא; *Ran* to 76b). Although, ex post facto, a woman who received an "outdated" *get* may remarry [and in this case the *get* has already been given], the wording of the mishnah implies that this is a *get* which is proper to use initially (*Ran*).

Others contend that if he were to have marital relations with her it would be tantamount to an explicit directive that the *get* be nullified (*Tos. Rid*).

Another interpretation of the mishnah is that *from before your face* is a euphemism for marital relations; that is, he declared that the *get* should take effect if he does not have relations with his wife for thirty days. Since they were not alone together during this period, the *get* takes effect (*Gem.* ibid.).

There is another version to the mishnah which reads: עַל מְנָת שֶׁאֶעֱבוֹר מִכְּנֶגֶד פָּנַיִךְ שְׁלֹשִׁים יוֹם, *on condition that I shall be away from your presence for thirty days.* According to this reading, the husband cannot nullify the *get* in the interim, because — if the condition is fulfilled — the *get* is retroactively effective from the time of delivery (see mishnah 5). Thus, the possibility which the mishnah tells us we need not fear is that the husband and wife will revoke the stipulation by common consent, thus rendering it impossible to fulfill and thereby invalidate the *get* (*Ramban*). *Ran* adds that revocation of such a stipulation is possible only in a case such as ours, in which the provision was made for the benefit of the wife [i.e., that if he is delayed, she should be able to remarry] and is therefore dependent upon her acquiescence.

8. [If one said:] "This is your *get* if I do not come within twelve months," and he died within twelve months, it is not a *get*.

[If he said:] "Here is your *get* from now if I do not come within twelve months," and he died within twelve months, it is a *get*.

YAD AVRAHAM

8.

„הֲרֵי זֶה גִּטֵּךְ אִם לֹא בָאתִי מִכָּאן וְעַד שְׁנֵים עָשָׂר חֹדֶשׁ״ — *[If one said:] "This is your get if I do not come within twelve months,"*

[A man gave his wife a *get* before leaving on a journey and stipulated that it take effect if he does not return within twelve months.]

וּמֵת בְּתוֹךְ שְׁנֵים עָשָׂר חֹדֶשׁ — אֵינוֹ גֵט. — *and he died within twelve months, it is not a get.*

Since the husband did not specify that the *get* should be retroactive, it would take effect only at the end of twelve months, at which time he already had died, and a *get* cannot become effective after its giver's death (*Rav;* see 1:6 and commentary ad loc.).

Although it has already been taught (mishnah 3) that a *get* which was designated to take effect if the husband dies is null, one might assume that this is so only in a case that the husband explicitly stated that the *get* is to take effect upon his death. Since this demonstrates that the purpose of the *get* is to free his wife from *yibum,* and that he is assuming that it can do so even after his death, there is no reason for him to want it to be effective prior to his death. In our case, however, the husband did not mention death, and it is conceivable that the *get* will be valid retroactively (*Tos. Yom Tov*), because a stipulation beginning with *if* can imply retroactivity (see mishnah 3).

According to R' Yose, who maintains that the date written on a document is considered a directive that it take effect on that day (*Bava Basra* 7:8), the *get* in this case would be retroactively effectual and would thus be valid (*Gem.* 76b).

„הֲרֵי זֶה גִּטֵּךְ מֵעַכְשָׁיו אִם לֹא בָאתִי מִכָּאן וְעַד שְׁנֵים עָשָׂר חֹדֶשׁ״, וּמֵת בְּתוֹךְ שְׁנֵים עָשָׂר חֹדֶשׁ — הֲרֵי זֶה גֵט. — *[If he said:] "Here is your get from now if I do not come within twelve months," and he died within twelve months, it is a get.*

[Since he stipulated that the *get* take effect retroactively from the time of its delivery, it is not considered to have been given after death, and hence, is valid.]

Although the principle that a *get* can become retroactively effective even after the giver's death has already been stated in mishnah 3, the *Tanna* tells us that it is valid in this case.

Otherwise, one might construe the fact that the husband did not mention death to be an indication that his intention is only to prevent her from waiting endlessly for his return, but that he did not have the possibility of death in mind, and thus the *get* should not be operative if that occurs (*Tif. Yis.*).

The *Gemara* (ibid.) raises the question as to whether the wife may remarry as soon as the husband dies, since the *get's* validity is now certain, or if she must wait until the twelve months have elapsed as a preventive measure, so that in cases in which the husband did not die, and the *get* is not valid until after the twelve months, the woman not be led to remarry earlier by confusing it with the other case (*Tos.* 76b s.v. דהא).

[ט] ,,אם לֹא בָאתִי מִכָּאן עַד שְׁנֵים עָשָׂר חֹדֶשׁ — כִּתְבוּ וּתְנוּ גֵט לְאִשְׁתִּי"; כָּתְבוּ גֵט בְּתוֹךְ שְׁנֵים עָשָׂר חֹדֶשׁ, וְנָתְנוּ לְאַחַר שְׁנֵים עָשָׂר חֹדֶשׁ — אֵינוֹ גֵט. ,,כִּתְבוּ וּתְנוּ גֵט לְאִשְׁתִּי אִם לֹא בָאתִי מִכָּאן עַד שְׁנֵים עָשָׂר חֹדֶשׁ"; כָּתְבוּ בְּתוֹךְ שְׁנֵים עָשָׂר חֹדֶשׁ וְנָתְנוּ לְאַחַר שְׁנֵים עָשָׂר חֹדֶשׁ — אֵינוֹ גֵט. רַבִּי יוֹסֵי אוֹמֵר: כָּזֶה גֵּט. כָּתְבוּ לְאַחַר שְׁנֵים עָשָׂר חֹדֶשׁ וְנָתְנוּ לְאַחַר שְׁנֵים עָשָׂר חֹדֶשׁ, וָמֵת: אִם הַגֵּט קָדַם לַמִּיתָה — הֲרֵי זֶה גֵט; וְאִם מִיתָה קָדְמָה לַגֵּט — אֵינוֹ גֵט. וְאִם אֵין יָדוּעַ — זוֹ הִיא

יד אברהם

Another possible reason for waiting is that the husband had not considered the possibility of death, and therefore, did not intend that the divorce take effect before the twelve months were over (*Ran*). The *Gemara* does not reach a conclusion.

9.

,,אם לֹא בָאתִי מִכָּאן עַד שְׁנֵים עָשָׂר חֹדֶשׁ — כִּתְבוּ וּתְנוּ גֵט לְאִשְׁתִּי"; — *[If one said:] "If I do not come within twelve months, write and give a get to my wife,"*

[A man who was setting out on a journey told two people to write a *get* and give it to his wife if he does not return within twelve months.]

כָּתְבוּ גֵט בְּתוֹךְ שְׁנֵים עָשָׂר חֹדֶשׁ, וְנָתְנוּ לְאַחַר שְׁנֵים עָשָׂר חֹדֶשׁ — אֵינוֹ גֵט. — *[and] they wrote a get within twelve months and gave [it] after twelve months, it is not a get.*

This is because his wording indicated his insistence that even the writing of the *get* be done after twelve months [since the time period was stated prior to the entire directive] (*Rav; Meiri*).

,,כִּתְבוּ וּתְנוּ גֵט לְאִשְׁתִּי אִם לֹא בָאתִי מִכָּאן עַד שְׁנֵים עָשָׂר חֹדֶשׁ"; כָּתְבוּ בְּתוֹךְ שְׁנֵים עָשָׂר חֹדֶשׁ וְנָתְנוּ לְאַחַר שְׁנֵים עָשָׂר חֹדֶשׁ — אֵינוֹ גֵט. — *[If he said:] "Write a get and give it to my wife if I do not come within twelve months," [and] they wrote [it] within twelve months and gave [it] after twelve months, it is not a get.*

Although his mentioning the writing of the *get* prior to the time period might possibly be interpreted to mean that he insisted only that the delivery — not the writing — of the *get* take place after twelve months, we nevertheless construe his statement to mean that both the delivery and the writing be done then (*Meiri*).

Since the *Tanna* rules in this case that the condition is effective although it had been

9. [If one said:] "If I do not come within twelve months, write and give a *get* to my wife," [and] they wrote a *get* within twelve months and gave [it] after twelve months, it is not a *get*.

[If he said:] "Write a *get* and give it to my wife if I do not come within twelve months," [and] they wrote [it] within twelve months and gave [it] after twelve months, it is not a *get*. R' Yose says: In such a case it is a *get*.

[If] they wrote [it] after twelve months and gave [it] after twelve months, and he died — if the *get* preceded [his] death, it is a *get;* if [his] death preceded the *get*, it is not a *get*. If it is not known, this is [the case regarding]

YAD AVRAHAM

stated after the directive in the husband's statements, it is obvious that he rejects the opinion of R' Meir, who maintains that the condition must precede the directive to be binding. In our case, for example, R' Meir would hold that the condition is binding only if he says, "If I do not come within twelve months, write a *get*..." (*Tos. Rid;* see commentary to mishnah 5 s.v. הרי זה גטך). Others contend that concerning instructions issued to an agent for the writing of a *get*, even R' Meir agrees that any manner in which a condition is conveyed is binding — even not in accordance with the rules which ordinarily govern stipulations — because the agent may do only that which the husband authorized (*Rashba* to 75a; *Ran* ibid.).

.רַבִּי יוֹסֵי אוֹמֵר: כָּזֶה גֵּט — *R' Yose says: In such a case it is a get.*

R' Yose disagrees with the first opinion, maintaining that the husband's choice of words does indicate that he insists only that the delivery of the *get* take place after twelve months, not its writing (*Gem.* 77a).

כָּתְבוּ לְאַחַר שְׁנֵים עָשָׂר חֹדֶשׁ וְנָתְנוּ לְאַחַר שְׁנֵים עָשָׂר חֹדֶשׁ, וָמֵת: — *[If] they wrote [it] after twelve months and gave [it] after twelve months, and he died —*

The agents followed the husband's instructions precisely, and then the husband died (*Meiri*).

אִם הַגֵּט קָדַם לַמִּיתָה — הֲרֵי זֶה גֵּט; וְאִם מִיתָה קָדְמָה לַגֵּט — אֵינוֹ גֵּט. — *if the get preceded [his] death, it is a get; if [his] death preceded the get, it is not a get.*

If he died after twelve months, but before the *get* was given, the divorce does not take effect (*Rambam, Hil. Gerushin* 9:22), since the *get* is not operative until it is delivered, at which time the husband had already died, and a divorce cannot take place after the husband's death (*Meiri*).

וְאִם אֵין יָדוּעַ — — *If it is not known,*

[If it is unknown whether the *get* preceded his death, or vice versa.]

שֶׁאָמְרוּ: מְגֹרֶשֶׁת וְאֵינָהּ מְגֹרֶשֶׁת.

יד אברהם

זוֹ הִיא שֶׁאָמְרוּ: מְגֹרֶשֶׁת וְאֵינָהּ מְגֹרֶשֶׁת. — *this is [the case regarding] which they said: She is divorced and not divorced.*

This is one of the cases concerning which the Rabbis ruled that her divorce remains in question (*Tos. Yom Tov*) [and another man who has relations with her must bring an אָשָׁם

7 which they said: She is divorced and not
9 divorced.

YAD AVRAHAM

תָּלוּי, *guilt-offering in case of doubt* (see commentary to mishnah 4 s.v. רַבִּי יוֹסֵי)]. Although the principle of *chazakah* (presumptive status) indicates that a person is presumed to be alive until it is proven otherwise, the fact that we now know that he has already died weakens the *chazakah* that he had been alive at the time the *get* was given (*Ran*).

פרק שמיני

Chapter Eight

[א] **הַזּוֹרֵק** גֵּט לְאִשְׁתּוֹ, וְהִיא בְתוֹךְ בֵּיתָהּ אוֹ בְתוֹךְ חֲצֵרָהּ — הֲרֵי זוֹ מְגֹרֶשֶׁת.
זְרָקוֹ לָהּ בְּתוֹךְ בֵּיתוֹ אוֹ בְתוֹךְ חֲצֵרוֹ, אֲפִלּוּ הוּא עִמָּהּ בַּמִּטָּה — אֵינָהּ מְגֹרֶשֶׁת.

ר' עובדיה מברטנורא

פרק שמיני – הזורק. (א) הזורק. הרי זו מגורשת. דכתיב (דברים כד, ג) ונתן בידה, ומדלא כתיב ובידה יתננו, משמע ונתן מכל מקום, בין בחצרה בין בגגה בין בקרפיפה. והוא שתהא עומדת בצד ביתה [או] בצד חצרה:

יד אברהם

1.

Although the passage regarding *gittin* (*Deut.* 24:1) states, *And he shall place [it] in her hand,* other methods of delivery are also valid if they conform to certain basic rules. This mishnah discusses such alternate methods.

הַזּוֹרֵק גֵּט לְאִשְׁתּוֹ, — *[If] one throws a get to his wife,*

In order to divorce his wife a man threw a *get* to her, rather than placing it into her hand, and it landed near her on the ground (*Rashi*).

וְהִיא בְתוֹךְ בֵּיתָהּ אוֹ בְתוֹךְ חֲצֵרָהּ — *and she is inside her house or inside her courtyard,*

The woman was standing inside a house or courtyard that were נִכְסֵי מְלוֹג, *melog* (*usufructuary*) *property* (*Rashi*). This term refers to those belongings which a wife brings into the marriage and are given to the husband for his use, but are still owned by the wife [as opposed to נִכְסֵי צֹאן בַּרְזֶל — *fixed-value property* — which are written in the *kesubah* and are considered the possession of the husband, since he is the one affected by their appreciation or depreciation (see *Yevamos* 7:1)]. This includes the possessions which she owned at the time of marriage and those which she inherited or were given to her as a gift afterward (*Rambam, Hil. Ishus* 16:2). [Anything else which she acquires after their marriage belongs to her husband and cannot be used for her receipt of a *get*.] The husband enjoys the dividends without having rights to the property itself, which reverts to her — in whatever condition it may be — upon their divorce or his death (*Rav, Rashi* to *Yevamos* 7:1; see General Introduction to ArtScroll *Yevamos*, p. 13).

The words *inside her house or inside her courtyard* are stated merely as an example; the same law applies if she is standing near the house or courtyard (*Tos. Yom Tov;* see below).

הֲרֵי זוֹ מְגֹרֶשֶׁת. — *she is divorced.*

This is derived from the verse (*Deut.* 24:1), *And he shall place [it] in her hand,* which is repeated in the Torah (ibid. v. 3) to indicate that he can also divorce her by placing a *get* into her property (*Gem.* 77a; *Ran; Meiri*). Nevertheless, the latter method is

1. [If] one throws a *get* to his wife, and she is inside her house or inside her courtyard, she is divorced.

[If] he threw it to her inside his house or inside his courtyard, even if it is with her in a bed she is not divorced.

YAD AVRAHAM

valid only if she is standing nearby at the time (*Rav* from *Gem.* 77b), because the courtyard in which she receives her *get* must be under her watch, similar to her hand, from which its validity is derived (*Gem.* ibid.).

Although a woman cannot receive a *get* by it being in her property unless the property is in her full possession, and even *melog* properties do not revert to her possession until after she is divorced or the husband dies [because whatever a woman acquires belongs to her husband (*Gem.* 77a)], since — at the moment she becomes divorced — the property reverts to her, the divorce and the possession of the property take effect simultaneously, and the *get* is valid (*Gem.* 77b).

Despite the fact that a person's property also has the status of an agent in regard to effecting acquisition of items on its owner's behalf, and hence, in our case, the property should acquire the *get* for the wife even without her knowledge, a *get* is considered detrimental to a woman (see 1:6) and therefore cannot be given to her through an agent without her being aware of it. Only when the courtyard functions as a substitute for her hand can it receive the *get* without her knowledge, but that requires her presence, as explained above (*Bava Metzia* 12a; see *Tos.* ad loc. s.v. חצר). However, if she told the husband to throw the *get* into her property in order to divorce her, she acquires the *get* if it is placed there even if she is not present, because the property then functions as her agent of receipt (*Ran* to 77b). Similarly, if the husband threw the *get* into his wife's property and then informed her that he had done so, and she said that the property should serve as an agent to receive it for her, it is valid (*Rashba* ibid.). This is not considered a *get* which was taken by the wife, rather than given by the husband (see General Introduction s.v. *The Divorce Process*), because the transfer to her — by virtue of the divorce — of the property and the *get* which is in it serves as the giving of the *get* (*Toras Gittin* to *Even HaEzer* 139).

זְרָקוֹ לָהּ בְּתוֹךְ בֵּיתוֹ אוֹ בְתוֹךְ חֲצֵרוֹ, אֲפִלּוּ הוּא עִמָּהּ בַּמִּטָּה — אֵינָהּ מְגֹרֶשֶׁת. — *[If] he threw it to her inside his house or inside his courtyard, even if it is with her in a bed she is not divorced.*

[If she was sitting on a bed in the property of the husband, and he threw the *get* onto the bed, it does not take effect, because it has not come into her possession. However, if the bed belonged to her, and it was ten handbreadths high, it is considered to be her separate domain, and the *get* in this case would be valid (*Gem.* 78a).]

If the bed was not ten handbreadths high, the validity of the *get* would remain in doubt, because the question of whether a utensil of a person can acquire an object on his behalf while in the property of the giver is an unresolved dispute (*Even HaEzer* 139:10).

לְתוֹךְ חֵיקָהּ אוֹ לְתוֹךְ קַלְתָּהּ — הֲרֵי זוֹ מְגֹרֶשֶׁת.

[ב] **אָמַר** לָהּ: „כְּנְסִי שְׁטָר חוֹב זֶה", אוֹ שֶׁמְּצָאַתּוּ מֵאֲחוֹרָיו, קוֹרְאָה וַהֲרֵי הוּא גִטָּהּ — אֵינוֹ גֵט, עַד שֶׁיֹּאמַר לָהּ: „הֵא גִטֵּךְ".

ר' עובדיה מברטנורא

קלתה. כלי שהנשים נותנות בו מטוה ומחטין: **הרי זו מגורשת.** ואפילו היא בתוך ביתו, דמקום חיקה וקלתה קנוי לה, שאין אדם מקפיד לא על מקום חיקה ולא על מקום קלתה: (ב) **או שמצאתו מאחוריו.** שהיה הגט על גבו, ועקם גבו לה כדי שתטלנו: **אינו גט עד שיאמר טלי גטך.** ולכי אמר טלי גטך מיהא הוי גט. אבל אם היה הגט על גבי קרקע, או על גבו, או בגופו, ולא עקם גבו, או לא המציא גופו לה כדי שתטלנו, אפילו אמר טלי גטך אינו גט: **קוראה והרי היא גיטה.** כשהיא קוראה בו רואה שהוא גטה:

יד אברהם

לְתוֹךְ חֵיקָהּ — *[If he threw it] into her lap*

[The wife was sitting on her husband's property, and he threw a *get* into her lap.] This is not exactly similar to placing it in her hand, because the clothing covering her lap was hanging down and dragging on the ground, and is thus not totally separate from his property. Therefore, it is necessary for the mishnah to tell us that, in this case too, the divorce is effected (*Tos.* 78a s.v. מקום חיקה).

אוֹ לְתוֹךְ קַלְתָּהּ, — *or into her basket,*

This is a type of basket in which women keep yarn and needles (*Rav*).

הֲרֵי זוֹ מְגֹרֶשֶׁת. — *she is divorced.*

This is because a man is not particular about the place where his wife sits or puts her basket, and he allows her to borrow that space for her use [thus rendering it like her own property regarding acquisition] (*Rav* from *Gem.* ibid.).

The same rule applies to any small items which the wife uses regularly (*Meiri*).

According to those who hold that a buyer can make acquisition of an article by placing it into his utensil although it is on the property of the seller (*Bava Basra* 85b), the *get* would be valid in this case even if the space in which the wife's basket sat had not been given to her for use (*Gem.* loc. cit.).

2.

[As explained in the General Introduction, the divorce procedure requires that the man give the *get* to his wife for the purpose of divorce, rather than her taking it from him.]

אָמַר לָהּ: „כְּנְסִי שְׁטָר חוֹב זֶה", — *[If] he said to her: "Take* (lit., *take in*) *this note of indebtedness,"*

A man gave his wife a *get* in the presence of two witnesses (*Meiri*) [but told her that it was a note of indebtedness].

The mishnah in *Maaser Sheni* 4:7 clearly indicates that when a man gives his wife a *get*, he must specify that he is giving her the document for the sake of divorce. Nevertheless, if they had been discussing divorce when he gave her the *get*, that suffices to clarify his intentions, and the divorce is valid (*Rav* ibid.; *Kiddushin* 6a).

[If he threw it] into her lap or into her basket, she is divorced.

2. [If] he said to her: "Take this note of indebtedness," or [if] she found it behind him, [and] she read it, and behold, it was her *get*, it is not a *get* until he will say to her: "This is your *get*."

YAD AVRAHAM

Some authorities therefore maintain that the case of the mishnah must be one in which they had been discussing divorce when he gave her the *get*. Otherwise, the *Tanna* could have stated that the *get* is void even if he is silent, and not only if he misled her into thinking that it was a monetary document (*Ramban* in *Milchamos Hashem; Ran*).

Others maintain that the *get* in this case was given without prior discussion of divorce (*Rambam, Hil. Ishus* 1:9; see *Lechem Mishneh* ad loc.). The fact that he misled her is mentioned because had he remained silent, the *get* would be invalidated only by Rabbinic law (*Rambam* ibid. 1:11), whereas in this case it is Biblically void (*Lechem Mishneh* loc. cit.; *Tos. R' Akiva Eiger*).

אוֹ שֶׁמְּצָאַתּוּ מֵאֲחוֹרָיו, — *[or] if she found it behind him,*

The *get* was on his back, which he turned toward her to allow her to take it (*Rav* from *Gem.* 78a). Had she taken it from him without his assistance, the requisite that he give her the *get* — derived from the phrase, *and he shall place it* (*Deut.* 24:1) — would be lacking, and even his subsequent declaration that it is a *get* (see below) would not validate the divorce (ibid.).

Others explain that the *get* was pressed against his hips; he tightened his muscles to force out the *get* and moved his body toward her. This is because both bringing the *get* closer to her and assisting her in taking it are necessary for the fulfillment of the requirement that he give her the *get*, rather than let her take it from him (*R' Chananel*, cited by *Rosh*).

Some maintain that, in this case, the husband and wife were discussing the possibility of divorce prior to the giving of the *get*. This discussion does not suffice to validate the divorce unless it is followed by a direct presentation of the *get* [which indicates clearly that the husband is acting upon their words], not by his giving it halfheartedly, such as in this case [which indicates hesitation, and thus, does not seem to be following up on their discussion] (*Ran*).

קוֹרְאָה וַהֲרֵי הוּא גִּטָּהּ — אֵינוֹ גֵט, — *[and] she read it, and behold, it was her get, it is not a get*

Upon reading it, she discovered that it was a *get* (*Rav*).

It is not valid because the Torah (*Deut.* ibid.) says: *and he shall place it in her hand, and he shall send her from his house,* which implies that, in giving the *get*, he must indicate that he is divorcing her (*Sifrei* ad loc.).

Others explain that by not indicating that he meant to divorce her, he created the impression that the document is not for that purpose, and thereby negate the *get's* capacity to effectuate a divorce (*Rashba; Ran; Meiri*).

If he told the witnesses that he is giving her a *get* and then told her that it is a note, the divorce is valid, because her agreement to the divorce is not necessary (*Gem.* 55a), and the witnesses can be relied upon to inform her afterward of the nature of the document, so that she will not return to her husband's house (*Tos.* 78a s.v. אינו גט; see 6:2).

עַד שֶׁיֹּאמַר לָהּ: ,,הֵא גִּטֵּךְ״. — *until he will say to her: "This is your get."*

If, after giving the *get* in either of

נָתַן בְּיָדָהּ וְהִיא יְשֵׁנָה; נֵעוֹרָה, קוֹרְאָה וַהֲרֵי הוּא גִטָּהּ — אֵינוֹ גֵט עַד שֶׁיֹּאמַר לָהּ: ,,הֵא גִטֵּךְ". הָיְתָה עוֹמֶדֶת בִּרְשׁוּת הָרַבִּים, וּזְרָקוֹ לָהּ: קָרוֹב

---

the aforementioned ways — telling her that it was a note, or turning his back to her — the husband informed her that it is a *get*, the divorce is valid (*Rav* from *Gem.* 78a), and he does not need to take it back and present it to her a second time (*Gem.* ibid.), as long as the *get* is still in her possession when he tells her (*Ramah*, cited by *Rosh*).

By the same token, if a man asked his wife to watch a *get* for him and later told her she should be divorced with it, or he placed a *get* in her property and afterward, when she was watching her property, he told her it is her *get*, it is not considered as if she took the *get* from him — which would invalidate the divorce — and the *get* takes effect. This is because the delivery of the *get* was done properly, and a subsequent declaration of divorce is sufficient to validate the *get* (*Ran*).

Others contend that the mishnah specifically chose a case in which the husband meant it to be a *get* from the outset but was hiding his intentions from her. However, if his original intention in giving the *get* was for a different purpose, a new delivery is necessary to validate it (*Tos. Rid*).

If he told her to acquire the note, rather that just to take it, she acquires it for the use of the paper, and it can no longer be valid as a *get* (*Ramah*, cited in *Tur Even HaEzer* 138) [unless he reacquires it from her and gives it back to her a second time].

נָתַן בְּיָדָהּ וְהִיא יְשֵׁנָה; נֵעוֹרָה, קוֹרְאָה וַהֲרֵי הוּא גִטָּהּ — אֵינוֹ גֵט — *[If] he placed [it] in her hand [when] she was sleeping, [and] she awoke [and] read it, and behold, it was her get, it is not a get*

Her receipt of the *get* is not valid, because the *get* was not guarded by her at that time (*Ran*) [and thus is not considered as having been given over to her].

Others explain that there is a Biblical requirement, derived from the juxtaposition of the words *a document of severance* with the words *and he shall place it in her hand* (*Deut.* 24:1), that the delivery of the *get* be for the sake of divorce (*Rambam, Hil. Gerushin* 1:9), with her awareness of this fact being on implicit requisite (*Oneg Yom Tov* 163 s.v. מיהו; *Avi Ezri* to *Hil. Gerushin* 10:23 s.v. ונראה; cf. *Even HaEzer* 136:4; *Beis Shmuel, Beur HaGra* ibid.).[1]

Even if they had been previously discussing the possibility of divorce, the *get* is not operative because his delivery was not valid (*Ran*).

עַד שֶׁיֹּאמַר לָהּ: ,,הֵא גִטֵּךְ". — *until he will say to her: "This is your get."*

[This would validate the divorce even without a new delivery, as explained above.]

הָיְתָה עוֹמֶדֶת בִּרְשׁוּת הָרַבִּים, וּזְרָקוֹ לָהּ: — *[If] she was standing in public property, and he threw it to her —*

A man threw his wife a *get* when she was standing in public property, or in any property that does not belong to either of them (*Meiri*).

קָרוֹב לָהּ — מְגֹרֶשֶׁת; — *[if it is] close to her, she is divorced;*

If the *get* lands in a place where the wife can guard it and the husband

1. [*Rambam* does not state explicitly that her awareness is necessary, but his application of the principle that the *get* be delivered for the sake of divorce to the case in which the wife is sleeping indicates as much.]

8 2 [If] he placed [it] in her hand [when] she was sleeping, [and] she awoke [and] read it, and behold, it was her *get*, it is not a *get* until he will say to her: "This is your *get*."

[If] she was standing in public property, and he threw it to her — [if it is] close to her,

YAD AVRAHAM

cannot [e.g., there is a stream between him and the *get* (*Rashi*)], the divorce is valid (*Rav* from *Gem.* 78a), even if it is closer to the husband (*Meiri*). Although the ability to guard an object which is not in one's property does not ordinarily constitute acquisition, the Rabbis validated a *get* given in such a manner in order to protect the woman from a situation which leaves her marital status unclear and would prevent her from remarrying. [Although the Rabbis do not have the authority to validate a divorce which is legally void] they can retroactively annul the original marriage, because its validity is subject to their continued approval (*Rosh;* see *Gem.* 33a, 73a and General Introduction s.v. *Rabbinic Annulment*). However, the *get* is invalid by Rabbinic law until she receives it in her hand (*Rav* from *Gem.* 78b). This is because we are apprehensive that people in such situations may miscalculate and assume that a *get* which is actually closer to the husband is closer to the wife; hence, they will assume that the divorce is valid when it is actually not, and will allow a married woman to marry another man (*Rashi* ad loc. s.v. עד דמטי).

Others opine that in order to be effectual, the *get* must be close enough to the woman so that she can bend down and take it. Even then, it is inoperative by Rabbinic law until she actually takes it (*Rambam, Hil. Gerushin* 5:13; *Even HaEzer* 139:13). There is another view that even placing the *get* in her private property is insufficient; rather, it must be placed in her hand (*Aruch* s.v. גט, cited in *Tos.* s.v. ואת; *R' Chananel,* cited by *Rosh; Rama* to *Even HaEzer* ibid. 14).

Another interpretation of the mishnah is that if the *get* landed within the four cubits surrounding the wife, the divorce is valid (*Gem.* 78a), because the four cubits around every person are considered his private domain for the purpose of acquisition (*Rashi* from *Bava Metzia* 10a). Although this form of acquisition is only a Rabbinic decree, once the Rabbis established it as the equivalent of private property by virtue of their authority over Jewish monetary possessions (see *Gem.* 36b), the acquisitions effected thereby are valid even by Biblical law (*Ran*).

Although there is a dispute whether this form of acquisition is applicable even in a public domain, those who maintain that it is not will interpret the mishnah to be referring to a סִימְטָא, *alleyway,* which is public property, but not a public thoroughfare (see *Rashi* to *Kesubos* 84b s.v. סימטא), regarding which everyone agrees that a person's four cubits therein are considered like his private domain for acquisition (*Ran*). Others contend that the acquisition of a *get* is more easily accomplished than other acquisitions, as evidenced by the fact that it can be given against the woman's will; therefore, everyone agrees that she can receive her *get* in her four cubits even in a public domain (*Meiri*).

Another view is that in a case in which the person can guard the article which is within his four cubits, everyone agrees that it is a valid acquisition even in a public

לָהּ — מְגֹרֶשֶׁת; קָרוֹב לוֹ — אֵינָהּ מְגֹרֶשֶׁת; מֶחֱצָה עַל מֶחֱצָה — מְגֹרֶשֶׁת וְאֵינָהּ מְגֹרֶשֶׁת.

[ג] **וְכֵן** לְעִנְיַן קִדּוּשִׁין, וְכֵן לְעִנְיַן הַחוֹב. אָמַר לוֹ בַּעַל חוֹבוֹ: „זְרֹק לִי חוֹבִי", וּזְרָקוֹ לוֹ: קָרוֹב לַמַּלְוֶה — זָכָה הַלֹּוֶה; קָרוֹב לַלֹּוֶה — הַלֹּוֶה

ר' עובדיה מברטנורא

קרוב לה מגורשת קרוב לו אינה מגורשת. כל שהיא יכולה לשמרו והוא אינו יכול לשמרו, זהו קרוב לה. וכל שהיא אינה יכולה לשמרו והוא יכול לשמרו, זהו קרוב לו. שניהם יכולים לשמרו, או שניהם אינם יכולים לשמרו, זהו מחצה על מחצה. ולענין פסק הלכה אינה מגורשת עד שיגיע גט לידה או לרשותה: (ג) **אמר לו בעל חובו זרוק לי חובי.** בגמרא (עח, ב) מוקמינן לה באומר זרוק לי חובי בתורת גטין, דכיון דאמר ליה הכי, הוה ליה לחוב זה דין גט, ואם זרק אותו הלוה קרוב למלוה ואבד, זכה הלוה ואינו חייב לשלם, ואם קרוב ללוה, הלוה חייב וכו'. אבל אם אמר לו זרוק לי חובי והפטר, מכיון שזרקו לו בכל ענין, פטור:

יד אברהם

established that space as his property, rather than hers (*Tos. HaRosh* ibid., s.v. ארבע אמות שלו).

מֶחֱצָה עַל מֶחֱצָה — מְגֹרֶשֶׁת וְאֵינָהּ מְגֹרֶשֶׁת. — *[if] half and half, she is divorced and not divorced.*

If the husband and wife are each able to guard the *get*, or if neither of them can guard it alone (*Rav*), but they can do so together (*Tos.* 78b, s.v. שנידהם), the validity of the *get* is questionable. [Therefore, the woman may not remarry without a new delivery of the *get*, and if her husband dies without children she must perform *chalitzah*.]

According to the other interpretation, this case is one in which one pair of witnesses testified that the *get* landed close to her, and another pair that it landed close to him (*Gem.* ibid.). Although by Biblical law, *chazakah* (presumptive status) should dictate that we presume that she is still married, the Rabbis decreed that a doubt arising from conflicting testimonies cannot be decided in such a manner (*Tos.* ad loc. s.v. והא א"א).

domain; and that is the case in our mishnah (*Tos.* 78b s.v. רבי יוחנן). A fourth opinion is that when an article is given over from one person to another, the involvement of the giver strengthens the recipient's acquisition, and the article can be acquired by its placement in the recipient's four cubits, even in a public domain (*Tos. HaRosh*).

קָרוֹב לוֹ — אֵינָהּ מְגֹרֶשֶׁת; — *[if] close to him, she is not divorced;*

If the *get* landed in a place where only the husband can guard it, it is not operative (*Rav* from *Gem.* 78b), even if it is close to the woman (*Meiri*). Even if the wife can guard it with the help of a third party — which would suffice to validate her acquisition — the husband's ability to guard it alone negates her possession of the *get*, and the divorce is null (*Tos. HaRosh* ibid., s.v. והיא אינה יכולה).

The other interpretation of the mishnah, mentioned above, explains this to mean that if the *get* landed within the husband's four cubits, it is not valid (*Gem.* 78a) even if it was also within her four cubits, as long as he had been there first and had thereby

she is divorced; [if] close to him, she is not divorced; [if] half and half, she is divorced and not divorced.

3. The same [is true] concerning *kiddushin,* and the same [is true] concerning a debt: [If] his creditor said to him: "Throw me my debt," and he threw it to him — [if it falls] close to the lender, the borrower gains; [if] close to the borrower, he is

YAD AVRAHAM

3.

וְכֵן לְעִנְיַן קִדּוּשִׁין, — *The same [is true] concerning kiddushin,*

Those rules, which were stated in the previous mishnah regarding a woman's receiving her *get* by virtue of it being placed close to her, also apply to *kiddushin* (or *erusin*), the first stage of marriage. This is derived from the verse, *And she went out ... and she was [married]* (*Deut.* 24:2), from which the Rabbis deduce exegetically that divorce and marriage correspond in every way that we can possibly compare them (*Meiri* from *Gem.* 78b).

וְכֵן לְעִנְיַן הַחוֹב: אָמַר לוֹ בַּעַל חוֹבוֹ: ,,זְרֹק לִי חוֹבִי", וּזְרָקוֹ לוֹ: — *and the same [is true] concerning a debt: [If] his creditor said to him: "Throw me my debt," and he threw it to him —*

A creditor said to his debtor, "Throw me my debt in accordance with the laws of *gittin*" (*Rav* from *Gem.* ibid.), thus indicating that if the debtor throws the money to the creditor, and it lands in a place which would suffice for a woman's receipt of her *get*, he is freed from his obligation (*Meiri*). If the creditor did not mention "the laws of *gittin*," his proximity to the money does not constitute an acquisition, and the debt remains in force (*Gem.* ibid.).

קָרוֹב לַמַּלְוֶה — זָכָה הַלֹּוֶה; — *[if it falls] close to the lender, the borrower gains;*

If the money lands close to the lender [i.e., the creditor] in a place where he can guard it and the borrower cannot (see previous mishnah)], the debt is canceled. If the money is then lost before the lender retrieves it, it is his loss (*Rav* from *Gem.* ibid.), because we do not assume that he had not been serious (*Gem.* ibid.).

[Although the version of the mishnah which is printed in our editions of the Talmud reads: זָכָה הַמַּלְוֶה, it is interpreted to mean not that *the lender gains*, but that *the lender acquires it*; i.e., that it is considered as if the lender had received it in regard to canceling the borrower's debt. Thus, both versions have the same meaning.]

There is another opinion that the case involves a debt which was not yet due, and the borrower changed his mind after throwing the money to the lender and decided that he does not wish to repay the loan now. If the acquisition is valid, it is too late for the borrower to change his mind; if it is not valid, he can retrieve the money until the debt is due (*Mordechai* 438).

קָרוֹב לַלֹּוֶה — הַלֹּוֶה חַיָּב; — *[if] close to the borrower, he is obligated;*

[If the money lands close to the borrower, the debt is not considered

חַיָּב; מֶחֱצָה עַל מֶחֱצָה — שְׁנֵיהֶם יַחֲלֹקוּ.
הָיְתָה עוֹמֶדֶת עַל רֹאשׁ הַגַּג, וּזְרָקוֹ לָהּ — כֵּיוָן שֶׁהִגִּיעַ לַאֲוִיר הַגַּג הֲרֵי זוֹ מְגֹרֶשֶׁת.
הוּא מִלְּמַעְלָה וְהִיא מִלְּמַטָּה, וּזְרָקוֹ לָהּ — כֵּיוָן שֶׁיָּצָא מֵרְשׁוּת הַגַּג, נִמְחַק אוֹ נִשְׂרַף, הֲרֵי זוֹ מְגֹרֶשֶׁת.

ר׳ עובדיה מברטנורא

לאויר הגג. לפחות משלשה סמוך לקרקעית הגג, דכלבוד דמי: **מרשות הגג.** יצא ממחיצת הגג ונכנס לתוך מחיצת המקום שהיא עומדת בו: **או נשרף [הרי זו] מגורשת.** והוא שקדמה זריקת הגט בחצר קודם שתהא הדליקה באויר החצר. שאם היתה הדליקה בחצר תחלה, מטיקרא לשריפה קאזיל ואינה מגורשת:

יד אברהם

paid; therefore, if it then becomes lost, the debt is still in force.]

If the creditor said: "Throw me my debt and be exempt," the debt is canceled as soon as the debtor throws him the money, regardless of where it lands (*Rav; Tur, Choshen Mishpat* 120; *Tos.* 78b s.v. אי הכי). Others contend that the debt is canceled only if the money lands close to the creditor, because when he told the debtor to throw him the money, he meant that he should throw it into his possession (*Rashba*).

מֶחֱצָה עַל מֶחֱצָה — שְׁנֵיהֶם יַחֲלֹקוּ. — *[if] half and half, they both divide [it].*

If it landed in a place where they can both guard it together, or either of them can do so alone (*Tif. Yis.*), half of the debt is considered paid, and if the money becomes lost, the debtor must pay the other half of the debt (*Rambam, Hil. Malveh* 16:1).

Although there is a general rule that הַמּוֹצִיא מֵחֲבֵרוֹ עָלָיו הָרְאָיָה, *if one seeks to exact something from another, the burden of proof is on him* (*Bava Kamma* 46b), we do not demand the same of the creditor in this case, who wishes to collect his debt. This is because, unlike the general rule — which applies when we are in doubt as to whom the item belongs — in this case, the mishnah's ruling that we divide it is not due to doubt, but rather because we know that they share possession of the money which the debtor threw to the creditor (*Tos.* 78b s.v. מחצה). However, according to the interpretation (mentioned in commentary to mishnah 2) that *half and half* means that there were conflicting testimonies, the division is indeed based on a doubt as to whom it belongs. Therefore, the mishnah must be understood like the explanation of *Mordechai* (see above), that the money thrown is still retrievable, and the borrower wants to change his mind and retract his early payment (*Maharsha* to 78b). [Thus, the issue is who has the right to this money which is in neither's possession, not whether the lender may collect money which is in the borrower's possession, and the general rule stated above, regarding exaction from another, pertains only to that which someone is seeking to exact from another's possession.]

הָיְתָה עוֹמֶדֶת עַל רֹאשׁ הַגַּג, — *[If] she was standing on top of the roof,*

I.e., a roof that belonged to her (*Gem.* 79a).

וּזְרָקוֹ לָהּ — *and he threw it to her,*

The husband was standing on the ground in his own property, and he

obligated; [if] half and half, they both divide [it].

[If] she was standing on top of the roof, and he threw it to her, once it reaches the airspace of the roof, she is divorced.

[If] he [was] above and she below, and he threw it to her, once it leaves the domain of the roof, [even if] it was erased or burnt, she is divorced.

YAD AVRAHAM

threw the *get* up to his wife (ibid.).

כֵּיוָן שֶׁהִגִּיעַ לַאֲוִיר הַגַּג הֲרֵי זוֹ מְגֹרֶשֶׁת. — *once it reaches the airspace of the roof, she is divorced.*

As soon as the *get* comes within three handbreadths of the roof, it is considered as if it had already landed, and she is divorced (*Rav* from *Gem.*).

Alternatively, if the roof was enclosed by a wall, as soon as the *get* comes within the walls and is no longer in danger of being blown away, it is considered to be in her guarded property, and she is divorced (*Gem.*).

הוּא מִלְמַעְלָה — *[If] he [was] above*

The husband was on a roof, which belonged to him (ibid.).

וְהִיא מִלְּמַטָּה, וּזְרָקוֹ לָהּ — *and she below, and he threw it to her,*

The wife was on the ground, on her property (ibid.) [and the husband threw the *get* down to her].

כֵּיוָן שֶׁיָּצָא מֵרְשׁוּת הַגַּג, — *once it leaves the domain of the roof,*

The *get* left the enclosure of the barriers around the roof and fell within those of the yard (*Rav*).

The *Gemara* construes the mishnah to be speaking of a case in which the walls of the courtyard rise above those of the roof which is within the yard. Thus, as soon as the *get* leaves the area of the roof, it immediately enters that of the yard. [Hence, the blanket statement of the mishnah that *once it leaves the domain of the roof ... she is divorced.*]

נִמְחַק — *[even if] it was erased*

The *get* became erased after it had begun to fall into the yard (*Gem.* ibid.); for example, it was erased by water (see *Rashi* ad loc. s.v. והא לא מינטר).

אוֹ נִשְׂרַף, — *or burnt,*

The *get* was consumed by a fire which began after the *get* had been thrown into the airspace of the yard (*Rav* from *Gem.*).

הֲרֵי זוֹ מְגֹרֶשֶׁת. — *she is divorced.*

This is because the entrance of the *get* into the enclosed airspace of her yard is equivalent to its landing on her guarded property, and she takes possession of it (*Gem.*).

However, while the *get* is still rising from the throw, it is not tantamount to its having landed on the ground, and therefore, if it becomes erased while it is rising, she is not divorced (ibid.). Similarly, if the fire had been burning before the *get* was thrown, the *get* is considered to have been thrown directly into the fire, and it is therefore not viewed as if it had landed on her property (*Rav* from *Gem.*).

The laws regarding the erasure or destruction of the *get* in this case apply also equally to the previous case of the mishnah, in which she was on the roof. However, since water [to erase the *get*] and fire are more prevalent on the ground than on a roof, the *Tanna* stated them in this case (*Rashba*).

Others contend that in the former case, if the *get* was erased or destroyed before

[ד] **בֵּית** שַׁמַּאי אוֹמְרִים: פּוֹטֵר אָדָם אֶת אִשְׁתּוֹ בְּגֵט יָשָׁן; וּבֵית הִלֵּל אוֹסְרִין. וְאֵיזֶהוּ גֵּט יָשָׁן? כֹּל שֶׁנִּתְיַחֵד עִמָּהּ אַחַר שֶׁכְּתָבוֹ לָהּ.

[ה] **כָּתַב** לְשׁוּם מַלְכוּת שֶׁאֵינָהּ הוֹגֶנֶת,

ר׳ עובדיה מברטנורא

(ד) **בגט ישן.** שכתב לגרש את אשתו ואחר שנכתב הגט נתייחד עמה. בית שמאי סברי, לא אמרינן גזירה שמא יאמרו גטה קודם לבנה, שמא ישהה את הגט שנה או שנתים בין כתיבה לנתינה ויהיו לה בנים ממנו בתוך זמן זה, ואחר כך יגרשנה בו, וכשיראו זמן הגט קודם ללידת הבן, יהיו סבורים שנתן לה גט משעת כתיבה, והוי פגם, שיאמרו מן הפנויה נולד. ופסק ההלכה, לא יגרש אדם את אשתו בגט ישן. ואם גרש והלך הבעל למדינה אחרת, תנשא בו לכתחלה: (ה) **כתב לשם מלכות שאינה הוגנת.** אם היה בבבל וכתב לחשבון שנות מלכות אדום, שאין להם מלכות במקום כתיבת הגט, תצא מזה ומזה. ונקראת מלכות [אדום] מלכות שאינה הוגנת, שאין לה לא כתב ולא לשון:

יד אברהם

landing, it is void (*Rambam, Hil. Gerushin* 5:3), because an upward throw is an unnatural form of movement and is thus contradictory to the natural direction of descent. Therefore, if it does not actually land, it cannot be considered tantamount to having done so. The point of the mishnah is only that if it does land, the divorce is effectual retroactive to when the *get* entered the enclosed airspace of the roof or came within three handbreadths of the ground (*Maggid Mishneh* ad loc.).

4.

בֵּית שַׁמַּאי אוֹמְרִים: פּוֹטֵר אָדָם אֶת אִשְׁתּוֹ בְּגֵט יָשָׁן; — *Beis Shammai say: A man may divorce his wife with an "old" get;*

[If a man was alone with his wife after having a *get* written for her (see below), he may still use that *get* to divorce her.]

וּבֵית הִלֵּל אוֹסְרִין. — *Beis Hillel, however, prohibit [it].*

They were concerned that the man and woman may have had marital relations after the *get* was written, which could lead to rumors that children born from those relations were conceived out of wedlock (*Rav* from *Gem.* 79b).

Yerushalmi explains that this dispute is based on another disagreement between Beis Shammai and Beis Hillel in 9:10. There, Beis Shammai maintain that a man may divorce his wife only if he found her to be adulterous; thus, if he wrote a *get* for that reason, it is not likely that he would subsequently desire intimacy with her. Beis Hillel, on the other hand, hold that he may divorce her for issues of much lesser magnitude; it is therefore feasible that he will still live with her (*Tos.* 79b s.v. בית שמאי).

Even according to Beis Hillel, if a man went ahead and did give his wife such a *get*, it is valid, and she may remarry (*Rav* from *Gem.* ibid.). This is not considered a predated *get*, which is invalid due to the negative repercussions which can come from confusion about the date of divorce (see 2:2 and commentary ad loc.), because in our

4. Beis Shammai say: A man may divorce his wife with an "old" *get;* Beis Hillel, however, prohibit [it]. What is an 'old' *get?* Any [time] he secludes himself with her after he wrote it for her.

5. [I]f] he wrote [the date of the *get*] according to [the reign of] a kingdom which is unworthy,

YAD AVRAHAM

case, the *get* was signed on the date which is written upon it and only the delivery was later (*Meiri*).

Others contend that it is valid ex post facto only if it was given through an agent who will generate publicity and thereby avoid the problems of a predated *get* (see *Gem.* 18a). However, even in such a case, Beis Hillel prohibits initially using such a *get* for fear of rumors that the children were conceived out of wedlock (*Rashba;* see *Rosh* to 17b, *Even HaEzer* 127:4).

Some authorities rule that she may remarry only if the husband has gone overseas and is thus unavailable to give another *get* (*Rashi; Ran*). Others do not make this distinction (*Rambam, Hil. Gerushin* 3:5; *Even HaEzer* 148:1; see *Beis Shmuel* ibid. 3).

Some maintain that if the husband wrote the *get* and sent it to her with an agent and was then alone with her before the agent reached her, she may not remarry without another *get*. She is permitted to do so only when the husband sent the *get* after their meeting, because we rely on the assumption that had they had relations, he would not have sent her a *get* which could create difficulties for his children (*Rama,* cited by *Rosh;* see *Korban Nesanel* ad loc.).

וְאֵיזֶהוּ גֵּט יָשָׁן? כָּל שֶׁנִּתְיַחֵד עִמָּהּ אַחַר שֶׁכְּתָבוֹ לָהּ. — *What is an "old" get? Any [time] he secludes himself with her after he wrote it for her.*

Even if the *get* was given after *erusin* (the first state of marriage [see 6:2]), we are concerned that they may have had relations, and he may not give her the *get* (*Rashba; Tos. R' Akiva Eiger*).

5.

In the time of the Mishnah, it was customary among the nations to date documents by the year of the reigning monarchy (*Meiri; Tos.* 80b s.v. וז), and Jewish divorce documents, which are considered to be of major significance (*Tos.* 80a s.v. מפני), were also dated in this manner for the sake of peaceful relations with the regime (*Rav* from *Gem.* ibid.). Accordingly, the Rabbis prohibited the dating of *gittin* by the reign of monarchies other than the one which ruled in that place at that time (*Rambam Commentary*). In our times, when the gentiles do not date their documents in this manner, it is no longer necessary for us to do so, and we therefore date all legal documents using the year from Creation (*Meiri; Tos.* ibid.).

כָּתַב לְשׁוּם מַלְכוּת שֶׁאֵינָהּ הוֹגֶנֶת, — *[If] he wrote [the date of the get] according to [the reign of] a kingdom which is unworthy,*

A man wrote a *get* for his wife in Babylonia and dated it by the years of

גיטין ח/ה

לְשׁוּם מַלְכוּת מָדַי, לְשׁוּם מַלְכוּת יָוָן, לְבִנְיַן הַבַּיִת, לְחֻרְבַּן הַבַּיִת; הָיָה בַמִּזְרָח, וְכָתַב: ,,בַּמַּעֲרָב״, בַּמַּעֲרָב, וְכָתַב: ,,בַּמִּזְרָח״ — תֵּצֵא מִזֶּה וּמִזֶּה, וּצְרִיכָה גֵט מִזֶּה וּמִזֶּה. וְאֵין לָהּ לֹא כְתֻבָּה, וְלֹא פֵרוֹת,

ר׳ עובדיה מברטנורא

או שכתב לשם מלכות מדי. לפי שלריך לכתוב לשם המלכות של מדינה שהגט נכתב בה, משום שלום מלכות, שיאמרו חשובים אנו בעיניהם שכותבים שטרותיהם בשמינו: **תצא מזה ומזה.** אם נשאת בגט זה, תלא מן הראשון ומן השני:

יד אברהם

the Roman Empire, which is an unworthy kingdom because it does not have its own language and alphabet (*Rav* from *Gem.* 80a), but adapted them from other nations (*Rashi* ad loc.). Despite this unworthiness, the regime in Babylonia would be provoked by the dating of *gittin* according to the years of the Roman Empire (*Tos.* 79b s.v. כתב).

Others explain that all other languages of antiquity were established at the time of the Tower of Babylon (*Gen.* 11:1) in accordance with the inherent spiritual characteristics of each nation; Latin, however, was developed by an individual named Latinus and has no innate connection to the Roman people (*Chasam Sofer* to 80a).

לְשׁוּם מַלְכוּת מָדַי, לְשׁוּם מַלְכוּת יָוָן, — *according to the kingdom of Media, according to the kingdom of Greece,*

It was forbidden to honor these kingdoms by dating a *get* according to their reigns, even though they were no longer in existence at the time, and it was less likely that doing so would arouse the jealousy of the current monarch (*Gem.* 80a).

לְבִנְיַן הַבַּיִת, — *to the construction of the Temple,*

Even dating a *get* by the years since the construction of the Temple, which is less likely to arouse jealousy than the honoring of a different sovereign, was prohibited (ibid.).

לְחֻרְבַּן הַבַּיִת; — *[or] to the destruction of the Temple;*

The Rabbis even prohibited dating *gittin* according to the destruction of the Temple, which was an expression of sorrow rather than homage (ibid.) [because doing so rather than dating according to the present regime might still arouse jealousy].

הָיָה בַמִּזְרָח, וְכָתַב: ,,בַּמַּעֲרָב״, בַּמַּעֲרָב, וְכָתַב: ,,בַּמִּזְרָח״, — *[or if] he was in the East, and he wrote: "in the West," [or] in the West, and he wrote: "in the East,"*

The scribe wrote the wrong location into the *get* (ibid.) — i.e., he wrote as the place in which it was drawn up a different city than the one in which the witnesses had signed it. However, it is not necessary for the text of the *get* to be written in the place stated within as long as the witnesses signed it here (*Rosh; Rambam, Hil. Gerushin* 1:25; *Mefaresh* ad loc.).

Others contend that the *get* must be written and signed in the place stated within the *get* as the location where it as drawn up (*Rama*, cited by *Tur, Even HaEzer* 128; see *Beis Yosef* ad loc.).

תֵּצֵא מִזֶּה וּמִזֶּה, — *she must leave both of them* (lit., *she must go out from this one and from this one*),

If the wife received a *get* with any of the aforementioned flaws, and then remarried, she becomes forbidden to

according to the kingdom of Media, according to the kingdom of Greece, to the construction of the Temple, [or] to the destruction of the Temple; [or if] he was in the East, and he wrote: "in the West," [or] in the West, and he wrote: "in the East," she must leave both of them, and she needs [to receive] a *get* from each of them. She is entitled neither to a *kesubah*, nor usufruct,

YAD AVRAHAM

both of the husbands (*Rav*); since the *get* was invalid, her intimacy with the second husband is considered the equivalent of adultery, in which case she is forbidden to both her husband and the adulterer (*Meiri*).

וּצְרִיכָה גֵט מִזֶּה וּמִזֶּה. — *and she needs [to receive] a get from each of them.*

If she wishes to marry a third man, she must receive a *get* from each of the first two (*Rashi* to *Yevamos* 88b). From the first husband, to whom she had been married legitimately, she requires a *get* by Biblical law, since the previous *get* was void. From the second, whose marriage to her was invalid, she is obligated by the Rabbis to receive a *get*, to avoid the possibility of people thinking that the first *get* — and hence, the second marriage — had been valid, and that she had married the third husband while still wed to the second (*Rashi; Meiri*).

The author of this mishnah is R' Meir, who holds that if a man gives his wife a *get* that deviates from the format dictated by the Rabbis, and she remarries, any child born of the second marriage is a *mamzer* (a person born from forbidden relations which are punishable by the death penalty or *kares* [spiritual excision and premature death]). Therefore, although the *gittin* discussed in the mishnah are void only by Rabbinic decree, the Rabbis revoked even their Biblical legality, thereby invalidating the second marriage completely. Thus, she requires a *get* from the second man (only because of) the reason mentioned above (*Tos. Yom Tov;* see *Pnei Yehoshua* to *Tos.* 80b s.v. וצריכא).

Others contend that these *gittin* are void only by Rabbinic law, but retain their Biblical validity (*Tos.; Ran; Tos Rid*). Thus, she requires another *get* from the first husband because of the Rabbinic decree which nullified the first, and one from the second husband because their marriage was Biblically valid (*Tos. Rid*).

וְאֵין לָהּ לֹא כְתֻבָּה, — *She is entitled neither to a kesubah,*

She does not receive payment of the *kesubah* (marriage contract), which a woman ordinarily collects upon divorce. This is because the purpose of the *kesubah* is to discourage men from divorcing their wives by imposing a financial burden on those who do; in our case, however, the Rabbis obligated the husbands to divorce (*Meiri; Tos. Rid* from *Yevamos* 89a). [As stated below, all the laws discussed here apply to both husbands.]

וְלֹא פֵרוֹת, — *nor usufruct,*

She is excluded from the Rabbinic ordinance which gives a husband the rights to the produce of his wife's fields in exchange for which he is obligated to redeem her if she is taken

וְלֹא מְזוֹנוֹת, וְלֹא בְלָאוֹת, לֹא עַל זֶה וְלֹא עַל זֶה; אִם נָטְלָה מִזֶּה וּמִזֶּה — תַּחֲזִיר. וְהַוָּלָד מַמְזֵר מִזֶּה וּמִזֶּה. וְלֹא זֶה וָזֶה מִטַּמְּאִין לָהּ, וְלֹא זֶה וָזֶה זַכָּאִין

ר׳ עובדיה מברטנורא

ואין לה לא פירות ולא בלאות וכו׳. כולה מתניתין מפרשה ביבמות פרק האשה רבה (צ״א, ב): **והולד ממזר מזה ומזה.** מתניתין רבי מאיר היא דאמר (פ, א) כל המשנה ממטבע שטבעו חכמים בגטין הולד ממזר. ואינה הלכה:

יד אברהם

captive [not an uncommon occurrence in those days] (*Rashi; Meiri; Tos. Rid;* see *Kesubos* 48b). This protection of the wife was ordained as a clause in the *kesubah;* in our case, since she is not entitled to her *kesubah,* this clause is also not in effect (*Meiri* from *Yevamos* ibid.). [Therefore, the husbands must reimburse her for any usufruct they enjoyed from her property, and if she is captured, they are not obligated to redeem her any more than any other Jew.]

Others explain that she is not remunerated for the produce of her property which the husbands consumed while they were married to her (*Ran* from *Yerushalmi* to *Yevamos* 10:1).

וְלֹא מְזוֹנוֹת, — *nor sustenance,*

She does not receive payment toward her food, nor is the husband obligated to reimburse a lender for money she had borrowed for food while they were still living together, with the stipulation that he would repay it (*Ran; Tos. Rid*). This, too, is an obligation stipulated in the *kesubah* and is therefore negated along with it (*Meiri* from *Yevamos* ibid.).

וְלֹא בְלָאוֹת, — *nor worn-out clothing,*

If any clothing from the wife's נִכְסֵי צֹאן בַּרְזֶל, *fixed-value property* (see commentary to 5:6 s.v. לָקַח מִן הָאִישׁ), or usufructuary property (see commentary to mishnah 1 s.v. וְהִיא) wore out completely, the husband is not obligated to replace the loss. However, he must return any such property still in hand (*Ran; Meiri; Rav* to *Yevamos* 10:1; *Rif* ibid.; *Rambam, Hil. Gerushin* 10:7). This is a fine levied on the woman for not taking the *get* to a Rabbi to clarify its validity (*Tos. Rid*).

Others contend that even worn clothing which is still usable need not be returned (*Rashi; Tos. Rid*).

לֹא עַל זֶה וְלֹא עַל זֶה; — *from either* (lit. *not upon this one nor upon this one*);

[She cannot claim any of these payments from either her first or second husband.]

אִם נָטְלָה מִזֶּה וּמִזֶּה — תַּחֲזִיר. — *if she took from either, she must return [it].*

[If she has already received any of the above payments from either of the two men, she must return it to them.]

וְהַוָּלָד מַמְזֵר מִזֶּה וּמִזֶּה. — [*Her*] *child by either is a mamzer.*

Any child from the second husband is a *mamzer* by Biblical law — since the divorce from the first husband was void (see commentary above s.v. וּצְרִיכָה גֵט) — and hence, may not marry a regular Jew (see *Deut.* 22:3). If she left the second husband without a *get* and returned to the first, any child born from that marriage is a *mamzer* by Rabbinic law — and is thus forbidden even to another *mamzer* — by virtue of the marriage to the second husband from which the

nor sustenance, nor worn-out clothing, from either; if she took from either, she must return [it]. [Her] child by either is a *mamzer.* Neither of them may contaminate himself to her, and neither has rights

Rabbis required a *get* (*Meiri*).

This is in accordance with the opinion of R' Meir, that if one deviates from the Rabbinically prescribed format of a *get,* it is totally void, and any child born to the wife from a subsequent marriage is a *mamzer* (*Rav* from *Gem.* 80a). The Sages, however, disagree, and the *halachah* follows their opinion that the child is legitimate (*Rav*).

According to those who maintain that the *get* is void only by Rabbinic law (see commentary above, loc. cit.), the ruling would be reversed. A child born from the first husband after she had already been married to the second man would be a *mamzer* by Biblical law, since the *get* — and thus, the second marriage — was Biblically valid. A child of the second husband would be Rabbinically illegitimate, because they invalidated the *get* (*Ran; Tos. Rid*).

The precise interpretation of the opinion of the Sages is a subject of dispute among the commentators. Some maintain that in both of the cases discussed in the mishnah — i.e., if the *get* was dated improperly, and if it had been written in a different place than indicated within it — the *get* is invalid, and she may not remarry without a new one (*R' Elchanan,* cited in *Tos.* 80b s.v. וז; *Ran*). Another view is that if the *get* was dated improperly, it is invalid, whereas if the location was incorrect, it may still be used (*Rashi* 80b s.v. הולד כשר; see *Rosh*). Others contend that the reverse is true: If the location written in the *get* is incorrect, this invalidates it, but the wrong date does not (*Tos.* ibid.).

וְלֹא זֶה וָזֶה מִטַּמְּאִין לָהּ, — *Neither of them may contaminate himself to her,*

A *Kohen* may not allow himself to become ritually contaminated by coming into contact with a corpse or being under the same roof with one (*Lev.* 21:1), except for close relatives, such as his wife (ibid., v. 2; see *Rashi* ad loc.). However, in a case in which marital relations between them is prohibited, the exemption for a wife does not apply. This is derived from the passage (ibid. v. 4): *A husband may not contaminate himself... when he is profaned* [i.e., when his wife is prohibited to him, and thus profanes him] (*Yevamos* 90b).

Since, in our case, both husbands are prohibited to her, if she dies, and either of them is a *Kohen,* he may not contaminate himself by coming in contact with her corpse (*Meiri*).

[This explanation is necessary only for the husband who is actually married to her by law; the other may not contaminate himself to her if he is a *Kohen,* because she is not his wife.]

וְלֹא זֶה וָזֶה זַכָּאִין לֹא בִמְצִיאָתָהּ, — *and neither has rights to her findings,*

[Neither man has the right to keep objects which she finds.]

The Rabbis gave every husband property rights over his wife's findings in order to avoid any resentment on his part over his obligation to support her (*Tos. HaRosh* to *Yevamos* ibid., s.v. טעמא). In our case, since his wife is forbidden to him, it is preferable to let him be resentful so that he should divorce her (*Meiri, Tos. Rid* from *Yevamos* ibid.).

[Here, too, the explanation is necessary only in reference to the one to whom she is actually married.]

לֹא בִמְצִיאָתָהּ, וְלֹא בְמַעֲשֵׂה יָדֶיהָ, וְלֹא בַהֲפָרַת נְדָרֶיהָ. הָיְתָה בַת יִשְׂרָאֵל — נִפְסֶלֶת מִן הַכְּהֻנָּה; בַּת לֵוִי — מִן הַמַּעֲשֵׂר; בַּת כֹּהֵן — מִן הַתְּרוּמָה. וְאֵין יוֹרְשָׁיו שֶׁל זֶה וְיוֹרְשָׁיו שֶׁל זֶה יוֹרְשִׁין כְּתֻבָּתָהּ. וְאִם מֵתוּ — אָחִיו שֶׁל זֶה וְאָחִיו שֶׁל זֶה חוֹלְצִין וְלֹא מְיַבְּמִין.

יד אברהם

וְלֹא בְמַעֲשֵׂה יָדֶיהָ, — *her handiwork,*

[Neither man has teh right to claim the products or profits of her work.]

The Rabbis awarded every husband the rights to his wife's handiwork as compensation for his obligation to support her. In our case, however, since there is no obligation of sustenance (see above), the husband has no rights to the products of her labor (*Meiri, Tos. Rid* from *Yevamos* ibid.).

וְלֹא בַהֲפָרַת נְדָרֶיהָ. — *or the revocation of her vows.*

[Neither man has the authority to revoke her vows.]

The Torah (*Num.* 30:14,17) empowers a husband to nullify his wife's vows, but only those which affect their mutual relationship, such as those which cause her distress (e.g., not to eat or bathe) or those which affect their conjugal relationship (e.g., not to be intimate with him) (*Nedarim* 79b). It is therefore understood that the reason for his authority is so that she should not become repulsive to him (*Yevamos* 90b; see *Rashi* ad loc.). In our case, since she is forbidden to these men, the Sages say, "Let her become repulsive to him so that he will divorce her" (*Meiri, Tos. Rid* from *Yevamos* ibid.).

הָיְתָה בַת יִשְׂרָאֵל — נִפְסֶלֶת מִן הַכְּהֻנָּה; — *[If] she was the daughter of a non-Kohen, she is disqualified from marrying a Kohen* (lit.. *from the priesthood*);

An adulterous cohabitation renders a woman a *zonah* (loosely, *harlot*), and prohibits her from ever marrying a *Kohen* (ibid.; see *Rambam, Hil. Issurei Biah* 18:1). Therefore, even if both men die without divorcing her, she is still prohibited to marry a *Kohen* (*Tif. Yis.*).

בַּת לֵוִי — מִן הַמַּעֲשֵׂר; — *[if] the daughter of a Levi, [she is disqualified] from the tithe;*

I.e., from eating מַעֲשֵׂר רִאשׁוֹן, *the first tithe*, which is given to *Leviim* (*Meiri* from *Yevamos* 91a). This is done to penalize her for not clarifying the validity of the *get* (*Tos. Rid*).

According to R' Meir, all non-*Leviim* are prohibited to eat the tithe; the Sages, however, permit them to eat it (*Yevamos* 85b). Either our mishnah follows R' Meir's opinion, the penalty here being that she is considered a non-*Levi*, and is thus forbidden to eat the tithe; or it follows the Sages' opinion as well, in which case the penalty is that the tithe is not given to her, although she is permitted to eat it (*Tos.* to *Yevamos* ibid., s.v. אמר רב ששת).

בַּת כֹּהֵן — מִן הַתְּרוּמָה. — *[and if] the daughter of a Kohen, [she is disqualified] from terumah.*

A *zonah* is disqualified from eating *terumah* (*Rashi* from *Sotah* 28a). The Rabbis fined her by prohibiting to her even the type of *terumah* which is only consecrated as such by Rabbinic

8
5
to her findings, her handiwork, or the revocation of her vows. [If] she was the daughter of a non-*Kohen*, she is disqualified from marrying a *Kohen;* [if] the daughter of a *Levi*, [she is disqualified] from the tithe; [and if] the daughter of a *Kohen*, [she is disqualified] from *terumah*. The heirs of both do not inherit her *kesubah*. If they died, the brother of each performs *chalitzah*, but not *yibum*.

YAD AVRAHAM

law [e.g., *terumah* from vegetables; see *Rambam, Hil. Terumos* 2:6] (*Tif. Yis.* from *Yevamos* ibid.).

Since the mishnah has already disqualified her from eating tithes, it is obvious that she also may not eat *terumah*, which is more sacred. Thus, the mishnah's seemingly superfluous statement that she is also prohibited to eat *terumah* must have been intended to include some novel ruling — i.e., her disqualification from even Rabbinical *terumah* (*Rashi* ad loc., s.v. בתרומה דרבנן).

וְאֵין יוֹרְשָׁיו שֶׁל זֶה וְיוֹרְשָׁיו שֶׁל זֶה יוֹרְשִׁין כְּתֻבָּתָהּ. — *The heirs of both do not inherit her kesubah.*

The Rabbis penalized not only her, but also her children from either of the two men, by depriving them of the special inheritance rights stipulated in the *kesubah* (*Yevamos* 91a). [The fact that they do not inherit the ordinary *kesubah* payments in case of her death is obvious, since it has already been stated that she receives no *kesubah*.]

One of the clauses of the *kesubah* is that if a woman dies during her husband's lifetime (at which time he inherits her estate), all of the money and property mentioned in the *kesubah* that are in his possession pass to their sons upon his death, and are not divided with any sons he may have had from another wife (see *Kesubos* 4:10). The mishnah informs us that, in this case, her sons do not have any such rights, and any property acquired by the husband through his marriage to her is divided equally among all his sons, regardless of who their mother is (*Rashi* from *Yevamos* ad loc.).

וְאִם מֵתוּ — *If they died,*

[If either of the two men should die without leaving offspring, and she falls before a surviving brother for *yibum*.]

אָחִיו שֶׁל זֶה וְאָחִיו שֶׁל זֶה חוֹלְצִין וְלֹא מְיַבְּמִין. — *the brother of each performs chalitzah, but not yibum.*

The brother of the first husband — to whom she was actually married — is obligated by Biblical law to perform *chalitzah* (*Rashi; Meiri*). The brother of the second man, too, must perform *chalitzah*, because people may think that the second marriage was valid, and that she therefore requires *yibum* or *chalitzah*. Neither the brother of the first nor that of the second[1] may perform *yibum*, as a penalty to the woman (*Rashi*).

1. [Actually, were the brother of the second husband to marry her, it would not constitute *yibum*, since she was never actually married to his brother. On the other hand, the Rabbinic decree which requires him to perform *chalitzah* could also be fulfilled through *yibum*, and

שִׁנָּה שְׁמוֹ וּשְׁמָהּ, שֵׁם עִירוֹ וְשֵׁם עִירָהּ — תֵּצֵא מִזֶּה וּמִזֶּה, וְכָל הַדְּרָכִים הָאֵלּוּ בָּהּ.

[ו] **כָּל** הָעֲרָיוֹת שֶׁאָמְרוּ צָרוֹתֵיהֶן מֻתָּרוֹת, הָלְכוּ הַצָּרוֹת הָאֵלּוּ וְנִשָּׂאוּ, וְנִמְצְאוּ אֵלּוּ אַיְלוֹנִיּוֹת — תֵּצֵא מִזֶּה וּמִזֶּה,

ר׳ עובדיה מברטנורא

(ו) **כל העריות שאמרו צרותיהן מותרות.** חמש עשרה עריות שאמרו חכמים שצרותיהן מותרות ליכנס לשוק בלא חליצה: **הלכו הצרות.** של עריות: **ונשאו.** לשוק: **ונמצאו.** העריות אילונית, ואיגלאי מלתא שהיו קדושי המת בטעות, ונמצא שלא היו אלו צרותיהן, ולא פטרום העריות האלו מן החליצה: **תצא מזה.** מבעל שניסאת לו, ומן היבם:

יד אברהם

Another reason the brother of the first may not perform *yibum* is that she is Rabbinically considered an adulteress, who is forbidden to her brother-in-law for *yibum* (*Tos. R' Akiva Eiger* to *Yevamos* 10:1; see *Gem.* ibid. 11a).

According to the view that the *get* and the second marriage are valid by Biblical law, the brother of the first husband is obligated to perform *chalitzah* by Rabbinic law [since the Rabbis invalidated the *get*] (*Ran*) [but he may not perform *yibum*, because the Biblical validity of the *get* renders her ineligible for *yibum* and she thus retains her status as the former wife of his brother, who is prohibited to him]. The *chalitzah* of the second husband is required by Biblical law (ibid.) [but he may not perform *yibum* as a penalty to her].

שִׁנָּה שְׁמוֹ וּשְׁמָהּ, — *[If] he changed his name or her name,*

[This is a new case.] An incorrect name for the husband or wife was written in the *get* (*Ritva; Tos. Rid;* see *Tos. Yom Tov*).

Another view is that the man or woman were called different names in different places, and the husband included in the *get* only the names which were used in the town where he wrote the *get* (*Tos.;* see 4:2; *Rav* ad loc.).

שֵׁם עִירוֹ וְשֵׁם עִירָהּ — *the name of his town or the name of her town,*

He wrote the wrong town in stating his or her residence (see *Pnei Yehoshua* to *Tos.* 80a s.v. שינה שמו).

Others explain that he wrote only one of the different names of the town in which he or she lived (*Tos.*, see 4:2).

תֵּצֵא מִזֶּה וּמִזֶּה, וְכָל הַדְּרָכִים הָאֵלּוּ בָּהּ. — *she must leave both of them, and all of these procedures apply to her.*

[All of the laws mentioned above apply in this case as well.]

The Sages agree with R' Meir in this case that any subsequent child that this woman bears from either husband is a *mamzer* (*Gem.* 80b), because a *get* such as this is Biblically invalid, and since she remarried based upon that *get*, and thereby caused her children from the second husband to be *mamzerim*, the Rabbis fined her and decreed the same for a child from the first husband (*Ran* to mishnah 6; see *Tos. Yom Tov*, ad loc.).

since she was never actually married to his brother, there is no prohibition of a brother's wife to prevent him from doing so. Therefore, *Rashi* explains the law that he may not do so as being a penalty to the woman.]

8
6 If he changed his name or her name, the name of his town or the name of her town, she must leave both of them, and all of these procedures apply to her.

6. [Concerning] all the *arayos* [about] which they said that their co-wives are permitted — if these co-wives went and were married, and these were found to be *ailoniyos*, she must leave both of

YAD AVRAHAM

6.

כָּל הָעֲרָיוֹת — *[Concerning] all the arayos*

[The term *ervah* (pl. *arayos*) refers to any of the twenty-one women who are Biblically prohibited to a man because of kinship, either by blood or by marriage (*Lev.* 18). Intimacy with any of these relatives is punishable by *kares*, if the transgression was deliberate, and marriage with any one of them does not take effect (see *Kiddushin* 3:12).]

שֶׁאָמְרוּ צָרוֹתֵיהֶן מֻתָּרוֹת, — *[about] which they said that their co-wives are permitted —*

In fifteen of these cases, it is possible for a woman to be an *ervah* to a man, but not to his brother. [For example, a woman is prohibited to marry her own father, but not her father's brother.] In such a case, if a man died, and his wife fell for *yibum* to his brother, to whom she is a *ervah*, not only she, but all her צָרוֹת, *co-wives*,[1] as well, are totally exempt from *yibum*, and may marry other men without even performing *chalitzah* (*Rav* from *Yevamos* 1:1).

הָלְכוּ הַצָּרוֹת הָאֵלּוּ וְנִשְּׂאוּ, — *if these co-wives went and were married,*

A man (e.g., Reuven) who was married to an *ervah* (e.g., Yocheved) of his brother (Levi) died without leaving children while his wife was still a minor (*Rashi* 80b s.v. ואי). Her co-wife (e.g., Sarah) assumed that she was exempt from *yibum* (since Yocheved was an *ervah* to Levi, and hence, should have freed her co-wives from *yibum*, as explained above) and married someone else (*Rav*).

וְנִמְצְאוּ אֵלּוּ אַיְלוֹנִיּוֹת — — *and these were found to be ailoniyos,*

The *ervah* (Yocheved) turned out to be an *ailonis* (a woman who cannot bear children [see 4:8]), which means that her marriage, having been based on a false premise — i.e., that she was capable of having children — was actually void. Thus, the other wife (Sarah) was never a co-wife of the *ervah* (Yocheved), since the latter was not really married to her husband, and it was prohibited for her (Sarah) to have remarried without performing *chalitzah* (*Rav*).

תֵּצֵא מִזֶּה וּמִזֶּה, — *she must leave both of them,*

She (Sarah) must leave both her new husband [by receiving a *get*] and

1. [Under Biblical law, a man may have more than one wife. The ban on bigamy was instituted by Rabbeinu Gershom Meor Hagolah early in the 11th century and was adopted by Ashkenazic, but not Sephardic, communities. See ArtScroll commentary to *Yevamos* 1:1, p. 14.]

וְכָל הַדְּרָכִים הָאֵלוּ בָּהּ.

[ז] **הַכּוֹנֵס** אֶת יְבִמְתּוֹ, וְהָלְכָה צָרָתָהּ וְנִשֵּׂאת לְאַחֵר, וְנִמְצֵאת זֹאת שֶׁהִיא אַיְלוֹנִית — תֵּצֵא מִזֶּה וּמִזֶּה, וְכָל הַדְּרָכִים הָאֵלוּ בָּהּ.

ר׳ עובדיה מברטנורא

וכל הדרכים האלו בה. וביבמות (כב, א) מוקמינן לה כרבי עקיבא דאמר יש ממזר מחייבי לאוין, ואינה הלכה: (ז) **ונשאת לאחר.** דקיימא לן ביאת האחת פוטרת צרתה. ונמצאת זו שנתיבמה אילונית, ואין יבומיה יבומין, ונמצא שלא נפטרה צרתה, ונשאת לשוק בלא חליצה: **תצא מזה ומזה.** מבעל זה ומיבמה הראשון:

יד אברהם

the *yavam* [through *chalitzah*] (*Rav*). The Rabbis decreed that she be forbidden to her husband because of the similarity between this case and one discussed in *Yevamos* (10:1). A man went overseas, and his wife remarried based on testimony that he had died, and the testimony was subsequently refuted. Since her second marriage is revealed to be adulterous, she becomes forbidden to both husbands (*Gem.* 80b; see *Rashba, Ritva*). In our case, the woman may also not marry the *yavam*, because people might think that he had performed *chalitzah*, after which it would have been prohibited to marry her (*Rashi* 80b s.v. זינו לא).

If she illicitly had relations with a man out of wedlock, she is not forbidden to the *yavam* (*Meiri* from *Sotah* 18b) because such acts are not publicized, and the few who know about it will also be aware that there had not been *chalitzah* (*Rashi* 80b, s.v. דמיחלפא). She is also permitted to the man with whom she had already had relations, because a case of illicit relations will not be confused with one of marriage, and the above decree does not apply (*Rashba*).

וְכָל הַדְּרָכִים הָאֵלוּ בָּהּ — *and all of these procedures apply to her.*

All of the laws listed in the previous mishnah apply to this case as well (*Meiri*). Although the co-wife assumed that there was no question of *yibum* whatsoever, she is still blamed for her plight (*Gem.* 80b), because she should have waited until the *ervah* had grown up and clarified her status before remarrying (*Rashi* ad loc. s.v. ואי).

This law is true only according to R' Akiva, who maintains that a child born from relations forbidden by any negative commandment — including the prohibition of remarrying a woman with whom one has performed *chalitzah* (*Deut.* 15:9; *Rashi* ad loc.) — is a *mamzer*. However, the *halachah* follows the opinion of the Sages, that only a child born of relations which carry the punishment of *kares* is a *mamzer* (*Rav* from *Yevamos* 92a). Therefore, although the other laws of the mishnah still apply, her children would be legitimate (*Rambam Commentary*).

them, and all of these procedures apply to her.

7. [If] one married his *yevamah*, and her co-wife went and was married to another, and it was discovered that this one is an *ailonis*, she must leave both of them, and all of these procedures apply to her.

YAD AVRAHAM

7.

If a man married several women and dies childless, once one of his widows has performed *yibum* or *chalitzah* with any of his surviving brothers, the other widows are free to marry other men (*Rav* from *Yevamos* 4:11). However, if it was subsequently discovered that the one who performed *yibum* or *chalitzah* had never actually been married to the brother who had died, one of the others must perform *yibum* or *chalitzah* before any of them may remarry.

הַכּוֹנֵס אֶת יְבִמְתּוֹ, — *[If] one married his yevamah,*

A man whose brother had died childless performed *yibum* with one of the widows while she was still a minor (*Rashi* 80b s.v. ואי).

וְהָלְכָה צָרָתָהּ וְנִשֵּׂאת לְאַחֵר, — *and her co-wife went and was married to another,*

[Another of the deceased's widows married a third man.]

וְנִמְצְאָה זֹאת שֶׁהִיא אַיְלוֹנִית — *and it was discovered that this one is an ailonis,*

[After the widow with whom *yibum* was performed had grown up, she was found to be an *ailonis*. This retroactively nullifies her original marriage and, consequently, her *yibum;* thus, the other woman actually required *yibum* or *chalitzah* and was married to the third man illegally (*Rav*).

תֵּצֵא מִזֶּה וּמִזֶּה, — *she must leave both of them,*

The co-wife must leave both her present husband [through a *get*] and the *yavam* [through *chalitzah*] (*Rav*). [She is forbidden to remain with either one of them for the reasons cited above (commentary to mishnah 6).]

וְכָל הַדְּרָכִים הָאֵלּוּ בָּהּ. — *and all of these procedures apply to her.*

[I.e., the procedures listed in mishnah 5.] Although this woman may have assumed that once *yibum* had been performed, she could immediately remarry, she is considered blameworthy (*Gem.* 80b) for not waiting until the *yevamah* had come of age, and her status had been clarified (*Rashi* ad loc. s.v. ואי).

In this case, too, the ruling is like the view of the Sages that if that woman had a child from her illegal marriage, it is not a *mamzer* (*Rav;* see commentary loc. cit. s.v. וכל הדרכים).

[ח] **כָּתַב** סוֹפֵר גֵּט לָאִישׁ וְשׁוֹבֵר לָאִשָּׁה, וְטָעָה וְנָתַן גֵּט לָאִשָּׁה וְשׁוֹבֵר לָאִישׁ, וְנָתְנוּ זֶה לָזֶה, וּלְאַחַר זְמַן הֲרֵי הַגֵּט יוֹצֵא מִיַּד הָאִישׁ וְשׁוֹבֵר מִיַּד הָאִשָּׁה — תֵּצֵא מִזֶּה וּמִזֶּה, וְכָל הַדְּרָכִים הָאֵלּוּ בָּהּ. רַבִּי אֱלִיעֶזֶר אוֹמֵר: אִם לְאַלְתַּר יָצָא — אֵין זֶה גֵּט; אִם לְאַחַר זְמַן יָצָא — הֲרֵי זֶה גֵּט, לֹא כָל הֵימֶנּוּ מִן הָרִאשׁוֹן לְאַבֵּד זְכוּתוֹ שֶׁל שֵׁנִי.

ר׳ עובדיה מברטנורא

(ח) **כתב סופר גט לאיש.** לגרש בו אשתו: **ושובר לאשה.** שתמסור לבעלה כשיפרע לה כתובתה: **וטעה הסופר.** כשמסר להן השטרות: **ונתן גט לאשה ושובר לאיש.** והם מסרו זה לזה, והלכה זו ונשאת, כסבורה שזה גט שמסר לה בעלה, וזה סבור שמסרה לו אשתו שובר. ורמב״ם גרים ונתן גט לאיש ושובר לאשה. ופירש ונתן, שחשב שנתן גט לאיש ושובר לאשה, אבל הוא לא עשה אלא בהפך. ודחוק הוא: **אם לאלתר.** כל זמן שלא נשאת יצא גט מתחת יד הבעל, אינו גט, וצריכה גט אחר. ואם לאחר שנשאת, הרי זה גט: **לא כל הימנו.** אין הכל כדבריו של זה הראשון להאמינו: **לאבד זכותו של שני.** שנשאה. דאמרינן קנוניא היה ביניהם, והחליפו השטרות לאחר שנשאת. והלכה כרבי אליעזר:

יד אברהם

8.

כָּתַב סוֹפֵר גֵּט לָאִישׁ — *[If] a scribe wrote a get for a man*

I.e., with which to divorce the latter's wife (*Rav*).

וְשׁוֹבֵר לָאִשָּׁה, — *and a receipt for a woman,*

To give to the husband upon receiving her *kesubah* payment (ibid.).

וְטָעָה וְנָתַן גֵּט לָאִשָּׁה וְשׁוֹבֵר לָאִישׁ, — *and he erred and gave the get to the woman and the receipt to the man,*

I.e., the husband later claimed that this is what had occurred (*Tos. Rid*).

וְנָתְנוּ זֶה לָזֶה, — *and they gave [them] one to another,*

The husband gave his wife the receipt thinking it was the *get*, and the wife gave him the *get* on the assumption that it was the receipt (*Tif. Yis.*). The woman then remarried, assuming that she was divorced (*Rav*).

Although a *get* given before witnesses who do not read it is invalid by Rabbinic law (*Gem.* 19b), a woman who was divorced with such a *get* and remarried is not compelled to leave her husband; the issue in this mishnah is only whether to force her to leave her new husband if it was discovered that the document given had been a receipt (*Tos.* ad loc. s.v. צריכי). Alternatively, the mishnah may be discussing a case in which there was a lapse between the time the witnesses read the *get* and the time it was given, and it was accidentally exchanged with the receipt in the interim (ibid.; *Ran*).[1]

1. [It is unclear how the mishnah could be discussing such a case, since it says explicitly that, according to the husband's claim, the scribe had exchanged the documents from the outset.]

8. [If] a scribe wrote a *get* for a man and a receipt for a woman, and he erred and gave the *get* to the woman and the receipt to the man, and they gave [them] one to another, and afterward, the *get* was found in the hand of the man and the receipt in the hand of the woman, she must leave both of them, and all of these procedures apply to her. R' Eliezer says: If it went out immediately, it is not a *get;* if it went out afterward, it is a *get,* [because] the first is not believed to abrogate the rights of the second.

YAD AVRAHAM

וּלְאַחַר זְמַן — *and afterward,*

I.e., after she remarried (*Tif. Yis.*).

הֲרֵי הַגֵּט יוֹצֵא מִיַּד הָאִישׁ וְשׁוֹבָר מִיַּד הָאִשָּׁה — *the get was found in* (lit., *went out from*) *the hand of the man and the receipt in the hand of the woman,*

[It was later discovered that the woman had the receipt, and her husband had the *get.*]

תֵּצֵא מִזֶּה וּמִזֶּה, וְכָל הַדְּרָכִים הָאֵלוּ בָּהּ. — *she must leave both of them, and all of these procedures apply to her.*

The husband's claim is accepted, and we suspect that the exchange did occur, and she was never divorced (*Tos. Rid*). [Therefore, she is considered to have had extramarital relations and is thus forbidden to both men, and all the other laws cited in mishnah 5 apply to her as well.]

רַבִּי אֱלִיעֶזֶר אוֹמֵר: אִם לְאַלְתַּר יָצָא — אֵין זֶה גֵּט; — *R' Eliezer says: If it went out immediately, it is not a get;*

If the mistake was discovered before she remarried, the *get* is invalid and she must receive a new divorce document from her husband (*Rav* from *Gem.* 90b).

Others contend that he can give her the same document that he had originally intended to give her, and it takes effect from when he gives it (*Meiri; Rambam, Hil. Gerushin* 10:11).

אִם לְאַחַר זְמַן יָצָא — הֲרֵי זֶה גֵּט, — *if it went out afterward, it is a get,*

If the mistake was not discovered until after she remarried, the husband is not believed that this is what had occurred, and the *get* remains in effect (ibid.).

There is another opinion that *immediately* means as long as their discussion concerning the divorce continued, and *afterward* means at any time after that (*Gem.* ibid.).

לֹא כָל הֵימֶנּוּ מִן הָרִאשׁוֹן לְאַבֵּד זְכוּתוֹ שֶׁל שֵׁנִי. — *[because] the first is not believed to abrogate the rights of the second.*

The first husband is not believed to invalidate the marriage of the second, because we suspect the former of plotting with the wife and exchanging the documents (*Rav*).

Although he has nothing to gain by doing this — since if we believe him, she becomes forbidden to both of them — he may not be aware of this and may have plotted accordingly (*Tos.* 91a s.v. לא).

כָּתַב לְגָרֵשׁ אֶת אִשְׁתּוֹ, וְנִמְלַךְ — בֵּית שַׁמַּאי אוֹמְרִים: פְּסָלָהּ מִן הַכְּהֻנָּה; וּבֵית הִלֵּל אוֹמְרִים: אַף עַל פִּי שֶׁנְּתָנוֹ לָהּ עַל תְּנַאי, וְלֹא נַעֲשָׂה הַתְּנַאי — לֹא פְסָלָהּ מִן הַכְּהֻנָּה.

[ט] **הַמְגָרֵשׁ** אֶת אִשְׁתּוֹ וְלָנָה עִמּוֹ בַּפֻּנְדְּקִי — בֵּית שַׁמַּאי אוֹמְרִים: אֵינָהּ צְרִיכָה הֵימֶנּוּ גֵּט שֵׁנִי; וּבֵית הִלֵּל אוֹמְרִים:

ר׳ עובדיה מברטנורא

(ט) **ולנה עמו בפונדקי.** ויש שם עדי יחוד ואין שם עדי ביאה. בית הלל סברי, הן הן עדי יחוד הן הן עדי ביאה, ואין אדם עושה בעילתו בעילת זנות, והרי קדשה בביאה. ובית שמאי סברי, לא אמרינן הן הן עדי יחוד הן הן עדי ביאה עד שיראוה שנבעלה:

יד אברהם

רֵיחַ הַגֵּט / The "Scent" of a Get

If a man gives his wife a *get* and says that she should be divorced from him but still not permitted to others, it is not valid; nevertheless, she thereby becomes forbidden to subsequently marry a *Kohen* if the husband dies. If the husband himself is a *Kohen,* he may not continue living with her (*Even HaEzer* 6:1). This is derived from the verse (*Lev.* 21:7): *And a woman divorced from her husband they shall not take,* which implies that even if she was given a *get* whose only purpose was to nullify her marriage to her husband, she becomes forbidden to a *Kohen* (*Gem.* 82b). This is referred to as רֵיחַ הַגֵּט, *the "scent" of a get* (*Yevamos* 52a).

Some authorities maintain that this law is Rabbinic in origin and the verse cited in the *Gemara* is only an אַסְמַכְתָּא, one which the Rabbis cite as a Scriptural basis for one of their enactments (*Rambam, Hil. Gerushin* 10:1; see *Maggid Mishneh* ad loc.).

כָּתַב לְגָרֵשׁ אֶת אִשְׁתּוֹ, וְנִמְלַךְ — *[If a man] wrote [a get] to divorce his wife and [then] changed his mind —*

And did not give her the *get* (*Rav*).

בֵּית שַׁמַּאי אוֹמְרִים: פְּסָלָהּ מִן הַכְּהֻנָּה; — *Beis Shammai say: He disqualified her from marrying a Kohen;*

They maintain that the mere writing of a *get* is considered *the "scent" of a get* (*Meiri*) by Rabbinic law (*Tos. Yom Tov*).

וּבֵית הִלֵּל אוֹמְרִים: אַף עַל פִּי שֶׁנְּתָנוֹ לָהּ עַל תְּנַאי, וְלֹא נַעֲשָׂה הַתְּנַאי — לֹא פְסָלָהּ מִן הַכְּהֻנָּה. — *Beis Hillel, however, say: Even if he gave it to her on a condition, and the condition was not met, he did not disqualify her from marrying a Kohen.*

Not only a *get* which was written and not given does not prohibit her to a *Kohen,* but even one which was actually given but did not take effect because its condition was not met (*Meiri*).

[If a man] wrote [a *get*] to divorce his wife and [then] changed his mind — Beis Shammai say: He disqualified her from marrying a *Kohen;* Beis Hillel, however, say: Even if he gave it to her on a condition, and the condition was not met, he did not disqualify her from marrying a *Kohen.*

9. One who divorced his wife, and [then] she lodged with him in an inn — Beis Shammai say: She does not need a second *get* from him; Beis Hillel, however, say:

YAD AVRAHAM

9.

Erusin and Nisuin

According to Biblical law, there are two stages to marriage. The first is known as אֵרוּסִין, *erusin,* or קִדּוּשִׁין, *kiddushin.* These terms describe both the first stages of marriage and the act that effects it. Following *erusin,* the couple is considered legally married in most respects. The wife may not be wed to anyone else; intimate relations with any other man is considered adultery and incurs the death penalty. In addition, *erusin* can be dissolved only by divorce (*Rambam, Hil. Ishus* 1:3). However, during this stage, the couple is not yet permitted to have relations (ibid. 10:1). The *erusin* can be legally established by any of the following methods, if they are done for the purpose of marriage: The man gives the woman either money (or any object of value, such as a ring) or a marriage document, or has relations with her (*Kiddushin* 1:1). The Rabbis forbade the last method (ibid. 12b); nevertheless, if one did perform *erusin* by having relations, it is valid (*Rambam* loc. cit. 3:21). The second and final stage of the marriage process is called נִשּׂוּאִין, *nisuin.*

הַמְגָרֵשׁ אֶת אִשְׁתּוֹ וְלָנָה עִמּוֹ בְּפֻנְדְּקִי — *One who divorced his wife, and [then] she lodged with him in an inn —*

And two witnesses attest that the man and his ex-wife had secluded themselves together, but did not see whether they had relations (*Rav* from *Gem.* 81b).

בֵּית שַׁמַּאי אוֹמְרִים: אֵינָהּ צְרִיכָה הֵימֶנּוּ גֵּט שֵׁנִי; — *Beis Shammai say: She does not need a second get from him;*

As long as the witnesses did not see that the couple had relations, they cannot assume that it occurred (ibid.). [Therefore, even if they did have relations, there is no new *erusin,* because there are no witnesses to validate it (see *Kiddushin* 65b).] However, if they did witness intimacy between them, a new *get* is required, because a man does not act promiscuous [when there is a permissible alternative], and he obviously intended that the relations should serve as *erusin* (*Gem.* 81b).

גיטין
ח/ט

צְרִיכָה הֵימֶנּוּ גֵּט שֵׁנִי. אֵימָתַי? בִּזְמַן שֶׁנִּתְגָּרְשָׁה מִן הַנִּשּׂוּאִין. וּמוֹדִים בְּנִתְגָּרְשָׁה מִן הָאֵרוּסִין שֶׁאֵינָהּ צְרִיכָה הֵימֶנּוּ גֵּט שֵׁנִי, מִפְּנֵי שֶׁאֵין לִבּוֹ גַּס בָּהּ.

כְּנָסָהּ בְּגֵט קֵרֵחַ — תֵּצֵא מִזֶּה וּמִזֶּה, וְכָל

ר׳ עובדיה מברטנורא

גט קרח. שקשריו מרובין מעדיו. דתקון רבנן גט מקושר משום כהנים קפדנים שהיו כותבים גט פתאום לנשותיהם, ומתחרטים, ולא היו יכולים להחזירן, ותקנו להם גט מקושר שאינו נוח ליכתב

יד אברהם

וּבֵית הִלֵּל אוֹמְרִים: צְרִיכָה הֵימֶנּוּ גֵּט שֵׁנִי. — *Beis Hillel, however, say: She needs a second get from him.*

Since there is a strong attachment between them, their encounter can be assumed to have included relations; thus, testimony to their secluding themselves is tantamount to testimony that they had relations. Since a man does not want his actions to be of a promiscuous nature, it can be further assumed that their intimacy was for the sake of marriage (ibid.; *Rosh* ad loc.).

Yerushalmi explains this dispute to be based on the disagreement between Beis Shammai and Beis Hillel as to whether a man may divorce his wife for reasons other than adultery (9:10). Beis Shammai maintain that he may not, and thus, one who divorced his wife is not likely to desire relations with her afterward. Beis Hillel hold that he may divorce her for less serious reasons, and therefore, we suspect that if they are secluded, they would have relations (*Tos.* 79b s.v. בית שמאי).

The question of a new *erusin* having taken place is applicable only if the man was aware of the witnesses' presence. Otherwise, since he knows that two witnesses are required for *erusin*, if he thinks there are none present, he obviously has no such intent (*Rashba* to 74a).

If the man was a *Kohen*, who is forbidden to marry a divorcee [even his own] (*Lev.* 21:7), we do not assume that they had intimacy, since we do not suspect that he would transgress a Biblical prohibition. The same is true if the woman had remarried after they had been divorced, and was subsequently widowed or divorced again. Since it is Biblically forbidden (*Deut.* 24:4) to remarry one's former wife if she had married someone else in the interim, we do not suspect that he would transgress a Biblical prohibition (*Meiri*).

אֵימָתַי? — *When?*

[When do we assume that *kiddushin* took place?]

בִּזְמַן שֶׁנִּתְגָּרְשָׁה מִן הַנִּשּׂוּאִין. — *When she was divorced from nisuin.*

[Only after having been divorced from *nisuin* — after which a couple is fully married and may live together (see preface) — is their relationship close enough, so that their seclusion together is presumed to have included intimacy.]

וּמוֹדִים בְּנִתְגָּרְשָׁה מִן הָאֵרוּסִין שֶׁאֵינָהּ צְרִיכָה הֵימֶנּוּ גֵּט שֵׁנִי, מִפְּנֵי שֶׁאֵין לִבּוֹ גַּס בָּהּ. — *They agree that [if] she was divorced from erusin, she does not need a second get from him because his heart is not close to her.*

[During *erusin*, their relationship is not yet at a point where intimacy can be presumed.] However, if intimacy was actually witnessed, it is considered to effect a new *erusin*, since he

8
9 She needs a second *get* from him. When? When she was divorced from *nisuin*. They agree that [if] she was divorced from *erusin*, she does not need a second *get* from him because his heart is not close to her.

[If a man] married a woman [on the basis of] a 'bald' *get*, she must leave both of them, and all of

would not indulge in promiscuous behavior, as stated above (*Rosh; Ran; Meiri; Rambam, Hil. Gerushin* 10:17).

Although in the case of an "old" *get* (mishnah 4), no distinction is made between a couple that already had *erusin* and one that had *nisuin*, that is because in that case, they are not yet divorced, and therefore, we suspect that they may have relations even after *erusin* (*Rashba* to 79b).

In addition, in our mishnah, the concern is whether there had been relations which would constitute a new marriage. Such relations would require witnesses, and thus, the assumption that there were marital relations must be strong enough to render those who observed them alone together as witnesses to their intimacy. Following a divorce from *erusin*, this assumption is not sufficiently strong. Therefore, even if they did happen to have relations, it is inconsequential, since the witnesses to the seclusion will not be considered witnesses to the relations. In the case of an "old" *get*, on the other hand, the concern is whether a rumor will spread that a child had been conceived illegitimately from the seclusion. The mere possibility of their having relations during that time is sufficient to give rise to such rumors (*Tos. R' Akiva Eiger* to mishnah 4).

Some authorities hold that, by the same reasoning, any man and woman who were witnessed having intimacy are presumed to have married thereby (*Geonim*, cited by *Rambam, Hil. Gerushin* 10:19). Others opine that this principle applies only if he had previously divorced her or had previously given her a conditional *erusin*. Only in these cases do we have grounds to assume that the intimacy was intended for the purpose of *erusin* (*Rashba; Ran*).

◆§ גֵּט מְקֻשָּׁר / A "Bound" Get

A גֵּט מְקֻשָּׁר is a *get* which is written one or two lines at a time; after each such unit, the *get* is folded over to cover the line(s), and is sewn together. On the outside of each fold, one witness must sign, with a minimum of three folds and three witnesses to each *get*.

This method of writing *gittin* was designed by the Rabbis in response to a situation in which short-tempered *Kohanim* were prone to divorce their wives in anger and subsequently regret it. They could not remarry them, however, because a divorcee is prohibited to a *Kohen*. Therefore, the Rabbis decreed that they may divorce their wives only with this type of *get*, which takes longer to prepare and thus allows the *Kohen* time to calm down and refrain from divorcing (*Rav* from *Bava Basra* 10:1; 160b).

— כְּנָסָהּ בְּגֵט קֵרֵחַ — *[If a man] married a woman* (lit., *her*) *[on the basis of] a "bald" get,*

A man married a woman who had

הַדְּרָכִים הָאֵלּוּ בָּהּ.

[י] **גֵּט** קֵרֵחַ — הַכֹּל מַשְׁלִימִין עָלָיו; דִּבְרֵי בֶן נַנָּס. רַבִּי עֲקִיבָא אוֹמֵר: אֵין מַשְׁלִימִין עָלָיו אֶלָּא קְרוֹבִים, הָרְאוּיִין לְהָעִיד בְּמָקוֹם אַחֵר.

ר׳ עובדיה מברטנורא

מהרה, שמא בתוך כך יתפייס. וכותב שטה אחת או שתים וכורכן על החלק ותופר, ועד אחד חותם על הכרך מבחוץ, וחוזר וכותב שני שיטין או יותר מבפנים וכורכן על החלק, וחותם עד שני על הכרך מבחוץ, וכן עד שלישי. ואם יש קשר כרוך ואין עד חתום מאחוריו, זהו קרח ופסול, דמסתמא למנין קשריו היו עדיו מתחלה, וחיישינן דלמא הבעל אמר להו כולכם חתומו, והרי אחד שלא חתם. ואם נשאת אשה בגט זה, תצא מזה ומזה, וכל הדרכים האלו בה. ומתניתין רבי מאיר היא, דאמר (פ, א) כל המשנה ממטבע שטבעו חכמים בגטין הולד ממזר. ואינה הלכה: (י) **הכל משלימין עליו.** ואפילו עבד, ואפילו פסול לעדות מחמת עבירה: **אלא קרוב שהוא ראוי להעיד בעדות אחרת.** שאין עליו פסול עדות אלא קורבה. אבל עבד או גזלן לא, עבד דלמא אתי לאסוקי ליוחסין, וגזלן דלמא אתו למימר עבד תשובה. אבל קרוב, כולי עלמא ידעי ליה דקרוב הוא. והלכה כבן ננס שהכל משלימין עליו, ומכל מקום אין חותם עליו אלא עד אחד פסול בלבד, והשאר צריך שיהיו כלם כשרים:

יד אברהם

been divorced with a "bald" *get* — i.e., a "bound" *get*, in which some of the folds had no witnesses signed on them. This is invalid by Rabbinic law, because it is normally assumed that the amount of witnesses the husband had asked to sign corresponds to the number of folds on the *get*. This leads us to believe that some of the witnesses the husband had asked to sign did not do so, which would make this case similar to one in which the husband told a group of people, "All of you sign my *get*," and only some signed. In that case, the *get* is invalid, because it was not prepared in accordance with the husband's instructions (6:7) (*Rav* from *Gem.* 91b; see below).

תֵּצֵא מִזֶּה וּמִזֶּה, — *she must leave both of them,*

Since the *get* was invalid, her remarriage was adulterous, and she is forbidden to both men (*Tos. R' Akiva Eiger*).

Even if we were to seek out the other people whom the husband had told to sign the *get* and they agreed to do so now, in which case the *get* would be valid (*Gem.* 18b), the divorce would take effect only from that day onward; her remarriage in the interim would still be considered adulterous (ibid.).

וְכָל הַדְּרָכִים הָאֵלּוּ בָּהּ. — *and all of these procedures apply to her.*

[All of the procedures listed in mishnah 5 apply to her.]

This, too, is in accordance with R' Meir's view that if one deviates from the Rabbinically dictated format of a *get* in divorcing a woman, the children born of subsequent relations with her are *mamzerim* (*Rav*). According to the Sages, however, only the other laws mentioned there apply, but the children are legitimate (*Meiri*).

Actually, this mishnah belongs together with the other cases in which she must leave

these procedures apply to her.

10. **A** "bald" *get* may be completed by anyone; [these are] the words of Ben Nannas. R' Akiva says: No one may complete it, except relatives, who are qualified to testify elsewhere.

YAD AVRAHAM

both husbands. However, upon mentioning the case of a scribe who exchanged a *get* and a receipt, the *Tanna* follows with another case of a *get* which was written but not delivered. Since that case is the subject of a dispute between Beis Shammai and Beis Hillel, the Mishnah then brings another one of their disputes in the case of a divorced couple lodging together in an inn (*Tos.* 81b s.v. בגט קרח).

10.

- גֵּט קֵרֵחַ — *A "bald" get*

A scribe, in preparing a "bound" *get*, made more folds in it than there were witnesses to sign. The *get* is not intrinsically invalid in this case, since — unlike in the case discussed in the previous mishnah — there are no witnesses who had been asked to sign but did not do so. Nevertheless, the *get* may not be used until all the folds are signed, because when it will be presented in another court, they will invalidate it for fear that not all of the witnesses had signed (*Ran*).

הַכֹּל מַשְׁלִימִין עָלָיו; דִּבְרֵי בֶן נַנָּס. — *may be completed by anyone; [these are] the words of Ben Nannas.*

Even slaves and thieves, who are disqualified from testifying in a court of law, may sign upon this *get* (*Rav*), because we only need their signatures to avoid giving the appearance that some witnesses had not signed; we do not need their testimony (*Rashi*).

Even witnesses who merely complete the *get* may sign only at the behest of the husband, because otherwise we are asking them to testify falsely (*Tos. Rid*) [since witnesses signed on a *get* do so before the divorce has taken place and attest only that the *get* had been written and signed on the husband's orders (see *Toras Gittin* to *Tos.* 67a s.v. אמרו לסופר)].

רַבִּי עֲקִיבָא אוֹמֵר: אֵין מַשְׁלִימִין עָלָיו, — *R' Akiva says: No one may complete it,*

[I.e., no person who is usually disqualified from testifying may do so in this case.]

אֶלָּא קְרוֹבִים, הָרְאוּיִין לְהָעִיד בְּמָקוֹם אַחֵר. — *except relatives, who are qualified to testify elsewhere.*

[I.e., who may testify when they are not related to those involved in the case.] Although this *get* does not require valid witnesses to complete it, if others see a slave or thief signed upon it, they may assume that the slave has been freed and the thief has repented, and they will erroneously rely on them for other testimony. Therefore only a relative may sign, since everyone knows he is a relative, and will not be led to accept his testimony in another case involving this person (*Gem.* 81b).

Even for the completion of a "bound" *get*, only one disqualified witness may be used. This is because if the authenticity of a "bound" *get* is challenged, it can be confirmed by the verification of any three of the signa-

וְאֵיזֶהוּ גֵט קֵרֵחַ? כֹּל שֶׁקְּשָׁרָיו מְרֻבִּין מֵעֵדָיו.

יד אברהם

In a case in which one of the three required witnesses to a "bound" *get* was a relative, there is a dispute in the *Gemara* whether the *get* is valid, since the third witness is required only by Rabbinic decree [for the sake of lengthening the process, as explained

tures. If two of the three signatures that are verified are those of disqualified witnesses, the confirmation will be meaningless, since we will not have verified the signature of two valid witnesses to this *get* (ibid., *Rashi* ad loc.).

8
10

What is a "bald" *get*? Any whose bindings are more than its witnesses.

YAD AVRAHAM

above], and not because his testimony is needed; or whether it is invalid, because the requirement for three witnesses to a "bound" *get* equates them to the two witnesses who must sign an ordinary *get*, and therefore, they must meet all the qualifications required of the latter (ibid.).

וְאֵיזֶהוּ גֵּט קֵרֵחַ? כָּל שֶׁקִּשְׁרָיו מְרֻבִּין מֵעֵדָיו. — *What is a "bald" get? Any whose bindings are more than its witnesses.*

[See commentary to mishnah 9 s.v. כְּנָסָהּ בְּגֵט קֵרֵחַ.]

פרק תשיעי

Chapter Nine

[א] **הַמְגָרֵשׁ** אֶת אִשְׁתּוֹ וְאָמַר לָהּ: „הֲרֵי אַתְּ מֻתֶּרֶת לְכָל אָדָם, אֶלָּא לִפְלוֹנִי״ — רַבִּי אֱלִיעֶזֶר מַתִּיר, וַחֲכָמִים אוֹסְרִין. כֵּיצַד יַעֲשֶׂה? יִטְּלֶנּוּ הֵימֶנָּה וְיַחֲזוֹר וְיִתְּנֶנּוּ לָהּ,

ר׳ עובדיה מברטנורא

פרק תשיעי – המגרש. (א) המגרש. רבי אליעזר מתיר. טעמא דרבי אליעזר, דכתיב (ויקרא כא, ז) ואשה גרושה מאישה לא יקחו, אפילו לא נתגרשה אלא מאישה, דאמר לה הרי את מגורשת ממני ואי את מותרת לכל אדם, פסולה לכהונה. אלמא גט הוא, והכא דשרייה לכל אדם חוץ מזה, מותרת לאחרים: **וחכמים אוסרים.** דאמרי איסור כהונה שאני, שרבה בהם הכתוב מצות יתירות, ואף על גב דהוה גט לפסלה לכהונה, לא הוי גט להתירה לאחרים. והלכה כחכמים. ולא אסרי רבנן אלא כשאמר הרי את מותרת לכל אדם אלא לפלוני, או חוץ מפלוני. אבל אי אמר לה הרי זה גטך על מנת שלא תנשאי לפלוני, מודו רבנן דהוי גט, שהרי התירה לכל אדם במסירת הגט, אלא שהתנה עמה שלא תנשא לאותו פלוני, והוה כשאר תנאי בעלמא. ואסרי רבנן למגרש לומר הרי זה גטך על מנת שתנשאי לפלוני, שלא יאמרו נשותיהן נותנים זה לזה במתנה. וכל תנאי שמתנה אדם בגט קודם כתיבת הגט, אף על פי שלא נכתב התנאי בתוכו, הגט פסול. אלא אחר שנתנו לידה, מתנה מה שהוא רוצה להתנות:

יד אברהם

1.

In order to be effective, a *get* must totally sever the marital relationship between the husband and wife (*Rambam, Hil. Gerushin* 1:3). If a man gives his wife a *get* which stipulates that her prohibition to specific men — which was caused by her *kiddushin* to him — be retained, there is a possibility that this is not considered total severance and that she is therefore not divorced. This issue is discussed in our mishnah.

הַמְגָרֵשׁ אֶת אִשְׁתּוֹ — *[If] one divorced his wife*

With a valid *get* which had no flaws (*Meiri*).

וְאָמַר לָהּ: — *and said to her:*

Upon giving her the *get* (*Rashi*).

„הֲרֵי אַתְּ מֻתֶּרֶת לְכָל אָדָם, אֶלָּא לִפְלוֹנִי״ — — *"You are permitted to every man, except So-and-so"* —

He qualified the *get* by dictating that the divorce take effect with regard to every man but one, to whom she shall still be prohibited (*Gem.* 82a).

רַבִּי אֱלִיעֶזֶר מַתִּיר, — *R' Eliezer permits [her];*

She is permitted to marry any man but the one specified (*Meiri*). He derives this from the verse (*Lev.* 21:7): *And a woman divorced from her husband he shall not take,* which indicates that even if a woman is only divorced from her husband, but not permitted to anyone else — i.e., he told her, "You are divorced from me, but are not permitted to any man" — she still assumes the status of a divorcee in regard to her prohibition to a *Kohen.* [Thus, if her husband subsequently died, she would be forbidden to a *Kohen.*] Apparently, even a *get* which precludes her marriage to all men is effective if only to some extent; certainly, then, the *get* in our case —

1. [If] one divorced his wife and said to her: "You are permitted to every man, except So-and-so" — R' Eliezer permits [her]; the Sages, however, prohibit [her]. What shall he do? He must take it from her and give it to her again,

YAD AVRAHAM

which excludes only one man from its effect — is valid (*Rav* from *Gem.* 82b).

In the case that the husband says: "You are divorced, but are not permitted to any man," since such a *get* permits her to no one, it is certainly not valid in any way except to prohibit her to a *Kohen* — and it is thus clear that the rules governing the capacity for a *get* to prohibit her to a *Kohen* differ from those governing its actual validity. Nevertheless, it is assumed that if any *get* with limited effect would not be valid, one which divorced her from her husband without permitting her to anyone else would be too far removed from legitimacy to even have the "scent" of a *get* (see commentary to 8:8) and prohibit her to a *Kohen.* Since we see that in the latter case, she does become forbidden to a *Kohen,* we may safely conclude that in our case — in which the husband specified that she be permitted to all but one man — the *get* is fully valid, except with regard to that man (*Tos.* 82b s.v. אפילו).

וַחֲכָמִים אוֹסְרִין. — *the Sages, however, prohibit [her].*

[From marrying anyone else.] She is not divorced at all (*Meiri*), because the fact that she is still prohibited as this man's wife to even one person negates the total severance which a *get* must accomplish, as implied by the verse (*Deut.* 24:3): *And he wrote for her a document of severance* (*Gem.* 82b).

The Sages hold that since *Kohanim* were given more commandments than the rest of the Jewish people, their laws are unique and not comparable to those which apply to all others. Therefore, the validity of a *get* is not related to its capacity to prohibit the woman to *Kohanim* (*Rav* from *Gem.* ibid.).

If a husband gave his wife a *get* on condition that she does not marry a certain man, even the Sages agree that it is valid. This is because the *get* itself actually permits her to marry any man, including this particular one; his stipulation that she not marry that person is equivalent to any condition that the husband may make (*Rav* from *Gem.* 82a).

In such a case, she is allowed to marry any other man. We do not fear that in the event that her new husband divorces her or dies, she would willfully break the condition and marry the one to whom the husband had forbidden her, thereby nullifying the *get* retroactively and rendering her current marriage illegitimate (*Tos.* 82b s.v. שרבי).

Some authorities contend that the Sages even disqualify a *get* if the husband stipulates whom she may or may not marry, since such a *get* is not totally effective in severing her from her husband (*Ran; Meiri*).

It is forbidden by Rabbinic law for a man to divorce his wife on condition that she marry a specific individual, because it appears as if he is presenting her to that man as a gift (*Rav* from *Gem.* 84a).

כֵּיצַד יַעֲשֶׂה? יִטְלֶנּוּ הֵימֶנָּה וְיַחֲזוֹר וְיִתְּנֶנּוּ לָהּ, — *What shall he do? He must take it from her and give it to her again,*

It is not sufficient to tell her that it should be her *get* with no conditions

וְיֹאמַר לָהּ: ,,הֲרֵי אַתְּ מֻתֶּרֶת לְכָל אָדָם״. וְאִם כְּתָבוֹ בְתוֹכוֹ — אַף עַל פִּי שֶׁחָזַר וּמְחָקוֹ, פָּסוּל.

[ב] ,,הֲרֵי אַתְּ מֻתֶּרֶת לְכָל אָדָם, אֶלָּא לְאַבָּא וּלְאָבִיךְ״, ,,לְאָחִי וּלְאָחִיךְ״, ,,לְעֶבֶד

יד אברהם

attached (see 8:2), because the *get* has already entered her possession, prohibiting her to a *Kohen*. Therefore, it is too late to restate the conditions of the *get* unless he reacquires it and presents it to her again (*Gem.* 84b).

וְיֹאמַר לָהּ: ,,הֲרֵי אַתְּ מֻתֶּרֶת לְכָל אָדָם״. — *and say to her: "You are permitted to every man."*

Or, "Here is you *get*" [without stating any qualifications] (*Tos. Rid; Rambam, Hil. Gerushin* 8:17).

Others maintain that it is valid only if he states explicitly that she is permitted to every man, because it is necessary for him to revoke the previously stated qualification that she is not permitted to a specific individual (*Ran*).

וְאִם כְּתָבוֹ בְתוֹכוֹ — *If he wrote it inside it,*

If he wrote in the *get* itself that a certain person is excluded from the effects of the divorce and may still not marry her (*Gem.* loc. cit.).

אַף עַל פִּי שֶׁחָזַר וּמְחָקוֹ, פָּסוּל. — *although he subsequently erased it, it is void.*

This is because the *get* was written based on this condition, which negates the total severance that it must effect in order to be valid, and it is therefore void (*Tos.* 84b s.v. אם). Even if this condition was included in the *get* after the תֹּרֶף [*toref*] (the part of the *get* which contains the specifics — see General Introduction) was written [and the writing of the *get*, which precedes the inclusion of this provision, was thus not affected by the stipulation], it is invalid, as a precautionary measure so that it not be confused with a case in which it was written before the *toref* [which is the primary portion of the *get*, and any stipulations upon which it is based define the essence of the *get*] (*Tos.* 85a s.v. דברי הכל).

The implication of the mishnah is that only writing such a condition in the *get* nullifies it, but stating it orally to the witnesses when the *get* is being written does not, and thus, if when he gives her the *get* he reverses himself and says that she should be permitted to all men, it would be valid. There is a dispute in the *Gemara* (ibid.) whether this is true only if he stated the condition after the *toref* had been written — since the validity of the *get* was already established without this stipulation (*Rashi* ad loc. s.v. והני מילי) — or that it is so even if he stated it beforehand, since the scribe writes the *get* with the intent that it be in accordance with the husband's final decision as to its provisions (*Tos.* ibid., s.v. מהו דתימהא). The *halachah* follows the former opinion (*Rav; Rosh*).

The Rabbis decreed that a *get* which contains any sort of stipulation written into it before the *toref* is void (*Rav* from *Gem.* 85a; *Rif; Rosh*). This was done as a preventive measure so that others not be led to write stipulations that limit the ability of the *get* in allowing her to marry any other man, in which case it would be Biblically void (*Tos.* ad loc. s.v. אבל). Some authorities explain that the disqualification is because any stipulation written into the *get* impedes the severance that it is required to effect (*Rambam* 8:4; *Even HaEzer* 147:2).

Rashi (84b s.v. פוסלין) holds that the

and say to her: "You are permitted to every man." If he wrote it inside it, although he subsequently erased it, it is void.

2. [If one said:] "You are permitted to every man, except Father and your father," "my brother and your brother," [or] "a slave and a

YAD AVRAHAM

stipulation disqualifies the *get* even if it is fulfilled. Others, however, contend that only if the condition is violated is the divorce invalidated (*Tos.* ad loc. s.v. כל; *Baal HaMaor*).

According to some commentators, the Sages' disqualification of a *get* to which any conditions were set prior to the writing of the *toref* applies even if the condition had been stated orally, without being written into the document (*Rav; Rashi* 85b s.v. שתוקי; *Tos.* 85a loc. cit.; *Rambam* loc. cit.; *Even HaEzer* loc. cit.). Others contend that an orally stated provision does not disqualify the *get* (*Baal HaMaor, Rashba; Ran*).

It can also be inferred from the mishnah that only if a provision which invalidates the *get* is erased does it affect the validity of the *get*, but not if anything else is erased. Nevertheless, it is customary to refrain from using a *get* with any erasures on it (*Tos.* 84b s.v. אם).

2.

This mishnah continues the discussion of the previous one regarding stipulations made to a *get* which limit its scope by prohibiting her to marry certain men.

"הֲרֵי אַתְּ מֻתֶּרֶת לְכָל אָדָם, — *[If one said:] "You are permitted to every man,*

[A man gave his wife a *get* and declared that she is permitted to every man except the following:]

אֶלָּא לְאַבָּא וּלְאָבִיךְ", "לְאָחִי וּלְאָחִיךְ", — *except Father and your father," "my brother and your brother,"*

To all of these relatives, this woman is an *ervah* — one who is prohibited for conjugal relations under penalty of *kares* [excision; Divinely decreed premature death] (*Lev.* 18; see commentary to 8:6); therefore, *kiddushin* (or *erusin*), the first stage of marriage, between any of them and this woman does not take effect (see *Kiddushin* 3:12; 65b).

"לְעֶבֶד — *[or] "a slave*

Marriage between a Jewish woman and a gentile slave does not take effect (*Yevamos* 45a). This is derived from the passage (*Gen.* 22:5) in which Abraham told Ishmael and Eliezer, his slave, *Stay here by yourselves with the donkey,* which the Rabbis interpret as denoting that a slave is compared to a donkey in that his marriage to a Jewess is void (*Kiddushin* 68a; see *Torah Temimah* to *Gem.* loc. cit.).

Although it is possible for this person to marry a Jewess if he is freed, in his present status he is forbidden to her (*Tif. Yis.* from *Gem.* 85a).

וּלְנָכְרִי", — *and a gentile,"*

A marriage between a Jew and a gentile has no validity. This is derived from the verse (*Deut.* 21:13) concerning a gentile woman taken captive in

וּלְנָכְרִי״, וּלְכָל מִי שֶׁאֵין לָהּ עָלָיו קִדּוּשִׁין — כָּשֵׁר. „הֲרֵי אַתְּ מֻתֶּרֶת לְכָל אָדָם, אֶלָּא...״, אַלְמָנָה, „לְכֹהֵן גָּדוֹל״; גְּרוּשָׁה וַחֲלוּצָה, „לְכֹהֵן הֶדְיוֹט״; מַמְזֶרֶת וּנְתִינָה, „לְיִשְׂרָאֵל״; בַּת יִשְׂרָאֵל, „לְמַמְזֵר וּלְנָתִין״; וּלְכָל מִי שֶׁיֵּשׁ לָהּ עָלָיו קִדּוּשִׁין, אֲפִלּוּ בַּעֲבֵרָה — פָּסוּל.

ר׳ עובדיה מברטנורא

(ב) **אלמנה לכהן גדול.** כיון דקדושין תופסים בחייבי לאוין, ולהאי לא תפסי משום איסור אישות שבה, אשתכח דשייר בגיטא:

יד אברהם

"You are permitted to every man except ..." — [if she was] a widow, "to the Kohen Gadol";

[A man gave a *get* to his wife, who had been previously widowed, and he stipulated that her divorce not take effect in regard to the *Kohen Gadol* (High Priest).] A widow is always prohibited to the latter (*Lev.* 21:14), but a marriage between them is effective ex post facto (*Kiddushin* 3:12).

גְּרוּשָׁה וַחֲלוּצָה, „לְכֹהֵן הֶדְיוֹט״; — *[or if she was] a divorcee or a chalutzah, "to an ordinary Kohen";*

[A man gave a *get* to his wife, who had previously been divorced or had performed *chalitzah*, and stipulated that it not permit her to marry a *Kohen.*] A divorcee is prohibited to a *Kohen* by Biblical law (*Lev.* 21:7), and a *chalutzah* is prohibited to one by Rabbinic law (*Yevamos* 24a). In both of these cases, marriage between them takes effect ex post facto (*Kiddushin* loc. cit.).

Even if the woman had not previously been widowed or divorced and had not performed *chalitzah*, she would be forbidden to a *Kohen* because of the present *get*. However, the mishnah also included these cases because they are used throughout the Talmud as the classical examples of mar-

war, about whom it is written that she must do certain actions (shave her head, cut her nails, etc.), and only *after this, she will be to you for a wife,* which implies that without this procedure, she cannot become his wife (*Kiddushin* 68b).

Similarly, the marriage of a gentile man and a Jewish woman is void (*Rashi* to *Yevamos* 45a).

וּלְכָל מִי שֶׁאֵין לָהּ עָלָיו קִדּוּשִׁין — *or anyone with whom she cannot have kiddushin,*

This comes to include all men to whom she is prohibited under penalty of *kares* [e.g., her son and his son] (*Gem.* 85a).

כָּשֵׁר. — *it is valid.*

If, upon divorcing his wife, a man stipulated that the *get* does not permit her to marry any of the above men, the *get* is valid, because his condition does not prohibit her to anyone whom she could otherwise have married (*Rashi*).

If he excluded a boy under thirteen years old, the *get* is null, because the boy will eventually come of age, at which time he would be able to marry her (*Gem.* ibid.).

„הֲרֵי אַתְּ מֻתֶּרֶת לְכָל אָדָם אֶלָּא ..״, אַלְמָנָה, „לְכֹהֵן גָּדוֹל״; — *[If he said:]*

9
2

gentile," or anyone with whom she cannot have *kiddushin*, it is valid.

[If he said:] "You are permitted to every man except ..." — [if she was] a widow, "to the *Kohen Gadol*"; [or if she was] a divorcee or a *chalutzah*, "to an ordinary *Kohen*"; [or if she was] a *mamzeres* or a Nesinite, "to a [regular] Jew"; [or if she was] the daughter of a [regular] Jew, "to a *mamzer* or a Nesinite"; or to anyone with whom she can have *kiddushin* — even illicitly — it is void.

YAD AVRAHAM

riages which are prohibited but still take effect (*Ran*).

מַמְזֶרֶת — *[or if she was] a mamzeres*

A *mamzeres* (fem. of *mamzer*) is the product of illicit relations which were prohibited under the penalty of *kares* or death inflicted by the court (see *Yevamos* 4:13). She is forbidden to marry anyone but a *mamzer*, a convert, or a freed slave (*Even HaEzer* 4:22; 24); nevertheless, her marriage to a legitimate Jew takes effect ex post facto (*Kiddushin* 3:12).

וּנְתִינָה, — *or a Nesinite,*

A woman descended from the Gibeonites, whom Joshua converted to Judaism (see ArtScroll commentary to *Yevamos* 2:4). נְתִינָה, *Nesinah* (fem. of *Nasin*), means *appointed one*. They were given this appellation because they were appointed by Joshua to be woodcutters and water-drawers for sacrificial purposes (*Joshua* 9:27). It is forbidden for a Jew to marry one of them, but such a marriage takes effect ex post facto (*Kiddushin* loc. cit.).

"לְיִשְׂרָאֵל"; — *"to a [regular] Jew";*

[A man gave a *get* to his wife who was a *mamzeres* or a Nesinite, but excluded a certain Jewish man from being permitted to marry her by virtue of that *get*.]

בַּת יִשְׂרָאֵל, "לְמַמְזֵר וּלְנָתִין"; — *[or if she was] the daughter of a [regular] Jew, "to a mamzer or a Nesinite";*

[A man gave his wife a *get*, but stipulated that it not take effect in regard to a certain *mamzer* or Nesinite.]

וּלְכָל מִי שֶׁיֵּשׁ לָהּ עָלָיו קִדּוּשִׁין, אֲפִלּוּ בַּעֲבֵרָה — *or to anyone with whom she can have kiddushin — even illicitly —*

[Any case in which the husband excluded someone to whom his wife is prohibited, but with whom her marriage takes effect ex post facto.] This includes any other relationship which is prohibited, but is not punishable by *kares* or the death penalty [e.g., relations between a Jew and an Ammonite or a Moabite] (*Gem.* 85a).

פָּסוּל. — *it is void.*

The *get* is not valid, because its qualification excludes these men from its effect and renders their marriage to the woman void; whereas without the qualification such a marriage would take effect. Therefore, it is a *get* which does not cause a total severance (*Rav*) [and thus is not valid, as explained in the commentary to mishnah 1].

[ג] **גּוּפוֹ** שֶׁל גֵּט: ,,הֲרֵי אַתְּ מֻתֶּרֶת לְכָל אָדָם". רַבִּי יְהוּדָה אוֹמֵר: ,,וְדֵין דְּיֶהֱוֵי לִיכִי מִינַּאי, סֵפֶר תֵּירוּכִין, וְאִגֶּרֶת שִׁבּוּקִין, וְגֵט פִּטוּרִין, לִמְהָךְ לְהִתְנַסְּבָא לְכָל גְּבַר דְּתִצְבְּיִין".
גּוּפוֹ שֶׁל גֵּט שִׁחְרוּר: ,,הֲרֵי אַתְּ בַּת חוֹרִין", ,,הֲרֵי אַתְּ לְעַצְמֵךְ".

ר' עובדיה מברטנורא

(ג) **גופו של גט.** עיקר כתב הגט, כך יכתבו בו: **ודין די יהוי ליכי מינאי.** שלריך להוכיח בתוכו שעל ידי ספר זה הוא מגרשה. ואי לא כתב ביה הכי, אתו למימר דבדיבור בעלמא גרשה, ושטר ראיה בעלמא. והלכה כרבי יהודה:

יד אברהם

3.

גּוּפוֹ שֶׁל גֵּט: — *The essence of a get [is]:*

I.e., the essential wording which must be written in a *get* for it to be valid (*Rav*), aside from the *toref*, the section which includes the names of the man and the woman, the place, and the date (*Tif. Yis.; Even HaEzer* 129:11).

Others contend that even if the names of the man and woman were not written in the *get*, it is still valid; only incorrect names invalidate a *get* (*Tos. Rid*).

,,הֲרֵי אַתְּ מֻתֶּרֶת לְכָל אָדָם". — *"You are permitted to every man."*

All other wording in the *get* is for the sake of elaboration and is not necessary for the *get* to be valid (*Meiri*).

רַבִּי יְהוּדָה אוֹמֵר: — *R' Yehudah says:*

The validity of the *get* requires the inclusion of the following words (*Meiri*).

,,וְדֵין, — *"And this,*

It must state explicitly that the document is what is effecting the divorce; otherwise, it is possible that he wants to effectuate it by his words at the time of delivery, with the document serving only as evidence of the divorce (*Rav* from *Gem.* 85b).

The Rabbis (the first, anonymous opinion in the mishnah), on the other hand, consider it a logical assumption that the divorce is being executed by means of the *get*, and therefore do not require that this be written into it (*Gem.* ibid.).

The word וְדֵן, *and this*, should be spelled without a *yud*, because with a *yud* it would read: וְדִין, *and the law*, which implies that he is divorcing her against his will because it is required by law (*Gem.* ibid., *Rashi* ad loc.), and such a *get* would not be valid (*Yevamos* 14:1).

דְּיֶהֱוֵי לִיכִי מִינַּאי, — *which shall be to you from me,*

It is necessary to specify that he is divorcing her from being married to him, so as to preclude the possibility that she is married to someone else, and he is divorcing her from that person (*Nedarim* 5b).

The Rabbis hold that this is not considered a serious possibility because it is self-evident that a man does not divorce someone else's wife (ibid.).

סֵפֶר תֵּירוּכִין, — *[is] a writ of divorce,*

3. The essence of a *get* [is]: "You are permitted to every man." R' Yehudah says: "And this, which shall be to you from me, [is] a writ of divorce, a letter of abandonment, and a bill of release, to go to be married to any man that you want."

The essence of a document of emancipation [is]: "You are a free woman," [or] "You are to yourself."

YAD AVRAHAM

The *vav* in the word תְּרוּכִין, *divorce*, should be elongated in the *get* to make clear that it is not a *yud*, because תְּרִיכִין means divorce in general, which would imply that the *get* is not meant to divorce this woman in particular (*Gem.* 85b, *Rashi* ad loc.).

Some maintain that the *vav* need not be longer than usual, only that the scribe must extend it enough so that it is clearly not a *yud*. Nevertheless, the custom is to write it a bit longer than usual (*Tos.* 85b s.v. ולורכיה).

וְאִגֶּרֶת שִׁבּוּקִין, — *a letter of abandonment,*

The word וְאִגֶּרֶת must be spelled without a *yud*, because אִיגֶּרֶת means *a roof* rather than *a letter* (*Gem.* loc. cit.). Here, too, the *vav* must be elongated (ibid.).

וְגֵט פִּטּוּרִין, — *and a bill of release,*

In the word פִּטּוּרִין, too, the *vav* must be elongated (*Tos.* ad loc. s.v. רבי יהודה).

These three terms for divorce written into the *get* signify the three basic marital obligations of food, clothing, and conjugal relations, from which the husband is released with this divorce (*Tif. Yis.*).

לִמְהָךְ — *to go*

This word must be written without a *yud*, because a *yud* would render it לְמִיהַךְ, *to me from this* (*Gem.*), implying that from this document she shall be his (*Rashi* ad loc.).

Care must be taken that the *hei* not look like a *ches*, which would read לְמֶחָךְ, *to joke* (*Gem.*).

לְהִתְנַסְּבָא לְכָל גְּבַר דְּתִצְבְּיִין". — *to be married to any man that you want."*

The word דְּתִצְבְּיִין must be spelled with three *yuden* between the *beis* and the *nun*; otherwise, it can be misconstrued to be speaking in the third person about women in general (*Gem.* ad loc.).

If any of the above instructions were not followed in a *get*, it is Rabbinically void (*Rambam, Hil. Gerushin* 4:14; *Maggid Mishneh* ad loc.; see *Rambam* ibid., 10:2). Others contend that it is invalidated only if the husband subsequently disputes the *get* by claiming that he intended the meaning implied by the flaw [e.g., he intended that it read לְמֶחָךְ, *to joke*, indicating that he was not serious] (*Ravad* ad loc.; *R' Hai Gaon*, cited by *Rosh*). A third opinion is that only if the husband wrote the *get* himself or dictated its wording can he dispute its validity in this manner. However, if he directed a scribe to write a *get* for his wife, and the scribe erred in one of these details, the *get* remains valid — even Rabbinically — and the husband's protest to the contrary is disregarded (*Baal HaIttur*, cited by *Rosh*).

גּוּפוֹ שֶׁל גֵּט שִׁחְרוּר: ,,הֲרֵי אַתְּ בַּת חוֹרִין", — *The essence of a document of emancipation [is]: "You are a free woman,"*

[The essential statement which must be written into a bill of emancipation is the fact that the slave is set free.]

In this version of the mishnah, the

[ד] **שְׁלֹשָׁה** גִּטִּין פְּסוּלִין; וְאִם נִשֵּׂאת — הַוָּלָד כָּשֵׁר: כָּתַב בִּכְתַב יָדוֹ, וְאֵין עָלָיו עֵדִים; יֵשׁ עָלָיו עֵדִים, וְאֵין בּוֹ זְמַן; יֵשׁ

ר׳ עובדיה מברטנורא

(ד) **כתב בכתב ידו ואין עליו עדים.** לרבי מאיר דאמר עדי חתימה כרתי, כתב ידו כמאה עדים דמי. ולרבי אלעזר דאמר עדי מסירה כרתי, הואיל וכתב ידו הוא, וכתב ונתן (דברים כד, א) קרינן ביה, ואף על גב דליכא עדי מסירה כשר מדאורייתא, וחכמים פסלוהו, דלמא אתי לאכשורי בכתב סופר: **ואין בו זמן.** דזמן תקנתא דרבנן הוא. אי משום פירות, אי משום שמא יחפה על בת אחותו, כדאמרינן בפרק [שני] (יז, א):

יד אברהם

feminine gender is used in order to be consistent with the first half of the mishnah. [However, the same rule would apply to a male slave.] Other versions read: בֶּן חוֹרִין, הֲרֵי אַתָּה לְעַצְמְךָ — הֲרֵי אַתָּה — in the masculine gender (*Rif; Meiri*).

הֲרֵי אַתְּ לְעַצְמֵךְ״. — *[or] "You are to yourself."*

[I.e., "You are under your own jurisdiction."]

It is unclear why R' Yehudah does not require a bill of emancipation to specify that the release is executed by the document and not by the words of the master, just as he does for a *get* (*Tos. Yom Tov*).

4.

שְׁלֹשָׁה גִּטִּין פְּסוּלִין; וְאִם נִשֵּׂאת — הַוָּלָד כָּשֵׁר: — *Three gittin are void; but if she married, the offspring is legitimate:*

The *gittin* listed below are void by Rabbinic law [and a woman may not rely upon them to remarry]. However, if she did, her children are legitimate (*Meiri*).

These *gittin* are set apart as different from all the others which were invalidated by the Rabbis, since, in all other cases, if she remarries, her second husband is obligated to divorce her unless they already had children; in these cases, however, he is permitted to continue living with her (*Ran* from *Gem.* 86a). The case of an "old" *get* (8:4) is also not included in this category, because in that case, the woman is fully permitted to remarry (*Gem.* loc. cit.).

The reason for the difference between these three *gittin* and all others which are Rabbinically invalid can be explained as follows. The Rabbinical requisites for a *get* comprise three general categories. The first is that of requirements which were enacted only for *gittin*, but not for other documents [e.g., a "bald" *get* (see 8:9)]. In these cases, the Rabbis were strict in their decrees and obligated her to leave both husbands in order to emphasize the gravity of *gittin* over all other legal documents [because it involves a prohibition whose punishment is *kares* — viz. that of living with a woman married to another man].

The second category includes basics required of all legal documents, without which they are invalid [e.g., writing the correct location (see 8:5)]. In such cases, the Sages were strict concerning *gittin* just as they were with all other documents.

The third category is that of Rab-

4. Three *gittin* are void; but if she married, the offspring is legitimate: [if] he wrote [it] with his handwriting, but there are no witnesses on it; [if] there are witnesses on it, but it has no date; [if] it

YAD AVRAHAM

binic ordinances which pertain to all legal documents, but whose noncompliance does not invalidate documents other than *gittin* [i.e., the cases in our mishnah]. In these instances, the Rabbis did not invalidate a *get* to the same extent as they did for noncompliance of other requirements, and they allowed the woman to continue living with her new husband, since these requisites are not as strict as the others (*Ramban; Ritva; Ran*).

Alternatively, this mishnah was written according to R' Meir, who holds that a *get* which deviates from the format dictated by the Rabbis is void, and any child born subsequently from a woman so divorced is a *mamzer* (see 8:5). In these cases, however, although her second husband must divorce her, her children are legitimate (*Gem.* ad loc.).

כָּתַב בִּכְתַב יָדוֹ, — *[if] he wrote [it] with his handwriting,*

The husband wrote the *get* himself, or he had it written by someone else and affixed his signature to it (ibid.).

וְאֵין עָלָיו עֵדִים; — *but there are no witnesses on it;*

There are no witnesses signed upon the *get* to validate it, as required by R' Meir (*Ran;* see General Introduction).

The *get* is Biblically valid even according to R' Meir, because a person's signature on his own document is the equivalent of the testimony of two witnesses (*Rav*). Nevertheless, the Rabbis prohibited using such a *get* initially, because people might confuse it with an unsigned *get* written by a scribe, which is void (*Rav; Rashi; Meiri; Tos. Rid*).

Alternatively, the Biblical validity of a *get* written by the husband is derived from the verse (*Deut.* 24:1), *And he shall write for her a document of severance,* which indicates that his writing alone is sufficient to validate the *get* (*Rashba* to *Kiddushin* 65b).

Another explanation of the Rabbinic invalidation of such a *get* is because there is no way to check the authenticity of the date (*Tos.* 3b s.v. כתב).

Others contend that this first, anonymous *Tanna* may even agree with R' Elazar, his disputant in the mishnah, that the witnesses who observe the delivery of the *get* are the ones who validate it. Although there were no such witnesses in this case, the *get* is Biblically valid because of the implication of the verse, cited above, that the husband can validate the *get* with his writing alone (*Rav; Rashi*).[1] [It is Rabbinically void, however, because of one of the reasons mentioned above.]

יֵשׁ עָלָיו עֵדִים, וְאֵין בּוֹ זְמַן; — *[if] there are witnesses on it, but it has no date;*

The *get* has witnesses signed on it, but it has no date, which is required by Rabbinic law. The date is necessary in order to prevent a man from covering up his wife's act of adultery by giving her a predated *get* with which she could

1. [According to this explanation, however, the nature of the dispute between the first *Tanna* and R' Elazar (see below) is unclear, since the former is discussing a case in which there were no witnesses to the delivery, and the latter a case in which there were.]

בּוֹ זְמַן, וְאֵין בּוֹ אֶלָּא עֵד אֶחָד. הֲרֵי אֵלּוּ שְׁלֹשָׁה גִּטִּין פְּסוּלִין; וְאִם נִשֵּׂאת — הַוָּלָד כָּשֵׁר. רַבִּי אֱלִיעֶזֶר אוֹמֵר: אַף עַל פִּי שֶׁאֵין עָלָיו עֵדִים, אֶלָּא שֶׁנְּתָנוֹ לָהּ בִּפְנֵי עֵדִים — כָּשֵׁר, וְגוֹבָה מִנְּכָסִים מְשֻׁעְבָּדִים, שֶׁאֵין הָעֵדִים חוֹתְמִין עַל הַגֵּט אֶלָּא מִפְּנֵי תִקּוּן הָעוֹלָם.

ר׳ עובדיה מברטנורא

ואין בו אלא עד אחד. איכא למאן דאמר אכתב ידו קאי, ורישא אשמעינן דאפילו אין בו עד, הולד כשר. והכא אשמעינן דאפילו יש בו עד אחד לכתחלה לא. ואיכא למאן דאמר אכתב סופר קאי, ואפילו הכי הולד כשר, דסופר הוה ליה במקום עד שני: **תקון העולם.** שמא ימותו עדי מסירה, ויבא הבעל ויערער לומר לא גרשתיה. והלכה כרבי אלעזר:

יד אברהם

claim that she had been divorced prior to the deed. Alternatively, the date is required in order to prevent him from selling the produce from his wife's fields after the divorce and claiming they were sold beforehand, while still under his jurisdiction (*Rav* from *Gem.* 17a; see commentary to 2:2).

Although a *get* must be dated by the reign of the monarchy in whose domain it was written for fear of agitating relations with the government (see 8:5), and if it is not so dated, it is void, a *get* with no date on it whatsoever would not be considered a lack of deference by the government and is therefore not invalidated by that decree (*Ran; Meiri*).

יֵשׁ בּוֹ זְמַן, וְאֵין בּוֹ אֶלָּא עֵד אֶחָד. — *[if] it has a date, but it has only one witness.*

The *get* was signed by one witness in addition to being written by the husband (*Meiri* from *Gem.* 86b; see *Rif, Rosh*). Although we already know from the first case that if a woman remarried on the strength of a *get* which was written or signed by the husband, the children of the subsequent marriage are legitimate, the mishnah now informs us that even if there is a witness signed on the *get* in addition to it having been written by the husband, it is still forbidden to initially use it for divorce (*Rav*).

Another opinion is that even if the *get* was written by a scribe and signed by one witness, it is valid by Biblical law (*Gem.* ibid.) [because the scribe's writing of the *get* is tantamount to testimony that he was ordered to do so by the husband]. We are not afraid that the scribe wrote this *get* for practice and then discarded it, and it was subsequently found by the woman who had one man sign upon it as witness, because scribes are generally careful not to leave *gittin* where they can be found by others. Nevertheless, their caution is not sufficient to be relied upon completely (*Tos.* 3b s.v. שלשה) [and therefore, the Rabbis prohibited such a *get*].

The same ruling would apply if there were no date on the *get;* the mishnah only specifies a dated *get* to tell us that although it is dated, the woman may not remarry when she receives it (*Tos.* ibid., s.v. יש בו זמן ואין וכו׳).

הֲרֵי אֵלּוּ שְׁלֹשָׁה גִּטִּין פְּסוּלִין; וְאִם נִשֵּׂאת — הַוָּלָד כָּשֵׁר. — *These three gittin are void; but if she married, the offspring is legitimate.*

This seemingly redundant statement comes to exclude a case of an agent who delivered a *get* from over-

9 4 has a date, but it has only one witness. These three *gittin* are void; but if she married, the offspring is legitimate. R' Elazar says: Although there are no witnesses on it, but he gave it to her in the presence of witnesses, it is valid, and one collects from mortgaged properties, because witnesses sign on a document only for the sake of the general good.

YAD AVRAHAM

seas without testifying that it was written and signed in his presence (see 1:1), in which case R' Meir holds that any child born subsequently to a woman so divorced is a *mamzer*, and the Sages disagree (*Gem.* 86a).[1] Since the agent can — and must — take back the *get* and redeliver it while giving the proper testimony (ibid.), there is more reason to assume leniency in this case, and it therefore must be excluded by an extra phrase of the mishnah (*Tos.* ad loc., s.v. מניינא).

רַבִּי אֱלְעָזָר אוֹמֵר: אַף עַל פִּי שֶׁאֵין עָלָיו עֵדִים, — *R' Elazar says: Although there are no witnesses on it,*

[There are no witnesses signed on the *get*.] Nor was it written or signed by the husband (*Rashi*).

אֶלָּא שֶׁנְּתָנוֹ לָהּ בִּפְנֵי עֵדִים — כָּשֵׁר. — *but he gave it to her in the presence of witnesses, it is valid,*

And the woman is permitted to remarry (ibid.).

וְגוֹבֶה מִנְּכָסִים מְשֻׁעְבָּדִים, — *and one collects from mortgaged properties,*

[Our translation and vowelization follow the interpretation of most commentators, who construe this phrase as referring not to *gittin*, but to notes of loans. Apparently, although the *Tanna* is discussing *gittin*, he mentions the case of a loan to teach that the ruling in that instance is parallel to that of a *get*. *Rashi* (3b s.v. וגובה) points out that the term *gittin* also includes notes of loans.]

R' Elazar maintains that a note for a loan without signed witnesses which is given over to the lender in the presence of witnesses is valid, and — when the debt becomes due and the borrower has no money to repay — the lender can collect from the mortgaged properties of the borrower (*Tos. Yom Tov; Ritva; Ran; Rashi* loc. cit., second version; *Tos.* ibid.).

Others explain this to be referring to a *get;* she can collect her *kesubah* from his mortgaged properties (*Tos. Rid; Rashi* loc. cit., first version). [According to this view, the mishnah should be read וְגוֹבָה, *and she collects.*]

שֶׁאֵין הָעֵדִים חוֹתְמִין עַל הַגֵּט אֶלָּא מִפְּנֵי תִקּוּן הָעוֹלָם. — *because witnesses sign on a document only for the sake of the general good.*

I.e., so that if the witnesses to the delivery of the *get* should die, and the

1. [According to R' Meir, the exclusion of that case from our mishnah indicates that if she subsequently married and had a child, he would be a *mamzer*. According to the Sages, the

[ה] **שְׁנַיִם** שֶׁשָּׁלְחוּ שְׁנֵי גִטִּין שָׁוִין, וְנִתְעָרְבוּ — נוֹתֵן שְׁנֵיהֶם לָזוֹ וּשְׁנֵיהֶם לָזוֹ; לְפִיכָךְ, אָבַד אֶחָד מֵהֶן — הֲרֵי הַשֵּׁנִי בָטֵל. חֲמִשָּׁה שֶׁכָּתְבוּ כְלָל בְּתוֹךְ הַגֵּט: „אִישׁ פְּלוֹנִי מְגָרֵשׁ פְּלוֹנִית, וּפְלוֹנִי פְּלוֹנִית״, וְהָעֵדִים מִלְּמַטָּה

ר׳ עובדיה מברטנורא

(ה) **שני גיטין שוין.** בשמותיהם: **הרי השני בטל.** דלא ידעינן דמאן ניהו: **כלל.** זמן אחד לכולן, בכך בשבת גירש פלוני פלונית ופלוני פלונית: **טופס לכל אחת.** זמן לכל אחת ואחת, בכך בשבת גירש פלוני לפלונית, והשליש הגט. ובכך בשבת גירש פלוני לפלונית, והשליש הגט, וכן כולם. והעדים מלמטן:

יד אברהם

husband disputes its validity, she has a signed *get* to prove that she was divorced (*Rav*).

The *Gemara* (86b) rules like R' Elazar, that witnesses to the delivery of a *get* suffice to validate it (*Rav*). The same is true of all other legal documents (*Tos.* 4a s.v. דקיימא; *Ramama, Hil. Malveh* 11:2; *Rosh*). Others contend that from the phrase (*Jer.* 43:44), *and written in a document and signed*, we derive that all other documents require signed witnesses to be valid (*Rif*, see *Ran; Meiri*).

There is a dispute among the commentators as to the validity of a *get* which was signed by witnesses but had no witnesses to its delivery. Some hold that even R' Elazar agrees that signed witnesses validate a *get;* he contends only that witnesses who observe the delivery are also sufficient (*Rif; Rambam, Hil. Gerushin* 1:16; *Ramban, Sefer HaZechus*). Thus, the benefit of witnesses signing a *get* is that their signature obviates the need for witnesses to the delivery (*Rif*).

Others maintain that only witnesses to the delivery of a *get* validate it, not those signed upon it. Nevertheless, if the divorce is disputed, we rely on the signed witnesses to attest to its validity on the assumption that if the *get* is in her hands, it must have been delivered properly (*R' Ephraim*, cited by *Ran; Baal HaMaor; Rosh; Tos.* loc. cit.).

A third view is that only witnesses to the delivery are effective. However, a *get* which is delivered with the signatures of two witnesses on it is tantamount to one delivered in the presence of witnesses. This is because the signatures attest that the *get* was written properly — i.e., at the behest of the husband — and the fact that it is now in her possession attests to its delivery (*Ran;* see *Ketzos HaChoshen* 90:7; *Nesivos HaMishpat* 28:7).

5.

As explained above (3:1), a *get* must be written with specific intent for the woman to whom it is subsequently given. Therefore, if the designated recipient of a *get* is not clearly identified, it is not valid.

שְׁנַיִם שֶׁשָּׁלְחוּ שְׁנֵי גִטִּין שָׁוִין, — *[If] two [men] sent two identical gittin,*

An agent was given a *get* by each of two men whose names were identical, and whose wives' names were also identical (*Rav*).

distinction between that case and the one in our mishnah is that in the former, the second husband would be coerced to divorce her, whereas in the latter, he is not (see commentary above s.v. שלשה גטין).

5. [If] two [men] sent two identical *gittin*, and they became mixed up, he gives both of them to this one and both of them to this one; therefore, [if] he lost one of them, the second is void.

[If] five wrote [as a] group in a *get*: "So-and-so is divorcing So-and-so, and So-and-so [is divorcing] So-and-so," and the witnesses are below,

YAD AVRAHAM

According to R' Meir, who holds that a *get* is validated by its signed witnesses, all information necessary for the *get's* validity must be written in the *get*, so as to be included in their testimony. Therefore, the mishnah must be discussing a case in which further identification which clearly identifies the designated recipient or the sender [e.g., the grandfathers' names] is included in each *get*, but the agent does not know which is which (*Tos.* 24b s.v. בעדי מסירה). Others maintain that even R' Meir agrees that outside sources can be relied upon to clarify the information in the *get*. Thus, the mishnah can be understood as stated — that the two *gittin* were totally identical (*Ran;* see commentary to 3:1).

— וְנִתְעָרְבוּ — *and they became mixed up,*

[And the agent does not know which *get* to give to which woman.]

נוֹתֵן שְׁנֵיהֶם לָזוֹ וּשְׁנֵיהֶם לָזוֹ; — *he gives both of them to this one and both of them to this one;*

[The agent gives both *gittin* to each of the women, thereby assuring that each one receives her *get*.]

[The witnesses to the delivery — who validate the *get* according to R' Elazar — do not know which is the appropriate *get* for each woman. Although when the agent hands a *get* to each of the women, it is unknown whether this delivery is valid for her divorce, this does not constitute non-compliance with the requirement derived from the phrase (*Deut.* 24:1), וְכָתַב לָהּ, *and he shall write for her,* which indicates that it must be clearly designated for her divorce, because this applies only to the writing of the *get*, not its delivery (*Gem.* 86b).

לְפִיכָךְ, אָבַד אֶחָד מֵהֶן — הֲרֵי הַשֵּׁנִי בָטֵל. — *therefore, [if] he lost one of them, the second is void.*

Because we do not know for which woman it was intended (*Rav*). However, if he gave the second *get* to either of the women, her marital status would be in doubt [since it may have been the *get* intended for her] (*Ran*).

חֲמִשָּׁה שֶׁכָּתְבוּ כְּלָל בְּתוֹךְ הַגֵּט; — *[If] five wrote [as a] group in a get:*

I.e., they included all of their *gittin* in one document — as described below — with one date for all of them (*Rav* from *Gem.* 86b).

,,אִישׁ פְּלוֹנִי מְגָרֵשׁ פְּלוֹנִית, וּפְלוֹנִי פְּלוֹנִית״, — *"So-and-so is divorcing So-and-so, and So-and-so [is divorcing] So-and-so,"*

The names were connected with the word *and.* However, if they were listed without *and* — i.e., *"So-and-so is divorcing So-and-so, So-and-so is..."* — it is the same as if a separate text had been written for each of them (*Gem.* 87a; see below).

— וְהָעֵדִים מִלְּמַטָּה — *and the witnesses are below,*

The remaining text of the *get* follows the listing of the names, and the witnesses are signed at the bottom of the document (*Meiri; Rambam, Hil. Gerushin* 4:18).

— כֻּלָּן כְּשֵׁרִין, וְיִנָּתֵן לְכָל אַחַת וְאֶחָת. הָיָה כָתוּב טֹפֶס לְכָל אַחַת וְאַחַת, וְהָעֵדִים מִלְּמַטָּה — אֶת שֶׁהָעֵדִים נִקְרִין עִמּוֹ כָּשֵׁר.

[ו] **שְׁנֵי** גִטִּין שֶׁכְּתָבָן זֶה בְּצַד זֶה, וּשְׁנַיִם עֵדִים עִבְרִים בָּאִים מִתַּחַת זֶה לְתַחַת זֶה,

ר׳ עובדיה מברטנורא

(ו) **שני גיטין שכתבן.** בשני דפין זה בלד זה, ושני עברים תחומים מתחת הגט, הראשון לתחת השני, שם העד תחת הראשון ושם אביו תחת השני, וכן עד שני תחתיו, וחזרו וחתמו תחתיהם שני ישראלים הדרים בארץ יון, וחתמו בכתב יוני, ודרך הכתב יוני שהולך מן השמאל אל הימין, נמצא שם העד תחת הגט שני, ושם אביו תחת הראשון:

יד אברהם

כֻּלָּן כְּשֵׁרִין, וְיִנָּתֵן לְכָל אַחַת וְאֶחָת. — *they are all valid, and it shall be given to each one.*

[The signatures of the witnesses are understood as applying to the entire document, and it is valid for each of the women.]

If the *get* reads: "We, So-and-so and So-and-so, are divorcing So-and-so and So-and-so ...," it is valid (*Meiri; Rambam* loc. cit.). Others opine that once the names have been written collectively in one *get*, it can no longer be divided into separate *gittin* to be validated (*Rif*, as cited by *Rashba;* see *Ran*).

הָיָה כָתוּב טֹפֶס — *[If] the text was written*

Although the term טֹפֶס, *tofes*, ordinarily refers to the standard wording of the *get* — as opposed to the תֹּרֶף, *toref*, the specific information pertaining to a particular *get* — it also has another connotation, referring to any portion of the document''s wording, when it is not mentioned in contrast to the *toref* (*Tos. Yom Tov*).

לְכָל אַחַת וְאַחַת, — *for each one,*

He dated each one separately — i.e., "On this day of the week, So-and-so is divorcing So-and-so, and he says to her ...; on this day of the week, So-and-so is divorcing So-and-so, and he says to her ..." (*Rav* from *Gem.* 86b).

If the dates were different, those with dates which precede the latest date are invalid, because they are predated *gittin* (*Gem.* 87a; see 2:2).

וְהָעֵדִים מִלְּמַטָּה — *and the witnesses are below,*

[The witnesses are signed after the last of these separate units.]

אֶת שֶׁהָעֵדִים נִקְרִין עִמּוֹ כָּשֵׁר. — *that with which the witnesses are read is valid.*

The last *get* written on the document is valid, because the signatures of the witnesses refer to it (*Rashi*). If the document is given to any of the women whose *gittin* are written earlier, her marital status would be in question (*Rambam* loc. cit.; *Even HaEzer* 130:9), because it is unclear if the signed testimony applies to her *get* as well (*Ran*).

Others contend that since there is no clear testimony to validate her *get*, it is definitely void (ibid.).

The rulings in this mishnah apply only if the *get* was given over to the women without witnesses; if it was

they are all valid, and it shall be given to each one. [If] the text was written for each one, and the witnesses are below, that with which the witnesses are read is valid.

6. [In a case of] two *gittin*, whose texts are alongside each other, and two Hebrew witnesses extend from beneath this one to beneath this one,

YAD AVRAHAM

given to each of them in the presence of witnesses, it is effective for all of them, because the *get* no longer requires signed testimony to be valid (*Rambam*, loc. cit.) [since the *Gemara*, following R' Elazar's view, rules that the *get* is validated by the witnesses to its delivery]. Although a *get* with invalid testimony signed on it is void even according to R' Elazar (*Gem.* 4a), in this case, where the flaw is obvious, and no one will rely on the signed testimony, this rule does not apply (*Ramban*).

Others contend that the invalid signed testimony disqualifies the *get* even in this case (*Ramach* in *Hasagos* to *Rambam, Hil. Gerushin* 4:22).

According to those who hold that R' Elazar requires a *get* to be given over in the presence of witnesses in order to be valid (see commentary to mishnah 4), the mishnah must be discussing such a case. Thus, all of the *gittin* in the document are validated by the witnesses to the delivery, and the difference between the last *get* in the document and the others is only that the document can be used as proof of the divorce recorded last, but not of the others (*Tos. Yom Tov*).

6.

It is customary for witnesses to a *get* (and other legal documents) to sign their name and their fathers' names, followed by the word עֵד, *witness;* for example, רְאוּבֵן בֶּן יַעֲקֹב, עֵד, *Reuven, the son of Yaakov, Witness.*

שְׁנֵי גִטִּין, שֶׁכְּתָבָן זֶה בְּצַד זֶה, — *[In a case of] two gittin, whose texts are alongside each other,*

Two *gittin* were written in two separate columns alongside each other (*Rav*) on the same sheet of parchment (*Rashi*).

וּשְׁנַיִם עֵדִים עִבְרִים בָּאִים מִתַּחַת זֶה לְתַחַת זֶה, — *and two Hebrew witnesses extend* (lit., *come*) *from beneath this one to beneath this one,*

Two witnesses signed their names in Hebrew under the two *gittin*, with their own names signed under the *get* on the right, and those of their fathers under the *get* on the left [Diagram A] (*Rav*).

Diagram A

וּשְׁנַיִם עֵדִים יְוָנִים בָּאִים מִתַּחַת זֶה לְתַחַת זֶה — אֶת שֶׁהָעֵדִים הָרִאשׁוֹנִים נִקְרָאִין עִמּוֹ כָּשֵׁר. עֵד אֶחָד עִבְרִי וְעֵד אֶחָד יְוָנִי, עֵד אֶחָד עִבְרִי וְעֵד

ר׳ עובדיה מברטנורא

את שהעדים הראשונים נקראים עמו כשר. אם העברים חתומים למעלה, שדרך כתב עברי שהולך מן הימין אל השמאל, ונמצא שם העד תחת הגט הימני, ושם אביו תחת הגט השמאלי, הימני כשר. ואם היונים חתומים למעלה, השמאלי כשר, ששמות העדים תחת השמאלי הם. וטעמא, דחיישינן שמא העדים האחרונים הפכו את כתבם לסדר שכתבו העדים הראשונים, שאם העברים היו חתומים למעלה שהם הולכים מן הימני אל השמאלי, וחתמו על הגט הימני, כשבאו שני היונים לחתום תחתיהם, הלכו גם הם מן הימני אל השמאלי כסדר כתיבת העברים, ונמצא שארבעתם חתמו על הגט הימני. וכן אם היונים חתומים למעלה, שמא הפכו העברים שבאו אחריהם סדר כתב עברי, והלכו מן השמאלי אל הימני, ונמצאו ארבעתם חתומים על השמאלי: **הכי גרסינן עד אחד עברי ועד אחד יוני עד אחד עברי ועד אחד יוני באים**

יד אברהם

וּשְׁנַיִם עֵדִים יְוָנִים בָּאִים מִתַּחַת זֶה לְתַחַת זֶה — *and two Greek witnesses extend from beneath this one to beneath this one,*

The Hebrew signatures are followed by the signatures of two Jewish men from Greece who signed the *get* in Greek. Since Greek is written from left to right, their own names appeared under the *get* to the left and their fathers' under the one to the right (*Rav; Rambam Commentary*).

Others explain that the witnesses from Greece also signed in Hebrew letters,[1] but they did so in the manner which was customary in Greece — to refer to their father's name before their own — i.e., רְאוּבֵן בֶּן יַעֲקֹב, meaning *Reuven's son, Yaakov.* Thus, in a case that the signatures extend across two *gittin* as described above, their father's names would be under the *get* on the right, and their own beneath the one on the left (*Rashi; Ran; Tos. Rid*).

אֶת שֶׁהָעֵדִים הָרִאשׁוֹנִים נִקְרָאִין עִמּוֹ כָּשֵׁר. — *that with which the first witnesses are read is valid.*

Only the *get* on the right — under which the first pair of witnesses signed their own names — is valid, but not the *get* on the left. Although the names under the latter *get* should be those of the Grecian witnesses

1. [*Rashi* first comments that they signed in the Greek language, and then goes on to explain the case in the manner described. Since Greek is written from left to right, his words appear self-contradictory. It is therefore likely that he means that they signed in the Greek language — using words which mean *Reuven's son, Yaakov* — but transliterated the words in Hebrew letters.]

2. It is difficult to comprehend how a signature could be written in Greek from right to left [or in Hebrew from left to right (as in the case below)] (*Tos. Yom Tov*). [Perhaps it means only that he wrote his father's name prior to his own in order to coincide with the previous signatures. Thus, "Reuven filius (Greek for *son of*) Yaakov" would be read backwards — *Yaakov filius Reuven* — and the name of the witness himself would be under the *get* to the right. By the same token, רְאוּבֵן בֶּן יַעֲקֹב would be read *Yaakov ben Reuven*, placing his own name under the *get* on the left.]

9 and two Greek witnesses extend from beneath this
6 one to beneath this one, that with which the first witnesses are read is valid. [If] one Hebrew witness and one Greek witness, one Hebrew witness and

themselves, we fear that they, too, may have signed from right to left[2] to conform with the Hebrew signatures preceding theirs, and thus, all four of the witnesses' own names are signed under the first *get* (*Rav* from *Gem.* 87b).

If the Greek signatures were first, the same principle would apply in reverse: Only the *get* on the left would be valid, but not the one on the right, for fear that the witnesses who signed in Hebrew signed from left to right in order to be consistent with the Greek signatures above theirs (ibid.).

According to the second interpretation mentioned above — that even the Grecian witnesses signed in Hebrew — the concern of the mishnah is that they may have signed in the style of the others — i.e., רְאוּבֵן בֶּן יַעֲקֹב, meaning *Reuven, the son of Yaakov* (*Rashi* ad loc.).

If a document is signed with the witness' name alone — e.g., *Reuven, Witness* — or with only his father's name — e.g., *the son of Yaakov, Witness* — the testimony is valid (mishnah 7). Thus, if the first *get* was signed *Reuven*, and the second was signed *the son of Yaakov, Witness*, it would be construed as two separate signatures, one for each *get*, with the word *Witness* referring to both of them, and both would be valid. Therefore, the case in our mishnah must be that under the first *get* the witness had signed *Reuven the son of*, which cannot be understood as a separate signature, and under the second one, *Yaakov, Witness*. We do not assume that the father, Yaakov, had signed the second *get*, and that his son, Reuven, had signed the first, using only his own name, and had relied on the presence of his father's signature alongside his own to complete the wording of his signature, because the mishnah is discussing a case in which it was clarified that the handwriting under the second *get* was not that of Reuven's father (*Meiri* from *Gem.* 87a; *Tos.* ad loc. s.v. וליתכשר).

Others explain that in a case that the second *get* was signed, "יַעֲקֹב, עֵד" ("*Yaakov, Witness*"), the words רְאוּבֵן בֶּן under the first would be interpreted to mean *the son of Reuven* and would be construed to be a separate signature. Therefore the *Gemara* explains that the signature under the second *get* was recognized as belonging to Reuven, the son of Yaakov, and not to Yaakov himself, thereby eliminating the above interpretation. Alternatively, the mishnah is discussing a case in which the signature read: "*Reuven, the son of Yaakov*," but did not include the word *Witness*. Since only a full signature containing one's name and that of his father is valid without the word *Witness* added at the end, but not a half-signature containing only the witness' name or that of his father, it is clear that this is all one signature which was extended across two *gittin* (*Meiri* from *Gem.* ibid.).

Rambam (*Hil. Gerushin* 4:21) states that signatures extended across two *gittin* are valid only for the first *get*, but he does not mention any of the distinctions discussed above. This is based on a Rabbinic enactment (*Gem.* 36a) requiring the witnesses to sign *gittin* explicitly, which *Rambam* interprets to mean that they are required to sign

אֶחָד יְוָנִי בָּאִין מִתַּחַת זֶה לְתַחַת זֶה — שְׁנֵיהֶן פְּסוּלִין.

ר׳ עובדיה מברטנורא

מתחת זה לתחת זה שניהם פסולין. וטעמא, דחיישינן שמא העד עברי הראשון חתם על הגט הימני הראשון כפי סדר כתב עברי, והעד היוני השני חתם על הגט השמאלי השני כפי סדר כתב יוני, שמתחילין מן השמאל, והעד השלישי העברי הפך כתב העברי, והתחיל גם הוא מהשמאל כמו היוני שלפניו, ונמצא גם הוא חתום על הגט השמאלי, והעד היוני האחרון חתם כדרכו מן השמאל אל הימין, וגם הוא חתום על השמאלי, ונמצאו שלשה עדים חתומים על השמאלי, ואחד בלבד חתום על הימני. או בהפך, שהעד השני היוני הפך כתבו לסדר כתב עברי, והתחיל מן הימין אל השמאל כמו שחתם העד עברי הראשון, והעד עברי השלישי חתם כדרכו מן הימין, ונמצאו שלשתן חתומים על הגט הימני הראשון, והעד היוני האחרון לבדו חתם כדרכו על הגט השמאלי. ומשום דלא ידעינן בהי מינייהו חתימו תלתא, ובהי מינייהו לא חתים אלא חד, שניהם פסולין:

יד אברהם

with their names and those of their fathers in order for their testimony to be accepted. Thus, the distinctions mentioned above are pertinent only to our mishnah, which was written before this decree, but they do not affect the final ruling (*Lechem Mishneh* ad loc.).

עֵד אֶחָד עִבְרִי וְעֵד אֶחָד יְוָנִי, עֵד אֶחָד עִבְרִי וְעֵד אֶחָד יְוָנִי בָּאִין מִתַּחַת זֶה לְתַחַת זֶה — *— [If] one Hebrew witness and one Greek witness, one Hebrew witness and one Greek witness extend from beneath this one to beneath this one,*

The first of the signatures which were written across both adjoining *gittin* was signed in Hebrew — from right to left — with the witness' own name under the right-hand *get*. The second was signed in Greek — from left to right — with the witness' own name beneath the left-hand *get*. The third was in Hebrew, and the fourth in Greek [see Diagram B??] (*Rav; Tos.* 87b s.v. עד אחד).

Diagram B

Text of Get	Text of Get

ראובן בן יעקב עד
Menashe filius Yosef, Witness
קהת בן לוי עד
Yachtzeail filius Naftali, Witness

There is another version to the mishnah, which reads, עֵד אֶחָד עִבְרִי וְעֵד אֶחָד יְוָנִי בָּאִין מִתַּחַת זֶה לְתַחַת זֶה, וְעֵד אֶחָד עִבְרִי וְעֵד אֶחָד יְוָנִי בָּאִין מִתַּחַת זֶה לְתַחַת זֶה — *One Hebrew witness and one Greek witness extend from beneath this one to beneath this one, and one Hebrew witness and one Greek witness extend from beneath this one to beneath this one,* implying that there was a Hebrew signature and a Greek signature written under each of the *gittin*. This would occur in a case in which the first witness signed in Hebrew in the regular manner, and the second signed in the Greek style,[1] with רְאוּבֵן בֶּן יַעֲקֹב

1. [This case could also be constructed according to those who understand the Grecian signature discussed by the mishnah to mean a signature in the Greek language. However, *Rashi* is the one who follows the alternate version of the text, and he interprets it as referring to the manner of signing.]

one Greek witness extend from beneath this one to beneath this one, they are both void.

YAD AVRAHAM

meaning *Reuven's son, Yaakov.* However, he wrote the name רְאוּבֵן on the end of the second line — under the *get* to the left — and the words בֶּן יַעֲקֹב, which include his own name, on the beginning of the third line. Thus, both of the first two witnesses' own names are signed on the first *get.* The third witness then signed his name in the Hebrew style — עַמְרָם בֶּן קְהָת, meaning *Amram, the son of Kehas* — but he wrote *Amram* on the end of the third line and *the son of Kehas* on the beginning of the fourth, thereby putting his own name beneath the second *get.* The fourth witness signed in the Greek style across the fifth line, so that his own name, too, is signed under the second *get* (*Rashi*). [Thus, each of the *gittin* is signed by one of the witnesses' own names in the Hebrew style, and one in the Greek (see Diagram C).]

Diagram C

.שְׁנֵיהֶן פְּסוּלִין — *they are both void.*

Both *gittin* are void, because any witness following another who had signed in a different manner may have altered the form of his signature in order to coincide with the one which preceded his (*Meiri*). Thus, it is possible that the second witness, who signed in Greek, signed from right to left in order to be consistent with the Hebrew signature above his — and thus, only the second Grecian witness' own name is signed below the second *get.*

Alternatively, it is possible that the first Greek signed in his normal manner, and the third witness — who signed in Hebrew — did so from left to right in order to align his signature with the Greek one preceding his, in which case the second *get* has sufficient testimony, but only the first witness' own name is signed beneath the first *get* (*Rav* from *Gem.,* loc. cit.).[1]

Here, too, as in the previous mishnah, if any of these *gittin* were delivered in the presence of two witnesses, they would be valid (*Tos. Yom Tov;* see commentary to mishnah 5 s.v. אֶת שֶׁהָעֵדִים).

1. [Although, in the previous mishnah, some commentators maintain that *gittin* in which it is unclear whether the witnesses' signatures applied to them or not are considered of questionable validity (see commentary ibid., s.v. אֶת שֶׁהָעֵדִים), whereas, in this case, the mishnah disqualifies them completely, perhaps we can differentiate between the two in the following manner. The previous mishnah is discussing a case in which it is clear that these are the signatures of the witnesses, only we are not certain whether they refer to any of the *gittin* other than the one directly above their signatures. In our case, however, it is unclear which names are those of the witnesses and which are those of their fathers. Thus, the uncertainty concerns not only the subject of the signed testimony but the identification of the signatures themselves. In such a case, the signatures do not constitute signed testimony at all, and both *gittin* are disqualified.]

[ז] **שִׁיֵּר** מִקְצָת הַגֵּט וּכְתָבוֹ בַּדַּף הַשֵּׁנִי, וְהָעֵדִים מִלְּמַטָּה — כָּשֵׁר. חָתְמוּ עֵדִים בְּרֹאשׁ הַדַּף, מִן הַצַּד, אוֹ מֵאַחֲרָיו בְּגֵט פָּשׁוּט — פָּסוּל.

הִקִּיף רֹאשׁוֹ שֶׁל זֶה בְּצַד רֹאשׁוֹ שֶׁל זֶה, וְהָעֵדִים בָּאֶמְצַע — שְׁנֵיהֶם פְּסוּלִין. סוֹפוֹ שֶׁל זֶה בְּצַד סוֹפוֹ שֶׁל זֶה, וְהָעֵדִים בָּאֶמְצַע — אֶת שֶׁהָעֵדִים נִקְרִין עִמּוֹ כָּשֵׁר.

ר׳ עובדיה מברטנורא

(ז) **בדף השני.** שאללו ברוחב המגילה: **מן הצד.** בגליון של ימין הגט, או בגליון השמאלי: **או מאחוריו בגט פשוט.** שעדיו בתוכו: **הקיף.** חבר זה אלל זה: **שניהם פסולים.** שאין נקראת החתימה לא עם זה ולא עם זה:

יד אברהם

7.

שִׁיֵּר מִקְצָת הַגֵּט — *[If] one left over part of the get*

[An unfinished *get* was written on the first column of a page.]

וּכְתָבוֹ בַּדַּף הַשֵּׁנִי, — *and wrote it on the second column,*

The remainder of the *get* was written on a second column alongside it (*Rav*).

וְהָעֵדִים מִלְּמַטָּה — *and the witnesses are at the bottom,*

The signatures of the witnesses were at the bottom of the second column (*Tif. Yis.*).

כָּשֵׁר. — *it is valid.*

The *get* is valid as long as it is evident that the document had not been cut at the bottom or top. Otherwise, it is void because of the possibility that they were two separate *gittin* which were combined into one in order to remove a provision which had been included in the first, or to change the date of the second (*Gem.* 88a).

Alternatively, if there is a blank space at the bottom of the first column and one at the top of the second, these fears would be allayed. However, there is still a possibility that the husband had ordered the *get* written, and then changed his mind in the middle [and the scribe had finished it on his own initiative (*Ran*) which would not be valid]. Therefore, it is valid only if the second column begins in midsentence, which renders the above possibility too unlikely to merit concern (*Gem.* ibid.).

חָתְמוּ עֵדִים בְּרֹאשׁ הַדַּף, — *[If] the witnesses signed at the top of the page,*

The *get* was written below the signatures of the witnesses (*Meiri*).

מִן הַצַּד, — *on the side,*

Or they signed on the margin of the page, on either side of the *get* (*Rav*).

אוֹ מֵאַחֲרָיו בְּגֵט פָּשׁוּט — *or on the back of an open get,*

The witnesses signed on the back of a standard *get*, which must be signed on the front (*Rav*) by Rabbinic law (*Rashi*) — as opposed to a bound *get* (see commentary to 8:9), which is signed on the back (*Tos. Rid*).

7. [If] one left over part of the *get* and wrote it on the second column, and the witnesses are at the bottom, it is valid. [If] the witnesses signed at the top of the page, on the side, or on the back of an open *get*, it is void.

[If] the top of this one was attached to the top of this one, [and] the witnesses are in between, they are both void. [If] at the end of this one [was attached] to the end of this one, [and] the witnesses are in between, that with which the witnesses are read is valid.

YAD AVRAHAM

פָּסוּל. — *it is void.*

The Rabbis decreed that witnesses must sign all legal documents beneath the text, and a document signed otherwise is void (*Tos.* to *Bava Basra* 160a s.v. פשוט).

הִקִּיף רֹאשׁוֹ שֶׁל זֶה בְּצַד רֹאשׁוֹ שֶׁל זֶה, וְהָעֵדִים בָּאֶמְצַע, — *[If] the top of this one was attached to the top of this one, [and] the witnesses are in between,*

Two *gittin* were attached together at the top of each, and the signatures of the witnesses were in the middle of the two *gittin* above their tops [Diagram A] (*Meiri*).

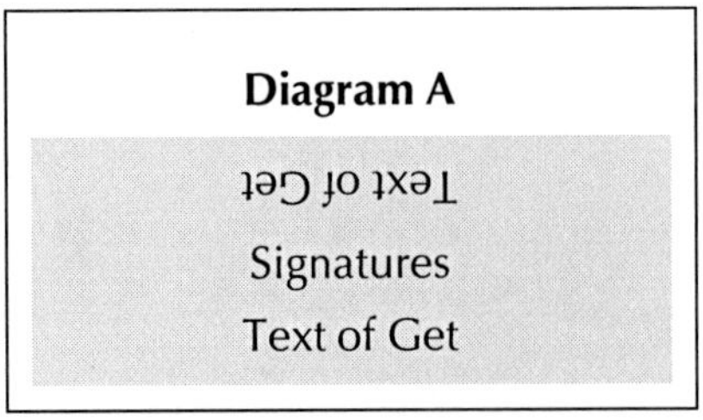

שְׁנֵיהֶם פְּסוּלִין. — *they are both void.*

Because the signatures are not read as part of either *get* (*Rav*) [since they are not beneath the text as required]. Even the *get* with whose text the top of the signatures' lettering is aligned — i.e., the one which is above the signatures when they are right side up — is invalid (*Tos.* 87b s.v. חתמו) [although it is similar to a standard signature in that respect].

סוֹפוֹ שֶׁל זֶה בְּצַד סוֹפוֹ שֶׁל זֶה, וְהָעֵדִים בָּאֶמְצַע, — *[If] the end of this one [was attached] to the end of this one, and the witnesses are in between,*

[Two *gittin* were attached at the bottom of each, and the witnesses were signed in between (Diagram B).]

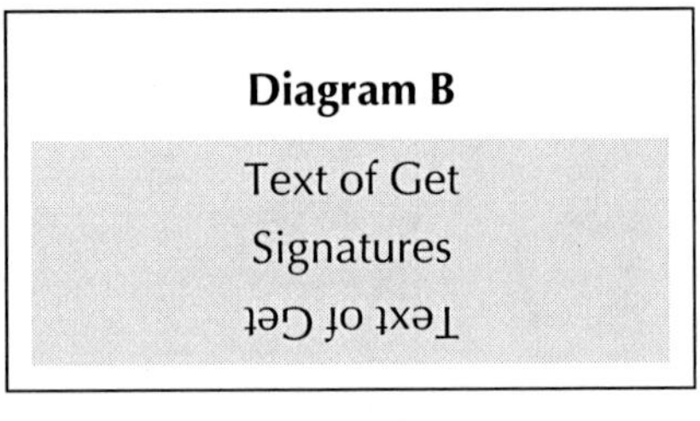

אֶת שֶׁהָעֵדִים נִקְרִין עִמּוֹ כָּשֵׁר. — *that with which the witnesses are read is valid.*

The *get* with whose writing the signatures are consistent — i.e., the top of the lettering of the signatures is aligned with the text in the usual manner — is valid (*Rashi*), and we do not say that since the signatures do not refer to one of the *gittin* they are

רֹאשׁוֹ שֶׁל זֶה בְּצַד סוֹפוֹ שֶׁל זֶה, וְהָעֵדִים בָּאֶמְצַע — אֶת שֶׁהָעֵדִים נִקְרִין בְּסוֹפוֹ כָּשֵׁר.

[ח] **גֵּט** שֶׁכְּתָבוֹ עִבְרִית, וְעֵדָיו יְוָנִית; יְוָנִית, וְעֵדָיו עִבְרִית; עֵד אֶחָד עִבְרִי, וְעֵד אֶחָד יְוָנִי; כְּתַב סוֹפֵר וְעֵד — כָּשֵׁר.

ר׳ עובדיה מברטנורא

את שהעדים נקרין בסופו. שכן חתימה כלפי סופו, ולא שרגלי חתימה כלפי ראשו, כשר: **(ח) כתב סופר ועד.** חתם סופר ועד. דהוי להו שני עדים. ואשמעינן מתניתין דלא חיישינן שמא הבעל לא צוה לכתוב לסופר, אלא אמר לשנים אמרו לסופר ויכתוב, ולפלוני ופלוני עדים ויחתומו, ואתו הנך עדים לכסופא דספרא, שיאמר איני בעיניו כשר לעדות, ואחתמוהו בלא רשותו דבעל, להא לא חיישינן:

יד אברהם

also not related to the other (*Tos.* loc. cit.).

רֹאשׁוֹ שֶׁל זֶה בְּצַד סוֹפוֹ שֶׁל זֶה, וְהָעֵדִים בָּאֶמְצַע — *[If] the top of this one [was attached] to the bottom of this one, and the witnesses are in between,*

[The bottom of one *get* was attached to the top of another, and the witnesses are signed in the middle of the two *gittin* (Diagram C).]

אֶת שֶׁהָעֵדִים נִקְרִין בְּסוֹפוֹ כָּשֵׁר. — *that with which the witnesses are read at its end is valid.*

The top *get*, below which the witnesses are signed, is valid, but not

Diagram C

Text of Get

Signatures

Text of Get

the bottom *get*, which is below the signatures (*Rav*).

In any of these cases, if the *get* was given over in the presence of two witnesses, it is valid (*Rambam, Hil. Gerushin* 4:2; see commentary to mishnah 5 s.v. אֶת שֶׁהָעֵדִים).

8.

The Mishnah continues its discussion of the laws governing the validity of the witnesses' signatures on a *get*.

גֵּט שֶׁכְּתָבוֹ עִבְרִית, וְעֵדָיו יְוָנִית; — *A get whose writing is [in] Hebrew, and whose witnesses [are in] Greek;*

A *get* written in Hebrew, but signed in Greek by Jewish witnesses (*Meiri*), is valid if the witnesses understand the language in which the *get* was written (ibid.; *Rambam, Hil. Gerushin* 4:7).

יְוָנִית, וְעֵדָיו עִבְרִית; — *[in] Greek, and its witnesses [in] Hebrew;*

[The *get* was written in Greek — since a *get* may be written in any language (ibid.) — and signed in Hebrew.]

However, the accepted custom is to write

9
8

[If] the top of this one [was attached] to the bottom of this one, [and] the witnesses are in between, that with which the witnesses are read at its end is valid.

8. A *get* whose writing is [in] Hebrew, and whose witnesses [are in] Greek; [in] Greek, and its witnesses [in] Hebrew; one witness [in] Hebrew and one witness [in] Greek; [or one which has] the writing of the scribe and a witness, is valid.

a *get* in Aramaic, and a *get* written in any other language may not be used except in pressing circumstances (*Even HaEzer* 126:1).

עֵד אֶחָד עִבְרִי, וְעֵד אֶחָד יְוָנִי; — *one witness [in] Hebrew, and one witness [in] Greek;*

[The witnesses signed in different languages.]

However, if part of the *get* was written in one language, and the other part in a second language, it is not valid (*Rambam,* loc. cit.; *Ran; Even HaEzer* 126:1). Others contend that this is true only if the witnesses signed in different languages; but if the witnesses signed in one language, that serves to unify the *get* and validate it (*Ravad, Hil. Gerushin* 4:7; *Rashba; Rama* to *Even HaEzer* loc. cit.; see *Chelkas Mechokek,* ibid. 3; *Beur HaGra,* ibid. 1).

כְּתַב סוֹפֵר וְעֵד — *[or one which has] the writing of the scribe and a witness,*

The *get* is signed by the scribe who wrote it and by another witness. We are not afraid that the husband asked two witnesses other than the scribe to sign, and that they asked the scribe to sign so he should not think that he is not considered fitting to be a witness (*Rav*) — which would invalidate his signature since it violated the husband's instructions (see 6:7) — because the mishnah holds like R' Yose (*Gem.* 88a), that an agent's assignment which does not include a tangible object cannot be transferred to another agent, and thus, the scribe would not sign the *get* unless instructed to do so by the husband (*Rashi* ad loc., 72a s.v. ר׳ יוסי היא; see commentary to 6:7 s.v. אף אנו).

There is another view that even if the scribe did not sign the *get,* his act of writing it is tantamount to testimony that he was ordered to do so by the husband [which is the point of signed testimony on a document (see *Nesivos HaMishpat* 28:7)]. Therefore, if one witness signed the *get,* it is valid (*Gem.* 86b; see commentary to mishnah 4 s.v. יש בו זמן). However, it is valid only if the scribe is an expert in the laws of *gittin* and can be relied upon to write a *get* only at the behest of the husband (*Gem.* ibid.; *Rashi* ad loc. s.v. ושמואל).

כָּשֵׁר. — *is valid.*

[All of these *gittin* are valid.]

„אִישׁ פְּלוֹנִי עֵד" — כָּשֵׁר. „בֶּן אִישׁ פְּלוֹנִי, עֵד" — כָּשֵׁר. „אִישׁ פְּלוֹנִי, בֶּן אִישׁ פְּלוֹנִי", וְלֹא כָתַב: „עֵד" — כָּשֵׁר; וְכָךְ הָיוּ נְקִיֵּי הַדַּעַת שֶׁבִּירוּשָׁלַיִם עוֹשִׂין. כָּתַב חֲנִיכָתוֹ וַחֲנִיכָתָהּ — כָּשֵׁר.

גֵּט מְעֻשֶּׂה: בְּיִשְׂרָאֵל — כָּשֵׁר; וּבְגּוֹיִם — פָּסוּל;

ר' עובדיה מברטנורא

חניכתו. שם לווי של משפחה: **מעושה.** בחזקה: **בישראל כשר.** אם אנסוהו בדין. כגון כל הנך דכופין להוציא, או שהיתה אסורה לו. ואם אנסוהו שלא כדין, פסול. ופוסל מן הכהונה, משום ריח גט: **ובנכרי.** כדין, פסול, ופוסל מן הכהונה. שלא כדין, אפילו ריח גט אין בו. ומי שחייב ליתן גט מן הדין, ואין כח בדייני ישראל לכופו, חובטין אותו על ידי נכרים, שאומרים עשה מה שישראל אומר לך, ונותן הגט על פי דייני ישראל:

יד אברהם

„אִישׁ פְּלוֹנִי, עֵד" — כָּשֵׁר. — *[A signature which reads:] "So-and-so, Witness" is valid.*

[If a witness signed his name to a *get*, but did not add his father's name — i.e., "the son of so-and-so" — it is valid, as long as he adds the word *Witness.*]

„בֶּן אִישׁ פְּלוֹנִי, עֵד" — כָּשֵׁר. — *[One which reads:] "The son of So-and-so, Witness"* is valid.

[Although he did not mention his own name.]

According to *Rambam* (*Hil. Gerushin* 4:21), the signature is not valid in these two cases due to a subsequent Rabbinic enactment requiring a full signature (*Lechem Mishneh* ad loc.; see commentary to mishnah 6, s.v. ושנים עדים עברים).

„אִישׁ פְּלוֹנִי, בֶּן אִישׁ פְּלוֹנִי", וְלֹא כָתַב: „עֵד" — כָּשֵׁר; — *[If he wrote:] "So-and-so, the son of So-and-so," and he did not write: "Witness," it is valid;*

[If he signed a full signature, it is valid even if he did not add the word *Witness.*]

וְכָךְ הָיוּ נְקִיֵּי הַדַּעַת שֶׁבִּירוּשָׁלַיִם עוֹשִׂין. — *and this is what the pure minded of Jerusalem used to do.*

Since they were careful to avoid unnecessary words, they did not add the word *Witness* to their signatures (*Rashi*).

In other versions of the Mishnah, this is stated after the next statement, and it refers to that (*Tos.* 88a s.v. וכך).

כָּתַב חֲנִיכָתוֹ וַחֲנִיכָתָהּ — כָּשֵׁר. — *[If] he wrote his surname or her surname, it is valid.*

If the husband, when writing his or his wife's name in the *get*, added a family name, rather than that of his or her father, it is valid (*Rav; Meiri*). Thus, if there was a distinguished individual in the family, members of that family might refer to that ancestor in their names — e.g., *Ibn Ezra* — rather than identifying themselves with their father's names (*Tos. Rid; Meiri*). However, this identification is valid only within three generations of the life of that ancestor (*Gem.* 88a; *Rashi* ad loc. s.v. עד; *Rosh*).

Another opinion is that the name may be used for ten generations (*Gem.* ibid.).

Others explain that the family name does not refer to a specific individual, but is simply a surname used by the family for identification. It is valid only if it has not

9
8

[A signature which reads:] "So-and-so, Witness" is valid. [One which reads:] "The son of So-and-so, Witness" is valid. [If he wrote:] "So-and-so, the son of So-and-so," and he did not write: "Witness," it is valid; and this is what the pure minded of Jerusalem used to do. [If] he wrote his surname or her surname, it is valid.

A *get* drawn up under coercion — [if] by a Jew, it is valid; but by a gentile, it is void;

YAD AVRAHAM

been in disuse for three (or ten, according to the alternate opinion) generations (*Meiri*).

There is another view that the names referred to in the mishnah are personal nicknames, not the family names described in the *Gemara* (*Tos.* loc. cit.). Although it is stated above (4:2) that a man must write his primary name in the *get* for it to be valid, the nickname discussed here is one which is familiar to all who know him and is therefore considered a primary name (*Ravad, Hil. Gerushin* 3:13; *Rosh* to 34b). Others explain this nickname to be one which is used in the same place as his proper name, not one used only in a different town (*Maggid Mishneh*, ad loc.). In such a case, there is a dispute whether, in a *get*, it is permitted to use only one of the names by which he is called in that place (*Rashba* to 34b), or whether he is obligated to include both (*Ramban* ad loc.). All agree, however, that if he used only one the divorce is valid (ibid.).

גֵּט מְעֻשֶּׂה: בְּיִשְׂרָאֵל — כָּשֵׁר; — *A get drawn up under coercion — [if] by a Jew, it is valid;*

If a man was compelled by a Jewish court (*Rambam Commentary*) to give a *get* to his wife, in a situation in which he was required by Jewish law to divorce her, it is valid (*Rav* from *Gem.* 88b). Although a *get* can be given only with the husband's consent (*Yevamos* 14:1), if he is pressured until he proclaims his desire to divorce her, it is legitimate (*Arachin* 5:6). This is because we assume that every Jew actually desires to heed the words of the Rabbis (*Bava Basra* 48a), and it is only the influence of his evil inclination which incites him to do otherwise. Thus, when this external desire is overcome by force, the person's declaration that he wants to comply with the law is an expression of his true will (*Rambam, Hil. Gerushin* 2:20).

If a Jew forced him to divorce his wife when he was under no obligation to do so, the *get* is not valid. However, she becomes prohibited to a *Kohen* (*Gem.* 88b) as a preventative measure so that other women — whose husbands were coerced to divorce them because the law required it — not be led to marry *Kohanim* (*Rashi* ad loc. s.v. כדין; *Meiri*).

וּבַגּוֹיִם — פָּסוּל; — *but by a gentile, it is void;*

If a gentile forces a Jew to give his wife a *get*, it is not valid. However, if the Jew is in fact obligated to divorce her, the *get* renders her prohibited to a *Kohen* (*Gem.* ad loc.), because if such a *get* is declared totally void, people may be led to assume that all *gittin* given under duress are not valid, even if imposed legally by a Jewish court (*Rashi* ad loc.; *Meiri*). If, however, he was under no obligation to divorce his

וּבַגּוֹיִם חוֹבְטִין אוֹתוֹ וְאוֹמְרִים לוֹ: ,,עֲשֵׂה מַה שֶּׁיִּשְׂרָאֵל אוֹמְרִים לְךָ״, וְכָשֵׁר.

[ט] **יָצָא** שְׁמָהּ בָּעִיר מְקֻדֶּשֶׁת — הֲרֵי זוֹ מְקֻדֶּשֶׁת; מְגֹרֶשֶׁת — הֲרֵי זוֹ מְגֹרֶשֶׁת; וּבִלְבַד שֶׁלֹּא יְהֵא שָׁם אֲמַתְלָא. אֵיזוֹ

ר׳ עובדיה מברטנורא

(ט) **יצא שמה בעיר מקודשת.** פנויה שיצא עליה קול, פלונית נתקדשה היום לפלוני. ולא קול הברה בלבד, אלא כגון שהיו נרות דולקות ומטות מוצעות, ובני אדם נכנסים ויוצאים ואומרים פלונית נתקדשה היום: **מגורשת הרי זו מגורשת.** ארישא קאי, האי איתתא דיצא עליה קול מקודשת, וחיישינן ליה, ואסרנוה לינשא אלא לאותו האיש, אם חזר ויצא עליה קול מגורשת, שגרשה אותו פלוני שיצא לה קול קדושין ממנו, הרי זו מגורשת ומותרת לכל, שהרי קול שחששנו לו

יד אברהם

wife, and the gentile coerced him to do so, the *get* is totally void (*Gem.* ibid.), because the illegal coercion of even a Jewish court prohibits her to a *Kohen* only by Rabbinic law and therefore does not warrant a preventative measure to reinforce it (*Rashi* ad loc.).

וּבַגּוֹיִם חוֹבְטִין אוֹתוֹ וְאוֹמְרִים לוֹ: ,,עֲשֵׂה מַה שֶּׁיִּשְׂרָאֵל אוֹמְרִים לְךָ״, וְכָשֵׁר. — *but they beat him through gentiles who say: "Do as the Jews say to you," and it is valid.*

A Jewish court may order a gentile to coerce a man to divorce his wife if he is so obligated (*Rav; Meiri*), because the gentile is then acting as the agent of the court (*Ran*).

Although a gentile cannot be an agent (see 2:5 and commentary, ad loc.), this is an act which does not require the legal status of an agent, only the assignment of the court to perform the function at their behest (*Tif. Yis.*).

Many versions of this mishnah do not include the word וְכָשֵׁר, *and it is valid;* nevertheless, that is certainly the intended implication (*Rif; Rosh; Tos.; Meiri*).

9.

יָצָא שְׁמָהּ בָּעִיר מְקֻדֶּשֶׁת — *[If] she was reported* (lit., *her name went out*) *in the town [to be] married,* —

A report was accepted in court that a certain single woman had been married (*Rav* from *Gem.* 89b). This occurs when two witnesses testify in court that they observed the factors which indicate a marriage celebration — i.e., lit candles, prepared couches, people coming and going in her house, and women rejoicing with her — and the witnesses heard the women say that this woman was married to So-and-so on this day (*Rambam, Hil. Ishus* 9:22; *Even HaEzer* 46:1 from *Gem.* 89a) and in this town (*Tif. Yis.; Rama* ad loc. from *Gem.* ibid.), and the testimony is investigated by the court and found to be plausible (*Rama* ibid. 2). However, if the husband's name was not specified, or they testified on a different day

but they beat him through gentiles who say: "Do as the Jews say to you," and it is valid.

9. [I]f] she was reported in the town [to be] married, she is married; [to be] divorced, she is divorced; as long as there is no qualification. What

YAD AVRAHAM

than the alleged marriage or in a different town, the report is not accepted (*Gem.* loc. cit.).

Alternatively, two witnesses testified that they heard from So-and-so, who had heard from So-and-so, that this woman was married to a certain man in the presence of two specified witnesses, who went overseas and are not available for questioning (*Rambam* loc. cit.; *Even HaEzer* 46:2 from *Gem.* 89a).

Others contend that only if the two witnesses quote two other witnesses who had actually seen the event themselves is their testimony accepted. However, this is valid even if each of them quotes only one witness (*Rosh; Rashba; Ran; Rama* loc. cit.). In this case, there is a dispute among the authorities whether their testimony must be given on the day of the alleged marriage and whether it must be given in the same town (*Beis Shmuel* 46:4).

In either of these cases, if the woman was already married — or even only betrothed — to someone else when this testimony was brought to court, it is disregarded (*Gem.* 89b).

If the report is later proven to be unfounded — e.g., the witnesses return from overseas and disclaim it — there is a dispute in the *Gemara* (98a) whether the report is officially refuted and its effects negated. The final ruling is debated among the authorities (*Ran; Rama* loc. cit. 4).

הֲרֵי זוֹ מְקֻדֶּשֶׁת; — *she is married;*

She is assumed to be married, and she must receive a *get* before marrying another man (*Meiri*).

If another man married her after this report, they must separate while the report is investigated. If it is confirmed, she needs no *get* from the second husband, since their marriage was void. If the report remains in doubt, the first man must divorce her, and she may marry the second. [They will have to perform the marriage once again due to the possibility that the report is true and their wedding was void.] She may not marry the first man, even after receiving a divorce from the second, because it will appear as if he is remarrying his divorcee who was married to someone else in the interim [which is forbidden] (*Gem.* 89b).

מְגֹרֶשֶׁת — הֲרֵי זוֹ מְגֹרֶשֶׁת; — *[to be] divorced, she is divorced;*

If the report of her marriage was followed by a report that she was subsequently divorced, it is accepted, and she is permitted to remarry, but is forbidden to a *Kohen* (*Rav* from *Gem.* 88b; *Rashi* ad loc. s.v. ה"ק).

Others contend that only if the report of her divorce accompanied the original report of her marriage is she permitted to remarry (*Ran* citing *Ravad; Even HaEzer* 46:7).

If a woman who was married to a *Kohen* was reported to have been divorced, it is disregarded, because she is not coerced to leave her husband on the strength of a mere report (*Rav, Tos. Yom Tov* from *Gem.* 88b, *Rashi* ad loc.).

וּבִלְבַד שֶׁלֹּא יְהֵא שָׁם אֲמַתְלָא. — *as long as there is no qualification.*

These reports of marriage or divorce are effectual only if they are not qualified, as explained below (*Rav*).

הִיא אֲמַתְלָא? ,,גֵּרֵשׁ אִישׁ פְּלוֹנִי אֶת אִשְׁתּוֹ עַל תְּנַאי״, ,,זָרַק לָהּ קִדּוּשֶׁיהָ, סָפֵק קָרוֹב לָהּ סָפֵק קָרוֹב לוֹ״ — זוֹ הִיא אֲמַתְלָא.

[י] **בֵּית** שַׁמַּאי אוֹמְרִים: לֹא יְגָרֵשׁ אָדָם אֶת אִשְׁתּוֹ אֶלָּא אִם כֵּן מָצָא בָהּ דְּבַר עֶרְוָה, שֶׁנֶּאֱמַר: ,,כִּי מָצָא בָהּ עֶרְוַת דָּבָר״. וּבֵית הִלֵּל אוֹמְרִים: אֲפִלּוּ הִקְדִּיחָה תַבְשִׁילוֹ, שֶׁנֶּאֱמַר: ,,כִּי מָצָא בָהּ עֶרְוַת דָּבָר״.

ר׳ עובדיה מברטנורא

תחלה שוברו עמו: **ובלבד שלא יהא שם אמתלא.** שלא יהא עם הקול של קדושין או של גרושין אמתלא, טעם שהוא שובר את כח הקול:

יד אברהם

אֵיזוֹ הִיא אֲמַתְלָא? ,,גֵּרֵשׁ אִישׁ פְּלוֹנִי אֶת אִשְׁתּוֹ עַל תְּנַאי״ — *What is a qualification? [If they said:] "So-and-so divorced his wife on a condition"*

[The report of the divorce included the fact that there had been a provision to the *get.*] Since the condition may not have been kept, the report of the divorce is disregarded (*Rashi*), and the report of marriage which preceded it [or accompanied it] is accepted (*Ran* citing *Ravad*).

There is another view that since knowledge of the marriage itself is based only upon a report, even the additional report of a divorce with a stipulation is sufficient to negate the assumption that she is married. Therefore, the case of a qualification negating a report of divorce is one in which a widow is reported to have been previously divorced, and is thus prohibited to a *Kohen.* If that report included the fact that there had been a provision to the *get,* it is disregarded[1] (*Ramban*).

,,זָרַק לָהּ קִדּוּשֶׁיהָ, סָפֵק קָרוֹב לָהּ סָפֵק קָרוֹב לוֹ״ — *[or] "He threw her kiddushin to her, [and there was] doubt [if] it was close to her or close to him"* —

Those who reported the marriage reported that he threw her the object or document with which he meant to marry her (see *Kiddushin* 1:1), but it was unclear whether it entered her jurisdiction in order for her to acquire it (see 8:3).

זוֹ הִיא אֲמַתְלָא. — *this is a disqualification.*

[This is a qualification which negates the effectuality of the report of marriage or divorce.]

If the qualifying factor was separately reported to the court after the report regarding the marriage or di-

1. *Ramban* cites cases mentioned in the *Gemara* (89a) in which reports of marriages are disregarded because of factors which only possibly invalidate those marriages to substantiate his view that as long as there is a legitimate doubt, the report of her marriage may be ignored. *Ran* disputes this proof, because the possibilities cited in those cases undermine the basic assumption of marriage; whereas in this case, the report of the marriage has been accepted, and the question at hand is only if the couple was subsequently divorced.

is a qualification? [If they said:] "So-and-so divorced his wife on a condition" [or] "He threw her *kiddushin* to her, [and there was] doubt [if] it was close to her or close to him" — this is a qualification.

10. Beis Shammai say: A man may not divorce his wife unless he found in her an act of adultery, as it says (*Deuteronomy* 24:1): *Because he found in her an adulterous thing.* Beis Hillel say: Even if she burnt his food, as it says: *Because he found in her an adulterous thing.*

YAD AVRAHAM

vorce, the qualification negates the effect of the first report only if it appears to the court that it is true (*Rambam, Hil. Ishus* 9:24; *Even HaEzer* 46:4).

10.

The *Tanna* concludes the tractate with a discussion of the acceptable reasons for a man to divorce his wife.

בֵּית שַׁמַּאי אוֹמְרִים: לֹא יְגָרֵשׁ אָדָם אֶת אִשְׁתּוֹ אֶלָּא אִם כֵּן מָצָא בָהּ דְּבַר עֶרְוָה, — *Beis Shammai say: A man may not divorce his wife unless he found in her an act* (lit., *a thing*) *of adultery,*

They maintain that it is forbidden for a man to divorce his wife unless two witnesses testify that she committed adultery (*Gem.* 90a).

There is a dispute among the authorities whether this prohibition applies also to a man who has performed *erusin*, but not completed the marriage with *nisuin* (*Mishneh LaMelech, Hil. Gerushin* 10:21).

שֶׁנֶּאֱמַר: ,,כִּי מָצָא בָהּ עֶרְוַת דָּבָר״. — *as it says* (*Deuteronomy* 24:1): *"Because he found in her an adulterous thing."*

In describing the divorce process, the verse tells us that the husband's reason for divorce is his discovery of adultery on her part; thus, only in such circumstances is divorce sanctioned.

וּבֵית הִלֵּל אוֹמְרִים: אֲפִלּוּ הִקְדִּיחָה תַבְשִׁילוֹ, — *Beis Hillel say: Even if she burnt his food* (lit., *cooked dish*),

He may divorce her even for burning his food or oversalting (*Rav*) when it is caused by a lack of care in attending to the needs of the household, or for any other manifestation of her rejection of his authority (*Meiri*). However, if he divorced her for no cause, the divorce is valid ex post facto, and he is not required to remarry her (ibid. from *Gem.* 90a).

Nevertheless, it is improper to divorce one's first wife (*Rambam, Hil. Gerushin* 10:21 from *Gem.* 90b) unless she conducts herself in an unchaste manner, in which case he is encouraged to divorce her (ibid. 22 from *Gem.*).

שֶׁנֶּאֱמַר: ,,כִּי מָצָא בָהּ עֶרְוַת דָּבָר״. — *as it says: "Because he found in her an adulterous thing."*

גיטין
ט/י

רַבִּי עֲקִיבָא אוֹמֵר: אֲפִלּוּ מָצָא אַחֶרֶת נָאָה הֵימֶנָּה, שֶׁנֶּאֱמַר: ,,וְהָיָה אִם לֹא תִמְצָא חֵן בְּעֵינָיו״.

סליקה לה מסכת גיטין

ר׳ עובדיה מברטנורא

(י) **אפילו הקדיחה תבשילו.** שרפתהו על ידי האור, או על ידי מלח. דדרשי בית הלל ערות דבר (דברים כד, א), או ערוה, או דבר, כלומר שאר דבר סרחון שאינו ערוה: **רבי עקיבא אומר אפילו מצא אחרת נאה ממנה.** ודריש קרא (דברים כד, א) הכי, אם לא תמצא חן של נוי בעיניו, או אם מצא בה ערוה, או דבר של סרחון, על כל אחד משלשה דברים הללו יכול לגרש. והלכה כבית הלל:

יד אברהם

[Since Scripture could have written only the word עֶרְוָה, *adultery*, and omitted the word דָּבָר, *thing*] the extra word indicates that he may also divorce her for any other disagreeable conduct aside from adultery (*Rav* from *Gem.* 90a). Adultery is mentioned specifically in order to disclose that even a woman who committed adultery is permitted to another man (*Gem.* ibid.), as stated in the next verse, *and she went and was married to another man* (*Tos. Yom Tov*).

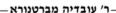

R' Akiva says: Even if he found another more beautiful than her, as it says (ibid.): *And it comes to pass that she does not find favor in his eyes.*

YAD AVRAHAM

The *halachah* follows the view of Beis Hillel (*Rav; Meiri*).

רַבִּי עֲקִיבָא אוֹמֵר: אֲפִלּוּ מָצָא אַחֶרֶת נָאָה הֵימֶנָּה, — *R' Akiva says: Even if he found another more beautiful than her,*

A man may divorce his wife simply because he desires to do so, even if he has found no fault in her actions (*Meiri*).

שֶׁנֶּאֱמַר: ,,וְהָיָה אִם לֹא תִמְצָא חֵן בְּעֵינָיו״. — *as it says (ibid.): "And it comes to pass that she does not find favor in his eyes."*

[I.e., that lack of favor is sufficient grounds for divorce.]

The verse continues: כִּי מָצָא בָהּ עֶרְוַת דָּבָר. The word כִּי has four meanings: *if, perhaps, except,* and *because.* R' Akiva translates כִּי in this verse to mean *if:* thus, the verse is interpreted: *If she does not find favor in his eyes [or] if he found in her an adulterous thing, and he shall write for her ...* Beis Shammai and Beis Hillel, on the other hand, render it *because;* hence: *she does not find favor in his eyes, because he found in her an adulterous thing* (*Gem.* 90a).

Glossary

ailonis אַיְלוֹנִית: a sexually underdeveloped woman who is incapable of childbearing. See commentary to 4:8.

bogeres, pl. **bogros** (בּוֹגְרוֹת) בּוֹגֶרֶת: a mature girl. This stage is usually reached at the age of twelve and a half years. See commentary to 6:3 s.v. נַעֲרָה.

chalitzah חֲלִיצָה: the procedure of taking off the shoe — a mechanism provided by the Torah to release the brothers and the widow of a deceased man when they do not wish to perform *yibum.* See General Introduction to ArtScroll *Yevamos.*

chazakah חֲזָקָה: (1) the rule that, unless proven otherwise, a person or thing is presumed to have retained its previous status; (2) possession.

Eretz Yisrael אֶרֶץ יִשְׂרָאֵל: the Land of Israel according to its halachically defined boundaries.

erusin אֵרוּסִין: the first stage of marriage, during which the couple is considered legally married in most respects. The term *betrothal,* albeit a poor and misleading translation, has sometimes been used for the sake of convenience. See preface to 8:9.

ervah, pl. **arayos** (עֲרָיוֹת) עֶרְוָה: one of the twenty-one women Biblically prohibited to a man because of kinship, either by blood or by marriage. See *Lev.* 18.

Gemara (abbr. **Gem.**) גְּמָרָא: the section of the Talmud that explains the Mishnah.

get, pl. **gittin** (גִּטִּין) גֵּט: (1) a bill of divorce; (2) any legal document. See General Introduction s.v. *The Get.*

halachah הֲלָכָה: (1) a religious law; (2) the accepted ruling; (3) [cap.] the body of Jewish law.

kares כָּרֵת: a form of excision meted out by the Heavenly Tribunal, sometimes as premature death, sometimes by one being predeceased by his children.

kesubah, pl. **kesubos** (כְּתוּבּוֹת) כְּתוּבָּה: (1) the agreement made between a man and his wife upon their marriage, whose foremost feature is the dower awarded her in the event of their divorce or his death; (2) the document upon which this agreement is recorded. See General Introduction to ArtScroll *Kesubos.*

kiddushin קִדּוּשִׁין: *erusin.*

Kohen, pl. **Kohanim** (כֹּהֲנִים) כֹּהֵן: a member of the priestly family descended from Aaron.

mamzer, fem. **mamzeres,** pl. **mamzerim** מַמְזֵר (מַמְזֶרֶת, מַמְזֵרִים): a person born from forbidden relations that are punishable by *kares* or the death penalty.

mikveh מִקְוֶה: ritual pool of water for the halachic cleansing of one who is ritually contaminated.

mishnah, pl. **mishnayos** (מִשְׁנָיוֹת) מִשְׁנָה: (1) [cap.] the section of the Talmud consisting of the collection of oral laws edited by R' Yehudah HaNasi (Judah the Prince); (2) an article of this section.

mitzvah pl. **mitzvos** (מִצְווֹת) מִצְוָה: a Biblical or Rabbinical precept.

naarah, pl. **naaros** (נְעָרוֹת) נַעֲרָה: a girl over the age of twelve years who has already grown two pubic hairs. This stage ends six months later when she becomes a *bogeres.* See commentary to 6:3.

neder, pl. **nedarim** (נְדָרִים) נֶדֶר: (loosely) a vow. In this tractate, the term always refers to the prohibitory *neder,* in which a person prohibits an item to himself or to others (see General Introduction to ArtScroll *Nedarim*).

nisuin נִשּׂוּאִין: the second and final stage of marriage. Cf. **erusin.**

Tanna, pl. **Tannaim** (תַּנָּאִים) תַּנָּא: a Sage quoted in the Mishnah or in works of the same period.

terumah תְּרוּמָה: a portion of the crop sanctified and given to a *Kohen* who — together with his household — may eat it, but only if both the one who eats the *terumah* and the *terumah* itself are ritually clean.

Torah תּוֹרָה: (1) The Five Books of Moses; (2) the entire Written and Oral Law.

yavam, pl. **yevamin** (יְבָמִין) יָבָם: the surviving brother upon whom the obligation of *yibum* falls.

yevamah יְבָמָה: a widow who falls to *yibum.*

yibum יִבּוּם: levirate marriage — i.e., the marriage prescribed by the Torah between a widow and her late husband's brother when the husband died childless. Cf. **chalitzah.** See General Introduction to ArtScroll *Yevamos.*

zuz זוּז: a type of silver coin, equivalent to one silver dinar.

מסכת קידושין
Tractate Kiddushin

Translation and anthologized commentary by

Rabbi Matis Roberts

Edited by

Rabbi Tzvi Arem

General Introduction to Kiddushin

◆§ *Erusin and Nisuin*

According to Biblical law, there are two stages to marriage. The first — known as אֵרוּסִין, *erusin*, or קִדּוּשִׁין, *kiddushin* — is the initial acquisition of the wife by the husband for the purpose of subsequent נִשּׂוּאִין, *nisuin* [full marriage] (see *Rambam, Hilchos Ishus* 1:1). Because *kiddushin* is described in Scripture as an act of acquisition, its execution is compared in many ways to the acquisition of monetary possessions (see *Gemara* 2a, 7a). [This analogy pertains only to the manner in which *kiddushin* is effected; its essence (and that of marriage), however, is in no way comparable to that of ownership.] As part of the marriage process, *kiddushin* is also a ritual act reflecting the sanctity of the marital bond; in fact, the terms קִדּוּשִׁין and הֶקְדֵּשׁ, *consecrated property*, are related. This facet, too, is manifest in its laws (see *Gem.* 7a; *Tosafos* ad loc. s.v. ונפשטו).

The terms *erusin* and *kiddushin* describe both the first stage of marriage and the act which effects it. We have sometimes translated them as *betrothal* only for lack of a better equivalent in English. The truth is, however, that *kiddushin* is very different from a mere engagement, in that during this stage — in most respects — the couple is considered legally married. The wife may not be wed to anyone else; intimate relations with any other man is considered adultery and incurs the death penalty. In addition, *erusin* can be dissolved only by divorce (*Rambam, Hil. Ishus* 1:3). However, during this stage of marriage, the couple is not yet permitted to have relations and several other laws pertaining to a married couple do not yet apply (ibid. 10:1). An engagement, on the other hand, has no legal significance, unless the man and woman obligate themselves to each other through other binding methods.

The second level of marriage, *nisuin*, takes place when the bride formally enters her husband's home or the bridal canopy (see *Yevamos* 3:10). This procedure is called חוּפָּה, *chupah*, and it completes the marriage process. If a man and woman who were already betrothed have conjugal relations for the sake of *nisuin*, this, too, completes the marriage process (*Rambam* ibid. 10:1).

In this volume, whenever someone is said to have married, it means that he has performed *nisuin* as well as *erusin*.

In earlier times, the period of *erusin* lasted a long time — usually a year (see *Kesubos* 5:2). Following the *kiddushin*, the bride returned to her father's home and remained there until the *nisuin*. Later, it became customary to perform both stages of the marriage at the wedding.

◆§ *Tractate Kiddushin*

As its name implies, this tractate deals with laws of the first stage of marriage. Nevertheless, the *Tanna* digresses into other topics as well, primarily that of how different forms of acquisition are executed, and that of the various genealogical classes among the Jewish people and their relationships with each other.

Tractate *Kiddushin* follows Tractate *Gittin* — which deals with divorce — despite the fact that their order of occurrence is obviously the other way around, because it follows the sequence in which these subjects are written in the verse (*Deuteronomy* 24:2): *And she shall go out from his house* [divorce], *and she shall go and be to another man* [marriage] (*Rambam, Introduction to Mishnah Commentary*).

⊰§ ***The Process of Kiddushin***

From the phrase (loc. cit. v. 1), כִּי יִקַּח אִישׁ אִשָּׁה, *When a man takes a wife*, it is derived that the acquisition of *kiddushin* must be one in which the husband acquires the wife, and not vice versa (*Gem.* 5b). In addition, the verse teaches us that the husband is the active party in the *kiddushin* process, and it is he who effects its execution (ibid. 4b). All that is required of the woman is that she consent to the act and allow it to take place (see *Ran* to *Nedarim* 30a s.v. ואשה).

From the juxtaposition of the subjects of divorce and *kiddushin* in the passage, the Sages derive that the two are analogous in every way that it is possible to compare them. Therefore, just as the divorce process is valid only if it includes the participation of two witnesses (see General Introduction to *Gittin*, s.v. *The Witnesses*), so, too, must *kiddushin* be performed in the presence of two witnesses.

The methods used to effect *kiddushin* are discussed in the first mishnah in the tractate.

⊰§ ***Kiddushin of a Minor***

Since the consent of the woman is requisite for the act of *kiddushin*, a minor — who is considered mentally incompetent — cannot accept *kiddushin*. However, the Torah gave a girl's father the authority to give her in betrothal — not only when she is a minor, but even when she is a *naarah* — a girl in her first six months after reaching the age of twelve and having grown two pubic hairs. This is derived from the verse concerning a *naarah* (*Deut.* 22:16), *My daughter I gave to this man for a wife* (*Gem.* 3b).

If a minor girl has no father, the Rabbis authorized her mother or brothers to give her in betrothal. However, when the girl comes of age, she may protest the *kiddushin* and thereby nullify it retroactively (see *Rambam, Hil. Ishus* 4:7,8 and ArtScroll Commentary to *Yevamos*, Chapter 8).

Notes Regarding the Commentary

As in the previous volumes of the Mishnah Series, every entry in the commentary has been carefully documented. Where the author has inserted a comment of his own, it is surrounded by brackets.

Untranslated Hebrew terms found in the Commentary are defined in the glossary at the end of the tractate.

פרק ראשון

Chapter One

הָאִשָּׁה נִקְנֵית בְּשָׁלשׁ דְּרָכִים, וְקוֹנָה אֶת עַצְמָהּ בִּשְׁתֵּי דְרָכִים: נִקְנֵית בְּכֶסֶף,

ר׳ עובדיה מברטנורא

פרק ראשון – האשה נקנית. (א) האשה נקנית. לפי שאין האשה מתקדשת אלא מדעתה, תנא האשה נקנית, ולא תנא האיש קונה. ואיידי דתנא רישא האשה נקנית, תנא סיפא היבמה נקנית, ואף על גב דיבמה נקנית ליבם בין מדעתה בין שלא מדעתה: **נקנית בכסף.** דגמרינן קיחה קיחה משדה עפרון, כתיב הכא (דברים כד, א) כי יקח איש אשה, וכתיב התם (בראשית כג, יג) נתתי כסף השדה קח ממני:

יד אברהם

1.

הָאִשָּׁה — *A woman*

The *Tanna* prefixes the word אִשָּׁה, *woman*, with the definite article — i.e., הָאִשָּׁה, *the woman*, referring to the woman who is discussed in the passage concerning marriage (*Deut.* 24:1ff): *If a man shall take a woman* ... (*Tos.* 2a).

נִקְנֵית — *is acquired*

She is acquired by her husband (*Rashi*), so that no other man can marry her as long as he is alive unless he gives her a *get* (divorce document). However, the acquisition discussed here is not a complete one, since these acts effect only the stage of *kiddushin*, not the full marital relationship of *nisuin* (*Meiri;* see General Introduction s.v. *Erusin and Nisuin*).

The mishnah uses the passive voice — *A woman is acquired* — rather than the active voice — *A man acquires a woman* [unlike the first mishnah in the second chapter which begins: A man betroths (*Rashi*)] — to indicate that *kiddushin* requires the woman's consent (*Rav* from *Gem.* 2b), just like all other acquisitions, which are valid only with the consent of the giver (*Meiri; Rashi* 44a s.v. קידושין).

In addition, the mishnah tells us that even if a man coerces a woman to consent to marry him, the marriage is not valid. Although other acquisitions effected in this manner are valid, the Rabbis negated such a *kiddushin* because of the man's improper behavior (*Rashba;* see *Bava Basra* 48b).

The word נִקְנֵית, *acquired*, from the root קִנְיָן, *kinyan* (acquisition), is used rather than מְקֻדֶּשֶׁת, *betrothed*, because one of the ways that the mishnah lists with which a woman can be acquired — viz. money — is derived hermeneutically from the verse (see below) which teaches us that money can be used to procure property, a transaction which is referred to as *kinyan* in the verse (*Gen.* 25:10): הַשָּׂדֶה אֲשֶׁר קָנָה אַבְרָהָם, *the field which Abraham acquired* (*Gen.* 2a).

בְּשָׁלשׁ דְּרָכִים; — *in three ways;*

The *Tanna* uses the word שָׁלשׁ, *three*, in the feminine gender, rather than the masculine form of שְׁלשָׁה, because this number is an adjective of the word דְּרָכִים, *ways*, whose gender is determined by the subject matter under discussion, which, in this case, is a woman (*Gem.* 2b).

Although we could easily count the number of ways that the mishnah proceeds to enumerate, the number is stated nevertheless to stress that only these methods of acquisition are valid for *kiddushin*, but not *chupah* (see General Introduction loc. cit.) or חֲלִיפִין, *chalifin* (exchange) (*Gem.* 3a).

1
1
1. A woman is acquired in three ways; she acquires herself in two ways: She is acquired with money,

YAD AVRAHAM

חֲלִיפִין/Chalifin

Chalifin is a form of acquisition whereby one who is acquiring an object from another person gives the latter another article [traditionally a handkerchief (see *Nedarim* 48b)] as a symbolic exchange (*Bava Metzia* 47a; *Rambam, Hil. Mechirah* 5:5; see mishnah 6). Usually, the one who receives the article that was used returns it to its owner, although he is not obligated to do so (*Nedarim* loc. cit.). Since *chalifin* can be executed with an object which is worth less than a *perutah* (the minimal unit of significant monetary value [see below]) it cannot be used for *kiddushin,* because a woman would not give herself over for betrothal for less than a *perutah* (*Gem.* 3a), since it is demeaning to her (*Rashi* 3b s.v. לא). Therefore, even if he betroths her through *chalifin* using an object which is worth a *perutah,* the *kiddushin* is not valid (ibid.), because the fact that the value of a *perutah* is not required renders the entire method of *chalifin* a degrading manner of acquisition (*Rashba;* cf. *Tos.* 3a s.v. ואשה; *Ramban; Ran*).

וְקוֹנָה אֶת עַצְמָהּ — *she acquires herself*

She returns to her own jurisdiction so that she may now marry another man (*Rashi*).

בִּשְׁתֵּי דְרָכִים: — *in two ways:*

Here, too, the mishnah tells us the number of ways in order to indicate that only these two methods are valid, to the exclusion of *chalitzah* [see below] (*Gem.* 3b). This is derived from the verse (*Deut.* 24:3): *And he wrote for her a document of severance,* which teaches us that severance from a husband must be brought about by a document, not by *chalitzah* (*Tos. Yom Tov* from *Gem.* 5a).

[The mishnah now lists the three methods by which *kiddushin* can be performed.]

נִקְנֵית בְּכֶסֶף, — *She is acquired with money,*[1]

A man gives money or an object of monetary value (see below) to a woman in the presence of two witnesses and declares — in such a way that she understands his intentions — that it is being given for the purpose of betrothing her to him (*Meiri*). It is customary to give a ring (*Rama* to *Even HaEzer* 27:1) and to say: "Behold, you are betrothed to me (*Gem.* 5a) by means of this (*Rambam, Hil. Ishus* 3:1; *Even HaEzer* loc. cit.) ring (*Baer Hatev* ibid. 3) according to the ritual of Moses and Israel" (*Rama* ibid.).

If, while the man and woman were discussing the issue of their marriage, he gave her money without explicitly declaring his intentions, it is considered self-evident that he means to betroth her, and the *kiddushin* takes effect (*Gem.* 6a).

That this form of acquisition may be used for *kiddushin* is derived hermeneutically by a comparison of a verse discussing *kiddushin* and one

1. [The translation of כֶּסֶף as *money* is used for the sake of simplicity, although there is disagreement among the commentators whether this term refers to money in general, or silver in particular. If the latter is assumed, coins of any other metal would be included in the category of objects of monetary value, which may be used in lieu of money, as the mishnah states below (see *Avnei Miluim* 27:1).

בִּשְׁטָר, וּבְבִיאָה.

א/א בְּכֶסֶף — בֵּית שַׁמַּאי אוֹמְרִים: בְּדִינָר וּבְשָׁוֶה דִינָר. וּבֵית הִלֵּל אוֹמְרִים: בִּפְרוּטָה וּבְשָׁוֶה פְרוּטָה.

ר׳ עובדיה מברטנורא

בשטר. כגון שכתב לה על הנייר, או על החרס, ואף על פי שאין בו שוה פרוטה, בתך מקודשת לי, בתך מאורסת לי, בתך לי לאנתו, ונתנו לה בפני עדים. וילפינן (דף ה, א) לה דכתיב (דברים כד, ב) ויצאה והיתה, מה יציאה בשטר, כדכתיב (שם פסוק א) וכתב לה ספר כריתות, אף הויה בשטר: **ובביאה.** בא עליה בפני עדים לשם קדושין, דכתיב (שם) כי יקח איש אשה ובעלה. ואף על פי שאין לך קדושין מפורשים בתורה יותר מקדושי ביאה, אמרו חכמים (דף יב, ב), שהמקדש בביאה מכין אותו מכת מרדות, שלא יהיו בני ישראל פרוצין: **בפרוטה.** היא חלי שעורה של כסף:

יד אברהם

discussing the acquisition of property with money. Both verses use a form of the word קִיחָה, *taking;* the one dealing with *kiddushin* is: *When a man takes a wife* (*Deut.* 24:1), and the one dealing with the acquisition of property is: *I have given the money for the field; take it from me* (*Gen.* 23:13). It is thus deduced that just as money may be used for the latter type of acquisition, it may be used for *kiddushin* as well (*Rav* from *Gem.* 4b).

Kiddushin with money is mentioned first in the mishnah, because most acquisitions are made with money (*Ran*). Alternatively, since the *Tanna* uses the word נִקְנֵית, *acquired,* because of the hermeneutical interpretation from which we derive that a woman can be acquired with money (see above), he mentions that method first (*Tos. Yom Tov*).

בִּשְׁטָר, — *with a document,*

In the presence of two witnesses, he gives her a document which states that she is betrothed to him. The document need not be worth a *perutah* (*Rav* from *Gem.* 9a; see *Tos. Yom Tov*). This is derived hermeneutically from the verse (*Deut.* 24:2): *And she left his house, and she went and was [married] to another man.* The juxtaposition of divorce and marriage in the same verse teaches us that they are analogous in every way feasible. Therefore, just as divorce is executed with a document (ibid. v. 1), so, too, is *kiddushin*[1] (*Rav* from *Gem.* 5a).

By the same token, just as a *get* must be written with specific intent for the woman to whom it is subsequently given (*Gittin* 3:1), so must a document of *kiddushin* (*Gem.* 9b).

This method of *kiddushin* is mentioned second because it, too, is a common form of acquisition (*Ran*).

When using a document for *kiddushin,* it is not necessary for the man to declare his intentions orally, since the purpose of the document is clearly stated within (*Meiri*).

Although a document for the acquisition of a field is given by the seller to the buyer, a document of *kiddushin* is given by the recipient (the man who is acquiring the woman) to the giver (the woman). This is because the verse (*Deut.* 24:1), *When a man takes a wife ...,* emphasizes the man as the active principal (*Tos. Yom Tov* from *Gem.* 9a; see *Tos.* ad loc., s.v. הלכתא).

1. [The document of *kiddushin* is not to be confused with the *kesubah* (marriage contract), which describes the husband's obligation to his wife and the dower awarded her in the event of their divorce or his death. The *kesubah* does not effect the marriage; it merely is given at that time (see General Introduction to ArtScroll *Kesubos*, p. 3).]

1 with a document, or with cohabitation.
1 With money — Beis Shammai say: With a *dinar* or with something worth a *dinar*. Beis Hillel, however, say: With a *perutah* or with something worth a

YAD AVRAHAM

וּבְבִיאָה. — *or with cohabitation.*

In the presence of two witnesses, a man tells a woman that he is marrying her through intimate relations, and the witnesses observe them going into a private place together (*Meiri*). That this is a form of effecting *kiddushin* is evident from the above verse, *When a man takes a wife, and has relations with her* (*Rav* from *Gem.* 4b). Although this is the only form of *kiddushin* mentioned explicitly in the Torah, the Rabbis decreed that a man who acquires a woman in this manner receive lashes because it is an immodest act (*Rav* from *Gem.* 12b). However, if he does so, the *kiddushin* is effective ex post facto (*Rambam, Hil. Ishus* 3:21).

If, while they were discussing the issue of their marriage, he secluded himself with her without declaring his intentions, the *kiddushin* is valid (*Chelkas Mechokek* to *Even HaEzer* 33:1), just as it is when betrothing with money. Others suggest that when betrothing with relations, the husband must explicitly declare his intentions for marriage, because the witnesses do not observe the actual act of marriage (*Beis Shmuel* ibid. 2).

The mishnah now proceeds to discuss the first method of *kiddushin* — with money — in more detail.

— בְּכֶסֶף — *With money* —

I.e., what is the amount of money necessary for *kiddushin?* (*Meiri*).

בֵּית שַׁמַּאי אוֹמְרִים: בְּדִינָר — *Beis Shammai say: With a dinar*

Although, by Biblical law, a man may use even a *perutah* (see below) for *kiddushin*, the Rabbis required that he use a *dinar* (*Rashi* 12a s.v. כהפקר), so that Jewish girls should not be viewed like public property because they are so inexpensive to acquire (*Gem.* ad loc.).

Others interpret the *Gemara* to mean that because of this reason, *kiddushin* requires a *dinar* by Biblical law (*Ritva*).

וּבְשָׁוֶה דִינָר. — *or with something worth a dinar.*

Since *kiddushin* requires the consent of both parties, it is a logical assumption that if they both agree that it be effected by an object of monetary value in lieu of money, it is valid (*Rav; Meiri*).

Others contend that the fact that an object of monetary value can be used must be based on a Biblical source, just as the *Gemara* (16a) requires a source for the validity of using such an object for redeeming a Jewish bondman (see commentary to mishnah 2). They conclude, however, that we deduce its validity for *kiddushin* from a comparison with the redemption of a Jewish bondman (*Tos.* 2a s.v. בפרוטה).

If the mishnah had said only *something worth a dinar*, it would be understood that a *dinar* itself is also included. Nevertheless, since it listed *money* among the forms of marital acquisition, it first mentions the amount of money required and then adds the fact that its equivalent is also acceptable (*Tos.* ibid.).

וּבֵית הִלֵּל אוֹמְרִים: בִּפְרוּטָה וּבְשָׁוֶה פְּרוּטָה. — *Beis Hillel, however, say: With a perutah or with something worth a perutah.*

A *perutah* is a copper coin (*Rashi*) and is the minimal unit of monetary value (*Meiri*).

קידושין
א/א

וְכַמָּה הִיא פְרוּטָה? אֶחָד מִשְּׁמוֹנָה בְּאִסָּר הָאִיטַלְקִי. וְקוֹנָה אֶת עַצְמָהּ בְּגֵט וּבְמִיתַת הַבַּעַל. הַיְבָמָה נִקְנֵית בְּבִיאָה, וְקוֹנָה אֶת עַצְמָהּ בַּחֲלִיצָה וּבְמִיתַת הַיָּבָם.

ר' עובדיה מברטנורא

היבמה נקנית. ליבם, להיות כאשתו לכל דבר, בביאה. אבל כסף ושטר לא מהנו בה מדאורייתא, אלא רבנן הוא דתקון דמהני בה מאמר לפסלה על שאר האחין, אבל לא לפטרה מן החליצה, ולא להטמא לה:

יד אברהם

If a man gave a woman an object worth less than a *perutah* for the purpose of betrothal, the validity of the *kiddushin* is in doubt (and she requires a *get* in order to marry another man), because this object may be worth a *perutah* in another locale, in which case it would be considered to have monetary value and the *kiddushin* would be valid (*Gem.* 12a, according to *Rashi* ad loc.). However, this is true only if the object can be taken to the place where it is worth a *perutah* without it spoiling (*Rambam, Hil. Ishus* 4:19).

Others contend that the object's innate value is based on its worth in that place alone. However, the Rabbis decreed that if a man — for the purpose of *kiddushin* — gives a woman an object that is worth less than a *perutah* in the locale where he gave it, he must divorce her before she may remarry (*Rosh; Ri,* cited by *Rosh*) out of apprehension that a person from a place where this object is worth a *perutah* will notice that a *kiddushin* made with it was disregarded and will apply that to similar instances in his town, where such a *kiddushin* would be valid (*Tos.,* cited by *Ran*). Accordingly, even if the article cannot be transferred to the place where it has value, the decree would apply (*Rosh; Ran*).

וְכַמָּה הִיא פְרוּטָה? — *How much is a perutah?*

The mishnah does not discuss the value of a *dinar,* because it was well known. In addition, it was deemed necessary to expound only upon the opinion of Beis Hillel, since theirs is the prevailing view (*Tos.*).

אֶחָד מִשְּׁמוֹנָה בְּאִסָּר הָאִיטַלְקִי. — *One-eighth of an Italian issar.*

An Italian *issar* was a silver coin which weighed as much as four grains of barley (*Rav* to *Eduyos* 4:7). Thus, a *perutah* is equal in value to an amount of silver weighing the same as half a grain of barley (*Rav*). This weight is estimated to be one-fortieth of a gram (*Chazon Ish* to *Yoreh Deah* 182:19).

וְקוֹנָה אֶת עַצְמָהּ בְּגֵט — *She acquires herself with a get*

A woman returns to her own jurisdiction [so that she may now marry another man (*Rashi*)] when she receives a bill of divorce from her husband, as the verse states (*Deut.* 24:1), *He shall write for her a document of severance ... and he shall send her from his house* (*Gem.* 13b).

The mishnah lists the possibility of divorce before that of the husband's death, because the former is mentioned explicitly in the verse (*Ran*).

וּבְמִיתַת הַבַּעַל.— *or with the death of the husband.*

This is derived exegetically from the verse (*Deut.* 24:3), *And the latter man hates her and he writes her a document of severance ... or if the latter man dies.*

The case of divorce and that of the husband's death are juxtaposed in the

1
1 *perutah.* How much is a *perutah?* One-eighth of an Italian *issar.*

She acquires herself with a *get* or with the death of the husband.

A *yevamah* is acquired with cohabitation, and acquires herself with *chalitzah* or with the death of the *yavam.*

YAD AVRAHAM

verse to indicate that the woman is released by the husband's death just as she is by a *get* (*Gem.* 13b; see *Torah Temimah* loc. cit.).

We do not say that it is only logical that a wife should be free to marry after her husband's death, for without the verse and its exegetical interpretation we might think that marrying a widow is similar to marrying one of those women related to a man by marriage [such as his stepmother or daughter-in-law (*Rashi*)], which is prohibited even after the death of her husband (ibid.).

◆§ יִבּוּם/Yibum (Levirate Marriage)

When a man dies childless, the Torah (*Deut.* 25:5) commands that one of his brothers (referred to as the *yavam*) marry his widow (the *yevamah*). The Torah also provides a mechanism by which the widow can be released from her legal attachment to the brothers in case they all refuse to marry her (ibid. v. 7ff). This procedure is known as *chalitzah* (taking off the shoe). See General Introduction to ArtScroll *Yevamos.*

הַיְבָמָה נִקְנֵית — *A yevamah is acquired*

She is acquired by the *yavam* to become his full wife [i.e., the equivalent of having performed both *kiddushin* and *nisuin*] (*Rav*).

Although a *yevamah* can be acquired even against her will (*Yevamos* 6:1), the mishnah uses the words, *A yevamah is acquired,* which could be misconstrued to indicate that her consent is required, rather than *A yavam acquires,* which intimates that the decision is his, in order to be consistent with the wording of the first half of the mishnah (*Rav* s.v. האשה from *Gem.* 2b).

בְּבִיאָה, — *with cohabitation;*

As stated explicitly in the verse (*Deut.* 25:5), *Her husband's brother shall come to her* [an expression denoting cohabitation] *and take her to himself for a wife* (*Rav* from *Gem.* 14a). The verse continues by concluding with the word וְיִבְּמָהּ, *and take her in yibum,* which also refers to intimacy (*Rashi* ad loc. s.v. ויבמה), to indicate that she can be acquired only with intimacy and not with money or a document (*Rav* from *Gem.*). Nevertheless, the Rabbis enacted that if a *yavam* gives a *yevamah* money or a document for the sake of *kiddushin,* it takes effect, and she becomes prohibited to the other brothers [and requires a *get*] if they choose not to complete the *yibum.* However, if he gives her a *get,* she still needs *chalitzah* as required by Biblical law. This Rabbinic marital acquisition is referred to as *maamar* (*Rav*).

וְקוֹנָה אֶת עַצְמָהּ בַּחֲלִיצָה — *and acquires herself with chalitzah*

To perform *chalitzah,* the Torah (*Deut.* 25:9) prescribes that the *yevamah* removes the *yavam's* shoe from

[ב] עֶבֶד עִבְרִי נִקְנֶה בְּכֶסֶף וּבִשְׁטָר, וְקוֹנֶה אֶת עַצְמוֹ בְּשָׁנִים, וּבְיוֹבֵל, וּבְגִרְעוֹן כֶּסֶף.

ר׳ עובדיה מברטנורא

(ב) עבד עברי נקנה בכסף. דכתיב (ויקרא כה, נא) מכסף מקנתו, מלמד שהוא נקנה בכסף: **ובשטר.** שנאמר באמה העבריה (שמות כא, י) אם אחרת יקח לו, הקישה הכתוב לאחרת, מה אחרת בשטר, אף האמה בשטר, וילמוד עבד עברי מאמה העבריה, דכתיב (דברים טו, יב) העברי או העבריה, מקיש עברי לעבריה: **בשנים.** לסוף שש שנים יצא חפשי. ואפילו היתה שמטה בתוך שש שנים, עובד, דכתיב (שמות כא, ב) שש שנים יעבוד ובשביעית, פעמים שהוא עובד בשביעית: **וביובל.** אם פגע יובל בתוך שש שנים, מוציאו: **ובגרעון כסף.** דכתיב באמה העבריה (שם פסוק ח) והפדה, והוקש עברי לעבריה, אם קנאו רבו בשש מנים והוא עתיד לצאת לסוף שש, נמצא קונה עבודת כל שנה במנה, כשבא לפדות עצמו, מגרע לו רבו מפדיונו דמי עבודת השנים שעבד:

יד אברהם

his foot, spits before him, and declares: "*So shall be done to the man who would not build his brother's house.*" She is thereby released from her status as a *yevamah*, as derived from the verse (ibid. v. 10), *And his name shall be called in Israel, "the house of one whose shoe was removed."* The superfluous word, *Israel*, teaches us that once *chalitzah* has taken place, she is permitted to all of Israel — i.e., she may marry other men (*Gem.* 14a).

.וּבְמִיתַת הַיָּבָם — *or with the death of the yavam.*

[If the *yavam* dies, the *yevamah* is permitted to remarry.] Since the death of a husband releases his wife from the stringent prohibition of adultery, which is punishable by *kares* (excision, Divinely decreed premature death), it certainly suffices to release a *yevamah* from the more lenient prohibition which restricts her from marrying anyone other than the *yavam*. By the same line of reasoning, we would deduce that a document, too, can be used to release her from *yibum*; however, the repetitive mention of the word *shoe* in the passage is interpreted as precluding the use of a document (ibid.; see *Tos.* s.v. אמר קרא).

[If there is more than one *yavam*, and neither *chalitzah* nor *yibum* has been performed, the death of one of them would not release the *yevamah*, since there is nothing to link her to that brother more than to the others. Even if he had performed *maamar* (see above), it has no effect in Biblical law, and she would remain prohibited to remarry until either *yibum* or *chalitzah* was performed with one of the remaining brothers.]

2.

After discussing the methods of acquiring a wife, the mishnah now goes on to discuss the methods of procuring other acquisitions. The first of these to be discussed is the acquisition of Jewish bondmen[1] (*Meiri*).

1. [We have rendered עֶבֶד עִבְרִי as *a Jewish bondman* and אָמָה עִבְרִיָּה as *a Jewish bondwoman* rather than giving the usual translation, *Jewish slave*, because the latter term implies that the person is the property of his master — similar to land, chattels, etc. — which is untrue of

1
2
2. **A** Jewish bondman is acquired with money or with a document, and acquires himself with years, or with *Yovel*, or with the deduction of money.

YAD AVRAHAM

There are four categories of Jewish bondmen discussed in the Torah: (1) a man who steals and cannot repay, in which case he is sold by the courts in order to pay the one who was robbed (*Ex.* 22:2; ibid. 21:1-6; *Deut.* 15:12-18); (2) a girl under the age of twelve who is sold by her father (*Ex.* 21:7-11; *Deut.* loc. cit.); (3) a man sold himself because of his poverty (*Lev.* 25:39-43); (4) a Jew who sells himself to a gentile (ibid. 47-55).

עֶבֶד עִבְרִי — *A Jewish bondman*

This refers to a Jewish man who was sold by the courts. Whether it also includes one who sold himself is dependent upon the dispute between the Rabbis and R' Elazar if that which is stated in the mishnah that a bondman goes free after six years of servitude applies to such a man as well (*Rashba* to 14b s.v. מוכר עצמו; see below).

נִקְנֶה — *is acquired*

[I.e., he comes under the proprietorship of his master in that he must work for him and that all rights to the profits from his work belong to his master. In addition] a bondman can be forced by his master to marry a Canaanite slave (see mishnah 3) in order to have children, who will be Canaanite slaves of the master (*Ex.* 21:4). However, this applies only to a bondman who was sold by the courts (*Gem.* 24b); one who sold himself is forbidden to a Canaanite slave (*Rashi* ad loc. s.v. אין רבו; *Rambam, Hil. Avadim* 3:3).

Others contend that even a bondman who sold himself is permitted to marry a Canaanite slave, but his master cannot force him to do so (*Ritva* to 24b).

בְּכֶסֶף — *with money*

I.e., the master gives money [or an object of monetary value (*Rambam, Hil. Avadim* 2:1)] to the bondman, if he is selling himself, or to the one who had been robbed, if the bondman is being sold by the courts and thereby acquires him (*Meiri*). This method is also effective for acquiring a Jewish bondwoman, in which case the money is given to her father (ibid.), and in acquisition of a Jewish bondman by a gentile (*Gem.* 14b).

This is derived from the words (*Lev.* 25:51), *from the money of his acquisition* (*Rav* from *Gem.* ibid.). Although this verse is discussing a Jew acquired by a gentile, the opening passage of that paragraph begins with the conjunctive *vav* — meaning *and* — to indicate that it is connected to the topic which precedes it, that of a Jew who sells himself to another Jew. The juxtaposition of the two cases is interpreted as teaching that the Jewish bondman can be acquired with money in both instances (*Gem.* 14b; see *Kesef Mishneh* to *Hil. Avadim* 4:3, *Lechem Mishneh* ad loc.).[1] Once this is

any Jew. This description does apply, however, to gentile slaves (see mishnah 3; cf. *Gem.* 16a, *Tos.* to *Yevamos* 70b s.v. אלמא).

1. [The *Gemara* (14b) mentions a different way to derive that a bondman can be acquired with money by another Jew. However, the fact that *Rav* gives the verse concerning the

established, it follows that a bondman sold by the courts, who is sold against his will (*Gem.* loc. cit.), and is thus more easily procured (*Rashi* ad loc. s.v. מכרוהו ב״ד), can also be acquired in the same manner (*Lechem Mishneh* loc. cit.).

Alternatively, a bondman sold by a court and one who sells himself are compared exegetically by virtue of the fact that Scripture uses the word שָׂכִיר, *hired hand,* regarding both of them (*Gem.* 14b).

Concerning a Jewish bondwoman, the verse says that a master *shall cause her to be redeemed* (*Ex.* 21:8), which indicates that he must take part in her redemption — i.e., when someone redeems her, the master does not receive his original purchase price, but must subtract from it the percentage of the price commensurate to the amount of time which she was in his servitude (*Gem.* loc. cit.). Thus, it is evident that the original acquisition can be effected with money (*Rashi* ad loc. s.v. שמגרעת; cf. *Ritva*). Since this is the source from where we derive that a bondwoman can be acquired with money, it is obvious that the original acquisition must be made with more than a *perutah,* so as to allow for the possibility of deducting for redemption (*Rambam, Hil. Avadim* 4:3 from *Gem.* 11b).

וּבִשְׁטָר, — *or with a document,*

The master gives the bondman a document which states that he is acquiring him (*Gem.* 16a; see *Tos. Yom Tov*). That this is effective is derived from the verse (*Ex.* 21:10), which states regarding a bondwoman: *If he* (the master) *will take another* [*woman*], from which we derive exegetically that the laws of a bondwoman are compared to those of a wife. Thus, just as a wife is acquired with a document (mishnah 1), so, too, is a bondwoman — i.e., with a document given to her father (*Rav* from *Gem.* 16a). From the phrase (*Deut.* 15:12), *If your brother shall be sold to you — the Jew or Jewess* — we learn that the laws of a bondman sold by the court and those of a bondwoman are analogous (*Rav* from *Gem.* 16a, 14b). The laws of a bondman who sells himself are derived from those governing one sold by the courts since Scripture uses the word שָׂכִיר, *hired hand,* regarding both of them (*Gem.* 14b). A gentile, however, cannot acquire a Jew with a document, because that method of acquisition is not available to gentiles at all (*Tos.* 14b s.v. הואיל).

Others contend that the bondman — or the bondwoman's father — gives the document, which states that he or she is entering the owner's possession, to the owner (*Meiri; Rambam, Hil. Avadim* 2:1 from *Gem.* 16a). Accordingly, the source for this is not from a document of *kiddushin* — which is given to the wife by the husband — but from the verse (*Ex.* 21:7), *She shall not go out like the slaves* [i.e., gentile slaves (*Rashi* ad loc.)]. From this we infer that although she cannot leave her master as gentile slaves do [i.e., if the owner knocks out their eye or tooth (ibid.)], she can be acquired in the same manner as they; i.e., with a document (*Gem.* loc. cit.).

וְקוֹנֶה אֶת עַצְמוֹ — *and acquires himself*

He leaves his master's possession, regaining the rights to the profits from his work, and he may no longer marry a Canaanite slave (*Meiri*).

bondman of a gentile as the source for our mishnah, which is discussing one that was acquired by a Jew (as is evident from the type of acquisition listed next — with a document — which cannot be done by a gentile), indicates that he agrees with the explanation of *Lechem Mishneh* that once the *Gemara* ascertained that the bondman of a Jew is compared to that of a gentile, that verse remains the primary source of derivation.]

בְּשָׁנִים, — *with years,*

A bondman goes free after six years of servitude, as stated in the verse (*Ex.* 21:2), *Six years he shall serve, and in the seventh he shall go free* (*Rav* from *Gem.* 16a).

According to the Rabbis, who hold that a man can sell himself for more than six years if he so desires (*Gem.* 14b), the mishnah is discussing only a bondman sold by the court. According to R' Elazar, however, who maintains that even one who sells himself — without specifying for how long — goes free after six years, the mishnah is discussing both types of bondmen (*Rashba* ibid.). The *halachah* follows the view of the Rabbis (*Rambam, Hil. Avadim* 2:3).

Others explain that according to both views, the term *years* could apply even to one who sold himself, because it can refer to a case in which a man sold himself for a specific number of years; when that time elapses, he goes free (*Tos. Yom Tov*).

A Jewish bondman belonging to a gentile does not go free after six years (*Gem.* 15b; *Rambam* loc. cit. 2:6).

וּבְיוֹבֵל, — *or with Yovel,*

All slaves are freed when the year of *Yovel* (Jubilee) — the fiftieth year which follows seven Sabbatical cycles — arrives, even if their six years have not been completed (*Rav*), as stated explicitly (*Lev.* 25:40): *Until the year of yovel, he shall work with you* (*Gem.* 16a).

This refers to a slave who sold himself. One who is sold by the court also goes free at *yovel*, as derived from the following verse (41), *and he shall return to his family* (*Gem.* 15a). The emancipation at *Yovel* of a slave belonging to a gentile is stated explicitly (loc. cit. v. 54).

וּבְגִרְעוֹן כֶּסֶף. — *or with the deduction of money.*

He can redeem himself — even without the master's consent (*Tos.* 16a s.v. לימא) — by deducting from his acquisition price the percentage commensurate to the amount of time he already worked, and paying the master the remainder. For example, if he was bought for six hundred *zuz* for a six-year period, each year's servitude is valued at one hundred (*Rav*). This is derived from the word (*Ex.* 22:8) וְהֶפְדָּהּ, *and he shall cause her to be redeemed* (ibid. from *Gem.* 16a), which indicates that the master takes part in the redemption process by deducting from her value the amount of time that she was in servitude (*Gem.* ibid.). [Application to the other categories of bondmen is derived from the hermeneutical process described above.]

He can also be ransomed with any object of monetary value, even against the master's will (*Ran* to mishnah 1). This is derived from the verse (*Lev.* 25:52), *according to his years he shall return his ransom,* in which the word יָשִׁיב, *he shall return,* is unnecessary for the plain meaning of the text [since it could have said his ransom is according to his years (*Rashi* 8a s.v. ישוב גאולתו)] and is added to include all objects of monetary value as well as money itself (*Gem.* loc. cit.).

If the bondman's value changes while he is in the master's possession, the price of his redemption is set according to whichever is less, his value at the time he was sold or his present value (*Gem.* 20a).

If a Jew sells himself as a bondman to a gentile, his closest relative who is capable of redeeming him is obligated to do so (*Rambam, Hil. Avadim*).

A bondman can also be set free with a document of emancipation (*Gem.* 16a), but the mishnah deletes this method, because it is discussing only those which take effect even without the master's consent (*Tos.* ad loc. s.v. לימא).

If the master dies, the bondman is inherited by the master's sons. If the master left no sons, the bondman goes free; he is

יְתֵרָה עָלָיו אָמָה הָעִבְרִיָּה שֶׁקּוֹנָה אֶת עַצְמָהּ בְּסִימָנִין.

הַנִּרְצָע נִקְנֶה בִּרְצִיעָה, וְקוֹנֶה אֶת עַצְמוֹ בְּיוֹבֵל וּבְמִיתַת הָאָדוֹן.

[ג] **עֶבֶד** כְּנַעֲנִי נִקְנֶה בְּכֶסֶף, וּבִשְׁטָר, וּבַחֲזָקָה.

ר' עובדיה מברטנורא

יתירה עליו אמה. שקונה עצמה בכל אלה, ובסימני נערות, כדילפינן (דף ד, א) מויצאה חנם (שמות כא, יא), ריבה לה יציאה לזו, שיוצאה בסימנים: **ובמיתת האדון.** דכתיב (שם פסוק ו) ועבדו לעולם, לו ולא לבן. אבל הנמכר ומת האדון בתוך שש, עובד לבן, דכתיב (שם פסוק ב) שש שנים יעבוד, בין לו בין לבנו. ודוקא לבן עובד כל שש אם מת האדון, אבל לבת ולאח ולשאר יורשים אינו עובד, דכתיב (דברים טו, יב) ועבדך שש שנים, לך ולא ליורשים. ואמה העבריה קונה עצמה במיתת האדון כנרצע, דכתיב גבי נרצע (שם פסוק יז) ואף לאמתך תעשה כן: (ג) **עבד כנעני נקנה בכסף ובשטר ובחזקה.** דכתיב (ויקרא כה, מו) והתנחלתם אותם לבניכם [אחריכם] לרשת אחוזה, הקיש עבדים לקרקעות, מה קרקע נקנה בכסף בשטר ובחזקה, אף עבד כנעני נקנה בכסף בשטר ובחזקה. וחזקת העבד, כגון שהתיר מנעל לרבו, או הנעילו, או הוליך כליו אחריו לבית המרחץ, הפשיטו, הרחיצו, סכו, גרדו, הלבישו, הגביהו, או שהגביה הרב את העבד, קנאו:

יד אברהם

not inherited by the daughters or any other relatives (*Rav* s.v. מיתת האדון, from *Gem.* 17b).

יְתֵרָה עָלָיו אָמָה הָעִבְרִיָּה — *A Jewish bondwoman has the advantage over him*

In addition to being able to be freed by any of the methods applicable to a bondman, she has the advantage of gaining her freedom in another manner as well (*Rav*).

שֶׁקּוֹנָה אֶת עַצְמָהּ בְּסִימָנִין. — *that she acquires herself with signs.*

She goes free as soon as she becomes a *naarah* — i.e., when she grows two pubic hairs after reaching the age of twelve years (*Tif. Yis.*). This is derived from the verse (*Ex.* 21:11), *And she shall go out for free, without money* — from which we derive exegetically that a bondwoman leaves her master's possession when she becomes a *naarah* (*Gem.* 4a).

She also goes free with the death of her master, and is not inherited by his sons (*Rav* s.v. ובמיתת האדון from *Gem.* 17b). However, the mishnah does not count this as an advantage over a bondman because he, too, goes free with the death of the master when the master leaves only daughters, but no sons (*Gem.* 18a).

Another way in which a bondwoman is freed is if her master marries her or he marries her off to his son, with the money which had been given for her initial acquisition serving as the money for *kiddushin,* in fulfillment of the Biblical commandment to do so (*Ex.* 21:8-9; *Rashi* ad loc.).

הַנִּרְצָע נִקְנֶה בִּרְצִיעָה, — *One who[se ear] is bored is acquired by the act of boring,*

If a slave who was sold by the court (*Rambam, Hil. Avadim* 3:6 from *Gem.* 14b) does not want to go free when his six years of servitude end, he may remain in slavery, but his master must bore a hole [with a metal tool (*Gem.* 21b)] through his right ear against a doorpost (*Ex.* 21:5-6; *Rashi* ad loc.).

A Jewish bondwoman has the advantage over him that she acquires herself with signs.

One who[se ear] is bored is acquired by the act of boring, and acquires himself with *Yovel* or with the death of the master.

3. **A** Canaanite slave is acquired with money, with a document, or with an act of possession.

YAD AVRAHAM

וְקוֹנֶה אֶת עַצְמוֹ בְּיוֹבֵל — *and acquires himself with Yovel*

The verse (ibid.) states, *And he shall serve him forever*, which actually means until *Yovel* (*Gem.* 21b). This is derived from that which is stated concerning *Yovel* (*Lev.* 25:10): *And you shall return, each man to his allotment and each man to his family*, which is interpreted hermeneutically as referring to a slave whose ear is bored (*Gem.* 15a).

וּבְמִיתַת הָאָדוֹן. — *or with the death of the master.*

As it says (loc. cit.), *And he shall serve him forever*, which means that the bondman who was bored must serve his master, but not the master's children (*Rav* from *Gem.* 17b).

3.

A Jew can acquire a gentile slave (*Lev.* 25:44), who becomes his monetary possession, to be kept permanently and inherited by his children (ibid. v. 46). When acquiring such a slave, the master must circumcise him and immerse him in a *mikveh* (ritual pool) for the purpose of enslaving him. With this, the slave becomes obligated in all of the commandments which Jewish women are obligated to do. If he is not willing to accept this, his master is given twelve months in which to convince him, after which he must sell him to a gentile (*Meiri*).

עֶבֶד כְּנַעֲנִי — *A Canaanite slave*

Any gentile slave is referred to as a Canaanite slave, because Canaan was cursed by his grandfather, Noah, that he be a slave [*Gen.* 9:25] (*Rashi* 22b s.v. שרה). [Similarly, any female gentile slave is referred to as a שִׁפְחָה כְּנַעֲנִית, *Canaanite female slave.*]

נִקְנֶה — *is acquired*

He can be bought from a Jew or a gentile who owned him previously or he can sell himself or his children into slavery (*Meiri*).

בְּכֶסֶף, וּבִשְׁטָר, — *with money, with a document,*

This is derived from the verse (*Lev.* 25:46), *And you shall bequeath them to your children after you to inherit an allotment.* By the use of the word אֲחֻזָּה, *allotment*, which generally refers to land, the verse equates the acquisition of slaves to that of land. Therefore, just as land is acquired with money, a document, or an act of possession (see mishnah 5), so, too, is a slave (*Rav* from *Gem.* 22b).

וּבַחֲזָקָה. — *or with an act of possession.*

I.e., by having the slave perform for him any service which is ordinarily performed by a slave for his master

וְקוֹנֶה אֶת עַצְמוֹ בְּכֶסֶף — עַל יְדֵי אֲחֵרִים, וּבִשְׁטָר — עַל יְדֵי עַצְמוֹ; דִּבְרֵי רַבִּי מֵאִיר. וַחֲכָמִים אוֹמְרִים: בְּכֶסֶף — עַל יְדֵי עַצְמוֹ,

ר' עובדיה מברטנורא

בכסף על ידי אחרים. שיתנוהו לרבו על מנת שיהיה זה בן חורין. אבל הוא עצמו לא יקבלנו מהם, ואפילו על מנת שאין לרבו רשות בו, דקסבר אין קנין לעבד בשום צד בלא רבו: **ובשטר על ידי עצמו.** דסבר חובה הוא לעבד שיצא מתחת ידי רבו לחירות, שאם עבד כהן הוא, פוסלו מלאכול בתרומה, ואם עבד ישראל הוא, אוסרו בשפחה. ומשום הכי קאמר דאינו יוצא לחירות בשטר על ידי אחרים, אלא על ידי עצמו, דכיון דחובה היא לו, אין חבין לאדם אלא בפניו. וכסף דעל ידי אחרים שאני, שכן קבלת רבו גרמה לו להשתחרר מאליו, ואין אחרים הללו חבין לו, אלא קבלת הרב, והרב אינו נעשה שלוחו, אלא לצורך עצמו, ומקנהו מאליו: **וחכמים אומרים בכסף על ידי עצמו.** דקסברי יש קנין לעבד בלא רבו, הלכך קונה את עצמו בכסף אפילו על ידי עצמו, וכל שכן על ידי אחרים:

יד אברהם

[thereby signifying that he is entering his servitude] (*Rambam, Hil. Mechirah* 2:2); e.g., to tie or untie his shoes, to carry his clothes to the bathhouse, to dress or undress him, wash him, rub him with oil, or carry him (*Rav* from *Gem.* loc. cit.).

This includes those services in which he receives physical benefit from the slave (e.g., dressing him) and those which are performed specifically by slaves (e.g., carrying his clothes to the bathhouse). However, any services which do not specifically indicate slavery (e.g., cooking for him) do not effect acquisition, just as making use of a field and not improving it is not a valid means of acquiring the field (*Ramban; Rashba; Ravad, Hil. Mechirah* 1:15).

Rambam (ibid.) states that making use of a field (e.g., spreading produce on it) does suffice to acquire it, and it therefore follows that according to him, a slave, too, could be acquired by making use of him (*Ran; Maggid Mishneh, Hil. Mechirah* 2:2). Others contend that this means of acquisition is valid only for a field, because at the time of usage it is clear that the field is his; the slave's act of cooking, however, offers no evidence as to whose work he is doing (*Kesef Mishneh* ad loc.).

Another valid act of acquisition would be the master carrying the slave (*Rav; Rambam, Hil. Mechirah* 2:2 from *Gem.* 22b). Others rule that this method is not valid (*Meiri*).

A slave can also be acquired with *chalifin* (see commentary to mishnah 1 s.v. בְּשָׁלֹשׁ) or by מְשִׁיכָה, *meshichah* (making him move) [see mishnah 4]. If the slave is a child, even causing him to walk by calling him is sufficient, because he does so solely in response to the command rather than on his own initiative. The mishnah deletes these methods of acquisition, however, because it lists only those which are unique to slaves and real estate (*Gem.* 22b).

Whether *chalifin* is valid for acquiring a slave from gentiles is controversial. Some maintain that gentiles cannot use this method of acquisition (*Meiri*), while others contend that they can (*Tos.* 2a s.v. ואשה).

וְקוֹנֶה אֶת עַצְמוֹ — *He acquires himself*

[He leaves the jurisdiction of his master] and becomes a full-fledged convert to Judaism (*Rambam, Hil. Issurei Biah* 13:12).

1
3

He acquires himself with money — through others, and with a document — on his own; [these are] the words of R' Meir. The Sages, however, say: With money — on his own,

YAD AVRAHAM

בְּכֶסֶף — עַל יְדֵי אֲחֵרִים, — *with money — through others,*

If another person gives the master money for the purpose of redeeming the slave, he goes free — even if it was done without the slave's consent. Although R' Meir — the author of this opinion — holds that manumission is considered detrimental to a slave (*Gittin* 1:6) because gentile female slaves — who tend to be unchaste and were therefore readily available for the satiation of his desires when he was a slave — become prohibited to him (commentary ad loc.), and another party cannot receive a document of emancipation on the slave's behalf without his consent (ibid.; see below), release through money is different. This is because it is the owner who effects the manumission by receiving the money — not the one who redeems him, and the owner is acting on his own behalf, not that of the slave (*Rav* from *Gem.* 23a).

Another reason is that money can be used to acquire a slave without his consent [by acquiring him from a previous owner], and therefore it can also be used to release him against his will. Although a document, too, can be used to acquire him against his will, that is an intrinsically different type of document than the one which is used to release him — since one describes an acquisition and the other an emancipation (*Rashi*) — and they are therefore not comparable (*Gem.* ibid.).

He cannot bring about his release with money on his own, because R' Meir holds that there is no way for a slave to acquire money without it transferring automatically to his owner (*Gem.* 23a).

וּבִשְׁטָר — עַל יְדֵי עַצְמוֹ; — *and with a document — on his own;*

[If his owner gives him a document of emancipation, even against his will, he goes free.] Although a slave cannot acquire anything for himself since everything he receives is automatically transferred to his owner, a document of emancipation is different, because his release and his ability to acquire the document for himself occur and take effect simultaneously (ibid.).

A third person can receive the document on the slave's behalf only with the latter's consent, because the detrimental aspects of emancipation disqualify anyone from accepting it for him on their own initiative (ibid.).

דִּבְרֵי רַבִּי מֵאִיר. — *[these are] the words of R' Meir.*

R' Meir holds that emancipation is considered detrimental, that a slave can have no acquisition which does not transfer to his master, and that the capacity for acquisition which is caused by a document of emancipation occurs simultaneously with the release itself (*Meiri*).

וַחֲכָמִים אוֹמְרִים: בְּכֶסֶף — עַל יְדֵי עַצְמוֹ, — *The Sages, however, say: With money — on his own,*

The Sages contend that a slave can acquire money without it transferring to the owner (see below); therefore, emancipation by money can be brought about by the slave himself as well as by others (*Rav* from *Gem.* 23a).

Others can release him with money even without his consent, because the Sages

וּבִשְׁטָר — עַל יְדֵי אֲחֵרִים, וּבִלְבַד שֶׁיְּהֵא הַכֶּסֶף מִשֶּׁל אֲחֵרִים.

[ד] **בְּהֵמָה** גַסָּה נִקְנֵית בִּמְסִירָה, וְהַדַּקָּה —

ר' עובדיה מברטנורא

ובשטר על ידי אחרים. דסברי, זכות הוא לעבד שילא מתחת ידי רבו לחירות, וזכין לאדם שלא בפניו. והלכה כחכמים. והעבד כנעני קונה עצמו, אם סימא רבו את עינו, או הפיל את שנו, או קטע ממנו אחד מעשרים וארבעה ראשי אברים, שהם [ראשי] אצבעות ידים, ואצבעות רגלים, וראשי אזנים, וראש החוטם, וראש הזכרות, וראשי שדים באשה. והא דלא חשיב להו במתניתין בכלל הדברים שהעבד קונה את עצמו, משום דהיוצא בראשי אברים, צריך גט שחרור מרבו, והיינו קונה את עצמו בשטר: **ובלבד שיהא הכסף משל אחרים.** דעבד אין לו כלום, דאף מציאה וקבלת מתנה, הכל לרבו. ואם בא להפדות על ידי עצמו, צריך להיות הכסף משל אחרים, שיתנהו לו על מנת שאין לרבו רשות בו: (ד) **במסירה.** בעלים מוסרין אותה ללוקח, באפסר או בשערה:

יד אברהם

consider emancipation a benefit, which can be effected by others (*Rif; Ramban;* see *Gittin* 1:6). However, if he explicitly says that he does not want to be released, it is considered a detriment and is not valid (see *Ran*). Some authorities maintain that the release is valid even in such a case, because the Sages do not dispute the reasons (stated above) that R' Meir validates emancipation through money even against the slave's will (*Ran;* see above).

וּבִשְׁטָר — עַל יְדֵי אֲחֵרִים, — *and with a document — through others,*

According to the Sages, a document of emancipation can be given even through a third party, because emancipation is considered a benefit and can be brought about without the slave's knowledge (*Rav*).

The *Gemara* (23a) rejects this interpretation of the mishnah, because — according to it — release by money and by document should have been written together: *With money and with a document — on his own or through others,* since they are both valid whether through the slave or a third person.

Rather, the mishnah is explained to be recording three different opinions on the subject. The first is that of R' Meir, as explained above. The second is that of the Sages — that money is valid when given by the slave, and certainly, by others. The fact that the same applies to a document is left unsaid, but is understood, since no such distinction is stated. The third opinion, stated in the words, *and with a document — through others,* is that of R' Shimon ben Elazar, who holds that emancipation by either document or money is valid only when done through a third party. This is because, with regard to money, he agrees with R' Meir that a slave can have no acquisition of his own; and, concerning a document, he does not accept the principle of emancipation and acquisition taking place simultaneously. Therefore, a document given to the slave merely reverts back to the master (*Rashi* 23a s.v. ושלש).

Others contend that according to R' Shimon ben Elazar, a slave can be released with money of his own as well as that of another (since he agrees with the Sages that a slave's acquisition of money is possible), but a document must be given to another person in order to be valid (because he does not accept the principle of simultaneous emancipation and acquisition). Accordingly, the second opinion stated in the mishnah concerning both money and a document is that of R' Shimon ben Elazar — viz. that release through money can be accomplished even by the slave, but that only a third party can receive a document of release for him. The mishnah attributes this statement to the Sages to indicate that they

and with a document — through others, as long as the money is from others.

4. A large animal is acquired by *mesirah,* and a

YAD AVRAHAM

concur with everything which is stated explicitly — viz. that money given by the slave and a document received by others effect his emancipation — and dispute only the implication thereof — i.e., that a document given to the slave himself is not valid (*Ramban; Ritva*).

וּבִלְבַד שֶׁיְּהֵא הַכֶּסֶף מִשֶּׁל אֲחֵרִים. — *as long as the money is from others.*

The Sages validate a slave's emancipation with money only if the money had been given to him on condition that the master have no jurisdiction over it (*Rav* from *Gem.* 23b; *Rabbeinu Tam,* cited by *Tos.* s.v. ורבי אלעזר). [Only in such a case does the slave acquire the money so that he can use it to redeem himself.]

Another opinion is that this method is valid only if the third party specifies that the money is being given on the condition that the slave be thereby emancipated. In such a case it does not transfer to the master, thereby losing the capacity to free the slave, because that would violate the terms of the gift and thereby nullify it (*Gem.* ibid.; *Rif; Rambam, Commentary* and *Hil. Avadim* 5:2; *Meiri*).

According to the first opinion, even R' Meir agrees that if it was explicitly stipulated that the owner not receive the money, it is valid for manumission. Nevertheless, he makes the blanket statement that emancipation with money can be done only *through others* because, even in the above case, the slave never fully acquires the money since he may use it only to give to the master for the sake of emancipation and not for any other purpose; therefore, it is included in the category of [emancipation] *through others* (*Tos.* loc. cit.).

4.

The mishnah now proceeds to discuss acceptable methods for the acquisition of movable property. One such method is through physical contact with the item itself. This can be done in one of three ways: הַגְבָּהָה, *lifting the object;* מְשִׁיכָה, *meshichah* [making it move] or מְסִירָה, *mesirah* [seizing it (*Meiri;* see below)]. There is a dispute in the *Gemara* (*Bava Metzia* 47b) whether the effectiveness of these methods of acquisition is of Biblical or Rabbinical origin (see commentary to mishnah 5, s.v. אינן נקנין). Each of these forms of acquisition is applicable for certain objects and situations, as will be discussed in this mishnah. The most effective of the three is that of lifting, followed by *meshichah,* and finally, by *mesirah.* [Others consider *mesirah* superior to *meshichah* (see below).] In any given situation, the most effective of the three must be employed in order for the acquisition to take effect (*Meiri*).[1]

בְּהֵמָה גַסָּה — *A large animal*

Such as a horse, mule, donkey, or ox (*Meiri*).

נִקְנֵית בִּמְסִירָה, — *is acquired by mesirah,*

The owner gives it over to the buyer

1. According to those who maintain that these methods are of Rabbinic origin, the Rabbis granted validity only to the best method available in each situation (*Ritva* to *Bava Basra* 76a). [If they are of Biblical origin, it is apparent that these acts demonstrate proprietorship only if the object is acquired in the most effective manner possible.]

בְּהַגְבָּהָה; דִּבְרֵי רַבִּי מֵאִיר וְרַבִּי אֱלִיעֶזֶר. וַחֲכָמִים אוֹמְרִים: בְּהֵמָה דַקָּה נִקְנֵית בִּמְשִׁיכָה.

ר' עובדיה מברטנורא

בהגבהה. ולא במשיכה: **נקנית במשיכה.** ואף על גב דאפשר בהגבהה, מכל מקום נקנית במשיכה, משום דמסרכא, שהיא מתחזקת בצפרניה תמיד ליאחז על גבי קרקע. ופסק ההלכה, בין בהמה דקה בין בהמה גסה נקנית במשיכה, וכל שכן בהגבהה. ומשיכה קונה בסימטא, שהיא זוית של רשות הרבים, ובחצר של שניהם. ומסירה קונה ברשות הרבים, ובחצר שאינה של שניהם. והגבהה קונה בכל מקום. וכל מה שדרכו בהגבהה, אינו נקנה אלא בהגבהה. ודבר הנקנה במסירה אינו נקנה במשיכה. וכן דבר הנקנה במשיכה אינו נקנה במסירה:

יד אברהם

— e.g., by handing him the reins or the animal's hair (*Rav; Rashi; Rambam Commentary*).

Others contend that to accomplish *mesirah,* it is sufficient for the buyer to grasp the animal upon the owner's instructions that he do so in order to acquire it (*Tos.; Ran; Meiri*).

Meshichah (see below) is a better method of acquisition than *mesirah* (*Rav; Tos.;* see *Tos. Yom Tov* s.v. וחכמים; *Rashbam* to *Bava Basra* 76b), because in so doing the buyer actively indicates that he is taking the object into his possession (*Ritva* to *Bava Basra* ad loc.). Nevertheless, it is valid only in a סִימְטָא, *simta* [an alleyway which is public property but not a public thoroughfare (*Rashi* to *Kesubos* 84b s.v. סימטא)], or in the common property of the buyer and seller (*Bava Basra* 76b), because this indication is appropriate only if the buyer owns the property into which the object is being drawn (*Ran*).[1] *Mesirah,* on the other hand, is used in a public domain or in property which belongs to neither the buyer nor the seller[2] (*Bava Basra* loc. cit.), but it is valid only for the acquisition of those objects which are too unwieldy to be acquired with *meshichah* (*Rambam, Hil. Mechirah* 3:3; *Ran*). Thus, the point of the mishnah is that large animals are considered unwieldy and may therefore be acquired through *mesirah,* but this applies only in public property or that of a third person (*Ran*).

Another opinion is that R' Meir and R' Eliezer consider the difference between acquisition with *meshichah* and *mesirah* to be dependent only upon the objects acquired and not upon the domain in which acquisition

1. According to the opinion that *mesirah* does not require that the original owner hand it over to the buyer (see below), every *meshichah* that is done by hand includes a *mesirah* — i.e., the grasping of the object by the buyer. Nevertheless, it is not valid in a public domain, because the fact that the buyer proceeded to perform *meshichah* indicates that he did not intend to effect the acquisition with *mesirah* alone, and it is therefore not effective (*Ran*).

2. *Mesirah* is limited to those areas because it is too weak a form of acquisition to be effective in an area where *meshichah* is appropriate (*Ran; Rashbam* to *Bava Basra* 76b). Also, since everyone has the right to place his possession in a *simta,* one who does so assumes temporary possession of that spot. Accordingly, when the seller placed his object in the *simta,* he became the temporary proprietor of the area in which it was placed, and the buyer's *mesirah* there is parallel to taking it within the seller's property, which is not valid. Therefore, the owner must move it from that spot with *meshichah* in order to acquire it (*Ran*).

small one by being lifted; [these are] the words of R' Meir and R' Eliezer. The Sages, however, say: A small animal is acquired by *meshichah.*

YAD AVRAHAM

takes place. Therefore, the acquisition of a large animal with *mesirah* is valid in a *simta* as well as in a public property, since it is too unwieldy to be acquired with *meshichah* (see *Ran*).

Others contend that the acquisition process of *mesirah* is superior to that of *meshichah* (*Rashi; Rabbeinu Tam*, cited by *Tos.*) because the seller actually participates in the process (*Tos.* to *Bava Basra* 76b s.v. ספינה; see above); accordingly, it can be used in a *simta* as well as in public property (*Rabbeinu Tam* ibid.). Thus, the mishnah is discussing both public property and such an alleyway, and the point is that in both of these areas only *mesirah* is valid, but not *meshichah* (*Rashi;* see *Ran*).

וְהַדַּקָּה — בְּהַגְבָּהָה; דִּבְרֵי רַבִּי מֵאִיר וְרַבִּי אֱלִיעֶזֶר. — *and a small one — by being lifted;* [*these are*] *the words of R' Meir and R' Eliezer.*

A small animal, which is normally moved by carrying it (*Meiri*), can be acquired only by being lifted off the ground, but not by *meshichah* [or *mesirah*] (*Rav*).

There is a dispute among the commentators whether it must be lifted three handbreadths off the ground (*Rashi*) or whether one handbreadth is sufficient (*Tos.* 26a s.v. אי נמי).

וַחֲכָמִים אוֹמְרִים: בְּהֵמָה דַקָּה נִקְנֵית בִּמְשִׁיכָה. — *The Sages, however, say: A small animal is acquired by meshichah.*

Meshichah (lit., *pulling*) is performed by pulling or riding the animal or even by calling it or hitting it and thereby making it go (*Rambam, Hil. Mechirah* 2:6 from *Gem.* 22b). Since even small animals plant their claws in the ground to resist being lifted, it is sufficiently difficult to lift them to warrant the validation of *meshichah* (*Rav*).

Whether *mesirah* is also valid depends upon the dispute stated above if it is superior to *meshichah* or not.

Those animals which are extremely light and easy to lift, such as ducks and roosters, are acquirable only by lifting them (*Meiri*).

A third opinion among the *Tannaim* is that both large and small animals are acquired by *meshichah* (*Gem.* 25b), since even small ones are too difficult to lift, and even the large ones are not too unwieldy for *meshichah* and can therefore not be acquired with *mesirah* (*Ran*). The *Gemara's* ruling (ibid.) follows this view. Therefore, any of these animals can be acquired in a *simta* or in jointly owned property of the buyer and seller by means of *meshichah.* However, in public property, where *meshichah* is not valid, they cannot be acquired except by being lifted (*Rambam* loc. cit. 5; *Ran*).

According to the second opinion cited above, that R' Meir validates *mesirah* even in a *simta,* the third opinion cited in the *Gemara* — that *meshichah,* and not *mesirah,* can be used to acquire a large or small animal — refers only to acquisition in a *simta.* In a public property, however, where *meshichah* is not valid, *mesirah* can be used to acquire even small animals. Thus, whereas R' Meir maintains that the designation of *meshichah* or *mesirah* as the valid form of acquisition depends entirely upon the nature of the object acquired — i.e., whether it is too unwieldy for *meshichah* —

[ה] **נְכָסִים** שֶׁיֵּשׁ לָהֶם אַחֲרָיוּת נִקְנִין בְּכֶסֶף, וּבִשְׁטָר, וּבַחֲזָקָה. וְשֶׁאֵין לָהֶם

ר׳ עובדיה מברטנורא

(ה) נכסים שיש להם אחריות. היינו קרקעות, שהמלוה את חבירו סומך עליהם, לפי שקיימים ועומדים. ופירוש אחריות, חזרה, שחוזר המלוה עליהם וטורף אותם מן הלקוחות כשלא ימצא כלום ללוה: **נקנין בכסף.** דכתיב (ירמיה לב, מד) שדות בכסף יקנו. והני מילי במקום שאין רגילין לכתוב שטר, אבל במקום שרגילין לכתוב שטר לא קנה עד שיכתוב שטר: **בשטר.** שכותב על הנייר או על החרס, שדי נתונה לך, שדי קנויה לך, ומוסרו לקונה. ודוקא במתנה נקנה הקרקע בשטר, אבל במכירה, עד שיתן את הכסף, אלא אם כן מוכר שדהו מפני רעתה, דהא קנה בשטר לחודיה. ומנלן דמקרקעי נקנין בשטר, דכתיב (שם) וכתוב בספר וחתום: **ובחזקה.** כגון שחפר בקרקע מעט, או נעל וגדר ופרץ כל שהוא בפני המוכר. ואם היה שלא בפניו, צריך שיאמר לו לך חזק וקני. ומנא לן שקרקע נקנה בחזקה, דכתיב (דברים יא, לא) וירשתם אותה וישבתם בה, במה ירשתם בישיבה:

יד אברהם

the *Gemara's* ruling is that it is dependent totally upon the area in which the acquisition is effected — i.e., anything for which lifting is not appropriate is acquired with *meshichah* in a *simta* and with *mesirah* in public property. Accordingly, the reasoning behind this opinion is not that large animals are not considered unwieldy, but that even unwieldy objects cannot be acquired by *mesirah* in a *simta,* only in public property (*Ran*).

Those who maintain that *mesirah* is preferable to *meshichah* understand the *Gemara's* conclusion to be that *meshichah,* as well as *mesirah,* is a valid form of acquisition for these animals (*Meiri*).

5.

נְכָסִים שֶׁיֵּשׁ לָהֶם אַחֲרָיוּת — *Possessions which can have a lien on them*

I.e., real properties which are mortgaged to a creditor, who relies upon their availability because they are permanent. The word אַחֲרָיוּת means *recourse* — i.e., that the lender can seize them as payment for his loan from buyers who bought them from the debtor after the loan was made (*Rav*).

The mishnah uses this term, rather than simply saying *land,* in order to include those things which are attached to the land; they are acquired in the same manner as the land itself (*Tif. Yis.*).

נִקְנִין — *are acquired*

I.e., as a gift, a sale, or for rental (ibid.).

בְּכֶסֶף, — *with money,*

The buyer gives the value of the land, or even a part of its value [as long as it is at least a *perutah*], to the seller for the purpose of acquisition (*Meiri*),[1] as stated in the verse (*Jer.* 32:44), *Fields with money they shall buy* (*Rav* from *Gem.* 26a). However, this is effective only in a place where it is not customary to write a document for the sale; where documents are written, the transfer is not finalized until the document is given (ibid.), unless it was explicitly stipulated that the transfer should take effect with

1. Some authorities maintain that money is valid for acquisition only if it is being given in payment for the land — whether in full or in part (*Sma* to *Choshen Mishpat* 190:1; *Avnei Miluim* 29:2). Others hold that money for acquisition is not necessarily connected to payment [and it can even be used to acquire a field which is being given as a gift, with no payment required] (*Turei Zahav* to *Choshen Mishpat* loc. cit.; *Nesivos Hamishpat* ibid. 2).

5. **P**ossessions which can have a lien on them are acquired with money, with a document, or with an act of possession, and [those] which cannot

money alone (*Gem.* ibid.). This is because the buyer does not feel secure until he receives a document as evidence of his purchase (*Rashi*).

Even if the custom is to use a document merely as evidence, but not for actual acquisition, the transfer of the field does not take place until the document is given. However, upon receipt of the bill of sale, the transfer takes effect retroactive to the time of payment, since that is the only method of acquisition which was employed (*Ran*). Others contend that only a document used for the actual acquisition must be given for the transfer to take effect, but not one used solely for evidence (see ibid.).

וּבִשְׁטָר, — *with a document,*

The owner writes on a paper or on earthenware that his field is being acquired by this person, and he hands it over to him (*Rav*), as stated in the verse (*Jer.* 32:11), *And I took the document of acquisition* (*Gem.* 26a).

Even if the document can be altered — in which case it usually is void — it is valid in this case, since it is being used for acquisition and not for evidence (*Meiri; Tos.* to *Gittin* 22b s.v. אבל).

This is valid only when land is given as a gift; land which is purchased cannot be acquired until payment is received (*Rav* from *Gem.* 26a) in full (*Ran*), because the seller's decision to sell is not finalized in his own mind until he receives payment (*Rashi*). Nevertheless, if he is selling the field because of its poor quality, the document itself can effect the sale (*Rav* from *Gem.* 26a), because the seller is anxious to close the deal before the buyer changes his mind (*Rashi*). Also, if it was explicitly stipulated that the document alone should effect the acquisition, it is valid (*Meiri*).

וּבַחֲזָקָה. — *or with an act of possession.*

For example, the buyer dug up part of the land, partially fenced it in, or locked up or breached the enclosure, in the presence of the seller. These may even be done in the seller's absence if he had directed the buyer to make the acquisition in that manner. This is derived from the verse (*Deut.* 11:31), *And you shall inherit it* [i.e., take possession of it from the Canaanite nations], *and you shall dwell in it,* which is interpreted to mean that it shall be inherited by dwelling in it [i.e., by showing possession] (*Rav* from *Gem.* 26a).

If the land cannot be possessed in any of the ways mentioned, the buyer can acquire it by using it for spreading out his produce or keeping his animal (*Rambam, Hil. Mechirah* 1:15). Others dispute this and maintain that in order to take possession, he must do something that improves the land itself (*Ravad* ad loc.).

This form of acquisition takes effect immediately, even if the seller did not yet receive payment or the bill of sale, because the buyer performed an act of acquisition in the field itself (*Ramban; Rosh; Ran; Meiri*) [unlike acquisition by money or a document]. Others contend that it does not take effect until the money and/or document are given (*Sheiltos* to *Behar; R' Chananel,* cited by *Rambam; Baal HaIttur,* cited by *Meiri*).

If a man bought several fields in several different places from one person, he can acquire all of them by performing an act of possession in only one of them, as long as he has paid for all of them (*Gem.* 27a). This is because all fields are considered attached, since all masses of land on earth are ulti-

אֲחֲרָיוּת אֵינָן נִקְנִין אֶלָּא בִמְשִׁיכָה. נְכָסִים שֶׁאֵין לָהֶם אַחֲרָיוּת נִקְנִין עִם נְכָסִים שֶׁיֵּשׁ לָהֶם אַחֲרָיוּת בְּכֶסֶף, וּבִשְׁטָר, וּבַחֲזָקָה; וְזוֹקְקִין נְכָסִים שֶׁאֵין לָהֶם אַחֲרָיוּת אֶת הַנְּכָסִים שֶׁיֵּשׁ לָהֶם אַחֲרָיוּת לִשָּׁבַע עֲלֵיהֶן:

ר׳ עובדיה מברטנורא

ושאין להם אחריות אין נקנין אלא במשיכה. דכתיב (ויקרא כה, יד) או קנה מיד עמיתך, דבר שאפשר לתתו מיד ליד אינו נקנה אלא בנתינה מיד ליד: **נקנין עם נכסים כו׳.** אם מכר מטלטלין עם הקרקע, כיון שקנה לוקח הקרקע באחת משלשה קניינים הללו נקנו מטלטלין עמה. והוא שיאמר לו קנה [הני] אגב קרקע. ונפקא לן מקרא דכתיב בדברי הימים (ב כא, ג) ויתן להם אביהם מתנות רבות לכסף ולזהב ולמגדנות עם ערי מצורות: **וזוקקין.** נכסים הללו שאין להם אחריות, את הנכסים שיש להם אחריות כו׳. אף על גב דאין נשבעין על הקרקעות, היכא דטענו מטלטלין וקרקעות ונתחייב לישבע על המטלטלין, זוקקין המטלטלין את הקרקעות לישבע עליהם על ידי גלגול שבועה. ולמדנו גלגול שבועה מסוטה, דכתיב (במדבר ה, כב) ואמרה האשה אמן אמן, אמן מאיש זה, אמן מאיש אחר. אמן שלא שטיתי ארוסה, אמן שלא שטיתי נשואה, שומרת יבם, וכנוסה:

יד אברהם

mately connected (ibid. 27b).

Real property can also be acquired with *chalifin* (*Rav* to mishnah 6). The mishnah does not list this method, however, because it is discussing only those methods of acquisition which are legitimate for fields, but not for movables (*Tos. R' Akiva Eiger*).

וְשֶׁאֵין לָהֶם אַחֲרָיוּת — and [*those*] *which cannot have a lien on them*

I.e., chattels (*Tif. Yis.*).

אֵינָן נִקְנִין אֶלָּא בִמְשִׁיכָה. — *are acquired only with meshichah.*

And similar methods of acquisition, such as *mesirah* and lifting[1] (*Ran; Meiri*), as opposed to the methods used for real property which are listed above. This is derived from the phrase (*Lev.* 25:14), *Or* [*you shall*] *acquire from the hand of your friend*, which indicates that something which is transferable from hand to hand must be acquired in such a manner (*Rav* from *Gem.* 26a); i.e., by *meshichah* (*Rashi* ad loc.) [or by the other similar methods].

According to the opinion that chattels can be acquired with money by Biblical law (*Bava Metzia* 47b), the mishnah is stating a Rabbinic enactment that requires *meshichah.* This was decreed for fear that once the seller has been paid, he will not bother to guard it properly even while it is still in his possession (ibid.; *Rashi* ad loc. 46b s.v. גזרה).

1. The mishnah specifies *meshichah* because that is the form of acquisition most commonly used. Alternatively, *meshichah* is the primary method of acquisition for movables for the following reasons: According to those who derive its effectiveness from the verse quoted above, the type of acquisition which best fits the description of the text is *meshichah*, because the buyer thereby takes it from the possession of the seller into that of his own. On the other hand, if the necessity for more than mere payment is a Rabbinic ordinance, *meshichah* affords the best protection for the item, because the buyer thereby takes it into his possession. The reason *mesirah* and lifting are also valid is that once the buyer has the object in his hand, he has only himself to blame if he then leaves it with the seller (*Ran*).

1
5 have a lien on them are acquired only with *meshichah.*

Possessions which cannot have a lien on them are acquired together with possessions which can have a lien on them with money, with a document, or with an act of possession; and possessions which cannot have a lien on them cause [one] to swear concerning possessions which can have a lien on them.

YAD AVRAHAM

נְכָסִים שֶׁאֵין לָהֶם אַחֲרָיוּת נִקְנִין עִם נְכָסִים שֶׁיֵּשׁ לָהֶם אַחֲרָיוּת בְּכֶסֶף, וּבִשְׁטָר, וּבַחֲזָקָה; — *Possessions which cannot have a lien on them are acquired together with possessions which can have a lien on them with money, with a document, or with an act of possession;*

If someone sold movable objects together with real property, when the buyer acquires the field through one of these procedures, he acquires the movable objects along with it (*Rav*), even if they are not found in the field itself (*Gem.* 27a). This is derived from the verse (*II Chronicles* 21:3), *And their father gave them many gifts of gold and silver and precious objects with fortified cities* (*Gem.* 26a). However, this method of acquisition is valid only if the seller told the buyer, "Acquire the movables אַגַּב (*by way of*) the real property" (*Rav* from *Gem.* 27a; *Ravad* to *Hil. Mechirah* 3:9; *Ran*).

Some authorities intimate that this formula is valid only if the term אַגַּב, *by way of*, is used [since it denotes that the chattels are being acquired in an incidental manner]; but if he told him, "Acquire the movables with the field," it is not valid (*Rashi* 27a s.v. אגב; see *Ran*). Others contend that as long as he specifies that they be acquired together with the field, the acquisition takes effect (*Ran; Meiri*).

Rambam (loc. cit.) holds that the seller must explicitly direct the buyer to acquire the movables together with the field only if the movables are not on the land. Otherwise, the acquisition is valid even without that directive, because once the field becomes the buyer's, he can acquire whatever is on it by virtue of their presence on his property (*Maggid Mishneh* ad loc.; *Ran;* see *Bava Metzia* 10b). Alternatively, when the seller consents to sell a field and the objects which are on it, it is self-evident that the intended method will have the buyer acquire the movables together with the field (*Kesef Mishneh* ad loc.).

This method of acquisition works only if the buyer has paid for the movables as well as the land. Otherwise, he can acquire only as much as he has paid for (*Gem.* 27a).

וְזוֹקְקִין נְכָסִים שֶׁאֵין לָהֶם אַחֲרָיוּת אֶת הַנְּכָסִים שֶׁיֵּשׁ לָהֶם אַחֲרָיוּת לִשָּׁבַע עֲלֵיהֶן. — *and possessions which cannot have a lien on them cause* [*one*] *to swear concerning possessions which can have a lien on them.*

Although oaths are not imposed by the court in cases regarding real property (*Shevuos* 6:5), if a man was sued for movables as well as land, and he was required to swear about the movables, he must also take an auxiliary oath concerning the land (*Rav*).

This principle is derived from the laws of a *sotah* (see mishnah 8), about whom it is written that the *Kohen* dictates to her an oath that she did not commit adultery, and she answers, "*Amen, amen*" (*Num.* 5:22). The dou-

[ו] **כָּל** הַנַּעֲשֶׂה דָמִים בְּאַחֵר, כֵּיוָן שֶׁזָּכָה זֶה — נִתְחַיֵּב זֶה בַּחֲלִיפָיו. כֵּיצַד?

ר' עובדיה מברטנורא

(ו) כל הנעשה דמים באחר. מפרש בגמרא (כח, א) כל הנשום דמים באחר, כל דבר שאם בא לתתו דמים באחר צריך לשומו, דהיינו כל מטלטלין בר ממטבע: **כיון שזכה זה.** כלומר, כיון שמשך האחד, נתחייב האחר בחליפיו בכל מקום שהם אם מתו או אבדו, ואף על פי שלא משך, לפי שבמשיכת המוכר את הסודר או את החפץ, נקנה המקח ללוקח בכל מקום שהוא, ואף על פי שאין בחפץ שקונים בו שוה פרוטה, ובלבד שלא יהיה מטבע או פירות, שאלו אין קונין בהם. וכל הדברים נקנים בחליפין, מטלטלין עבדים וקרקעות, חוץ מהמטבע שאינו נקנה בחליפין, משום דדעתיה דאינש אצורתא דמטבע לא על גופיה, וצורתא עבידא דבטלה. לפיכך אם לקח אדם מטבע בלא משקל ובלא מנין, ואמר אלו חלופי שדה פלונית, או עבד פלוני, או חפץ פלוני, כיון שמשך זה, נתחייב האחר בחליפיו, דהא גלי דעתיה דלאו אצורתא קפיד, הואיל ולא שקל ולא מנה. ואין שום דרך שיועיל בקניית המטבע היכא דליתיה בעיניה, אלא להקנותו אגב קרקע:

יד אברהם

not have been obligated to take even the primary oath (*Tos.* ad loc. s.v. הכי). From this we derive that in monetary issues too, an auxiliary oath can be imposed even regarding those things which never require a primary oath — i.e., real property (*Gem.* 28a).

An auxiliary oath can be imposed even for a claim about which the claimant himself is unsure — just as the auxiliary oath of a *sotah* is not based upon any certainty (ibid.). Nevertheless, there must be some reasonable basis for the claim (*Tos.* ad loc. s.v. אמרה).

ble response denotes that she had no intimacy with her alleged adulterer nor with any other man, neither following her *nisuin* nor during her *erusin* (*Sotah* 2:4). Thus, although there was no basis upon which to require an oath regarding other acts of adultery, it is nevertheless imposed upon her as an adjunct to the primary oath (*Gem.* 27b). She must even swear that she did not commit adultery during the stage of *erusin*, when the laws of *sotah* do not apply, and regarding which she normally would

6.

חֲלִיפִין/Chalifin

Chalifin, exchange, is a method of acquisition derived from the verse (*Ruth* 4:7), *Formerly, this was done in Israel in cases of redemption and exchange transactions to validate all matters: one would remove his shoe and give it to another* (*Bava Metzia* 47a).

There are two categories of *chalifin*: One is an even exchange of two objects [in which each is in place of payment for the other, as well as its means of acquisition], which is referred to in the verse by the word *exchange transactions;* the other is uneven exchange [often referred to as קִנְיַן סוּדָר (lit., *acquisition by handkerchief*), in which the article given as the means of acquisition is not being used in place of payment and is generally returned (see *Nedarim* 48b)], which is derived from the words *to validate all matters* (*Tos.* to *Bava Metzia* 47a s.v. גאולה).

1
6

6. **A**nything which is used as payment for another [object], once this one takes possession — that one becomes liable for its exchange. How?

YAD AVRAHAM

כָּל הַנַּעֲשֶׂה דָמִים בְּאַחֵר, — *Anything which is used as payment for another [object],*

Anything whose value must be evaluated in order to be used as payment for another object — i.e., any movable object[1] aside from money, whose value is clearly defined (*Rav* from *Gem.* 28a; *Rashi* ad loc.). Real property can also be used for this method of acquisition, but the mishnah specifies movables, because they are commonly used for that purpose (*Ran*).

The simple translation of the mishnah would be that it refers to money, which is used as payment for other objects. However, this would indicate that money can be used for *chalifin* (*Gem.* loc. cit.), and the ruling is that it cannot (*Rav* from *Bava Metzia* 47a). The reason for this is that one who accepts money takes it for the sake of the legal value of the coin, which can be negated by the government (*Rav* from ibid. 46b). Therefore, it does not have a definitive value and cannot be used for *chalifin* (*Rashi* from ibid. 47a). However, if he accepted coins without ascertaining their value, he obviously took them for the sake of the metal itself and not for their legal value, and they are valid for *chalifin* (*Rav; Rambam Commentary*).

[Any article which is not defined as a כְּלִי, *useful utensil,* is defined in regard to *chalifin* as a פְּרִי, *fruit* (i.e., something designated for consumption rather than usage], and is not included among the movables which are acceptable for this method of acquisition (*Rav* from *Bava Metzia* 47a).

Others interpret the mishnah to mean: *Anything which must be evaluated to be used in exchange for another article* — i.e., for *chalifin.* They thereby deduce that although it is not necessary to exchange objects of equal value, the worth of each object must nevertheless be assessed in order to be used for *chalifin* (*Rabbeinu Chananel,* cited by *Ran*). Others dispute this conclusion (*Ran*).

Another approach is that the mishnah is discussing the evaluation of one article in terms of the value of another item. For example, "This field is worth such and such an amount of peppers" (*Rambam Commentary*). [This explains the statement of the mishnah that all movables can be used for *chalifin,* implying that even fruits are acceptable because] the mishnah is referring to an even exchange, for which all movables are valid (*Rambam, Hil. Mechirah* 5:1), whereas the word נַעֲלוֹ, *his shoe,* in the verse (*Ruth* 4:7) from which *chalifin* is derived — that precludes the use of fruits — refers to an uneven exchange (ibid. 5; see *Tos. Yom Tov*).

כֵּיוָן שֶׁזָּכָה זֶה — נִתְחַיֵּב זֶה בַּחֲלִיפָיו. — *once this one takes possession, that one becomes liable for its exchange.*

As soon as one party takes possession of the article he is acquiring, the other obtains the object for which the former is being exchanged. Thus, if the second article is lost or damaged, its new owner suffers the loss even if he has not yet taken possession (*Rav*).

כֵּיצַד? — *How?*

[What is an example of acquisition by *chalifin?*]

1. [It is not clear why these commentators understand the mishnah to be referring only to movables. Indeed, *Ritva* interprets it to be discussing real property as well, with the movables mentioned below used only as examples.]

קידושין
א/ו

הֶחֱלִיף שׁוֹר בְּפָרָה, אוֹ חֲמוֹר בְּשׁוֹר, כֵּיוָן שֶׁזָּכָה זֶה — נִתְחַיֵּב זֶה בַּחֲלִיפָיו.

רְשׁוּת הַגָּבוֹהַּ — בְּכֶסֶף, וּרְשׁוּת הַהֶדְיוֹט — בַּחֲזָקָה. אֲמִירָתוֹ לַגָּבוֹהַּ כִּמְסִירָתוֹ לַהֶדְיוֹט.

ר׳ עובדיה מברטנורא

רשות הגבוה בכסף. גזבר שנתן מעות בבהמה לצורך הקדש, אפילו היא בסוף העולם, קנה. ובהדיוט לא קנה אלא בחזקה, כלומר עד שימשוך. ואם נתן ההדיוט דמים על החפץ, כל זמן שלא משך החפץ לא קנה, ומחזיר המוכר את הדמים אם חוזר בו ממכירת החפץ, וצריך לקבל עליו מי שפרע. אבל אם משך הלוקח החפץ, אף על פי שעדיין לא נתן הדמים שהתנה, אין שום אחד מהם יכול לחזור בו. ואם לא נתן דמים ולא משך החפץ, אלא שנתפשרו על המקח בפני עדים, ונתרצה זה שיקנה בכך וכך, ונתרצה חבירו למכור בכך ובכך, אפילו אמר אתם עדי, אין באלה הדברים כלום, ואפילו מי שפרע אין כאן: **אמירתו לגבוה כמסירתו להדיוט.** האומר שור זה עולה, בית זה הקדש, אפילו בסוף העולם, קנה. ובהדיוט לא קנה עד שימשוך בבהמה, ויחזיק בבית:

יד אברהם

הֶחֱלִיף שׁוֹר בְּפָרָה, אוֹ חֲמוֹר בְּשׁוֹר, — [*If one*] *exchanged an ox for a cow, or a donkey for an ox,*

The point is that this holds true even if the exchanged articles are not of the same type (*Tif. Yis.*).

כֵּיוָן שֶׁזָּכָה זֶה — נִתְחַיֵּב זֶה בַּחֲלִיפָיו. — *once this one takes possession — that one becomes liable for its exchange.*

[The other person automatically acquires the animal being given in exchange and suffers the loss if it dies or is lost or damaged, even if he has not yet taken possession.] Although an animal cannot technically be defined as a utensil, it is included in that category in regard to *chalifin*, because it can be used for labor (*Tos.* 28b s.v. הכי קאמר; *Meiri*).

The example given — in which one article is exchanged for another one — implies that if someone exchanged a cow for both an ox and a donkey, the cow is not transferred to the other party until the first takes possession of both the ox and the donkey (*Tif. Yis.*).

Another opinion is that animals are not included under the category of utensils in regard to *chalifin*. Accordingly, the mishnah is not discussing *chalifin* — for which the animals mentioned would be disqualified — but rather acquisition with money. The point is that there are times when money can be used for acquisition in the same manner as *chalifin*. An example of this is if someone sold another an ox, and the buyer took possession of the ox, but did not yet pay. The seller subsequently requested to be given the buyer's cow in payment rather than the money, and [if the buyer agrees] he would acquire the cow with the money that the buyer owed him. Since money can be used to acquire movables by Biblical law, but was invalidated by Rabbinic decree (see commentary to mishnah 5 s.v. אֵינָן נִקְנִין), this is valid, because the Rabbis did not extend the decree to unusual cases of acquisition such as this one (*Gem.* 28b, *Rashi* ad loc.).

רְשׁוּת הַגָּבוֹהַּ — בְּכֶסֶף, — *Possession by the Temple treasury* (lit., *the Most High*) — *is with money,*

If the Temple treasurer pays for movable objects, they become the possession of the Temple immedi-

1
6
[If one] exchanged an ox for a cow, or a donkey for an ox, once this one takes possession — that one becomes liable for its exchange.

Possession by the Temple treasury is with money, and possession by a private person is with an act of possession. Its oral dedication to the Temple is like its delivery to a private person.

YAD AVRAHAM

ately, even without any other act of acquisition (*Rav* from *Gem.* ad loc.), because the Rabbinic enactment invalidating acquisition of movables with money was not applied to Temple property (*Meiri*).

According to the view that money is void for the acquisition of movables by Biblical law (see commentary to mishnah 5 loc. cit.), the exception for Temple property is derived from the verse (*Psalms* 24:1), *HASHEM'S Is the earth,* which indicates that everything in the world is His, and He can therefore take possession of anything without the normally required procedure (*Yerushalmi,* cited by *Meiri*).

Accordingly, if the Temple treasurer paid for an object and it then increased in value, he may take it for the Temple without paying for the increase. Nevertheless, if it decreased in value before he took possession he pays only the lower price. This is because the Temple cannot hold a position inferior to that of a private person, and the latter would acquire the objects for the lower price, because his acquisition does not take effect with payment alone (*Gem.* 29a).

Although the transfer of an object to the Temple can be accomplished with a mere declaration to that effect (see below), that is only when it is given as a gift or at a bargain price. However, when someone sells an object to the Temple, he is unwilling to sell it at a loss, and thus does not want it to be transferred until he is paid (*Tos.* 29a s.v. משכן). Others explain that although the seller becomes committed to the sale with words alone, the Temple's commitment does not take place until the time of payment, and before that time the treasurer can change his mind (*Meiri*).

וּרְשׁוּת הַהֶדְיוֹט — בַּחֲזָקָה. — *and possession by a private person — is with an act of possession.*

A private person can acquire movables only by an act of possession, such as *meshichah*[1] (see mishnah 5). If he paid for the article but did not take possession, the seller has the right to return the money and keep the article; however, he is cursed by the judges for reneging on his commitment (*Rav* from *Bava Metzia* 4:2). If only an oral commitment was made, it is not binding, and even the curse is not given (*Rav*).

אֲמִירָתוֹ לַגָּבוֹהַּ כִּמְסִירָתוֹ לַהֶדְיוֹט. — *Its oral dedication to the Temple is like its delivery to a private person.*

For example, if someone says, "This ox is a burnt-offering," or "This house belongs to the Temple," his words

1. The mishnah could not be dealing with land, in which case the term *act of possession* would refer to improving the land — as it does in mishnah 5 — because land can be acquired with money by a private person as well as by the Temple, and the contrast stated in the mishnah would not hold true (*Meiri*).

[ז] כָּל מִצְוֹת הַבֵּן עַל הָאָב — אֲנָשִׁים חַיָּבִין וְנָשִׁים פְּטוּרוֹת; וְכָל מִצְוֹת הָאָב עַל הַבֵּן

ר׳ עובדיה מברטנורא

(ז) **כל מצות הבן על האב.** כל מלות הבן המוטלות על האב לעשות לבנו. והן ששה דברים, למולו, לפדותו אם הוא בכור, ללמדו תורה, ללמדו אומנות, להשיאו אשה, להשיטו בנהר: **אנשים חייבים.** האב חייב במלות הללו לבנו, והאם פטורה: **וכל מצות האב.** המוטלות על הבן לעשות לאביו, שהם מורא וכבוד. מורא, לא ישב במקומו, ולא יסתור את דבריו, ולא יכריע את דבריו. כבוד, מאכיל ומשקה, מלביש ומכסה, מכניס, ומוליא:

יד אברהם

take effect immediately — even if the object is not in his hands — just as a private person acquires things with an act of possession (*Rav*).

7.

Having mentioned *kiddushin* — which is connected to the precept of propagation, in which only men are obligated — the Mishnah now defines those categories of commandments in which women are obligated and those in which they are not (*Meiri*).

כָּל מִצְוֹת הַבֵּן עַל הָאָב — *All commandments involving the son* [*incumbent*] *on the father* —

Namely: to circumcise him, to redeem him if he is the firstborn, to teach him Torah, to marry him off, to teach him a trade, and to teach him how to swim (*Rav* from *Gem.* 29a).

The wording מִצְוַת הַבֵּן — literally, *commandment of the son* — indicates that if the father did not fulfill his responsibility in any of these areas, the son is obligated to do so himself, as explained in the *Gemara* (ibid.) (*Tos. Yom Tov*).

אֲנָשִׁים חַיָּבִין — *men are obligated*

A father is obligated to fulfill these commandments involving his son (*Rav*).

The obligation to circumcise one's son is derived from the verse (*Gen.* 21:4), *And Abraham circumcised Isaac his son ... as God commanded him,* since the use of the word *command* always denotes that it was decreed upon all generations (*Gem.* 29a).

He is obligated in the redemption of his firstborn, by virtue of the verse (*Ex.* 34:20), *Every firstborn of your sons you shall redeem* (*Gem.* loc. cit.).

He must teach him Torah until he is sufficiently proficient in it to be able to fulfill the commandments properly (*Meiri*), as it is stated (*Deut.* 11:19), *Teach them to your sons* (*Gem.* 29b).

He is obligated to marry off his son, as stated in the verse (*Jer.* 29:6), *And take wives for your sons* (*Gem.* 30b).

The responsibility to teach him a trade is derived from the verse (*Ecc.* 9:9), *See life with the woman whom you love.* The word *life* refers to the trade from which one derives a livelihood, and the woman mentioned is meant either literally or as a figurative reference to Torah. Thus, a trade is compared either to a woman or to Torah, indicating that the father is obligated to teach his son a trade just as he is responsible to find him a wife and teach him Torah (*Gem.* loc. cit.).

The obligation to teach him how to swim is based on the fact that this skill

7. All commandments involving the son [incumbent] on the father — men are obligated and women are exempt; and all commandments involving the father [incumbent] on the son —

YAD AVRAHAM

could save his life (ibid.) [and it is therefore included in the word *life* in the aforementioned verse].

וְנָשִׁים פְּטוּרוֹת; — *and women are exempt;*

A mother is not obligated to fulfill these commandments involving her son (*Rav*).

The very verse (*Gen.* 21:4) which tells us of the father's obligation to circumcise his son also exempts the mother from it by concluding: *as God commanded him,* which is interpreted to mean *him,* and not *her* (*Gem.* 29a).[1]

The *Gemara* (ibid.) derives exegetically that the parental obligation to redeem the firstborn is imposed only upon one who must redeem himself if he is the firstborn and was not redeemed by his father. Since a woman is not included in that obligation (see ibid.), she also does not have the responsibility to redeem her son (ibid.). The same process of derivation exempts a woman from the responsibility to teach her son Torah (*Gem.* 29b).

She is not responsible to marry off her son, because the verse in which that obligation is stated begins: *Take for yourselves wives* (*Jer.* 29:6), obviously addressing only men (*Tos. Yom Tov*). Moreover, a woman is not included in the commandment to propagate [*Gen.* 1:28] (*Yevamos* 65b), and is therefore not obligated to concern herself with marriage (*Meiri; Nimukei Yosef* to 30b; *Shitah Lo Noda Lemi* ibid.; see *Ran*).

A mother is also not obligated to teach her son a trade, because this is derived either from the obligation to teach him Torah or from that of finding him a wife (see above), neither of which apply to the mother (*Shitah Lo Noda Lemi* loc. cit.). [For the same reason, she does not have to teach him how to swim.]

וְכָל מִצְוֹת הָאָב עַל הַבֵּן — — *and all commandments involving the father [incumbent] on the son —*

This refers to the obligation to fear him (*Lev.* 19:3) — e.g., to refrain from sitting in his regular place, contradicting his words, or expressing an opinion as to whom is correct in a dispute between his father and another (see *Rashi* 31b s.v. ולא מכריעו) — and to honor him (*Ex.* 20:12) — e.g., to feed him and clothe him, dress him,

1. This exemption is necessary, even though circumcision is a positive commandment with a set time — the eighth day — from which women are always exempt (see below), because the obligation of circumcision remains in effect even when that time passed (*Tos.* ad loc. s.v. אותו; cf. *Ran*). Alternatively, since the eighth day from birth can occur on any given day, it is not considered a precept with a set time (*Tos. Rid*).

However, the verse is required only according to those who maintain that circumcision may be performed at night. According to the prevailing view that it may be done only by day, this in itself sets a time for the commandment, and women are automatically exempt (*Tos.* loc. cit.). Others contend that the parental obligation is not that they must personally perform the circumcision, but only that they must arrange for it, and that can be done by night as well as by day (*Tos. Rid*).

— אֶחָד אֲנָשִׁים וְאֶחָד נָשִׁים חַיָּבִין.

וְכָל מִצְוַת עֲשֵׂה שֶׁהַזְּמָן גְּרָמָהּ — אֲנָשִׁים חַיָּבִין וְנָשִׁים פְּטוּרוֹת; וְכָל מִצְוַת עֲשֵׂה שֶׁלֹּא הַזְּמַן גְּרָמָהּ — אֶחָד אֲנָשִׁים וְאֶחָד נָשִׁים חַיָּבִין.

וְכָל מִצְוַת לֹא תַעֲשֶׂה — בֵּין שֶׁהַזְּמַן גְּרָמָהּ, בֵּין שֶׁלֹּא הַזְּמַן גְּרָמָהּ — אֶחָד אֲנָשִׁים וְאֶחָד נָשִׁים חַיָּבִין, חוּץ מִבַּל תַּשְׁחִית, וּבַל תַּקִּיף,

ר׳ עובדיה מברטנורא

אחד אנשים ואחד נשים חייבים. הבנים והבנות חייבים: **וכל מצות עשה שהזמן גרמה.** שהזמן גרם למצוה שתבא, כגון שופר, סוכה, לולב, וציצית: **שלא הזמן גרמה.** כגון מזוזה, מעקה, אבדה, ושלוח הקן. והני תרי כללי לאו דוקא, כדקיימא לן (לד, א) אין למדין מן הכללות אפילו במקום שנאמר בהם חוץ, שהרי מצה בליל הפסח, ושמחה במועדים, והקהל בחג הסוכות, כולן מצות עשה שהזמן גרמה הן, ונשים חייבות. ותלמוד תורה, ופריה ורביה, ופדיון הבן, ממצות עשה שלא הזמן גרמה הן, ונשים פטורות. אבל כללא בתרא דכל מצות לא תעשה אחד אנשים ואחד נשים חייבים, חוץ מבל תקיף, ובל תשחית, ובל תטמא למתים, כללא דוקא הוא, וילפינן ליה מדכתיב (במדבר ה, ו) איש או אשה כי יעשו מכל חטאת האדם, השוה הכתוב אשה לאיש לכל עונשין שבתורה: **חוץ מבל תקיף ובל תשחית.** דכתיב (ויקרא יט, כז) לא תקיפו פאת ראשכם, ולא

יד אברהם

and escort him (*Rav* from *Gem.* 31b).

Even to confirm his father's words is forbidden, because it implies that they need his confirmation (*Tos. Yom Tov*).

אֶחָד אֲנָשִׁים וְאֶחָד נָשִׁים חַיָּבִין. — *both men and women are obligated.*

Sons and daughters are both obligated in these commandments (*Rav*), since the word תִּירָאוּ, *You shall fear* [your parents] (*Lev.* 19:3), is stated in the plural form (*Gem.* 30b), and we derive that the same is true regarding the precept of fearing them (*Shitah Lo Noda Lemi* ad loc.).

וְכָל מִצְוַת עֲשֵׂה שֶׁהַזְּמַן גְּרָמָהּ — *Every positive commandment which time causes* (lit., *which the time caused it*) —

I.e., that a certain time brings about the onset of the obligation — e.g., *shofar, lulav, succah,* etc. (*Rav* from *Gem.* 33b; cf. *Rambam Commentary*).

אֲנָשִׁים חַיָּבִין וְנָשִׁים פְּטוּרוֹת; — *men are obligated and women are exempt;*

The exemption of women from these commandments is derived from the fact that they are exempt from the precept of *tefillin* [phylacteries] (*Berachos* 3:3), which is derived hermeneutically from the juxtaposition of the verse regarding the commandment of *tefillin* to that of Torah study, from which women are exempt, as explained above. The verses (*Deut.* 6:7,8) read: *Teach them thoroughly to your sons ... Bind them as a sign upon your arm ...* (*Gem.* 34a).

Exceptions to this include the obligations to eat matzah on Passover (*Ex.* 12:18; see *Pesachim* 43b), to rejoice [by partaking of the festival offerings] on the festivals (*Deut.* 16:11), and to assemble in the courtyard of the Temple on the festival of Succos in *Shemittah* (the Sabbatical year) to hear

1 both men and women are obligated.
7 Every positive commandment which time causes — men are obligated and women are exempt; and every positive commandment which time does not cause — both men and women are obligated.

Every negative commandment — whether time causes [it], or time does not cause [it] — both men and women are obligated, except for the prohibition of destroying [one's beard], the prohibition of rounding [one's head], and the prohibition of

YAD AVRAHAM

the public reading of the Torah (ibid. 31:12) — all of which include women (*Rav* from *Gem.* loc. cit.; cf. *Rambam Commentary*).

וְכָל מִצְוַת עֲשֵׂה שֶׁלֹּא הַזְּמַן גְּרָמָהּ — אֶחָד אֲנָשִׁים וְאֶחָד נָשִׁים חַיָּבִין. — *and every positive commandment which time does not cause — both men and women are obligated.*

This category includes the obligations to affix *mezuzos* (*Deut.* 6:9), to put a fence around a roof (ibid. 22:8), and to send away a bird from her nest before removing her offspring (ibid. v. 7) (*Rav* from *Gem.* 34a). Exceptions to this rule include Torah study, the obligation to propagate, and the redemption of the firstborn — all of which do not apply to women (see above), although they have no set time (ibid.).

Although the precept of putting up a fence on one's roof is dictated also by the negative commandment (*Deut.* 22:8), *You shall not place blood in your house*, the issue of a woman's inclusion in the positive commandment would be pertinent if she had built the house with the intention of enclosing the roof, in which case she would not transgress the negative commandment. If she later changed her mind and refused to enclose the roof, she would be violating only the positive commandment. The same applies to sending away a mother bird, which is required also by the prohibition (ibid. v. 6), *You shall not take the mother with the children.* If a woman would take the mother bird before taking her young with the intention of chasing her away, she would thereby avoid transgressing the prohibition. Nevertheless, she would still be bound by the positive commandment to actually send the bird away (*Tos.* 34a s.v. מעקה).

Others contend that regarding any precept that is dictated by both negative and positive commandments, a woman is obligated by the positive commandment by virtue of her inclusion in the negative commandment. However, in these cases, the negative and positive commandments are not parallel, because even after transgressing the prohibitions by building a house with the intent of leaving the roof unprotected and by taking the mother bird with the intent of keeping her, one is still bound by the positive commandments to build a fence and release the bird (*Ran*).

וְכָל מִצְוַת לֹא תַעֲשֶׂה — בֵּין שֶׁהַזְּמַן גְּרָמָהּ, בֵּין שֶׁלֹּא הַזְּמַן גְּרָמָהּ — אֶחָד אֲנָשִׁים וְאֶחָד נָשִׁים חַיָּבִין, — *Every negative commandment — whether time causes [it], or time does not cause [it] — both men and women are obligated,*

As derived from the verse (*Num.* 5:6), *A man or woman who shall do any of the sins of a person* — which equates men and women in regard to all punishments in the Torah (*Rav* from

וּבַל תִּטַּמֵּא לַמֵּתִים.

[ח] הַסְּמִיכוֹת, וְהַתְּנוּפוֹת, וְהַהַגָּשׁוֹת, וְהַקְּמִיצוֹת, וְהַהַקְטָרוֹת,

ר׳ עובדיה מברטנורא

תשחית את פאת זקנך. כל שישנו בהשחתה ישנו בהקפה, וכל שאינו בהשחתה אינו בהקפה. והני נשי, הואיל וליתנהו בהשחתה, ליתנהו בהקפה. ומנלן דליתנהו בהשחתה, דכתיב (ויקרא יט, כז) פאת זקנך, ולא כתיב פאת זקנכם, מאי זקנך, זקנך ולא זקן אשתך: **ובל תטמא למתים.** דכתיב (שם כא, א) אמור אל הכהנים בני אהרן, בני אהרן ולא בנות אהרן: **(ח) הסמיכות והתנופות.** אינה סומכת, ואינה מניפה, ואינה מגשת מנחה בקרן מערבית דרומית כמשפטה אם היא כהנת,

יד אברהם

Gem. 35a), i.e., those negative commandments that are punishable by lashes (*Rashi* ad loc.).

This rule has no exceptions besides the three listed below (*Rav*).

חוּץ מִבַּל תַּשְׁחִית, — *except for the prohibition of destroying* [*one's beard*],

The Torah (*Lev.* 19:27) states: *You shall not destroy the corners of your beard,* in the singular form, despite the fact that the first half of the verse is written in the plural form. This is meant to stress that it refers to *your beard,* and not your wife's beard (*Rav* from *Gem.* 35b) — i.e., even if she grows a beard and cuts it [she has not transgressed] (*Rashi* ad loc.).

וּבַל תַּקִּיף, — *the prohibition of rounding* [*one's head*] (*ibid.*),

The same verse begins, *You shall not round the corners of your heads* — i.e., to make the hairline even all around, so that there is no hair beneath the temples (*Rashi* to *Lev.* 19:27). From the juxtaposition of this prohibition with that of cutting the beard, we derive that only those who are forbidden to destroy their beards are also prohibited to round out their hairlines — thus excluding women (*Rav* from *Gem.* loc. cit.).

וּבַל תִּטַּמֵּא לַמֵּתִים. — *and the prohibition of becoming contaminated for the dead.*

[This is a commandment applying exclusively to *Kohanim,* prohibiting them from coming in contact with the dead and thereby ritually contaminating themselves.] The verse (*Lev.* 21:1) begins: *Say to the ... sons of Aaron,* from which we infer the exclusion of the daughters of *Kohanim* (*Rav* from *Gem.* 35b).

8.

הַסְּמִיכוֹת, — *The* [*rites of*] *semichah,*

A man who offers an animal [but not a bird] for any sacrifice, except a firstborn and a paschal lamb, is required to place his hands on the animal's head and lean on it with all his strength before it is slaughtered (*Meiri* from *Lev.* 1:4). This ritual is called *semichah* (leaning). A woman who offers a sacrifice is exempt from this obligation, because the Torah specifies that it applies to בְּנֵי יִשְׂרָאֵל, *the Children* (lit., *Sons*) *of Israel,* thus excluding women (*Gem.* 36a).

Despite the fact that many verses containing negative and positive commandments with no specified times are prefaced with these same words, they are not interpreted to

becoming contaminated for the dead.

8. The [rites of] *semichah,* waving, bringing close, *kemitzah,* burning, *melikah*

YAD AVRAHAM

exempt women from those precepts, because we derive from other passages that women, too, are included in them (see mishnah 7). Therefore, the phrase בְּנֵי יִשְׂרָאֵל, *the Children of Israel,* in these verses is interpreted as excluding gentiles (*Ritva*).

Although women should be exempt from all commandments involving offerings since the latter have a set time — they may be brought only during the day (*Zevachim* 98a) — were it not for the Torah's specific exclusion of women, we would derive from the juxtaposition in one verse of the commandments of *semichah* and slaughtering (*Lev.* 3:2) that just as a woman is qualified to slaughter an animal for an offering (*Zevachim* 3:1), she is also qualified — and therefore obligated — to perform *semichah* on it (*Tos.* 36a s.v. הקבלות). Alternatively, we might assume that if a woman brings an offering, since she cannot perform *semichah* for herself, a man must do it for her; the verse teaches us that no *semichah* is necessary for a woman's offering (*Pnei Yehoshua*).

וְהַתְּנוּפוֹת — *waving,*

When a man brings a שְׁלָמִים, *peace-offering,* he must take the chest and thigh of the animal [and those entrails which are to be burnt on the Altar (*Menachos* 61b)] and, together with the *Kohen,* wave them away from him, back toward him, and up and down (*Meiri* from *Lev.* 7:30). When a woman brings the offering, the *Kohen* performs this ritual (ibid.), since this passage, too, is prefaced by the words (ibid. v. 29), *Speak to the Children (Sons) of Israel* (*Gem.* 36a).

A special exemption for women is necessary despite the fact that the precept has a set time, because we would otherwise compare all such cases to those listed at the end of the mishnah, in which the waving by a woman is explicitly required (*Tos.* ad loc.).

וְהַהַגָּשׁוֹת, — *bringing close,*

The procedure for bringing a מִנְחָה, *meal-offering,* requires that after it has been inserted in the proper utensil, and oil and spices have been placed upon it, it is given to a *Kohen,* who brings it close to the southwest corner of the Altar (*Meiri* from *Sotah* 14b). The daughter of a *Kohen* may not perform this service, as derived from the verse (*Lev.* 6:7), *The sons of Aaron shall bring it close,* which excludes women (*Gem.* 36a).

Women must be specifically disqualified from this procedure — and those listed below — although they all have set times (see above), to teach us that not only are they not obligated to perform these rituals, but their doing so invalidates the sacrifice (*Tos.* ibid.; *Meiri*).

וְהַקְּמִיצוֹת, — *kemitzah,*

When bringing a meal-offering, the *Kohen* must take a handful of grain and remove the excess, until he is left with only that which is enclosed in his three middle fingers while they are bent over his palm (*Lev.* 2:2; *Menachos* 11a). This procedure is called *kemitzah,* and it is valid only when performed by a male *Kohen,* as the verse begins, *And he shall bring it to the sons of Aaron* (*Gem.* 36a).

וְהַהַקְטָרוֹת, — *burning,*

The burning of all offerings on the Altar may be performed only by a male *Kohen,* as it says (*Lev.* 3:5), *And the sons of Aaron shall burn it on*

וְהַמְּלִיקוֹת, וְהַהַזָּאוֹת וְהַקַּבָּלוֹת — נוֹהֲגוֹת בָּאֲנָשִׁים וְלֹא בַנָּשִׁים, חוּץ מִמִּנְחַת סוֹטָה וּנְזִירָה, שֶׁהֵן מְנִיפוֹת.

[ט] **כָּל** מִצְוָה שֶׁהִיא תְלוּיָה בָאָרֶץ — אֵינָהּ נוֹהֶגֶת אֶלָּא בָאָרֶץ; וְשֶׁאֵינָהּ תְּלוּיָה בָאָרֶץ — נוֹהֶגֶת בֵּין בָּאָרֶץ בֵּין בְּחוּצָה לָאָרֶץ,

ר' עובדיה מברטנורא

ואינה קומלת, ולא מקטרת, ואינה מולקת עוף, ואינה מקבלת דם במזרק, ואינה מזה דם: **חוץ מסוטה ונזירה שהן מניפות.** מנחתן בעלמן, שמנחתן טעונה תנופה בבעלים: **(ט) כל מצוה שאינה תלויה בארץ.** כל מלוה שהיא חובת הגוף מיקריא אינה תלויה בארץ, ושהיא חובת

יד אברהם

the Altar (ibid.).

וְהַמְּלִיקוֹת — *melikah,*

When a bird is brought as an offering, the *Kohen* kills it by cutting its neck with his fingernail (*Lev.* 1:15). Since the verse juxtaposes the description of this procedure with that of offering the animal on the Altar, it teaches us that *melikah,* too, may be performed only by a male *Kohen* (*Gem.* ibid.).

וְהַהַזָּאוֹת — *sprinkling,*

This refers to the sprinkling of the blood of a bird-offering on the Altar (*Gem.* 36b). The exclusion of women from this service is derived from their exclusion from the ritual of placing the blood of a sheep offered on the Altar. Since a sheep, which does not require slaughtering by a *Kohen,* must have its blood placed on the Altar by a male *Kohen* [as derived from the verse (*Lev.* 1:11), *And the sons of Aaron shall place its blood on the Altar* (*Rashi* 36b, s.v. להזאתו)], it follows that a bird-offering, which may be slaughtered only by a male *Kohen,* must certainly have its blood sprinkled on the Altar by a male *Kohen* (*Gem.* ibid.).

וְהַקַּבָּלוֹת — *and receiving —* —

I.e., receiving the blood [which flows from the animal when it is slaughtered] in a pan (*Rav*). This is derived from the verse (*Lev.* 1:5), *And the sons of Aaron shall bring the blood,* which the Rabbis interpret as referring to the receiving of the blood (*Zevachim* 4a).

This verse refers also to the carrying of the blood to the Altar (ibid.), and thus, a woman is excluded from performing that service as well (*Tos.* 36a s.v. הקבלות).

נוֹהֲגוֹת בָּאֲנָשִׁים וְלֹא בַנָּשִׁים — *pertain to men and not to women,*

[Only men are qualified to perform these services, as explained above.]

חוּץ מִמִּנְחַת סוֹטָה — *except for the meal-offering of a sotah*

The term סוֹטָה, *sotah,* refers to a woman who was warned by her husband against being alone with a specific man and was subsequently observed in seclusion with him by two witnesses, who do not know if the man and woman had intimacy. As described in Scripture (*Num.* 5:11*ff*), such a woman must undergo a complex procedure, which includes bringing a meal-offering, taking an oath that she did not commit adultery, and

sprinkling, and receiving — pertain to men and not to women, except for the meal-offering of a *sotah* and a female Nazirite, [in which cases] they wave [them].

9. Every commandment which is dependent on land applies only in the Land; that which is not dependent on land applies both in the Land and outside the Land, except for *orlah*

YAD AVRAHAM

drinking a specially prepared mixture which would prove fatal to her if she was guilty, but beneficial to her if she was innocent.

Regarding her meal-offering, it says (ibid. v. 25), *And the Kohen shall take from the hand of the woman... and he shall wave the meal-offering before* HASHEM. From the word *hand*, we derive hermeneutically that this case is analogous to that of a peace-offering, concerning which the word *hand* is also used — *His hand shall bring it* (*Lev.* 7:30). Thus, just as one who offers a peace-offering must participate in the rite of waving (see above), so too must the *sotah* (*Gem.* 36b).

וּנְזִירָה, שֶׁהֵן מְנִיפוֹת. — *and a female Nazirite, [in which cases] they wave [them].*

Because Scripture uses the term כַּף, *palm*, with regard to both the *sotah* (*Num.* 5:18) and the Nazirite (ibid. 6:19), we derive hermeneutically that just as a *sotah* participates in the rite of waving, so too does a woman Nazirite (*Gem.* loc. cit.).

9.

Having discussed the distinction between the obligation of a man and those of a woman, the mishnah goes on to discuss the distinction between precepts which are limited to Eretz Yisrael and those which are not (*Meiri*).

כָּל מִצְוָה שֶׁהִיא תְלוּיָה בָאָרֶץ — *Every commandment which is dependent on land* —

I.e., an obligation concerning land (*Rav* from *Gem.* 37a) or its produce — e.g., tithes, *terumah* and *challah* [portions of one's crop and dough, respectively, which must be given to a *Kohen* (see preface to *Gittin* 3:7 and footnote to ibid. 5:9)] (*Rashi* 37a).

The mishnah uses the more ambiguous wording, *dependent on land*, rather than an *obligation involving land*, in order to include commandments which relate to produce of land, as well as those relating to land itself (*Tos. Yom Tov*).

אֵינָהּ נוֹהֶגֶת אֶלָּא בָאָרֶץ; — *applies only in the Land;*

[Such commandments are applicable only in Eretz Yisrael.]

וְשֶׁאֵינָהּ תְּלוּיָה בָאָרֶץ — נוֹהֶגֶת בֵּין בָּאָרֶץ בֵּין בְּחוּצָה לָאָרֶץ, — *that which is not dependent on land applies both in the Land and outside the Land,*

A commandment which does not concern land is binding both in Eretz Yisrael and in the Diaspora (*Rav* from *Gem.* loc. cit.), even those which the Torah associates with the entrance of

חוּץ מִן הָעָרְלָה וְהַכִּלְאָיִם. רַבִּי אֱלִיעֶזֶר אוֹמֵר: אַף מִן הֶחָדָשׁ.

[י] **כָּל הָעוֹשֶׂה** מִצְוָה אַחַת — מְטִיבִין

ר' עובדיה מברטנורא

קרקע מיקריא תלויה בארץ: **חוץ מן הערלה.** שנוהגת בחוצה לארץ הלכה למשה מסיני, וכלאי הכרם בחוצה לארץ מדרבנן, וכלאי זרעים מותרין לזרעם בחוץ לארץ: **רבי אליעזר אומר אף החדש.** אסור בחוץ לארץ מן התורה, אף על פי שהוא חובת קרקע, שנאמר (ויקרא כג, יד) בכל מושבותיכם, בכל מקום שאתם יושבים. והלכה כרבי אליעזר: (י) **כל העושה מצוה אחת.** יתירה על זכיותיו, כדי שיהיו זכיותיו מרובין מעונותיו:

יד אברהם

the Jewish people into the Holy Land [e.g., *tefillin* (see *Ex.* 13:11,16)] (*Meiri*).

This distinction is based on the verse (*Deut.* 12:1), *These are the decrees and the laws which you must guard to do in the land which* HASHEM, *the God of your fathers, has given you to inherit, all of the days which you live on the earth.* The final phrase obligates us to fulfill the commandments even outside the Holy Land, yet the earlier words of the verse indicate that they are appli-cable only within it. Since the topic which the Torah proceeds to discuss is that of idolatry, it is derived that just as that prohibition — which does not concern land — is applicable in all lands, so too are all such commandments applicable in all lands. Accordingly, the words which limit the laws of the Torah to the land are understood as referring only to obligations concerning land (*Gem.* 37a).

חוּץ מִן הָעָרְלָה — *except for orlah*

This is the commandment prohibiting any benefit from the fruit which a tree bears for the first three years after it is planted (*Lev.* 19:23; see *Rashi* ad loc.). Although this is an obligation concerning land, it is הֲלָכָה לְמֹשֶׁה מִסִּינַי, *a tradition* [*transmitted orally*] *to Moses at Sinai,* that it is binding everywhere, not only in the Holy Land (*Rav* from *Gem.* 38b).

Others contend that its application outside of Eretz Yisrael is a Rabbinic ordinance which the Jews who lived in the Diaspora accepted upon themselves (*Meiri* from *Gem.* ibid.).

וְהַכִּלְאָיִם. — *and kilayim.*

This refers to the prohibition of כִּלְאֵי הַכֶּרֶם, the sowing of two different species of seeds together with those of grapes (*Deut.* 22:9; *Gem.* 39a), which is prohibited even outside the Holy Land by Rabbinic law (*Rav* from *Gem.* ibid.).

The prohibition of כִּלְאֵי זְרָעִים — seeding any two different species together, even without grapes (*Lev.* 19:19) — is applicable only in Eretz Yisrael (*Rav* from *Gem.* 38b). This distinction is due to the fact that the type of *kilayim* mentioned above — in which two species are sown together with grapes — is forbidden by Biblical law for any benefit whatsoever, whereas this type of *kilayim* is forbidden only to eat. Therefore, the Rabbis were stricter in their decrees concerning the former than those concerning the latter (*Gem.* ibid.).

A third prohibition of *kilayim* — grafting trees of different species [which is also included in the verse (*Lev.* loc. cit.), *Your field you shall not plant in a mixture*

and *kilayim.* R' Eliezer says: Also *chadash.*

10. Whoever fulfills one commandment is

(*Rambam, Hil. Kilayim* 1:5)] — is prohibited even outside Eretz Yisrael by Biblical law (*Gem.* 38b).

Although the obligation to separate *challah* — a portion of dough to be given also to a *Kohen* — is applicable outside the Holy Land (*Challah* 4:8), the mishnah does not mention it, because it lists only those precepts which are pertinent to the produce grown by a gentile as well as that of a Jew (*Yerushalmi,* cited by *Tos.* 36b s.v. כל). It is thus apparent that the prohibitions of *orlah* and *kilayim* apply even to produce grown by a gentile, since they are mentioned in the mishnah (*Tos.* ibid.).

רַבִּי אֱלִיעֶזֶר אוֹמֵר: אַף מִן הֶחָדָשׁ. — *R' Eliezer says: Also chadash.*

[Just as *orlah* and *kilayim* are commandments concerning land which are applicable outside of Eretz Yisrael, so too is *chadash.*] This is the prohibition against eating new grain from the annual crop until the *omer*-offering is brought on the second day of Passover (*Lev.* 23:14). The fact that it applies everywhere is derived from the phrase (ibid.), *in all your dwelling places* (*Rav* from *Gem.* 37a).

The first, anonymous opinion in the mishnah explains these words to indicate that the precept of *chadash* became applicable only after the Holy Land had been conquered and settled (*Gem.* ibid.).

There is another version which leaves out the word אַף, *also,* according to which R' Eliezer maintains that only *chadash* is forbidden in the Diaspora, but not *orlah* and *kilayim* (*Gem.* 39a; *Tos.* ad loc. s.v. תני).

The *halachah* follows R' Eliezer's view that *chadash* is prohibited even outside Eretz Yisrael by Biblical law (*Rav; Rif; Rambam, Commentary* and *Hil. Maachalos Asuros* 10:2; *Rosh; Meiri; Yoreh Deah* 293:2; see *Beur Halachah* to *Orach Chaim* 489:10 s.v. אף בזמן הזה).

Others contend that it is prohibited only outside the Holy Land by Rabbinic law, and, therefore, food which is only suspected of being *chadash* is permitted (*Baal HaTerumos,* cited by *Rosh,* Responsum 2; *Or Zarua* 328; see *Aruch HaShulchan* to *Yoreh Deah* loc. cit. 5).

10.

Having discussed different facets of the commandments, the mishnah now dwells on the subject of their importance.

כָּל הָעוֹשֶׂה מִצְוָה אַחַת — *Whoever fulfills one commandment* —

I.e., one more than his sins, so that his merit outweighs his guilt (*Rav* from *Gem.* 39b). This balance is not weighed by quantity alone, but is rather dependent upon the qualitative importance of his deeds (*Meiri; Rambam, Hil. Teshuvah* 3:2).

The mishnah does not explain that it refers to one good deed more than the number of his sins, because, in reality — as the mishnah states — every commandment which a person fulfills earns him the reward stated. However, it can be negated if his merits are outweighed by his sins (*Maharal*).

If a person overcomes a desire to sin, it is tantamount to actively fulfilling a commandment (*Gem.* 39b).

לוֹ, וּמַאֲרִיכִין לוֹ יָמָיו, וְנוֹחֵל אֶת הָאָרֶץ; וְכָל שֶׁאֵינוֹ עוֹשֶׂה מִצְוָה אַחַת — אֵין מְטִיבִין לוֹ, וְאֵין מַאֲרִיכִין לוֹ יָמָיו, וְאֵינוֹ נוֹחֵל אֶת הָאָרֶץ.

כָּל שֶׁיֶּשְׁנוֹ בַּמִּקְרָא וּבַמִּשְׁנָה וּבְדֶרֶךְ אֶרֶץ — לֹא בִמְהֵרָה הוּא חוֹטֵא, שֶׁנֶּאֱמַר: „וְהַחוּט הַמְשֻׁלָּשׁ לֹא בִמְהֵרָה יִנָּתֵק"; וְכָל שֶׁאֵינוֹ לֹא בַמִּקְרָא וְלֹא בַמִּשְׁנָה וְלֹא בְדֶרֶךְ אֶרֶץ — אֵינוֹ מִן הַיִּשּׁוּב.

ר' עובדיה מברטנורא

מטיבין לו ומאריכין את ימיו. לעולם הבא: **ונוחל את הארץ.** ארץ החיים: **וכל שאינו עושה מצוה אחת.** שהיו עונותיו מרובין מזכיותיו, ואינו עושה מצוה אחת שיהיה מחצה זכאי ומחצה חייב, אלא נשארו עונותיו מרובין: **ולא בדרך ארץ.** שאין משאו ומתנו בנחת עם הבריות: **אינו מן הישוב.** אינו מועיל לישובו של עולם, והוי מושבו מושב לצים, ופסול לעדות:

יד אברהם

מְטִיבִין לוֹ, — *is benefited,*

In the World to Come (*Rav;* see *Pnei Yehoshua* s.v. משנה), which is completely good (*Gem.* loc. cit.). That which the Torah (*Deut.* 11:13*ff.*, et al.) guarantees worldly reward for fulfillment of the commandments and punishment for their transgression is only in reference to the relative merit and guilt of the nation as a whole (*Maharsha, Chidushei Aggados* to 59b s.v. שכר מצוה). The rewards specified for the fulfillment of individual commandments such as honoring one's parents (*Deut.* 5:16) and sending away the mother bird (ibid. 22:7) is also construed as referring to the World to Come (*Gem.* 39b).

Others explain the mishnah as referring to benefits in this world (*Rashi; Rambam Commentary; Meiri; Maharal*) which are bestowed upon the righteous in order to facilitate their service of God and thereby increase their reward in the World to Come (*Rambam, Hil. Teshuvah* 9:1).

Although we often find in this world that the righteous suffer and the wicked prosper, that is in order to enhance the reward of the righteous and increase the punishment of the wicked in the next world (*Meiri* from *Gem.* loc. cit.; *Rashi* ad loc. s.v. מתני'; cf. *Sefer Halkarim* 4:12,13).

The mishnah (*Peah* 1:1) which states that if a person fulfills certain precepts, he earns reward in this world as well as the next — implying that for all other commandments, the reward is limited to the next world — refers to the special capacity of those specific commandments to tip the scales to the side of merit even when they are actually evenly balanced (*Gem.* 39b). This is of greater value than when God tips the scales toward the side of merit (see below), because that which a person earns on his own is greater than receiving a gift (*Tos.* ad loc. s.v. שאם; *Tos. Yom Tov*).

וּמַאֲרִיכִין לוֹ יָמָיו, — *his days are prolonged,*

In the World to Come (*Rav*), which is everlasting (*Gem.* 39b).[1]

1. [According to this interpretation, the dual reward of benefits and prolonged days does not refer to two separate blessings, but to the two outstanding characteristics of the World to Come; its complete goodness and its eternalness.]

1 benefited, his days are prolonged, and he inherits
10 the land; and whoever does not fulfill one commandment is not benefited, his days are not prolonged, and he does not inherit the land.

Whoever is [involved] in the [study of] Scripture and Mishnah and conducts himself properly will not easily sin, as it says (*Ecclesiastes* 4:12): *A three-ply cord is not easily severed;* and whoever is [involved] neither in [the study of] Scripture nor Mishnah and does not conduct himself properly is not part of civilization.

YAD AVRAHAM

Others contend that this, too, refers to a long life in this world (*Rambam Commentary; Meiri; Maharal*), which is also bestowed for the purpose of providing more opportunity to earn eternal reward (*Rambam, Hil. Teshuvah* 9:1).

;וְנוֹחֵל אֶת הָאָרֶץ — *and he inherits the land;*

This refers to the land of the living (*Rav*) — i.e., the World to Come (*Rashi; Rambam Commentary*).

The previously stated rewards, which *Rav* also explains as dealing with the hereafter, refer to that which is done to a righteous person in this world in order to enhance his ultimate reward — e.g., punishment which atones for his sins (*Tos. Yom Tov*).

[Although a person is rewarded for every good deed and punished for every sin (see *Eccl.* 12:14 and ArtScroll commentary ibid.), and so, even if his sins outweigh his merits, he will still be rewarded for every good deed — the difference between one's merit outweighing his guilt and vice versa lies in the manner in which his reward and punishment are given. If his merits are greater, his retribution will be handled in a way which will benefit him as much as possible in the World to Come. One such method is that mentioned by *Tos. Yom Tov* above — he receives the punishment in this world rather than in the next world (see *Rambam, Shaar HaGemul; Derech Hashem* 2:2; *Kochvei Or* 4).]

וְכָל שֶׁאֵינוֹ עוֹשֶׂה מִצְוָה אַחַת — אֵין מְטִיבִין לוֹ, וְאֵין מַאֲרִיכִין לוֹ יָמָיו, וְאֵינוֹ נוֹחֵל אֶת הָאָרֶץ. — *and whoever does not fulfill one commandment is not benefited, his days are not prolonged, and he does not inherit the land.*

This refers to someone whose sins outweigh his merits, and he does not fulfill one commandment to balance them (*Rav; Rambam Commentary*).

If his merit and guilt are equally balanced, God, in His kindness, "tips the scales" in his favor (*Tos. Yom Tov, Maharsha* in *Chidushei Aggados* from *Rosh Hashanah* 17b).

כָּל שֶׁיֶּשְׁנוֹ בַּמִּקְרָא וּבַמִּשְׁנָה וּבְדֶרֶךְ אֶרֶץ — לֹא בִמְהֵרָה הוּא חוֹטֵא, שֶׁנֶּאֱמַר: ,,וְהַחוּט הַמְשֻׁלָּשׁ לֹא בִמְהֵרָה יִנָּתֵק״; — *Whoever is [involved] in [the study of] Scripture and Mishnah and conducts himself properly* (lit., *the way of the land*) *will not easily sin, as it says* (*Ecclesiastes* 4:12): *"A three-ply cord is not easily severed."*

דֶּרֶךְ אֶרֶץ means dealing with others in a pleasant manner (*Rav* s.v. ולא; *Rambam Commentary*).

These three categories represent the basic areas of a Jew's obligations. In Scripture we find the fundamentals of our faith; the Mishnah contains the details of all the laws, and the entire scope of character refinement is included in the realm of pleasant dealings with others (*Tif. Yis.*).

וְכָל שֶׁאֵינוֹ לֹא בַמִּקְרָא וְלֹא בַמִּשְׁנָה וְלֹא בְדֶרֶךְ אֶרֶץ — *Whoever is [involved] neither in [the study of] Scripture nor Mishnah and does not conduct himself properly* —

He does not possess any of these attributes (ibid.).

אֵינוֹ מִן הַיִּשּׁוּב. — *is not part of civilization.*

He is of no value to society (*Rav*); rather, his departure from civilization would be beneficial (*Rambam Commentary*). His company is the company of idlers (*Rav* from *Gem.* 41a), and he is not acceptable as a witness (ibid. from *Gem.* 39b), because he is not careful about his deeds and has no shame (*Rashi* ad loc.).

פרק שני

Chapter Two

[א] **הָאִישׁ** מְקַדֵּשׁ בּוֹ וּבִשְׁלוּחוֹ. הָאִשָּׁה מִתְקַדֶּשֶׁת בָּהּ וּבִשְׁלוּחָהּ. הָאִישׁ מְקַדֵּשׁ אֶת בִּתּוֹ כְּשֶׁהִיא נַעֲרָה, בּוֹ וּבִשְׁלוּחוֹ.

ר׳ עובדיה מברטנורא

פרק שני – האיש מקדש. (א) האיש מקדש בו ובשלוחו. בו תחלה ואחר כך בשלוחו, שמצוה בו יותר מבשלוחו, דכי עסיק גופו במצוה מקבל שכר טפי. וילפינן (מא, ב) שלוחו של אדם כמותו מקרא, דכתיב (שמות יב, ו) ושחטו אותו כל קהל עדת ישראל, וכי כל ישראל שוחטין, אלא מכאן ששלוחו של אדם כמותו: **האיש מקדש את בתו בשהיא נערה.** וכל שכן כשהיא קטנה, והאי דנקט נערה, אורח ארעא אשמועינן, שאסור לאדם לקדש את בתו כשהיא קטנה, עד

יד אברהם

1.

הָאִישׁ מְקַדֵּשׁ — *A man betroths [a woman]*

Having previously (1:1) used the verb נִקְנֵית, *acquired,* which stems from the Biblical term קִנְיָן, *kinyan,* the Mishnah now uses the Rabbinic terminology מְקַדֵּשׁ, *betroths,* from קִדּוּשִׁין, *kiddushin,* which means that she becomes prohibited to the rest of the world like an object of הֶקְדֵּשׁ, *Temple property* (*Gem.* 2b).

בּוֹ — *by himself*

It is preferable that he perform the *kiddushin* himself, because the reward for fulfilling any commandment is increased when one does it himself (*Rav* from *Gem.* 41a).

וּבִשְׁלוּחוֹ. — *or through his agent.*

[An agent can effect *kiddushin* by giving a woman money [or an item of monetary value] or a document, as described in commentary to 1:1 on behalf of another man.]

From the wording of the verse (*Deut.* 24:1), *and he shall send her from his house*, rather than *and he shall divorce her*, we derive that a *get* can be delivered by an agent. From the juxtaposition of the subjects of *kiddushin* and divorce in the verse (ibid. 2), *and she left his house, and she went and was to another man,* we learn that *kiddushin* and divorce are analogous in every way feasible. Therefore, *kiddushin,* too, may be performed through an agent (*Gem.* loc. cit.).

Another source proving that an agent may legally be appointed to act on one's behalf is that which is written regarding the paschal lamb (*Ex.* 12:6) — *And all of the Congregation of Israel shall slaughter it* — despite the fact that the slaughtering of an offering may not be done by more than one person (*Ran* from *Chullin* 29b). It is thus evident that the slaughtering done by one person is attributed to all those on whose behalf he acted, by virtue of his being their agent (*Gem.* 42a).

From this verse we would know that an agent is effective for matters of Temple property; the verse concerning divorce serves as a basis for the validity of an agent in nonsacred matters. Between the two sources, we apply the concept of a legal agent to all areas of Jewish law (*Gem.* 41b).

If the man has never met the woman, it is forbidden for him to marry her through an agent, because she may turn out to be despicable in his eyes (*Tif. Yis.* from *Gem.* 41a). However, if he did so, the *kiddushin* takes effect ex post facto (*Meiri*).

הָאִשָּׁה מִתְקַדֶּשֶׁת בָּהּ — *A woman is betrothed by herself*

The woman, too, should accept *kiddushin* on her behalf, rather than through an agent, in order to perform

1. A man betroths [a woman] by himself or through his agent. A woman is betrothed by herself or through her agent. A man gives his daughter in *kiddushin* when she is a *naarah*, by himself or through his agent.

YAD AVRAHAM

the *mitzvah* personally (*Gem.* loc. cit.).

Although a woman is not included in the commandment of propagation, her part in bringing about its fulfillment by the man also earns her reward. In addition, she is partially included in that precept (*Meiri*) [by virtue of her inclusion in the exhortation (*Isaiah* 45:18), *He created it not a waste; to be inhabited he formed it* (see commentary to *Gittin* 4:5)].

וּבִשְׁלוּחָהּ. — *or through her agent.*

[An agent may receive the *kiddushin* on her behalf.] She is not prohibited to use an agent, even if she has never seen the man, because a woman's desire to be wed is so great that if she sent an agent to accept *kiddushin* on her behalf, it is safe to assume that she will be happy with whoever marries her (*Gem.* 41a).

The legitimacy of an agent accepting *kiddushin* for the woman is based upon the fact that he can accept a *get* on her behalf (see above), which is derived from the extra suffix meaning *her*, in the word (*Deut.* 24:1) וְשִׁלְּחָהּ, *And he shall send her* (*Gem.* ibid.; see General Introduction to *Gittin* and footnote ad loc.).

A separate verse is needed to allow an agent for this purpose, because a *get* [as well as money or a document for *kiddushin*] must be placed in the woman's possession to be effective. Therefore, it is necessary for the Torah to tell us that the agent's receipt of the *get* on the woman's behalf is considered as if she had received it herself (*Pnei Yehoshua* to 41a).

הָאִישׁ מְקַדֵּשׁ אֶת בִּתּוֹ כְּשֶׁהִיא נַעֲרָה, — *A man gives his daughter in kiddushin when she is a naarah,*

A man retains the authority over his daughter with regard to *kiddushin* through the age of *naarus* — i.e., until six months after she reaches the age of twelve years and grows two pubic hairs (*Tif. Yis.*; see 1:2) — and during this period, he can marry her off even against her will (*Meiri*).

Since the money for her *kiddushin* belongs to her father — as is derived from the verse (*Num.* 30:17), *in her naarus, in the house of her father,* which teaches us that all profits of her *naarus* belong to her father — it is clear that his authority is still in force during this period (*Gem.* 3b).

The father can also marry off his daughter when she is a minor; the mishnah specifies *naarus* to indicate that it is initially prohibited to marry off a daughter until she comes of age and can consent to the choice of a husband (*Rav* from *Gem.* 41a).

Although a woman is assumed to prefer marriage to any man rather than remaining single (see above), this applies only when she originally agrees to the marriage; we are not afraid that she will change her mind. However, when the *kiddushin* had been without her consent from the onset, her satisfaction cannot be taken for granted (*Tos.* ad loc. s.v. אסור).

Others contend that even when betrothed without her consent, she will be happy to be married; a minor, however, could be influenced by others to reject her husband, and therefore, she should not be married off before she matures (*Meiri*).

בּוֹ וּבִשְׁלוּחוֹ. — *by himself or through his agent.*

Here, too, it is preferable that the

קידושין
ב/א

הָאוֹמֵר לְאִשָּׁה: ,,הִתְקַדְּשִׁי לִי בִּתְמָרָה זוֹ, הִתְקַדְּשִׁי לִי בְּזוֹ״, אִם יֵשׁ בְּאַחַת מֵהֶן שָׁוֶה פְרוּטָה — מְקֻדֶּשֶׁת; וְאִם לָאו — אֵינָהּ מְקֻדֶּשֶׁת. ,,בְּזוֹ, וּבְזוֹ, וּבְזוֹ״, אִם יֵשׁ שָׁוֶה פְרוּטָה בְּכֻלָּן — מְקֻדֶּשֶׁת; וְאִם לָאו — אֵינָהּ מְקֻדֶּשֶׁת. הָיְתָה אוֹכֶלֶת רִאשׁוֹנָה רִאשׁוֹנָה — אֵינָהּ מְקֻדֶּשֶׁת, עַד שֶׁיְּהֵא בְּאַחַת מֵהֶן שָׁוֶה פְרוּטָה.

ר׳ עובדיה מברטנורא

שתגדיל ותאמר בפלוני אני רוצה: **ואם לאו אינה מקודשת.** דכיון דאמר התקדשי, התקדשי, כל חד הוי קדושין באפי נפשייהו: **עד שיהא באחת מהן שוה פרוטה.** האי אחת מהן לא מיתוקמא אלא באחרונה שבהן, דכי אמר לה התקדשי לי בזו, ובזו, ובזו, והיתה אוכלת אחת אחת, כל אותן שאכלה הוו מלוה גבה, וכי מטיא אחרונה שבה נגמרים הקדושין, אי אית בה שוה פרוטה הוה ליה מקדש במלוה ופרוטה, וקיימא לן (מו, א), המקדש במלוה ופרוטה, דעתה אפרוטה, ומקודשת. אבל אי לית באחרונה שוה פרוטה, אף על גב דאיכא בקמאי שוה פרוטה, כי מטי גמר קדושין הוה ליה מקדש במלוה, והמקדש במלוה אינה מקודשת:

יד אברהם

father marry her off himself, so as to bring about the fulfillment of the commandment of propagation through his own efforts (*Meiri*).

הָאוֹמֵר לְאִשָּׁה: ,,הִתְקַדְּשִׁי לִי בִּתְמָרָה זוֹ, הִתְקַדְּשִׁי לִי בְּזוֹ״, — [*If*] *one says to a woman: "Be betrothed to me with this date; be betrothed to me with this one"* —

He applies the term *kiddushin* for each piece of fruit separately, thus indicating that each one is being given independently to effect *kiddushin* on its own (*Rav*).

אִם יֵשׁ בְּאַחַת מֵהֶן שָׁוֶה פְרוּטָה — מְקֻדֶּשֶׁת; — *if one of them has the value of a perutah, she is betrothed;*

Since he indicated that they are being given for separate acts of *kiddushin*, their value cannot be combined to total a *perutah* (*Meiri*), which is the minimum amount of money acceptable for *kiddushin* according to the prevailing opinion of Beis Hillel (1:1; *Rambam, Hil. Ishus* 3:1). [Therefore, only if one of them is worth a *perutah* by itself is the *kiddushin* valid.]

וְאִם לָאו — אֵינָהּ מְקֻדֶּשֶׁת. — *if not, she is not betrothed.*

However, because of the possibility that the date may be worth a *perutah* elsewhere, in which case the *kiddushin* would be valid, she requires a *get* in order to marry another man (*Rambam* ibid., 5:26 from *Gem.* 12a; see commentary to 1:1 s.v. ובית הלל).

,,בְּזוֹ, וּבְזוֹ, וּבְזוֹ״, — [*If he says:*] *"With this, and with this, and with this"* —

[He said: "Be betrothed to me with this and with this," without using the term *kiddushin* for each one separately.] Even if he did not use the word *and*, but simply said, "With this, with this," the ruling stated below would apply (*Meiri*).

If he said: "With this and also with this," or he identified different items

2
1 [If] one says to a woman: "Be betrothed to me with this date; be betrothed to me with this one" — if one of them has the value of a *perutah,* she is betrothed; if not, she is not betrothed.

[If he says:] "With this, and with this, and with this" — if there is the value of a *perutah* in all of them — she is betrothed; if not, she is not betrothed. [If] she was eating [them] one by one, she is not betrothed, unless one of them has the value of a *perutah.*

YAD AVRAHAM

— e.g., "With a pomegranate, with a nut" — the same would apply (ibid. from 47a).

אִם יֵשׁ שָׁוֶה פְרוּטָה בְּכֻלָּן — מְקֻדֶּשֶׁת; וְאִם לָאו — אֵינָהּ מְקֻדֶּשֶׁת. — *if there is the value of a perutah in all of them, she is betrothed; if not, she is not betrothed.*

The separate items are assessed; if their total value is a *perutah* or more, the *kiddushin* is valid (*Meiri*).

This is the opinion of R' Shimon, who maintains that when a person lists several items, his intention is construed as being that they should be combined together, unless he explicitly separates them (*Gem.* 46a). Other *Tannaim* hold that even if he did not mention *kiddushin* with regard to each item, he is understood to mean each one separately (see *Gem.* 44a). [Therefore, at least one of them must be worth a *perutah* by itself in order for the *kiddushin* to take effect.]

הָיְתָה אוֹכֶלֶת רִאשׁוֹנָה רִאשׁוֹנָה — *[If] she was eating [them] one by one,*

He handed her each of the dates, indicating that it was being given for the purpose of *kiddushin,* and she consumed it before receiving the next one (*Meiri*).

אֵינָהּ מְקֻדֶּשֶׁת, — *she is not betrothed,*

Even though he did not apply the word *kiddushin* to each date separately (*Gem.* loc. cit.).

עַד שֶׁיְּהֵא בְּאַחַת מֵהֶן שָׁוֶה פְּרוּטָה. — *unless one of them has the value of a perutah.*

If the last one which he gave her is valued at a *perutah,* the *kiddushin* is valid. However, if one of those given earlier was worth a *perutah,* but the last one was not, the *kiddushin* does not take effect. This is because she became indebted to him for the value of the date when she consumed it, before he finished the act of *kiddushin* — i.e., the giving of all the dates.[1] Therefore, when the *kiddushin* is to take place, it is not the date itself which is being used to effect it — since that is no longer extant — but the annulment of the debt which was caused by its consumption, and the annulment of a debt is not acceptable for *kiddushin* (*Rav* from *Gem.* 46a).

However, when the last fruit is worth a *perutah,* the *kiddushin* is valid, because the date was not yet consumed when the *kiddushin* took effect.

1. This is due to the fact that when someone gives money for the sake of *kiddushin* he is giving it only for that purpose, and if the *kiddushin* is invalidated, the money must be returned. Therefore, as long as the *kiddushin* has not taken effect, she has no rights to the date, and if she ate it, she must reimburse him for its value (*Gem.* 46b; *Rashi* ad loc.).

[ב] „הִתְקַדְּשִׁי לִי בְּכוֹס זֶה שֶׁל יַיִן", וְנִמְצָא שֶׁל דְּבַשׁ; „שֶׁל דְּבַשׁ", וְנִמְצָא שֶׁל יַיִן; „בְּדִינָר זֶה שֶׁל כֶּסֶף", וְנִמְצָא שֶׁל זָהָב; „שֶׁל זָהָב", וְנִמְצָא שֶׁל כֶּסֶף; „עַל מְנָת שֶׁאֲנִי עָשִׁיר", וְנִמְצָא עָנִי; „עָנִי", וְנִמְצָא עָשִׁיר — אֵינָהּ מְקֻדֶּשֶׁת. רַבִּי שִׁמְעוֹן אוֹמֵר: אִם הִטְעָהּ לְשֶׁבַח — מְקֻדֶּשֶׁת.

ר' עובדיה מברטנורא

(ב) **של זהב ונמצא של כסף כו'.** דאיכא דניחא לה בהא, ואיכא דניחא לה בהא: **רבי שמעון אומר אם הטעה לשבח הרי זו מקודשת.** לא פליג רבי שמעון אלא על שבח דממון, דמסתמא דניחא לה בההוא שבח. אבל על שבח דיוחסין, כגון לוי ונמצא כהן, מודה רבי שמעון דאפילו הטעתו, או הטעה הוא אותה לשבח, אינה מקודשת, דלא ניחא לה בשבחו, מפני שמתגאה עליה. ואין הלכה כרבי שמעון:

יד אברהם

[Although he is also offering her the annulment of the debts she incurred by having eaten the other dates, and if that is the basis of her acceptance, the *kiddushin* is not valid] we assume that her consent is based primarily upon the new gift to her (ibid.).

If he said, "Be betrothed to me with these," and handed them to her one at a time, even if she consumed each date before receiving the next one, the *kiddushin* is valid. Since he already finished his declaration that he is giving them to her for *kiddushin*, she acquires each one for that purpose as soon as she receives it, and no debt is incurred (*Gem.* 47a; see *Tos. R' Akiva*).

There is another opinion that this last statement of the mishnah refers to the first case, in which he identified each date as the basis for a separate *kiddushin* by using the word *kiddushin* for each one. The mishnah tells us that although she benefited from them immediately by eating them, they are still not valid for *kiddushin* unless one of them is worth a *perutah* by itself (*Gem.* 46a; *Tos.* ad loc. s.v. אימא).

2.

[The next two mishnayos deal with the case of a man who betrothed a woman under false pretenses, because *kiddushin* requires the consent of the woman in order to be valid (1:1), if her consent was due to a misconception, the *kiddushin* is void.]

„הִתְקַדְּשִׁי לִי בְּכוֹס זֶה שֶׁל יַיִן", — [*If a man said to a woman:*] *"Be betrothed to me with this cup of wine,"*

She accepted it on the assumption that it was wine, since this occurred at night when she could not see (*Meiri*), or when the cup was covered up (*Even HaEzer* 38:24). If she could clearly see that it was honey, and she accepted it nonetheless, the *kiddushin* is valid (*Meiri; Teshuvos HaRashba* 1186). Nevertheless, he should perform the act of *kiddushin* again since there is no clear source for this ruling (*Teshuvos HaRashba* ad loc.).

וְנִמְצָא שֶׁל דְּבַשׁ; — *and it was found to*

2. [If a man said to a woman:] "Be betrothed to me with this cup of wine," and it was found to be of honey; [or] "of honey," and it was found to be of wine; "with this dinar of silver," and it was found to be of gold; [or] "of gold," and it was found to be of silver; "on condition that I am a rich man," and he was found to be a poor man; [or] "a poor man," and he was found to be a rich man — she is not betrothed. R' Shimon say: If he deceived her to [her] advantage, she is betrothed.

YAD AVRAHAM

be of honey;

Although honey is more valuable than wine, she might interested in obtaining only wine (*Meiri*).

,,שֶׁל דְּבַשׁ", וְנִמְצָא שֶׁל יַיִן; — [or] *"of honey," and it was found to be of wine;*

[He said that it was filled with honey, but actually, it contained wine, which is worth less than honey.]

,,בְּדִינָר זֶה שֶׁל כֶּסֶף", וְנִמְצָא שֶׁל זָהָב; — *"with this dinar of silver," and it was found to be of gold;*

[He described the coin he gave her as being of silver, but it was actually gold] and it is possible that she requires silver for some purpose (*Tos. Yom Tov* from *Rambam Commentary*) — e.g., she needs it to complete a silver adornment (*Tos.* 48b s.v. איכא).

,,שֶׁל זָהָב", וְנִמְצָא שֶׁל כֶּסֶף; — [or] *"of gold," and it was found to be of silver;*

[Which is of less value than gold.]

,,עַל מְנָת שֶׁאֲנִי עָשִׁיר", וְנִמְצָא עָנִי; — *"on condition that I am a rich man," and he was found to be a poor man;*

[He stipulated the *kiddushin* on the fact that he was rich, but actually, he was poor.]

,,עָנִי," וְנִמְצָא עָשִׁיר — — [or] *"a poor man," and he was found to be a rich man —*

She might not want a rich husband, because he will be busy with his possessions (*Yerushalmi* to 2:3, cited by *Rosh* to *Gem.* 49a). Alternatively, she may want a stronger position in her marriage than she could attain if she married a rich man (*Meiri*).

אֵינָהּ מְקֻדֶּשֶׁת. — *she is not betrothed.*

Any time the circumstances are different from that which was claimed by the man, the *kiddushin* is not valid (*Meiri*) [because her consent — which is necessary for the validity of the *kiddushin* — was based on a false assumption].

However, if he stated that he was performing *kiddushin* with one coin and he gave her two, there is no conceivable reason for her to object, and the *kiddushin* is valid (*Beis Shmuel, Even HaEzer* 38:45).

רַבִּי שִׁמְעוֹן אוֹמֵר: אִם הִטְעָהּ לְשֶׁבַח מְקֻדֶּשֶׁת. — *R' Shimon says: If he deceived her to [her] advantage, she is betrothed.*

This refers to a case in which she sent an agent to accept *kiddushin* on her behalf and told him that the man had said he would betroth her with silver. If he gave the agent gold instead, R' Shimon maintains that the *kiddushin* is valid, because she did not mean to rule out gold, but only

קידושין [ג] ,,עַל מְנָת שֶׁאֲנִי כֹהֵן", וְנִמְצָא לֵוִי; ,,לֵוִי",
ב/ג וְנִמְצָא כֹהֵן; ,,נָתִין", וְנִמְצָא מַמְזֵר;
,,מַמְזֵר", וְנִמְצָא נָתִין; ,,בֶּן עִיר", וְנִמְצָא בֶּן כְּרַךְ;
,,בֶּן כְּרַךְ", וְנִמְצָא בֶּן עִיר; ,,עַל מְנָת שֶׁבֵּיתִי קָרוֹב
לַמֶּרְחָץ", וְנִמְצָא רָחוֹק; ,,רָחוֹק", וְנִמְצָא קָרוֹב;
,,עַל מְנָת שֶׁיֶּשׁ לִי בַת", אוֹ ,,שִׁפְחָה גַּדֶּלֶת",

ר' עובדיה מברטנורא

(ג) **שפחה גודלת.** קולעת שער הנשים. פירוש אחר, דברנית ובעלת לשון, כמו שנאמר (יחזקאל לה, יג) ותגדילו עלי בפיכם:

יד אברהם

false, the *kiddushin* is not valid notwithstanding that the truth is to her advantage (ibid.).

If the issue was one of stature rather than value — e.g., he claimed to be a *Levi* and turned out to be a *Kohen* — even R' Shimon agrees that we assume she is insistent upon his being a *Levi.* This is because she may prefer a mate who is appropriate to her station in life (*Gem.* 49a) so that he should not feel superior to her (*Rashi* ad loc. s.v. אבל בשבח יוחסין).

to indicate that even silver was acceptable to her. This is in dispute with the first, anonymous *Tanna* in the mishnah, who maintains that even in such a case we assume that the woman insists upon receiving silver, as she stated, and gold is therefore not valid (*Gem.* 48b).

However, if she accepted *kiddushin* directly from the man, R' Shimon agrees that if the claims he made are

3.

,,עַל מְנָת שֶׁאֲנִי כֹהֵן", — *"[Be betrothed to me] on condition that I am a Kohen,"*

[A man betrothed a woman and stipulated that it be valid only if he is a *Kohen.*]

וְנִמְצָא לֵוִי, — *and he was found [to be] a Levi;*

[Which is of less stature than a *Kohen* and thus not as appealing to the woman.]

,,לֵוִי," וְנִמְצָא כֹהֵן; — *[or] "a Levi," and he was found [to be] a Kohen;*

[He stipulated that the *kiddushin* is valid only if he is a *Levi,* and it turned out that he was a *Kohen.*] The woman may consider herself inappropriate for someone of such stature (*Gem.* 49a; see mishnah 2). Alternatively, she may not want a husband who bears the burden of the priesthood (*Yerushalmi,* cited by *Rosh* to *Gem.* 49a).

,,נָתִין", — *"a Nesinite,"*

[He stipulated that the *kiddushin* be valid if he was a Nesinite.]

A Nesinite is a descendant of the Gibeonites whom Joshua converted to Judaism (see commentary to 4:1 s.v. גֵּרֵי, and to *Yevamos* 2:4). The term נָתִין literally means *appointed one.* They were given this name because Joshua appointed them to be woodcutters and water carriers for sacrificial purposes (*Josh.* 9:27). It is forbidden for a legitimate Jew to marry a Nesinite, but such a marriage takes effect ex post facto (3:12).

וְנִמְצָא מַמְזֵר; — *and he was found [to be] a mamzer;*

2
3

3. "[Be betrothed to me] on condition that I am a *Kohen*," and he was found [to be] a *Levi;* [or] "a *Levi*," and he was found [to be] a *Kohen;* "a Nesinite," and he was found [to be] a *mamzer;* [or] "a *mamzer*," and he was found [to be] a Nesinite; "a townsman," and he was found [to be] a city dweller; [or] 'a city dweller," and he was found [to be] a townsman; "on condition that my house is close to the bathhouse," and it was found [to be] distant; [or] "distant," and it was found [to be] close; "on condition that I have a daughter," or "a slave who makes braids,"

YAD AVRAHAM

A *mamzer* is the product of the illicit relations of two people between whom *kiddushin* cannot take effect because of their prohibition to each other (3:12). A *mamzer* may only marry another *mamzer*, a convert, or a freed slave (*Even HaEzer* 4:22,24); nevertheless, if one does marry a legitimate Jew, the marriage takes effect ex post facto (3:12).

A *mamzer* is of higher stature than a Nesinite, because he comes from fully legitimate Jews (*Meiri*). Nevertheless, a woman may prefer a Nesinite because he will be less likely to feel superior to her (ibid. from *Gem.* 49a).

„מַמְזֵר", וְנִמְצָא נָתִין; — [*or*] "*a mamzer*," *and he was found* [*to be*] *a Nesinite;*

[She may not be willing to marry someone of that lineage.]

„בֶּן עִיר", וְנִמְצָא בֶּן כְּרַךְ, — "*a townsman*," *and he was found* [*to be*] *a city dweller,*

He betrothed her on condition that he was a townsman, and it turned out that he lived in a city, which is crowded and busy, and prices therein are expensive (*Rashi*).

„בֶּן כְּרַךְ", וְנִמְצָא בֶּן עִיר; — [*or*] "*a city dweller*," *and he was found to be a townsman;*

He lived in a town, where commodities are not as easily available as in a city (*Kesubos* 110b; see ArtScroll commentary ibid. 13:10).

„עַל מְנָת שֶׁבֵּיתִי קָרוֹב לַמֶּרְחָץ", וְנִמְצָא רָחוֹק; — '*on condition that my house is close to the bathhouse*," *and it was found* [*to be*] *distant,*

[He stipulated that the *kiddushin* is valid only if he lives near a bathhouse, and it turned out that he did not, which is an inconvenience.]

„רָחוֹק", וְנִמְצָא קָרוֹב; — [*or*] "*distant*," *and it was found* [*to be*] *close;*

Although he deceived her to her advantage, she may prefer living farther from the bathhouse (*Meiri*) [e.g., for the sake of privacy].

„עַל מְנָת שֶׁיֵּשׁ לִי בַת", — "*on condition that I have a daughter*,"

Who can help with the housework (*Meiri*).

אוֹ „שִׁפְחָה גַּדֶּלֶת", — *or* "*a slave who makes braids*,"

She is trained in this or any other

וְאֵין לוֹ; אוֹ „עַל מְנָת שֶׁאֵין לִי", וְיֵשׁ לוֹ; „עַל מְנָת שֶׁאֵין לִי בָּנִים", וְיֵשׁ לוֹ; אוֹ „עַל מְנָת שֶׁיֵּשׁ לִי", וְאֵין לוֹ; וּבְכֻלָּם, אַף עַל פִּי שֶׁאָמְרָה: „בְּלִבִּי הָיָה לְהִתְקַדֵּשׁ לוֹ אַף עַל פִּי כֵן" — אֵינָהּ מְקֻדֶּשֶׁת. וְכֵן הִיא שֶׁהִטְעַתּוּ.

[ד] **הָאוֹמֵר** לִשְׁלוּחוֹ: „צֵא וְקַדֵּשׁ לִי אִשָּׁה פְּלוֹנִית בְּמָקוֹם פְּלוֹנִי", וְהָלַךְ וְקִדְּשָׁהּ בְּמָקוֹם אַחֵר — אֵינָהּ מְקֻדֶּשֶׁת. „הֲרֵי

ר׳ עובדיה מברטנורא

אף על פי שאמרה בלבי היה להתקדש בו׳. דדברים שבלב אינם דברים: (ד) **והלך וקדשה במקום אחר בו׳.** דמראה מקום הוא לו, ואין זה תנאי:

יד אברהם

trade (*Meiri*) [and is therefore an asset].

This interpretation assumes that גַּדֶּלֶת comes from the word גְּדִיל, *braid* (*Rav; Tos.* 49a s.v. מאי). Others contend that it comes from the word גָּדוֹל, *large*, and refers to the fact that she is an older girl who can be of help (*Gem.* ad loc.) or to the fact that she has great status [and is thus an honored possession] (*Gem.* ibid.; *Rashi*). Another opinion is that it refers to the verse (*Ezekiel* 35:13): וַתַּגְדִּילוּ עָלַי בְּפִיכֶם, *And you have magnified yourselves against Me with your mouths*, and means that she is talkative [and thus, good company] (*Rav*).

וְאֵין לוֹ; — *and he does not;*

[And the condition to the *kiddushin* was thus negated.]

אוֹ „עַל מְנָת שֶׁאֵין לִי", וְיֵשׁ לוֹ; — *or "on condition that I do not have," and he has;*

The woman may not want an older girl in the house who will prevent her from running the household in her own way (*Meiri*). Nor does she want a slave who has a trade and will gossip about matters of their home to her customers (*Tos.* 49a, loc. cit.).

Each of the other interpretations regarding the slave also includes a negative facet. If she is grown up, she may hinder the running of the household, just like an older daughter (*Meiri*). If she is of stature, she may feel comfortable with the neighbors to the point that she will gossip with them about the home (*Rashi* 49a, s.v. לא ניחא לי). [The undesirability of a garrulous slave is obvious.]

„עַל מְנָת שֶׁאֵין לִי בָּנִים", וְיֵשׁ לוֹ; — *"on condition that I have no sons," and he does have;*

[The man claimed to have no sons, but actually had. This could be undesirable to the woman for a number of reasons — e.g., she fears they will not accept he and will hinder her relationship with her husband.]

אוֹ „עַל מְנָת שֶׁיֵּשׁ לִי," וְאֵין לוֹ; — *or "on condition that I have," and he does not —*

[She may be relying on the assistance which would be suitable from such sons.]

וּבְכֻלָּם, אַף עַל פִּי שֶׁאָמְרָה: „בְּלִבִּי הָיָה לְהִתְקַדֵּשׁ לוֹ אַף עַל פִּי כֵן", — *in all these cases, although she said: "I intended* (lit., *it was in my heart*) *to be betrothed*

2
4 and he does not; or "on condition that I do not have," and he has; "on condition that I have no sons," and he does have; or "on condition that I have," and he does not; in all these cases, although she said: "I intended to be betrothed to him nonetheless," she is not betrothed. The same [applies if] she deceived him.

4. [If] one says to his agent: "Go out and betroth So-and-so for me in such and such a place," and he went and betrothed her in a different place, she is not betrothed. [If he said:] "She is

YAD AVRAHAM

to him nonetheless" —

I.e., even if his stated condition is untrue [she still wants the *kiddushin* to take effect] (*Rashi*).

.אֵינָהּ מְקֻדֶּשֶׁת — *she is not betrothed.*

Because intentions that are not stated explicitly have no effect in Jewish law (*Rav* from *Gem.* 49b).

However, if at the time of *kiddushin*, she declared explicitly that she accepts it whether or not the stated condition is true, it is valid (*Meiri*).

The rule that unstated intentions have no effect does not apply in a case in which it is self-evident that those intentions exist. This is the reason for the statement of the *Gemara* (*Bava Basra* 132a) that if someone, after hearing that his son had died, gave his possessions to another, and it was subsequently discovered that the son was alive, the gift is void because it is obvious that he gave it to him because he thought his son was dead (*Meiri* to 49b).

.וְכֵן הִיא שֶׁהִטְעַתּוּ — *The same [applies if] she deceived him.*

The same rule is applicable if a man betrothed a woman on condition that her claim about herself was true, and it turned out to be otherwise — the *kiddushin* is void even if he says that he intended to betroth her in any case (*Meiri*).

Others contend that in such a case, the condition would be an explicit stipulation to the *kiddushin*, and thus not analogous to the cases listed above in which her intention that his claim be a condition to the betrothal is only assumed. Therefore, they construe this last case of the mishnah as one in which she told him to betroth her on condition that her claim was true [but he betrothed her without mentioning the stipulation] (*Haflaah, Kuntres Acharon* 38:24) [in which case we assume that his intention was in accordance with his instructions, and the claim must prove true for the *kiddushin* to be binding].

4.

הָאוֹמֵר לִשְׁלוּחוֹ: ,,צֵא וְקַדֵּשׁ לִי אִשָּׁה פְּלוֹנִית בְּמָקוֹם פְּלוֹנִי״, וְהָלַךְ וְקִדְּשָׁהּ בְּמָקוֹם אַחֵר, — *[If] one says to his agent: "Go out and betroth So-and-so for me in such-and-such a place," and he went and betrothed her in a different place,*

The agent went against his sender's instructions and betrothed her elsewhere (*Tos. Yom Tov* to 3:1).

.אֵינָהּ מְקֻדֶּשֶׁת — *she is not betrothed.*

Because we assume that the man desired that the *kiddushin* be per-

הִיא בְּמָקוֹם פְּלוֹנִי״, וְקִדְּשָׁהּ בְּמָקוֹם אַחֵר — הֲרֵי זוֹ מְקֻדֶּשֶׁת.

[ה] **הַמְקַדֵּשׁ** אֶת הָאִשָּׁה עַל מְנָת שֶׁאֵין עָלֶיהָ נְדָרִים, וְנִמְצְאוּ עָלֶיהָ נְדָרִים — אֵינָהּ מְקֻדֶּשֶׁת. כְּנָסָהּ סְתָם, וְנִמְצְאוּ עָלֶיהָ נְדָרִים — תֵּצֵא שֶׁלֹּא בִכְתֻבָּה. עַל מְנָת שֶׁאֵין בָּהּ מוּמִין, וְנִמְצְאוּ בָהּ מוּמִין

ר׳ עובדיה מברטנורא

(ה) **תצא שלא בכתובה.** דאמר אי אפשי באשה נדרנית, אבל גיטא בעיא מספק כיון דלא פירש, דלמא דעתיה נמי אנדרנית:

יד אברהם

formed specifically in that place, since he has friends there who will speak well of him if she inquires about his character (*Gem.* 50a) [and an act of *kiddushin* performed by one's agent in violation of his instructions is not valid, since he is not authorized to perform the betrothal under those circumstancse].

״הֲרֵי הִיא בְּמָקוֹם פְּלוֹנִי״, וְקִדְּשָׁהּ בְּמָקוֹם אַחֵר — [*If he said:*] *"She is in such and such a place," and he betrothed her in a different place,*

[The man told the agent that the woman is to be found in a certain place, and the agent encountered her elsewhere and performed the *kiddushin* on behalf of the sender in that place.]

הֲרֵי זוֹ מְקֻדֶּשֶׁת. — *she is betrothed.*

Because he only meant to inform the agent of her whereabouts, not to insist upon a specific location where the *kiddushin* must take place (*Rav*).

Both of these rulings also apply when a woman sends an agent to accept *kiddushin* on her behalf (*Meiri*).

5.

This mishnah is also found in *Kesubos* 7:7, and the commentators there expound it at length. It is repeated here because of the cases in which the *kiddushin* is void; those discussing the husband's exemption from paying the *kesubah* are mentioned incidentally (*Gem.* 50a).

הַמְקַדֵּשׁ אֶת הָאִשָּׁה עַל מְנָת שֶׁאֵין עָלֶיהָ נְדָרִים, וְנִמְצְאוּ עָלֶיהָ נְדָרִים — [*If*] *one betroths a woman on condition that she is not under any vows* (lit., *there are no vows on her*), *and it is found that she is under vows,*

This refers to vows to which people generally object, such as those obligating abstinence from eating meat, drinking wine, or wearing colored dresses. Abstaining from such pleasures constitutes self-denial, and she will become repugnant to her husband (*Rav* to *Kesubos* 7:7 from *Gem.* ibid. 72b).

As a rule, only such vows, which

in such and such a place," and he betrothed her in a different place, she is betrothed.

5. [If] one betroths a woman on condition that she is not under any vows, and it is found that she is under vows, she is not betrothed. [If] he married her without making any stipulations, and it is found that she is under vows, she may be divorced without a *kesubah.*

[If he betrothed her] on condition that she has no [bodily] defects, and [such] defects were found

YAD AVRAHAM

involve self-denial, are considered objectionable, and not others. Since he did not specify which vows he meant, we assume that he referred only to these. Should he stipulate that he objects to a particular vow other than these, the same ruling applies (*Tos.* ad loc. s.v. ומידי).

Rif rules that all other vows besides those enumerated above are not considered objectionable even if they involve self-denial, unless the husband specifically stated his disapproval of them (*Tos. R' Akiva* loc. cit.).

.אֵינָהּ מְקֻדֶּשֶׁת — *she is not betrothed.*

The betrothal is retroactively invalidated; therefore, she requires no divorce and may marry someone else (*Rashba, Ran* ibid.).

Others — based on *Yerushalmi* — rule that she may not remarry without first receiving a divorce from her first husband, because of the possibility that she may go to a sage, who will retroactively annul her vows (see *Kesubos* 74b), thereby validating her first *kiddushin* once again (*Rabbeinu Yerucham*).

.כְּנָסָהּ סְתָם, וְנִמְצְאוּ עָלֶיהָ נְדָרִים — תֵּצֵא שֶׁלֹּא בִכְתֻבָּה — *[If] he married her without making any stipulations, and it is found that she is under vows, she may be divorced without a kesubah.*

This is a continuation of the first part of the mishnah: If he had betrothed her on condition that she is not under any vows and subsequently married her without making such a stipulation — which may have been an indication that he had waived the condition — he may nevertheless divorce her without a *kesubah.* This is because — in pecuniary matters — the burden of proof always lies on the one who seeks to exact money from the other. Therefore, in order for her to collect her *kesubah,* she would have to prove that he had waived the condition, which is impossible to do in our case. She does, however, require a divorce, because of the possibility that he had indeed waived his condition, in which case the *erusin* and marriage were valid. Since this involves a possible prohibition — her marrying someone else while still being married to the first man — we follow the more stringent alternative and require a divorce from the first man (*Tos. Yom Tov* to *Kesubos* 7:7 from ibid. 72b).

.עַל מְנָת שֶׁאֵין בָּהּ מוּמִין, וְנִמְצְאוּ בָהּ מוּמִין, אֵינָהּ מְקֻדֶּשֶׁת — *[If he betrothed her] on condition that she has no [bodily]*

— אֵינָהּ מְקֻדֶּשֶׁת. כְּנָסָהּ סְתָם, וְנִמְצְאוּ בָהּ מוּמִין — תֵּצֵא שֶׁלֹּא בִכְתֻבָּה. כָּל הַמּוּמִין הַפּוֹסְלִים בְּכֹהֲנִים — פּוֹסְלִים בְּנָשִׁים.

[ו] **הַמְקַדֵּשׁ** שְׁתֵּי נָשִׁים בְּשָׁוֶה פְרוּטָה, אוֹ אִשָּׁה אַחַת בְּפָחוֹת מִשָּׁוֶה פְרוּטָה, אַף עַל פִּי שֶׁשָּׁלַח סִבְלוֹנוֹת לְאַחַר מִכָּאן

ר' עובדיה מברטנורא

הפוסלים בכהנים. מפורש בכתובות (דף עה, א): (ו) **סבלונות.** דורונות שדרך חתן לשלוח לארוסתו:

יד אברהם

defects were found upon her, she may be divorced without a kesubah.

This is true even if he had betrothed her on the condition that she has no bodily defects (*Tif. Yis.* ibid.; see above).

[Just as in the first part of the mishnah, although she cannot collect her *kesubah*, she requires a divorce.]

The *Tanna* did not combine the cases of vows and bodily defects in one sentence, but chose to state each case separately. *Tiferes Yisrael* (ibid.) theorizes that he did so because of the halachic difference between the two cases. The *Gemara* (ibid. 74b) tells us that in the case of vows, if she consulted a sage who retroactively annulled her vows before her husband was even aware of them, the betrothal is valid, since it is as if the vow never existed. In the case of bodily defects, however, if she visited a physician who cured them even before the husband became aware of them, the *erusin* is nevertheless invalid, since the defects were in existence at the time of the *kiddushin.*

כָּל הַמּוּמִין הַפּוֹסְלִים בְּכֹהֲנִים — *All [bodily] defects that disqualify Kohanim*

defects, and [such] defects were found upon her, she is not betrothed.

[If she had one of the defects described below, the *kiddushin* is retroactively nullified.]

This stipulation is, in fact, superfluous, since the same applies even if he makes no such stipulation, as evidenced by the ruling in *Kesubos* 5:3 (see ArtScroll commentary there) that a daughter of a non-*Kohen* betrothed to a *Kohen* may not eat *terumah*, lest he discover a bodily defect upon her that will invalidate the betrothal. The mishnah states this only to teach us that even if he made such a condition at the time of betrothal, if he proceeds to marry without any stipulation, and such defects were found on her, she requires a divorce (*Tos.* ibid. 72b, s.v. על מנת).

Tosafos conclude, however, that if he betrothed her without stipulating, she requires a divorce by Rabbinic enactment — or perhaps even by Biblical law — because of the possibility [that he would have betrothed her even if he would have been aware of the defects] (*Tos. Chadashim* ibid. 7:7).

כְּנָסָהּ סְתָם, וְנִמְצְאוּ בָהּ מוּמִין — תֵּצֵא שֶׁלֹּא בִכְתֻבָּה. — *[If] he married her without making any stipulations, and [bodily]*

upon her, she is not betrothed. [If] he married her without making any stipulations, and [bodily] defects were found upon her, she may be divorced without a *kesubah*. All [bodily] defects that disqualify *Kohanim*, [also] disqualify women.

6. [If] one betroths two women with the value of a *perutah* or one woman with less than the value of a *perutah* — even though he sent gifts afterwards

YAD AVRAHAM

These are enumerated in *Bechoros* Chapter 7 (*Rav* loc. cit.). [They disqualify a *Kohen* from participating in the sacrificial service in the Temple, based on *Leviticus* 21:16-24; e.g,. if his eyes are unusually low or high on the face.]

.פּוֹסְלִים בַּנָּשִׁים — [*also*] *disqualify women.*

[If found on a woman, her betrothal is void.] The *Gemara* also adds the following other bodily defects of a woman that would invalidate her *erusin*, although they do not disqualify a *Kohen*: excessive perspiration; bad breath, or a vile odor from another part of the body; a harsh voice, different from that of other women; a dog bite that healed and formed a scar; and breasts that are a handbreadth larger than usual or have a handbreadth of space between them. Also included is a mole on her forehead which is covered when she wears a hat; one that is always exposed is not in this category, however, since he certainly saw it and accepted it (*Rav* ibid. from *Gem.* ibid. 75a).

6.

The *halachah* follows the view of Beis Hillel (1:1) that if a man wishes to betroth a woman by giving her money, he must give her at least a *perutah* or an item worth that much (*Rambam, Hil. Ishus* 3:1).

,הַמְקַדֵּשׁ שְׁתֵּי נָשִׁים בְּשָׁוֶה פְרוּטָה — [*If*] *one betroths two women with the value of a perutah*

[A man betrothed two women simultaneously,[1] but gave something which was worth one *perutah* to cover both betrothals — each of which requires a *perutah* to be valid (see 1:1).]

,אוֹ אִשָּׁה אַחַת בְּפָחוֹת מִשָּׁוֶה פְרוּטָה — *or one woman with less than the value of a perutah —*

The invalidity of the *kiddushin* is even more obvious than that of the previous case, since he did not give the value of a *perutah* at all (*Gem.* 50b).

אַף עַל פִּי שֶׁשָּׁלַח סִבְלוֹנוֹת לְאַחַר מִכָּאן — *— even though he sent gifts afterwards —*

He sent the type of gifts which are customary for a groom to send his

1. [According to a Biblical law, a man may be married to more than one wife at the same time. The *cherem* (ban) on bigamy was instituted by Rabbeinu Gershom Meor Hagolah in the 11th century and was adopted by Ashkenazic, but not Sephardic, communities.]

קידושין — אֵינָהּ מְקֻדֶּשֶׁת, שֶׁמֵּחֲמַת קִדּוּשִׁין הָרִאשׁוֹנִים שָׁלַח. וְכֵן קָטָן שֶׁקִּדֵּשׁ.

[ז] **הַמְקַדֵּשׁ** אִשָּׁה וּבִתָּהּ, אוֹ אִשָּׁה וַאֲחוֹתָהּ כְּאַחַת — אֵינָן מְקֻדָּשׁוֹת. וּמַעֲשֶׂה

ר' עובדיה מברטנורא

אינה מקודשת. ולא אמרינן יודע היה שאין קדושיו קדושין, וגמר ושלח סבלונות לשם קדושין, אלא אמרינן, מחמת קדושין הראשונים שלח: **ובן קטן שקידש.** ושלח סבלונות משהגדיל: **(ז) אינן מקודשות.** דאמר קרא (ויקרא יח, יח) ואשה אל אחותה לא תקח לצרור, בשעה שנעשו צרות זו לזו, אין לך לקוחין אפילו באחת מהן. והוא הדין לכל שאר עריות שיש בהן כרת, שאין קדושין תופסין בהם:

יד אברהם

bride (*Rav*), in the presence of witnesses, without specifying explicitly that they were sent as gifts and not for *kiddushin* (*Meiri*).

The word סִבְלוֹנוֹת comes from the word סַבָּל, *one who bears a burden,* since they are carried from the groom to the bride (*Rambam Commentary*).

,אֵינָהּ מְקֻדֶּשֶׁת — *she is not betrothed,*

We assume that he did not realize that the original *kiddushin* was invalid and therefore, did not send those gifts for the sake of a second attempt at effecting *kiddushin* (*Rav*).

.שֶׁמֵּחֲמַת קִדּוּשִׁין הָרִאשׁוֹנִים שָׁלַח — *because he sent* [*them*] *on account of the original kiddushin.*

[We assume that he was still relying on the validity of the first *kiddushin* and was sending her the customary gifts of a groom to his bride.]

Although he is undoubtedly aware of the possibility that his *kiddushin* is not valid, he continues to rely upon his original assumption, and sends gifts, because there is no harm done even if they are not betrothed (*Ran*). However, if he has relations with her, it is understood that he means to perform a second act of *kiddushin,* because a man would not allow his intimacy to be illicit (*Rif, Meiri* from *Kesubos* 74b), and even the possibility thereof is sufficient motivation to induce him to designate his act of intimacy for the purpose of *kiddushin* (*Ran*).

.וְכֵן קָטָן שֶׁקִּדֵּשׁ — *The same* [*applies to*] *a minor who betrothed.*

Although it is even more well known that the *kiddushin* of a minor is void (*Gem.* 50b), if he sends the customary gifts to the woman after he comes of age, we do not assume that he intends them to serve as *kiddushin,* but rather that he has maintained his misconception that the original *kiddushin* was valid (*Tif. Yis.*).

The mishnah cites this case separately from the other two, because in the previous cases she requires a *get* before marrying again, since the article which was given for *kiddushin* may have sufficient value elsewhere, thereby rendering the *kiddushin* valid (*Tos. R' Akiva;* see commentary to 1:1 s.v. ובית הלל) [whereas there is no way for the *kiddushin* of a minor to be valid].

7.

This mishnah is based on the fact that *kiddushin* with an עֶרְוָה, *ervah* — one with whom relations are prohibited under penalty of *kares* (Divinely decreed excision) — does not take effect (3:12).

— she is not betrothed, because he sent [them] on account of the original *kiddushin.* The same [applies to] a minor who betrothed.

7. [If] one betroths a woman and her daughter, or a woman and her sister simultaneously, they are not betrothed. It happened that [there

YAD AVRAHAM

הַמְקַדֵּשׁ אִשָּׁה וּבִתָּהּ, אוֹ אִשָּׁה וַאֲחוֹתָהּ — כְּאַחַת — *[If] one betroths a woman and her daughter, or a woman and her sister simultaneously,*

A man gave two perutos to either of these pairs of women (Meiri) and said, "You are both hereby betrothed to me" (Rashi).

אֵינָן מְקֻדָּשׁוֹת. — *they are not betrothed.*

Neither *kiddushin* takes effect, and neither woman requires a *get* in order to marry someone else (*Meiri*). This is derived from the verse (*Lev.* 18:18), *Do not take a woman to her sister to be co-wives* — i.e., if they are being made into co-wives with each other you cannot acquire even one of them (*Rav, Rambam Commentary* from *Gem.* 50b). The same applies to all who fall under the category of *ervah* which are punishable by *kares* [similar to a wife's sister] (*Rav*) — since they are all interconnected by virtue of the verse (ibid. v. 25), *All who shall do any of these abominations — their souls shall be cut off from the midst of their nation* (*Gem.* 67b).

Those conjugal prohibitions that are punishable only by lashes — e.g., a divorcee to a *Kohen* (*Lev.* 21:7) — do not prevent *kiddushin* from taking effect ex post facto despite Scripture's use of the words *You shall not take* with regard to them. This is derived from the verse (*Deut.* 21:15), *If a man shall have two wives, one who is loved and one who is hated.* The *Gemara* (68a) explains that the wife who is hated is one who is forbidden to her husband by virtue of a Biblical prohibition punishable by lashes. Thus, we see that the *kiddushin* of such a woman does take effect (*Tos. Yom Tov*).

The *Gemara* (50a) rejects this approach, concluding that the verse is discussing one's *kiddushin* to the sister of a woman previously betrothed to him, and not one betrothing two sisters simultaneously. The reason *kiddushin* with two sisters together is void is because of the principle that any two acts which cannot take effect one after the other can also not be effected simultaneously (ibid.).

If he gave a *perutah* to two sisters simultaneously, or to one of them who had been appointed an agent by the other, and he said that one of them should be betrothed to him, they both require a *get* before marrying another man (*Rav* from *Gem.* 52a). Although the question of whom the man had actually betrothed prohibits him to have intimacy with either of them — since each is possibly his wife's sister — the *kiddushin* to one of them is valid. However, since we do no know to which one, he must divorce both of them (*Gem.* ibid.).

However, if he said that the one who is eligible to have marital relations with him should be betrothed, neither *kiddushin* takes effect, because the fact that they both become prohibited to him with this act — since each may be his wife's sister —

בְּחָמֵשׁ נָשִׁים, וּבָהֶן שְׁתֵּי אֲחָיוֹת, וְלִקֵּט אֶחָד כַּלְכָּלָה שֶׁל תְּאֵנִים, וְשֶׁלָּהֶן הָיְתָה, וְשֶׁל שְׁבִיעִית הָיְתָה, וְאָמַר: „הֲרֵי כֻּלְּכֶם מְקֻדָּשׁוֹת לִי בְּכַלְכָּלָה זוֹ״, וְקִבְּלָה אַחַת מֵהֶן עַל יְדֵי כֻלָּן — וְאָמְרוּ חֲכָמִים: אֵין הָאֲחָיוֹת מְקֻדָּשׁוֹת.

ר׳ עובדיה מברטנורא

ושלהן היתה. שמעינן מהא מתניתין, דהמקדש בגזל, ואפילו בגזל דידה, אינה מקודשת, ולא אמרינן מדקבילתיה אחילתיה, מדקתני, ושלהן היתה, ושל שביעית היתה, משום דשל שביעית היתה שהפירות הפקר משום הכי הנשים מקודשות, אלא שאין אחיות מקודשות, אבל אם לא היתה שביעית, הואיל ושלהן היתה, לא היו קדושין תופסים באחת מהן, ודוקא בגזל שלפני יאוש בעלים אמרינן דלא הוה קדושין, אבל המקדש בגזל שלאחר יאוש, קדושיו קדושין. ושמעינן נמי, שהמקדש בפירות שביעית מקודשת, ולא אמרינן אינן ממונו לזכות בהן, אלא כיון שזכה בהן, ממונו הם לכל דבר. ושמעינן נמי, שאשה נעשית שליח לחברתה, ואפילו במקום שנעשית לה צרה, ואף על גב דבכל עדות שהאשה כשרה לה אין הצרה כשרה לה, שליחותה מיהא כיון דעבדא עבדא. דהא הכא בקדושין הללו הן נעשות צרות על ידי זו שקבלתה, וקתני אין האחיות מקודשות, הא נכריות מקודשות. ומתניתין מתרצה בגמרא (מא, ב) אליבא דהלכתא הכי, המקדש אשה ובתה, או אשה ואחותה, שתיהן כאחת אינן מקודשות, הא אחת מאשה ובתה, אחת מאשה ואחותה, כגון שאמר לשתיהן אחת מכם מקודשת לי, ולא פירש לאיזו מהן מקדש, וקבלה אחת מהן הקדושין על ידי חברתה, או שתיהן קבלו קדושין כאחת, מקודשות, ושתיהן צריכות גט. ואם אמר הראויה מכם לביאה מקודשת לי, אינן מקודשות, דכל אחת מהן איכא לספוקה באחות אשתו, ואין שום אחת מהן ראויה לביאה. ומעשה נמי בחמש נשים ובהן שתי אחיות, ולקט אחד כלכלה של תאנים, ואמר הראויה מכם לביאה תתקדש לי, ואמרו חכמים אין אחיות מתקדשות, הא נכריות שהיו ראויות לביאה, מתקדשות, אבל אם אמר כולכם מתקדשות לי, לא היתה שום אחת מהן מקודשת, דכי היכי דאין אחיות מקודשות כך אין האחרות מקודשות היכי דאמר כולכם:

יד אברהם

renders both of them ineligible (*Rav* from *Gem.* 57b).

וּמַעֲשֶׂה בְּחָמֵשׁ נָשִׁים, וּבָהֶן שְׁתֵּי אֲחָיוֹת, — *It happened that* [*there were*] *five women, among whom were two sisters,*

The mishnah relates an incident which illustrates the fact that if a man performs an act of *kiddushin* with two sisters and proclaims that he is betrothing the one with whom he may have marital relations, neither is betrothed (ibid.).

וְלִקֵּט אֶחָד כַּלְכָּלָה שֶׁל תְּאֵנִים, וְשֶׁלָּהֶן הָיְתָה, וְשֶׁל שְׁבִיעִית הָיְתָה, — *and someone gathered a basket of figs* [*which*] *were theirs and were from Shemittah,*

Since this occurred during *Shemittah* (the Sabbatical year), when all produce must be left in the fields for all to take (*Lev.* 25:4), they did not belong to the owner of the field but are rather public property. Therefore, anyone who takes them possesses them (*Rav* from *Gem.* 52a). Although it is forbidden to make transactions with such produce, if one did so it is valid ex post facto (*Tos.* ad loc., s.v. המקדש).

Others entertain the possibility that it is permitted to use such produce for *kiddushin,* because the Rabbis were lenient in this regard for the sake of the precept of

2 7 were] five women, among whom were two sisters, and someone gathered a basket of figs [which] were theirs and were from *Shemittah*, and he said: "All of you are betrothed to me with this basket," and one of them accepted it for all of them — and the Sages said: The sisters are not betrothed.

YAD AVRAHAM

propagation (*Tos.* to *Avodah Zarah* 62a, s.v. נמצא; see *Tos. R' Akiva*).

וְאָמַר: ,,הֲרֵי כֻּלְּכֶם מְקֻדָּשׁוֹת לִי בְּכַלְכָּלָה זוֹ", — *and he said: "All of you are betrothed to me with this basket,"*

The *Gemara* (51b) explains that he said, "Those among you who are permissible for relations with me are hereby betrothed to me with this basket" (*Rav*). [The mishnah cannot be understood in its simple sense, because in such a case, none of the betrothals would take effect, as explained below.]

Had they not been figs of *Shemittah*, which are available to the general public, the *kiddushin* would be null because of the fact that they were stolen from the women (*Rav* from *Gem.* loc. cit.). However, had there been a previous engagement to be betrothed between the man and one of the women, her acceptance of the figs would be interpreted as consent to his acquisition of them and his subsequent use of them for *kiddushin* (*Gem.* 52b, *Rashi* ad loc. s.v. בדשדיך) [and she would thereby become betrothed to him even if this occurred in a non-*Shemittah* year].

וְקִבְּלָה אַחַת מֵהֶן עַל יְדֵי כֻלָּן — *and one of them accepted it for all of them* —

Although a woman is not trusted to testify concerning her co-wife [because of the usual enmity between them (see *Yevamos* 15:4)], she can nevertheless accept *kiddushin* on behalf of another woman together with her own from the same man, thereby rendering them co-wives (*Rav* from *Gem.* 52a).

Even if she does not state that she is accepting *kiddushin* on behalf of the other woman, she is assumed to be doing so, as long as she was designated by them to be an agent for that purpose and did not refuse (*Rosh*).

וְאָמְרוּ חֲכָמִים: אֵין הָאֲחָיוֹת מְקֻדָּשׁוֹת. — *and the Sages said: The sisters are not betrothed.*

[The sisters are not betrothed, because each one's *kiddushin* would render the other an *ervah* to the man. Since neither can be identified as having been included in the *kiddushin* more than the other, they are both excluded. The others are betrothed, however, because he explicitly stated that those who are fitting for relations with him should be betrothed to him (see above).]

However, if he said that he was betrothing all of them, none of the betrothals would take effect, because he made them all dependent upon one another, and if one is void, all the others are also invalidated (*Rav* from *Gem.* 51a).

Although the ruling is that if someone gives one gift to both a person and a fetus, the fact that the gift to the fetus does not take effect because it cannot acquire anything does not negate the gift to the one already born; this applies only when he

[ח] הַמְקַדֵּשׁ בְּחֶלְקוֹ, בֵּין קָדְשֵׁי קָדָשִׁים בֵּין קָדָשִׁים קַלִּים — אֵינָהּ מְקֻדֶּשֶׁת; בְּמַעֲשֵׂר שֵׁנִי, בֵּין שׁוֹגֵג בֵּין מֵזִיד —

ר׳ עובדיה מברטנורא

(ח) המקדש בחלקו. שחלק עם אחיו הכהנים: **אינה מקודשת.** דכהנים משלחן גבוה קא זכו, ואמר קרא (במדבר יח, ט) (ו)זה יהיה לך מקדש הקדשים מן האש, מה אש אין אתה משתמש בו אלא לאכילה, כך מתנות הללו לא תשתמש בהן אלא לאכילה, ובמעשר כתיב (ויקרא כז, ל) לה׳ הוא, בהווייתו יהא:

יד אברהם

Others contend that the reasoning behind the law concerning a gift is pertinent to our mishnah as well, and even if he said, "All of you are betrothed to me," the ruling of the mishnah applies and the invalidity of one does not negate the others. According to this opinion, the mishnah can be interpreted as stated — that he said, "All of you are betrothed," rather than referring to a case in which he specified those who are permissible to him (*Rif;* see *Rosh, Ran*).

stated each one separately — i.e., "I am giving this to you and the fetus together." In case, however, if he included all of the women with the words "All of you," the betrothals cannot be separated one from the other so that some will be valid and not the others (see *Rosh*). Alternatively, when one is giving a gift, his intention toward each recipient is separate; whereas when making a purchase [or, in this case, *kiddushin*] he may be interested only if he acquires the entire group as stated (*Ran*).

8.

[The mishnah now focuses on sanctified objects, discussing which of them can be used to betroth a woman by virtue of their monetary value.]

הַמְקַדֵּשׁ בְּחֶלְקוֹ, — [*If*] *someone betroths with his portion,*

[A *Kohen* who receives his share of a sacrificial offering — which is divided among the *Kohanim* (*Rav*) — gave it to a woman for the purpose of *kiddushin.*]

When someone offers a sacrifice, part of the atonement [as in the case of a חַטָּאת, *sin-offering*] or appeasement [as in the case of an עוֹלָה, *elevation-offering*] which it effects is accomplished by the *Kohanim* eating the portions of the animal which are allotted to them (*Pesachim* 59b), as specified in the Torah (*Num.* 18:5-20). The *Kohanim* who are appointed to serve in the Temple that day (see *Rambam, Hil. Klei HaMikdash* 4:3) divide the portions of the sacrifices which are offered there (*Lev.* 7:9, *Rashi* ad loc.).

The mishnah's use of the wording, *with his portion,* indicates that he betrothed her after the blood of the sacrifice had been offered on the Altar, since only then is the animal apportioned among the *Kohanim,* and not before it is slaughtered. This is to avoid dispute with R' Yose, who maintains that animals designated for sacrifices of lesser sanctity (see below) belong to the owner until they are slaughtered, and if the owner gave them for *kiddushin* before that time it would be valid (*Gem.* 52b).

בֵּין קָדְשֵׁי קָדָשִׁים — *whether from the most holy offerings* (lit., *holies of holies*)

8. [If] someone betroths with his portion, whether from the most holy offerings or offerings of lesser holiness, she is not betrothed; with the second tithe, whether inadvertently or intentionally,

YAD AVRAHAM

These are sacrifices, such as sin-offerings and guilt-offerings (*Meiri*), which must be slaughtered in the northern part of the Temple Courtyard (*Zevachim* 5:1). Only *Kohanim* may partake of them, and they may be eaten only in the Courtyard (ibid. 3:5).

בֵּין קָדָשִׁים קַלִּים — *or offerings of lesser holiness* (lit., *light holies*),

These are sacrifices, such as peace-offerings (*Meiri*), which may be slaughtered anywhere in the Temple courtyard (loc. cit. 6-8). Generally, portions of these sacrifices are given to the *Kohanim* and the rest of the meat which is not offered on the Altar is eaten by the owner. Both the *Kohanim's* and owner's portions may be eaten anywhere within the walls of Jerusalem (ibid.).

In this case, the statement of the mishnah refers to both a *Kohen* who gave his share to a woman for *kiddushin* and a man who offered a sacrifice and betrothed a woman with the part which he may eat (*Meiri;* cf. *Rambam, Hil. Me'ilah* 4:8; *Mishneh LaMelech* ad loc.).

אֵינָהּ מְקֻדֶּשֶׁת; — *she is not betrothed;*

Because even these portions of the sacrifices which may be eaten do not belong to the *Kohanim* [or owner (*Rashi*)]. Rather, it is considered as if they are eating from the "table of God" — i.e., Divinely owned possessions from which these individuals are permitted to partake (*Rav* from *Gem.* 5a,b), but may not use them for the monetary transactions (*Meiri*).

This is derived from the verse (*Num.* 18:9), *This shall be to you of the most holy offerings from the fire,* which compares the sacrifices to fire to indicate that just as fire is used only for purposes of eating, so too are the portions of the *Kohanim* given to them only for consumption (*Rav* from *Gem.* ibid.; see *Tos. Yom Tov*).

Others interpret the word *fire* in the verse to refer to those parts of the offering which are burnt on the Altar. Just as they are designated for consumption, so are the portions of the *Kohanim* (*Rashi* ad loc.).

From the juxtaposition of the verse concerning the most holy offerings (*Lev.* 7:10) with the one discussing those of lesser sanctity (ibid. v. 11), we derive that the two are analogous, and the former also does not become the possession of those to whom they are allotted for consumption (*Gem.* 53a).

Although a man can betroth a woman with the benefit he causes her, even if he does not give her anything tangible (*Gem.* 63a) [and in this case she received the benefit of the food he gave her], that is only if he has the right to charge money for that benefit and he gives it to her for *kiddushin* instead. In our case, however, what he gave her is not his, and he cannot collect payment for it; therefore, it cannot effect *kiddushin* (*Tos.* 52b s.v. המקדש).

בְּמַעֲשֵׂר שֵׁנִי, — *with the second tithe,*

[This is a new case. A man betrothed a woman with the second tithe.]

[In the first, second, fourth, and fifth years of the seven-year *Shemittah* cycle, a second tithe is separated from one's produce in addition to the first, which is given to the *Levi.* The

לֹא קִדֵּשׁ; דִּבְרֵי רַבִּי מֵאִיר. רַבִּי יְהוּדָה אוֹמֵר: בְּשׁוֹגֵג — לֹא קִדֵּשׁ; בְּמֵזִיד — קִדֵּשׁ.

וּבַהֶקְדֵּשׁ: בְּמֵזִיד — קִדֵּשׁ; וּבְשׁוֹגֵג — לֹא קִדֵּשׁ; דִּבְרֵי רַבִּי מֵאִיר. רַבִּי יְהוּדָה אוֹמֵר: בְּשׁוֹגֵג — קִדֵּשׁ; בְּמֵזִיד — לֹא קִדֵּשׁ.

ר' עובדיה מברטנורא

רבי יהודה אומר מזיד קדש. במעשר שני, הואיל ויולא לחולין על ידי פדיון, והרי הוליאו לחולין על ידי קדושין הללו, ורבי מאיר סבר לית דרך חלול בכך: **ובהקדש.** של בדק הבית: **מזיד קדש.** שכיון שידע שהוא הקדש, והוליאו לחולין בכוונה, נתחללה קדושתו: **ובשוגג.** דלא ידע שהוא הקדש, ולא ניחא ליה דלתחלל הקדש על ידיה, לא נתחללה קדושתו, ואינה מקודשת, ורבי יהודה סבר איפכא. והלכה כרבי מאיר במעשר, וכרבי יהודה בהקדש:

יד אברהם

second tithe must be brought to Jerusalem and eaten there or redeemed by money which is taken there and used for the purchase of food.]

בֵּין שׁוֹגֵג בֵּין מֵזִיד — לֹא קִדֵּשׁ; דִּבְרֵי רַבִּי מֵאִיר. — *whether inadvertently or intentionally, the kiddushin is not valid* (lit., *he did not betroth*); [*these are*] *the words of R' Meir.*

R' Meir maintains that the second tithe is considered to be Divinely owned (*Gem.* 54b; 24a), as derived from the verse (*Lev.* 27:30), *And every tithe of the land — from the seeds of the land or from the fruit of the tree — is to God* (*Meiri;* cf. *Tos. Yom Tov; Tos. R' Akiva*). Therefore, he cannot use it to betroth a woman (*Gem.* 53a).

רַבִּי יְהוּדָה אוֹמֵר: בְּשׁוֹגֵג — לֹא קִדֵּשׁ; — *R' Yehudah says:* [*If*] *inadvertently, the kiddushin is not valid;*

If the woman was unaware that the produce she was receiving was of the second tithe, the *kiddushin* is not valid, because we assume that since she must take it to Jerusalem in order to eat it, had she realized its status, she would not have accepted it (*Meiri* from *Gem.* 53b). However, if he gave it to her in Jerusalem, the *kiddushin* is valid, since there is no effort involved (*Meiri*).

Some are of the opinion that even in a case in which the man was not aware of the fact that the object he gave her for *kiddushin* was from the second tithe, the *kiddushin* would be invalid. This is because he would not want to risk alienating her by giving her something for *kiddushin* which places a burden upon her — viz., the burden of carrying it to Jerusalem (*Gem.* ibid.; see *Tos.* s.v. איהו).

בְּמֵזִיד — קִדֵּשׁ. — [*if*] *intentionally, it is valid.*

If she realized that he was giving her produce of the second tithe, the *kiddushin* is valid, because R' Yehudah maintains that such produce is the monetary possession of the owner, and a transaction which it effects is valid (*Meiri* from *Gem.* 54b).

Others explain that it is valid for *kiddushin*, because it is divested of its sanctity by virtue of the transaction, and it therefore becomes the woman's private possession (*Rav;* see *Tos. R' Akiva*).

The *halachah* regarding produce of the second tithe follows the view of R' Meir (*Rav* from *Gem.* 54b).

וּבַהֶקְדֵּשׁ: — *And with hekdesh:*

A man betrothed a woman with *hekdesh* — that which is designated

2 8 the *kiddushin* is not valid; [these are] the words of R′ Meir. R′ Yehudah says: [If] inadvertently, the *kiddushin* is not valid; [if] intentionally, it is valid.

And with *hekdesh:* [if] intentionally, the *kiddushin* is valid; [if] inadvertently, it is not valid. [These are] the words of R′ Meir. R′ Yehudah says: [If] inadvertently, it is valid; [if] intentionally, it is not.

YAD AVRAHAM

for the needs of the Temple (*Rav*) [as opposed to portions from the offerings themselves].

בְּמֵזִיד — קִדֵּשׁ; — [*if*] *intentionally, the kiddushin is valid;*

If he gave the object to the woman despite his awareness that it belonged to the Temple, the *kiddushin* is valid, because Temple property that is used in a transaction is thereby removed from the Temple's possession (*Rav*). Although the guilt-offering imposed upon one who misuses sacred property [which is the primary source for the fact that a transaction with such an object removes it from the possession of the Temple and divests it of its sanctity] is only for one who does so inadvertently (*Lev.* 5:15), one who misuses sacred property intentionally also divests it of sanctity (*Meiri*). This is derived from the use in that verse of the words כִּי תִמְעֹל מַעַל, *who shall commit a trespass,* which denotes an intentional act, as evidenced by the use of the same word with regard to a *sotah* (*Num.* 5:12), whose action was intentional (*Tos.* 53b s.v. אף).

וּבְשׁוֹגֵג, לֹא קִדֵּשׁ; דִּבְרֵי רַבִּי מֵאִיר. — [*if*] *inadvertently, it is not valid.* [*These are*] *the words of R′ Meir.*

R′ Meir holds that it can be assumed that if the man had realized he was misusing sacred property with his act, he would not have done it. Thus, the *kiddushin* was based on misunderstanding and is therefore void (*Rav* from *Gem.* 53b).

[Similarly, any transaction which was made inadvertently with an object belonging to the Temple does not strip the object of its sanctity, since the transaction is void.] That which an offering is required for inadvertently removing an article from the possession of *hekdesh* (see above) is only for something which was eaten or destroyed and was thereby lost to *hekdesh* (*Gem.* 54b).

Some hold that even if it was the woman who was misled, the *kiddushin* is null, even though she is not the one who is misusing the object, because she would not have consented to be a party to the desecration of sacred property (ibid.).

רַבִּי יְהוּדָה אוֹמֵר: בְּשׁוֹגֵג — קִדֵּשׁ; — *R′ Yehudah says:* [*If*] *inadvertently, it is valid;*

R′ Yehudah contends that any inadvertent use of sacred property divests it of its sanctity, and the *kiddushin* is therefore valid (*Meiri*). [He does not accept as a certainty the assumption that they would not want the *kiddushin* if they realized he had used a sacred object to effect it.]

בְּמֵזִיד — לֹא קִדֵּשׁ. — [*if*] *intentionally, it is not.*

הַמְקַדֵּשׁ בְּעָרְלָה, בְּכִלְאֵי הַכֶּרֶם, בְּשׁוֹר הַנִּסְקָל, וּבְעֶגְלָה עֲרוּפָה, בְּצִפֳּרֵי

ר׳ עובדיה מברטנורא

(ט) **המקדש בערלה וכו׳ אינה מקודשת.** דכולהו איסורי הנאה נינהו. ערלה, דכתיב (ויקרא יט, כג) לא יאכל, אחד איסור אכילה ואחד איסור הנאה במשמע: **ובכלאי הכרם.** דכתיב (דברים כב, ט) פן תקדש, פן תוקד אש: **ובשור הנסקל.** דכתיב ביה (שמות כא, כח) ולא יאכל את בשרו: **ובעגלה ערופה.** דכתיב ביה כפרה כקדשים, שנאמר (דברים כא, ח) ונכפר להם הדם: **בציפורי מצורע.** דתניא (נז, א), נאמר מכשיר ומכפר בפנים, אשמו של מצורע שהוא מכשיר אותו לאכול בקדשים, וחטאתו שמכפר, ושניהם נעשים בפנים. ונאמר מכשיר ומכפר בחוץ, מכשיר, צפרי מצורע שמכשירין המצורע לבא אל תוך המחנה, ומכפר, עגלה ערופה, שנאמר בה ונכפר להם הדם, ושניהם נעשים חוץ לעזרה. מה מכשיר ומכפר האמור בפנים, שהם אשמו וחטאתו של מצורע, עשה בו מכשיר כמכפר, דתרווייהו קדשים נינהו ואסורים בהנאה, אף מכשיר ומכפר האמורים בחוץ, שהם צפרי מצורע ועגלה ערופה, עשה בו מכשיר כמכפר להיות אסורים בהנאה. ומאימתי אסורין צפורי מצורע בהנאה, משעת שחיטה, והצפור השחוטה בלבד היא שאסורה בהנאה, ועגלה ערופה, ירידתה אל נחל איתן אוסרתה:

יד אברהם

If he used an object for *kiddushin* despite his awareness that it belongs to the Temple, the *kiddushin* is not valid, because the intentional use of sacred items does not alter its status. Therefore, the article still belongs to the Temple and not the woman (*Rav* from *Gem.* 54b).

The *halachah* regarding *hekdesh* follows the view of R' Yehudah (ibid.).

9.

[This mishnah continues the discussion of which articles may be used as the equivalent of money for *kiddushin.*]

הַמְקַדֵּשׁ בְּעָרְלָה, — [*If*] *one betroths with orlah,*

[A man gave produce of *orlah* (see 1:9) to a woman for the purpose of *kiddushin.*]

It is forbidden to benefit from *orlah* in any way, as stated in the verse (*Lev.* 19:23): *Three years it shall be restricted for you; it shall not be eaten.* This refers to the prohibition of any benefit as well as that of eating (*Rav* from *Gem.* 56b), as derived from the verse (*Deut.* 14:21), *You shall not eat any* [*unslaughtered*] *carcass; to the stranger who is within your gates you may give it that he may eat it, or* [*you may*] *sell it to a gentile.* From the fact that permission to sell the prohibited item had to be specified, it is evident that a prohibition against eating something ordinarily includes all other benefits as well (*Gem.* loc. cit.).

Although it is permitted to benefit from *orlah* in an irregular manner (*Pesachim* 24b), and it thus has a monetary value, in this case the woman accepted it on the assumption that she could use it in the normal fashion, and the *kiddushin* is thus based on a misconception (*Tos.* 56b s.v. המקדש). Others contend that benefiting from *orlah* even in an irregular manner is permitted only to one who is ill (*Ran*).

בְּכִלְאֵי הַכֶּרֶם, — *with kilayim of the vineyard,*

Kilayim of the vineyard (see 1:9) are also prohibited for any benefit, as derived from the words (*Deut.* 22:9) ,פֶּן

9. [If] one betroths with *orlah*, with *kilayim* of the vineyard, with an ox which was [condemned to be] stoned, with a calf whose neck is [to be] broken, with the birds of a *metzora*,

תוּקְדַּשׁ, *lest it be rendered abominable* (*Rashi* ad loc.) — which are exegetically interpreted to mean פֶּן תּוּקַד אֵשׁ — *lest it be burnt by fire* [i.e., it shall become forbidden for any benefit, and thus be fit only to be destroyed] (*Rav* from *Gem.* 56b).

בְּשׁוֹר הַנִּסְקָל, — *with an ox which was [condemned to be] stoned,*

An ox condemned to die by the courts for killing a man (*Ex.* 21:28) is prohibited for benefit, as derived from the words (ibid.), *its flesh shall not be eaten* (*Rav* from *Gem.* 56b; cf. *Tos., Kereisos* 24a). Even if it was not stoned but slaughtered by *shechitah*, its meat is still forbidden (*Gem.*).

According to many authorities, the ox is prohibited for benefit as soon as the verdict is handed down. However, *Rabbeinu Tam* states that it becomes prohibited only upon its death (see *Tos., Bava Kamma* 45a s.v. מכור, *Sanhedrin* 79b s.v. בשור, *Zevachim* 70b s.v. אפילו).

וּבְעֶגְלָה עֲרוּפָה, — *with a calf whose neck is [to be] broken,*

If the victim of a murder is found outside a city and it is not known who killed him, the elders of the city nearest the corpse must take a calf to a valley of unworked ground, where its neck is broken (*Deut.* 21:1-4). The passage prescribes a prayer to be recited by the elders of the town, which includes the words (ibid. v. 8), *Forgive Your nation, Israel.* With these words, the calf is compared to offerings in the Temple, which also effect atonement. The calf is therefore considered analogous to Temple property in that it is prohibited to use even for benefits other than eating (*Rav* from *Gem.* 57a). This prohibition takes effect from the moment the calf is taken down to the valley (ibid.).

בְּצִפֳּרֵי מְצֹרָע, — *with the birds of a metzora,*

[A *metzora* (commonly mistranslated *leper*) is the victim of a skin disease of a specific nature which renders him *tamei* (see *Lev.* 13). Once cured, he must undergo a complex purification process. The first part of this procedure requires two birds. One is slaughtered, and the other is dipped into its blood and used to sprinkle the blood on the *metzora*, after which it is set free (*Lev.* 14:1-7).]

The first bird is prohibited for benefit from the time it is slaughtered, as derived in the following manner. Temple sacrifices fall into two categories — atonement offerings, such as most sin-(*chatas*) and guilt-(*asham*) offerings; and qualifying offerings, such as the *metzora's* guilt-offering and the sin-offering of a *zavah*, which serve to qualify their owner to eat *kodashim*. Objects used in rites outside the Temple can also be divided this way: the *metzora's bird* qualifies him to enter the city, while the *calf whose neck is broken* and *the goat sent away to Azazel* (on Yom Kippur) atone. Now both types of Temple sacrifices are analogous in being prohibited for benefit. A similar analogy should exist for the categories used outside the Temple: Just as the *calf whose neck is broken* and the *goat sent*

קידושין ב/ט

מְצֹרָע, וּבִשְׂעַר נָזִיר, וּבְפֶטֶר חֲמוֹר, וּבְבָשָׂר בְּחָלָב, וּבְחֻלִּין שֶׁנִּשְׁחֲטוּ בָעֲזָרָה — אֵינָהּ מְקֻדֶּשֶׁת. מְכָרָן וְקִדֵּשׁ בִּדְמֵיהֶן — מְקֻדֶּשֶׁת.

ר׳ עובדיה מברטנורא

ובשער הנזיר. דאמר קרא (במדבר ו, ה) קדש יהיה גדל פרע שער ראשו, גדל פרע שער ראשו יהיה קדוש: **ופטר חמור.** נאמר בו (שמות יג, יג) וערפתו, ונאמר בעגלה ערופה (דברים כא, ד) וערפו, מה עגלה ערופה אסורה בהנאה, אף פטר חמור אסור בהנאה, ואינו אסור בהנאה אלא אחר עריפה: **ובבשר בחלב.** נאמר שלש פעמים (שמות כג, יט; שם לד, כו; דברים יד, כא) לא תבשל גדי בחלב אמו, אחד לאסור אכילה, ואחד לאסור הנאה, ואחד לאסור בשול: **ובחולין שנשחטו בעזרה.** דכתיב (דברים יב, כא) כי ירחק ממך המקום וזבחת, ברחוק מקום אתה זובח ואי אתה זובח בקרוב מקום. יכול לא יאכלנו אבל ישליכנו לכלבים, תלמוד לומר (שמות כב, ל) לכלב תשליכון אותו, אותו אתה משליך לכלב, ואי אתה משליך לכלב חולין שנשחטו בעזרה: **מכרן וקדש בדמיהן מקודשת.** שאין לך דבר שתופס את דמיו להיות כמוהו, אלא עבודה זרה ושביעית. עבודה זרה, שנאמר (דברים ז, כו) והיית חרם כמוהו, כל מה שאתה מהוה ממנו הרי הוא כמוהו, ושביעית, שנאמר (ויקרא כה, יב) קדש היא, תופסת דמיה כהקדש, והוו עבודה זרה ושביעית שני כתובים הבאים כאחד, וכל שני כתובים הבאין כאחד אין מלמדין:

יד אברהם

to Azazel which atone are forbidden for any use, so too the qualifying bird of the *metzora* should be forbidden for use (*Rav* and *Rambam Comm.* from *Gem.* 57a; see *Chullin* 140a and *Kereisos* 25a, *Rashi*).

There is actually a dispute in the *Gemara* (ibid.) whether the prohibition takes effect from the time of slaughtering, as explained above, or from the time the birds are designated for this ritual, in which case the second bird is also prohibited until it is sent away (*Rashi* ad loc. s.v. משעת לקיחתו).

Others contend that even according to the view that the prohibition takes effect from the time the first bird is slaughtered, it still pertains to the second bird as well. This is evidenced by the mishnah's use of the plural form — *birds of a metzora* — in contrast with all the other items, which are listed in the singular form (*Tos.* 57a s.v. משעת שחיטה).

וּבִשְׂעַר נָזִיר — *with the hair of a Nazirite,*

A Nazirite is forbidden to cut his hair for the duration of his vow (*Num.* 6:5). Upon fulfilling his vow, he must shave off all his hair as part of the concluding ritual. The Nazirite's hair is forbidden for benefit both during the vow and after being shaved at the vow's conclusion. Concerning his hair, the Torah says (ibid.): קָדֹשׁ יִהְיֶה, *it shall be sanctified,* to indicate that it is prohibited for any benefit (*Rav* from *Gem.* 57b).

The use of the word קָדֹשׁ, which means *sanctified,* rather than קֹדֶשׁ — which refers to the status of *hekdesh* (*Rashi*) — indicates that it is not comparable to *hekdesh* completely and, if sold, one may benefit from the payment for it (*Gem.* ibid.; see below).

וּבְפֶטֶר חֲמוֹר, — *with the firstborn of a donkey,*

The Torah says (*Ex.* 13:13), *Every first issue donkey you shall redeem with a lamb or kid; if you do not redeem it, then you must axe the back of its neck.* From the word וַעֲרַפְתּוֹ, *and axe the back of its neck,* we derive that it is compared to a calf whose neck is to be broken [see above] and is prohibited

2 with the hair of a Nazirite, with the firstborn of a
9 donkey, with meat and milk, or with *chullin* slaughtered in the Courtyard, she is not betrothed. [If] he sold them and betrothed with their payment, she is betrothed.

YAD AVRAHAM

for any benefit (*Rav* from *Bechoros* 9b).

There is a dispute among the *Tannaim* whether this prohibition takes effect as soon as the donkey is born or only after its neck is broken (*Gem.* 57b).

וּבְבָשָׂר בְּחָלָב, — *with meat and milk,*

The verse, *You shall not cook a kid in the milk of its mother*, is stated three times (*Ex.* 23:19; ibid. 34:26; *Deut.* 14:21) — once to prohibit cooking meat and milk together, once to prohibit eating such a mixture, and once to forbid any benefit from it (*Rav* from *Gem.* ad loc.).

וּבְחֻלִּין שֶׁנִּשְׁחֲטוּ בָּעֲזָרָה — *or with chullin slaughtered in the Courtyard,* —

[*Chullin* refers to nonsacred animals, food, etc.] The Torah (*Deut.* 12:21) says, *When the place which HASHEM your God, has chosen shall be distant from you ... and you will slaughter from your cattle.* From this we derive that one may slaughter nonsacred cattle only when he is distant from the Temple, but not when he is in its Courtyard (*Gem.* ibid.).

If one transgressed, and slaughtered *chullin* in the Temple Courtyard, it is prohibited for any benefit, as derived from the verse (*Ex.* 22:30), *You shall not eat flesh which is torn apart in the field; to the dog you shall throw it,* which is interpreted by the *Gemara* (*Chullin* 68a) to mean that a fetus whose leg emerged from the womb is not made kosher with the slaughtering of its mother, but it is permitted for benefit and may be fed to one's dog. This case is contrasted to that of *chullin* slaughtered outside the Temple Courtyard, in that the former emerged from within its boundaries — i.e., it emerged partially from the womb before it was ready to emerge completely — whereas the latter entered beyond its boundaries — i.e., it was brought within a proscribed area. We therefore derive that only the fetus, which emerged from within its boundary, is permitted for benefit; but *chullin* slaughtered in the Courtyard, which entered beyond its allotted boundary, is not (*Gem.* 58a; *Rashi* s.v. ואי אתה משליך).

אֵינָהּ מְקֻדֶּשֶׁת. — *she is not betrothed.*

[If a man used any of the aforementioned items to betroth a woman, the *kiddushin* is not valid, because one cannot use an item from which it is forbidden to benefit for the purpose of *kiddushin* (see mishnah 8).

However, if a man, for the purpose of *kiddushin*, gave a woman something which is forbidden for benefit by Rabbinic law, the *kiddushin* takes effect, unless it is a Rabbinic ordinance which is rooted in a Biblical prohibition (*Rosh*). Others contend that even Rabbinically prohibited items cannot effect *kiddushin* (*Ran; Meiri;* cf. *Rambam, Hil. Ishus* 5:1; *Maggid Mishneh, Kesef Mishneh* ad loc.).

מְכָרָן וְקִדֵּשׁ בִּדְמֵיהֶן — מְקֻדֶּשֶׁת. — *[If] he sold them and betrothed with their payment, she is betrothed.*

If a man sold any of the items listed

[י] **הַמְקַדֵּשׁ** בִּתְרוּמוֹת, וּבְמַעַשְׂרוֹת, וּבְמַתָּנוֹת, וּבְמֵי חַטָּאת, וּבְאֵפֶר חַטָּאת — הֲרֵי זוֹ מְקֻדֶּשֶׁת, וַאֲפִלּוּ יִשְׂרָאֵל.

ר׳ עובדיה מברטנורא

(י) **המקדש בתרומות.** תרומה גדולה ותרומת מעשר: **ובמעשרות.** מעשר ראשון, ומעשר עני: **ומתנות.** הזרוע, והלחיים, והקיבה: **ובמי חטאת.** ובמי אפר חטאת. וראויים למכרם לטמאים, ליקח מהם שכר הבאה ושכר מלוי המים, אבל שכר הזאה ושכר קדוש, והוא נתינת האפר במים, אסור: **ואפילו ישראל.** הכי קאמר, ואפילו ישראל שנפלו לו תרומות ומתנות מבית אבי אמו כהן, שזכה בהם, ויכול למכרם לכהנים, אם קדש בהם את האשה, מקודשת. ואפילו לא נפלו לו תרומות, אלא טבלים שעדיין לא הורמו, הואיל ומורישו כהן, היה עומד להרימם, והתרומות שלו, וזה הישראל שירש אותם, כמי יפריש מהם התרומה והיא שלו, ויכול למכרה לכהנים, דמתנות שלא הורמו כמי שהורמו דמו:

יד אברהם

above and gave that which he received in payment to a woman for the sake of *kiddushin*, the *kiddushin* is valid, because only the prohibitions of something used for idolatry and of produce of *Shemittah* carry over to their payments as well. This is based on the fact that both of the above are specified explicitly as applying to their payments (*Lev.* 22:12; *Deut.* 7:26; see *Gem.* loc. cit.), and any law which is written in two separate places [when one could theoretically have been derived from the other] cannot be applied further (*Rav* from *Gem.* ibid.).

Although if someone sells a forbidden item to another, the sale is not valid and he must return the money [and his *kiddushin* with that payment should be void because it is not his], the mishnah is discussing a case in which the man sold one of these items to a gentile [to whom they are not prohibited] or to someone who was aware of their status and is thus understood to have given the payment as a gift (*Rosh*). Alternatively, although the seller must repay the buyer, since the sale is void, he acquires the money which was given in payment, but is obligated to compensate the buyer for that amount (*Ran*).

Despite the fact that the payment used to buy *orlah* is prohibited for benefit by Rabbinic law, the woman can be betrothed with it, since it is not prohibited to her. It is prohibited only to the one who sold the *orlah*. Although the man is thereby benefiting from that money, the Rabbis were lenient in this case because of the precept of propagation (*Rashi* to *Avodah Zarah* 54b s.v. למעוטי). Alternatively, although they are forbidden for benefit, if one transgressed and used them for a transaction, it is valid (*Rosh;* see above).

10.

הַמְקַדֵּשׁ בִּתְרוּמוֹת, — [*If*] *one betroths with terumos,*

Someone gave a woman *terumah* — the portion which one must separate from his produce to give to a *Kohen* (see commentary to *Gittin* (3:7) — or *terumah* from the tithe — i.e., a tenth of the tithe that the Levite receives, which he must separate and give to a *Kohen* (ibid.) — for the sake of *kiddushin* (*Rav*).

Unlike the *Kohen's* share in offer-

10. [If] one betroths with *terumos*, with tithes, with gifts, with the waters of purification, or with the ashes of purification, she is betrothed, and even a non-*Kohen*.

YAD AVRAHAM

ings (see mishnah 8), *terumos* belong to the *Kohen* himself [and he may use them for the transaction] (*Tos. Yom Tov*).

וּבְמַעַשְׂרוֹת, — *with tithes,*

He gave the woman from מַעֲשֵׂר רִאשׁוֹן, *the first tithe*, or from מַעֲשֵׂר עָנִי, *the tithe for the poor given in* the third and sixth year of the Sabbatical cycle, which is given to the poor [see commentary to *Gittin* 3:7] (*Rav*).

וּבְמַתָּנוֹת, — *with gifts,*

I.e., the right foreleg, the cheeks, and the stomach of every animal that one slaughters, which he must give to a *Kohen* (*Tif. Yis.* from *Deut.* 18:3).

וּבְמֵי חַטָּאת — *with the waters of purification,*

The water which is drawn for the sake of mixing it with the ashes of the Red Cow (*Tif. Yis.*; see below).

וּבְאֵפֶר חַטָּאת, — *or with the ashes of purification,*

The ashes of the Red Cow, which are mixed with water and sprinkled upon one who became ritually contaminated through contact with a corpse (*Tif. Yis.* from *Num.* 19).

Both of the above may be sold to those who are contaminated, because although it is forbidden to take payment for performing the *mitzvah* of mixing the ashes with the water or sprinkling the mixture on the contaminated person, it is permitted to exact compensation for the exertion involved in carrying the ashes and filling the container with water (*Rav*; *Rambam, Hil. Ishus* 5:3). Therefore, when he betroths her with either of these items, she gains the benefit of being able to collect money from those who need them, in exchange for the exertion (*Maggid Mishneh* ad loc.).

Others explain that he betrothed her with the payment for these exertions (*Rashi* 58a s.v. בשכר הבאה; *Ravad* loc. cit.).

הֲרֵי זוֹ מְקֻדֶּשֶׁת — *she is betrothed,*

[All of these items belong completely to their owners and can be used to betroth a woman.]

וַאֲפִלּוּ יִשְׂרָאֵל. — *and even a non-Kohen.*

Even a non-*Kohen*, who inherited from his maternal grandfather — who was a *Kohen* — produce from which *terumos* and tithes were not yet separated, may use these for the purpose of *kiddushin*. This is because the portions of the produce of a *Kohen* which were not yet separated are considered as if already apportioned, since he may keep them for himself [and it is therefore tantamount to having inherited these portions after they were separated] (*Rav* from *Gem.* 58a). However, he cannot effect *kiddushin* by giving a woman the right to allot the *terumos* and tithes of his produce to whichever *Kohen* she chooses, because that privilege is not considered to be of monetary value (*Gem.* ibid.; *Rambam, Hil. Ishus* 5:6).

Others contend that the right to choose the recipient of these portions is indeed considered to be of monetary value, and thus, the mishnah is discussing a man who used that privilege to betroth a woman (*R' Chananel*; *Rosh*).

פרק שלישי

Chapter Three

[א] **הָאוֹמֵר** לַחֲבֵרוֹ: „צֵא וְקַדֵּשׁ לִי אִשָּׁה פְּלוֹנִית", וְהָלַךְ וְקִדְּשָׁהּ לְעַצְמוֹ — מְקֻדֶּשֶׁת. וְכֵן הָאוֹמֵר לָאִשָּׁה: „הֲרֵי אַתְּ מְקֻדֶּשֶׁת לִי לְאַחַר שְׁלֹשִׁים יוֹם", וּבָא אַחֵר וְקִדְּשָׁהּ בְּתוֹךְ שְׁלֹשִׁים יוֹם — מְקֻדֶּשֶׁת לַשֵּׁנִי.

ר' עובדיה מברטנורא

פרק שלישי – האומר. (א) האומר לחבירו צא וקדש לי אשה פלונית והלך וקדשה לעצמו. אמרינן בגמרא (נח, ב) מאי והלך, שהלך ברמאות. ולהכי תנן האומר לחברו ולא תנן האומר לשלוחו, לאשמועינן דאף על גב דלא עשאו שליח מתחלה לכך, אלא שאמר לו קדש לי אשה פלונית, אם קדשה לעצמו קרינן ביה שהלך ברמאות, ורמאי הוי: **ובא אחר וקדשה בתוך שלשים יום מקודשת לשני.** ויכול לכנסה אפילו בתוך אלו השלשים יום:

יד אברהם

1.

הָאוֹמֵר לַחֲבֵרוֹ: — [*If*] *one says to another:*

The mishnah chose the word *another*, rather than *agent*, to indicate that although the man did not appoint him as an agent to seek out the woman and betroth her to him, but only requested that he do so if he should happen to be in her vicinity, he is, nevertheless, considered deceitful if he betroths her to himself (*Rav* from *Gem.* 59a; *Rashi* ad loc. s.v. דקתני לשלוחו האמר).

„צֵא וְקַדֵּשׁ לִי אִשָּׁה פְּלוֹנִית", — *"Go and betroth So-and-so to me,"*

The term *go* denotes that she is to be found elsewhere, and that reaching her entails effort. Were this not the case, the man would be expected to perform the act of *kiddushin* himself, since it is always better for a person to perform a *mitzvah* by himself rather than have someone else do it for him (*Tif. Yis.*; see 2:1).

וְהָלַךְ וְקִדְּשָׁהּ לְעַצְמוֹ — *and he went and betrothed her to himself,*

The other person went deceitfully [in violation of his agreement with the sender] (*Rav* from *Gem.* 59b) and betrothed her to himself with his own money (*Mordechai*).

מְקֻדֶּשֶׁת. — *she is betrothed.*

She is betrothed to the other person and does not require a *get* from the man who sent him, since we are not concerned that had she known that the latter sent the former to betroth her, she would have refused the *kiddushin* of the messenger and accepted that of the sender (*Meiri; Ran*).

Some commentators explain the mishnah to be discussing a case in which the messenger first told the woman that he had been sent by the sender to betroth her and subsequently said, "You are betrothed to me." The mishnah tells us that we do not assume that she understood him to be speaking of the name of the sender, and accepted the *kiddushin* on that basis, but rather that she realized his intent and consented to his own *kiddushin* (*Tos.* 58b s.v. האומר).

וְכֵן הָאוֹמֵר לָאִשָּׁה: „הֲרֵי אַתְּ מְקֻדֶּשֶׁת לִי לְאַחַר שְׁלֹשִׁים יוֹם", — *Similarly,* [*if*] *one says to a woman: "You are betrothed to me after thirty days,"*

[A man gave money to a woman

3
1

1. [If] one says to another: "Go and betroth So-and-so to me," and he went and betrothed her to himself, she is betrothed. Similarly, [if] one says to a woman: "You are betrothed to me after thirty days," and another came and betrothed her within thirty days, she is betrothed to the second.

YAD AVRAHAM

and said that she should become betrothed to him with that money after thirty days.] This is a legitimate form of *kiddushin*, and it takes effect even if she no longer has the money when the thirty days elapse. Although if he had given her money for safekeeping and she lost it, he could not betroth her with it, that is because it was not yet hers when it was lost [and thus she never actually received anything which could serve as the money for *kiddushin*]. In our case, however, the money became hers as soon as she received it, and it is therefore valid for *kiddushin*. It is also not comparable to betrothing a woman with money that was previously given to her as a loan, which is not valid since he is not giving her anything new at the time of *kiddushin*, because in our case the money was given from the outset for the sake of *kiddushin* (*Gem.* 59a).

If the woman retracted her consent before the thirty days had ended, the *kiddushin* is void, and she must return the money, because something which is based on mere words [since the *kiddushin* was not yet finalized] can be reversed with words (ibid.). The man can also reverse himself (*Ran; Meiri*), but he cannot reclaim his money if he does [since he is the one who reneged on their agreement] (*Ran*).

If a man betrothed a woman — on condition that it take effect after thirty days — with cohabitation or with a document which was lost before the thirty days were over, there is a dispute among the authorities whether the *kiddushin* takes effect. These cases are not comparable to that of betrothal in this manner with money, because in the latter case if she changes her mind, she must reimburse him for the money he gave her [and its effect is thus still extant], whereas the document and cohabitation are no longer extant (*Meiri*).

וּבָא אַחֵר וְקִדְּשָׁהּ בְּתוֹךְ שְׁלֹשִׁים יוֹם — מְקֻדֶּשֶׁת לַשֵּׁנִי. — *and another came and betrothed her within thirty days, she is betrothed to the second.*

He may even perform *nisuin* (full marriage) with her within the thirty days (*Rav*).

Since the first man's *kiddushin* was not yet completed when the second one betrothed her, the latter's is valid. Accordingly, when the time arrives for the first *kiddushin* to take effect, it is prevented from doing so by virtue of the fact that she is already betrothed to the second (*Rambam, Hil. Ishus* 7:11).

Rambam's wording implies that if the second man who betrothed her died or divorced her before the thirty days were over, the first *kiddushin* takes effect, since she is no longer the wife of another man. Her acceptance of the second *kiddushin* does not constitute a retraction of her

בַּת כֹּהֵן לְיִשְׂרָאֵל — תֹּאכַל בַּתְּרוּמָה. "מֵעַכְשָׁיו וּלְאַחַר שְׁלֹשִׁים יוֹם", וּבָא אַחֵר וְקִדְּשָׁהּ בְּתוֹךְ שְׁלֹשִׁים יוֹם — מְקֻדֶּשֶׁת וְאֵינָהּ מְקֻדֶּשֶׁת. בַּת

ר' עובדיה מברטנורא

בת כהן לישראל. אם בת כהן היא זאת שנתקדשה לאחר שלשים יום, כל אותן שלשים יום תאכל בתרומה, שלא נפסלה מלאכול בתרומת בית אביה. ואם בת ישראל לכהן היא, לא תאכל בתרומה, שעדיין אינה אשת כהן: **מקודשת.** וצריכה גט מתרווייהו:

יד אברהם

consent to the first, because it allows for the possibility of the first one being reinstated if the second one is terminated before the end of the thirty days, and there is thus no indication that she intended otherwise (*Ran*).

Others contend that acceptance of a second *kiddushin* does constitute rejection of the first, and the first does not take effect even if the second is negated (*Rosh; Rashba*).

בַּת כֹּהֵן לְיִשְׂרָאֵל — תֹּאכַל בַּתְּרוּמָה. — *The daughter of a Kohen* [*betrothed*] *to a non-Kohen may eat terumah.*

A non-*Kohen* is prohibited by Biblical law from eating *terumah* (*Lev.* 22:10). The Torah adds (ibid. v. 11), however, that *If a Kohen will acquire a soul* [*as*] *the acquisition of his money, he shall eat of it.* This verse refers basically to the Canaanite slave of a *Kohen* (*Rashi* ad loc.), but it also includes the *Kohen's* wife who may eat *terumah* from the time of their *kiddushin* (*Gem.* 5a). However, the Rabbis decreed that she may not partake of it until after their *nisuin* (ibid.). On the other hand, the daughter of a *Kohen* who is betrothed to a non-*Kohen* becomes Biblically forbidden to eat *terumah* (*Lev.* 22:12; *Yevamos* 9:4).

The mishnah is telling us here that if the daughter of a *Kohen* was betrothed by a non-*Kohen* on condition that it take effect after thirty days, she may continue to eat *terumah* (see 2:10) during that time, since the *kiddushin* did not yet take effect. By the same token, if the daughter of a non-*Kohen* was betrothed in this manner to a *Kohen*, she may not eat *terumah* during the thirty-day period[1] (*Rav; Rambam Commentary;* see *Ran*).

Another version of the mishnah (followed by the *Yachin U'Boaz* ed.) reads בַּת יִשְׂרָאֵל לְכֹהֵן תֹּאכַל בַּתְּרוּמָה, *The daughter of a non-Kohen to a Kohen may eat terumah,* and it refers to the mishnah's previous case, in which the woman was betrothed by a second man during the thirty-day period. If that second man was a *Kohen*, she may eat *terumah*, since we disregard the first *kiddushin* (*Ran*). The mishnah's statement applies according to the Biblical law that the betrothed of a *Kohen* may eat *terumah*, or — even after the Rabbinical decree

1. [Actually, even after the period of thirty days elapses, she may not eat *terumah*, because — as stated above — the Rabbis decreed that the daughter of a non-*Kohen* who is betrothed to a *Kohen* may not eat *terumah* until they are fully married, due to the fear that she may share it with her brothers and sisters (*Gem.* 5a). Nevertheless, *Rav's* statement is applicable in Biblical law. Alternatively, it is pertinent in a case in which they were also married within the thirty days, and she is thus permitted to eat *terumah* when the thirty days elapse, and the marriage takes effect (cf. *Tos. Ri HaZaken*).]

3
1

The daughter of a *Kohen* [betrothed] to a non-*Kohen* may eat *terumah*. [If he said:] "From now and after thirty days," and another came and betrothed her within thirty days, she is betrothed and not betrothed. The daughter of a

YAD AVRAHAM

prohibiting this — if they were also married within the thirty days (*Tos. Ri HaZaken*).

,,מֵעַכְשָׁיו וּלְאַחַר שְׁלשִׁים יוֹם,'' — [*If he said:*] "*From now and after thirty days,*"

If a man betrothed a woman and said, "It should take effect from now and after thirty days," it is unclear whether his latter words were meant to retract his statement that it take effect immediately or merely to add a stipulation that it not be finalized until after thirty days, at which time it should take effect retroactively (*Meiri* from *Gem.* 59b).

Although any other condition which he may set is not understood to be a reversal of his original statement that it take effect immediately, a stipulation such as this, which affects only the time of *kiddushin* and is not dependent upon any other action or occurrence, strongly suggests that he meant to change the time of the effectuality of the *kiddushin* (*Meiri*).

וּבָא אַחֵר וְקִדְּשָׁהּ בְּתוֹךְ שְׁלשִׁים יוֹם - מְקֻדֶּשֶׁת וְאֵינָהּ מְקֻדֶּשֶׁת. — *and another came and betrothed her within thirty days, she is betrothed and not betrothed.*

I.e., she requires a *get* from one of them in order to marry the other [for which a new *kiddushin* is required, since the validity of both betrothals is in question], and from both if she wants to marry a third man (*Ran*). If the time span of thirty days was meant only as a stipulation to the originally stated *kiddushin*, its retroactive validity from the time of betrothal nullifies the *kiddushin* of the second man. If it was a retraction, however, and the *kiddushin* is not valid until after thirty days, the second man's *kiddushin* takes effect first, and prevents the first man's from taking effect. Since, from the first man's words, it is not clear which of these meanings he had intended,[1] she requires a *get* from both men, even after the thirty days have elapsed (*Gem.* loc. cit.).

If one man betrothed her, stipulating that the *kiddushin* take effect "from now and after thirty days," and then a second man betrothed her "from now and after twenty days," and a third man "from now and after ten days", she would not need a *get* from the second man, because his *kiddushin* certainly did not take effect for the following reason: If the second half of this type of statement is understood to be a reversal of its first half, and the *kiddushin* does not take effect at all until after the time specified, the third *kiddushin*, which became effective after ten days, is the first to take effect, and it nullifies the others. If it is understood to mean that the *kiddushin* not be finalized until the later date, but is effective retroactively from the time of the betrothal, the first *kiddushin* takes effect retroactively at the end of thirty days and nullifies the others (*Gem.* 60a).

There is another view in the *Gemara* (ibid.) that the ruling of the mishnah is not due to uncertainty as to the man's inten-

1. [What he had in mind at the time is irrelevant if he did not convey it in words, since, in Jewish law, unspoken intentions are disregarded (see commentary to *Gittin* 4:1 s.v. הֲרֵי).

יִשְׂרָאֵל לְכֹהֵן אוֹ בַּת כֹּהֵן לְיִשְׂרָאֵל — לֹא תֹאכַל בַּתְּרוּמָה.

[ב] **הָאוֹמֵר** לָאִשָּׁה: „הֲרֵי אַתְּ מְקֻדֶּשֶׁת לִי עַל מְנָת שֶׁאֶתֵּן לָךְ מָאתַיִם זוּז" — הֲרֵי זוֹ מְקֻדֶּשֶׁת, וְהוּא יִתֵּן. „עַל מְנָת שֶׁאֶתֵּן

ר' עובדיה מברטנורא

(ב) **הרי את מקודשת לי.** בפרוטה זו על מנת שאתן לך מאתים זוז: **ויתן.** ומשיתן נתקדשה למפרע, דכל האומר על מנת כאומר מעכשיו דמי:

יד אברהם

tions, but to the fact that the first man left room for the *kiddushin* of the second, and they are therefore both partially valid. Consequently, if the second stipulated that his *kiddushin* take effect "from now and after twenty days," and the third — "from now and after ten days" — they are all partially valid, and she requires a *get* from each of them. Even if the second man stipulated that his *kiddushin* take effect "from now and after forty days," it is still effectual, since the first *kiddushin* allowed for its validity (*Ran*).

Although a man cannot betroth half a woman (*Gem.* 7a), that is because he is leaving the other half of her without *kiddushin,* and a woman cannot be only half-betrothed. In this case, however, he stipulated that the *kiddushin* be finalized after thirty days, and his betrothal thus applies to the entire woman (*Tos.* 60a s.v. אפילו).

בַּת יִשְׂרָאֵל לְכֹהֵן אוֹ בַּת כֹּהֵן לְיִשְׂרָאֵל — לֹא תֹאכַל בַּתְּרוּמָה. — *The daughter of a non-Kohen to a Kohen or the daughter of a Kohen to a non-Kohen may not eat terumah.*

If a *Kohen* betrothed the daughter of a non-*Kohen* "from now and after thirty days," the *kiddushin* is not finalized until the end of the thirty days, and she may not eat *terumah* (see footnote to commentary above s.v. בַּת כֹּהֵן). On the other hand, if a non-*Kohen* betrothed the daughter of a *Kohen* in this manner, she is immediately disqualified from *terumah* [since his intention might have been that the *kiddushin* take effect retroactively from that time, and she will have illegally eaten *terumah* as the wife of a non-*Kohen*] (*Ran,* quoting *Rambam*).

Others explain the mishnah to be discussing the previous case, in which a second man betrothed her before the thirty days were over. The uncertainty as to which *kiddushin* is valid is applied not only to the more stringent issue of divorce, requiring that she receive a *get* from each, but also to the more lenient prohibition of *terumah,* and disqualifies her from eating it (*Ran*).

2.

[This mishnah deals with the subject of a *kiddushin* with a stipulation, similar to the discussion of the same issue concerning a *get* in *Gittin* 7:5.]

הָאוֹמֵר לָאִשָּׁה: „הֲרֵי אַתְּ מְקֻדֶּשֶׁת לִי — [*If*] *one says to a woman: "You are betrothed to me"*

"With this *perutah*" (*Rav*) — [i.e.,

non-*Kohen* to a *Kohen* or the daughter of a *Kohen* to a non-*Kohen* may not eat *terumah.*

2. [I]f] one says to a woman: "You are betrothed to me on condition that I will give you two hundred *zuz*," she is betrothed, and he gives [it]. "On condition that I will give

YAD AVRAHAM

he clearly indicated that the medium for *kiddushin* was the *perutah* he was handing her and not the money mentioned in the stipulation that follows].

עַל מְנָת שֶׁאֶתֵּן לָךְ מָאתַיִם זוּז" — *on condition that I will give you two hundred zuz,"* —

The mishnah chose this amount as an example, because it is considered sufficient funds for a person to purchase food and clothes for one year, as evidenced by the fact that one who has two hundred *zuz* may not collect *peah* — the corners of the field which are left uncut for the poor to gather [*Peah* 8:8, *Rav* ad loc.] (*Rishon LeTzion*).

There is a dispute among the authorities whether or not he must state the condition in a dual manner — i.e., "If the condition is met, the *kiddushin* takes effect; if not, it does not" (see preface to mishnah 4 and commentary to *Gittin* 7:5).

הֲרֵי זוֹ מְקֻדֶּשֶׁת, וְהוּא יִתֵּן. — *she is betrothed, and he gives* [*it*].

This does not mean that he is compelled to give her the money and fulfill his condition (*Meiri*); rather, it means that when he gives it to her the *kiddushin* takes effect retroactively from the moment of betrothal (see 1:1), because the words עַל מְנָת, *on condition,* imply that the fulfillment of the provision should validate the *kiddushin* retroactively (*Rav* from *Gem.* 60a). Therefore, if she was betrothed to another man in the interim, the fulfillment of the stipulation to the first *kiddushin* would negate the second *kiddushin* entirely (*Gem.* ibid.).

If the man died before fulfilling his condition the *kiddushin* is void, and there is no question of *yibum* (see 1:1), even if his heirs give the woman two hundred *zuz*. This is because he stipulated, "On condition that I will give," which means only he himself, but not his heirs. For the same reason, if the woman died, there is no question of his becoming prohibited to her relatives (see 2:6) even if he gives the money to her heirs in order to fulfill the condition, because his stipulation to give her the money does not include her heirs (*Meiri;* cf. *Avnei Miluim* 38:10).

There is disagreement among the commentators as to whether or not the man can retract the *kiddushin* before fulfilling the condition. If he cannot, the *kiddushin* remains as stipulated, and if he fulfills the condition at any time it takes effect retroactively (*Meiri; Beis Shmuel, Even HaEzer* 38:60).

There is another view that the words *on condition* do not indicate that the *kiddushin* should take effect retroactively, but rather, that it should become valid when the condition is met. Accordingly, if she is betrothed by another in the interim, that *kiddushin* is effective, and the first is nullified (*Gem.* 60a).

לָךְ מִכָּאן וְעַד שְׁלֹשִׁים יוֹם״: נָתַן לָהּ בְּתוֹךְ שְׁלֹשִׁים — מְקֻדֶּשֶׁת; וְאִם לָאו — אֵינָהּ מְקֻדֶּשֶׁת. ,,עַל מְנָת שֶׁיֶּשׁ לִי מָאתַיִם זוּז״ — הֲרֵי זוֹ מְקֻדֶּשֶׁת, וְיֶשׁ לוֹ. ,,עַל מְנָת שֶׁאַרְאֵךְ מָאתַיִם זוּז״ — הֲרֵי זוֹ מְקֻדֶּשֶׁת, וְיַרְאֶה לָהּ. וְאִם הֶרְאָהּ עַל הַשֻּׁלְחָן — אֵינָהּ מְקֻדֶּשֶׁת.

[ג] ,,**עַל** מְנָת שֶׁיֶּשׁ לִי בֵּית כּוֹר עָפָר״ — הֲרֵי זוֹ מְקֻדֶּשֶׁת, וְיֶשׁ לוֹ. ,,עַל מְנָת שֶׁיֶּשׁ לִי

ר׳ עובדיה מברטנורא

הרי זו מקודשת ויש לו. אם יש עדים שיש לו. ואם לא נודע שיש לו הרי זו מקודשת מספק, שמא יש לו ומתכוין לקלקלה: **ו[אם] הראה על השלחן.** שהיה שולחני, והראה על השלחן מעות שאינן שלו, אינה מקודשת: (ג) **בית כור.** מקום הראוי לזרוע כור, שהוא שלשים סאין: **ויש לו.** אם יש עדים שיש לו מקודשת ודאי. ואם אין ידוע שיש לו מקודשת מספק, ולא אמרינן, זוזי דעביד איניש דמצנעי, חיישינן דלמא אית ליה ומתכוין לקלקלה, אבל ארעא לא חיישינן דלמא אית ליה, דאם איתא דאית ליה ארעא, קלא אית ליה:

יד אברהם

,,עַל מְנָת שֶׁאֶתֵּן לָךְ מִכָּאן וְעַד שְׁלֹשִׁים יוֹם״: נָתַן לָהּ בְּתוֹךְ שְׁלֹשִׁים — מְקֻדֶּשֶׁת; וְאִם לָאו — אֵינָהּ מְקֻדֶּשֶׁת. — *"On condition that I will give* [*it*] *to you from now until thirty days" —* [*if*] *he gave* [*it*] *to her within thirty* [*days*], *she is betrothed; if not, she is not betrothed.*

[If the man stipulated that he must give her the money within a specific period of time, he must give it to her within that time in order for the *kiddushin* to be valid.] We do not assume that he set the time limit only in order to motivate himself to fulfill the condition expeditiously (*Gem.* 60b).

,,עַל מְנָת שֶׁיֶּשׁ לִי מָאתַיִם זוּז״ — הֲרֵי זוֹ מְקֻדֶּשֶׁת, וְיֶשׁ לוֹ. — [*If he says:*] *"On condition that I have two hundred zuz," she is betrothed* [*provided*] *he has* [*it*].

If he betrothed her on condition that he has two hundred *zuz,* the *kiddushin* is finalized if there are witnesses that he has the money (*Rav* from *Gem.* ibid.), even if he has it in a different land (*Ran*).

If it cannot be ascertained whether or not he has the money, the validity of the *kiddushin* remains in doubt (*Rav* from *Gem.* ibid.), because it is possible that he has the money, but is not producing it because he wishes to harm her [by causing her to remarry illicitly on the assumption that her *kiddushin* to him is void] (*Rav*).

,,עַל מְנָת שֶׁאַרְאֵךְ מָאתַיִם זוּז״ — הֲרֵי זוֹ מְקֻדֶּשֶׁת, וְיַרְאֶה לָהּ. — *"On condition that I will show you two hundred zuz," she is betrothed* [*provided*] *he shows* [*it to*] *her.*

Since he stipulated that he will show her the money, she must see it herself in order for the *kiddushin* to be valid, and it is not sufficient to establish through the testimony of witnesses that he possesses it (*Ramah,*

[it] to you from now until thirty days" — [if] he gave [it] to her within thirty [days], she is betrothed; if not, she is not betrothed.

[If he says:] "On condition that I have two hundred *zuz*," she is betrothed [provided] he has [it]. "On condition that I will show you two hundred *zuz*," she is betrothed [provided] he shows [it to] her. If he showed [it] to her on the table, she is not betrothed.

3. [If he said:] "On condition that I have a *beis kor* of land," she is betrothed [provided] he has [it]. "On condition that I have [it] in a specific

YAD AVRAHAM

cited in *Tur Even HaEzer* 38).

וְאִם הֶרְאָהּ עַל הַשֻּׁלְחָן — *If he showed* [*it*] *to her on the table,*

He was a money changer, and he showed her money which was in his possession but did not belong to him (*Rav*), even money in whose profits he has a right to share (*Gem.* 60b; *Rashi*).

.אֵינָהּ מְקֻדֶּשֶׁת — *she is not betrothed.*

Because his condition is understood to mean that he will show her money which belongs to him (*Meiri*).

If the money was lent to him, the *kiddushin* is valid, because money which a person borrows becomes his entirely, and his obligation to the lender is only that he reimburse him, not that he return the same money (*Tos. R' Akiva*).

3.

״עַל מְנָת שֶׁיֵּשׁ לִי בֵּית כּוֹר עָפָר״ — [*If he said*:] *"On condition that I have a beis kor of land,"*

A man betrothed a woman and stated that the *kiddushin* is valid if he owns an area of land within which one can plant a *kor*, which is thirty *seah* (*Rav*). [The area for the planting of a *seah* is given as 2500 square cubits[1] (*Rashi*). Thus, a *beis kor* would be 75,000 square cubits of land.]

.הֲרֵי זוֹ מְקֻדֶּשֶׁת, וְיֵשׁ לוֹ — *she is betrothed* [*provided*] *he has* [*it*].

If witnesses testify that he owns that amount of land, the *kiddushin* takes effect. However, if it cannot be ascertained whether or not he owns that amount of land, the validity of the *kiddushin* remains questionable, because he might be hiding the fact of his possession in order to harm her [see mishnah 2]. We do not assume that, since land cannot be hidden, he would not be able to keep his ownership of the land secret (*Rav* from *Gem.* 60b).[2]

1. [There are different opinions as to the precise measurement of a cubit, ranging from eighteen inches to twenty-four (see General Introduction to ArtScroll *Eruvin*, p. 12).]

2. This is derived from the Mishnah's parallelization of the case of the land to that of the two hundred *zuz* (mishnah 2). Since no new statement was required for a case in which the

בְּמָקוֹם פְּלוֹנִי״: אִם יֵשׁ לוֹ בְּאוֹתוֹ מָקוֹם — מְקֻדֶּשֶׁת; וְאִם לָאו — אֵינָהּ מְקֻדֶּשֶׁת. ,,עַל מְנָת שֶׁאַרְאֵךְ בֵּית כּוֹר עָפָר״ — הֲרֵי זוֹ מְקֻדֶּשֶׁת, וְיַרְאֶנָּה. וְאִם הֶרְאָהּ בְּבִקְעָה — אֵינָהּ מְקֻדֶּשֶׁת.

[ד] **רַבִּי** מֵאִיר אוֹמֵר: כָּל תְּנַאי שֶׁאֵינוֹ כִתְנַאי

ר׳ עובדיה מברטנורא

ואם הראה בבקעה. שאינה שלו, ואף על גב דנחת בה לחכירות או לקבלנות אינה מקודשת: **(ד) כל תנאי.** שאינו כפול וכו׳ אינו תנאי, ואף על פי שלא נתקיים התנאי נתקיימו הדברים:

יד אברהם

,,עַל מְנָת שֶׁיֵּשׁ לִי בְּמָקוֹם פְּלוֹנִי״: אִם יֵשׁ לוֹ בְּאוֹתוֹ מָקוֹם — מְקֻדֶּשֶׁת; וְאִם לָאו — אֵינָהּ מְקֻדֶּשֶׁת. — *"On condition that I have [it] in a specific place" — if he has [it] in that place, she is betrothed; if not, she is not betrothed.*

If he betrothed her on condition that he owns a *beis kor* of land in a specific place, he must own that amount of land in that place for the *kiddushin* to be valid. [Although we assume that the only reason the woman would insist on the land being in a specific place is so she will have access to its produce] even if he is willing to bring the produce from the field to his house the *kiddushin* is void (*Gem.* ibid.) [because the condition which he stated must be met (see 2:2)].

If we do not find land belonging to him in that place, the validity of the *kiddushin* remains in question, because he may be concealing his ownership in order to harm her (*Rambam, Hil. Ishus* 7:3; see mishnah 2).

Others contend that it is not possible to conceal one's ownership once the specific location is known, and the *kiddushin* is therefore void (*Hagahos Ramach* ibid.).

Some maintain that if the man has land which is as close to his home as the area specified, the *kiddushin* is valid, because if the effort involved in bringing home produce from the field is the same, there is no reason for the woman to insist on one location over the other[1] (*Rashba*). Others contend that this is not different than the cases in the previous chapter (2:2*f.*), in which any inaccuracy in what the husband claims at the time of *kiddushin* invalidates the betrothal, even if it involves something which people usually do not care about (*Ran; Maggid Mishneh, Hil. Ishus* 7:3).[2]

veracity of his claim is clear, the parallel is understood to indicate that they are analogous in a case of uncertainty as well (*Gem.* ibid.).

1. [This is not analogous to a case in which the field was further but he is willing to bring the produce home (see above). In that case, the situation of the field itself is not in accordance with his stipulation; but there is another factor which can rectify that — his willingness to bring the produce home. In this case, however, the location of the field itself is what renders the situation analogous to that which he stipulated; therefore, the condition is considered as having been met.]

2. *Lechem Mishneh* (ad loc.) explains *Rashba's* reasoning to be that only in those cases in which the inaccuracy pertains to the primary facet of the stipulation is the *kiddushin* void. In this case, however, the major issue is the husband's possession of the land; the location is secondary. Therefore, we do not assume that she would insist on the accuracy of the location.

3 place" — if he has [it] in that place, she is betrothed;
4 if not, she is not betrothed. "On condition that I will show you a *beis kor* of land" — she is betrothed [provided] he will show [it to] her. If he showed [it to] her in a valley, she is not betrothed.

4. **R**' Meir says: Any condition which is not like

YAD AVRAHAM

If he betrothed her on condition that he has a sum of money in a specific place, the ruling would be analogous to that of our mishnah (*Rambam* ad loc.; *Rosh; Meiri*).

,,עַל מְנָת שֶׁאַרְאֵךְ בֵּית כּוֹר עָפָר" — הֲרֵי זוֹ מְקֻדֶּשֶׁת, וְיַרְאֶנָּה. — *"On condition that I will show you a beis kor of land," she is betrothed [provided] he will show [it to] her.*

He must show her a tract of land of that size which belongs to him (*Gem.* 60b). [The testimony of witnesses to that effect will not suffice (see mish-nah 2).]

וְאִם הֶרְאָהּ בְּבִקְעָה — אֵינָהּ מְקֻדֶּשֶׁת. — *If he showed [it to] her in a valley, she is not betrothed.*

If he shows her land which does not belong to him in a valley full of fields, even if he rents it or is a sharecropper there, the *kiddushin* is not valid (*Rav* from *Gem.* ibid.).

Even if the position of sharecropper of this field has been held by his family for generations, it is not considered his (*Ran*).

4.

תְּנַאי כָּפוּל/The Double Stipulation

The Torah (*Num.* 32) relates that the tribes of Gad and Reuven requested permission from Moses to settle in the Land of Gilead, on the eastern side of the Jordan River. After some discussion, Moses agreed to their request, but stipulated that they must first lead the battle to conquer the Land of Canaan. When informing Elazar and the other leaders of the people of his decision, he said (ibid. v. 29): *If the children of Gad and the children of Reuven will cross the Jordan with you with all zealousness at the front of [the army] of Hashem, and the Land shall be conquered before you, then you shall give them the Land of Gilead as an allotment. But if they will not cross zealously with you, they shall inherit in your midst in the Land of Canaan* (see *Targum Onkelos, Rashi* ad loc.).

[This type of stipulation is referred to as "the condition of the children of Gad and the children of Reuven," and it is used by R' Meir as a source from which to derive the rules which govern the validity of all stipulations in Jewish law. The primary issue in this mishnah is whether we derive from this passage that when stipulating a condition, it must be explicitly stated that if the condition is met, the agreement is valid; and if the condition is not met, it is not valid.]

רַבִּי מֵאִיר אוֹמֵר: — *R' Meir says:*

R' Meir disputes the previous mish-nayos, which discussed conditions that were stipulated without stating

בְּנֵי גָד וּבְנֵי רְאוּבֵן אֵינוֹ תְנַאי, שֶׁנֶּאֱמַר: ,,וַיֹּאמֶר
מֹשֶׁה אֲלֵהֶם: אִם יַעַבְרוּ בְנֵי גָד וּבְנֵי רְאוּבֵן",
וּכְתִיב: ,,וְאִם לֹא יַעַבְרוּ חֲלוּצִים". רַבִּי חֲנִינָא בֶּן
גַּמְלִיאֵל אוֹמֵר: צָרִיךְ הָיָה הַדָּבָר לְאָמְרוֹ,

───────────── ר' עובדיה מברטנורא ─────────────

אם יעברו ואם לא יעברו. וְאִי לָא כְפָל הַדְּבָרִים הָיְתָה מַתְנָתוֹ קַיֶּמֶת, וְהָיוּ נוֹחֲלִים אֶת אֶרֶץ
הַגִּלְעָד אַף עַל פִּי שֶׁלֹּא הָיוּ עוֹבְרִים, וְאַף עַל גַּב דְּאָמַר אִם יַעַבְרוּ אִתְּכֶם, לֵית לַן מִכְּלָל הֵין אַתָּה
שׁוֹמֵעַ לָאו. וְשַׁמְעִינַן מִינֵּיהּ נַמִי, דִּבְטֵינַן תְּנָאֵי קוֹדֶם לְמַעֲשֶׂה, מִדְּלֹא אָמַר תְּנוּ לָהֶם אִם יַעַבְרוּ, מַשְׁמַע
דְּאִי הֲוָה אָמַר הָכִי, לֹא אָתֵי תְנָאָה וּמְבַטֵּל מַעֲשֶׂה דְמַתְנָה דְקַדְמֵיהּ. וְשָׁמַע מִינָּהּ נַמִי, דִּבְטֵינַן הֵין
קוֹדֶם לְלָאו, דְּלֹא אָמַר תְּחִלָּה אִם לֹא יַעַבְרוּ אַל תִּתְּנוּ, וְאִם יַעַבְרוּ וְנִתְתֶּם: **רבי חנינא בו'.** אִתְּנָאֵי
כְּפוּל פָּלִיג, דְּאֵין צָרִיךְ לִכְפּוֹל, דְּמִכְּלַל הֵין נִשְׁמַע לָאו, וְזֶה שֶׁכְּפָלוֹ מֹשֶׁה, צוֹרֶךְ הָיָה הַדָּבָר. וְלָעִנְיַן פְּסַק
הֲלָכָה, אִם אָמַר עַל מְנָת, אֵין צָרִיךְ תְּנָאֵי כָּפוּל, וְלֹא הֵין קוֹדֶם לְלָאו, וְלֹא תְנָאָי קוֹדֶם לְמַעֲשֶׂה, אֶלָּא
הַתְּנָאֵי קַיֶּם. וְאִם לֹא אָמַר עַל מְנָת, צָרִיךְ כָּל הָנֵי דְּאָמְרִינַן, וְאִם לָאו, הַתְּנָאֵי בָּטֵל וְהַמַּעֲשֶׂה קַיֶּם.
וְלֹא שְׁנָא בִּתְנָאֵי שֶׁבְּדִינֵי מָמוֹנוֹת וְלֹא שְׁנָא בִּתְנָאֵי שֶׁבְּגִיטִּין וְקִדּוּשִׁין, הַכֹּל שָׁוֶה לְדָבָר זֶה:

יד אברהם

both alternatives, and the *Tanna*
recognized them as valid (*Rambam
Commentary; Tos. Ri HaZaken*).

[According to the opinion that the need
for a double stipulation does not apply to
conditions whose fulfillment validates the
deed retroactively (see below, s.v. שֶׁאֶלְמָלֵא),
this mishnah is not directly related to the
previous mishnayos. Presumably, it was
placed here simply because it is pertinent to
the discussion above concerning stipulations.]

— כָּל תְּנַאי שֶׁאֵינוֹ כִּתְנַאי בְּנֵי גָד וּבְנֵי רְאוּבֵן
*Any condition which is not like the
condition of the children of Gad and the
children of Reuven*

I.e., if both the alternatives and their
consequences are not stated (*Rav*).

אֵינוֹ תְנַאי, — *is not a condition,*

The condition is not binding and
the agreement is valid even if the
condition is not met (*Rav*). This is
because we assume that the fact that
the one who made the condition did
not state both alternatives indicates
that [although he desires the fulfillment of the stipulation] he wants the

agreement to be in force in any event
(*Ran* to mishnah 5).

If it is self-evident that the intent of the
person stipulating the condition is that if
the latter is not fulfilled, the agreement
should not be in force, the condition is
binding even if both alternatives were not
stated (*Tos.* 6b s.v. לא; 49b s.v. דברים). For
example, if a man gives another person his
esrog to use on the first day of Succos [when
it is necessary to perform the precept with
one's own *esrog*] on condition that he return
it afterward, the condition is binding even
if it is not stated from both sides, because it
is obvious that he is giving it to him only for
the purpose of fulfilling the precept (*Tos.* 6b,
loc. cit.).

שֶׁנֶּאֱמַר: ,,וַיֹּאמֶר מֹשֶׁה אֲלֵהֶם: אִם יַעַבְרוּ בְנֵי
גָד וּבְנֵי רְאוּבֵן", וּכְתִיב: ,,וְאִם לֹא יַעַבְרוּ
חֲלוּצִים." — *as it says* (Num. 32:29):
"And Moses said to them: If the
children of Gad and the children of
Reuven will cross ...," and it is written
(ibid. v. 30): "But if they will not cross
zealously ..."

From the second half of Moses'
statement — that if they do not cross
the Jordan to help conquer the Land of

3 the condition of the children of Gad and the
4 children of Reuven is not a condition, as it says (*Num.* 32:29): *And Moses said to them: If the children of Gad and the children of Reuven will cross ...*, and it is written (ibid. v. 30): *But if they will not cross zealously ...* R' Chanina ben Gamliel says: It was necessary for the matter to be stated,

YAD AVRAHAM

Canaan, they will not receive the land they requested in Gilead — it is evident that, without those words, they would have received the land whether or not they crossed, even though Moses had already stipulated that they will receive it if they cross over and join the battle. It is thus clear that a stipulation must explicitly include both alternatives, and we cannot assume from the condition itself that if it is not met, the agreement is void (*Rav*).

This principle — that a stipulation must be analogous to the one made regarding the descendants of Gad and Reuven in order to be binding — is the source for the following other laws as well (*Meiri; Rambam, Hil. Ishus* 6:2):

Just as Moses said, "*If they shall cross the Jordan ... you shall give them the Land of Gilead,*" so too must every condition be stated prior to the act [e.g., "If you give me a gift, you are betrothed to me"] and not vice versa (*Rav;* cf. *Rambam* loc. cit. 4; see *Bava Metzia* 7:11).

Also, the positive facet of the condition — i.e., that which renders the agreement valid (*Meiri*) — must be stated prior to the negative facet [e.g., "If you do this, the *kiddushin* is valid; if not, it is not"] — and not the opposite way, just as Moses first stated that if they fulfill the condition, they will receive the land and afterwards said that if they do not cross over, they will not receive it (*Rav*).

In addition, the condition must deal with something other than the agreement itself, just as the condition of helping conquer the Land of Canaan dealt with an event separate from the allocation of the Land of Gilead. It also may not be a contradiction to the agreement (*Ran*) — e.g., "If you return this to me, it will be yours" (*Meiri;* see *Tos.* 6b s.v. לא).

רַבִּי חֲנִינָא בֶּן גַּמְלִיאֵל אוֹמֵר: צָרִיךְ הָיָה הַדָּבָר לְאָמְרוֹ, — *R' Chanina*[1] *ben Gamliel says: It was necessary for the matter to be stated,*

He maintains that, ordinarily, a stipulation need not be stated with both alternatives because merely stating that if the condition is fulfilled, the agreement is in effect implies that the opposite is also true. In the Biblical incident discussed above, however, it was necessary for Moses to use a double stipulation for a different reason, as explained below (*Rav*).

Some commentators maintain that R' Chanina disputes only the necessity for stating a condition from both sides, but he agrees with the other requisites (mentioned above) for the validity of a stipulation (*Rashi*). Others contend that he disagrees with all of them (*Tos.*). He specifies that he disputes the need for a double stipulation only because he considers that to be the only one of these requisites which could possibly be derived from the condition of the descendants of Gad and Reuven by virtue

1. [Some versions read: רַבִּי חֲנַנְיָא *R' Chananya.*]

שֶׁאִלְמָלֵא כֵן — יֵשׁ בְּמַשְׁמַע שֶׁאֲפִלּוּ בְּאֶרֶץ כְּנַעַן לֹא יִנְחָלוּ.

[ה] **הַמְקַדֵּשׁ** אֶת הָאִשָּׁה וְאָמַר: ,,כְּסָבוּר הָיִיתִי שֶׁהִיא כֹהֶנֶת, וַהֲרֵי הִיא לְוִיָּה", ,,לְוִיָּה, וַהֲרֵי הִיא כֹהֶנֶת"; ,,עֲנִיָּה, וַהֲרֵי הִיא עֲשִׁירָה", ,,עֲשִׁירָה, וַהֲרֵי הִיא עֲנִיָּה" — הֲרֵי זוֹ מְקֻדֶּשֶׁת, מִפְּנֵי שֶׁלֹּא הִטְעַתּוּ.

יד אברהם

of the seeming redundancy of Moses' words. However, there is no indication at all that the other factors were necessary for the validity of the stipulation (*Ran*).

שֶׁאִלְמָלֵא כֵן — יֵשׁ בְּמַשְׁמַע שֶׁאֲפִלּוּ בְּאֶרֶץ כְּנַעַן לֹא יִנְחָלוּ. — *because otherwise, it is implicit that even in the Land of Canaan they shall not inherit.*

Had Moses not stated explicitly that if the tribes of Gad and Reuven did not fulfill the condition — although they would not be given the land they requested east of the Jordan — they would still share in the allocation of the land of Canaan, it would be assumed that they would not receive a portion on either side of the Jordan (*Gem.* 61a), since they rejected the Land of Canaan when they requested to be allowed to settle in the Land of Gilead (*Rashi* ad loc.).

The *Gemara* (ibid.) explains that R' Meir disagrees, maintaining that this would have been understood even if Moses had said only, *But if they will not ... they shall inherit in your midst*, without adding the words *in the Land of Canaan*. These extra words indicate that even to exclude them from the Land of Gilead, it was necessary for Moses to make a double stipulation.

R' Chanina, however, contends that without the extra words, it would be implied only that if they did not help to conquer the Land of Canaan, they would receive a share in the Land of Gilead which they helped conquer [i.e., the share which would be coming to them if Gilead were divided among all the tribes — as opposed to the entire area, which they actually received], but not in the Land of Canaan. It was therefore necessary to state explicitly that they would also receive their share in the Land of Canaan (*Rashi* 61a; cf. *Tos.* ad loc. s.v. אי).

The *halachah* follows the view of R' Meir, that a stipulation must be similar in all the ways described above to the condition of the descendants of Gad and Reuven in order to be binding, whether it involves a religious matter or a monetary matter (*Rav; Rambam, Hil. Zechiyah* 3:8; *Tos.* 49b s.v. דברים). However, if one used the term עַל מְנָת, *on condition*, which implies that the agreement be effective retroactively when the condition is met (see mishnah 2), it is valid even without these requisites (*Rav;* see commentary to *Gittin* 7:5).

Others contend that these rules apply to religious matters, but not to pecuniary matters (*Rashba* to *Bava Basra* 137b s.v. ואם לאו), while a third view opines that they pertain only to *gittin* and *kiddushin* (*Rif*, responsum 31; see *Ravad* to *Hil. Zechiyah* loc. cit.).

3
5 because otherwise, it is implicit that even in the Land of Canaan they shall not inherit.

5. [I]f] one betrothed a woman and said: "I thought that she is the daughter of a *Kohen,* and lo, she is the daughter of a *Levi*"; [or] "the daughter of a *Levi,* and lo, she is the daughter of a *Kohen*"; "a poor woman, and lo, she is a rich woman"; [or] "a rich woman, and lo, she is a poor woman" — she is betrothed, because she did not deceive him.

YAD AVRAHAM

5.

The first portion of this mishnah deals with the principle stated above (2:3), that unexpressed intentions have no effect in Jewish law. It is mentioned here in order to clarify that even R' Chanina, who maintains in the previous mishnah that a stipulation does not need to be expressed with both alternatives, agrees that it must nevertheless be stated explicitly to be effective (*Ran; Meiri*).

[The second portion discusses the issue of a man betrothing a woman who is not presently eligible to be betrothed to him, to take effect on a later date when she will be eligible. It is connected to the broader question of acquiring something before it comes into existence.]

הַמְקַדֵּשׁ אֶת הָאִשָּׁה — *[If] one betrothed a woman*

[Without stating that the *kiddushin* was based on any assumptions regarding her status.]

וְאָמַר: — *and said:*

[He subsequently claimed that his *kiddushin* had been based on one of the following misconceptions:]

,,כְּסָבוּר הָיִיתִי שֶׁהִיא כֹהֶנֶת, וַהֲרֵי הִיא לְוִיָּה", — *"I thought that she is the daughter of a Kohen, and lo, she is the daughter of a Levi";*

[He meant to betroth her only if her father was a *Kohen,* which is a more prestigious status than that of a *Levi.*]

,,לְוִיָּה, וַהֲרֵי הִיא כֹהֶנֶת"; — [*or*] *"the daughter of a Levi, and lo, she is the daughter of a Kohen";*

[He claims that he betrothed her on the assumption that her father was a *Levi,* and would not have done so had he known that he was a *Kohen.*]

Although a *Kohen* is of greater stature, he may prefer a wife of lesser stature (see 2:3).

,,עֲנִיָּה, וַהֲרֵי הִיא עֲשִׁירָה", ,,עֲשִׁירָה, וַהֲרֵי הִיא עֲנִיָּה" — *"a poor woman, and lo, she is a rich woman";* [*or*] *"a rich woman, and lo, she is a poor woman"* —

[He betrothed her under the false assumption that she was poor, or, alternatively, that she was rich.]

הֲרֵי זוֹ מְקֻדֶּשֶׁת, מִפְּנֵי שֶׁלֹּא הִטְעַתּוּ. — *she is betrothed, because she did not deceive him.*

Rather, he deceived himself by

הָאוֹמֵר לָאִשָּׁה: הֲרֵי אַתְּ מְקֻדֶּשֶׁת לִי לְאַחַר שֶׁאֶתְגַּיֵּר", אוֹ ,,לְאַחַר שֶׁתִּתְגַּיְּרִי"; ,,לְאַחַר שֶׁאֶשְׁתַּחְרֵר", אוֹ ,,לְאַחַר שֶׁתִּשְׁתַּחְרְרִי"; ,,לְאַחַר שֶׁיָּמוּת בַּעְלֵיךְ", אוֹ ,,לְאַחַר שֶׁתָּמוּת אֲחוֹתֵיךְ"; ,,לְאַחַר שֶׁיַּחֲלוֹץ לִיךְ יְבָמִיךְ" — אֵינָהּ מְקֻדֶּשֶׁת.

יד אברהם

making groundless assumptions, and since he did not express this condition orally, it is ineffective and does not negate the *kiddushin* (*Rashi*).

If she deceived him by making a false claim, his *kiddushin* would be based on that assumption and would therefore be void. Even R' Meir — who ordinarily requires a stipulation to be expressed with both alternatives (mishnah 4) — would agree in this case. This is because R' Meir's ruling is based on his opinion that if someone does not state a condition with both alternatives, it indicates that he wants the agreement to be in effect whether or not the condition is met. However, when he states that the *kiddushin* is based entirely on a certain assumption, it is clear that he wants the *kiddushin* to take effect only if that assumption is true (*Ran;* cf. *Ran* to *Gittin* 75b s.v. אתקין שמואל).

הָאוֹמֵר לָאִשָּׁה: ,,הֲרֵי אַתְּ מְקֻדֶּשֶׁת לִי לְאַחַר שֶׁאֶתְגַּיֵּר", — *[If] one says to a woman: "You are betrothed to me after I will be converted,"*

[A gentile man who was planning to convert to Judaism gave money to a Jewish woman for the purpose of betrothing her when his conversion takes place.]

The *kiddushin* does not take effect — as stated below — even if the money was still in her possession at the time of his conversion. This is because she cannot be betrothed to him in his present situation (*Meiri*), since *kiddushin* between a Jew and a gentile is not valid (mishnah 12) [and a legal act whose validity is based upon a situation which is not yet existent does not take effect]. If it were completely within his ability to bring about the conversion, that would suffice to validate the *kiddushin.* This is not the case, however, since conversion requires the participation of three men forming a religious court, and it is possible that he may not find three men willing to participate (*Gem.* 62b).

Although a male proselyte can be circumcised and immersed in a *mikveh* (ritual pool) [two of the necessary steps in conversion to Judaism] without the participation of three men, his acceptance of the authority of the Torah [a third prerequisite to conversion] must be made before a court (*Tos.* 62b s.v. גר). Others contend that even if he undergoes the entire conversion process on his own, it is valid, but he may not marry a Jewish woman unless he immerses in a *mikveh* in the presence of three Jewish men (*Meiri*).

אוֹ ,,לְאַחַר שֶׁתִּתְגַּיְּרִי"; — *or "after you will be converted";*

[A Jewish man gave money to a gentile woman who was planning to convert to Judaism, for the purpose of betrothing her after she becomes Jewish.] The *kiddushin* does not take effect, since it is not in his power to convert her and render her eligible for

3
5

[If] one says to a woman: "You are betrothed to me after I will be converted," or "after you will be converted"; "after I become freed," or "after you become freed"; "after your husband shall die," or "after your sister shall die"; "after your *yavam* shall give you *chalitzah*" — she is not betrothed.

YAD AVRAHAM

kiddushin, as explained above (*Meiri*).[1]

„לְאַחַר שֶׁאֶשְׁתַּחְרֵר", — *"after I become freed,"*

[A Canaanite slave (see 1:3) performed *kiddushin* with a free Jewish woman to take effect after his release, at which time he becomes a full-fledged Jew (ibid.).] It cannot take effect immediately, since *kiddushin* between a free Jew and a Canaanite slave is void (mishnah 12), and it is not in his power to effect his freedom (*Meiri*). [Therefore, the *kiddushin* is not valid, as stated below.]

אוֹ „לְאַחַר שֶׁתִּשְׁתַּחְרְרִי"; — *or "after you become freed";*

[A free Jewish man betrothed a Canaanite slave (see 1:3), in order that the *kiddushin* take effect after she is released.] Since it is not within his power to secure her release, the *kiddushin* is not valid (*Meiri*).

He cannot even betroth his own slave in this manner, even though he is able to release her and render her eligible for *kiddushin,* because a slave is compared in Scripture to a beast, as derived from Abraham's directive to Eliezer, his slave (*Gen.* 22:5), *Stay here ... with the donkey.* The necessity for such a major change as one from a beast to a human invalidates the *kiddushin,* because after her release, she is considered to be an entirely different being from the one he betrothed (*Gem.* ibid.).

„לְאַחַר שֶׁיָּמוּת בַּעְלִיךְ", — *"after your husband shall die,"*

[A man betrothed a married woman, stipulating that the *kiddushin* take effect after the death of her present husband.]

אוֹ „לְאַחַר שֶׁתָּמוּת אֲחוֹתִיךְ"; — *or "after your sister shall die";*

[A man betrothed his wife's sister — who is forbidden to him as long as his wife is alive (*Lev.* 18:18) — stipulating that the *kiddushin* take effect after his wife dies.]

„לְאַחַר שֶׁיַּחֲלֹץ לִיךְ יְבָמִיךְ" — *"after your yavam shall give you chalitzah"* —

[A man betrothed a *yevamah* — who is prohibited to anyone but the *yavam* (see 1:1) — stipulating that the *kiddushin* take effect after her release through *chalitzah.*]

אֵינָהּ מְקֻדֶּשֶׁת. — *she is not betrothed.*

In all of the above cases, the woman is not betrothed, because the situation which allows for the validity of the *kiddushin* is not yet in existence, and it

1. [*Meiri's* wording implies that even if the woman were able to convert completely on her own, the *kiddushin* would not be valid, since the man is not able to bring it about. Apparently, because the man is the active principal in the execution (see General Introduction s.v. The Process of Kiddushin), it must be within his power to render her eligible in order for the *kiddushin* to be valid after the condition is fulfilled.]

וְכֵן הָאוֹמֵר לַחֲבֵרוֹ: „אִם יָלְדָה אִשְׁתְּךָ נְקֵבָה הֲרֵי הִיא מְקֻדֶּשֶׁת לִי" — אֵינָהּ מְקֻדֶּשֶׁת. אִם הָיְתָה אֵשֶׁת חֲבֵרוֹ מְעֻבֶּרֶת, וְהֻכַּר עֻבָּרָהּ — דְּבָרָיו קַיָּמִין, וְאִם יָלְדָה נְקֵבָה — מְקֻדֶּשֶׁת.

[ו] **הָאוֹמֵר** לָאִשָּׁה: „הֲרֵי אַתְּ מְקֻדֶּשֶׁת לִי עַל מְנָת שֶׁאֲדַבֵּר עָלַיִךְ לַשִּׁלְטוֹן", וְ„אֶעֱשֶׂה עִמָּךְ כְּפוֹעֵל":

ר' עובדיה מברטנורא

(ה) **והוכר עוברה דבריו קיימין.** כתב רמב"ם דאין לו לבא עליה עד שיקדשנה קדושין שניים, שאין אדם מקנה דבר שלא בא לעולם, ולא אמרו דבריו קיימים אלא להחמיר עליה שאסורה ליכנס לאחרים: (ו) **ואעשה עמך כפועל.** בפעולת יום אחד, ולאו דמקדש לה בשכר פעולה, דכיון דקיימא לן (סנ, א) ישנה לשכירות מתחילה ועד סוף, נמצא כשגמר פעולתו הוי שכירותו מלוה אצלה, והמקדש במלוה אינה מקודשת, אלא דמקדש לה השתא בפרוטה על מנת שיעשה אחר כך עמה כפועל:

יד אברהם

Shmuel, that the validity of *kiddushin* with a *yevamah* is an unresolved question. Therefore, if a man betrothed a *yevamah*, stipulating that the *kiddushin* should take effect after *chalitzah*, the validity of that *kiddushin* would remain in doubt [and she would require a *get* from the betrother before getting married to another man] (*Ran; Even HaEzer* 40:6).

Another view is that since if he were to betroth her in order that the *kiddushin* take effect immediately, it would possibly be valid and would necessitate a *get* before she could marry another man, that is sufficient grounds to consider such a *kiddushin* as more than merely something dependent upon a non-existent situation. Therefore, her status as a *yevamah* does not prevent the effectuality of *kiddushin* which is to take effect after *chalitzah*, and such a *kiddushin* is valid (*Rambam, Hil. Ishus* 7:15, *Kesef Mishneh* ad loc.; *Meiri*).

וְכֵן הָאוֹמֵר לַחֲבֵרוֹ: „אִם יָלְדָה אִשְׁתְּךָ נְקֵבָה הֲרֵי הִיא מְקֻדֶּשֶׁת לִי" — אֵינָהּ מְקֻדֶּשֶׁת. — *Likewise, [if] one says to another: "If your wife bears a female, she is*

is not within the man's power to bring it about on his own (*Rashi*).

There is a dispute among the *Tannaim* (*Yevamos* 4:13) whether all marital relationships which are Biblically prohibited are void, or only those which are punishable by *kares*. There is a further dispute among the *Amoraim* (ibid. 92b) whether, according to the prevailing latter opinion, the prohibition against marrying a *yavam* — which is not punishable by *kares* — is an exception, so that such a *kiddushin*, too, would be void. According to Rav (the Talmudic sage), who holds that it is void, our mishnah — which implies that *kiddushin* with a *yevamah* does not take effect — is consistent with the prevalent ruling. Shmuel, however, maintains that whether or not *kiddushin* with a *yevamah* takes effect is an unresolved question. Accordingly, our mishnah — which assumes that such a *kiddushin* is void — follows the opinion of R' Akiva, that *kiddushin* with any woman who is Biblically prohibited is void (*Ran; Tos. R' Akiva Eiger*).

The *halachah* follows the view of

3
6

Likewise, [if] one says to another: "If your wife bears a female, she is betrothed to me," she is not betrothed. If the other's wife was pregnant and her fetus was discernible, his words are effective; and if she bore a female, she is betrothed.

6. [If] one says to a woman: "You are betrothed to me on condition that I will speak on your behalf to the ruler," or "I will work for you like a

YAD AVRAHAM

betrothed to me," she is not betrothed.

[If a man gave money to another for the purpose of betrothing his daughter when she will be born, the *kiddushin* is not valid, because she is not yet in existence.]

אִם הָיְתָה אֵשֶׁת חֲבֵרוֹ מְעֻבֶּרֶת, וְהֻכַּר עֻבָּרָהּ — דְּבָרָיו קַיָּמִין, וְאִם יָלְדָה נְקֵבָה — מְקֻדֶּשֶׁת. — *If the other's wife was pregnant and her fetus was discernible, his words are effective; and if she bore a female, she is betrothed.*

[As soon as the daughter is born, she is betrothed to him.]

However, he must perform *kiddushin* with her again when she is born, because the fact that the fetus is discernible is not really considered as if the child were already present. The mishnah means only because the *kiddushin* is similar enough to one which is valid, the Sages prohibited her to other men (*Rav; Rambam Commentary*).

Rambam writes elsewhere (*Hil. Ishus* 7:16) that the *kiddushin* is actually valid, since the child is considered present as soon as the fetus is discernible (*Maggid Mishneh* ad loc.). Nevertheless, he should betroth her again after she is born so that the *kiddushin* should be beyond question.

Alternate versions of the mishnah do not include this last statement (*Tos. Yom Tov*); indeed, other commentators maintain that even if the fetus is discernible, the *kiddushin* is void (*Ravad*, loc. cit.; *Meiri*).

6.

הָאוֹמֵר לָאִשָּׁה: ,,הֲרֵי אַתְּ מְקֻדֶּשֶׁת לִי עַל מְנָת שֶׁאֲדַבֵּר עָלַיִךְ לַשִּׁלְטוֹן", — *[If] one says to a woman: "You are betrothed to me on condition that I will speak on your behalf to the ruler,"*

A man betrothed a woman with a *perutah* (*Gem.* 63a) on condition that he intervene with a ruler to prevent the latter from molesting her (*Tos. Yom Tov*).

וְ,,אֶעֱשֶׂה עִמָּךְ כְּפוֹעֵל": — *or "I will work for you like a laborer"* —

[He betrothed her on condition that he work for her like a laborer] for one day (*Rav*).

If he betrothed her with the value of the work itself, the *kiddushin* is not valid. This is because payment for services becomes due — *perutah* by *perutah* — as the work is being done, and remains a debt to the employee until he is paid. Therefore, by the time his work is finished the payment is already past due. Accordingly, if he betroths her with that value, he is

דִּבֵּר עָלֶיהָ לַשִּׁלְטוֹן, וְעָשָׂה עִמָּהּ כְּפוֹעֵל — מְקֻדֶּשֶׁת; וְאִם לָאו — אֵינָהּ מְקֻדֶּשֶׁת.

,,עַל מְנָת שֶׁיִּרְצֶה אַבָּא״: רָצָה הָאָב — מְקֻדֶּשֶׁת; וְאִם לָאו — אֵינָהּ מְקֻדֶּשֶׁת. מֵת הָאָב — הֲרֵי זוֹ מְקֻדֶּשֶׁת; מֵת הַבֵּן — מְלַמְּדִין אֶת הָאָב לוֹמַר שֶׁאֵינוֹ רוֹצֶה.

ר׳ עובדיה מברטנורא

על מנת שירצה אבא. בגמרא (סג, ב) מפרש שלא ימחה אבא, וכשקבע זמן למחאתו, כגון שאמר שלא ימחה אבא כל שלשים יום. הלכך רצה האב, שעברו שלשים יום ולא מיחה, הרי זו מקודשת, לא רצה, שמיחה בתוך שלשים, אינה מקודשת: **מת האב.** תוך שלשים, הרי זו מקודשת, דאמרינן מאן מחי: **מת הבן.** בתוך שלשים, מלמדים את האב שימחה, כדי שלא תהא זקוקה ליבם:

יד אברהם

actually waiving her debt to him rather than giving her something new, and this is not valid for *kiddushin* (*Rav* from *Gem.* 63a).

דִּבֵּר עָלֶיהָ לַשִּׁלְטוֹן, וְעָשָׂה עִמָּהּ כְּפוֹעֵל — מְקֻדֶּשֶׁת; וְאִם לָאו — אֵינָהּ מְקֻדֶּשֶׁת. *[if] he spoke on her behalf to the ruler or he worked for her like a laborer, she is betrothed; if not, she is not betrothed.*

Although the fact that a *kiddushin* can be based on a condition has already been stated many times, the mishnah uses these examples to teach us that only if the services were offered as a condition is the *kiddushin* valid, but not if they were rendered in order to serve as the equivalent of money for the *kiddushin* itself [as stated above] (*Ran*).

If he did not specify exactly what he will do for her, but stated only that he will seek her benefit from the ruler, or that he will work for her, whatever service he performs in this manner is sufficient to fulfill the condition, and she cannot say that she wanted him to accomplish something else [since she consented to the condition as stated at the time of *kiddushin*] (*Rosh*; *Chelkas Mechokek* to *Even HaEzer* 38:12). Others contend that she can nevertheless say that this was not the service she desired (*Beis Yosef* ad loc.).

,,עַל מְנָת שֶׁיִּרְצֶה אַבָּא״: רָצָה הָאָב — מְקֻדֶּשֶׁת; וְאִם לָאו — אֵינָהּ מְקֻדֶּשֶׁת. *[If he said:] "On condition that Father will consent" — [if] the father consented, she is betrothed; if not, she is not betrothed.*

If a man betrothed a woman on condition that his father does not protest the *kiddushin* within a set period of time, the condition is binding, and the *kiddushin* is valid only if his father does not protest it within that time (*Rav* from *Gem.* 63b).

Another explanation given in the *Gemara* is that *on condition that Father will consent* means that he must consent explicitly in order for the *kiddushin* to be valid, and as long as he does not do so, it is not finalized (*Ran*).

A third interpretation is that the *kiddushin* was made on condition that his father will be silent (*Gem.* 63b) at the moment he hears of it (*Rashi*). In such a case, if the father is silent, the *kiddushin* is valid; if he protests, it is void (ibid.).

3
6

laborer" — [if] he spoke on her behalf to the ruler or he worked for her like a laborer, she is betrothed; if not, she is not betrothed.

[If he said:] "On condition that Father will consent" — [if] the father consented, she is betrothed; if not, she is not betrothed. [If] the father dies, she is betrothed; [if] the son dies, they instruct the father to say that he does not consent.

YAD AVRAHAM

מֵת הָאָב — הֲרֵי זוֹ מְקֻדֶּשֶׁת; — *[If] the father dies, she is betrothed;*

If his father dies [without protesting the *kiddushin*] before the allotted time passes, the *kiddushin* is valid, because it is no longer possible for him to protest (*Rav*).

According to the interpretation that the stipulation requires that the father actively consent in order to validate the *kiddushin*, this statement of the mishnah must be discussing a different case, because if the father dies, it is obviously no longer possible for him to consent. Therefore, the mishnah is either discussing the first case mentioned above, in which the man stipulated that his father's protest would negate the *kiddushin* (*Gem.* 63b), or the situation described below.

According to the opinion that the condition was that the father remain silent at the moment he hears of the *kiddushin*, this statement of the mishnah is referring to a case in which the father died before hearing of the *kiddushin*. Since such a stipulation indicates that the son's primary intent is that his father should not protest the *kiddushin*, but not that he must explicitly approve, once the father's death precludes any such protest, the *kiddushin* is valid (*Ran*).

מֵת הַבֵּן — מְלַמְּדִין אֶת הָאָב לוֹמַר שֶׁאֵינוֹ רוֹצֶה. — *[if] the son dies, they instruct the father to say that he does not consent.*

If the son died within thirty days [and he had no children], they instruct the father to say that he does not consent — thereby invalidating the *kiddushin*, so that the woman should not fall to *yibum* (*Ran*).

In this case, the condition must be one which stipulates that the protest of the father can nullify the *kiddushin*. For if it were a case in which the son had stipulated that his father be silent at the time he hears of the *kiddushin*, and he had already done so, a subsequent protest would not help to nullify it (*Gem.* 63b). Indeed, the mishnah's words *they instruct the father to say* imply that he already heard of the *kiddushin* without reacting, and is now being advised what to do at this point (*Ran*). If the son had stipulated that the *kiddushin* is valid if the father consents, the latter's protest cannot free her from *yibum*, because if he later consents, the condition will then be fulfilled, which will retroactively validate the *kiddushin* (ibid.). Therefore, the only possible interpretation of this case is that he stipulated that if the father protests, the *kiddushin* should be nullified, and they therefore instruct him to do so (*Gem.* loc. cit.).

[ז] ,,קִדַּשְׁתִּי אֶת בִּתִּי, וְאֵינִי יוֹדֵעַ לְמִי קִדַּשְׁתִּיהָ", וּבָא אֶחָד וְאָמַר: ,,אֲנִי קִדַּשְׁתִּיהָ" — נֶאֱמָן. זֶה אָמַר: ,,אֲנִי קִדַּשְׁתִּיהָ", וְזֶה אָמַר: ,,אֲנִי קִדַּשְׁתִּיהָ" — שְׁנֵיהֶם נוֹתְנִים גֵּט. וְאִם רָצוּ — אֶחָד נוֹתֵן גֵּט, וְאֶחָד כּוֹנֵס.

[ח] ,,קִדַּשְׁתִּי אֶת בִּתִּי", ,,קִדַּשְׁתִּיהָ וְגֵרַשְׁתִּיהָ כְּשֶׁהִיא

ר' עובדיה מברטנורא

(ז) אני קדשתיה נאמן. לכנסה, דלא חציף למימר קמיה דאב שקבל הקדושין, אני הוא, אם לא היה אמת, דמרתת דלמא מכחיש ליה:

יד אברהם

7.

קִדַּשְׁתִּי אֶת בִּתִּי,, — [*If a man said:*] *"I gave my daughter in kiddushin,*

A man has the authority to accept *kiddushin* for his daughter when she is a minor and when she is a *naarah* (see 2:1). In addition, he is believed not only to say that he did so — which prohibits her to all other men (mishnah 8) — but even to say to whom he betrothed her (*Gem.* 64a), as stated in the verse (*Deut.* 22:18), *I gave my daughter to this man.*

There is a dispute in the *Gemara* (63b) whether the father's declaration that he accepted *kiddushin* for his daughter is sufficient evidence for a court to execute someone who has intimacy with her, or whether it suffices only to prohibit her to other men.

וְאֵינִי יוֹדֵעַ לְמִי קִדַּשְׁתִּיהָ" — *but I do not know to whom I gave her in kiddushin,"*

She is thus prohibited to every man (*Meiri*) [because she might be betrothed to another man].

וּבָא אֶחָד וְאָמַר: ,,אֲנִי קִדַּשְׁתִּיהָ" — נֶאֱמָן. — *and one came and said: "I betrothed her," he is believed.*

If a man claimed that he is the one who had betrothed her, he is believed, because he would be afraid to lie in front of her father, who might contradict him. Therefore, he is permitted to marry her (*Rav* from *Gem.* 63b).

Although the testimony of two witnesses is ordinarily required in order to permit a woman to marry, that is only when they testify to a change in the status quo [e.g., she was previously married to Reuven and they testify that he divorced her, which would permit her to remarry]. In this case, however, the man's statement is not changing the status quo; rather, he is revealing that he is the unknown man to whom it has been established that she is betrothed. Therefore, his testimony alone is sufficient (*Ran*).

There is another opinion in the *Gemara* that he is believed only to the extent that if he gives her a *get*, she becomes permitted to marry another man, because a man would not sin — by causing someone to marry a

7. [If a man said:] "I gave my daughter in *kiddushin*, but I do not know to whom I gave her in *kiddushin*," and one came and said: "I betrothed her," he is believed. [If] this one said: "I betrothed her," and this one said: "I betrothed her," they both give a *get*. If they want, one gives a *get* and one marries.

8. [If a man said:] "I gave my daughter in *kiddushin*," [or] "I gave her in *kiddushin*

YAD AVRAHAM

woman when she is actually another man's wife — if he derives no benefit from it. However, he himself is not allowed to marry her, for fear that he will lie for that purpose.

If a woman declared that she had accepted *kiddushin* for herself but does not recall from who, all agree that one who claims to be the husband may not marry her, because he may be confident enough of his appeal to her to assume that she will cover up for him, and he is therefore not afraid of being contradicted (*Gem.* ibid.). Nevertheless, he is believed to the extent that if he gives her a *get*, she becomes permitted to all others, since he is not likely to lie if he does not benefit from it. He himself may not remarry her, however (*Rambam, Hil. Ishus* 9:14), for fear that he will lie about the *kiddushin* and then give her a *get* in order to subsequently marry her (*Ran*).

זֶה אָמַר: „אֲנִי קִדַּשְׁתִּיהָ", וְזֶה אָמַר: „אֲנִי קִדַּשְׁתִּיהָ" — שְׁנֵיהֶם נוֹתְנִים גֵּט. — *[If] this one said: "I betrothed her," and this one said: "I betrothed her," they both give a get.*

Since one of them is definitely lying, we cannot trust either to allow him to marry her. Nevertheless, we permit her to remarry upon receiving *gittin* from both of them, and we are not concerned with the possibility that they are both lying, and she had actually been betrothed to a third man (*Meiri*).

וְאִם רָצוּ — אֶחָד נוֹתֵן גֵּט, וְאֶחָד כּוֹנֵס. — *If they want, one gives a get and one marries.*

After one of the two has given a *get*, the other one may marry her, since the only other person whom we suspect may have betrothed her has now divorced her. Nevertheless, he must first perform another act of *kiddushin* with her, since it may have been the other man who had originally betrothed her (*Ran; Meiri*).

If one man claimed that he was the one who had betrothed her, and he was then given permission to marry her, and after their marriage, another man came and claimed that he was her true husband, the latter is not believed to prohibit her to her present husband (*Meiri; Rambam, Hil. Ishus* 9:13).

8.

„קִדַּשְׁתִּי אֶת בִּתִּי" — *[If a man said:] "I gave my daughter in kiddushin,"* —

This refers to a daughter who is a minor or a *naarah* (*Meiri*). [A man has

קְטַנָּה״, וַהֲרֵי הִיא קְטַנָּה — נֶאֱמָן.
,,קִדַּשְׁתִּיהָ וְגֵרַשְׁתִּיהָ כְּשֶׁהִיא קְטַנָּה״, וַהֲרֵי הִיא גְדוֹלָה — אֵינוֹ נֶאֱמָן.
,,נִשְׁבֵּית וּפְדִיתִיהָ״: בֵּין שֶׁהִיא קְטַנָּה בֵּין שֶׁהִיא גְדוֹלָה — אֵינוֹ נֶאֱמָן.
מִי שֶׁאָמַר בִּשְׁעַת מִיתָתוֹ: ,,יֵשׁ לִי בָנִים״ —

ר׳ עובדיה מברטנורא

(ח) **וגרשתיה.** קבלתי את גטה: **והרי היא קטנה.** עכשיו כשאמר עליה כך: **נאמן.** לפסלה מן הכהונה, שהאב נאמן על בתו כל זמן שהיא קטנה, דכתיב (דברים כב, טז) את בתי נתתי לאיש הזה, כשאמר לאיש, אסרה על הכל, שאין אנו יודעים למי, כשחזר ואמר לזה, התירה לו: **והרי היא גדולה.** ואם לאחר שגדלה אמר כך, ובקטנותה לא אמר, אינו נאמן: **נשבית ופדיתיה וכו׳ אינו נאמן.** לפסלה מן הכהונה, דכשואין הימניה רחמנא לאב, לשבויה לא הימניה: **יש לי בנים.** ואין אשתי זקוקה ליבם:

יד אברהם

the authority to marry off his daughter during these stages and is believed to say he did so, as explained in the previous mishnah.]

Other versions read: *I gave my daughter, the minor, in kiddushin* (*Rif; Rosh; Meiri*), but the ruling nevertheless applies to a *naarah* as well (*Meiri*).

[*or*] — ,,קִדַּשְׁתִּיהָ וְגֵרַשְׁתִּיהָ כְּשֶׁהִיא קְטַנָּה״, *"I gave her in kiddushin and accepted her divorce when she was a minor,"*

A father also has the authority to accept a *get* on behalf of his daughter during these stages, as long as she has only had *kiddushin* (*Kesubos* 4:4). Once she has had *nisuin* (full marriage), however, she leaves his jurisdiction entirely (ibid. 4:5).

Here, too, the mishnah mentions a minor, but the same ruling would apply to a *naarah* (*Meiri*).

וַהֲרֵי הִיא קְטַנָּה — *and she is a minor,* —

She is a minor [or a *naarah* (*Meiri*)] at the time of his testimony (*Rav*).

נֶאֱמָן. — *he is believed.*

He is believed to establish her as a divorcee, thereby disqualifying her from marrying a *Kohen* (*Rav;* see *Lev.* 21:7).

The fact that a father is believed about the *kiddushin* and divorce of his daughter who is a minor or a *naarah* is derived from the verse, discussing a *naarah* (*Deut.* 22:16), *I gave my daughter to this man for a wife.* Upon saying, *"I gave my daughter,"* the father prohibits her to every man; when he adds, *"to this man,"* he is thereby permitting her to him (*Rav* from *Gem.* 64a) [and we can therefore conclude that he is also believed to permit her to remarry by stating that he accepted her divorce].

Nevertheless, he is only believed that she was divorced if he says so immediately after attesting to her *kiddushin.* Otherwise, once her *kiddushin* has been established by his word, he is not believed to testify that she was divorced, since the passage does not specifically grant him credibility with regard to her divorce (*Ran*). [Were it not for the special

and accepted her divorce when she was a minor," and she is a minor, he is believed.

[If he said:] "I gave her in *kiddushin* and accepted her divorce when she was a minor," and she is an adult, he is not believed.

[If he said:] "She was abducted and I ransomed her" — whether she is a minor or she is an adult — he is not believed.

One who said at the time of his death: "I have

YAD AVRAHAM

credibility granted him by the Torah, he would not be believed to testify as an ordinary witness, because one witness alone cannot effect a change in the status quo — e.g., to establish a hitherto married woman as unmarried or vice versa.]

„קִדַּשְׁתִּיהָ וְגֵרַשְׁתִּיהָ כְּשֶׁהִיא קְטַנָּה", וַהֲרֵי הִיא גְדוֹלָה — אֵינוֹ נֶאֱמָן. — *[If he said:] "I gave her in kiddushin and accepted her divorce when she was a minor," and she is an adult, he is not believed.*

If after she became a *bogeres* (usually at the age of twelve and a half years; see commentary to *Gittin* 6:2 s.v. נַעֲרָה) — at which time she attains full adulthood and leaves her father's jurisdiction completely — he testified that she had been betrothed and divorced as a minor, he is not believed (*Rav*) [because the credibility granted him by the Torah pertains only to a daughter who is a minor or a *naarah* at the time of his testimony].

„נִשְׁבֵּית וּפְדִיתִיהָ": בֵּין שֶׁהִיא קְטַנָּה בֵּין שֶׁהִיא גְדוֹלָה — אֵינוֹ נֶאֱמָן. — *[If he said:] "She was abducted and I ransomed her" — whether she is a minor or she is an adult — he is not believed.*

He is not believed to disqualify her from marrying a *Kohen* by virtue of the possibility that she was molested by the gentile who abducted her, thereby prohibiting her to a *Kohen* (see *Rambam, Hil. Issurei Biah* 18:1). This is because the Torah only granted him credibility regarding her marriage, but not her abduction (*Rav* from *Gem.* 64a; see *Ran*).

After discussing the credibility of a father concerning his daughter, the mishnah now goes on to discuss the issue of a man's credibility regarding his wife's status with respect to *yibum* (see *Meiri*).

מִי שֶׁאָמַר בִּשְׁעַת מִיתָתוֹ: — *One who said at the time of his death:*

The same would be true if he said it at any other time; the mishnah mentions *the time of death* only because that is the time when a man is likely to concern himself with his wife's status regarding *yibum* (*Rashbam* to *Bava Basra* 134b s.v. בשעת מיתתי).

„יֵשׁ לִי בָנִים" — — *"I have sons,"*

"And therefore, my wife is not eligible for *yibum* upon my death" (see 1:1) [which applies only to the wife of a man who dies without children] (*Rav*).

The mishnah is discussing a case in which the man was not known to have sons or brothers (*Gem.* 64a), and thus, it is presumed that his wife is not

נֶאֱמָן. ,,יֵשׁ לִי אַחִים" — אֵינוֹ נֶאֱמָן.
הַמְקַדֵּשׁ אֶת בִּתּוֹ סְתָם — אֵין הַבּוֹגְרוֹת בִּכְלָל.

[ט] **מִי** שֶׁיֵּשׁ לוֹ שְׁתֵּי כִתֵּי בָנוֹת מִשְּׁתֵּי נָשִׁים, וְאָמַר: ,,קִדַּשְׁתִּי אֶת בִּתִּי הַגְּדוֹלָה,

ר' עובדיה מברטנורא

יש לי אחים. ואשתי זקוקה ליבם, ועד עכשיו היתה בחזקת שאינה זקוקה: **אין הבוגרות בכלל.** לפי שאינן ברשות האב לקדשן, ואף על פי שעשאתו הבוגרת שליח לקבל קדושיה, אמרינן לא שביק איניש מצוה דרמיא עליה ועביד מצוה דלא רמיא עליה, אבל הקטנות והנערות כולן צריכות גט מספק, דלא ידעינן איזו מהם קדש: **(ט) קדשתי את בתי גדולה.** איצטריך תנא לאשמועינן פלוגתא דרבי מאיר ודרבי יוסי בקדשתי את הגדולה ובקדשתי את הקטנה. דאי אשמועינן בקדשתי את הגדולה, הוה אמינא בהא קאמר רבי מאיר, דכיון דאיכא דזוטרא מינה,

יד אברהם

,,יֵשׁ לִי אַחִים" — אֵינוֹ נֶאֱמָן. — [*If he said:*] *"I have brothers," he is not believed.*

He is not believed to render his wife bound to *yibum*, because he is directly contradicting her presumptive status which dictates that she is not bound (*Rav*).

If he was presumed to have brothers — thus making her bound to *yibum* — and he declared that he has none, there is a dispute among the authorities whether or not he is believed to contradict the presumed status quo by virtue of the fact that he could give her a *get* (see footnote 1) (*Rosh; Ran*).

הַמְקַדֵּשׁ אֶת בִּתּוֹ סְתָם — [*If*] *one gives his daughter in kiddushin without specification,*

[A man who had more than one daughter (*Tif. Yis.*) accepted *kiddushin* on behalf of his daughter, but neither he nor the betrother specified which of them was being betrothed.]

אֵין הַבּוֹגְרוֹת בִּכְלָל. — *the bogros are not included.*

The possibility of having been the one who was betrothed — which bound to *yibum* [since there was no brother to whom to be bound] (*Rashi* ad loc. s.v. דלא מוחזק לן).

נֶאֱמָן. — *is believed.*

Because his statement coincides with her presumptive status of being free from *yibum*. Therefore, if someone should later come and claim to be the man's brother, he is not believed [to alter her status to be that of a woman requiring *yibum* and thereby negate the basis for the husband's credibility] since the husband's statement has already been accepted (ibid.).

The mishnah in *Bava Basra* (8:6) makes a statement similar to that of our mishnah in order to add that if the husband was presumed to have brothers, but it was not known if he had sons, and he stated that he did have sons — thus freeing her from *yibum* — he is believed. Since he is not directly contradicting the presumed status quo, which relates to the question of brothers rather than sons, he is believed to free her from *yibum* by virtue of the fact that he could have given her a *get* and avoided the entire issue[1] (*Bava Basra* 134b; see *Tos. Yom Tov*).

1. [This is based on the principle of מִיגּוֹ, *miggo* [lit., *since*] — i.e., since he would have been able to achieve his objective without making this statement, he had no reason to do so unless it is true.]

sons,'' is believed. [If he said:] ''I have brothers,'' he is not believed.

[If] one gives his daughter in *kiddushin* without specification, the *bogros* are not included.

9. [If] one has two groups of daughters from two wives, and he said: ''I gave my elder daughter

YAD AVRAHAM

prohibits his daughters from marrying without a *get* — does not pertain to those who have already reached the stage of a *bogeres* (see above) since they are not under the father's jurisdiction, and he is unable to accept *kiddushin* for them (*Rav*).

Even if they had appointed him to accept *kiddushin* on their behalf, they do not require a *get* in this case,[1] because it is assumed that he would not ignore a responsibility which is incumbent upon him [i.e., to marry off his daughter when he has the authority to do so, as stated in the verse (*Jer.* 29:6), *And your daughters give to them*] and pursue a *mitzvah* which is not his responsibility [i.e., to marry off his daughters who have reached the stage of a *bogeres* and are therefore under their own jurisdiction] (*Rav* from *Gem.* 64b).

According to those who maintain that *kiddushin* which does not allow for intimacy is not valid (see commentary to 2:7), even those under his jurisdiction would not be betrothed, since each of them is forbidden to the man, because she may be his wife's sister. Therefore, the mishnah must be discussing a case in which the father had only two daughters — one who was a minor [or a *naarah*] and one who was a *bogeres*. Since the *bogeres* is certainly excluded from the *kiddushin*, the second daughter — who is still under her father's jurisdiction — is clearly identified as the one whom he gave in *kiddushin*. The plural form *bogros* is used, because the mishnah is discussing *bogros*, in general, who could be involved in such an incident (*Gem.* 64b). Indeed, some versions of the mishnah read: *bogeres* (*Shinuyei Nuschaos*).

9.

מִי שֶׁיֵּשׁ לוֹ שְׁתֵּי כִתֵּי בָנוֹת מִשְּׁתֵּי נָשִׁים, — *[If] one has two groups of daughters from two wives,*

This refers to a case in which he married his second wife after the first had died [or after he had divorced her] and thus, all of the daughters from the first wife were older than those from the second (*Rashi*).

וְאָמַר: ,,קִדַּשְׁתִּי אֶת בִּתִּי הַגְּדוֹלָה, — *and he said: ''I gave my elder daughter in kiddushin,*

All the daughters were still under his jurisdiction; or were all *bogros*, but

1. This is inferred because otherwise the statement of the mishnah is self-evident and superfluous — it is obvious that they are excluded, because the father cannot accept *kiddushin* on their behalf. The only alternative interpretation of the mishnah's statement is that only the *bogros* are excluded, but the others are not — even though they may not have intimacy with the man (see below). However, if that were the case, the mishnah would have said so outright rather than focusing on the *bogros* (*Tos. Yom Tov*).

וְאֵינִי יוֹדֵעַ אִם גְּדוֹלָה שֶׁבַּגְּדוֹלוֹת, אוֹ גְדוֹלָה שֶׁבַּקְּטַנּוֹת, אוֹ קְטַנָּה שֶׁבַּגְּדוֹלוֹת, שֶׁהִיא גְדוֹלָה מִן הַגְּדוֹלָה שֶׁבַּקְּטַנּוֹת" — כֻּלָּן אֲסוּרוֹת חוּץ מִן הַקְּטַנָּה שֶׁבַּקְּטַנּוֹת; דִּבְרֵי רַבִּי מֵאִיר. רַבִּי יוֹסֵי אוֹמֵר: כֻּלָּן מֻתָּרוֹת חוּץ מִן הַגְּדוֹלָה שֶׁבַּגְּדוֹלוֹת.

„קִדַּשְׁתִּי אֶת בִּתִּי הַקְּטַנָּה, וְאֵינִי יוֹדֵעַ אִם קְטַנָּה שֶׁבַּקְּטַנּוֹת, אוֹ קְטַנָּה שֶׁבַּגְּדוֹלוֹת, אוֹ גְדוֹלָה שֶׁבַּקְּטַנּוֹת, שֶׁהִיא קְטַנָּה מִן הַקְּטַנּוֹת שֶׁבַּגְּדוֹלוֹת" — כֻּלָּן אֲסוּרוֹת חוּץ מִן הַגְּדוֹלָה שֶׁבַּגְּדוֹלוֹת; דִּבְרֵי רַבִּי מֵאִיר. רַבִּי יוֹסֵי אוֹמֵר: כֻּלָּן מֻתָּרוֹת חוּץ מִן הַקְּטַנָּה שֶׁבַּקְּטַנּוֹת.

ר' עובדיה מברטנורא

להך גדולה קרי לה, דשבח הוא לאדם לקרות בתו בלשון גדולה אף על פי שהיא קטנה, כשיש קטנה למטה ממנה. אבל קטנה, אימא מודי ליה לרבי יוסי, דכל שהוא יכול לקרות אותה גדולה אין קורא אותה קטנה. ואי אתמר בהא, בהא קאמר רבי יוסי, אבל בהך אימא מודי ליה לרבי מאיר, לכך הוצרכו שתיהן. והלכה כרבי יוסי בשתיהן:

יד אברהם

had appointed him to accept *kiddushin* on their behalf (*Tos. Yom Tov;* see mishnah 8).

Even if the man who had made the *kiddushin* subsequently identified which of them he had betrothed, he is not believed, because he is thereby removing the others from their status of being possibly married, and that requires two witnesses (*Tos. Yom Tov; Tos. R' Akiva*).

וְאֵינִי יוֹדֵעַ אִם גְּדוֹלָה שֶׁבַּגְּדוֹלוֹת, אוֹ גְדוֹלָה שֶׁבַּקְּטַנּוֹת, אוֹ קְטַנָּה שֶׁבַּגְּדוֹלוֹת, שֶׁהִיא גְדוֹלָה מִן הַגְּדוֹלָה שֶׁבַּקְּטַנּוֹת" — *and I do not know if [it was] the elder of the older ones, or the elder of the younger ones, or the younger of the older ones, who is older than the elder of the younger ones,"*

[He remembered that he had accepted *kiddushin* on behalf of his elder daughter, but he was not certain whether he had been referring to the eldest of all his daughters, one of those from the older group, or the eldest of the younger group.]

כֻּלָּן אֲסוּרוֹת חוּץ מִן הַקְּטַנָּה שֶׁבַּקְּטַנּוֹת; דִּבְרֵי רַבִּי מֵאִיר. — *they are all prohibited except for the younger of the younger ones; [these are] the words of R' Meir.*

[All of those who could possibly be referred to as *the elder* are prohibited to marry until they receive a *get* from the husband, because each of them may be the one who was betrothed.]

The mishnah is discussing a case in which the younger group included only two daughters. If there were more, only the eldest of them would be under consideration, because he would not refer to any of the others as *the elder*. However, the first group

3 in *kiddushin*, and I do not know if [it was] the elder
9 of the older ones, or the elder of the younger ones, or the younger of the older ones, who is older than the elder of the younger ones," they are all prohibited except for the younger of the younger ones; [these are] the words of R' Meir. R' Yose says: They are all permitted except for the elder of the older ones.

[If he said:] "I gave my younger daughter in *kiddushin*, and I do not know if [it was] the younger of the younger ones, or the younger of the older ones, or the elder of the younger ones, who is younger than the younger of the older ones," they are all prohibited except for the elder of the older ones; [these are] the words of R' Meir. R' Yose says: They are all permitted except for the younger of the younger ones.

YAD AVRAHAM

could include any number of girls, because any of them might be referred to as *the elder* by virtue of their being from the older group (*Gem.* 65a).

According to those who hold that *kiddushin* which does not allow for intimacy is void (see commentary to 2:7), the mishnah is discussing a case in which the identity of the daughter who was betrothed was clear at the time of *kiddushin*, but was later forgotten. Otherwise, the fact that it was unclear at the time of *kiddushin* would prohibit each of them to the husband, because of the possibility that he might have betrothed her sister, and the *kiddushin* would thus be void (*Gem.* 51b).

רַבִּי יוֹסֵי אוֹמֵר: כֻּלָּן מֻתָּרוֹת חוּץ מִן הַגְּדוֹלָה שֶׁבַּגְּדוֹלוֹת. — *R' Yose says: They are all permitted except for the elder of the older ones.*

R' Yose maintains that a person would not place himself in a situation which allows for ambiguity. It is therefore assumed that he would refer only to the eldest of all his daughters as *the elder daughter* (*Ran, Meiri* from *Gem.* 64b).

,,קִדַּשְׁתִּי אֶת בִּתִּי הַקְּטַנָּה, וְאֵינִי יוֹדֵעַ אִם קְטַנָּה שֶׁבַּקְּטַנּוֹת, אוֹ קְטַנָּה שֶׁבַּגְּדוֹלוֹת, אוֹ גְדוֹלָה שֶׁבַּקְּטַנּוֹת, שֶׁהִיא קְטַנָּה מִן הַקְּטַנּוֹת שֶׁבַּגְּדוֹלוֹת" — כֻּלָּן אֲסוּרוֹת חוּץ מִן הַגְּדוֹלָה שֶׁבַּגְּדוֹלוֹת; דִּבְרֵי רַבִּי מֵאִיר. רַבִּי יוֹסֵי אוֹמֵר: כֻּלָּן מֻתָּרוֹת חוּץ מִן הַקְּטַנָּה שֶׁבַּקְּטַנּוֹת. — *[If he said:] "I gave my younger daughter in kiddushin, and I do not know if [it was] the younger of the younger ones, or the younger of the older ones, or the elder of the younger ones, who is younger than the younger of the older ones," they are all prohibited except for the elder of the older ones; [these are] the words of R' Meir. R' Yose says: They are all permitted except for the younger of the younger ones.*

The mishnah repeats the dispute of R' Meir and R' Yose in this second

קידושין
ג/י

[י] **הָאוֹמֵר** לְאִשָּׁה: „קִדַּשְׁתִּיךְ", וְהִיא אוֹמֶרֶת: „לֹא קִדַּשְׁתַּנִי" — הוּא אָסוּר בִּקְרוֹבוֹתֶיהָ, וְהִיא מֻתֶּרֶת בִּקְרוֹבָיו. הִיא אוֹמֶרֶת: „קִדַּשְׁתַּנִי", וְהוּא אוֹמֵר: „לֹא קִדַּשְׁתִּיךְ" — הוּא מֻתָּר בִּקְרוֹבוֹתֶיהָ, וְהִיא אֲסוּרָה בִּקְרוֹבָיו.

ר' עובדיה מברטנורא

(י) **האומר לאשה קדשתיך וכו'.** איצטריך לאשמועינן באומר קדשתיך ובאומרת קדשתני. דאי אשמועינן באומר לאשה קדשתיך שהוא אסור בקרובותיה והיא מותרת בקרוביו, הוה אמינא, דינא הוא דלא מתסרא איהי בקרוביו, דאיהו שקורי קא משקר, דגברא לא איכפת ליה אם אוסר עצמו הנס בקרובותיה, ומשקר ואמר קדשתיך אף על גב דלא קדשה. אבל איהי כי אמרה קדשתני, דאסרה נפשה אכולי עלמא עד שיתן לה גט, אי לאו דקים לה לא הוה אמרה, ונתסר איהו על פיה בקרובותיה, ואפילו יהב לה גט, קא משמע לן: **קדשתיך והיא אומרת לא**

יד אברהם

case, because we might otherwise assume that R' Meir maintains that a man would only use a term like *elder daughter* ambiguously, because it is a laudatory description, but he would not refer to any but his youngest daughter as *the younger.*

By the same token, this second case alone would not suffice, because we might assume that even R' Yose agrees that a father would use the description of *elder daughter* loosely (*Rav* from *Gem.* 64b).

The *halachah* in both of these cases follows the view of R' Yose (*Rav*).

10.

When a man betroths a woman, several of her relatives become Biblically prohibited to him. These include her mother, her grandmothers, her sisters, and her daughters and granddaughters from a previous marriage (*Lev.* 18:17*f.*). Her sister becomes permitted to him if his wife dies, whereas the others remain forbidden forever (ibid.). In addition, the Rabbis prohibited the wife's great-grandmother and her great-granddaughter (*Yevamos* 21a).

By the same token, she becomes Biblically prohibited to his father, his sons from a previous marriage, his brothers, and his brothers' sons (loc. cit. vs. 7, 14-16). She also becomes Rabbinically prohibited to his grandsons, his grandfathers, and his sisters' sons, among others (*Yevamos* loc. cit.).

הָאוֹמֵר לְאִשָּׁה: „קִדַּשְׁתִּיךְ", — *[If] one says to a woman: "I betrothed you,"*

A man claimed to have betrothed a woman in the presence of two witnesses (*Gem.* 65b) who are not available to testify because they died or went overseas, or because he does not remember who they are (*Meiri*).

וְהִיא אוֹמֶרֶת: „לֹא קִדַּשְׁתַּנִי" — *and she says: "You did not betroth me,"*

10. [If] one says to a woman: "I betrothed you," and she says: "You did not betroth me," he is forbidden to [marry] her relatives, but she is permitted to [marry] his relatives. [If] she says: "You betrothed me," and he says: "I did not betroth you," he is permitted to [marry] her relatives, but she is forbidden to [marry] his relatives.

YAD AVRAHAM

However, if she agreed that he had betrothed her in the presence of witnesses, their claim would be believed (ibid.).

הוּא אָסוּר בִּקְרוֹבוֹתֶיהָ, — *he is forbidden to [marry] her relatives,*

By claiming that he betrothed her [which would forbid him to marry her relatives,] he has actually rendered them prohibited to him [although we do not know if the claim is true] (*Rashi*).

There is discussion among the commentators whether the basis of this principle — that one renders something prohibited to himself simply by claiming that it is so — is because a person is believed in everything he says to his own detriment, just as in monetary matters (*Gem.* 65b), or because it is tantamount to a vow prohibiting that object to himself (*Shaar Hamelech* to *Hil. Ishus* 9:15).

וְהִיא מֻתֶּרֶת בִּקְרוֹבָיו. — *but she is permitted to [marry] his relatives.*

Because she contests his claim, and there are no witnesses to support it (*Meiri*).

הִיא אוֹמֶרֶת: „קִדַּשְׁתַּנִי", וְהוּא אוֹמֵר: „לֹא קִדַּשְׁתִּיךְ" — הוּא מֻתָּר בִּקְרוֹבוֹתֶיהָ, — *[If] she says: "You betrothed me," and he says: "I did not betroth you," he is permitted to [marry] her relatives,*

Since her claim renders her forbidden to marry until receiving a *get* from him [which he is not obligated to provide (see below)], we might assume that she would not place herself in such a position unless it were true and she is believed. Therefore, the mishnah tells that despite this theory, she is not believed, and her relatives remain permitted to him (*Rav* from *Gem.* 65a).

וְהִיא אֲסוּרָה בִּקְרוֹבָיו. — *but she is forbidden to [marry] his relatives.*

[Since she claims that they are forbidden to her by virtue of having been betrothed to him.]

In addition, she is forbidden to marry at all until he gives her a *get* (*Meiri*), and we therefore request from him that he do so (*Rav* to mishnah 11 from *Gem.* 65a). However, we cannot force him to do so, because in giving her a *get* he becomes prohibited to marry her relatives (*Gem.* ibid.) by Rabbinic law, since it would look like he was marrying the relative of his divorcee, which is prohibited (*Ran*).

If he gives her a *get* on his own initiative, he is obligated to pay her *kesubah* (marriage contract),[1] because his action attests to the veracity

1. Since the mishnah is discussing a woman who claims that she was only betrothed — not fully married — some commentators deduce from this that the obligation of the *kesubah* is

,,קִדַּשְׁתִּיךְ״, וְהִיא אוֹמֶרֶת: ,,לֹא קִדַּשְׁתָּ אֶלָּא בִתִּי״ — הוּא אָסוּר בִּקְרוֹבוֹת גְּדוֹלָה, וּגְדוֹלָה מֻתֶּרֶת בִּקְרוֹבָיו; הוּא מֻתָּר בִּקְרוֹבוֹת קְטַנָּה, וּקְטַנָּה מֻתֶּרֶת בִּקְרוֹבָיו.

[יא] ,,**קִדַּשְׁתִּי** אֶת בִּתֵּךְ״, וְהִיא אוֹמֶרֶת: ,,לֹא קִדַּשְׁתָּ אֶלָּא אוֹתִי״ — הוּא אָסוּר בִּקְרוֹבוֹת קְטַנָּה, וּקְטַנָּה מֻתֶּרֶת בִּקְרוֹבָיו; הוּא מֻתָּר בִּקְרוֹבוֹת גְּדוֹלָה, וּגְדוֹלָה אֲסוּרָה בִּקְרוֹבָיו.

ר׳ עובדיה מברטנורא

קדשת אלא בתי וכו׳. משום דהוה סלקא דעתין לומר, מאחר שהאב נאמן על בתו מן התורה, תהיה האם נאמנת על בתה מדרבנן, קא משמע לן דאינה נאמנת: **(יא) קדשתי את בתך וכו׳.** איידי דתנא להני בבי דלעיל, תנא נמי להא, ואף על פי שהיא משנה שאינה לריכה. ובכל הני דהיא אומרת קדשתני, מבקשים ממנו ליתן גט כדי להתירה, ואם מעלמו נתן גט, כופין אותו ליתן כתובה:

יד אברהם

of her claim (*Gem.* loc. cit.). However, if at the time he gave her the *get* he explained that he is doing so only to free her to remarry, he is believed [and he does not become obligated to pay the *kesubah*] (*Ran*).

,,קִדַּשְׁתִּיךְ״, וְהִיא אוֹמֶרֶת: ,,לֹא קִדַּשְׁתָּ אֶלָּא בִתִּי״ — — [*If he says:*] *"I betrothed you," and she says, "You betrothed my daughter,"*

The mishnah is telling us that although a father is believed about the *kiddushin* of his daughter by Biblical law (see mishnah 9), her mother is not given that credibility, even by Rabbinic law (*Rav* from *Gem.* 65a).

הוּא אָסוּר בִּקְרוֹבוֹת גְּדוֹלָה, וּגְדוֹלָה מֻתֶּרֶת בִּקְרוֹבָיו; — *he is forbidden to [marry] the relatives of the elder, but the elder is permitted to [marry] his relatives.*

The elder refers to the mother (*Meiri*). [Her relatives are prohibited to him, since he claims to have betrothed her, but she is permitted to his relatives, because she denies having been betrothed to him.]

הוּא מֻתָּר בִּקְרוֹבוֹת קְטַנָּה, וּקְטַנָּה מֻתֶּרֶת בִּקְרוֹבָיו. — *he is permitted to [marry] the relatives of the younger, and the younger is permitted to [marry] his relatives.*

incurred by the husband from the time of *kiddushin* (*Tos.* 64a; *Ran;* see General Introduction to ArtScroll *Kesubos*, p. 6). Those who disagree construe the mishnah's case as taking place in a town where the custom was to write a *kesubah* prior to the *kiddushin*. The alleged husband claims that he had indeed written the *kesubah*, but had not betrothed her (*Tos. Yom Tov*).

3
11

[If he says:] "I betrothed you," and she says: "You betrothed my daughter," he is forbidden to [marry] the relatives of the elder, but the elder is permitted to [marry] his relatives; he is permitted to [marry] the relatives of the younger, and the younger is permitted to [marry] his relatives.

11. [If a man says:] "I betrothed your daughter," and she says: "You betrothed me," he is forbidden to [marry] the relatives of the younger, and the younger is permitted to [marry] his relatives; he is permitted to [marry] the relatives of the elder, and the elder is forbidden to [marry] his relatives.

YAD AVRAHAM

The younger refers to *the daughter* (ibid.). [She made no claim whatsoever, and is therefore not prohibited from marrying his relatives. The man is permitted to marry any relatives of hers who are not forbidden to him by virtue of their being relatives of her mother — e.g., half sister from her father — since he claims to have betrothed the mother, and not the daughter.]

11.

This mishnah adds no new information which could not be deduced from the previous one. It was written only for the sake of rounding out the discussion of the cases mentioned above (*Rav* from *Gem.* 65a).

,,קִדַּשְׁתִּי אֶת בִּתֵּךְ״ — [*If a man says:*] *"I betrothed your daughter,"*

[A man claims that he betrothed a certain woman's daughter] and that her father had accepted the *kiddushin* on her behalf (*Meiri*) [since a mother does not have the authority to do so].

Alternatively, it is referring to a daughter who is a *bogeres* (see mishnah 8) and had appointed her mother to accept *kiddushin* on her behalf (*Tos. Yom Tov*).

וְהִיא אוֹמֶרֶת: ,,לֹא קִדַּשְׁתָּ אֶלָּא אוֹתִי״ — הוּא אָסוּר בִּקְרוֹבוֹת קְטַנָּה, וּקְטַנָּה מֻתֶּרֶת בִּקְרוֹבָיו; הוּא מֻתָּר בִּקְרוֹבוֹת גְּדוֹלָה, וּגְדוֹלָה אֲסוּרָה בִּקְרוֹבָיו. — *and she says: "You betrothed me," he is forbidden to* [*marry*] *the relatives of the younger, and the younger is permitted to* [*marry*] *his relatives; he is permitted to* [*marry*] *the relatives of the elder, and the elder is forbidden to* [*marry*] *his relatives.*

[He is permitted to marry those relatives of the mother who are not prohibited to him by virtue of being relatives of the daughter.]

[יב] **כָּל** מָקוֹם שֶׁיֵּשׁ קִדּוּשִׁין וְאֵין עֲבֵרָה — הַוָּלָד הוֹלֵךְ אַחַר הַזָּכָר. וְאֵיזֶה זוֹ? כֹּהֶנֶת, לְוִיָּה, וְיִשְׂרְאֵלִית שֶׁנִּשְּׂאוּ לְכֹהֵן, וּלְלֵוִי, וּלְיִשְׂרָאֵל. וְכָל מָקוֹם שֶׁיֵּשׁ קִדּוּשִׁין וְיֵשׁ עֲבֵרָה, הַוָּלָד הוֹלֵךְ אַחַר הַפָּגוּם. וְאֵיזוֹ זוֹ? אַלְמָנָה לְכֹהֵן גָּדוֹל, גְּרוּשָׁה וַחֲלוּצָה לְכֹהֵן הֶדְיוֹט, מַמְזֶרֶת וּנְתִינָה לְיִשְׂרָאֵל, בַּת יִשְׂרָאֵל לְמַמְזֵר וּלְנָתִין.

ר׳ עובדיה מברטנורא

(יב) **כל מקום שיש קדושין ואין עבירה.** שקדושין תופסין בה, ואין עבירה בנשואיה. והאי כללא לאו דוקא, שהרי גר שנשא ממזרת יש קדושין ואין עבירה, דקהל גרים לא אקרי קהל, ואף על פי כן אין הולד הולך אחר הזכר, שהולד ממזר, אחד גר שנשא ממזרת ואחד ממזר שנשא גיורת:

יד אברהם

12.

This mishnah discusses the different categories of marital relations and the status of the offspring thereof.

כָּל מָקוֹם שֶׁיֵּשׁ קִדּוּשִׁין וְאֵין עֲבֵרָה — *In every case in which there is kiddushin and there is no transgression,*

If a man marries a woman with whom his *kiddushin* takes effect and with whom marital relations are permitted to him (*Rav*).

The words *every case* are meant to include examples which are not listed in the mishnah — e.g., a non-*Kohen* who marries a חֲלָלָה, *chalalah* [a woman forbidden to *Kohanim* who had intimacy with one, or a female child born from such a relationship (*Rambam, Hil. Issurei Biah* 19:1)], who is prohibited to a *Kohen* (*Lev.* 21:7). The child of such a marriage follows the father and does not inherit the mother's status (*Gem.* 67a). Thus, if the child is a girl, she is permitted to a *Kohen* (*Rashi* ad loc. s.v. והרי ישראל).

הַוָּלָד הוֹלֵךְ אַחַר הַזָּכָר. — *the offspring follows the male.*

[The child assumes the status of the father rather than that of the mother] as it is written (*Num.* 1:18), *to their families, to the house of their fathers* (*Rashi*).

וְאֵיזֶה זוֹ? — *Which is this?*

[What are examples of this principle?]

These words indicate that there are exceptions to this rule (*Gem.* 67a). One of these is when a proselyte marries a *mamzeres,* in which case the relationship is permitted and the *kiddushin* takes effect, but the child is nevertheless a *mamzer,* following the mother (*Rav* from *Gem.* ibid.).

Another exception is a חָלָל, *chalal* [a male child born from a relationship between a *Kohen* and a woman forbidden to him (*Rambam* loc. cit. 3)], who married a regular Jewess. Our mishnah accepts the opinion of R' Dustai, who maintains that the child of such a marriage is not a *chalal,* because Jewish daughters are compared to a *mikveh* in that they purify their children from inheriting *chalal* states (*Gem.* ibid.).

3
12 **12.** In every case in which there is *kiddushin* and there is no transgression, the offspring follows the male. Which is this? [This is] the daughter of a *Kohen*, a *Levi*, or a *Yisrael* who was married to a *Kohen*, a *Levi*, or a *Yisrael*.

In every case in which there is *kiddushin* and there is transgression, the offspring follows the defective one. Which is this? [This is] a widow to a *Kohen Gadol*, a divorcee or a *chalutzah* to an ordinary *Kohen*, a *mamzeres* or a Nesinite to a regular Jew, [or] the daughter of a regular Jew to a *mamzer* or a Nesinite.

YAD AVRAHAM

כֹּהֶנֶת, לְוִיָּה, וְיִשְׂרְאֵלִית שֶׁנִּשְּׂאוּ לְכֹהֵן, וּלְלֵוִי, וּלְיִשְׂרָאֵל. — *[This is] the daughter of a Kohen, a Levi, or a Yisrael, who was married to a Kohen, a Levi, or a Yisrael.*

[The term *Yisrael* here refers to a Jew who is neither a *Kohen* nor a *Levi*. In each of these cases, the children assume the status of their father.]

וְכָל מָקוֹם שֶׁיֵּשׁ קִדּוּשִׁין וְיֵשׁ עֲבֵרָה, — *In every case in which there is kiddushin and there is transgression,*

Any marriage in which marital relations are prohibited, but the *kiddushin* takes effect nevertheless (*Meiri*).

The words, *In every case*, are added here only to be consistent with the wording of the mishnah's first statement; there are no examples of this rule beyond the ones listed (*Gem.* ibid.; cf. *Tos. Yom Tov*, s.v. ואיזו זו; *Likkutim* ad loc.).

הַוָּלָד הוֹלֵךְ אַחַר הַפָּגוּם. — *the offspring follows the defective one.*

[The offspring assumes the status of the defective parent.]

וְאֵיזוֹ זוֹ? — *Which is this?*

This wording, too, is included only for the sake of symmetry with the previous case; there are no exceptions to this rule (ibid.).

אַלְמָנָה לְכֹהֵן גָּדוֹל, גְּרוּשָׁה וַחֲלוּצָה לְכֹהֵן הֶדְיוֹט, — *[This is] a widow to a Kohen Gadol, a divorcee or a chalutzah to an ordinary Kohen,*

A widow is Biblically prohibited to a *Kohen Gadol* [High Priest] (*Lev.* 21:14) as is a divorcee to any *Kohen* (ibid. v. 7). A *chalutzah* — a woman whose *yavam* released her through the process of *chalitzah* rather than marrying her with *yibum* (see 1:1) — is forbidden to a *Kohen* by Rabbinic law (*Yevamos* 24a), because of her similarity to a divorcee (*Rambam, Hil. Issurei Biah* 17:7).

In each of these cases, the woman becomes a *chalalah* upon having intimacy, but the *Kohen* does not become a *chalal*; the offspring follows the mother and becomes a *chalal* or *chalalah* (*Meiri*).

This mishnah follows the accepted opinion of R' Shimon Hatimni, who holds that the product of illicit relations is a *mamzer* only if the prohibitions forbidding those relations is punishable by *kares*, and only in such a case is the *kiddushin* void (*Tos.* 66b s.v. כל; see *Tos.* 67b).

מַמְזֶרֶת וּנְתִינָה לְיִשְׂרָאֵל, בַּת יִשְׂרָאֵל לְמַמְזֵר וּלְנָתִין. — *a mamzeres or a Nesinite to a regular Jew, [or] the daughter of a*

קידושין
ג/יב

וְכָל מִי שֶׁאֵין לָהּ עָלָיו קִדּוּשִׁין, אֲבָל יֵשׁ לָהּ עַל אֲחֵרִים קִדּוּשִׁין — הַוָּלָד מַמְזֵר. וְאֵיזֶה זֶה? הַבָּא עַל אַחַת מִכָּל הָעֲרָיוֹת שֶׁבַּתּוֹרָה.

וְכָל מִי שֶׁאֵין לָהּ לֹא עָלָיו וְלֹא עַל אֲחֵרִים קִדּוּשִׁין — הַוָּלָד כְּמוֹתָהּ. וְאֵיזֶה זֶה? וְלַד שִׁפְחָה וְנָכְרִית.

ר׳ עובדיה מברטנורא

וכל מי שאין לה עליו קדושין וכו׳ הולד ממזר. ביבמות (מט, א) נפקא לן מקרא דכתיב (דברים כג, א) לא יקח איש את אשת אביו, וסמיך ליה לא יבא ממזר, ומוקמינן לה בשומרת יבם של אביו, שהיא אשת אחי אביו שהיא עליו בכרת: **על אחת מכל העריות.** של חייבי כריתות: **ולד שפחה ונכרית.** דכתיב בשפחה (שמות כא, ד) האשה וילדיה תהיה לאדוניה, ובנכרית כתיב (דברים ז, ד) כי יסיר את בנך מאחרי, ומדלא כתיב כי תסיר, שמע מינה הכי קאמר, בתך לא תתן לבנו, כי יסיר בעל בתך את בנך אשר תלד לו בתך, מאחרי. אבל אבתו לא תקח לבנך לא מהדר, שאין הבן הבא מן הנכרית קרוי בנך אלא בנה:

יד אברהם

regular Jew to a mamzer or a Nesinite.

Marriage between a legitimate Jew and a *mamzer* — an illegitimate Jew who is the product of relations which are punishable by *kares* (see 2:3) — is prohibited by Biblical law (*Deut.* 23:3). The prohibition against marrying a Nesinite — a descendant of the Gibeonites who deceived Joshua into accepting them as proselytes (see 2:3) — is the subject of a dispute as to whether it is of Biblical origin or Rabbinic origin (*Tos.* to *Kesubos* 28a s.v. אלו נערות, and ArtScroll commentary ibid. p. 50, footnote 1).

[In each of these cases, the child assumes the pedigree of the defective parent.]

וְכָל מִי שֶׁאֵין לָהּ עָלָיו קִדּוּשִׁין, אֲבָל יֵשׁ לָהּ עַל אֲחֵרִים קִדּוּשִׁין — [*In a case of*] *anyone who cannot have kiddushin with him but can have kiddushin with others,*

[A man married a woman who is eligible for *kiddushin* with other men but is forbidden to him by a prohibition which prevents their *kiddushin* from taking effect.]

הַוָּלָד מַמְזֵר. — *the offspring is a mamzer.*

The prohibition against marrying a *mamzer* (*Deut.* 23:3) is written near the verse (ibid. v. 1) that is interpreted as prohibiting one from marrying the wife of his father's brother, which is subject to the penalty of *kares* (*Lev.* 18:14; ibid. v. 29). From this juxtaposition, we derive that the offspring of a man and woman between whom relations are punishable by *kares* — and hence, between whom *kiddushin* does not take effect (see below) — is a *mamzer* (*Rav* from *Yevamos* 49a).

וְאֵיזֶה זֶה? הַבָּא עַל אַחַת מִכָּל הָעֲרָיוֹת שֶׁבַּתּוֹרָה. — *Which is this?* [*This is*] *one who has relations with any of the arayos which are in the Torah.*

Kiddushin with any of the Biblical *arayos* [sing. *ervah*] (*Lev.* 18) — women with whom conjugal relations are prohibited under penalty of *kares*

3
12

[In a case of] anyone who cannot have *kiddushin* with him but can have *kiddushin* with others, the offspring is a *mamzer*. Which is this? [This is] one who has relations with any of the *arayos* which are in the Torah.

[In a case of] anyone who cannot have *kiddushin* with him or with others, the offspring is like her. Which is this? [This is] the offspring of a slave and a gentile woman.

YAD AVRAHAM

(*Rav*) — is void. This is derived from the verse (*Lev.* 18:18): *And a woman with her sister you shall not take* (*Gem.* 67b), which is construed to mean that you are not able to take her, because *kiddushin* with her does not take effect (*Rashi* ad loc. s.v. לא יקח and s.v. מאחות אשה). We derive that the same holds true for all *arayos* by virtue of the verse (loc. cit., v. 29), *Whoever shall do any of these abominations shall be cut off*, which refers to all of the *arayos*. The fact that they are all included together in one verse teaches us that their laws can be derived from one another (*Gem.* loc. cit.).

[The offspring of such relations is a *mamzer*, as explained above.]

The exception to this rule is a *niddah* (a woman who has not immersed in a *mikveh* to purify herself from the ritual contamination which comes from menstruation), who is prohibited under penalty of *kares*, but is nonetheless eligible for *kiddushin* (*Gem.* 68a).

וְכָל מִי שֶׁאֵין לָהּ לֹא עָלָיו וְלֹא עַל אֲחֵרִים קִדּוּשִׁין — הַוָּלָד כְּמוֹתָהּ. — *[In a case of] anyone who cannot have kiddushin with him or with others, the offspring is like her.*

[The offspring of any woman who is not eligible for *kiddushin* with any Jewish man assumes the mother's status.]

וְאֵיזֶה זֶהוּ? וְלַד שִׁפְחָה — *Which is this? [This is] the offspring of a slave*

The child of a gentile female slave (see commentary to 1:3) assumes her status, as derived from the verse (*Ex.* 21:4), *The woman and her children shall be to her master* (*Rav* from *Gem.* 68b). Since her child always assumes her status [even if the father was of a lower status — e.g., a *mamzer* (*Tos. Yom Tov*)], it is apparent that the mother is one with whom *kiddushin* cannot take effect (*Ran*). [Otherwise, the child would assume the lower status of the two, as dictated by the second rule of the mishnah.]

In other versions of the *Gemara*, the fact that a female slave is disqualified from *kiddushin* is derived from the verse (*Gen.* 22:5), *Stay here with the donkey*, which compares a slave to a donkey in that there can be no *kiddushin* with him (*Rashi*); and the same applies to a female slave (*Rashi* to *Yevamos* 45a s.v. חייבי לאוין).

Even if *kiddushin* with a slave could take effect, her child from a Jewish father would be a slave, because intimacy between them is forbidden and it is thus included in the second category of the mishnah. However, the mishnah is teaching us that not only

רַבִּי טַרְפוֹן אוֹמֵר: יְכוֹלִין מַמְזֵרִים לִטַּהֵר. כֵּיצַד? מַמְזֵר שֶׁנָּשָׂא שִׁפְחָה — הַוָּלָד עֶבֶד; שִׁחְרְרוֹ — נִמְצָא הַבֵּן בֶּן חוֹרִין. רַבִּי אֱלִיעֶזֶר אוֹמֵר: הֲרֵי זֶה עֶבֶד מַמְזֵר.

ר׳ עובדיה מברטנורא

(יג) **ממזר שנשא שפחה.** ואפילו לכתחלה יכול ממזר לישא שפחה כדי לטהר את בניו. והלכה כרבי טרפון. ומודה רבי טרפון שעבד שנשא ממזרת הולד ממזר, שעבד אין לו ייחס:

יד אברהם

does the child have the status of a slave, but he is not considered the father's child in regard to any area of Jewish law — e.g., inheritance (*Tos.* 68b s.v. ולדה).

.וְנָכְרִית — *and a gentile woman.*

This is derived from the verse (*Deut.* 7:3f.), *Your daughter you shall not give to his son, and his daughter you shall not take for your son, because he will turn your son away from Me.* The words, *He will turn your son away from Me,* refer to the gentile husband of your daughter, which indicates that their offspring is still considered your offspring — i.e., they are Jewish. No such statement is made concerning the case in which a Jewish man married a gentile girl, because the offspring of such a marriage follows the mother and is not Jewish (*Rav* from *Gem.* loc. cit.).

The *Gemara* (ibid.) concludes that this verse refers to all gentiles only according to a minority opinion. According to the Sages, however, it is discussing only the Seven Nations from whom the Jews conquered the Land of Canaan. They derive that there can be no *kiddushin* with any gentile from that which the Torah (*Deut.* 21:13) says regarding a Jewish man who captured a gentile woman in battle, and did certain actions enumerated in the passage — i.e., shaved her head, cut her nails, etc. *And after this you shall come to her and have relations with her and she will be to you for a wife.* From this we infer that only under such circumstances can there be *kiddushin* between a Jew and a gentile.

Scripture says further (ibid., v. 15), *If a man will have two wives ... and they will bear him sons.* The *Gemara* (ibid.) derives from this that only when there can be *kiddushin* between them are the sons considered his; otherwise, they follow the mother.

13.

.רַבִּי טַרְפוֹן אוֹמֵר: יְכוֹלִין מַמְזֵרִים לִטַּהֵר — *R' Tarfon says: Mamzerim can be purified.*

A *mamzer* can be purified so that he does not transmit his illegitimacy to his children (*Rashi*).

כֵּיצַד? מַמְזֵר שֶׁנָּשָׂא שִׁפְחָה — *How? [If] a mamzer married a slave,*

A *mamzer* is permitted to marry a gentile slave (*Rav* from *Gem.* 69a). This is because the prohibition to marry a female slave is derived from the verse (*Deut.* 23:18), *And there shall not be a kadesh* [קָדֵשׁ] (immoral man) *among the Sons of Israel,* which is rendered by *Targun Onkelos* as: *And a Jewish man shall not marry a slave* (see *Rashi* ad loc.). However, since a *mamzer* is the product of illicit relations, the negative connotation of the word *kadesh* already applies to him, and he is therefore exempt from a

3
13

13. R' Tarfon says: *Mamzerim* can be purified. How? [If] a *mamzer* married a slave, the offspring is a slave; [if] he freed him, the son becomes a freeman. R' Eliezer says: This is a slave who is a *mamzer.*

prohibition which is based upon the fact that it causes that blemish (*Ran* citing *Rabbeinu Tam*).

הַוָּלָד עֶבֶד; — *the offspring is a slave;*

He is a slave and not a *mamzer,* because the offspring of a female slave assumes the genealogical status of the mother (*Rashi;* see mishnah 12).

שִׁחְרְרוֹ — נִמְצָא הַבֵּן בֶּן חוֹרִין. — *[if] he freed him, the son becomes a freeman.*

Since a gentile slave who is freed becomes a full proselyte to Judaism (*Rambam, Hil. Issurei Biah* 13:12).

This plan would not work for a *mamzeres,* since the child of a male slave does not assume his father's status (*Rav* from *Gem.* 69a), because the comparison in Scripture between a slave and a beast (see commentary to mishnah 12 s.v. ואיזה? זה ולד) teaches us that there is no paternal pedigree among slaves.[1] Therefore, if a *mamzeres* were to marry a slave, their child would still be a *mamzer* (*Rashi*).

If a *mamzer* married a gentile, their child can become a legitimate Jew through conversion. However, such an approach is not recommended by the mishnah, because a *mamzer* — just like all other Jews — is prohibited to marry a gentile woman (*Meiri*).

רַבִּי אֱלִיעֶזֶר אוֹמֵר: הֲרֵי זֶה עֶבֶד מַמְזֵר. — *R' Eliezer says: This is a slave who is a mamzer.*

He maintains that the genealogy of a *mamzer* cannot be changed, as derived from the verse (*Deut.* 23:3), *Also the tenth generation shall not come to him in the Congregation of* HASHEM. The extra word, לוֹ, *to him,* teaches us that the next generation retains his illegitimacy under all circumstances (*Gem.* 69a).

R' Tarfon contends that the verse pertains only to a legitimate Jew who married a *mamzeres,* teaching us that in such a case the rule of paternal lineage does not apply, and the child assumes the status of the mother. However, a child in the womb of a slave has no genealogical connection to the father whatsoever (*Gem.* ibid.).

The *halachah* follows the view of R' Tarfon (*Rav*).

1. [Although a female slave is also compared to a beast (see mishnah 12 loc. cit.), the child is apparently hers by virtue of her having borne it, and therefore assumes her pedigree.]

פרק רביעי

Chapter Four

קידושין ד/א

[א] **עֲשָׂרָה** יוֹחֲסִין עָלוּ מִבָּבֶל: כַּהֲנֵי, לְוִיֵּי, יִשְׂרְאֵלֵי, חֲלָלֵי, גֵּרֵי, וַחֲרוּרֵי, מַמְזֵרֵי, נְתִינֵי, שְׁתוּקֵי, וַאֲסוּפֵי. כַּהֲנֵי, לְוִיֵּי,

ר' עובדיה מברטנורא

פרק רביעי – עשרה יוחסין. (א) עשרה יוחסין עלו מבבל. שהפריש עזרא כל הפסולים שהיו בבבל והוליכן עמו, כדי שלא יתערבו עם המיוחסין, מאחר שאין שם בית דין: **חללי.** כהנים שנולדו מן הפסולות לכהונה, כגון אלמנה לכהן גדול, גרושה חללה זונה לכהן הדיוט: **חרורי.** עבדים משוחררים: **נתיני.** גבעונים שמלו בימי יהושע, ונאסרו לבא בקהל: **שתוקי ואסופי.** מפרש להו ואזיל:

יד אברהם

1.

Having initiated a discussion regarding genealogical status in the previous chapter, the Mishnah goes on to discuss ten distinct genealogical classes among the Jewish people, and the laws governing their intermarriage.

עֲשָׂרָה יוֹחֲסִין עָלוּ מִבָּבֶל: — *Ten genealogical classes went up from Babylon:*

They went up to the Land of Israel together with Ezra [who directed the construction of the Second Temple] (*Gem.* 69a). The mishnah uses the words *went up*, rather than just saying that they went to the Land, to teach us that the Holy Land is the highest of all lands (ibid.).[1]

Ezra was apprehensive that, since there was no Sanhedrin (High Court) in Babylonia to clarify one's genealogical status, marriages between members of different classes who are prohibited to each other would occur. He therefore brought with him all Jews of tainted pedigree [who are prohibited to either *Kohanim* or to Jews of pure pedigree because of their status] (*Rav*).

These ten classes embody ten distinct levels of spiritual sanctity within the Jewish people (*Maharsha*).

כַּהֲנֵי, לְוִיֵּי, יִשְׂרְאֵלֵי, — *Kohanim, Leviim, Yisraelim,*

As it is written (*Ezra* 2:70), *The Kohanim and Leviim and some of the people, and the singers, gatekeepers, and Nesinites settled in their cities, and all of Israel in their cities* (*Gem.* 69b).

[The term *Yisraelim* in our mishnah refers to all Jews who are neither *Kohanim* nor *Leviim*, and are not among the other classes listed.]

Although in a later verse (8:15), Ezra states: *But I could find no Leviim*, that is because he found only those who had amputated their thumbs,[2] and were therefore unable to perform the Temple service by playing the lyre in accompaniment to

1. Since the world is a sphere, any designation of one area as the highest — i.e., the center of the sphere, which is closest to Heaven — is totally arbitrary. Therefore, the designation of Eretz Yisrael as the highest land is meant in a spiritual sense (*Maharal*).

2. During the Babylonian exile, the captives were ordered to entertain their captors with songs and music of the songs of Zion (*Psalms* 137;2). To avoid carrying out this order [which would be degrading to the Temple service] they amputated their thumbs, so that they would no longer be able to pluck the strings of the lyre (*Rashi*).

4
1

1. Ten genealogical classes went up from Babylon: *Kohanim, Leviim, Yisraelim, chalalim,* proselytes, freedmen, *mamzerim,* Nesinites, *shesukim,* and foundlings. *Kohanim, Leviim,* and

YAD AVRAHAM

the service of the *Kohanim* (*Rashi* ad loc.; *Tos.* ibid. s.v. ומבני לוי).

Others explain that he did not find any *Leviim* on that day, but he subsequently returned to Babylon and gathered *Leviim* to accompany him (*Meiri; Tos. Yom Tov*). According to those who maintain that the service of the *Leviim* in the Temple could be performed even by singing alone without the use of instruments, only this second explanation is valid (*Tos. Yom Tov*).

חֲלָלֵי, — *chalalim,*

Children born from relations between a *Kohen* and a woman who is prohibited to him because he is a *Kohen* — e.g., a widow to a *Kohen Gadol* (High Priest) or a divorcee, a *chalalah,* or a *zonah* [loosely, *harlot*] (see *Rambam, Hil. Issurei Biah* 18:1) to an ordinary *Kohen*[1] (*Rav;* see commentary to mishnah 6).

They, too, immigrated to Eretz Yisrael together with Ezra, as derived from the verse (*Ezra* 2:61f.), *Of the children of the Kohanim ... These searched for their genealogical record, but they could not be found, and they were banned from the priesthood* (*Gem.* 69b).

גֵּרֵי, וַחֲרוּרֵי, — *proselytes, freedmen,*

I.e., freed gentile slaves (see 1:3) — who become full-fledged Jews when they are released (*Rambam, Hil. Issurei Biah* 14:19). Converts also accompanied Ezra, as it says (loc. cit. 6:21), *everyone who had separated himself from the defilement of the nations of the land* (*Gem.* 70a).

מַמְזֵרֵי, — *mamzerim,*

A *mamzer* is an illegitimate Jew, the child of a man and a woman between whom *kiddushin* cannot take effect (see 3:12). He is prohibited to marry a legitimate Jew (*Deut.* 23:3).

Mamzerim, too, emigrated with Ezra from Babylonia, as derived from the verse (*Ezra* 2:59), *The following went up from Tel Melach and Tel Charsha ... but they could not state whether they were of Israelite ancestry.* Since these are the only Babylonian cities mentioned in the chapter, the Rabbis understood that they refer homiletically to the nature of the immigrants rather than the places from where they came (*Maharsha*). *Tel Melach* [lit., *mound of salt*] refers to those who were certainly illegitimate, having descended from people likened to the immoral inhabitants of Sodom, which was turned into a mound of salt (*Gem.* loc. cit.). According to the Sodomite legal code, a man guilty of striking another's wife and causing her to miscarry was required to compensate for the crime by impregnating the victim (*Sanhedrin* 109b). In so doing, he fathered an illegitimate child (*Rashi*).

1. [The term *chalalah* applies also to a woman who, although prohibited to a *Kohen,* had intimacy with one (*Rambam* ibid. 19:1). Nevertheless, *Rav* (as well as *Rashi, Ran,* and *Meiri*) mentions only the offspring of such relations in defining the term, because the mishnah is dealing with classes of genealogical status, which include only those whose status is the result of their parentage.]

וְיִשְׂרְאֵלִי מֻתָּרִים לָבֹא זֶה בָזֶה; לְוִיֵּי, יִשְׂרְאֵלֵי, חֲלָלֵי, גֵּרֵי, וַחֲרוּרֵי מֻתָּרִים לָבוֹא זֶה בָזֶה; גֵּרֵי, וַחֲרוּרֵי, מַמְזֵרֵי, וּנְתִינֵי, שְׁתוּקֵי, וַאֲסוּפֵי כֻּלָּם מֻתָּרִין לָבֹא זֶה בָזֶה.

ר׳ עובדיה מברטנורא

גיורי וחרורי ממזרי כו׳ כולם מותרין לבא זה בזה. דקהל גרים לא אקרי קהל, ולא הוזהרו ממזרים לבא בקהל גרים, אבל לויי וישראלי בממזרי לא. ושתוקי ואסופי ספק ממזרים הם, ומותרין להתערב בממזר ודאי, דאמרינן (עג, א), בקהל ודאי הוא דלא יבא, הא בקהל ספק יבא:

יד אברהם

נְתִינֵי, — *Nesinites,*

These are descendants of the Gibeonites, who deceived Joshua into accepting them as proselytes (see 2:3), and were prohibited to intermarry with Jews of untainted pedigree (*Rav*). They are mentioned explicitly as having gone to Eretz Yisrael with Ezra (*Ezra* 8:20).

Some authorities consider Nesinites to be Biblically prohibited by virtue of the verse (*Deut.* 7:3): *Do not intermarry with them* [i.e., members of the seven Canaanite nations] (*Tos.* to *Kesubos* 29a s.v. אלו). Others contend that the Biblical prohibition no longer applies after their conversion to Judaism (*Rashi* ad loc.; *Rambam, Hil. Issurei Biah* 12:22). According to these authorities, their prohibition is due to a Rabbinic decree (*Ran*). There is a third view, that although the Biblical proscription is still in effect despite their conversion, it pertains only to Canaanite converts themselves, but not to their descendants; the prohibition against marrying their descendants is of Rabbinic origin (*Ritva*).

שְׁתוּקֵי, — *shesukim,*

[This word stems from the term שְׁתִיקָה, *silence*, and means *those who are silenced*.]

These are children of Jewish mothers whose fathers are unidentified (mishnah 2); hence, they are possibly *mamzerim* (*Meiri*). They, too, went up with Ezra, as derived homiletically from the term (loc. cit. 2:59) *Tel Charsha* [lit., *the mound of the mute*], which alludes to those who did not know their fathers and were therefore muted — or silenced — by their mothers when they called any specific man their father (*Gem.* 70a; *Rashi* to mishnah).

וַאֲסוּפֵי. — *and foundlings.*

This refers to children found in the streets, both of whose parents are unidentified (mishnah 2), and whose legitimacy is therefore in doubt (*Meiri*). Their ascent to the Holy Land is derived from the end of the verse (loc. cit.), *but they could not state whether they were of Yisrael ancestry* (*Gem.* 70a) — i.e., whether they were Jews or gentiles (*Rashi*), since a person is born Jewish only if his mother is Jewish (3:12).

כֹּהֲנֵי, לְוִיֵּי, וְיִשְׂרְאֵלִי מֻתָּרִים לָבֹא זֶה בָזֶה; — *Kohanim, Leviim, and Yisraelim may intermarry;*

[There are no prohibitions restricting intermarriage among these three classes. However,] all the other listed in the mishnah are prohibited to a *Kohen* (*Meiri;* see below).

לְוִיֵּי, יִשְׂרְאֵלֵי, חֲלָלֵי, גֵּרֵי, וַחֲרוּרֵי מֻתָּרִים

4
1
Yisraelim may intermarry; *Leviim, Yisraelim, chalalim,* proselytes, and freedmen may intermarry; proselytes, freedmen, *mamzerim,* Nesinites, *shesukim,* and foundlings may all intermarry.

YAD AVRAHAM

לָבֹא זֶה בָּזֶה; — *Leviim, Yisraelim, chalalim, proselytes, and freedmen may intermarry;*

Women of the last three categories are forbidden to marry a *Kohen.* Scripture explicitly prohibits a *Kohen* from marrying a *chalalah* (*Lev.* 21:7), and a female proselyte and freedwoman are included in the category of *zonah* mentioned there (*Meiri; Ran; Rambam, Hil. Issurei Biah* 18:3; cf. *Ravad, Maggid Mishneh* ad loc.). The mishnah teaches that *Leviim* and *Yisraelim,* however, are not subject to any of the Kohanic prohibitions.

Both a male proselyte and *chalal* are permitted to marry the daughter of a *Kohen* (*Gem.* 72b).

גֵּרֵי, וַחֲרוּרֵי, מַמְזֵרֵי, וּנְתִינֵי, שְׁתוּקֵי, וַאֲסוּפֵי כֻּלָּם מֻתָּרִין לָבֹא זֶה בָּזֶה. — *proselytes, freedmen, mamzerim, Nesinites, shesukim, and foundlings may all intermarry.*

In discussing the marital prohibitions which are based on genealogical status, the Torah (*Deut.* 23) uses the word קָהָל, *Congregation,* five times. Three of these are written to prohibit the above classes to the Congregations of *Kohanim, Leviim,* and those *Yisraelim* who were born Jewish and have no genealogical blemishes which would render them prohibited to other non-*Kohanim.* Another teaches us that a *mamzer* is forbidden only to someone who is definitely a member of the "congregation" of legitimate Jews, but not someone whose legitimacy is in doubt. Thus, a *shesuki* and a foundling are permitted to a *mamzer.* From the fifth, we derive that only one who is definitely a *mamzer* is prohibited to a legitimate Jew, not one whose legitimacy is uncertain. [However, these individuals are prohibited to members of the Congregation by Rabbinic law (see mishnah 2).] Since there is no further mention of the word *Congregation,* we deduce that proselytes and freedmen [who comprise a distinct genealogical class] are not prohibited to marry *mamzerim* [or possible *mamzerim*] (*Gem.* 73a).

Even according to the view that Nesinites may not enter the Congregation by Biblical law, their marriage to other classes excluded from the Congregation is still permissible. Although the prohibition against marrying a Nesinite is derived from the verse which prohibits intermarriage with gentiles (*Deut.* 7:3; see above s.v. נְתִינֵי) — a prohibition which applies even to those of defective lineage — the inclusion in this prohibition of those who have already converted, such as Nesinites, does not ban them to any greater degree than the prohibition of *mamzerim;* thus it applies only to members of the Congregation, whose genealogical purity would become tainted by such relations. Only actual gentiles are forbidden even to those who are prohibited to enter the Congregation because Scripture ties this stricture to the fear that they may draw them away from God (ibid. v. 4). This is not applicable to a Nesinite, since he is subject to all the commandments of

[ב] **וְאֵלּוּ** הֵם שְׁתוּקֵי: כֹּל שֶׁהוּא מַכִּיר אֶת אִמּוֹ וְאֵינוֹ מַכִּיר אֶת אָבִיו; אֲסוּפֵי: כָּל שֶׁנֶּאֱסַף מִן הַשּׁוּק וְאֵינוֹ מַכִּיר לֹא אָבִיו וְלֹא אִמּוֹ. אַבָּא שָׁאוּל הָיָה קוֹרֵא לִשְׁתוּקֵי: בְּדוּקֵי.

[ג] **כָּל** הָאֲסוּרִים לָבֹא בַקָּהָל מֻתָּרִים לָבֹא זֶה

ר׳ עובדיה מברטנורא

(ב) **שתוקי.** כל שהוא מכיר את אמו, שקורא אבא, ואמו משתקתו: **בדוקי.** שבודקין את אמו, אם אמרה לכשר נבעלתי, הולד כשר. והלכה כאבא שאול: (ג) **כל האסורים לבא בקהל.** אף על גב דתנינן לה ברישא (במשנה א), ממזרי ונתיני וכו׳ מותרים לבא זה בזה, הא קא משמע לן, כגון גר עמוני ומואבי עם ממזר שתוקי ואסופי:

יד אברהם

If someone who was born Jewish marries a proselyte, their child is prohibited to a *mamzer* (*Rambam, Hil. Issurei Biah* 15:9). Others contend that if the father is a proselyte, the child assumes his status and is permitted to those who may not enter the Congregation (*Ran*). All agree, however, that once a descendant of proselytes is no longer identified by people as such, he is prohibited to marry a *mamzer* by Rabbinic law (*Gem.* 75a; *Rambam* ad loc. 8).

Although the halachah is in accordance with the opinion of R' Tarfon — that a *mamzer* is permitted to marry a slave even if the latter has not been freed (see 3:13) — the mishnah mentions only freedmen in this list, because they are permitted to all of those listed, whereas a slave is prohibited to all but *mamzerim* (*Ran*).

the Torah just like any other Jew (*Rashba;* cf. *Ran*).

According to those who maintain that Nesinites are prohibited only by Rabbinic law, they are forbidden to marry anyone who may not enter the Congregation, since by Biblical law they are fully legitimate Jews. The mishnah mentions Nesinites among the others listed here, only because they are always grouped with *mamzerim* and are therefore mentioned together [since they are both Biblically prohibited to members of the Congregation] as one class, but not because they are permitted to the others (*Tos.* to *Yevamos* 79a, s.v. ונתינים; *Kesef Mishneh, Hil. Issurei Biah* 12:22).

2.

וְאֵלּוּ הֵם שְׁתוּקֵי: כָּל שֶׁהוּא מַכִּיר אֶת אִמּוֹ וְאֵינוֹ מַכִּיר אֶת אָבִיו; — *These are shesukim: Anyone who recognizes his mother, but does not recognize his father;*

His mother is known but his father is not identified, and therefore, when he calls a man his father, his mother silences him. Because of his uncertain parentage, the possibility that he is a *mamzer* must be considered (*Rav* from *Gem.* 70a). Although he is permitted to enter into the Congregation by Biblical law (see commentary to previous mishnah, s.v. גֵּרֵי), the Rabbis prohibited such a marriage for the sake of maintaining the genealogical purity of members of the Congregation (*Gem.* 73a).

אֲסוּפֵי: כָּל שֶׁנֶּאֱסַף מִן הַשּׁוּק וְאֵינוֹ מַכִּיר לֹא

2. These are *shesukim:* Anyone who recognizes his mother, but does not recognize his father; foundlings: Anyone who was taken in from the street and does not recognize his father or his mother. Abba Shaul called *shesukim: bedukim.*

3. All who are prohibited to enter into the Congregation are allowed to intermarry

YAD AVRAHAM

.אָבִיו וְלֹא אִמּוֹ — *foundlings: Anyone who was taken in from the street and does not recognize his father or his mother.*

[The term אֲסוּפִי, *foundling,* is related to אֲסִיפָה, *gathering,* or *taking in.*]

He, too, is forbidden to enter the Congregation by Rabbinic law for the reason mentioned above (ibid.).

If there is evidence that the child's parents were concerned for his welfare — e.g., he was circumcised or found in a protected place — it is assumed that he is legitimate (*Gem.* 73b) and that his parents abandoned him because they did not have the means to provide for his needs. Had the child been illegitimate, they would not have bothered to do these things, since they intended to discard him in any case (*Rashi* ibid. s.v. אין בו).

If a man and woman declare that they are the parents of the child before he is taken in from the street, they are believed. Once he has been taken in, however, his legal status as a foundling takes effect, and they are no longer able to alter it. Nevertheless, if he was found during a famine, they are believed (*Gem.* ad loc.), since it is likely that they wanted him to be cared for by someone who had the means to do so (*Rambam, Hil. Issurei Biah* 15:30).

.אַבָּא שָׁאוּל הָיָה קוֹרֵא לִשְׁתוּקֵי: בְּדוּקֵי — *Abba Shaul called shesukim: bedukim.*

[The expression בְּדוּקִי, *beduki,* is related to the term בְּדִיקָה, *investigation,* and means *one who is investigated.*]

They investigate by asking the mother about the father's identity. If she states that he was someone to whom she was permitted, she is believed, and the son is accepted as legitimate (*Rav* from *Gem.* 74a). She is believed even in a situation where the probability is that their intimacy was prohibited (*Gem.* ibid.) — e.g., she was betrothed, and she claimed to have had intimacy with the man to whom she was betrothed [who is only one person, as opposed to all of the many others who it could have been, to whom she was forbidden under penalty of *kares* due to her *kiddushin*] (*Rashi*).

The *halachah* is in accordance with the opinion of Abba Shaul (*Rav* from *Gem.* ibid.).

3.

This mishnah continues the discussion concerning Jews who are disqualified from entering into the Congregation.

כָּל הָאֲסוּרִים לָבֹא בַקָּהָל מֻתָּרִים לָבֹא זֶה בָזֶה; — *All who are prohibited to enter into the Congregation are allowed to intermarry with each other;*

בָּזֶה; רַבִּי יְהוּדָה אוֹסֵר. רַבִּי אֱלִיעֶזֶר אוֹמֵר: וַדָּאָן בְּוַדָּאָן — מֻתָּר. וַדָּאָן בִּסְפֵקָן, וּסְפֵקָן בְּוַדָּאָן, וּסְפֵקָן בִּסְפֵקָן — אָסוּר. וְאֵלּוּ הֵן הַסְּפֵקוֹת: שְׁתוּקִי, אֲסוּפִי, וְכוּתִי.

ר׳ עובדיה מברטנורא

רבי יהודה אוסר. מפרש בגמרא (עד, ב) דהכי קאמר, אפילו רבי יהודה שאוסר גר בממזרת, הני מילי גר של שאר נכרים שמותר לבא בקהל, הוא דאסור בממזרת לרבי יהודה, דסבירא ליה קהל גרים אקרי קהל, אבל גר עמוני ומואבי שאסור לבא בקהל, מודה רבי יהודה שמותר בממזרת: **ודאן בודאן מותר.** כגון ממזרי בנתיני: **ודאן בספיקן.** ממזרי ונתיני בשתוקי ואסופי: **ספיקן בספיקן.** שתוקי בשתוקית, ואסופי באסופית, ואסופי בשתוקית. אף על פי שזה ספק וזה ספק, אסור, שמא זה כשר וזה פסול. והלכה כרבי אליעזר: **כותי.** הוי ספיקייהו לפי שאין בקיאין בתורת גטין וקדושין. והאידנא עשאום כנכרים גמורים לכל דבריהם:

יד אברהם

Although this has already been made clear in the first mishnah, the *Tanna* is now discussing a Moabite or Ammonite proselyte to Judaism [who is disqualified from marrying into the Congregation (*Deut.* 23:4)], who was not mentioned previously. The mishnah teaches us that they are permitted to intermarry with the other prohibited classes even according to R' Yehudah, as explained below (*Rav* from *Gem.* 74b).

.רַבִּי יְהוּדָה אוֹסֵר — *R' Yehudah prohibits* [*it*].

These words refer to R' Yehudah's opinion concerning other proselytes, and the mishnah is understood as follows: Even R' Yehudah — who prohibits proselytes to intermarry with those classes who are disqualified from entering the Congregation (*Gem.* 72b) — agrees that Moabite and Ammonite proselytes are permitted to do so. Since they are prohibited to enter into the Congregation, and are thus not included within it, the interdiction proscribing other disqualified classes from marrying into the Congregation does not forbid them to these proselytes (*Rav* from *Gem.* ibid.).

The *Gemara* must explain R' Yehudah in this manner, because it is inconceivable that he should prohibit a *mamzer* to these proselytes, since the latter are clearly not included in the Congregation (*Gem.* ibid.).

.רַבִּי אֱלִיעֶזֶר אוֹמֵר: וַדָּאָן בְּוַדָּאָן — מֻתָּר — *R' Eliezer says: Those who are definite*[*ly unfit*] *with those who are definite*[*ly unfit*] *is permitted.*

This refers to all of those classes who are disqualified from entering into the Congregation — those listed in the first mishnah as well as the Ammonite and Moabite proselytes mentioned above (*Meiri*). [In this, R' Eliezer's opinion concurs with the other *Tannaim* — that intermarriage between members of these classes is permissible.]

,וַדָּאָן בִּסְפֵקָן — *Those who are definite*[*ly unfit*] *with those who*[*se status*] *is doubtful,*

Marriage between any of those listed above with one whose eligibility to enter into the Congregation is in doubt is prohibited (*Rav*), because R' Eliezer maintains that the Rabbis enacted decrees to guard the genealogical purity of even those whose status

4 with each other; R′ Yehudah prohibits [it]. R′
3 Eliezer says: Those who are definite[ly unfit] with those who are definite[ly unfit] is permitted. Those who are definite[ly unfit] with those who[se status is doubtful, those who[se status] is doubtful with those who are definite[ly unfit], and those who[se status] is doubtful with those who[se status] is doubtful are prohibited. Those who[se status] is doubtful are: a *shesuki*, a foundling, and a Cuthean.

YAD AVRAHAM

is in question (*Meiri*).

וְסָפֵק בְּוַדָּאן, — *those who[se status] is doubtful with those who are definite[ly unfit],*

This seems to be the same as the previous case, and it is therefore excluded from some versions of the text (*Shinuyei Nuschaos*). *Tiferes Yisrael* suggests that it refers to a situation in which there was intermarriage between a group of people who were definitely unfit and a group of those whose eligibility was doubtful, and it was not known which members of subsequent generations from the group whose eligibility was doubtful descended from those marriages. In questioning the eligibility of any given descendant to enter the Congregation, the probability is that he is unfit. First of all, the original group whose status was questionable may have been disqualified. Even if this were not so, this individual may descend from those who intermarried with those who were definitely disqualified. Despite this probability, these descendants are prohibited to one who is definitely unfit.

וְסָפֵק בְּסָפֵק — אָסוּר. — *and those who[se status] is doubtful with those who[se status] is doubtful are prohibited.*

Those of doubtful status may not even marry each other, because one may be legitimate and the other illegitimate (*Rav*).

וְאֵלּוּ הֵן הַסְּפֵקוֹת: שְׁתוּקִי, אֲסוּפִי, וְכוּתִי. — *Those who[se status] is doubtful are: a shesuki, a foundling, and a Cuthean.*

Shesukim and foundlings are possibly *mamzerim*, as explained in the previous mishnah. Cutheans (or Cuthites) — also known as Samaritans — are members of a group of people who were resettled by King Sennacherib in the Land of Israel and eventually converted to Judaism (see commentary to *Gittin* 1:5). They, too, are considered by R′ Eliezer to be of doubtful status, because they were not well versed in the laws of marriage and divorce, and the possibility of *mamzerim* due to adulterous marriages was thus a serious concern (*Rav* from *Gem.* 76a).

The Rabbis subsequently declared the Cutheans to be considered as gentiles (*Rav*), because they reverted to idolatry (*Chullin* 6a).

The *halachah* is in accordance with the view of R′ Eliezer (*Rav*).

[ד] **הַנּוֹשֵׂא** אִשָּׁה כֹּהֶנֶת צָרִיךְ לִבְדּוֹק אַחֲרֶיהָ אַרְבַּע אִמָּהוֹת שֶׁהֵן שְׁמוֹנֶה: אִמָּהּ, וְאֵם אִמָּהּ, וְאֵם אֲבִי אִמָּהּ וְאִמָּהּ, וְאֵם אָבִיהָ וְאִמָּהּ, וְאֵם אֲבִי אָבִיהָ וְאִמָּהּ.

ר׳ עובדיה מברטנורא

(ד) **ארבע אמהות.** שתים מצד האב, ושתים מצד האם: **שהם שמנה.** ארבע מן האב, וארבע מן האם, ואלו הן, אמה, אם אמה, אם אבי אמה, אם אם אבי אמה, אם אביה, אם אם אביה, אם אבי אביה, אם אם אבי אביה, בודקים בהם שלא היה באחת מהן מן הפסולות. ואם היתה לויה וישראלית, וכהן בא לכנסה, מוסיפין עליהן עוד אחת, אם אחת בכל זוג וזוג, כגון אמה, ואם אמה, ואם אם אמה, וכן כולם. והא דבדקינן באמהות, ולא בדקינן באבות שמא יש פסול באביה או באבי אביה, משום דדרך האנשים, כשמגנין זה את זה מתוך קטטה, מגנין ביוחסין, ואם היה שום פסול מצד האבות היה ידוע, אבל הנשים, אין זו מגנה את זו בפסול יחס אלא בזנות, וכי

יד אברהם

4.

◆§ Preserving the Pure Pedigree of Kohanim

In order to help preserve genealogical purity among *Kohanim,* the Rabbis ordained that a *Kohen* must investigate the status of a woman's ancestors in the manner described below before he marries her, in order to be certain that she has no genealogical defect which would prohibit her to him (see *Rashi* 76a s.v. לא הוזהרו).

Some commentators contend that the Rabbis were primarily concerned with the possibility of the woman being a *chalalah,* since the identity of *mamzerim* is usually well known. However, once they required the investigation, they extended its scope to include the possibility of her being a *mamzeres* as well (*Tos.* ad loc. s.v. צריך).

R' Meir holds that this applies to any woman whom a *Kohen* wishes to marry. The Rabbis, however, maintain that it pertains only to a woman whose eligibility to marry him has been placed in doubt (*Gem.* 76b). This occurs, according to one view, when two witnesses testify that they heard rumors of her disqualification (*Rashi* ad loc.). Others explain that witnesses testify that someone with a genealogical blemish — e.g., a *mamzer,* a *chalal,* or a slave — had married into her family in earlier generations, but they do not know whether she descends from that individual (*Meiri; Rambam, Hil. Issurei Biah* 19:18).

Some authorities contend that when a question of illegitimacy arises concerning a woman, even a non-*Kohen* may not marry her without investigating her lineage (ibid.; see *Maggid Mishneh* ad loc.; cf. *Tos. Yom Tov*). Others opine that the decree requiring this investigation was imposed only upon *Kohanim* (*Rav; Rashi* 76a loc. cit.; *Tos.* ibid. s.v. הנושא; *Tos. Yom Tov*).

The daughter of a *Kohen* was not required to investigate her prospective

4
4

4. One who marries the daughter of a *Kohen* must investigate her through four mothers who are eight; her mother, her mother's mother, her mother's father's mother and her mother, her father's mother and her mother, and her father's father's mother and her mother.

YAD AVRAHAM

husband's pedigree in this manner, because she is not forbidden to marry a *chalal* (*Gem.* 76a). She is not even required to make certain that there were no *mamzerim* in his family, because the Rabbis demand this extra degree of caution only from male *Kohanim*, who are required by Biblical law to maintain a special measure of genealogical purity [i.e., they are more restricted in their choice of wives than other Jews] (*Rashi* loc. cit.).

Rabbeinu Tam is of the opinion that the investigation described in the mishnah is not a prerequisite to the marriage itself, but only to the qualification of their children to serve in the Temple (*Tos.* 76a s.v. צריך). However, this applies only according to the opinion of R' Meir, who requires this investigation even when the woman's validity is not in question. On the other hand, when a doubt has been raised, even marriage itself is prohibited without scrutiny (*Tos. Yom Tov*).

הַנּוֹשֵׂא אִשָּׁה כֹּהֶנֶת — *One who marries the daughter of a Kohen*

A *Kohen* who desires to marry the daughter of a *Kohen*, whose eligibility to him has been placed in doubt (*Rav;* see preface).

צָרִיךְ לִבְדּוֹק אַחֲרֶיהָ — *must investigate her*

To clarify her genealogical status (*Rav*).

אַרְבַּע אִמָּהוֹת — *through four mothers*

Two from her mother's side and two from her father's side (ibid.).

שֶׁהֵן שְׁמֹנֶה: — *who are eight:*

The mother of each of the four must also be scrutinized, in order for the investigation to be effective (*Rav*). [Hence, a total of eight mothers are investigated.]

Only her female ancestors must be investigated, not the male ones, because when men quarrel, they tend to insult each other by aspersing the other's pedigree. Therefore, had there been any question regarding the status of the men, it would have already been brought to light. Women, however, tend to insult each other by maligning the other's morality, and questions of genealogical purity may never have been uncovered (*Rav* from *Gem.* 76a).

אִמָּהּ, וְאֵם אִמָּהּ, וְאֵם אֲבִי אִמָּהּ וְאִמָּהּ, — *her mother, her mother's mother, her mother's father's mother and her mother,*

The last term refers to the mother of her mother's father's mother (*Rav*).

וְאֵם אָבִיהָ וְאִמָּהּ. — *her father's mother and her mother,*

I.e., the mother of her father's mother (ibid.).

וְאֵם אֲבִי אָבִיהָ וְאִמָּהּ. — *and her father's father's mother and her mother.*

I.e., the mother of her father's father's mother (ibid.).

לְוִיָּה וְיִשְׂרְאֵלִית — מוֹסִיפִין עֲלֵיהֶן עוֹד אֶחָת.

[ה] **אֵין** בּוֹדְקִין לֹא מִן הַמִּזְבֵּחַ וּלְמַעְלָה, וְלֹא מִן הַדּוּכָן וּלְמַעְלָה, וְלֹא מִן סַנְהֶדְרִין וּלְמַעְלָה.

ר' עובדיה מברטנורא

איכא בהו מילתא בפסול יוחסין לית ליה קלא. ולא נאמרה חיוב בדיקה זו אלא במשפחה שקרא עליה ערער, אבל משפחה שאין בה חשד אינו צריך לבדוק, שכל המשפחות בחזקת כשרות הן עומדות. והאיש בלבד הוא שצריך לבדוק כשבא לישא אשה ממשפחה שיש בה חשד, אבל כהנת שבאת לינשא אינה צריכה לבדוק אחר האיש, שלא הוזהרו כשרות לינשא לפסולים, וכהנת מותרת לכתחלה להנשא לגר ולחלל, וכל שכן לויה וישראלית: (ה) **אין בודקין מן המזבח ולמעלה.** התחיל לבדוק באמהות, ומצא שאבי אביה שמש על גבי המזבח, אין צריך לבדוק אחר אם אבי אביה, דכיון דכהן שמש על גבי המזבח, בידוע שמיוחס היה: **ולא מן הדוכן ולמעלה.** אם מצא שהיה משורר על הדוכן: **ולא מן הסנהדרין ולמעלה.** ודוקא מן הסנהדרין שבירושלים, ואפילו מאותן שדנין דיני ממונות בלבד, שלא היו מעמידין מן הסנהדרין בירושלים אלא כהן ולוי וישראל מיוחס, שנאמר (במדבר יא, טז) והתיצבו שם עמך, בדומין לך ביחס ובחכמה:

יד אברהם

לְוִיָּה וְיִשְׂרְאֵלִית — *[If she is] the daughter of a Levi or a Yisrael,*

And a *Kohen* wanted to marry her (*Rav;* see preface).

מוֹסִיפִין עֲלֵיהֶן עוֹד אֶחָת. — *one more is added to them.*

He is required to investigate one earlier generation in addition to teach of the four pairs of women mentioned above (*Rav* from *Gem.* 76a) — i.e., the mother of her mother's mother, the mother of her mother's father's mother, the mother of her father's mother's mother, and the mother of her father's father's mother's mother (*Tis. Yis.*), which makes a total of twelve women who must be investigated (*Gem.* ibid.). This is necessary, because marriage with those who are disqualified to marry a *Kohen,* as well as those prohibited to all Jews, was more prevalent among non-*Kohanim* than among *Kohanim* (*Rambam Commentary; Meiri*) [and a broader investigation was therefore required for women from that group].

According to another opinion in the *Gemara* (76b), the mishnah means that to each of the four pairs of women whom *Kohanim* must investigate, they add one more pair — viz., the four women mentioned above and each of their mothers — adding up to a total of sixteen women.

Others explain that only the woman's mother's mother's mother and her father's mother's mother are added, making a total of ten women (*Rambam, Hil. Issurei Biah* 19:19).

There is another version of this phrase in the mishnah which reads לְוִיִּים וְיִשְׂרְאֵלִים מוֹסִיפִים עוֹד אַחַת, *Leviim and Yisraelim add one more.* This means that, although the possibility of a woman being a *chalalah* — who is prohibited only to a *Kohen* — requires the investigation of only eight women, non-*Kohanim* who wish to marry a woman must extend their investigation further, in order to ascertain that she is not ineligible to enter into the Congregation. This was enacted in order to motivate men to marry women from their own tribe with whom they are familiar [and thereby

[If she is] the daughter of a *Levi* or a *Yisrael,* one more is added to them.

5. From the Altar and upward is not investigated, nor from the Platform and upward, nor from the Sanhedrin and upward.

YAD AVRAHAM

avoid the possibility of prohibited marriages taking place inadvertently] rather than undertaking the cumbersome process of investigating the family of a stranger. Since *Kohanim* were more careful in choosing their wives, the Rabbis were more lenient with them in this decree (*Yerushalmi;* see *Meiri;* cf. *Ran*).

5.

This mishnah is a continuation of the previous one, which requires the investigation of a woman's antecedents before marrying her. The *Tanna* tells us that if evidence of genealogical purity is found among her male ancestors no further scrutiny of their mothers is necessary.

אֵין בּוֹדְקִין לֹא מִן הַמִּזְבֵּחַ וּלְמַעְלָה, — *From the Altar and upward is not investigated,*

If a man began to investigate a woman's ancestors (see previous mishnah), and discovered that her father's father had served on the Altar of the Temple, the status of that grandfather's mother need not be investigated further (*Rav*), because no one was allowed to serve on the Altar unless his pedigree was clarified by the High Court (*Gem.* 76b). The same applies to her other male antecedents [i.e., her father and her mother's father], the status of whose mothers must usually be investigated (*Tos. Yom Tov*).

Some commentators explain that the mishnah is referring even to those rites for which non-*Kohanim* are qualified, such as slaughtering animals for offerings and skinning them. Although these rites may be performed even by slaves, they were generally reserved for those of genealogical purity (*Tos.;* cf. *Tos. Yom Tov*).

Some authorities maintain that if the investigation was required because the woman's eligibility had been aspersed (see preface to previous mishnah), this ruling does not apply, and a full scrutiny is required (*Meiri*).

וְלֹא מִן הַדּוּכָן וּלְמַעְלָה, — *nor from the Platform and upward,*

[If it is established that her father, her mother's father, or her father's father was among the *Leviim* who stood on the Platform in the Temple to provide musical accompaniment to the Temple service — for which the *Leviim* were designated — their mother need not be investigated] because the High Court scrutinized the pedigree of all *Leviim* before allowing them to perform this service (*Gem.* 76b).

Some commentators explain that the mishnah refers also to *Kohanim* who stood on the Platform to bless the nation (*Tos.* to *Kesubos* 24b s.v. חד).

וְלֹא מִן סַנְהֶדְרִין וּלְמַעְלָה. — *nor from the Sanhedrin and upward.*

If he had served on a *Sanhedrin* — a court of twenty-three judges which was qualified to try cases involving

וְכָל שֶׁהֶחְזְקוּ אֲבוֹתָיו מִשּׁוֹטְרֵי הָרַבִּים וְגַבָּאֵי צְדָקָה — מַשִּׂיאִין לַכְּהֻנָּה, וְאֵינוֹ צָרִיךְ לִבְדּוֹק אַחֲרֵיהֶן. רַבִּי יוֹסֵי אוֹמֵר: אַף מִי שֶׁהָיָה חָתוּם עֵד בְּעַרְכֵי הַיְשָׁנָה שֶׁל צִפּוֹרִי. רַבִּי חֲנִינָא בֶּן אַנְטִיגְנוֹס אוֹמֵר: אַף מִי שֶׁהָיָה מֻכְתָּב בְּאִסְטְרַטְיָא שֶׁל מֶלֶךְ.

ר׳ עובדיה מברטנורא

וגבאי צדקה. כיון דמנצו בהדי אנשי, שממשכנין על הצדקה ואפילו בערב שבת, אי הוה בהו מלתא, קלא הוה להו: **בערכי ישנה של צפורי.** בסנהדראות של עיר ששמה ישנה, הסמוכה לצפורי: **ערכי.** סנהדראות שהיו עורכין ומסדרין היוחסין: **אסרטיא של מלך.** בחלוקת חדש בחדש לצאת למלחמת בית דוד, משפחה פלונית בחדש פלוני. ולא היו יוצאים למלחמה אלא מיוחסין, שתהא זכותן וזכות אבותן מסייעתן:

יד אברהם

capital punishment (*Tos. Yom Tov;* see *Rashi* 76b s.v. מכל מום and s.v. שוטרי הרבים) — his genealogical purity is established, because no one with an imperfect lineage may sit on such a court. This is derived from the verse regarding the judges appointed by Moses (*Ex.* 18:22): *They shall bear* [the burden of judgment] *with you.* The extra word אִתָּךְ, *with you,* denotes those who are similar to you — i.e., those who are of similar genealogical purity (*Gem.* loc. cit.).

וְכָל שֶׁהֶחְזְקוּ אֲבוֹתָיו מִשּׁוֹטְרֵי הָרַבִּים — *Anyone whose ancestors were known to have been from the public officials*

This refers to those who judged monetary cases in Jerusalem. Although Jews of any genealogical class are qualified to sit on such a court, in Jerusalem they allowed only those of untainted pedigree to do so (*Gem.* 76b).

וְגַבָּאֵי צְדָקָה — *or from the charity collectors*

These collectors had the authority to take collaterals for uncollected charity obligations — even on Fridays, when people were busy preparing for Shabbos [and did not want to be disturbed] (*Rashi*). Therefore, they were often involved in arguments, and any genealogical flaws they may have had would certainly have been uncovered (*Rav* from *Gem.* ibid.).

מַשִּׂיאִין לַכְּהֻנָּה, וְאֵינוֹ צָרִיךְ לִבְדּוֹק אַחֲרֵיהֶן. — *may marry off* [*their daughters*] *to a Kohen* (lit., *to the priesthood*), *and it is not necessary to investigate their descent.*

[The descendants of these men may marry off their daughters to *Kohanim* without any scrutiny of the pedigree of those ancestors' mothers.]

רַבִּי יוֹסֵי אוֹמֵר: אַף מִי שֶׁהָיָה חָתוּם עֵד בְּעַרְכֵי הַיְשָׁנָה שֶׁל צִפּוֹרִי. — *R' Yose says: Also one who is signed as a witness in the court of Yeshanah near Sephoris.*

In the town of Yeshanah, which was near the city of Sephoris, they allowed only those of genealogical purity to testify (*Rambam Commen-*

4
5 Anyone whose ancestors were known to have been from the public officials or from the charity collectors may marry off [their daughters] to a *Kohen*, and it is not necessary to investigate their descent. R' Yose says: Also one who is signed as a witness in the court of Yeshanah near Sephoris. R' Chanina ben Antignos says: Also one who is listed in the king's army.

tary). [Therefore, if someone was signed as a witness on a document drawn up under the auspices of the court of Yeshanah, he required no further investigation.]

In other versions, the word עֵד, *witness*, is not included in the text, and the mishnah is referring to one who is signed on the registry of the courts. In that town, they allowed only those of unflawed pedigree to serve as judges, and they kept a registry to record all those whose genealogy had been investigated and found to be untainted, thus rendering them eligible for the judiciary (*Rashi*; see *Tos. Yom Tov*).

רַבִּי חֲנִינָא בֶּן אַנְטִיגְנוֹס אוֹמֵר: אַף מִי שֶׁהָיָה מֻכְתָּב בְּאִסְטְרַטְיָא שֶׁל מֶלֶךְ. — *R' Chanina ben Antignos says: Also one who is listed in the king's army.*

This refers to the army of King David, in which they accepted only those of genealogical purity so that their merit and that of their fathers would aid them (*Rav* from *Gem.* 76b).

6.

Regarding a *Kohen Gadol*, the Torah states (*Lev.* 21:15), *And he shall not profane his seed in his nation*, from which it is derived that if he has relations with any of the women who are prohibited to him because of his status as a *Kohen* (see *Gem.* 77b), their child is a *chalal*, one who is disqualified from the sanctity of the priesthood (*Gem.* 77a). However, the precise connotation of the words לֹא יְחַלֵּל, *he shall not profane*, denotes someone whom he is degrading from a previous status through his actions, rather than one who was born with that defect. Therefore, we derive that the forbidden woman with whom the *Kohen Gadol* had relations becomes a *chalalah* (ibid.).

The Torah prohibits a *zonah* to all *Kohanim* (loc. cit. v. 7) and repeats the prohibition upon discussing the laws of a *Kohen Gadol* (ibid. v. 14). The *Gemara* (77b) derives from this redundancy that the two types of *Kohanim* are compared, and a child born of relations between a *Kohen* and a woman who is prohibited to him because he is a *Kohen* is likewise a *chalal* [and the woman becomes a *chalalah*].

A *chalal* is prohibited to eat *terumah* (*Gem.* ibid.). A male *chalal* is also ineligible to serve in the Temple (see *Gem.* 66b; *Rambam, Hil. Issurei Biah* 19:10); a female *chalalah* is forbidden to a *Kohen* (*Lev.* 21:7).

[ו] **בַּת** חָלָל זָכָר פְּסוּלָה מִן הַכְּהֻנָּה לְעוֹלָם. יִשְׂרָאֵל שֶׁנָּשָׂא חֲלָלָה — בִּתּוֹ כְּשֵׁרָה לַכְּהֻנָּה. חָלָל שֶׁנָּשָׂא בַּת יִשְׂרָאֵל — בִּתּוֹ פְּסוּלָה לַכְּהֻנָּה.

רַבִּי יְהוּדָה אוֹמֵר: בַּת גֵּר זָכָר כְּבַת חָלָל זָכָר.

ר׳ עובדיה מברטנורא

(ו) **בת חלל זכר פסולה מן הכהונה לעולם.** בת בנו, או בת בן בנו, עד סוף כל הדורות, אבל בת בתו מישראל כשרה לכהונה, דבת חלל[ה] עלמה מישראל כשרה לכהונה: **בת גר זכר.** אפילו מישראלית, פסולה לכהונה כבת חלל זכר:

יד אברהם

בַּת חָלָל זָכָר פְּסוּלָה מִן הַכְּהֻנָּה — *The daughter of a male chalal is disqualified from marrying a Kohen*

[Any child born to a male *chalal* assumes his father's status (see 3:12); a daughter is prohibited to a *Kohen.*]

R' Dustai ben R' Yehudah disputes this mishnah, maintaining that if the child's mother is not a *chalalah,* he assumes her untainted status rather than that of his father (*Gem.* 77a).

לְעוֹלָם. — *forever.*

The daughter of the male *chalal's* son and that of his son's son, ad infinitum, are also *chalalos* (*Rav*), unlike an Egyptian or Edomite convert, who is forbidden along with his children to enter into the Congregation, but whose grandchildren are permitted (*Gem.* loc. cit.; *Deut.* 23:8,9). The daughter of a male *chalal's* daughter, on the other hand, is permitted to a *Kohen,* as stated below (*Rav*).

יִשְׂרָאֵל שֶׁנָּשָׂא חֲלָלָה — בִּתּוֹ כְּשֵׁרָה לַכְּהֻנָּה. — [*If*] *a non-Kohen married a chalalah, his daughter is qualified to marry a Kohen.*

This is derived exegetically in the following manner: The verse (*Lev.* 21:15): *He shall not profane his seed in his nation* is compared to the verse (ibid. v. 4), *He, a husband in his nation, shall not become contaminated.* Just as the prohibition against ritual contamination applies only to male *Kohanim* (see *Sotah* 3:7), the *seed* mentioned in this verse as becoming profaned by his act refers only to male children. However, Scripture's choice of the term *seed* in this verse, rather than *son,* indicates that this distinction applies only to the grandchild of the *Kohen,* but not to his child, who is rendered a *chalal* by his act whether the child is a boy or a girl. Furthermore, the inclusion of the father and the child in the same verse teaches us that they are compared: Just as the father's seed — whether male or female — is a *chalal,* so is his son's. Therefore, the distinction between a son and a daughter, which is derived from the comparison to the laws of ritual contamination, can apply only to the children of the *Kohen's* daughter when she is a *chalalah,* and teaches us that her son is a *chalal* but her daughter is not (*Gem.* loc. cit.).

All this applies only to a *chalalah* who married a non-*Kohen.* The daughter of a *chalalah* and a *Kohen* is a *chalalah* by virtue of the fact that

6. The daughter of a male *chalal* is disqualified from marrying a *Kohen* forever.

[If] a non-*Kohen* married a *chalalah*, his daughter is qualified to marry a *Kohen*. [If] a *chalal* married the daughter of a non-*Kohen*, his daughter is disqualified from marrying a *Kohen*.

R' Yehudah says: The daughter of a male proselyte is like the daughter of a male *chalal*.

YAD AVRAHAM

her parents' relationship was forbidden, since her mother was a *chalalah*, and she is therefore profaned (*Rashi*).

חָלָל שֶׁנָּשָׂא בַּת יִשְׂרָאֵל — בִּתּוֹ פְּסוּלָה לַכְּהֻנָּה. — [*If*] *a chalal married the daughter of a non-Kohen, his daughter is disqualified from marrying a Kohen.*

This was already stated above, but the mishnah repeats it in order to parallel the previous statement, for the sake of symmetry (*Gem.* loc. cit.).

רַבִּי יְהוּדָה אוֹמֵר: בַּת גֵּר זָכָר כְּבַת חָלָל זָכָר. — *R' Yehudah says: The daughter of a male proselyte is like the daughter of a male chalal.*

[I.e., she, too, may not marry a *Kohen*.]

Even if her mother was born Jewish, the daughter has the status of a proselyte like her father (*Rav*) even after several generations [in which the father of each generation was a descendant of that proselyte, similar to the law of a *chalal* stated above] (*Meiri*).

This is derived from the verse regarding *Kohanim* (*Ezek.* 44:22): *A widow and a divorcee they shall not take for themselves as wives, only virgins from the seed of the House of Israel.* R' Yehudah holds that this refers to the main source of the seed — i.e., the father (see 3:12) — who must be from the House of Israel and not a proselyte in order for his daughter to be permitted to a *Kohen* (*Gem.* 78a; *Rashi* ad loc.).[1]

Although the beginning of the verse, which prohibits a widow, refers only to a *Kohen Gadol*, the rest of it pertains to all *Kohanim* (ibid.).

7.

This mishnah is a continuation of the discussion, begun in the previous mishnah, concerning the eligibility of the daughter of a proselyte to marry a *Kohen*.

1. Obviously, this verse also disqualifies a proselyte herself from marrying a *Kohen*. Those who maintain that she is prohibited because she is a *zonah* (see commentary to mishnah 1, s.v. לְוִיִּי) interpret the passage to be teaching us that she is disqualified, without giving the reason for it (*Maggid Mishneh* to *Hil. Issurei Biah* 18:3).

[ז] **רַבִּי** אֱלִיעֶזֶר בֶּן יַעֲקֹב אוֹמֵר: יִשְׂרָאֵל שֶׁנָּשָׂא גִיּוֹרֶת — בִּתּוֹ כְּשֵׁרָה לַכְּהֻנָּה; וְגֵר שֶׁנָּשָׂא בַת יִשְׂרָאֵל — בִּתּוֹ כְּשֵׁרָה לַכְּהֻנָּה. אֲבָל גֵּר שֶׁנָּשָׂא גִיּוֹרֶת — בִּתּוֹ פְּסוּלָה לַכְּהֻנָּה. אֶחָד גֵּר וְאֶחָד עֲבָדִים מְשֻׁחְרָרִים, אֲפִלּוּ עַד עֲשָׂרָה דוֹרוֹת, עַד שֶׁתְּהֵא אִמּוֹ מִיִּשְׂרָאֵל. רַבִּי יוֹסֵי אוֹמֵר: אַף גֵּר שֶׁנָּשָׂא גִיּוֹרֶת בִּתּוֹ כְּשֵׁרָה לַכְּהֻנָּה.

[ח] **הָאוֹמֵר:** "בְּנִי זֶה מַמְזֵר" — אֵינוֹ נֶאֱמָן.

ר׳ עובדיה מברטנורא

(ז) **רבי אליעזר בן יעקב אומר כו׳.** מסקינן בגמרא (עח, ב), שהבא לימלך מורין לו כרבי אליעזר בן יעקב, שלא ישא כהן בת גר וגיורת. אבל אם נשא, הלכה כרבי יוסי, ואין מוציאין אותה מידו, וזרעו ממנה כשר: (ח) **האומר בני זה ממזר הוא אינו נאמן.** דקרוב הוא אצלו, ואין קרוב כשר להעיד:

יד אברהם

רַבִּי אֱלִיעֶזֶר בֶּן יַעֲקֹב אוֹמֵר: יִשְׂרָאֵל שֶׁנָּשָׂא גִיּוֹרֶת — בִּתּוֹ כְּשֵׁרָה לַכְּהֻנָּה; — *R' Eliezer ben Yaakov says: [If] a non-Kohen married a proselyte, his daughter is qualified to marry a Kohen;*

[However, if a *Kohen* married a proselyte, their child would be a *chalal,* since the *Kohen* was forbidden to marry her (see mishnah 1).]

וְגֵר שֶׁנָּשָׂא בַת יִשְׂרָאֵל — בִּתּוֹ כְּשֵׁרָה לַכְּהֻנָּה. אֲבָל גֵּר שֶׁנָּשָׂא גִיּוֹרֶת — בִּתּוֹ פְּסוּלָה לַכְּהֻנָּה. — *[if] a proselyte married the daughter of a regular Jew, his daughter is qualified to marry a Kohen. However, [if] a proselyte married a proselyte, his daughter is disqualified from marrying a Kohen.*

[He maintains that as long as either of the parents is of Jewish descent — i.e., has the legal status of a regular Jew, and not that of a proselyte (see commentary to mishnah 6 s.v. רבי יהודה) — their daughter is permitted to a *Kohen.*] This is because he interprets the phrase (*Ezek.* 44:22), *from the seed of the House of Israel,* to include anyone who has even one parent of Jewish descent (*Gem.* 77a).

[The term יִשְׂרָאֵל in this phrase does not exclude a *Kohen,* since a proselyte is permitted to the daughter of a *Kohen* (see *Gem.* 76b).]

אֶחָד גֵּר וְאֶחָד עֲבָדִים מְשֻׁחְרָרִים, — [*This applies to*] *both a proselyte and freedmen,*

[A gentile slave owned by a Jew and then freed becomes a full-fledged Jew, and is thus included in the category of proselytes (see mishnah 1).]

אֲפִלּוּ עַד עֲשָׂרָה דוֹרוֹת, — *even until ten generations,*

[The status of a proselyte remains for all generations, as long as both parents in each generation are descendants of proselytes.] The mishnah specifies *ten generations,* because that is the number given in Scripture (*Deut.* 23:3), when it states that the

7. R' Eliezer ben Yaakov says: [If] a non-*Kohen* married a proselyte, his daughter is qualified to marry a *Kohen;* [if] a proselyte married the daughter of a regular Jew, his daughter is qualified to marry a *Kohen.* However, [if] a proselyte married a proselyte, his daughter is disqualified from marrying a *Kohen.* [This applies to] both a proselyte and freedmen, even until ten generations, unless his mother is of Jewish descent. R' Yose says: Even [if] a proselyte married a proselyte, his daughter is qualified to marry a *Kohen.*

8. One who says: "This son of mine is a *mamzer,*"

YAD AVRAHAM

status of a *mamzer* remains forever (*Tos. Yom Tov* to *Bikkurim* 1:5).

עַד שֶׁתְּהֵא אִמּוֹ מִיִּשְׂרָאֵל. — *unless his mother is of Jewish descent.*

[If the wife of a proselyte was of Jewish descent, their son assumes her status rather than the defective status of his father, and his daughter is permitted to a *Kohen.*] Obviously, the same applies to one whose father was of Jewish descent but whose mother was a proselyte (*Tif. Yis.*), since the father is considered the primary parent in this matter (see previous mishnah).

רַבִּי יוֹסֵי אוֹמֵר: אַף גֵּר שֶׁנָּשָׂא גִיּוֹרֶת בִּתּוֹ כְּשֵׁרָה לַכְּהֻנָּה. — *R' Yose says: Even [if] a proselyte married a proselyte, his daughter is qualified to marry a Kohen.*

R' Yose interprets the phrase, *from the seed of the House of Israel,* to mean one who was seeded — i.e., conceived — in *the House of Israel.* Thus, as long as the girl's parents were Jewish at the time she was conceived, she is permitted to a *Kohen* (*Gem.* 77a).

The *Gemara* (78b) rules that a *Kohen* should initially refrain from marrying the daughter of two proselytes — in accordance with the opinion of R' Eliezer ben Yaakov — but if he did marry such a woman, he is not required to divorce her, and his children are legitimate *Kohanim* (*Rav*).

8.

הָאוֹמֵר: ,,בְּנִי זֶה מַמְזֵר'' — *One who says: "This son of mine is a mamzer,"* —

A man asserts that a certain person is his son, but declares that he was born from a woman who was prohibited to him under penalty of *kares* (excision; Divinely decreed premature death) and is therefore a *mamzer* (*Meiri*).

Others interpret that he declares about someone who was assumed to be his son that he is in fact not his son, but rather a *mamzer* — born to his wife from a different father (*Tif. Yis.;* see *Pnei Yehoshua*).

וַאֲפִלּוּ שְׁנֵיהֶם אוֹמְרִים עַל הָעֻבָּר שֶׁבְּמֵעֶיהָ: ,,מַמְזֵר הוּא" — אֵינָם נֶאֱמָנִים. רַבִּי יְהוּדָה אוֹמֵר: נֶאֱמָנִים.

ר' עובדיה מברטנורא

אפילו שניהם. הבעל והאשה, ולא מבעיא כשהאב לבדו מעיד שהוא ממזר דלא מהימן, דלא קים ליה בגויה, אלא אפילו אמו דקים ליה בגויה אינה נאמנת, אפילו על עובר שבמעיה שלא היה לעולם בחזקת כשרות: **רבי יהודה אומר נאמנים.** טעמא דרבי יהודה דכתיב (דברים כא, יז) יכיר, יכירנו לאחרים, מכאן שהאב נאמן לפסול את בנו, ואין האם נאמנת על בנה. ודוקא על בנו הוא נאמן, אבל לא על בן בנו, שאם היו לבן זה בנים אינו נאמן לפסלם. והלכה כרבי יהודה:

יד אברהם

אֵינוֹ נֶאֱמָן. — *is not believed.*

This is because he is his son's relative, and a person cannot testify concerning his relative[1] (*Rav; Rashi*).

In addition, since the son had been assumed to be legitimate, the word of one witness is not sufficient to alter his status (*Ran*).

Others explain that in order to be believed about his son, he must also be believed that he committed a transgression, and a person's testimony about his own sin is not accepted in court (*Meiri*).

וַאֲפִלּוּ שְׁנֵיהֶם אוֹמְרִים — *Even if they both say,*

The mother, whose knowledge of the facts concerning her children is more certain than that of the father, supports his testimony that the child is a *mamzer* (*Rav* from *Gem.* 78b).

עַל הָעֻבָּר שֶׁבְּמֵעֶיהָ: — *concerning the fetus in her womb:*

Who has no presumptive status of legitimacy, since he was not yet born (ibid.).

,,מַמְזֵר הוּא" — — *"He is a mamzer,"* —

I.e., he was fathered by someone other than his mother's husband (*Rashi; Meiri*).

אֵינָם נֶאֱמָנִים. — *they are not believed.*

Since most of a woman's conjugal relations are assumed to have been with her husband, any statement to the effect that a child was fathered by another man is in conflict with the majority factor; therefore, they are not believed[2] (*Sefer Hamiknah*).

1. *Pnei Yehoshua* explains that although in matters of religious law, such as this, one witness is believed and even a relative is qualified to testify, the mishnah is discussing a case in which most of the women in the town are permitted to him. In such a situation, one witness is not believed to declare the son a *mamzer*, because he is in conflict with the rule of רֹב, *the majority factor*, which dictates that we assume that which is probable. *Rashi* adds that even if there is another witness who affirms the father's testimony, it does not suffice, since the testimony of a relative is void and cannot be combined with that of another witness.

Alternatively, in this case, the man's wife disputes his statement and claims that the son is legitimate. If he were a valid witness, her claim would be disregarded, because a disqualified witness — such as a woman — cannot dispute the testimony of a valid witness, even in those areas where the testimony of a disqualified witness is acceptable. However, since the man is a relative, he too is a disqualified witness, and his testimony is neutralized by her statement to the contrary (*Sefer Hamiknah*).

2. [Although two witnesses are believed to contradict a majority factor, that is only when

is not believed. Even if they both say, concerning the fetus in her womb: "He is a *mamzer*," they are not believed. R' Yehudah says: They are believed.

YAD AVRAHAM

.רַבִּי יְהוּדָה אוֹמֵר: נֶאֱמָנִים — *R' Yehudah says: They are believed.*

Both a man who says his own son is a *mamzer* and one who says that his wife's child is illegitimate, having been fathered by another man, are believed (*Tos. Yom Tov*). This is because it is written in the Torah (*Deut.* 21:17) concerning a man with two wives: *The firstborn, the son of the hated woman, he shall recognize to give him a double portion* [*of inheritance*]. From the extra expression, *he shall recognize* (*Meiri*), R' Yehudah derives that a father is believed in his recognition of his son — i.e., to identify him — whether to single him out as the firstborn or to declare him illegitimate (*Rav* from *Gem.* 89b).

Although the passage is explicitly discussing the father's identification of his firstborn son, the *Gemara* derives that he is also believed to disqualify him. This is because if the father identified the younger of his wife's two sons as his firstborn, he has thereby stated that the older son is from a different father, which [in a case in which it was known that he was born to this man's wife after they were married] renders him illegitimate. Alternatively, the *Gemara* (68a) explains that the *hated woman* mentioned in this verse refers to one whom he married illicitly, such as a divorcee to a *Kohen*. Thus, his credibility includes identification of his son as being born to this woman, and hence, a *chalal* (*Tos.* 74a s.v. כשם). It can be assumed that he is similarly believed concerning other disqualifications[1] (*Tos. Yom Tov*).

The mother is not believed on her own [because the verse grants credibility only to the father] (*Rav*).

Although a woman is believed to say that her son is legitimate (mishnah 2), that is because one whose genealogy is unknown is permitted to enter into the Congregation by Biblical law. Although the Rabbis prohibited such a person to do so, they granted his mother credibility concerning that prohibition. Her claim that he is a *mamzer*, however, contradicts his presumed Biblical status of legitimacy, and she is therefore not believed (*Ran* to mishnah 2; cf. *Tos. R' Akiva Eiger* here).

The passage grants a man credibility only concerning his son, but not his grandson. Therefore, if the son has children of his own, who would be affected by the testimony of the grandfather, the latter is no longer believed (*Rav* from *Yevamos* 47a), even concerning his sons (*Ran*).

The *halachah* is in accordance with the view of R' Yehudah (*Rav; Rambam, Hil. Issurei Biah* 15:15).

they are valid witnesses; in this case, however, the mother — being a woman, as well as a relative — is disqualified from testifying.]

1. [According to the first explanation, it is clear in the passage that a father is believed to say about someone who is assumed to be his son that he is actually not. According to the second approach, however, which derives from the passage only that he is trusted concerning the status of his son, no reason is given as to why he is also trusted to say that a certain person is not his child. It is therefore apparent that the *Gemara* considers the establishment of whether or not someone is one's son analogous to clarifying a son's status.]

קידושין
ד/ט

[ט] מִי שֶׁנָּתַן רְשׁוּת לִשְׁלוּחוֹ לְקַדֵּשׁ אֶת בִּתּוֹ, וְהָלַךְ הוּא וְקִדְּשָׁהּ: אִם שֶׁלּוֹ קָדְמוּ — קִדּוּשָׁיו קִדּוּשִׁין; וְאִם שֶׁל שְׁלוּחוֹ קָדְמוּ — קִדּוּשָׁיו קִדּוּשִׁין; וְאִם אֵינוֹ יָדוּעַ — שְׁנֵיהֶם נוֹתְנִים גֵּט. וְאִם רָצוּ — אֶחָד נוֹתֵן גֵּט וְאֶחָד כּוֹנֵס.

וְכֵן הָאִשָּׁה שֶׁנָּתְנָה רְשׁוּת לִשְׁלוּחָהּ לְקַדְּשָׁהּ, וְהָלְכָה וְקִדְּשָׁה אֶת עַצְמָהּ: אִם שֶׁלָּהּ קָדְמוּ — קִדּוּשֶׁיהָ קִדּוּשִׁין; וְאִם שֶׁל שְׁלוּחָהּ קָדְמוּ — קִדּוּשָׁיו קִדּוּשִׁין; וְאִם אֵינוֹ יָדוּעַ — שְׁנֵיהֶם נוֹתְנִין לָהּ גֵּט. וְאִם רָצוּ — אֶחָד נוֹתֵן לָהּ גֵּט וְאֶחָד כּוֹנֵס.

ר׳ עובדיה מברטנורא

(ט) **וכן האשה שנתנה רשות לשלוחה.** אצטריך תנא לאשמועינן באב שעשה שליח לקדש את בתו, ובאשה שעשתה שליח לקדש את עצמה. דאי אשמועינן באב, הוה אמינא, אב דקים ליה ביוחסין, וכשמצא מיוחס זה קדשה לו, הוא דאמרינן דבטל את השליח, אבל אשה דלא קים לה ביוחסין, אף על גב דקדשה את עצמה, לא סמכה על קדושיה ולא בטלה את השליח, דסברה דלמא משכח שליח אדם מיוחס מזה. ואי אשמועינן בדידה, הוה אמינא משום דאשה דייקא ומנסבא, כי קדשה עצמה בטלה את השליח, אבל אב דלא קפיד על בתו אם תנשא לבטל כל דהו, לא בטליה לשליחות דשליח, והאי דקדים וקדשה, סבר דלמא לא משכח, צריכא:

יד אברהם

9.

This mishnah is based on the principle stated above (2:1) that a father can give his daughter in *kiddushin* when she is a *naarah* — and certainly when she is a minor — and he can also appoint an agent to accept *kiddushin* on her behalf. Similarly, a woman who is already a *bogeres* can appoint an agent to accept her *kiddushin.*

מִי שֶׁנָּתַן רְשׁוּת לִשְׁלוּחוֹ לְקַדֵּשׁ אֶת בִּתּוֹ, — [*If*] *someone authorized his agent to give his daughter in kiddushin,*

I.e., his daughter who was a minor or a *naarah* (*Meiri*).

וְהָלַךְ הוּא וְקִדְּשָׁהּ: — *and he went and gave her in kiddushin —*

The father himself gave her in betrothal to someone other than the man to whom the agent had given her (*Tif. Yis.*).

אִם שֶׁלּוֹ קָדְמוּ — קִדּוּשָׁיו קִדּוּשִׁין; — *if his was first, his kiddushin is valid;*

If the father's betrothal preceded the agent's, it takes effect, and the agent's authorization is nullified. Although he did not nullify it explicitly it is automatically void, because her betrothal by the father precludes the validity of any subsequent *kiddushin* brought about through the agent (*Meiri*).

4
9

9. [I]f someone authorized his agent to give his daughter in *kiddushin*, and he went and gave her in *kiddushin* — if his was first, his *kiddushin* is valid; if that of his agent was first, his *kiddushin* is valid; if it is not known, they both give a *get*. If they desire, one may give a *get* and the other may marry [her].

Similarly, [if] a woman authorized an agent to accept her *kiddushin*, and she went and accepted her own *kiddushin* — if hers was first, her *kiddushin* is valid; if her agent's was first, his *kiddushin* is valid; if it is not known, they both give her a *get*. If they desire, one may give her a *get* and the other marry [her].

YAD AVRAHAM

וְאִם שֶׁל שְׁלוּחוֹ קָדַם — קִדּוּשָׁיו קִדּוּשִׁין; — *if that of his agent was first, his kiddushin is valid;*

[The *kiddushin* of the agent is valid, because once he gave her in betrothal, the father can no longer give her to another man.]

וְאִם אֵינוֹ יָדוּעַ — שְׁנֵיהֶם נוֹתְנִים גֵּט. — *if it is not known, they both give a get.*

If it cannot be ascertained which of the two occurred first, she must receive a *get* from both the man who betrothed her through the father and the one who did so through the agent before she can marry a third man (*Rashi*).

וְאִם רָצוּ — אֶחָד נוֹתֵן גֵּט וְאֶחָד כּוֹנֵס. — *If they desire, one may give a get and the other may marry* [*her*].

[Once one of these men has given a *get*, the other may marry her. However, he must first betroth her again, since the validity of his first *kiddushin* is in question.]

וְכֵן הָאִשָּׁה שֶׁנָּתְנָה רְשׁוּת לִשְׁלוּחָהּ לְקַדְּשָׁהּ, וְהָלְכָה וְקִדְּשָׁה אֶת עַצְמָהּ: אִם שֶׁלָּהּ קָדַם — קִדּוּשֶׁיהָ קִדּוּשִׁין; וְאִם שֶׁל שְׁלוּחָהּ קָדַם — קִדּוּשָׁיו קִדּוּשִׁין; וְאִם אֵינוֹ יָדוּעַ — שְׁנֵיהֶם נוֹתְנִים לָהּ גֵּט. וְאִם רָצוּ — אֶחָד נוֹתֵן לָהּ גֵּט וְאֶחָד כּוֹנֵס. — *Similarly,* [*if*] *a woman authorized an agent to accept her kiddushin, and she went and accepted her own kiddushin — if hers was first, her kiddushin is valid; if her agent's was first, his kiddushin is valid; if it is not known, they both give her a get. If they desire, one may give her a get and the other marry* [*her*].

The mishnah discusses both this case and that of the father, because neither of them could be derived from the other. If only the case of the father's betrothal had been mentioned, we might think that the father meant his betrothal to be binding — to the point of precluding that of the agent — because he is likely to be aware of the husband's genealogical status and he therefore decided at the time of *kiddushin* that this man is acceptable to him. The woman her-

קידושין
ד/י

[י] **מִי** שֶׁיָּצָא הוּא וְאִשְׁתּוֹ לִמְדִינַת הַיָּם, וּבָא הוּא וְאִשְׁתּוֹ וּבָנָיו, וְאָמַר: אִשָּׁה שֶׁיָּצְאת עִמּוֹ לִמְדִינַת הַיָּם הֲרֵי הִיא זוֹ, וְאֵלּוּ בָנֶיהָ — אֵינוֹ צָרִיךְ לְהָבִיא רְאָיָה לֹא עַל הָאִשָּׁה וְלֹא עַל הַבָּנִים. ,,מֵתָה, וְאֵלּוּ בָנֶיהָ" — מֵבִיא רְאָיָה עַל הַבָּנִים, וְאֵינוֹ מֵבִיא רְאָיָה עַל הָאִשָּׁה.

ר׳ עובדיה מברטנורא

(י) **אינו צריך להביא ראיה על האשה.** שהיא מיוחסת, שכבר בדקה כשנשאה: **ולא על הבנים.** בבנים קטנים שכרוכים אחרי אמן:

יד אברהם

matter to him which *kiddushin* takes effect; he accepted *kiddushin* only because of the possibility that the agent will not succeed in doing so, but he did not intend that it be finalized, thereby invalidating the subsequent betrothal of the agent. Therefore, the mishnah tells us that whichever *kiddushin* is made first is binding (*Rav* from *Gem.* 79a).

self, however, is generally not certain of a man's status, and she may have intended that her *kiddushin* be held in abeyance until the relative status of the two men is clarified. Therefore, the mishnah must tell us that her *kiddushin* is binding.

Had the mishnah stated only the second ruling, we might assume that the father's primary concern is that his daughter be betrothed, but it does not

10.

The Mishnah now returns to the topic of genealogical classes, and to the issue of a man's credibility regarding his children's status.

Although the *halachah* follows the opinion of the Rabbis (see commentary to mishnah 4), that we do not need to investigate a person's genealogical purity, if it has not been aspersed, members of those families who were already established through investigation as being eligible to marry a *Kohen* could not marry a woman who had not been scrutinized if they wished their children to retain that status (*Maggid Mishneh* to *Hil. Issurei Biah* 20:5; *Tos. Yom Tov*).

מִי שֶׁיָּצָא הוּא וְאִשְׁתּוֹ לִמְדִינַת הַיָּם, — *Someone who went overseas with his wife*

And her pedigree had already been scrutinized before he married her (*Tis. Yis.*) [and she had been discovered to be eligible to marry a *Kohen*].

וּבָא הוּא וְאִשְׁתּוֹ — *and then came with his wife*

He returned with his wife after a long time, and no one knew if she was the woman with whom he had left (ibid.).

וּבָנָיו, — *and his children,*

I.e., small children who clung to his wife as children to a mother (*Gem.* 79b).

וְאָמַר: אִשָּׁה שֶׁיָּצְאת עִמּוֹ לִמְדִינַת הַיָּם הֲרֵי

10. Someone who went overseas with his wife and then came with his wife and his children, and said that this is the woman who went overseas with him and these are her children need not bring proof concerning the woman nor concerning the children. [If he said:] " She died and these are her children," he must bring proof concerning the children, but he need not bring proof concerning the woman.

YAD AVRAHAM

הִיא זוֹ, — *and said that this is the woman who went overseas with him*

[And her eligibility to marry a *Kohen* is therefore already established.]

וְאֵלּוּ בָנֶיהָ — *and these are her children*

[And their status is also confirmed, since these are their parents.]

אֵינוֹ צָרִיךְ לְהָבִיא רְאָיָה לֹא עַל הָאִשָּׁה — *need not bring proof concerning the woman*

He does not need to establish her pedigree, since it has already been done [because he is believed that she is the wife with whom he left] (*Rav*).

Others interpret this to mean that he does not have to establish that she is the mother of these children, since they cling to her (*Tos.*).

וְלֹא עַל הַבָּנִים. — *nor concerning the children.*

They are assumed to be the children of this man and woman because of their obvious attachment to her. Therefore, if the man is a *Kohen*, the children may eat *terumah*, and the girls among them — as well as the daughters which any of them subsequently have — are permitted to *Kohanim* (*Meiri* from *Gem.* 80a; *Rashi* ad loc. s.v. אבל ליוחסין).

Others construe this as meaning that he is believed that they are his children (*Tos.*).

"מֵתָה, וְאֵלּוּ בָנֶיהָ" — [*If he said:*] *"She died and these are her children,"*

[His wife did not return with him, and he claimed that she had died, and that the children who were with him were from her, their status having thus been already established.]

מֵבִיא רְאָיָה עַל הַבָּנִים, — *he must bring proof concerning the children,*

He must prove that these are her children (*Rashi*) [since the evidence of their attachment to her is not present].

Even according to R' Yehudah, who holds that a man is believed about the status of his son (mishnah 8), the Rabbis required proof in this case for the sake of maintaining genealogical purity (*Tos. Yom Tov*).

וְאֵינוֹ מֵבִיא רְאָיָה עַל הָאִשָּׁה. — *but he need not bring proof concerning the woman.*

He need not establish her genealogical status, since it has already been done (*Rashi; Meiri*).

Others explain that he must prove that these are the children of his wife who died overseas, but he is believed that the woman who died was the same as the one with whom he left — whose status has already been established (*Tos.*, according to *Maharsha, Tos. Yom Tov;* cf. *Maharshal*).

[יא] „**אִשָּׁה** נָשָׂאתִי בִּמְדִינַת הַיָּם הֲרֵי הִיא זוֹ, וְאֵלּוּ בָנֶיהָ״ — מֵבִיא רְאָיָה עַל הָאִשָּׁה, וְאֵינוֹ צָרִיךְ לְהָבִיא רְאָיָה עַל הַבָּנִים.

„מֵתָה, וְאֵלּוּ בָנֶיהָ״ — צָרִיךְ לְהָבִיא רְאָיָה עַל הָאִשָּׁה וְעַל הַבָּנִים.

[יב] **לֹא** יִתְיַחֵד אָדָם עִם שְׁתֵּי נָשִׁים, אֲבָל

ר׳ עובדיה מברטנורא

(יב) **לא יתיחד איש אחד עם שתי נשים.** מפני שדעתן קלה, ושתיהן נוחות להתפתות:

יד אברהם

11.

„אִשָּׁה נָשָׂאתִי בִּמְדִינַת הַיָּם הֲרֵי הִיא זוֹ, וְאֵלּוּ בָנֶיהָ״ — *[If one says: "I married a woman overseas; this is she and these are her children,"*

A man returned from overseas with a wife, and with young children who cling to her (*Gem.* 79b) [and he claims that she is his wife and they are their children].

מֵבִיא רְאָיָה עַל הָאִשָּׁה, — *he must bring proof concerning the woman,*

He must establish his wife's pedigree in order for her children to be permitted to marry *Kohanim* (*Meiri*).

וְאֵינוֹ צָרִיךְ לְהָבִיא רְאָיָה עַל הַבָּנִים. — *but he need not bring proof concerning the children.*

He need not prove that these are her children, for their attachment to her is sufficient evidence (ibid.).

„מֵתָה, וְאֵלּוּ בָנֶיהָ״ — [*If he says:*] *"She died, and these are her children,"*

If he returned with children but no wife, and he stated that his wife had died and these are their children (ibid.).

צָרִיךְ לְהָבִיא רְאָיָה עַל הָאִשָּׁה וְעַל הַבָּנִים. — *he must bring proof concerning the woman and the children.*

He must prove that his wife's pedigree was such that her children are permitted to marry *Kohanim*, and that these are her children (ibid.).

12.

יחוד — The Prohibition of Secluding Oneself With a Woman

It is Biblically prohibited for a man to be alone with an *ervah* — a woman with whom he is prohibited to have conjugal relations under penalty of *kares* (see 3:10). This is derived from the verse (*Deut.* 13:7), *If your brother, the son of your mother, shall convince you* ... From Scripture's unusual description of one's *brother as the son of your mother*, we derive that a son may be alone with his mother [who is an *ervah*], but not with any other *ervah* (*Gem.* 80b).[1]

1. *Pnei Yehoshua* explains that although this derivation seems extremely far-fetched, since there is no apparent indication that the verse is discussing the seclusion of a man and a

11. [If one says:] " I married a woman overseas; this is she and these are her children," he must bring proof concerning the woman, but he need not bring proof concerning the children.

[If he says:] " She died, and these are her children," he must bring proof concerning the woman and the children.

12. A man may not be alone with two women,

YAD AVRAHAM

Seclusion with an unmarried woman who is not an *ervah* was prohibited by the court of King David (*Sanhedrin* 21b), and seclusion with a gentile was prohibited by the decree of Shammai and Hillel (*Avodah Zarah* 36b).

The Rabbis ordained that one who secludes himself with a woman receives forty lashes. However, this does not apply if she is married, because people will suspect her of having committed adultery and will cast aspersion on the legitimacy of her children (*Gem.* 81a).

לֹא יִתְיַחֵד אָדָם עִם שְׁתֵּי נָשִׁים, — *A man may not be alone with two women,*

It is forbidden for even a virtuous man [over the age of nine (*Rambam, Hil. Issurei Biah* 22:10)] to be secluded with one or even two women [over the age of three (ibid.)], even if the women are virtuous. This is because the man may be overcome by his lust if there is no other man present to discourage him, and the women might frivolously ignore the prohibition because of an emotional incentive. The woman who was seduced could then persuade the others to cover up for her or even to duplicate her act (*Meiri*).

According to some authorities, this applies only to one or two women; if there are three or more women present, a man is permitted to be alone with them (ibid.; *Rashi* 82a s.v. לא יתיחד). Others contend that it is prohibited for a man to be alone with any number of women (*Rambam* loc. cit. 8).

If the two women are co-wives, the wives of two brothers, stepmother and stepdaughter, mother-in-law and daughter-in-law, or sisters-in-law, a man is permitted to be alone with them. Since each of them is assumed to bear animosity toward the other (see commentary to *Gittin* 2:7), she will avoid transgressing, because she does not rely on the other to refrain from revealing her misdeed (*Rav, Rambam* loc. cit. 9 from *Gem.* 81b).

If one of the two women is a child who understands what cohabitation is, but does not yet desire it, a man is permitted to be alone with them, because the child will not be persuaded to participate and is likely to divulge what occurred (*Rav* from *Gem.* ibid.).

woman, it is based upon the next part of the verse: *your son, your daughter, your wife, or your friend ... secretly* [i.e., in seclusion]. From the fact that the verse does not mention a sister as well as a brother, we derive that a man may not be secluded with any *ervah* other than his daughter (who is mentioned in the verse) or his mother (who is alluded to in the beginning of the verse), as stated in the *Gemara.*

אִשָּׁה אַחַת מִתְיַחֶדֶת עִם שְׁנֵי אֲנָשִׁים. רַבִּי שִׁמְעוֹן אוֹמֵר: אַף אִישׁ אֶחָד מִתְיַחֵד עִם שְׁתֵּי נָשִׁים בִּזְמַן שֶׁאִשְׁתּוֹ עִמּוֹ. וְיָשֵׁן עִמָּהֶם בַּפֻּנְדְּקִי, מִפְּנֵי שֶׁאִשְׁתּוֹ מְשַׁמַּרְתּוֹ.

מִתְיַחֵד אָדָם עִם אִמּוֹ וְעִם בִּתּוֹ, וְיָשֵׁן עִמָּהֶם בְּקֵרוּב בָּשָׂר. וְאִם הִגְדִּילוּ — זוֹ יְשֵׁנָה בִּכְסוּתָהּ וְזֶה יָשֵׁן בִּכְסוּתוֹ.

ר׳ עובדיה מברטנורא

אבל אשה אחת מתיחדת עם שני אנשים. שהאחד בוש מחברו. ופסק הלכה, לא תתיחד אשה אחת עם שני אנשים, וכל שכן איש אחד עם שתי נשים, אלא אם כן היו שתי הנשים צרות או יבמות, או אשה ובת בעלה, או אשה וחמותה, או אשה עם תינוקת שיודעת טעם ביאה ואינה מוסרת עצמה לביאה, לפי שאלו שונאות זו את זו, ומתיראות זו מזו, וכן היא מתיראה מן הקטנה שמא תראה ותגיד. ומלקים על יחוד הפנויה, ועל יחוד עם הערוות, חוץ מאשת איש, שאין מלקין עליה שלא להוציא לעז על בניה. ומותר להתיחד עם הבהמה ועם הזכר, שלא נחשדו ישראל על הזכור ועל הבהמה: **הגדילו זו ישנה בכסותה וכו׳.** (ו)הוא שתהיה הבת משתים עשרה שנה ויום אחד, והבן משלש עשרה שנה ויום אחד. ובזמן שהיא בושה לעמוד לפניו ערומה, אפילו בפחות מכן יכניס הוא בבגדו והיא בבגדה:

יד אברהם

אֲבָל אִשָּׁה אַחַת מִתְיַחֶדֶת עִם שְׁנֵי אֲנָשִׁים. — *but one woman may be alone with two men.*

Because each of the men will be ashamed to give in to his desires in the presence of the other (*Rav*). The *Gemara* (80b) concludes that this applies only to men of high moral character, but others are prohibited to seclude themselves with one woman even if there are other men present. Therefore, the *halachah* is that it is prohibited (*Rav; Rambam,* loc. cit. 8), since people today do not possess that level of morality (see *Ran*).

Others contend that the ruling of the mishnah applies to the average person, and only those who are unusually immoral are prohibited in a group (*Ran; Meiri;* see *Even HaEzer* 22:5; *Rema* ibid.).

רַבִּי שִׁמְעוֹן אוֹמֵר: אַף אִישׁ אֶחָד מִתְיַחֵד עִם שְׁתֵּי נָשִׁים בִּזְמַן שֶׁאִשְׁתּוֹ עִמּוֹ. — *R' Shimon says: Even one man may be alone with two women when his wife is with him.*

[When a man's wife is with him, he may seclude himself with two other women, because his wife will watch him, as stated below.]

He is even permitted to seclude himself with only one other woman when his wife is with him. The mishnah mentions two women only because that is the case being discussed (*Hagahos HaGra*).

According to another version of the mishnah, R' Shimon is discussing the case of the first *Tanna,* in which the man is not with his wife; R' Shimon contends that one man is permitted to be alone with two women [the prohibition applies only to one

but one woman may be alone with two men. R' Shimon says: Even one man may be alone with two women when his wife is with him. He may sleep with them in an inn, because his wife watches him.

A man may be alone with his mother or with his daughter, and he may sleep with them with bodily contact. If they grew up, she sleeps in her clothes and he sleeps in his clothes.

YAD AVRAHAM

man with one woman]. According to this version, the words *when his wife is with him* are part of the next statement (*Tos.; Rif; Meiri*).

וְיָשֵׁן עִמָּהֶם בַּפֻּנְדְּקִי, מִפְּנֵי שֶׁאִשְׁתּוֹ מְשַׁמַּרְתּוֹ. — *He may sleep with them in an inn, because his wife watches him.*

R' Shimon maintains that even to sleep in an inn (see *Tif. Yis.*) at night with another woman is permitted when his wife is present, because she will be cautious in this situation and will be easily awakened if anything untoward occurs (*Meiri*).

According to the alternate version of the mishnah cited above, this is not part of R' Shimon's statement, but is rather true according to everyone (*Tos.; Meiri*).

מִתְיַחֵד אָדָם עִם אִמּוֹ וְעִם בִּתּוֹ, — *A man may be alone with his mother or with his daughter,*

The permissibility of the seclusion of a man and his mother is derived from Scripture (see preface), and that of a father with his daughter is considered a parallel situation (*Ran;* cf. *Pnei Yehoshua* cited loc. cit.). In both cases, there is little fear that they will be led to have relations, and therefore they are allowed to live together even on a regular basis (*Meiri*).

A brother and sister are also permitted to be alone together (*Gem.* 81b), because they are not likely to come to intimacy. However, it is forbidden for them to live together on a regular basis (*Rashi* ibid.; *Rosh; Chelkas Mechokek* to *Even HaEzer* 22:1; *Aruch HaShulchan* ibid.; cf. *Beis Shmuel* ibid.).

וְיָשֵׁן עִמָּהֶם בְּקֵרוּב בָּשָׂר. — *and he may sleep with them with bodily contact.*

It is also permitted for them to hug and kiss (*Tif. Yis.; Even HaEzer* 21:7).

וְאִם הִגְדִּילוּ — *If they grew up,* —

They reached adulthood — i.e., a boy at thirteen years and a girl at twelve (*Rav* from *Gem.* 81b) — or even if they reached puberty earlier (*Meiri*). This also applies to a younger girl if she is embarrassed to stand naked before her father (*Rav* from *Gem.* ibid.).

זוֹ יְשֵׁנָה בִּכְסוּתָהּ וְזֶה יָשֵׁן בִּכְסוּתוֹ. — *she* (lit., *this one*) *sleeps in her clothes and he sleeps in his clothes.*

[They may still sleep together, but not with bodily contact.] However, they are still permitted to hug and kiss (*Beis Shmuel* to *Even HaEzer* 21:15).

[יג] **לֹא** יִלְמַד אָדָם רַוָּק סוֹפְרִים, וְלֹא תִלְמַד אִשָּׁה סוֹפְרִים. רַבִּי אֱלִיעֶזֶר אוֹמֵר: אַף מִי שֶׁאֵין לוֹ אִשָּׁה לֹא יִלְמַד סוֹפְרִים.

[יד] **רַבִּי** יְהוּדָה אוֹמֵר: לֹא יִרְעֶה רַוָּק בְּהֵמָה, וְלֹא יִישְׁנוּ שְׁנֵי רַוָּקִים בְּטַלִּית אַחַת; וַחֲכָמִים מַתִּירִין.

כָּל שֶׁעִסְקוֹ עִם הַנָּשִׁים לֹא יִתְיַחֵד עִם הַנָּשִׁים.

ר׳ עובדיה מברטנורא

(יג) **רווק.** פנוי בלא אשה: **לא ילמד סופרים.** לא ירגיל עלמו להיות מן הסופרים, כלומר מלמד תינוקות, מפני אמותיהן של תינוקות שמלויות אללו להביא את בניהן אל בית הספר: **אף מי שאין לו אשה.** אף על פי שאינו פנוי, אלא יש לו אשה ואינה שרוייה עמו, לא ילמד סופרים. ואין הלכה כרבי אליעזר: (יד) **וחכמים מתירין.** והלכה כחכמים, שלא נחשדו ישראל על הזכור: **כל שאומנתו בין הנשים.** שמלאכת אומנתו נעשית לנשים, והנשים לריכות לו: **לא יתיחד עם הנשים.** ואפילו עם הרבה נשים, לפי שלבן גס בו ומחפות עליו. ואילו אינש אחרינא, עם שתי נשים תנן (משנה יב) דלא, שלש וארבע שפיר דמי. ורמב״ם פירש, דלא שרינן [אפילו] משום כדי חייו להתיחד עם הנשים הואיל ופרנסתו מהן:

יד אברהם

13.

לֹא יִלְמַד אָדָם רַוָּק סוֹפְרִים, — *A bachelor may not accustom himself to be among the teachers,*

A man who is not married may not be a teacher of children (*Rav; Chelkas Mechokek, Even HaEzer* 22:20), because he will be in constant contact with their mothers (*Gem.* 82a) and may be sexually aroused by them (*Meiri*).

Others contend that this refers only to one who has never been married (*Meiri;* see *Beis Shmuel, Even HaEzer* 22:19).

וְלֹא תִלְמַד אִשָּׁה סוֹפְרִים. — *and a woman may not accustom herself to be among the teachers.*

A woman may not teach children, because she may come to be secluded with their fathers (*Meiri; Rambam, Hil. Issurei Biah* 22:13).

Some authorities maintain that this applies only to an unmarried woman (*Perishah* to *Even HaEzer* 22:26). Others contend that even a married woman is prohibited unless her husband is in the same city (*Chelkas Mechokek* loc. cit. 21). A third view is that even if her husband is in that city, she may not teach them (*Turei Zahav, Yoreh Deah* 245:7).

רַבִּי אֱלִיעֶזֶר אוֹמֵר: אַף מִי שֶׁאֵין לוֹ אִשָּׁה לֹא יִלְמַד סוֹפְרִים. — *R' Eliezer says: Also one whose wife is not living with him* (lit., *who has no wife*) *may not accustom himself to be among the teachers.*

Even someone who is married is prohibited to teach children if his wife is presently not living with him (*Gem.* loc. cit.).

The *halachah* is in accordance with

13. A bachelor may not accustom himself to be among the teachers, and a woman may not accustom herself to be among the teachers. R' Eliezer says: Also one whose wife is not living with him may not accustom himself to be among the teachers.

14. R' Yehudah says: A bachelor may not herd cattle, and two bachelors may not sleep in one garment; the Sages, however, permit [it].

Anyone whose business is with women may not be alone with women. A man should not

YAD AVRAHAM

the opinion of the first *Tanna* — that the prohibition applies only to a bachelor [or one who has never been married] (*Rav;* cf. *Maggid Mishneh* loc. cit.; *Chelkas Mechokek* loc. cit. 19).

14.

The Mishnah continues the discussion concerning measures which were enacted by the Rabbis to prevent prohibited relations. This leads to the topic of trades which one should avoid because they cause excessive contact with women, and, in turn, to a discussion concerning different means of livelihood.

רַבִּי יְהוּדָה אוֹמֵר: לֹא יִרְעֶה רַוָּק בְּהֵמָה, — *R' Yehudah says: A bachelor may not herd cattle,*

For it may lead to bestiality (*Meiri*).

וְלֹא יִישְׁנוּ שְׁנֵי רַוָּקִים בְּטַלִּית אַחַת; — *and two bachelors may not sleep in one garment;*

Because they may be drawn to homosexual acts (*Rashi; Meiri*).

וַחֲכָמִים מַתִּירִין. — *the Sages, however, permit* [*it*].

Because the Jewish people are not suspected of homosexuality (*Rav* from *Gem.* 82a) or bestiality (*Gem.* ibid.).

The *halachah* follows the view of the Sages (*Rav*).

כָּל שֶׁעִסְקוֹ עִם הַנָּשִׁים לֹא יִתְיַחֵד עִם הַנָּשִׁים. — *Anyone whose business is with women may not be alone with women.*

Although seclusion with women is prohibited to all men, that is only when there are no more than two women involved. However, someone whose trade is one in which he provides for the needs of women is prohibited to seclude himself with even more than two women, because — due to their friendliness with him — they will refrain from relating his misdeed to others (*Rav; Rashi*).

Others maintain that all men are prohibited from being alone with more than two women (see commentary to mishnah 12 s.v. לֹא יִתְיַחֵד). The unique stringency of

וְלֹא יְלַמֵּד אָדָם אֶת בְּנוֹ אֻמָּנוּת בֵּין הַנָּשִׁים. רַבִּי מֵאִיר אוֹמֵר: לְעוֹלָם יְלַמֵּד אָדָם אֶת בְּנוֹ אֻמָּנוּת נְקִיָּה וְקַלָּה, וְיִתְפַּלֵּל לְמִי שֶׁהָעֹשֶׁר וְהַנְּכָסִים שֶׁלּוֹ, שֶׁאֵין אֻמָּנוּת שֶׁאֵין בָּהּ עֲנִיּוּת וַעֲשִׁירוּת, שֶׁלֹּא עֲנִיּוּת מִן הָאֻמָּנוּת, וְלֹא עֲשִׁירוּת מִן הָאֻמָּנוּת; אֶלָּא הַכֹּל לְפִי זְכוּתוֹ.

רַבִּי שִׁמְעוֹן בֶּן אֶלְעָזָר אוֹמֵר: רָאִיתָ מִיָּמֶיךָ חַיָּה וָעוֹף שֶׁיֵּשׁ לָהֶם אֻמָּנוּת? וְהֵן מִתְפַּרְנְסִין שֶׁלֹּא בְצַעַר.

יד אברהם

one whose business is with women is that it is forbidden even if his wife is with him (*Tos.*; see *Radal*).

According to some authorities, the point of the mishnah is that even one whose livelihood depends on women may not be alone with them. Rather he must either bring his wife along with him, or seek another trade (*Rambam, Hil. Issurei Biah* 22:8).

Another interpretation is that one may not be alone with women even when he is involved in his business, and his mind is concentrating on that (*Meiri; R' Chananel,* cited by *Rosh*).

וְלֹא יְלַמֵּד אָדָם אֶת בְּנוֹ אֻמָּנוּת בֵּין הַנָּשִׁים. — *A man should not teach his son a trade* [*which involves being*] *among women.*

Because he will become accustomed to being very friendly with them (*Meiri*).

Others explain that he should not teach a trade to boys and girls together, because they will become accustomed to excessive interaction with each other (ibid.).

רַבִּי מֵאִיר אוֹמֵר: לְעוֹלָם יְלַמֵּד אָדָם אֶת בְּנוֹ אֻמָּנוּת נְקִיָּה וְקַלָּה, — *R' Meir says: A man should always teach his son a clean and light trade,*

I.e., a trade which is not degrading and does not require heavy labor — e.g., sewing and weaving (*Meiri*).

Some commentators note that sewing and weaving are trades which usually involve interaction with women. They therefore explain that R' Meir disagrees with the first *Tanna,* and contends that it is preferable to choose a light and clean trade, even if it will cause involvement with women (*Likkutim*).

Another interpretation of the mishnah is that the trade should be *clean* from theft — i.e., one which does not lend itself to dishonesty — and *light,* in that it does not involve loss of money [i.e., risky investments] (*Aruch* s.v. תלם).

Others explain that he should teach him a trade which is *light,* in that it does not require excessive involvement, so that he can spend most of his time studying Torah (*Maharsha*).

וְיִתְפַּלֵּל לְמִי שֶׁהָעֹשֶׁר וְהַנְּכָסִים שֶׁלּוֹ, — *and he should pray to the One to Whom wealth and possessions belong,*

[I.e., he should pray to God] that he be successful in his trade (*Meiri*), and not assume that this trade [which is light and clean] cannot bring him wealth (*Rashi*).

Maharsha explains that he should not be afraid to limit his involvement in his trade in order to spend more time learning Torah (see above), but he should do so, and rely on God, Who is the Master of all wealth and possessions.

teach his son a trade [which involves being] among women.

R' Meir says: A man should always teach his son a clean and light trade, and he should pray to the One to Whom wealth and possessions belong, because there is no trade which does not include poverty and wealth, since poverty is not from the trade, nor is wealth from the trade; rather, all is in accordance with one's merit.

R' Shimon ben Elazar says: Have you ever seen a wild animal or a bird which has a trade? Yet they are sustained without difficulty.

YAD AVRAHAM

שֶׁאֵין אֻמָּנוּת שֶׁאֵין בָּהּ עֲנִיּוּת וַעֲשִׁירוּת, — *because there is no trade which does not include poverty and wealth,*

He should not be afraid to seek a light and clean trade and rely on God for his livelihood, because among the practitioners of every trade, there are wealthy men and poor men; thus, no matter what his trade, he must rely on God (*Tif. Yis.*).

שֶׁלֹּא עֲנִיּוּת מִן הָאֻמָּנוּת, וְלֹא עֲשִׁירוּת מִן הָאֻמָּנוּת; — *since poverty is not from the trade, nor is wealth from the trade;*

[The true cause of a person's financial status is not the nature of his trade.]

אֶלָּא הַכֹּל לְפִי זְכוּתוֹ. — *rather, all is in accordance with one's merit.*

And with God's mercy (*Meiri*) [which can be invoked through prayer].

Although a person's station is dictated by his מַזָּל, *mazal* (*Moed Katan* 28a) — the lot which is destined for him from the time he is conceived (*Tif. Yis.* from *Niddah* 16b) — this can be altered by one's merit or by the combination of merit and prayer (*Tos. Yom Tov*).

Others explain that the mishnah is actually referring to a person's *mazal*, not his merit (*Tos.*). The word זְכוּת is not used here to mean *merit*, but rather *acquisition*, as it is used in many places in the Talmud (e.g., *Gittin* 1:6). Thus, the mishnah is stating that all which a person's lot encompasses, including his *mazal*, as well as that which he achieves through merit or prayer, decides his financial status (*Likkutim*).

Another interpretation is that a person should realize that despite all his work and prayers, his potential for prosperity is limited in accordance with his destined lot, and he should therefore not lose faith in God if those endeavors do not bring the desired results (*Tif. Yis.*).

רַבִּי שִׁמְעוֹן בֶּן אֶלְעָזָר אוֹמֵר: רָאִיתָ מִיָּמֶיךָ חַיָּה וָעוֹף שֶׁיֵּשׁ לָהֶם אֻמָּנוּת? וְהֵן מִתְפַּרְנְסִין שֶׁלֹּא בְצַעַר. — *R' Shimon ben Elazar says: Have you ever seen a wild animal or a bird which has a trade? Yet they are sustained without difficulty.*

He does not mention domesticated animals, because they generally rely on human beings for their sustenance (*Radal*).

וַהֲלֹא לֹא נִבְרְאוּ אֶלָּא לְשַׁמְּשֵׁנִי, — *But they were created only* (lit., *were not*

קידושין
ד/יד

וַהֲלֹא לֹא נִבְרְאוּ אֶלָּא לְשַׁמְּשֵׁנִי, וַאֲנִי נִבְרֵאתִי לְשַׁמֵּשׁ אֶת קוֹנִי, אֵינוֹ דִין שֶׁאֶתְפַּרְנֵס שֶׁלֹּא בְצַעַר? אֶלָּא שֶׁהֲרֵעוֹתִי מַעֲשַׂי וְקִפַּחְתִּי אֶת פַּרְנָסָתִי.

אַבָּא גוֹרְיָן אִישׁ צַדְיָן אוֹמֵר מִשּׁוּם אַבָּא גוֹרְיָא: לֹא יְלַמֵּד אָדָם אֶת בְּנוֹ חַמָּר, גַּמָּל, סַפָּן, רוֹעֶה, וְחֶנְוָנִי, שֶׁאֻמָּנוּתָן אֻמָּנוּת לִסְטִים. רַבִּי יְהוּדָה אוֹמֵר מִשְּׁמוֹ: הַחַמָּרִין רֻבָּן רְשָׁעִים; וְהַגַּמָּלִין רֻבָּן כְּשֵׁרִים; הַסַּפָּנִין רֻבָּן חֲסִידִים; טוֹב שֶׁבָּרוֹפְאִים לְגֵיהִנֹּם; וְהַכָּשֵׁר שֶׁבַּטַּבָּחִים שֻׁתָּפוֹ שֶׁל עֲמָלֵק.

ר׳ עובדיה מברטנורא

חמר גמל וספן. כל אלו אומנות לסטות, כשלנין בדרכים נכנסים ולוקטים עצים ופירות מן הכרמים, ועוד, שנשכרים לבני אדם ומעבירין על תנאם: **רועה.** [בהמות שלו], שמעביר הבהמות לרעות בשדה אחרים: **חנוני.** מלומד באונאה, להטיל מים ביין, וצרורות בחיטין. שחייב אדם ללמד את בנו אומנות נקיה:

יד אברהם

created, except) to serve me,

The negative sentence structure — *were not created, except* — denotes that they have no choice but to fulfill that function, since they do not have free will (*Maharsha*).

וַאֲנִי נִבְרֵאתִי לְשַׁמֵּשׁ אֶת קוֹנִי, — *and I was created to serve my Master.*

Through the proper use of my free will to choose to do so (ibid.),

אֵינוֹ דִין שֶׁאֶתְפַּרְנֵס שֶׁלֹּא בְצַעַר? אֶלָּא שֶׁהֲרֵעוֹתִי מַעֲשַׂי וְקִפַּחְתִּי אֶת פַּרְנָסָתִי. — *does it not follow that I should be sustained without difficulty? However, I have corrupted my deeds and curtailed my sustenance.*

With Adam's sin, mankind lost the privilege of being sustained without effort (*Maharsha; Pnei Yehoshua*).

Alternatively, one who corrupts his deeds loses the privilege to have his livelihood provided by others so that he can involve himself exclusively in Torah study (*Pnei Yehoshua*).

אַבָּא גוֹרְיָן אִישׁ צַדְיָן אוֹמֵר מִשּׁוּם אַבָּא גוֹרְיָא: לֹא יְלַמֵּד אָדָם אֶת בְּנוֹ חַמָּר, גַּמָּל, סַפָּן, — *Abba Guryon of Tzadyan* [or *Tzaydan,* as is the reading in accurate editions of the Mishnah], *quoting Abba Gurya, says: A man should not teach his son* [*to be*] *a donkey driver, a camel driver, a sailor,*

Practitioners of these trades tend to be thieves, because they steal supplies from nearby properties when they lodge, and they violate the terms of their agreements with their employers [since they travel for long distances and cannot be overseen] (*Rav*).

Some versions of the mishnah add קַדָּר, [or קָרָר (*Kol HaRamaz; cf. Tos. HaRosh to Bava Metzia 75a*)] *a wagon driver* (*Tos. Yom Tov*) [who tends to be dishonest for the same reason]

Another reason given for the disdain toward these trades is that they force a

4
14

But they were created only to serve me, and I was created to serve my Master. Does it not follow that I should be sustained without difficulty? However, I have corrupted my deeds and curtailed my sustenance.

Abba Guryan of Tzadyan, quoting Abba Gurya, says: A man should not teach his son [to be] a donkey driver, a camel driver, a sailor, a shepherd, or a storekeeper, because their trade is the trade of robbers. R' Yehudah, quoting him, says: Most donkey drivers are evildoers; and most camel drivers are righteous men; most sailors are pious men; the best of doctors to *Gehinnom*; and the most righteous of animal-slaughterers is a partner with Amalek.

YAD AVRAHAM

person to spend so much time away from home (*Maharsha*).

,רוֹעֶה — *a shepherd,*

One who tends his own sheep and often allows them to graze in the fields of others (*Rav*).

,וְחֶנְוָנִי — *or a storekeeper,*

Who often practices deceit by mixing water in his wine, and pebbles in his grain (ibid.).

.שֶׁאֻמָּנוּתָן אֻמָּנוּת לִסְטִים — *because their trade is the trade of robbers.*

[I.e., these trades lend themselves to dishonesty.]

:רַבִּי יְהוּדָה אוֹמֵר מִשְּׁמוֹ — *R' Yehudah, quoting him, says:*

R' Yehudah quoted Abba Gurya (*Rashi*).

;הַחַמָּרִין רֻבָּן רְשָׁעִים — *Most donkey drivers are evildoers;*

Because their trade lends itself to dishonesty, as explained above, and they do not travel far enough to be affected in the manner described below, regarding camel drivers (*Meiri*).

;וְהַגַּמָּלִין רֻבָּן כְּשֵׁרִים — *and most camel drivers are righteous men;*

Since they travel in deserts which are full of dangers, their fear is aroused, and they humble themselves before God (*Rashi*).

This refers to those who lead camels on foot. Those who ride them, however, are mostly evildoers (*Niddah* 14a), because their bodies rub against the camel, which causes sexual arousal (*Tos.* ad loc.).

;הַסַּפָּנִין רֻבָּן חֲסִידִים — *most sailors are pious men;*

Their travels are even more fraught with danger, and they are therefore deeply moved to fear God (*Rashi*).

;טוֹב שֶׁבָּרוֹפְאִים לְגֵיהִנֹּם — *the best of doctors to Gehinnom;*

They do not fear sickness, and are therefore not humble to God; at times they cause death; and they refuse to heal the poor who cannot pay them (*Rashi*).

The mishnah specifies *the best of doctors,* not *the most righteous.* This is because the

רַבִּי נְהוֹרַאי אוֹמֵר: מַנִּיחַ אֲנִי כָּל אֻמָּנוּת שֶׁבָּעוֹלָם וְאֵינִי מְלַמֵּד אֶת בְּנִי אֶלָּא תוֹרָה, שֶׁאָדָם אוֹכֵל מִשְּׂכָרָהּ בָּעוֹלָם הַזֶּה, וְהַקֶּרֶן קַיֶּמֶת לָעוֹלָם הַבָּא. וּשְׁאָר כָּל אֻמָּנוּת אֵינָן כֵּן: כְּשֶׁאָדָם בָּא לִידֵי חֹלִי, אוֹ לִידֵי זִקְנָה, אוֹ לִידֵי יִסּוּרִין, וְאֵינוֹ יָכוֹל לַעֲסוֹק בִּמְלַאכְתּוֹ — הֲרֵי הוּא מֵת בְּרָעָב. אֲבָל הַתּוֹרָה אֵינָהּ כֵּן, אֶלָּא מְשַׁמַּרְתּוֹ מִכָּל רַע בְּנַעֲרוּתוֹ, וְנוֹתֶנֶת לוֹ אַחֲרִית וְתִקְוָה בְּזִקְנוּתוֹ. בְּנַעֲרוּתוֹ מַה הוּא אוֹמֵר? „וְקוֵֹי ה׳ יַחֲלִיפוּ כֹחַ״. בְּזִקְנוּתוֹ מַהוּ אוֹמֵר? „עוֹד יְנוּבוּן בְּשֵׂיבָה״. וְכֵן הוּא אוֹמֵר בְּאַבְרָהָם אָבִינוּ, עָלָיו הַשָּׁלוֹם:

יד אברהם

It is clear that R' Nehorai is not coming to dispute the statement of R' Meir, and to say that no one should pursue a trade, since the *Gemara* (*Eruvin* 13b) says that R' Nehorai was another name for R' Meir (*Meleches Shlomo*). Rather, he is saying that someone who is capable of achieving lofty levels of Torah scholarship and piety is permitted to abandon all avenues of financial endeavor in order to pursue only spiritual goals, and his needs will be provided by others. Since he saw these qualities in his own son, he raised him in that manner (*Pnei Yehoshua*).

Others explain that anyone whose faith in God is complete, and is able to rely on Him for all his needs without anxiety, may pursue only Torah, and his needs will be provided for. Those who are unable to maintain this degree of faith must take time from their Torah studies to earn a living (*Sefer HaMiknah;* see *Berachos* 35b).

שֶׁאָדָם אוֹכֵל מִשְּׂכָרָהּ בָּעוֹלָם הַזֶּה, וְהַקֶּרֶן קַיֶּמֶת לָעוֹלָם הַבָּא. — *for a man benefits from its rewards in this world, and the*

best doctors often rely completely on their own judgment and refuse to consult others, which can bring tragic results (*Maharsha; Tif. Yis.*).

וְהַכָּשֵׁר שֶׁבַּטַּבָּחִים שֻׁתָּפוֹ שֶׁל עֲמָלֵק. — *and the most righteous of animal-slaughterers is a partner with Amalek.*

One who slaughters animals is constantly faced with questions of *kashrus,* and he often bases his decision on his financial need (*Rashi*). In this he is comparable to Elifaz, the father of Amalek, who took away all of Jacob's money when the latter was traveling to the house of Laban (*Meiri*).

Others explain that his constant involvement in slaughtering animals causes him to become hardened and cruel, like Amalek, who was the first nation to attack the Jewish people after the exodus from Egypt (*Tos. Yom Tov; Tif. Yis.*).

רַבִּי נְהוֹרַאי אוֹמֵר: מַנִּיחַ אֲנִי כָּל אֻמָּנוּת שֶׁבָּעוֹלָם וְאֵינִי מְלַמֵּד אֶת בְּנִי אֶלָּא תוֹרָה, — *R' Nehorai says: I abandon every trade in the world and I teach my son only Torah,*

R' Nehorai says: I abandon every trade in the world and I teach my son only Torah, for a man benefits from its rewards in this world, and the principal remains for the World to Come. All other trades are not so; when a man becomes sick, old, or afflicted, and he cannot engage in his work, he dies of starvation. But Torah is not so; rather, it guards him from all evil in his youth, and it provides him with benefit and hope in his old age. Regarding his youth, what does it say? *And those whose hope is in* HASHEM shall renew their strength (*Isaiah* 40:31). Regarding his old age, what does it say? *They will still be fruitful in old age* (*Psalms* 92:15). And likewise it says regarding

YAD AVRAHAM

principal remains for the World to Come.

[I.e., the rewards for Torah last not only in this world, but eternally, in the next world.]

וּשְׁאָר כָּל אֻמָּנוּת אֵינָן כֵּן: — *All other trades are not so:*

Their rewards are temporary, and provide benefit only at the time when they are earned (*Meiri*).

כְּשֶׁאָדָם בָּא לִידֵי חֹלִי, אוֹ לִידֵי זִקְנָה, אוֹ לִידֵי יִסּוּרִין, — *when a man becomes sick, old, or afflicted,*

I.e., with emotional afflictions, such as worry and anger (*Tif. Yis.*).

וְאֵינוֹ יָכוֹל לַעֲסוֹק בִּמְלַאכְתּוֹ — הֲרֵי הוּא מֵת בְּרָעָב. — *and he cannot engage in his work, he dies of starvation.*

[No trade provides a guarantee of livelihood for all contingencies.]

אֲבָל הַתּוֹרָה אֵינָהּ כֵּן, אֶלָּא מְשַׁמַּרְתּוּ מִכָּל רַע בְּנַעֲרוּתוֹ, וְנוֹתֶנֶת לוֹ אַחֲרִית וְתִקְוָה בְּזִקְנוּתוֹ. — *But Torah is not so; rather, it guards him from all evil in his youth, and it provides him with benefit and hope in his old age.*

Even one who is incapacitated and cannot study continues to benefit from the rewards of his previous studies (*Rashi; Tif. Yis.*).

בְּנַעֲרוּתוֹ מַה הוּא אוֹמֵר? ,,וְקוֵֹי ה׳ יַחֲלִיפוּ כֹחַ״. — *Regarding his youth, what does it say? "And those who hope is in* H*ASHEM shall renew their strength"* (*Isaiah* 40:31).

I.e., before one surge of energy wanes, God provides him with another to replace it (*Ibn Ezra* ad loc.).

בְּזִקְנוּתוֹ מַהוּ אוֹמֵר? ,,עוֹד יְנוּבוּן בְּשֵׂיבָה״. — *Regarding his old age, what does it say? "They will still be fruitful in old age"* (*Psalms* 92:15).

I.e., their reward shall come to fruition in their old age (*Rashi* 82b).

וְכֵן הוּא אוֹמֵר בְּאַבְרָהָם אָבִינוּ, עָלָיו הַשָּׁלוֹם: ,,וְאַבְרָהָם זָקֵן . . . וַה׳ בֵּרַךְ אֶת אַבְרָהָם בַּכֹּל״. — *And likewise it says regarding our forefather Abraham — peace upon*

„וְאַבְרָהָם זָקֵן ... וַה׳ בֵּרַךְ אֶת אַבְרָהָם בַּכֹּל״. מָצִינוּ שֶׁעָשָׂה אַבְרָהָם אָבִינוּ אֶת כָּל הַתּוֹרָה כֻּלָּהּ עַד שֶׁלֹּא נִתְּנָה, שֶׁנֶּאֱמַר: „עֵקֶב אֲשֶׁר שָׁמַע אַבְרָהָם בְּקֹלִי וַיִּשְׁמֹר מִשְׁמַרְתִּי, מִצְוֹתַי, חֻקּוֹתַי, וְתוֹרֹתָי״.

סליקא לה מסכת קידושין
הדרן עלך סדר נשים

יד אברהם

מָצִינוּ שֶׁעָשָׂה אַבְרָהָם אָבִינוּ אֶת כָּל הַתּוֹרָה כֻּלָּהּ עַד שֶׁלֹּא נִתְּנָה, שֶׁנֶּאֱמַר: „עֵקֶב אֲשֶׁר שָׁמַע אַבְרָהָם בְּקֹלִי וַיִּשְׁמֹר מִשְׁמַרְתִּי, מִצְוֹתַי, חֻקּוֹתַי, וְתוֹרֹתָי״. — *We find that our forefather Abraham fulfilled the entire Torah before it*

him (Gen. 24:1): *"And Abraham was old ... and Hashem blessed Abraham with everything."*

We find that Abraham was rewarded in his old age more than in his earlier years (*Tosefta*).

4
14

our forefather Abraham — peace upon him (*Gen.* 24:1): *And Abraham was old ... and HASHEM blessed Abraham with everything.* We find that our forefather Abraham fulfilled the entire Torah before it was given, as it says (ibid. 26:5): *Because Abraham obeyed My voice and safeguarded My Ordinances, My Commandments, My Decrees, and My Teachings.*

YAD AVRAHAM

was given, as it says (ibid. 26:5): *"Because Abraham obeyed My voice and safeguarded My Ordinances, My Commandments, My Decrees, and My Teachings."*

This is added so that one should not think that Abraham's reward could not have been for fulfilling the Torah, since it had not yet been given in his day (*Tif. Yis.*).

Glossary

Amora, pl. **Amoraim** (אֲמוֹרָאִים) אֲמוֹרָא: a Sage of the post-Mishnaic era quoted in the *Gemara* or other works of the same period.

bogeres, pl. **bogeres** (בּוֹגְרוֹת) בּוֹגֶרֶת: a mature girl. This stage is usually reached at the age of twelve and a half years. See commentary to *Gittin* 6:3, s.v. נַעֲרָה. Cf. **naarah.**

chalifin חֲלִיפִין: an exchange of two objects made for the purpose of acquiring one or both of them. See preface to 1:6.

chalitzah חֲלִיצָה: the procedure of taking off the shoe — a mechanism provided by the Torah to release the brothers and the widow of a deceased man when they do not wish to perform *yibum*. See General Introduction to ArtScroll *Yevamos*.

chazakah חֲזָקָה: (1) an act of possession; (2) the rule that, unless proven otherwise, a person or thing is presumed to have retained its previous status.

chupah חוּפָּה: (1) the procedure by which *nisuin* is effected; (2) a canopy used for this purpose.

dinar דִּינָר: a type of coin. A silver dinar equals one *zuz*.

erusin אֵרוּסִין: the first stage of marriage, during which the couple is considered legally married in most respects. The term *betrothal*, albeit a poor and misleading translation, has sometimes been used for the sake of convenience. See General Introduction.

ervah, pl. **arayos** (עֲרָיוֹת) עֶרְוָה: one of the twenty-one women Biblically prohibited to a man because of kinship, either by blood or by marriage. See *Lev.* 18.

Gemara (abbr. **Gem.**) גְּמָרָא: the section of the Talmud that explains the Mishnah.

get, pl. **gittin** (גִּטִּין) גֵּט: (1) a bill of divorce; (2) any legal document. See General Introduction, s.v. *The Get*.

halachah הֲלָכָה: (1) a religious law; (2) the accepted ruling; (3) [cap.] the body of Jewish law.

kares כָּרֵת: a form of excision meted out by the Heavenly Tribunal, sometimes as premature death, sometimes by one being predeceased by his children.

kesubah, pl. **kesubos** (כְּתוּבּוֹת) כְּתוּבָּה: (1) the agreement made between a man and his wife upon their marriage, whose foremost feature is the dower awarded her in the event of their divorce or his death; (2) the document upon which this agreement is recorded. See General Introduction to ArtScroll *Kesubos*.

kiddushin קִדּוּשִׁין: *erusin*.

Kohen, pl. **Kohanim** (כֹּהֲנִים) כֹּהֵן: a member of the priestly family descended from Aaron.

mamzer, fem. **mamzeres,** pl. **mamzerim** מַמְזֵר (מַמְזֶרֶת, מַמְזֵרִים): a person born from forbidden relations that are punishable by *kares* or the death penalty.

mishnah, pl. **mishnayos** (מִשְׁנָיוֹת) מִשְׁנָה: (1) [cap.] the section of the Talmud consisting of the collection of oral laws edited by R' Yehudah HaNasi (Judah the Prince); (2) an article of this section.

mitzvah pl. **mitzvos** (מִצְוֹת) מִצְוָה: a Biblical or Rabbinical precept.

naarah, pl. **naaros** (נְעָרוֹת) נַעֲרָה: a girl over the age of twelve years who has already grown two pubic hairs. This stage ends six months later when she becomes a *bogeres*. See commentary to 6:3.

nisuin נִשּׂוּאִין: the second and final stage of marriage. Cf. **erusin.** See General Introduction.

perutah פְּרוּטָה: the minimal unit of significant monetary value. See commentary to 1:1 s.v. אֶחָד.

Tanna, pl. **Tannaim** (תַּנָּאִים) תַּנָּא: a Sage quoted in the Mishnah or in works of the same period.

terumah תְּרוּמָה: a portion of the crop sanctified and given to a *Kohen* who — together with his household — may eat it, but only if both the one who eats the *terumah* and the *terumah* itself are ritually clean.

Torah תּוֹרָה: (1) The Five Books of Moses; (2) the entire Written and Oral Law.

yavam, pl. **yevamin** (יְבָמִין) יָבָם: the surviving brother upon whom the obligation of *yibum* falls.

yevamah יְבָמָה: a widow who falls to *yibum*.

yibum יִבּוּם: levirate marriage — i.e., the marriage prescribed by the Torah between a widow and her late husband's brother when the husband died childless. Cf. **chalitzah.** See General Introduction to ArtScroll *Yevamos*.

הַדְרָן לְסֵדֶר נָשִׁים

Upon the סִיּוּם, *completion,* of the study of an entire *seder* of the Mishnah, a festive meal (which has the status of a *seudas mitzvah*) should be eaten — preferably with a *minyan* in attendance. The following prayers of thanksgiving are recited by one who has completed the learning.

[The words in brackets are inserted according to some customs.]

The first paragraph is recited three times.

הַדְרָן עֲלָךְ סֵדֶר נָשִׁים וְהַדְרָךְ עֲלָן; דַּעְתָּן עֲלָךְ סֵדֶר נָשִׁים וְדַעְתָּךְ עֲלָן; לָא נִתְנְשֵׁי מִנָּךְ סֵדֶר נָשִׁים וְלָא תִתְנְשֵׁי מִנָּן, לָא בְּעָלְמָא הָדֵין וְלָא בְּעָלְמָא דְאָתֵי.

הַעֲרֶב נָא יי אֱלֹהֵינוּ אֶת דִּבְרֵי תוֹרָתְךָ בְּפִינוּ וּבְפִי עַמְּךָ בֵּית יִשְׂרָאֵל, וְנִהְיֶה [כֻּלָּנוּ,] אֲנַחְנוּ וְצֶאֱצָאֵינוּ [וְצֶאֱצָאֵי צֶאֱצָאֵינוּ] וְצֶאֱצָאֵי עַמְּךָ בֵּית יִשְׂרָאֵל, כֻּלָּנוּ יוֹדְעֵי שְׁמֶךָ וְלוֹמְדֵי תוֹרָתֶךָ [לִשְׁמָהּ]. מֵאֹיְבַי תְּחַכְּמֵנִי מִצְוֹתֶךָ, כִּי לְעוֹלָם הִיא לִי. יְהִי לִבִּי תָמִים בְּחֻקֶּיךָ, לְמַעַן לֹא אֵבוֹשׁ. לְעוֹלָם לֹא אֶשְׁכַּח פִּקּוּדֶיךָ, כִּי בָם חִיִּיתָנִי. בָּרוּךְ אַתָּה יי, לַמְּדֵנִי חֻקֶּיךָ. אָמֵן אָמֵן אָמֵן, סֶלָה וָעֶד.

מוֹדֶה אֲנִי לְפָנֶיךָ יי אֱלֹהַי וֵאלֹהֵי אֲבוֹתַי, שֶׁשַּׂמְתָּ חֶלְקִי מִיּוֹשְׁבֵי בֵּית הַמִּדְרָשׁ, וְלֹא שַׂמְתָּ חֶלְקִי מִיּוֹשְׁבֵי קְרָנוֹת. שֶׁאֲנִי מַשְׁכִּים וְהֵם מַשְׁכִּימִים, אֲנִי מַשְׁכִּים לְדִבְרֵי תוֹרָה, וְהֵם מַשְׁכִּימִים לִדְבָרִים בְּטֵלִים. אֲנִי עָמֵל וְהֵם עֲמֵלִים, אֲנִי עָמֵל וּמְקַבֵּל שָׂכָר, וְהֵם עֲמֵלִים וְאֵינָם מְקַבְּלִים שָׂכָר. אֲנִי רָץ וְהֵם רָצִים, אֲנִי רָץ לְחַיֵּי הָעוֹלָם הַבָּא, וְהֵם רָצִים לִבְאֵר שַׁחַת, שֶׁנֶּאֱמַר: וְאַתָּה אֱלֹהִים, תּוֹרִדֵם לִבְאֵר שַׁחַת, אַנְשֵׁי דָמִים וּמִרְמָה לֹא יֶחֱצוּ יְמֵיהֶם, וַאֲנִי אֶבְטַח בָּךְ.

יְהִי רָצוֹן מִלְּפָנֶיךָ יְיָ אֱלֹהַי וֵאלֹהֵי אֲבוֹתַי, כְּשֵׁם שֶׁעֲזַרְתַּנִי לְסַיֵּם סֵדֶר נָשִׁים, כֵּן תַּעַזְרֵנִי לְהַתְחִיל סְדָרִים אֲחֵרִים וּלְסַיְּמָם, לִלְמֹד וּלְלַמֵּד מִתּוֹךְ הָרְחָבָה, לִשְׁמֹר וְלַעֲשׂוֹת וּלְקַיֵּם אֶת כָּל דִּבְרֵי תַלְמוּד תּוֹרָתֶךָ בְּאַהֲבָה. וּזְכוּת כָּל הַתַּנָּאִים וְתַלְמִידֵי חֲכָמִים הַנִּזְכָּרִים בְּסֵדֶר נָשִׁים וּבְכָל הַסְּפָרִים שֶׁלָּמַדְתִּי, יַעֲמֹד לִי וּלְזַרְעִי וּלְזֶרַע זַרְעִי, שֶׁלֹּא תָמוּשׁ הַתּוֹרָה הַקְּדוֹשָׁה מִפִּי וּמִפִּי זַרְעִי וְזֶרַע זַרְעִי מֵעַתָּה וְעַד עוֹלָם. וִיקֻיַּם בִּי מִקְרָא שֶׁכָּתוּב: בְּהִתְהַלֶּכְךָ תַּנְחֶה אֹתָךְ, בְּשָׁכְבְּךָ תִּשְׁמֹר עָלֶיךָ, וַהֲקִיצוֹתָ הִיא תְשִׂיחֶךָ. כִּי בִי יִרְבּוּ יָמֶיךָ, וְיוֹסִיפוּ לְךָ שְׁנוֹת חַיִּים. אֹרֶךְ יָמִים בִּימִינָהּ, בִּשְׂמֹאולָהּ עֹשֶׁר וְכָבוֹד. יְיָ עֹז לְעַמּוֹ יִתֵּן, יְיָ יְבָרֵךְ אֶת עַמּוֹ בַשָּׁלוֹם.

לְהוֹדוֹת לְהַלֵּל לְשַׁבֵּחַ לְפָאֵר לְרוֹמֵם לְהַדֵּר וּלְנַצֵּחַ לְבָרֵךְ לְעַלֵּה וּלְקַלֵּס, עַל כָּל דִּבְרֵי שִׁירוֹת וְתִשְׁבְּחוֹת דָּוִד בֶּן יִשַׁי עַבְדְּךָ מְשִׁיחֶךָ. בַּעֲצָתְךָ תַנְחֵנִי; וְאַחַר, כָּבוֹד תִּקָּחֵנִי. וְהוּא רַחוּם יְכַפֵּר עָוֹן וְלֹא יַשְׁחִית, וְהִרְבָּה לְהָשִׁיב אַפּוֹ, וְלֹא יָעִיר כָּל חֲמָתוֹ. אַשְׁרֵי הַגֶּבֶר אֲשֶׁר תְּיַסְּרֶנּוּ יָּהּ, וּמִתּוֹרָתְךָ תְלַמְּדֶנּוּ. וַאֲנִי בְּחַסְדְּךָ בָטַחְתִּי, יָגֵל לִבִּי בִּישׁוּעָתֶךָ, אָשִׁירָה לַיְיָ, כִּי גָמַל עָלָי. שׂוֹשׂ אָשִׂישׂ בַּיְיָ, תָּגֵל נַפְשִׁי בֵּאלֹהַי, כִּי הִלְבִּישַׁנִי בִּגְדֵי יֶשַׁע, מְעִיל צְדָקָה יְעָטָנִי; כֶּחָתָן יְכַהֵן פְּאֵר, וְכַכַּלָּה תַּעְדֶּה כֵלֶיהָ. וְיִבְטְחוּ בְךָ יוֹדְעֵי שְׁמֶךָ, כִּי לֹא עָזַבְתָּ דֹּרְשֶׁיךָ, יְיָ. שִׂמְחוּ בַיְיָ, וְגִילוּ צַדִּיקִים, וְהַרְנִינוּ כָּל יִשְׁרֵי לֵב. נֵר לְרַגְלִי דְבָרֶךָ, וְאוֹר לִנְתִיבָתִי. אוֹדְךָ כִּי עֲנִיתָנִי, וַתְּהִי לִי לִישׁוּעָה.

הַשִּׁיר שֶׁהַלְוִיִּם הָיוּ אוֹמְרִים בְּבֵית הַמִּקְדָּשׁ. בַּיּוֹם הָרִאשׁוֹן הָיוּ אוֹמְרִים: לַיְיָ הָאָרֶץ וּמְלוֹאָהּ, תֵּבֵל

וְיֹשְׁבֵי בָהּ. בַּשֵּׁנִי הָיוּ אוֹמְרִים: גָּדוֹל יי וּמְהֻלָּל מְאֹד, בְּעִיר אֱלֹהֵינוּ הַר קָדְשׁוֹ. בַּשְּׁלִישִׁי הָיוּ אוֹמְרִים: אֱלֹהִים נִצָּב בַּעֲדַת אֵל, בְּקֶרֶב אֱלֹהִים יִשְׁפֹּט. בָּרְבִיעִי הָיוּ אוֹמְרִים: אֵל נְקָמוֹת יי, אֵל נְקָמוֹת הוֹפִיעַ. בַּחֲמִישִׁי הָיוּ אוֹמְרִים: הַרְנִינוּ לֵאלֹהִים עוּזֵּנוּ, הָרִיעוּ לֵאלֹהֵי יַעֲקֹב. בַּשִּׁשִּׁי הָיוּ אוֹמְרִים: יי מָלָךְ גֵּאוּת לָבֵשׁ, לָבֵשׁ יי עֹז הִתְאַזָּר, אַף תִּכּוֹן תֵּבֵל בַּל תִּמּוֹט. בַּשַּׁבָּת הָיוּ אוֹמְרִים: מִזְמוֹר שִׁיר לְיוֹם הַשַּׁבָּת. מִזְמוֹר שִׁיר לֶעָתִיד לָבֹא, לְיוֹם שֶׁכֻּלּוֹ שַׁבָּת וּמְנוּחָה לְחַיֵּי הָעוֹלָמִים.

If a *minyan* is present, the following version of the Rabbis' *Kaddish* is recited by one or more of those present.
It may be recited even by one whose parents are still living.

יִתְגַּדַּל וְיִתְקַדַּשׁ שְׁמֵהּ רַבָּא. (Cong.—אָמֵן.) בְּעָלְמָא דִּי הוּא עָתִיד לְאִתְחַדָּתָא, וּלְאַחֲיָאָה מֵתַיָּא, וּלְאַסָּקָא יָתְהוֹן לְחַיֵּי עָלְמָא, וּלְמִבְנֵא קַרְתָּא דִירוּשְׁלֵם, וּלְשַׁכְלָלָא הֵיכְלֵהּ בְּגַוַּהּ, וּלְמֶעְקַר פָּלְחָנָא נֻכְרָאָה מִן אַרְעָא, וְלַאֲתָבָא פָּלְחָנָא דִּי שְׁמַיָּא לְאַתְרֵהּ, וְיַמְלִיךְ קֻדְשָׁא בְּרִיךְ הוּא בְּמַלְכוּתֵהּ וִיקָרֵהּ, [וְיַצְמַח פֻּרְקָנֵהּ וִיקָרֵב מְשִׁיחֵהּ (Cong.— אָמֵן)] בְּחַיֵּיכוֹן וּבְיוֹמֵיכוֹן וּבְחַיֵּי דְכָל בֵּית יִשְׂרָאֵל, בַּעֲגָלָא וּבִזְמַן קָרִיב. וְאִמְרוּ: אָמֵן.

(Cong.– אָמֵן. יְהֵא שְׁמֵהּ רַבָּא מְבָרַךְ לְעָלַם וּלְעָלְמֵי עָלְמַיָּא.)

יְהֵא שְׁמֵהּ רַבָּא מְבָרַךְ לְעָלַם וּלְעָלְמֵי עָלְמַיָּא.

יִתְבָּרַךְ וְיִשְׁתַּבַּח וְיִתְפָּאַר וְיִתְרוֹמַם וְיִתְנַשֵּׂא וְיִתְהַדָּר וְיִתְעַלֶּה וְיִתְהַלָּל שְׁמֵהּ דְּקֻדְשָׁא בְּרִיךְ הוּא (Cong.– בְּרִיךְ הוּא) °לְעֵלָּא מִן כָּל (Rosh Hashanah to Yom Kippur substitute— °לְעֵלָּא וּלְעֵלָּא מִכָּל) בִּרְכָתָא וְשִׁירָתָא תֻּשְׁבְּחָתָא וְנֶחֱמָתָא, דַּאֲמִירָן בְּעָלְמָא. וְאִמְרוּ: אָמֵן. (Cong.– אָמֵן.)

עַל יִשְׂרָאֵל וְעַל רַבָּנָן, וְעַל תַּלְמִידֵיהוֹן וְעַל כָּל תַּלְמִידֵי תַלְמִידֵיהוֹן, וְעַל כָּל מָאן דְּעָסְקִין בְּאוֹרַיְתָא, דִּי בְאַתְרָא הָדֵין וְדִי בְכָל אֲתַר וַאֲתַר. יְהֵא לְהוֹן וּלְכוֹן שְׁלָמָא רַבָּא, חִנָּא וְחִסְדָּא וְרַחֲמִין, וְחַיִּין אֲרִיכִין, וּמְזוֹנֵי רְוִיחֵי, וּפֻרְקָנָא מִן קֳדָם אֲבוּהוֹן דִּי בִשְׁמַיָּא [וְאַרְעָא]. וְאִמְרוּ: אָמֵן. (Cong.— אָמֵן.)

יְהֵא שְׁלָמָא רַבָּא מִן שְׁמַיָּא, וְחַיִּים [טוֹבִים] עָלֵינוּ וְעַל כָּל יִשְׂרָאֵל. וְאִמְרוּ: אָמֵן. (Cong.— אָמֵן.)

Take three steps back. Bow left and say . . . עֹשֶׂה; bow right and say . . . הוּא; bow forward and say וְעַל כָּל . . . אָמֵן. Remain standing in place for a few moments, then take three steps forward.

עֹשֶׂה שָׁלוֹם בִּמְרוֹמָיו, הוּא בְּרַחֲמָיו יַעֲשֶׂה שָׁלוֹם עָלֵינוּ, וְעַל כָּל יִשְׂרָאֵל. וְאִמְרוּ: אָמֵן. (Cong.— אָמֵן.)

This volume is part of
THE ARTSCROLL® SERIES
an ongoing project of
translations, commentaries and expositions on
Scripture, Mishnah, Talmud, Midrash, Halachah,
liturgy, history, the classic Rabbinic writings,
biographies and thought.

For a brochure of current publications visit your local
Hebrew bookseller or contact the publisher:

Mesorah Publications, ltd

313 Regina Avenue / Rahway, New Jersey 07065
(718) 921-9000 / www.artscroll.com